ALBERTI'S TEN BOOKS ON ARCHITECTURE

SUMMO DECORE NITESCAT.

B. Picart sculpsit. 1726.

TEN BOOKS

ON

ARCHITECTURE

by

LEONE BATTISTA ALBERTI

Translated into *Italian*

By *COSIMO BARTOLI*

And into *English*

By *JAMES LEONI*, VENETIAN ARCHITECT

Edited by

JOSEPH RYKWERT

1955
ALEC TIRANTI LTD.
72 *Charlotte Street*
LONDON, W.I

BIBLIOGRAPHICAL NOTE

The Leoni edition appeared in 1726, 1739
and 1755.

The present is a complete reprint of the *Ten Books on Architecture*
from the 1755 edition, with the addition of
the ' Life ' from the 1739 edition.

The Editor has appended footnotes on pages 241ff.
These are keyed to the main text by marginal references.

Made and printed in the United Kingdom

Editor's Foreword

HE LAWS of nature, the lost wisdom of the ancients, and the common sense of planning : every philosopher of the art of architecture seems bound to judge contemporary practice by these three criteria. But any change in the way of life, any shift in the interpretation of history or new development of cosmology create so different an historical condition that even the short passage of time between two generations forces a revaluation or, at least, a restatement of existing theory.

Such has been the situation since the fifteenth century, at any rate. Only one systematic treatise has survived from earlier times : Vitruvius' *Ten Books on Architecture*. Unfortunately Vitruvius was not particularly distinguished as an architect, a grammarian or a stylist. But his was the only work on architecture to have been preserved until the revival of learning during the reign of Charlemagne ; and from then on its survival was assured.

Manuscripts of the Ten Books were constantly re-copied during the Middle Ages, and about 1415 the whole text was thoroughly revised after Poggio's famous visit to the library of S. Gall. It is now difficult to assess what use Mediaeval architects had made of Vitruvius' precepts. His work was certainly valued both for its cosmological information and for practical advice about engineering problems. In his own time he seems to have been something of a reactionary, harking back not only to Greek theory of art, but also to Greek building practice, little interested in structural invention and transmitting the wisdom he had extracted from his predecessors—much of it probably from the forty or so treatises which he mentions in the preface to his Seventh Book—in a half-hearted and often rather confused way.

When Alberti, after a lapse of thirteen centuries, set out to establish a completely new way of building consonant with his thought and his way of life, he did so—for all his veneration of Antiquity—without any illusions about the merits of the ancient treatise. He respected Vitruvius' learning and made frequent acknowledgements to him. But he found the book badly written, confused, and considered the nomenclature—which is full of Greek terms—quite useless. Alberti's attitude to the architectural teaching of antiquity cannot, therefore, be measured by his criticism of Vitruvius. He appealed over the authority of one technician, to the whole body of classical writing. And beyond the writings, to the practice of ancient builders.

Indeed, Alberti believed firmly in the greatness of Rome, and had an almost Virgilian belief in the superiority of Italy. The ruins of ancient Rome, so long neglected, had already moved Petrarch to tears and sonnets, and Cola di Rienzi to rebellion. But to Alberti, and to Brunelleschi before him, they had become—with the aid of these writings without which they could not have been interpreted—the guide and standard of all new buildings, of an architecture worthy of a new and great Rome.

Alberti's contemporaries accepted his book enthusiastically. He had expounded, justified and developed the new way of building which had been initiated by Brunelleschi. When he presented his treatise to Pope Nicholas V in 1452—it was then in all probability in a rather rudimentary form—his reputation as a scholar and as a writer of great distinction already stood very high. He came to be regarded as one of the leading thinkers and stylists of the day. ' Who else in our time,' writes one of his admirers, not without exaggeration, ' has been so profoundly initiated into the Platonic mysteries as our Leo ? ' And later writers such as Paolo Giovio, himself a scholar and a critic, admired his prose and his learning, particularly in his treatment of architecture, a subject so alien to the normal concerns of rhetoric.

The original Latin text of Alberti's *Ten Books* was first printed in Florence in 1485 ; it was prefaced by a dedicatory letter, addressed to Lorenzo de' Medici by Angelo Poliziano. This Latin edition was reprinted twice : in Paris in 1512 (this is the edition in which the books were first subdivided into chapters), and in Strasbourg in 1541. The first Italian translation—by Pietro Lauro—appeared in Venice in 1546. In 1550 Cosimo Bartoli, who in 1568 was to publish the first edition of Alberti's Italian works (an anthology of his translations from the Latin of Alberti and texts written in Italian by Alberti himself), printed his translation of the *Ten Books* which, from then on, became the most widely read text. This was also the first edition to be illustrated. Jean Martin, the translator of Vitruvius and of the *Hypnerotomachia Polyphili*, translated the *Ten Books* into French. This translation was published in Paris in 1553, after Martin's death, and was prefaced by an elegy by Ronsard. A Spanish translation was printed in 1582 ; a Portuguese translation made in the sixteenth century, has remained in manuscript.

Giacomo Leoni (1686–1746), a Venetian architect who came to England some time before 1715, published a sumptuous edition of his translation of the *Ten Books on Architecture*, the *Three Books on Painting*, and the *Book on Sculpture*, in 1726. (This last had already appeared in English in John Evelyn's edition of Fréart de Chambray's *Parallel of the Orders* of 1664.) Leoni had previously (in 1715–16) published an even more splendid edition of Palladio, though his authority was not, in the end, accepted by the English Palladian group. Little is known so far about the circumstances in which the translation of Alberti was prepared, or who Leoni's English collaborator was. (Nicholas Dubois had collaborated in the translation of Palladio.) The illustrations, as in the case of the edition of Palladio, were engraved by a French artist, Bernard Picart (1673–1733) from Leoni's drawings which in their turn were based on the woodcuts in the Bartoli edition of 1550. The last translation to appear was the German one, prepared from the original Latin text by Max Theuer, a Viennese architect, and supplied with valuable notes and introduction.

Although the flaccid, whiggified and not-quite-Augustan prose of Leoni's version misses the sharp definition and classic roundness of the original, it is still the only easily accessible source for the doctrine of the great quattrocento master, whose teaching has become increasingly relevant in the last few years. The search for a rationale, for an expressive method, which prompted le Corbusier's invention of the Modulor, has now progressed further, and issues long forgotten —such as the language of symbolic form in architecture—arouse a new and urgent interest. Although no one would expect Alberti to provide the younger generation of architects with a ready-made answer to their problems, there is much in this book which will appear not only stimulating, but even directly relevant.

My thanks are due in the first place to Professor Rudolf Wittkower. I should also like to express my gratitude to Miss Barbara Flower, Mr. Cecil Grayson, Dr. L. Ettlinger, Miss Pamela Fieldes, Miss Sheila Somers and Dr. C. H. Talbot, who have helped me in the preparation of this edition.

The Contents

The text printed here is a translation of the *Ten Books on Architecture* from Leoni's third edition of 1755, which printed the English translation only. Previous editions had the English translation and Bartoli's Italian version in parallel columns. Included here is the life of Alberti by Raphael du Fresne which appeared only in the two earlier editions. Du Fresne's bibliography, which Leoni had also taken from the Leonardo-Alberti anthology of 1651, has, however, not been included. The commentary is based on Max Theuer's annotations to his German translation of 1911 to which I have referred in the prefatory note; use has also been made of more recent research. Alberti's whole teaching has been systematized and discussed in a standard work by Paul-Henri Michel, *Un Ideal Humain au XVme Siècle; La Pensée de L.B. Alberti*, Paris 1930. A recent contribution to the study of Alberti's thought is Mario Petrini's essay *L'Uomo di Alberti*, in BELFAGOR, VI, 1951, pp. 665–74. There is another essay of importance dealing exclusively with Alberti's theory of art: *Die Begründung der modernen Aesthetik und Kunstwissenschaft durch Lèon Battista Alberti*, by W. Flemming, Leipzig 1916. A short thesis by Paul Hoffmann, *Studien zu Leon Battista zehn Büchern De Re Aedificatoria*, Frankenberg i.S 1883, contains several helpful suggestions.

By far the most important study of Alberti's work as an architect in relation to his teaching will be found in *Principles of Architecture in the Age of Humanism*, by Rudolf Wittkower, 2nd edition, London 1952. Also of great interest are the two recent essays: *The Imagery of the Tempio Malatestiano* by Charles Mitchell in STUDI ROMAGNOLI, II (1951), pp. 77–90, and *The Project of Nicholas V for re-building the Borgo Leonino in Rome*, by Torgil Magnuson in the ART BULLETIN, June 1954, XXXVI, 2, pp. 89–115, which should be compared with Georg Dehio's *Die Bauprojekte Nicolaus V* in REPERTORIUM FUER KUNSTWISSENSCHAFT, III (1880), pp. 241–257. Cf. also *Leone Battista Alberti als Kunstphilosoph*, by Irene Behn, Strasbourg 1911, and Maria Luisa Gengaro, *Leon Battista Alberti Teorico e Architetto del Rinascimento*, Milano 1939.

For illustrations of Alberti's architectural works, see particularly *Leon Battista Alberti Architetto*, by Corrado Ricci, Torino 1917, and *L. B. Alberti*, by Adolfo Venturi, Roma 1923, in the series BIBLIOTECA D'ARTE ILLUSTRATA. The definitive life of Alberti is that by Girolamo Mancini, second edition, Firenze 1911. The most comprehensive bibliography of Alberti's writings and studies relating to him will be found in Michel, pp. 11–46. This may be supplemented, for more recent material, by reference to Wittkower's book. Cf. also C. Grayson: *Notes on the Texts of some Vernacular Works of Leon Battista Alberti*, and *Studi su Leon Battista Alberti*, both in RINASCIMENTO (III, 1952, pp. 211–44, and IV, 1953, pp. 45–62).

For information on Giacomo Leoni, cf. J. Summerson, *Architecture in Britain 1530–1830*, London 1953; H. M. Colvin, *Biographical Dictionary of English Architects 1660–1840*, London 1954; and Rudolf Wittkower.

The Life of Alberti is taken from the *Trattato della Pittura di Lionardo da Vinci ... con la Vita dell'istesso autore scritta da Raffaello du Fresne. Ci sono giunti i tre libri della Pittura, ed il trattato della Statua di Leon-Battista Alberti, con la Vita del medesimo*, Paris 1651.

THE

PREFACE.

O UR Anceſtors have left us many and various Arts tending to the Pleaſure and Conveniency of Life, acquired with the greateſt Induſtry and Diligence: Which Arts, though they all pretend, with a Kind of Emulation, to have in View the great End of being ſerviceable to Mankind; yet we know that each of them in particular has ſomething in it that ſeems to promiſe a diſtinct and ſeparate Fruit: Some Arts we follow for Neceſſity, ſome we approve for their Uſefulneſs, and ſome we eſteem becauſe they lead us to the Knowledge of Things that are delightful. What theſe Arts are, it is not neceſſary for me to enumerate; for they are obvious. But if you take a View of the whole Circle of Arts, you ſhall hardly find one but what, deſpiſing all others, regards and ſeeks only its own particular Ends: Or if you do meet with any of ſuch a Nature that you can in no wiſe do without it, and which yet brings along with it Profit at the ſame Time, conjoined with Pleaſure and Honour, you will, I believe, be convinced, that Architecture is not to be excluded from that Number. For it is certain, if you examine the Matter carefully, it is inexpreſſibly delightful, and of the greateſt Convenience to Mankind in all Reſpects, both publick and private; and in Dignity not inferior to the moſt excellent. But before I proceed further, it will not be improper to explain what he is that I allow to be an Architect: For it is not a Carpenter or a Joiner that I thus rank with the greateſt Maſters in other Sciences; the manual Operator being no more than an Inſtrument to the Architect. Him I call an Architect, who, by ſure and wonderful Art and Method, is able, both with Thought and Invention, to deviſe, and, with Execution, to compleat all thoſe Works, which, by means of the Movement of great Weights, and the Conjunction and Amaſſment of Bodies, can, with the greateſt Beauty, be adapted to the Uſes of Mankind: And to be able to do this, he muſt have a thorough Inſight into the nobleſt and moſt curious Sciences. Such muſt be the Architect. But to return.

Some have been of Opinion, that either Water or Fire were the principal Occaſions of bringing Men together into Societies; but to us, who conſider the Uſefulneſs and Neceſſity of Coverings and Walls, it ſeems evident, that they were the chief Cauſes of aſſembling Men together. But the only Obligation we have to the Architect is not for his providing us with ſafe 2 and pleaſant Places, where we may ſhelter ourſelves from the Heat of the Sun, from Cold and Tempeſt, (though this is no ſmall Benefit); but for having beſides contrived many other Things, both of a private and publick Nature of the higheſt Uſe and Convenience to the Life of Man. How many noble Families, reduced by the Calamity of the Times, had been utterly loſt, both in our own native City, and in others, had not their paternal Habitations preſerved and cheriſhed them, as it were, in the Boſom of their Forefathers. *Dædalus* in his Time was 3 greatly eſteemed for having made the *Selinuntians* a Vault, which gathered ſo warm and kindly a Vapour, as provoked a plentiful Sweat, and thereby cured their Diſtempers with great Eaſe and Pleaſure. Why need I mention others who have contrived many Things of the like Sort conducive to Health; as Places for Exerciſe, for Swimming, Baths and the like? Or why ſhould I inſtance in Vehicles, Mills, Time-meaſures, and other ſuch minute Things, which nevertheleſs are of great Uſe in Life? Why ſhould I inſiſt upon the great Plenty of Waters brought from the moſt remote and hidden Places, and employed to ſo many different and uſeful Purpoſes? Upon Trophies, Tabernacles, ſacred Edifices, Churches and the like, adapted

to

to divine Worſhip, and the Service of Poſterity ? Or laſtly, why ſhould I mention the Rocks
cut, Mountains bored through, Vallies filled up, Lakes confined, Marſhes diſcharged into the
Sea, Ships built, Rivers turned, their Mouths cleared, Bridges laid over them, Harbours formed,
not only ſerving to Men's immediate Conveniencies, but alſo opening them a Way to all Parts
of the World ; whereby Men have been enabled mutually to furniſh one another with Proviſions, Spices, Gems, and to communicate their Knowledge, and whatever elſe is healthful or
pleaſurable. Add to theſe the Engines and Machines of War, Fortreſſes, and the like Inventions neceſſary to the Defending the Liberty of our Country, Maintaining the Honour, and En-
creaſing the Greatneſs of a City, and to the Acquiſition and Eſtabliſhment of an Empire. I
am really perſuaded, that if we were to enquire of all the Cities which, within the Memory of
Man, have fallen by Siege into the Power of new Maſters, who it was that ſubjected and over-
came them, they would tell you, the Architect ; and that they were ſtrong enough to have
deſpiſed the armed Enemy, but not to withſtand the Shocks of the Engines, the Violence of
the Machines, and the Force of the other Inſtruments of War, with which the Architect diſ-
treſſed, demoliſhed and ruinated them. And the Beſieged, on the contrary, would inform
you, that their greateſt Defence lay in the Art and Aſſiſtance of the Architect. And if you
were to examine into the Expeditions that have been undertaken, you would go near to find
that moſt of the Victories were gained more by the Art and Skill of the Architects, than by the
Conduct or Fortune of the Generals ; and that the Enemy was oftener overcome and conquered
by the Architect's Wit, without the Captain's Arms, than by the Captain's Arms without the
Architect's Wit : And what is of great Conſequence is, that the Architect conquers with a
ſmall Number of Men, and without the Loſs of Troops. Let this ſuffice as to the Uſefulneſs
of this Art.

But how much the Study and Subject of Building delights, and how firmly it is rooted in
the Mind of Man, appears from ſeveral Inſtances, and particularly from this ; that you ſhall
find no body who has the Means but what has an Inclination to be building ſomething : And
if a Man has happened to think of any Thing new in Architecture, he is fond of communicat-
ing and divulging it for the Uſe of others, as if conſtrained thereto by Nature. And how often
does it fall out, that even when we are employed upon other Things, we cannot keep our
Thoughts and Imaginations, from Projecting ſome Edifice ? And when we ſee other Men's
Houſes, we immediately ſet about a careful Examination of all the Proportions and Dimenſions,
and, to the beſt of our Ability, conſider what might be added, retrenched or altered ; and preſently give our Opinions how it might be made more compleat or beautiful. And if a Building be well laid out, and juſtly finiſhed, who is he that does not view it with the utmoſt Pleaſure and Delight ? But why need I mention not only how much Benefit and Delight, but how
much Glory to Architecture has brought to Nations, which have cultivated it both at home
and abroad ? Who that has built any publick Edifice does not think himſelf honoured by it,
when it is reputable to a Man only to have built a handſome Habitation for himſelf ? Men of
publick Spirits approve and rejoice when you have raiſed a fine Wall or Portico, and adorned
it with Portals, Columns, and a handſome Roof, knowing you have thereby not only ſerved
yourſelf, but them too, having by this generous Uſe of your Wealth, gained an Addition of
great Honour to yourſelf, your Family, your Deſcendants, and your City. The Sepulchre of
Jupiter was the firſt Step to the ennobling the Iſland of *Crete* ; and *Delos* was not ſo much
reſpected for the Oracle of *Apollo*, as for the beautiful Structure of the City, and the Majeſty of
the Temple. How much Authority accrued to the *Roman* Name and Empire from their
Buildings, I ſhall dwell upon no further, than that the Sepulchres and other Remains of the
ancient Magnificence, every where to be found, are a great Inducement and Argument with us
for believing many Things related by Hiſtorians, which might otherwiſe have ſeemed incredible.
Thucydides extreamly commends the Prudence of ſome Ancients, who had ſo adorned their City
with all Sorts of fine Structures, that their Power thereby appeared to be much greater than it
really was. And what potent or wiſe Prince can be named, that among his chief Projects for
eternizing his Name and Poſterity, did not make Uſe of Architecture. But of this enough.
The Concluſion is, that for the Service, Security, Honour and Ornament of the Publick, we
are exceedingly obliged to the Architect ; to whom, in Time of Leiſure, we are indebted for
Tranquility,

Tranquility, Pleafure and Health, in Time of Bufinefs for Affiftance and Profit; and in **both**, for Security and Dignity. Let us not therefore deny that he ought to be praifed and efteemed, and to be allowed a Place, both for the wonderful and ravifhing Beauty of his Works, and for the Neceffity, Serviceablenefs, and Strength of the Things which he has invented, among the Chief of thofe who have deferved Honour and Rewards from Mankind. The Confideration of thefe Things induced me, for my Diverfion, to look a little further into this Art and its Operations, from what Principles it was derived, and of what Parts it confifted: And finding them of various Kinds, in Number almoft infinite, in their Nature marvellous, of Ufe incredible, infomuch that it was doubtful what Condition of Men, or what Part of the Commonwealth, or what Degree in the City, whether the Publick or Private, Things facred or profane, Repofe or Labour, the Individual or the whole human Species, was moft obliged to the Architect, or rather Inventor of all Conveniencies; I refolved, for feveral Reafons, too tedious here to repeat, to collect all thofe Things which are contained in thefe Ten Books. In treating of which, we fhall obferve this Method: We confider that an Edifice is a Kind of Body confifting, like all other Bodies, of Defign and of Matter; the firft is produced by the Thought, the other by Nature; fo that the one is to be provided by the Application and Contrivance of the Mind, and the other by due Preparation and Choice. And we further reflected, that neither the one nor the other of itfelf was fufficient, without the Hand of an experienced Artificer, that knew how to form his Materials after a juft Defign. And the Ufe of Edifices being various, it was neceffary to enquire whether one and the fame Kind of Defign was fit for all Sorts of Buildings; upon which Account we have diftinguifhed the feveral Kinds of Buildings: Wherein perceiving that the main Point was the juft Compofition and Relation of the Lines among themfelves, from whence arifes the Height of Beauty, I therefore began to examine what Beauty really was, and what Sort of Beauty was proper to each Edifice. And as we often meet with Faults in all thefe Refpects, I confidered how they might be altered or amended. Every Book therefore has its Title prefixed to it, according to the Variety of the Subject: The Firft treats of Defigns; the Second, of Materials; the Third, of the Work; the Fourth, of Works in general; the Fifth, of Works in particular; the Sixth, of Ornaments in general; the Seventh, of the Ornaments proper for facred Edifices; the Eighth, of thofe for publick and profane ones; The Ninth, of thofe for the Houfes of private Perfons; the Tenth, of Amendments and Alterations in Buildings: To which is added, a various Hiftory of Waters, and how they are found, and what Ufe is to be made of the Architect in all thefe Works: As alfo Four other Books, Three of which treat of the Art of Painting; and the Fourth, of Sculpture.

The

The Life of
LEONE BATTISTA ALBERTI
by Raphael du Fresne

OW ancient, noble and powerful the family of the *Albertis* was in *Florence*, we may be satisfied by History; and *Scipio Ammirato*, who for certain reasons had a mind to exalt the name of the *Concinis*, cou'd think of no better nor more effectual method to do it, than by putting it in company with the *Albertis*, and deducing both families from the same origin. All we shall say of them is, that even so early as in the year 1304. they were already in great authority in *Florence*, and favoured the party of the *Bianchis*; and in the year 1384. upon the festival which was celebrated in *Florence* upon account of the acquisition of *Arezzo*, the Figure which the *Albertis* made was so magnificent, that it seemed more befitting some great Prince, than any private persons. In the Registers of the Commonwealth we find that the *Albertis* nine times possessed the Gonfalonership, which was the highest degree of honour and power to which the *Florentines* cou'd aspire. But in the frequent storms and troubles wherein the publick affairs were tossed, fortune did not always shine upon them. In 1387. *Cyprian* and *Benedict de Alberti* were driven out of their Country, and afterwards in 1411. all that family, even to the very children, were banished by edict: but in 1428. their sentence of banishment was taken off, and they were all again allowed to return and live freely at *Florence*. The above-named *Cyprian* was father of *Alberto*, *Lorenzo* and *John*. *Alberto Alberti* was first Canon, and afterwards, in the year 1437, Bishop of *Camerino*: and Pope *Eugenius*, who was received by the *Florentines* in their City in so pompous and affectionate a manner, having,

at the time when he held his Council there, made trial of this Prelate's virtues, did then, as a mark of his gratitude towards his Nation, and as a reward due to his merit, honour him with the Cardinalship. *Lorenzo*, the brother of this *Alberto*, left several sons, particularly *Bernardo*, *Carlo*, and *Leone Battista*, whose rare qualities will afford us ample matter of praise in this short discourse. With how much care and exactness these brothers were educated by their father in their youth, we may read in the treatise which the same *Leone Battista* wrote of the conveniences and inconveniences of Learning: wherein he tells us, that all the hours in the day were in such a manner allotted to their particular studies, that there was no time for idleness. When they had attained a riper age, besides the study of letters, *Carlo* took upon him the care of all the domestic concerns; but *Leone Battista*, despising every thing but books, gave himself up entirely to the improvement of his mind, and made so great a progress in the sciences, that he outstript all the great men of that age who were most famous for their learning.

THE first taste he gave of the vivacity and acuteness of his wit, was by imposing upon the judgment of the men of letters of that age, by a learned and ingenious piece of raillery, and with more success than *Sigonius* did afterwards: for when he was but twenty years old, at the University of *Bologna*, he privately composed a Fable called *Philodoxios*, under the name of *Lepidus* the Comick Poet, which he afterwards published as an antique piece, which he had newly discovered by accident in an old manuscript. And indeed, in this performance *Alberti* so happily imitated the ancient style of the *Latin* Comick Writers, that falling into the hands of *Aldus Manutius*, who was universally allowed to be an excellent Judge of the truest and purest *Latin* style, he printed it at *Lucca* in the year 1588. dedicating it to *Ascanius Persius*, a person also of profound learning, as the performance of an ancient Author. *Lepidam Lepidi, antiqui comici, quisquis ille sit, fabulam ad te mitto, eruditissime Persi, quæ cum ad manus meas pervenerit, perire nolui : & antiquitatis rationem habendam esse duxi. Multa sunt in eâ observatione digna, quæ tibi, totius vetustatis solertissimo indagatori, non displicebunt, mihi certè cum placuerint, &c.* But that *Alberti* wrote this fable in the twentieth year of his age, he himself thought fit to declare in the prologue : *Non quidem cupio, non peto in laudem trahi, quod hac vigesima annorum meorum ætate, hanc ineptius scripserim fabulam. Verum expecto inde haberi apud vos hoc persuasionis, non vacuum me scilicet, non exundique incuriè meos obivisse annos.* *Alberti* having thus made trial of his own strength at so early an age, there was no science but what he studied and attained, not suffering a single day to pass without reading or composing something, as he himself affirms : and he was of so ready an apprehension, that he seemed equally born for all sorts of studies : nor is it easy to determine whether he was a better Orator or Poet, whether he wrote more excellently in *Latin* or *Italian*, whether he was more versed in the practical sciences or the speculative, or whether he cou'd discourse of important matters with more weight, or of common and mean things with more pleasantness and politeness.

7   WE are told that once *Lorenzo de Medicis*, the true *Mecænas* of that age, in order to make the hottest part of the summer pass off as agreeably as possible, got together into the Grove of *Camaldoli* an assembly of persons illustrious in all sorts of literature, among whom *Marsilio Ficino, Donato Acciaioli, Leone Battista Alberti, Alamanno Rinuccino* and *Christophero Landino* were the chief. What was the conversation among such great men, every one may imagine. But none gained so much admiration as *Alberti*, who in several sublime discourses full of the most exalted learning, clearly shewed that in the *Æneid*, under the veil of a great many beautiful fictions, there lay concealed the highest secrets of Philosophy, and that *Virgil* was a true and real Philosopher, only fantastically habited like a Poet. These sound reasonings made such an impression upon the minds of the hearers,

that *Christoforo Landino* (who upon this occasion chose to be Secretary to the Assembly) recorded them all in a book, and out of them afterwards composed that Work which we see printed in *Latin*, under the title of the *Camaldoline Questions* : wherein towards the end *Landino* (known better to us by the name of *Landinus*) has the following words : *Hæc sunt quæ de plurimis longeque excellentioribus, quæ Leo Baptista Albertus memoriter, dilucide, ac capiose, in tantorum virorum concessu disputavit, meminisse volui.* 8

ALBERTI left a great many fine compositions both in *Latin* and *Italian*, whereof we have subjoined a copious list at the end of this life. Among his *Latin* Works there is one truly worthy of immortality, and which may be paralell'd with all antiquity, which is that entitled *Momus*, which for its excellency, in the same year 1520. was twice re-printed at *Rome*. And indeed in this Work he very beautifully and in a way entirely new, with the finest raillery and pleasantness lays open, in four books, all those things which others in a grave severe style had wrote of moral Philosophy, but still proposing to himself to insist chiefly upon those points which relate to the forming a perfect Prince, and knowing the characters of those that are about him. There is another little piece of his which is very pretty called, *Trivia*, or of the Causes under the Jurisdiction of the Senators, and another which he entitled *de Jure*, concerning the administration of Justice, which for I know not what reason *Cosimo Bartoli*, who translated into *Italian* and published in one Volume several little pieces of *Leone Battista Alberti*, printed as the fifth and sixth books of the *Momus* or *Prince*. He wrote a little Book of FABLES, wherein he is said in variety of invention to have excelled even *Æsop*. He also composed a treatise of the life 9 and manners of his Dog, and another upon the Fly, having a surprizing genius for playing with the gravest and most exalted Subjects, and philosophizing upon the lowest and meanest. He left three books of OECONOMY in *Italian*, and some amorous things both in prose and verse, and was the first (as *George Vasari* informs us in his life) that endeavoured to reduce the common *Italian* verse to the measure of the *Latins*, as in this epistle :

Questa pur estrema miserabile pistola mando
   A te che spregi miseramente noi, &c.

BUT while I am giving this account of *Alberti's* wonderful Genius for all sorts of polite literature, and of the rank he held among the men of learning; I think I hear myself called upon by people of other professions, namely Painters and Architects, who pretend to him for their own, and shewing me what great things he has done in Painting and Architecture, pull me back, and as if I were to write the character of another *Alberti*, oblige me to pass from speculative Sciences to practical and mechanical Arts. And indeed so great was the capacity and so extensive the Genius of our *Alberti*, that he not only attain'd a general knowledge of all arts and sciences, but even descended to the particulars of every one of them; and whatever it was that he applied himself to, he cou'd make men fancy, that he had never turned his noble disposition to any thing else, equalling and even excelling those that were at the top of each profession. In his days the study of Architecture was in a manner lost; or if any notices of it remained, they were so corrupted and so different from the greatness and politeness of the ancient *Roman* times, that the Works produced by them were very mean. *Leone Battista Alberti* was the first that endeavoured to bring back this art to its ancient purity, and that clearing it of the barbarisms of the *Gothick* ages, restored it to order and proportion; insomuch that he was universally called the *Florentine Vitruvius*. His fame induced Pope *Nicholas* V. to employ him in the ordering a great many Buildings at *Rome*; and he confided the more heartily in his counsels, as he was particularly informed of his extraordinary qualities by *Biondo Forlivese*, a man of great merit and his familiar friend.

10

AT the desire of *Sigismondo Pandolfo Malatesta*, Lord of *Rimino*, he drew the plan of the Church of St. *Francis*, which was begun in the year 1447. and proved one of the most stately and sumptuous in all *Italy*. It was brought to the perfection in which we now

11   see it in the year 1550. And since *Vasari*, tho' upon occasions of less moment he is prolix enough, has been sparing of his words in the description of this Church, tho' by

means of the abode he made in *Rimino*, where he painted the St. *Francis* which is over the great Altar in the same Building, he had an opportunity of taking exact notice of every part of it; we, in order in some measure to supply his negligence, and to do the greater honour to the memory of the Architect, shall set down here such things as, upon a frequent view of it, we thought most worthy of observation. To begin therefore with the Front, we shall take notice that it rises upon a noble basement, all of *Istrian* marble, which runs clear round the whole building, having for its cornice a handsome ornament of foliages and the *Pandolpho* arms, very curiously interwreathed together. Upon this stand four half Columns of the composite order, fluted. The interstices are filled with three Niches, whereof the middle one makes the great Gate, which opens a little way within the Nich, adorned with very beautiful foliages: next to these are the architrave, freeze and cornice, over which just answering to the Gate, are two Pilasters of the same Order with a Nich between them, which, if the design had been quite compleated, wou'd have served to have given light to the middle Isle and to set the Statue of our Lord in. In the sides of the Church without, is a very stately and noble invention, being seven great Arches, and under them as many Tombs designed for the great men of *Rimini*. The inside of the Fabrick does not in the least fall short of the outside either in greatness of design, nor delicacy of ornaments, which, tho' they have I know not what in them of *Gothick*, if we consider the rudeness of that age, are not altogether without their merit. There is a great profusion of Marble both within and without; and we read, in the life of *Sigismund*, that passing by *Ravenna* with his train, he upon this occasion stript the ancient Churches of St. *Severus* and *Classi*, taking away all their incrustation, and removing to *Rimino* every thing that he thought might be serviceable for the compleating the Structure he was about; insomuch that he was justly blamed for it by Pope *Pius* the second, and held guilty of little less than sacrilege. In one of the Chapels, which are in number six, are the Tombs of *Sigismund* and *Isotta* his wife, very rich and handsome, and over one of them (as *Vasari* writes) the Portrait of that Lord, and in another part of the same Building that of *Leone Battista.*

IN the year 1551. *Lewis Gonzaga*, Marquiss of *Mantua*, who had a very great devotion for the *Annuntiata* of *Florence*, upon account of a vow made to her by his Spouse, for a happy delivery, built the Choir or high Altar which we now see in that Church, with the arms of the *Gonzaga* family all round it, according to a design given by *Leone Battista*: which as it shews the magnificence of that Prince, so it is an instance of the skill of the Architect who in a very odd and difficult manner contrived that Structure after the model of a Rotunda with nine Chapels round it. And because there are some things in it which do not satisfy the eye so well as might be expected, the arches of the Chapels seeming by the sweep of the fabrick, when viewed in profile, to fall in backwards, we shall refer the Reader to *Vasari's* account of it.

THE same Marquiss having a mind, in his own City, to rebuild quite from the foundations, the Church of St. *Andrew*, venerable upon account of the blood of Christ which is preserved in it, in the year 1472. sent for *Alberti*, and having made him acquainted with his intention to adorn *Mantua* with a noble and costly Temple, got him to make the Model of the new Church which we now see there. It is all of Brick in the shape of a Cross; the lower part of which is formed by one single vaulted Roof which covers the whole great Body of the Church, 208 foot long and 80 broad, without a single chain either of iron or wood to keep it together. The whole Fabrick is of the composite order, with three large Chappels on each side, and as many small ones. In each arm of the Cross are two Chapels, opposite one to the other. The middle of the Square, over which the Cupola is to be, is about 80 foot in breadth. Beyond this Square is the Choir, which is of an oval form, 104 foot long and of the same breadth as the body of the Church, which together with the aforesaid square in the year of our Lord 1600. was finished quite to the upper Cornice, according to *Alberti's* old model. The front is divided into three Doors, the biggest whereof, which is in the middle, is adorned with white marble, with beautiful foliages curiously carved, and the smaller Doors on each side are of grey marble,

adorned in the same manner. Whoever has a mind for a more particular description, may find it in *Donesmond's* sixth book of the Ecclesiastical History of *Mantua*, from whence we have taken the short account we have given of it. *Mario Equicola* in the History of *Mantua*, informs us that the same *Alberti* began the Church of St. *Sebastian* in the same City. He had for his Assistant and the faithful Executor of his designs at *Mantua*, one *Luke* a *Florentine*, who had worked for him before at *Florence* in the structure of the Choir of the *Annuntiata.*

BUT whatever *Rome*, *Rimino* and *Mantua* may owe to the industry and ingenuity of *Leone Battista*, his Country is no less obliged to him for contributing not a little to its adorning. The Front of the Church of St. *Maria Novella* was built under his direction, and very curiously embellished with a beautiful mixture of black and white marble suitably to the greatness of the whole Body of the Fabrick. He gave *Cosimo Rucellai* the design of the Palace which he built in the Street called the Vineyard; and in the Church of St. *Brancacius*, is a Chapel of his contrivance. He directed a great many other Works, which for brevity we omit. He left very few performances in Painting. *Paulus Jovius*, who wrote his Elogium, and ranked him among the men illustrious for Learning, commends the Portrait which he drew of himself; which at the time when *Vasari* wrote, was in the house of *Palla Rucellai*, with some other Paintings by the same *Alberti.*

IT appears from what has been already said, that for the knowledge of Letters, and skill in Design, *Leone Battista Alberti* may with the highest justice be recorded among the men famous in both those professions. And in order to unite them more closely together, he resolved that the language of the one shou'd serve to illustrate the operations of the other, giving speech to those Arts which before had always been in a manner dumb, and committing their precepts to writing in a very fine style in *Latin*. Sculpture was the first which he undertook to treat of, in a little book in *Latin* intitled of *Statuary*. He afterwards wrote three Books of Painting, in the same language, which are highly commended by all the Connoisseurs, as well for their noble and clear style, as for the importance of their precepts. In the first he lays open the Principles of the Art, drawn from Geometry. The second contains those certain Rules, from which a Painter ought never to depart, either in his Composition, Drawing or Colouring, which are the three heads to which all considerations relating to Painting may be reduced. In the third Book he treats of the duty of a Painter, and the end he ought to propose to himself in his labours.

THE last Work of *Leone Battista Alberti*, and that which has the most merit in it, as having cost him the most labour and study, is the Book which he wrote of ARCHITECTURE, in which with exquisite method and great perspicuity, he discovers all the secrets of that Art, which before lay hid in the obscure Writings of *Vitruvius*; nor was it published till after his death, by his brother *Bernardo*, who dedicated it to *Lorenzo de Medicis*, as the Author intended to have done himself. It was translated into *Italian*, and illustrated with Designs, by *Cosimo Bartoli* a *Florentine* Gentleman, who dedicated it to *Cosimo de Medicis* in the year 1550. The same *Bartoli* also translated his Books of Painting and Sculpture, and printed them in the year 1568. with the other small Works of *Alberti*. There was another Version of the Treatise of Painting, done before by *Domenichi*, and printed in the year 1547.

HAVING thus in *Italian*, a language foreign to my birth, given some account of the extraordinary Genius of *Leone Battista* and admired the excellent fruits of it, I have nothing further to add but that it were to be wished, for the honour of so great a Man, and yet more for the service of the publick and the glory of Learning, that all his Works might some time or other be collected together: for which purpose I shall here subjoin a list of them. *Alberti* died in *Florence*, the place of his nativity, and was buried in the Church of the *Holy Cross*.

The TABLE of CONTENTS.

CHAP.

CHAP.

THE

THE

ARCHITECTURE

OF

Leone Batiſta Alberti.

BOOK I. CHAP. I.

Of Deſigns; their Value and Rules.

BEING to treat of the Deſigns of Edifices, we ſhall collect and tranſcribe into this our Work, all the moſt curious and uſeful Obſervations left us by the Ancients, and which they gathered in the actual Execution of theſe Works; and to theſe we ſhall join whatever we ourſelves may have diſcovered by our Study, Application and Labour, that ſeems likely to be of Uſe. But as we deſire, in the handling this difficult, knotty, and commonly obſcure Subject, to be as clear and intelligible as poſſible; we ſhall, according to our Cuſtom, explain what the Nature of our Subject is; which will ſhew the Origin of the important Matters that we are to write of, at their very Fountain-Head, and enable us to expreſs the Things that follow, in a more eaſy and perſpicuous Style. We ſhall therefore firſt lay down, that the whole Art of Building conſiſts in the Deſign, and in the Structure. The whole Force and Rule of the Deſign, conſiſts in a right and exact adapting and joining together the Lines and Angles which compoſe and form the Face of the Building. It is the Property and Buſineſs of the Deſign to appoint to the Edifice and all its Parts their proper Places, determinate Number, juſt Proportion and beautiful Order; ſo that the whole Form of the Structure be proportionable. Nor has this Deſign any thing that makes it in its Nature inſeparable from Matter; for we ſee that the ſame Deſign is in a Multitude of Buildings, which have all the ſame Form, and are exactly alike as to the Situation of their Parts and the Diſpoſition of their Lines and Angles; and we can in our Thought and Imagination contrive perfect Forms of Buildings entirely ſeparate from Matter, by ſettling and regulating in a certain Order, the Diſpoſition and Conjunction of the Lines and Angles. Which being

B   granted,

granted, we shall call the Design a firm and graceful pre-ordering of the Lines and Angles, conceived in the Mind, and contrived by an ingenious Artist. But if we would enquire what a Building is in its own Nature, together with the Structure thereof, it may not be amiss, to consider from what Beginnings the Habitations of Men, which we call Edifices, took their Rise, and the Progress of their Improvement: Which unless I am mistaken, may be resolved as follows.

CHAP II.

Of the first Occasion of erecting Edifices; of how many Parts the Art of Building consists, and what is necessary to each of those Parts.

IN the Beginning Men looked out for Settlements in some secure Country; and having found a convenient Spot suitable to their Occasions, they there made themselves a Habitation so contrived, that private and publick Matters might not be confounded together in the same Place; but that they might have one Part for Sleep, another for their Kitchen, and others for their other necessary Uses. They then began to think of a Covering to defend them from Sun and Rain; and in order thereto, they erected Walls to place this Covering upon. By this means they knew they should be the more compleatly sheltered from piercing Colds, and stormy Winds. Lastly, in the Sides of the Walls, from Top to Bottom, they opened Passages and Windows, for going in and out, and letting in Light and Air, and for the Conveniency of discharging any Wet, or any gross Vapours, which might chance to get into the House. And whosoever it was, whether the Goddess *Vesta*, Daughter of *Saturn*, or *Euryalus* and *Hyperbius*, the two Brothers, or *Gellio*, or *Thraso*, or the Cyclop *Typhinchius*, that first contrived these Things: I am persuaded the first Beginnings of them were such as I have described, and that Use and Arts have since improved them to such a Pitch, that the various Kinds of Buildings are become almost infinite: Some are publick, some private, some sacred, some profane, some serve for Use and Necessity, some for the Ornament of our Cities, or the Beauty of our Temples: But no body will therefore deny, that they were all derived from the Principles abovementioned: Which being so, it is evident, that the whole Art of Building consists in six Things, which are these: The Region, the Seat or Platform, the Compartition, the Walling, the Covering and the Apertures; and if these Principles are first thoroughly conceived, that which is to follow will the more easily be understood. We shall therefore define them thus, the Region with us shall be the whole large open Place in which we are to build, and of which the Seat or Platform shall be only a Part: But the Platform shall be a determined Spot of the Region, circumscribed by Walls for Use and Service. But under the Title of Platform, we shall likewise include all those Spaces of the Buildings, which in walking we tread upon with our Feet. The Compartition is that which sub-divides the whole Platform of the House into smaller Platforms, so that the whole Edifice thus formed and constituted of these its Members, seems to be full of lesser Edifices: By Walling we shall understand all that Structure, which is carried up from the Ground to the Top to support the Weight of the Roof, and such also as is raised on the Inside of the Building, to separate the Apartments; Covering we shall call not only that Part, which is laid over the Top of the Edifice to receive the Rain, but any Part too which is extended in length and breadth over the Heads of those within; which includes all Ceilings, half-arched Roofs, Vaults, and the like. Apertures are all those Outlets, which are in any Part of the Building, for the Convenience of Egress and Regress, or the Passage of Things necessary for the Inmates. Of these therefore we shall treat, and of all the Parts of each, having first premised some Things, which whether they are Principles, or necessary Concomitants of the Principles of this Work which we have undertaken, are certainly very much to our Purpose: For having considered, whether there was any Thing that might concern any of those Parts which we have enumerated; we found three Things by no means to be neglected, which relate particularly to the Covering, the Walling, and the like; Namely, that each of them be adapted to some certain and determinate Conveniency, and above all, be wholesome.

That

That they be firm, solid, durable, in a Manner eternal, as to Stability: And as to Gracefulness and Beauty, delicately and justly adorned, and set off in all their Parts. Having laid down these Principles as the Foundations of what we are to write, we proceed to our Subject.

CHAP. III.

Of the Region, of the Climate or Air, of the Sun and Winds, which affect the Air.

THE Ancients used the utmost Caution to fix upon a Region that had in it nothing noxious, and was furnished with all Conveniences; and especially they took particular Care that the Air was not unwholesome or intemperate; in which they shewed a great Deal of Prudence; for they knew that if the Earth or Water had any Defect in them, Art and Industry might correct it; but they affirmed, that neither Contrivance nor Multitude of Hands was able sufficiently to correct and amend the Air. And it must be allowed, that, as what we breathe is so conducive to the Nourishment and Support of Life, the purer it is, the more it must preserve and maintain our Health. Besides, how great an Influence the Air has in the Generation, Production, Aliment, and Preservation of Things, is unknown to nobody. It is even observed, that they who draw a pure Air, have better Understandings than those who breathe a heavy moist one: Which is supposed to be the Reason that the *Athenians* had much sharper Wits than the *Thebans*. We know that the Air, according to the different Situation and Position of Places, affects us sometimes in one Manner, and sometimes in another. Some of the Causes of this Variety we imagine we understand; others by the Obscurity of their Natures are altogether hidden and unknown to us. We shall first speak of the manifest Causes, and consider afterwards of the more occult; that we may know how to chuse a Region commodious and healthful. The Ancient Theologists called the Air *Pallas*. *Homer* makes her a Goddess, and names her *Glaucopis*, which signifies an Air naturally clear and transparent. And it is certain, that Air is the most healthy, which is the most purged and purified, and which may most easily be pierced by the Sight; the clearest and lightest, and the least Subject to Variations. And on the contrary we affirm the Air to be pestiferous, where there is a continued Collection of thick Clouds and stinking Vapours, and which always hangs like a great Weight upon the Eyes, and obstructs the Sight. The Occasion of this Difference proceeds from several Causes, but chiefly I take it, from the Sun and Winds. But we are not here to spend Time in these physical Enquiries, how the Vapours by the Power of the Sun are raised from the most profound and hidden Parts of the Earth, and drawn up to the Sky, where gathering themselves together in vast Bodies in the immense Spaces of the Air, either by their own huge Weight, or by receiving the Rays of the Sun upon their rarified Parts, they fall and thereby press upon the Air and occasion the Winds; and being afterwards carried to the Ocean by their Drought, they plunge, and having bathed and impregnated themselves with Moisture from the Sea, they once more ascend through the Air, where being pressed by the Winds, and as it were squeezed like a Sponge, they discharge their Burthen of Water in Rains, which again create new Vapours. Whether these Conjectures be true, or whether the Wind be occasioned by a dry Fumosity of the Earth, or a hot Evaporation stirred by the Pressure of the Cold; or that it be, as we may call it, the Breath of the Air; or nothing but the Air itself put into Agitation by the Motion of the World, or by the Course and Radiation of the Stars; or by the generating Spirit of all Things in its own Nature active, or something else not of a separate Existence, but consisting in the Air itself acted upon and inflamed by the Heat of the higher Air; or whatever other Opinion or Way of accounting for these Things be truer or more ancient, I shall pass it over as not making to my Purpose. However, unless I am mistaken, we may conceive from what has been laid already, why some Countries in the World enjoy a pleasant chearful Air, while others, close adjoyning to them, and as it were laid by Nature in the same Lap, are stupified and afflicted with a heavy and dismal Climate. For I suppose, that this happens from no other Cause, but their being ill disposed for the Operation of the Sun and Winds. *Cicero* tells us, that *Syracuse* was so placed, that the Inhabitants never missed seeing the Sun every Day in the Year; a Situation very seldom to be met with

with, but when Neceſſity or Opportunity will allow of it to be deſired above all Things. That Region therefore is to be choſen, which is moſt free from the Power of Clouds and all other heavy thick Vapours. Thoſe who apply themſelves to theſe Enquiries have obſerved, that the Rays and Heat of the Sun act with more Violence upon cloſe denſe Bodies, than upon thoſe of a looſer Contexture, upon Oil more than Water, Iron more than Wool ; for which Reaſon they ſay the Air is moſt groſs and heavy in thoſe Places, which are moſt ſubject to great Heats. The *Ægyptians* contending for Nobility with all the other Nations in the World, boaſted, that the firſt Men were created in their Country, becauſe no Place was ſo fit to plant the firſt Race of Men in, as there, where they might live the moſt healthily ; and that they were bleſſed by the Gods with a Kind of perpetual Spring, and a conſtant unchangeable Diſpoſition of Air above all the Reſt of the Word. And *Herodotus* writes, that among the *Ægyptians*, thoſe chiefly who lived towards *Libia*, are the moſt healthy, becauſe they enjoy continual gentle Breezes. And to me the Reaſon why ſome Cities, both in *Italy* and in other Parts of the World, are perpetually unhealthy and peſtilential, ſeems plainly to be the ſudden Turns and Changes in the Air, from Hot to Cold, and from Cold to Hot. So that it very much concerns us to be extremely careful in our Obſervation, what and how much Sun the Region we pitch upon is expoſed to ; that there be neither more Sun nor more Shade than is neceſſary. The *Garamantes* curſe the Sun, both at it's Riſing and it's Setting, becauſe they are ſcorched with the long Continuation of it's Beams. Other Nations look pale and wan, by living in a Kind of perpetual Night. And theſe Things happen not ſo much, becauſe ſuch Places have the Pole more depreſſed or oblique, tho' there is a great deal in that too, as becauſe they are aptly ſituated for receiving the Sun and Winds, or are skreened from them, I ſhould chuſe ſoft Breezes before Winds, but even Winds, though violent and bluſtering, before a Calm, motionleſs, and conſequently, a heavy Air. Water, ſays *Ovid*, corrupts, if not moved : And it is certain the Air, to uſe ſuch an Expreſſion, wonderfully exhilerated by Motion : For I am perſuaded, that thereby the Vapours which riſe from the Earth are either diſſipated, or elſe growing warm by Action are

concocted as they ſhould be. But then I would have theſe Winds come to me, broken by the Oppoſition of Hills and Woods, or tired with a long Journey. I would take heed that they did not bring any ill Qualities along with them, gathered from any Places they paſſed through. And for this Reaſon we ſhould be careful to avoid all Neighbourhoods from which any noxious Particles may be brought : In the Number of which are all ill Smells, and all groſs Exhalations from Marſhes, and eſpecially from ſtagnating Waters and Ditches. The Naturaliſts lay it down for certain, that all Rivers that uſe to be ſupplied by Snows, bring cold foggy Winds : But no Water is ſo noiſome and pernicious, as that which rots and putrifies for want of Motion. And the Contagion of ſuch a Neighbourhood, will be ſtill more miſchievous, according as it is more or leſs expoſed to unwholeſome Winds : For we are told, that the very Winds themſelves are in their own Natures ſome more wholeſome than others. Thus *Pliny* from *Theophraſtus* and *Hippocrates* informs us, that the *North* is the beſt for reſtoring and preſerving of Health ; and all the Naturaliſts affirm, that the *South* is the moſt noxious of all to Mankind ; nay further, that the very Beaſts may not ſafely be left in the Fields while that Wind blows ; and they have obſerved, that at ſuch Times the Stork never flies, and that the Dolphins in a *North* Wind, if it ſtands fair towards them, can hear any Voice, but in a *South*, they are more ſlow in hearing it, and muſt have it brought to them oppoſite to the Wind. They ſay too, that in a *North* Wind an Eel will live ſix Days out of Water, but not ſo in a *South*, ſuch is the Groſſneſs and unwholeſome Property of that Wind ; and that as the *South* Wind brings Catarrhs and Rheums, ſo the *North-Weſt* is apt to give Coughs. They likewiſe find Fault with the Neighbourhood of the *Mediterranean*, upon this Account chiefly, becauſe they ſuppoſe, that a Place expoſed to the Reflection of the Sun's Rays, does in effect ſuffer two Suns, one ſcorching them from the Heavens, and the other from the Water ; and ſuch Places upon the Setting of the Sun feel the greateſt and moſt ſenſible Alterations in the Air when the cold Shadows of Night come on. And there are ſome who think, that the *Weſtern* Reverberations or Reflections of the Sun, either from the Sea or any other Water, or from the Mountains, moleſt us moſt

of

of all: Becaufe they double the Heat of a Place already fufficiently warmed by whole Day's Sun. And if it happens, that with all this Sun the heavy grofs Winds have free Accefs to you, what can be more annoying or intollerable? The early Morning Breezes too, which bring the Vapours crude juft as they are raifed, are certainly to be avoided. Thus we have briefly fpoken of the Sun and Winds, by which the Air is altered and made healthy and noxious, as much as we thought neceffary here: And in their Places we fhall difcourfe of them more diftinctly.

C H A P. IV.

Which Region is, and which is not commodious for Building.

IN chufing the Region it will be proper to have it fuch, that the Inhabitants may find it convenient in all Refpects, both as to its natural Properties, and as to the Neighbourhood and its Correfpondence with the reft of Mankind. For certainly I would never build a City upon a fteep inacceffible Cliff of the *Alps*, as *Caligula* intended; unlefs obliged by the utmoft Extremity: Nor in a folitary Defart, as *Varro* defcribes that Part of *France* to have been which was beyond the *Rhine*, and as *Cæfar* paints *England* in his Days. Neither fhould I be pleafed to live, as in *Ægina*, only upon the Eggs of Birds, or upon Acorns, as they did in fome Parts of *Spain* in *Pliny*'s Time. I would if poffible have nothing be wanting that could be of Ufe in Life. For this Reafon, more than any other, *Alexander* was perfectly in the right in not building a City upon Mount *Athos* (though the Invention and Defign of the Architect *Policrates* muft needs have been wonderful) becaufe the Inhabitants could never have been well fupplied with Conveniences. *Ariftotle* was indeed beft pleafed with a Region that was difficult of Accefs, and efpecially to build a City in: And we find there have been fome Nations, which have chofe to have their Confines quite ftript and laid into a Defart for a great Way together, only in order to diftrefs their Enemies. Whether this Method is to be approved or blamed, we fhall examine in another Place. If it is of Service in a publick Regard, I cannot find Fault with it: But for the Situation of other Buildings, I fhould much rather chufe a Region that had many and different Ways of Accefs, for the eafy bringing in all Manner of Neceffaries, both by Land-Carriage and Water-Carriage, as well in Winter as in Summer. The Region itfelf likewife fhould neither be too moift through too great abundance of Water, nor too much parched with Drought, but be kindly and temperate. And if we cannot find one exactly in all Refpects as we would have it, let us chufe it rather fomewhat cold and dry, than warm and moift: For our Houfes, our Cloaths, Fires, and Exercife, will eafily overcome the Cold; neither is it believed, that the Drynefs of a Soil can have any thing in it very noxious, either to the Bodies or Mind, only that by Drynefs Men's Bodies are hardened, and by Cold perhaps made fomewhat rougher: But it is held for certain, that all Bodies corrupt with too much Humidity, and are relaxed by Heat. And we find that Men either in cold Weather, or that live in cold Places, are more healthy and lefs fubject to Diftempers; though it is allowed, that in hot Climates Men have better Wits, as they have better Conftitutions in cold. I have read in *Appian* the Hiftorian, that the *Numidians* are very long lived, becaufe their Winters are never too cold. That Region therefore will be far the beft, which is juft moderately warm and moift, becaufe that will produce lufty handfome Men, and not fubject to Melancholy. Secondly, that Region will be moft eligible, which being placed among Countries liable to Snow, enjoys more Sun than its Neighbours; and among Countries burnt by the Sun, that which has moft Humidity and Shade. But no Building, let it be what it will, can be placed more unfightly or inconveniently, than in a Valley down between two Hills; becaufe, not to infift upon more manifeft Reafons, an Edifice fo placed has no Manner of Dignity, lying quite hid; and it's Profpect being interrupted can have neither Pleafure nor Beauty. But what is this to thofe greater Mifchiefs which will fhortly happen, when the Houfe is overwhelmed by Floods and filled with Waters that pour in upon it from the adjoining Hills; and imbibing continual Wet, rots and decays, and always exhales Vapours extreamly noxious to the Health of its Inhabitants. In such a Place, the Understanding can never be clear, the Spirits being damps and stupified; nor will any Kind of Bodies endure long. The Books will grow mouldy and rot; the Arms will rust, nothing in the Storehouse will keep, and in short, the Excess of Moisture will spoil and destroy every Thing. If the Sun shines in, you will be scorched insufferably by the frequent Reflection of his Rays, which will be beat back upon you from every Side, and if it does not, you will be dried and withered by the continual Shade. Add to this, that if the Winds gets in, being confined as it were in a Channel, it will rage there with greater Fury than in other Places; and if it never enters, the Air for want of Motion will grow thick and muddy; such a Valley may not improperly be called a Puddle, or Bog of Air. The Form of the Place therefore in which we intend to build, ought to be graceful and pleasant, not mean and low, as if it were buried below the rest of the Earth, but lofty, and as it were a Hawk to look clear round about, and constantly refreshed on every Side with delightful Breezes. Besides this, let there be Plenty of every Thing necessary, either to the Convenience or Pleasure of Life, as Water, Fire and Provisions: But Care must be taken, that there is nothing in any of these Things prejudicial to the Health. The Springs must be opened and tasted, and the Water tried by Fire, that there be no Mixture in it of mucous, viscous or crude Particles, that may affect the Constitutions of the Inhabitants. I omit the ill Effects that often proceed from Water, as breeding Wens in the Throat, and giving the Stone; as likewise those other more wonderful Effects of Water, which *Vitruvius* the Architect has learnedly and elegantly summed up. It is the Opinion of the Physician *Hipocrates*, that they who drink Water not well purged, but heavy and ill-tasted, grow Cholicky, and to have large swelled Bellies, while the rest of their Members, their Arms, their Shoulders and their Faces become thin and extenuated. Add to this, that though the Fault of the Spleen ill digesting of the Blood, they fall into several Kinds of Distempers, some even pestilential. In Summer, Fluxes of the Belly by the stirring of the Choler, and the dissolving of the Humours waste all their Strength; and all the Year round they are continually liable to heavy

and tedious Infirmities, such as the Dropsy, Asthma and Pleurify. The young lose their Senses by melancholy Bile; the old are burnt by the Inflammation of the Humours; the Women with Difficulty conceive, and with more Difficulty bring forth: In a Word, every Age and every Sex will fall by early and untimely Deaths, destroyed and worn away by Diseases; nor will they enjoy a single Day while they live, without being tormented with Melancholy or black Humours, and fretted with Spleen and Vapours; so that their Minds will never be free from Vexation and Uneasiness. Many other Things might be said of Water, which have been observed by the ancient Historians, very curious and remarkable, and of extream Efficacy to the Health of Mankind; but they are uncommon, and might seem rather intended to make a Shew of Knowledge than for actual Use; besides that we shall speak more copiously of Waters in their proper Place. Thus much certainly is not to be neglected, and is most manifest, namely, that Water gives Nourishment to all Plants, Seeds, and every Thing else that has the vegetative Life, with the Plenty of whose Fruits Men are refreshed and supported. If all this be granted, certainly we ought very carefully to examine what Veins of Water the Country is furnished with, in which we intend to dwell. *Diodorus* tells us, that the *Indians* are generally lusty strong Men, and very sharp witted, which he imputes to their having a wholesome Air and good Water. Now that Water we conceive to be the best tasted which has no Taste, and that is best coloured which has no Colour at all. It is agreed, that the best Water is clear, transparent and light, such as being poured upon a white Cloth leaves no Stain; and upon boiling has no Sediment, and which does not cover the Bed it flows in with Moss or Slime, nor especially the Stones which it runs over. A further Proof of the Goodness of Water is, when boiling any Kind of Pulse in it makes them tender, and when it makes good Bread. Neither should we be less careful to examine and note, whether the Region ingenders nothing pestiferous or venemous, that the Inhabitants may be in no Danger. I pass over some Things, which are recorded by the Ancients, to wit, that in *Colchos* there distills from the Leaves of the Trees a Honey, which whosoever tastes falls senseless, and for a whole Day seems to be dead: As also what is said to have happened in *Antony*'s Army, occasioned by

certain

certain Herbs, which the Soldiers eating for want of Bread, grew besotted, and employed themselves in nothing but digging Stones out of the Ground, till their Choler being stirred they fell down dead ; nor was any Remedy found against this Plague, as we are informed by *Plutarch*, but drinking of Wine; these Things are commonly known. But good Heavens! what shall we say to what has happened in our own Days in *Apulia* in *Italy* ; what incredible Effects of Poison have we seen there! the Bite of a small Earth Spider, commonly called a *Tarantula*, throwing Men into various Kinds of Madness, and even Fury ; a Thing strange to be told. No Swelling, no livid Spot appearing in any Part of the Body from the sharp Bite or Sting of the venomous Beast; but suddenly losing their Senses, they fall piteously to bewail themselves, and if no Assistance is given them they die. They cure this Distemper with *Theophrastus*'s Remedy, who says, that Persons bit by Vipers used to be cured by the Sound of Pipes. The Musi-

cians therefore with different Kinds of Harmony try to asswage the Pain, and when they hit upon the Kind proper to the Patient, immediately, as if he were suddenly awakened, he starts up, and transported with Joy, falls to bestirring himself to the Musick with all his Strength, in whatever his Fancy prompts him to. Some that are thus bit, you shall see exercise themselves in Dancing, others in Singing, and others stirring in other Motions, just as their Inclination or Madness guides them, till through mere Weariness they are forced to give over. And thus without giving themselves the least Rest, they will sweat themselves for some Days, and so recover their Health merely by their Madness having quite spent itself. We read too of something like this that happened among the *Albanians*, who fought against *Pompey* with such a Power of Horse ; that there was a Sort of Cobweb among them, which whoever touched surely died, some Laughing, and others on the contrary Weeping.

CHAP. V.

By what Marks and Characters we are to know the Goodness of the Region.

NOR are those Things alone sufficient for the chusing of the Region, which are obvious and manifest of themselves; but we must weigh every Circumstance, and consider the most occult Tokens. Thus it will be a good Sign of an excellent Air and of good Water, if the Country produces Plenty of good Fruits, if it fosters a good Number of Men of a good old Age, if it abounds with lusty handsome Youth, if the People are fruitful, and if the Births are natural and never monstrous. I have myself seen some Cities, which out of Respect to the Times I forbear to name, where there is scarce a Woman, but what sees herself at the same Instant, the Mother both of a Man and of a Monster. Another City I know in *Italy*, where there are so many People Humpbacked, Squint-eyed, Crooked and Lame, that there is scarce a Family, but what has Somebody in it defective or distorted. And certainly, where we see such frequent and great Inequalities of Body to Body, and Member to Member; we may well conclude, that it proceeds from some Defect in the Climate or Air, or from some more hidden Cause of the Corruption of Nature. Nor is it foreign to our

Purpose what has been observed, that in a gross Air we are more inclined to Hunger, and in a thin One to Thirst: and we may not improbably draw some Conjectures from the Shape and Looks of other Animals, what Constitutions the Men will have in the same Place ; for if the Cattle look lively, fat and large, you may not unreasonably hope to have Children that will be so too. Neither will it be amiss to gather Notice of the Air and Winds, even from other Bodies not endued with animal Life; thus if the Walls of the neighbouring Buildings are grown rusty and rugged, it shews that some malignant Influence has Power there. The Trees too bending all one Way, as if by general Consent, shew that they have suffered the Force of high rough Winds ; and the very Stones, whether growing in their native Seats, or placed in Buildings, if their Tops are any thing considerably rotted, shew the Intemperature of the Air, sometimes too hot and sometimes over cold. A Region so exposed to the furious Assaults of Tempests is to be avoided, as the very worst of all ; for if the Bodies of Men are seized with too excessive Cold or Heat, the whole Frame and Contexture

ture of all the Parts is presently broken and diffolved, and falls into dangerous Diftempers and immature old Age. A City ftanding at the Foot of a Hill, and looking towards the fetting Sun, is accounted unhealthy, more for this Reafon than any other, that it feels too fuddenly the cold chilling Breezes of the Night. It may likewife be convenient by looking back into Times paft, according to the Obfervations of the Wife, to examine into Properties yet more hidden, if there be fuch in the Place: For there are Countries which have in their Nature fome Secret undifcovered Qualities, which confer Happinefs or Unhappinefs. *Locris* and *Crotona* are faid to have never been infected with any Plague. In the Ifle of *Candia* there is no mifchievous Creature. In *France* very few Monfters are born; in other Places, the Naturalifts fay, that in the Middle either of Summer or Winter it never Thunders: But in *Campania*, according to *Pliny*, it Thunders at thofe very Times over thofe Cities that ftand to the South; and the Mountains near *Albania* are faid to be called *Ceraunia*, from the frequent Lightnings that fall upon it. The Ifle of *Lemnos* too being very fubject to Lightning, was the Reafon, *Servius* informs us, of the Poets feigning that *Vulcan* fell there from Heaven. About the Streights of *Gallipoli* and the *Effedones*, it was never known either to Thunder or Lighten. If it Rains in *Ægypt* it is reckoned a Prodigy. Near the *Hydafpes* in the Beginning of Summer it Rains continually. They fay that in *Lybia* the Air is fo feldom ftirred by Winds, that it grows fo thick, that feveral Kinds of Vapours are vifible in the Sky: And on the Contrary, in moft Parts of *Galatia*, the Winds blow in Summer with fo much Violence, that it drives along the very Stones

like Sand. In *Spain* near the *Ebro*, they fay the North-Weft Wind blows fo hard, that it overturns Carts heavy laden. In *Æthiopia* we are told the South never blows, and Hiftorians write, that this Wind in *Arabia* and the Country of the *Troglodites* burns up every Thing that is green: And *Thucydides* affirms, that *Delos* was never troubled with Earthquakes, but always ftood firm upon the fame Rock, though the other Iflands all about it were often laid in Ruins by Earthquakes. We ourfelves fee, that the Part of *Italy*, which runs from the *Selva dell' Aglio* below *Rome*, all along the Ridge of Hills of the *Campagna di Roma* quite to *Capua*, is perpetually ftript and almoft quite laid wafte by Earthquakes. Some believe *Achaia* was fo called from its frequent Inundations of Water. I find that *Rome* was always fubject to Agues, and *Galen* takes thofe Agues to be a new Kind of double Tertian, which muft have various and almoft direct Remedies applied to it at different Seafons. It is an old Fable among the Poets, that *Typho* the Giant being buried in the Ifland of *Prochyta*, often turns himfelf about, and with his turning fhakes the whole Ifland from its very Foundation. The Reafon of this Fiction of the Poets was, becaufe that Ifland was fo tormented with Earthquakes and Eruptions, that the *Erythreans* and *Chalcidians*, who inhabited it, were forced to fly for it. And again, afterwards thofe who were fent by *Hiero* of *Syracufe* to build a new City there, frightened with the continual Danger of Deftruction, deferted it too. Wherefore all Things of this Nature are to be fifted out from long Obfervation, and examined and compared by other Places, in order to come at a clear and full Knowledge of every Particular. 23

C H A P. VI.

Of fome more hidden Conveniencies and Inconveniencies of the Region which a wife Man ought to enquire into.

WE ought further to enquire carefully, whether the Region is ufed to be molefted with any more hidden Inconveniency. *Plato* believed, that in fome Places the Influence of Spirits often reigned, and was at fometimes mifchievous, and at others propitious to the Inhabitants. It is certain there are fome Places where Men are very fubject to run mad,

others where they are eafily difpofed to do themfelves a Mifchief, and where they put an End to their own Lives by Halters or Precipices, Steel or Poifon. It is therefore very neceffary to examine by the moft occult Traces of Nature, every Thing that can be attended with fuch Effects. It was an ancient Cuftom brought down even from *Demetrius's* Time, 24

not

not only in laying the Foundations of Cities and Towns, but also in marking out Camps for the Armies, to inspect the Entrails of the Beast that grazed upon the Place, and to observe both their Condition and Colour. In which if they chanced to find any Defect, they avoided that Place as unhealthy. *Varro* informs us of his own Knowledge, that in some Places the Air was full of minute Animalcules as small as Atoms, which being received together with the Breath into the Lungs, fastened upon the Intestines, and gnawing upon them, caused dreadful raging Diseases, and at length Plagues and Death. Nor ought we to forget that there are some Places, which, though in their own Nature, they are subject to no Inconvenience or Mischief whatsoever, yet are so situated, that by the Arrival of Foreigners they will often be infected with pestilential Distempers. And this shall happen, not only by Means of Armies of Enemies endeavouring to do you all the Mischief they can, as befals those Nations which are exposed to inhuman Barbarians; but by a friendly Reception and Entertainment of them you shall expose yourself to extreme Calamities. Others by having Neighbours desirous of Innovations, have by their Broils and Destruction fallen into great Dangers themselves. *Pera* a City upon the *Pontus*, a Colony of the *Genoese*, is continually afflicted with the Plague, by their giving daily Admission to Slaves, both infirm in Mind, and almost quite rotten and worn away with mere Filth and Nastiness. Some likewise will have it, that it is the Part of a prudent and wise Man to enquire by Augury and the Observation of the Heavens, what Fortune he shall have in such a Place. Which Arts, provided they are not incompatiable with our Religion, I own I do not despise. Who can deny that what they call Fortune, whatever she be, has a very great Power over human Affairs? Can we venture to affirm, that the publick Fortune of *Rome* had not a great Share in the Enlargement of the Empire? The City of *Iolaus* in *Sardinia*, built by a Grandson of *Hercules*, though often attacked both by the *Carthaginians* and the *Ro-*

mans, yet as *Diodorus* writes, always preserved its Liberty. Can we suppose that the Temple at *Delphos*, first burnt by *Flegias*, should afterwards in *Sylla*'s Time be consumed by Fire, the third Time, without the particular ill Fortune of that Place? What shall we say of the Capitol? How often has that been in Flames? The City of the *Sybarites*, after repeated Calamities, often deserted and often restored, at length quite ruined, was utterly abandoned; nay, those who fled from it were pursued by ill Fortune, nor could they, by removing their Dwellings and leaving the ancient Name of their City, ever save themselves from Misery and Destruction: For new Inhabitants coming in upon them, all their most ancient and principal Families, their sacred Edifices and their whole City, were utterly laid waste and destroyed with Fire and Sword. But we need not dwell upon these Things which Historians are full of. Our whole Design is to shew, that it is the Part of a wise Man to do every thing which may make him secure, that the Trouble and Expence of his Building shall not be in vain, and that his Work itself may be permanent. And certainly to omit no Precaution which may effect so great a Design, is the Business of every prudent Man. Or will you say, that it is not of the utmost Importance both to you and yours to execute an Undertaking, that brings with it Health, Dignity and Pleasure, and recommends your Name with Reputation to Posterity? Here you are to apply yourselves to your Studies, here you are to breed your dear Children and live with your Family, here you are to spend your Days both of Labour and Rest, here all the Schemes of your whole Life are to be executed; so that I do not think any Thing in the World can be named, except Virtue, which can deserve more Care and Application, than to fix a good and convenient Habitation for yourself and Family. And who can be sure of having such a one, who despises the Precautions before-mentioned? but of these enough. Come we now to the Seat or Platform.

CHAP. VII.

Of the Seat or Platform, and of the several Sorts of Lines.

IN chusing the Platform, we ought to observe all the same Rules that we have laid down about the Region; for as the Region is a determinate and select Part of the whole

Country, fo the Platform is a certain determinate Part of the Region taken up by the Building; and for this Reafon, any Thing that may annoy or be of Service to the Region, may do the fame to the Platform. But though this be fo, yet our Difcuffion and Confiderations here will offer us fome Precepts, which feem particularly to regard the Platform only; and fome again which do not feem fo properly to belong to the Seat as in a great Meafure to the Region; which are thefe. It is neceffary to confider what Work we are taking in Hand, publick or private, facred or profane, and fo of the Reft, which we fhall treat of diftinctly in their proper Places. For one Situation and one Space is to be allotted to an Exchange, another to a Theatre, another to a *Palæftra*, or Place of Exercife, and another to a Temple; fo that we muft have regard to the Quality and Ufe of every Edifice in the Determining of its Situation and Form. But to proceed here only in a general Difcuffion of thefe Things as we began, we fhall touch only upon thofe Points which we judge neceffary: Firft faying fomething of Lines, which may be of Service for underftanding what follows. For being to treat of the Defign of the Platform, it will not be inconvenient to explain thofe Things firft whereof that Defign confifts. Every Defign therefore is compofed of Lines and Angles; the Lines are that extreme Defign which includes the whole Space of the Platform. That Part of the Superficies of this Defign, which is contained between two Lines touching at fome certain Point, is called an Angle. The Interfection therefore or croffing of two Lines over each other form four Angles. If each of thefe Angles be equal to all and each of the other three, they are called right Angles; if they are lefs, they are called acute, and the greater obtufe. Of Lines too fome are ftrait

and others curve; of involved winding Lines it is not neceffary to fpeak here. The ftrait Line is a Line drawn from one Point to another, the fhorteft Way that poffibly can be. The curve Line is Part of a Circle; a Circle is a Draught made from one of two Points, and turned upon the fame Superficies in fuch a Manner, that in its whole Circumference it is never nearer nor farther from that immoveable Point the Centre, than it was at the firft Turn. But to this it is neceffary to add, that the curve Line, which was faid to be Part of the Circle, among us Architects, for its Similitude, is called an Arch. And the ftrait Line, which is drawn from the two extreme Points of the curve Line, for the fame Reafon is called a Chord. And that Line, which goes from the middle Point of the Chord up to the Arch, leaving equal Angles on each Side, is called the *Sagitta*. And that which is carried from the fixed immoveable Point within the Circle to the curve Line of the Circle, is called the *Radius*. And that immoveable Point in the Middle is called the Centre. And the Line which paffes through the Centre and touches both Sides of the Circumference, is called the Diameter. Arches too are different, for fome are entire, fome are imperfect, and fome are compofite. The entire is that which is the full Half of a Circle, or that whofe Chord is the Diameter of the whole Circle. The Imperfect is that whofe Chord is lefs than a Diameter, fo that this imperfect Arch is Part of a Semi-circle. The compofite Arch is formed of two imperfect Arches, and fo the joyning of thofe two Arches, interfecting each other, makes an Angle at Top, which never happens either in the entire or imperfect Arch. Thefe Things being premifed, we proceed as follows.

25

C H A P. VIII.

Of the Kinds of Platforms, their Forms and Figures, and which are the moft serviceable and lasting.

OF Platforms, fome are angular and others circular; of the angular, fome confift all of right Lines, and fome of right Lines and curve mixed together. But I do not remember among the Buildings of the Ancients to have met with any angular Defign, compofed of feveral curve Lines, without any Mixture of ftrait Lines at all: But in this we fhould have regard to thofe Things, which being wanting in all Parts of the Structure, are greatly blamed; and which, where they are, make the Edifice handfome and convenient.

It

It is that the Angles, the Lines and all the Parts have a certain Variety, but not too much nor too little of it, but so ordered both for Use and Beauty, that the entire Parts may answer to the entire, and like Parts to like. Right Angles are very convenient; the Acute are never used even in mean inconsiderable Platforms, unless upon absolute Necessity, or the Constraint of the Nature and Manner of the Situation, or to make some other Part of the Platform more graceful. The obtuse Angles, have been thought very convenient, but it has always been observed as a Rule never to place them any where in unequal Numbers. The circular Platform is esteemed to be the most capacious of all, and the least expensive to enclose either with Wall or Rampart. The nearest to this is said to be that which has several Sides, but then they must be all alike and answerable to each other, and equal throughout the whole Platform. But those are commended most of all, which are most convenient for raising the Wall to the just Heighth of the Work, as are those which have six and eight Sides. I have seen a Platform of ten Angles very commodious and majestick. You may make them very well of twelve, nay, sixteen Angles. I myself have seen one of twenty-four; but these are very rare. The Side Lines ought to be so ordered, that those which are opposite may be equal to them, nor should we ever in any Work apply a long Line to correspond to a short one; but let there be a just and reasonable Proportion, according to the Degree of the Thing, among all the Parts. We would have the Angles set towards that Side, which either any Weight of Earth, or the Violence and Assaults of Waters or Winds may threaten and endanger; to the Intent that the Force and Shock that beats upon the Edifice may be broken and split into several Parts, resisting the Attack (to use such an Expression) with the stout Corner of the Wall, and not with one of the weak Sides. But if the other Lineaments of the Structure hinder you from disposing of such an Angle in such a Part as you could desire, at least make use of a curve Line; that being a Part of a Circle, and the Circle itself according to the Philosophers being all Angles. Further, the Seat must be either upon a Plain, or on the Side or Top of a Hill; if it is on a Plain, it is necessary to raise the Earth and make something of an Eminence; for besides that, such a Situation in a Plain adds much of Dignity, if you neglect to do it, you will find very great Inconveniences. For the overflowing of Rivers and Rains generally leaves Mud upon level Grounds, which by degrees raises the Earth higher and higher, which still increases, if through Negligence the Rubbish and Dirt, which gathers every Day be not removed. *Frontinus* the Architect used to say, that several Hills were risen in *Rome* in his Time by the continual Fires. But we in our Days see it in a Manner quite buried under Ground with Filth and Rubbish. In the Dutchy of *Spoletto*, I have seen a small ancient Temple, which at first was built in a Plain, that is now almost wholly buried by the raising of the Earth; that Plain reaching to the Foot of the Hills. But why should I mention Buildings that stand under Mountains? That noble Temple by the Wall of *Ravenna*, which has for its Covering a Cup of Stone of one single Piece, though it be near the Sea and far enough from the Hills, is above a fourth Part sunk in the Earth, through the Injury of Time. But how high this Eminence ought to be raised for each Platform, shall be shewn in due Time, when we come to treat of that Subject more particularly, and not summarily as we do here. It is certain every Situation should be made strong, either by Nature or Art. And therefore it is not amiss to follow their Method, who advise first to try the Goodness of the Earth by digging in several Places at some Distance the one from the other, whether it be firm or loose, or soft, fit or unfit to bear the Weight of the Wall. For if it stands upon a Descent, we must have a Care that the upper Part does not lie too heavy and break down the lower; or that the lower Part, if any Accident should shake it, does not pull the upper down along with it. I would have this Part of the Building, which is intended to be the Basis of all the Rest, particularly strong and tightly knit together in all its Parts. If the Seat be upon the Summit of an Hill, either it should be raised where it is not even, or else be made level by plaining away the Top. But here we are to consider, that we should always chuse that Way (though still with a due Regard to the Dignity of the Work) which is least troublesome and expensive. Perhaps it may be proper to pare away some of the Top of the Hill, and enlarge and add to the Sides. For which Reason that Architect, whoever he was, shewed a great deal of Contrivance, that built *Alatro*, a Town of the *Campagna di Roma*, seated upon a Rocky Hill; for he so ordered it, it, that the Foundations of the Citadel or Temple (whatever it was) which are all that now remain, the Superstructure being quite demolished, should be supported and fortified beneath by the Pieces of Stone cut off in plaining the Top of the Rock. And there is another Thing in that Work that I am extremely pleased with; namely, that he set the Angle of the Platform towards that Side on which the Rock has the most precipitate Descent, and fortified that Angle with huge Pieces of the Fragments piled up one upon the other, and contrived by the joyning of the Stones to make the Structure beautiful with a very little Ex-

28 pence. I am likewise very much pleased with the Contrivance of that other Architect, who not having a sufficient Quantity of Stone, in order to keep up the Weight of the Hill, made a Fence of a great Number of Semi-circles, putting the Backs of the Curves within the Hill; which besides that it looked handsome to the Eye, was extremely strong and very cheap; for it makes a Wall, which though not solid, was as firm as if it had been solid, and of the Thickness of the *Sagitta* of those Curves. I like *Vitruvius*'s Method too, which I find was observed by the ancient Architects all over

29 *Rome*, and especially in *Tarquin*'s Wall, of making use of Buttresses; though they did not every where mind to make the Distance between one Buttress and another, to be the same as the Heighth of the Wall; but as the Strength or Weakness of the Hill required it, they placed them sometimes closer and sometimes further off. I have taken Notice too, that the ancient Architects were not contented with making one Slope for their Platform, but raised several like so many Steps, which strengthened and secured the Sides of the Hill quite down to the very Root of it. Nor can I disapprove their Method herein. That Stream at *Perugia*, which runs under Mount *Lucino* and the Hill the Town stands upon, continually undermining and eating away the Root of the Mountain, by degrees brings down all the impending Weight; by which means a great Part of the Town drops and falls to

Ruin. I am mightily pleased with that Number of little Chapels, which are fixed about the *Area* of the great Church in the Vatican; for of these, such as are placed in the Hollows of the Mountains close against the Wall of the Church, are of great Service both as to Strength and Convenience, in supporting the Weight of the Hill, which continually grows heavier and heavier, and in intercepting the Wet, which falls from the Top of the Cliff, and keeping it from getting into the Church; by which means the principal Wall of it keeps dry and sound. And those Chapels, which are placed on the other Side at the lowest Decline of the Hill, serve with their Arches to close the Plain, which is made above, and preventing the Earth from crumbling keeps it from falling in. And I have observed that the Architect, who built the Temple of *Latona* in *Rome*, contrived his 30 Work and his Structure very ingeniously; for he so placed the Angle of the Platform within the impending Hill, that two upright Walls supported the incumbent Weight, and divided and broke the Pressure by setting that Angle against it. But since we have begun to celebrate the Praises of the Ancients that contrived their Buildings prudently, I will not omit one Thing which I recollect, and which is very much to the present Purpose. In the Church of St. *Mark* at *Venice* is a very useful Precaution of the Architect, who having made the Foundation of the Temple very strong, left every here and there a Hole, that if by chance any subterraneous Vapour or Wind should be gathered there, it might easily find a Passage out. To conclude, all the Plains that you make which are to be under any Covering, must be laid exactly level, but those which are to be left open, should have just Slope enough for the Rain to run off; but of this we have said enough, and perhaps more than was requisite in this Place; because most of these Things respect the Walling. But as they happened to fall naturally together, we did not think proper to separate them in our Discourse. It remains that we treat of the Compartition.

CHAP. IX.

Of the Compartition, and of the Origin of Building.

THE whole Force of the Invention and all our Skill and Knowledge in the Art of Building, is required in the Compartition: Because the distinct Parts of the entire Building, and, to use such a Word, the Entireness of each of those Parts, and the Union and Agreement of all the Lines and Angles in the Work, duly ordered for Convenience, Pleasure and Beauty, are disposed and measured out by the Compartition alone: for if a City, according to the Opinion of Philosophers, be no more than a great House, and, on the other Hand, a House be a little City; why may it not be said, that the Members of that House are so many little Houses; such as the Court-yard, the Hall, the Parlour, the Portico, and the like? And what is there in any of these, which, if omitted by Carelessness or Negligence, will not greatly take from the Praise and Dignity of the Work. Great Care and Diligence therefore is to be used in well considering these Things, which so much concern the whole Building; and in so ordering it, that even the most inconsiderable Parts may not be uncomformable to the Rules of Art, and good Contrivance. What has been already said above of the Region and Platform, may be of no small use in doing of this aptly and conveniently; and as the Members of the Body are correspondent to each other, so it is fit that one Part should answer to another in a Building; whence we say, that great Edifices require great Members. Which indeed was so well observed by the Ancients, that they used much larger Bricks, as well as other Materials, about publick and large Buildings, than in private ones. To every Member therefore ought to be allotted its fit Place and proper Situation; not less than Dignity requires, not greater than Conveniency demands; not in an impertinent or indecent Place, but in a Situation so proper to itself, that it could be set no where else more fitly. Nor should the Part of the Structure, that is to be of the greatest Honour, be thrown into a remote Corner; nor that which ought to be the most publick, into a private Hole; nor that which should be most private, be set in too conspicuous a Place. We should besides have re-

gard to the Seasons of the Year, and make a great deal of Difference between hot Places and cold, both in Proportions and Situation. If Rooms for Summer are large and spacious, and those for Winter more compact, it will not be at all amiss; the Summer ones shady and open to the Air, and the Winter ones to the Sun. And here we should provide, that the Inhabitants may not be obliged to pass out of a cold Place into a hot one, without a Medium of temperate Air; or out of a warm one into one exposed to Cold and Winds; because nothing is so prejudicial to human Bodies. And these ought to agree one Member with another to perfect and compose the main Design and Beauty of the whole; that we may not so lay out our whole Study in adorning one Part, as to leave the rest neglected and homely in Comparison of it; but let them bear that Proportion among themselves, that they may appear to be an entire and perfect Body, and not disjointed and unfinished Members. Moreover in the forming of these Members too, we ought to imitate the Modesty of Nature; because in this, as well as in other Cases, the World never commends a Moderation, so much as it blames an extravagant Intemperance in Building. Let the Members therefore be modestly proportioned, and necessary for your Uses. For all Building in general, if you consider it well, owes it's Birth to Necessity, was nursed by Convenience, and embellished by Use; Pleasure was the last Thing consulted in it, which is never truly obtained by Things that are immoderate. Let your Building therefore be such, that it may not want any Members which it has not, and that those which it has, may not in any Respect deserve to be condemned. Nor would I have the Edifice terminated all the Way with even continued Lines void of all manner of Variety; for some please us by their Largeness, others with being little, and others moderate. One Part therefore should be terminated with strait Lines, another with curve, and another again with strait and curve mixed together; provided you observe the Caution I have so often given you, to avoid falling into the Error of Excess, so as to seem

E   to

to have made a Monster with Limbs difproportionable: Variety is without Difpute a very great Beauty in every Thing, when it joins and brings together, in a regular manner, Things different, but proportionable to each other; but it is rather fhocking, if they are unfuitable and incoherent. For as in Mufick, when the Bafe anfwers the Treble, and the Tenor agrees with both, there arifes from that Variety of Sounds an harmonious and wonderful Union of Proportions which delights and enchants our Senfes; fo the like happens in every thing elfe that ftrikes and pleafes our Fancy. Laftly, thefe Things muft be fo executed, as Ufe or Conveniency requires, or according to the approved Practice of Men of Skill; becaufe deviating from eftablifhed Cuftom, generally robs a Thing of its whole Beauty, as conforming to it, is applauded and attended with Succefs. Neverthelefs, tho' other famous Architects feem, by their Practice, to have determined this or that Compartition, whether *Doric,* or *Ionic,* or *Corinthian,* or *Tufcan,* to be the moft convenient of any; yet they do not thereby tie us down to follow them fo clofely, as to tranfcribe their very Defigns into this Work of ours; but only ftir us up by their Inftructions to produce fomething of our own Invention, and to endeavour to acquire equal or greater Praife than they did. But of thefe Things we fhall fpeak more diftinctly in their proper Places, when we come to confider in what manner a City and its Members ought to be difpofed, and every thing neceffary for the Convenience of each.

C H A P. X.

Of the Columns and Walls, and fome Obfervations relating to the Columns.

WE are now to treat fummarily of the Difpofition of the Wall. But here I muft not omit what I have obferved among the Ancients; namely, that they conftantly avoided drawing any of the outer Lines of the Platform quite ftrait, fo as to let any great Length go on without being interrupted by the Concavity of fome curve Line, or the Interfection of fome Angle; and the Reafon why thofe wife Men did this is plain, that the Wall, having, as it were, Props joined to it to reft againft, might be fo much the ftronger. In treating of the Walling, we fhould begin with the moft noble Parts of it. This Place therefore naturally leads us to fpeak of the Columns, and of the Things belonging to them; a Row of Columns being indeed nothing elfe but a Wall open and difcontinued in feveral Places. And having occafion to define a Column, it would not be at all improper to fay, that it is a certain ftrong continued Part of the Wall, carried up perpendicular from the Foundation to the Top, for fupporting the Covering. In the whole Compafs of the Art of Building, you will find nothing, that either for Workmanfhip, Expence or Beauty, deferves to be preferred before the Columns. But thefe Columns having fome Particulars in which they differ from one another; in this Place we fhall fpeak only of their Agreement; becaufe that regards the Genus of them; but as to their Difference, which relates to their Species, we fhall handle it in its proper Place. To begin therefore as we may fay from the Root, every Column has its Foundation; this Foundation being brought up to a Level with the Plane of the *Area,* it was ufual to raife thereupon a kind of little Wall, which we fhall call the Plinth, others perhaps may call it the Dye; upon the Plinth ftood the Bafe, on the Bafe, the Column; and over the Column the Capital; their Proportion was, that from the middle downwards, they were fomewhat bigger, and from thence upwards grew more and more taper, and that the Foot was fomething larger than the Top of all. I make no doubt, that at firft the Column was invented to fupport the Covering. Afterwards Men's Thoughts being ftirred up to worthy Attempts, they ftudied, tho' themfelves were mortal, to make their Buildings in a Manner immortal and eternal; and for this Reafon they made Columns, Architraves, Intablatures, and Coverings all of Marble. And in doing thefe Things, the ancient Architects always kept fo clofe to Nature, as to feem, if poffible, never to have confulted any Thing but mere Convenience in Building, and at the fame Time made it their Care, that their Works fhould be not only ftrong and ufeful, but

but also pleasant to the Sight. Nature at first certainly gave us Columns made of Wood, and of a round Figure, afterwards by Use they came in some Places to be cut square. Thereupon, if I judge right, seeing in these wooden Columns certain Rings of Circles of Brass or Iron, fasten'd about the Top and Bottom, that the continual Weight which they are made to bear, might not split them; the Architects too left at the Foot of their Columns of Marble, a little Ring like a sort of Binding; whereby they are defended from any Drops of Rain that might dash up again upon them. And at the Top too they left another little Band, and over that an Astragal or Collar; with which helps they observ'd the Columns of Wood to be fortified. In the Bases of their Columns it was their Rule, that the under Part should consist of strait Lines and right Angles, but that their upper Superficies should terminate circularly to answer to the Round of the Pillar; and they made this Base on every Side broader than high, and wider than the Column by a determinate Part of itself; and the under Superficies of the Base they made broader than the upper; the Plinth too they would have a certain Proportion broader than the Base, and the Foundation again a determinate Part wider than the Plinth. And all these Parts thus placed one upon the other, they erected perpendicular from the Center of the Foundation. On the other hand, the Capitals all agree in this, that their under Parts imitate their Columns, but their upper End in a Square; and consequently the upper Part of the Capital must always be somewhat broader than the under. This may suffice here as to the Columns. The Wall ought to be raised with the same Proportions as the Columns; so that if it is to be as high as the Column and its Capital, its Thickness ought to be the same with that of the bottom of the Column. And they also observed this Rule, that there shou'd be neither Pillar, nor Base, nor Capital, nor Wall, but what should in all respects correspond with every thing else of the same Order, in Heighth, Thickness, Form and Dimension. But tho' both are Faults, either to make the Wall too thin or too thick, higher or lower than the Rule and Proportion requires; yet of the two I wou'd chuse to offend on that Side, where we shou'd have occasion to take away rather than to add. And here I think it will not be amiss to take notice of some Errors in Buildings, that we our selves may be the more circumspect: in as much as the chief Praise is to be exempt from Blame. I have observed therefore in St. *Peter*'s Church at *Rome* what indeed the thing itself demonstrates, that it was ill advised to draw a very long and thick Wall over so many frequent and continued Apertures, without strength'ning it with any curve Lines or any other Fortification whatsoever. And what more deserves our Notice, all this Wing of Wall, under which are too frequent and continued Apertures, and which is raised to a great Heighth, is exposed as a Butt to the impetuous Blasts of the North-East: by which means already thro' the continual Violence of the Winds it is swerved from its Direction above two Yards: and I doubt not that in a short time, some little accidental shock will throw it down into Ruins; and if it were not kept in by the Timber Frame of the Roof, it must infallibly have fallen down before now. But the Architect may not be so much in Fault, because consulting only the Necessity of his Situation, he might perhaps imagine that the Neighbourhood of the Mountain, which overlooks the Church, might be a sufficient Shelter against the Winds. Nevertheless it is certain, those Wings ought to have been more strengthned on both Sides.

C H A P. XI.

Of the great Usefulness of the Coverings both to the Inhabitants and the other Parts of the Building, and that being various in their Natures, they must be made of various Sorts.

THE Covering for Usefulness far exceeds any other Part of the Building. It not only secures the Health of the Inhabitants by defending them from the Night, from the Rain, and especially from the burning Rays of the Sun; but it also preserves all the rest of the Edifice. Take away the Covering and the Materials rot, the Wall moulders and splits,

and

and in short the whole Structure falls to Ruin. The very Foundations themselves, which you will hardly believe, are secured by the Protection of the Covering: nor have so many Buildings been destroyed by Fire, Sword, War, by Multitude of Enemies, and all other Calamities put together, as have gone to Ruin by being left naked and uncovered thro Negligence. It is certain the Coverings are the defensive Arms of the Building against the Assaults and Violence of Storms and Tempests. Wherefore our Ancestors in this as in other things acted very laudably, in ascribing so much Honour to the Covering, that they spent their whole Art and Study in adorning and beautifying it. For some of their Coverings we see of Brass, others of Glass, some of Gold with gilded Beams and Rafters, and richly adorned with Cornishes of Flowers and Statues. Of Coverings some are open to the Air, others not: the open are those which are not for walking upon, but only for receiving the Rain. Those not open to the Air, are the Roofs and Coves that are between the Covering and the Foundations, so that one House seems to stand upon another. By this means it comes to pass that the same Work, which is the Covering to the Apartments below, is the *Area* to those above. Of these Coverings those above our Heads we call Roofs, or Cielings; and those which we tread upon with our Feet, *Areas*. Whether the uppermost Covering, which lies to the open Air, is to be reckoned as an *Area* or Pavement, we shall examine in another Place. But the Covering to the open Air, tho' it be of a plain Superficies, ought never to lie even with respect to the *Area* which it covers below; but shou'd always incline of one Side to throw off the Rain. But the Coverings within, that are of a plain Superficies, should be in all Parts equally distant from the Floor. All Coverings must answer in Lines and Angles to the Form and Shape of the Platform and Wall which they are to cover: And as those are various, some being all of curve Lines, others all of strait, and others of both mixed together, the Coverings too are therefore various, and of several kinds. But tho' they have this natural Difference, and that some are hemispherical; others made up of four Arches; others vaulted;

others consisting of Parts of several Arches; some sloping or ridged like ordinary mean Houses: yet which-soever of these kinds we chuse it is absolutely necessary, that all Coverings shou'd be so disposed as to shelter and shade the Pavement, and throw off all Water and Rain, defending the whole Edifice upon which it is placed for a Covering. For Rain is always prepared to do Mischief, and whereover there is the least Crack never fails to get in and do some Hurt or other: By its Subtility it penetrates and makes its way by its Humidity rots and destroys, by its Continuance loosens and unknits all the Nerves of the Building, and in the End ruins and lays Waste the whole Structure to the very Foundations. And for this Reason prudent Architects have always taken care that the Rain should have a free Slope to run off; and that the Water should never be stop'd in any Place, or get into any Part where it cou'd do Hurt. And therefore they advised, that in Places subject to much Snow, the Coverings should have a very steep Slope, rising even to an acute Angle, that the Snow might never rest and gather upon them, but fall off easily; but in more Summerish Climates (to use such an Expression) they laid their Covering less oblique. Lastly we should endeavour if possible, without Prejudice to the Lights or Wall, to have the whole Structure overlaid with one equal Covering in a manner all of one Piece, and so far jutting out, that the Water falling from the Gutters may not wet or soak into the Wall: and all the Coverings should be so disposed, where there are more than one, that one may not spout upon the other. The Space of Covering too that the Water is to run over should never be too large, because upon Rains the Water gathering in the Gutters in too great Abundance would wash back again and flow into the House; which would greatly prejudice the whole Work. Where the *Area* therefore is very large, the Covering should be divided into several Slopes, and the Rain flow off in different Places; and this is not only attended with Convenience, but Beauty too. If you are obliged in any Place to have several Coverings, let them join one to another in such a Manner, that when you are once under one, you may pass from that to all the rest always under shelter.

C H A P. XII.

Of the Apertures in the Building, that is to say of the Windows and Doors, and of those which do not take up the whole Thickness of the Wall, and their Number and Sizes.

WE are now come to treat of the Apertures, which are of two Sorts, the one serving for the Admission of Light and Air, and the other for the Entrance and Passage of the Inhabitants, and of all Manner of Conveniencies all thro' the House. Those for Light are the Windows; those for Passage, the Doors, Stairs, and the Spaces between the Columns : Those too which are for the carrying away of Water and Smoak, as Wells, Sinks, the Gullets, as we may call them of Chimneys, the Mouths of Ovens and Furnaces are also called Apertures. No Room ought to be without a Window, by which the inclosed Air may be let out and renew'd, because else it will corrupt and grow unwholesome. *Capitolinus* the Historian relates, that in the Temple of *Apollo* at *Babylon* there was found a little Gold Casket of very great Antiquity, upon opening of which there issued a Steam of Air, corrupted by Length of Time, and so poisonous, that spreading itself abroad, it not only killed every body that was near, but infected all *Asia* with a most dreadful Plague quite as far as *Parthia*. In the History of *Ammianus Marcellinus*, we read, that in *Seleucia* in the Time of *Mark Anthony* and *Verus*, after the Plunder and Spoiling of the Temple, and carrying away the Image of the *Conic Apollo* to *Rome*, they discovered a little Hole which had been formerly stop'd up by the *Chaldean* Priests : Which being opened by the Soldiers, out of a greedy Desire of Plunder, sent forth a Vapour so dreadfully pestilential and infectious, that from the Confines of *Persia* quite to *Gaul*, the whole Country was tainted with a mortal and loathsome Distemper. Every Room therefore should have Windows, not only to let in the Light, but to renew the Air ; and they ought to be so accommodated to Convenience and the Thickness of the Wall, as not to admit more remote than Use and Necessity requires. Morevover we are to take notice what Winds our Windows are to stand open to ; because those which look towards a healthy Air may be allow'd to be large every Way ; and it will not be amiss to open them in such Manner that the Air

may go clear round the Bodies of the Inhabitants; which may easily be contrived, if the Jambs of the Windows are made so low, that you may both see and be seen from the Inside into the Street. But such Windows as are exposed to Winds not altogether so healthy, ought to be so proportion'd as to admit what Light is requisite, but not any Thing larger than is just necessary for that Use; and they should likewise be set high, that the Wall may break the Winds before they reach us : Because by this means we shall have Wind enough to renew our Air, but so interrupted as to take off from the ill Effects of it. We should also observe what Suns our House stands to, and according to various Conveniencies make the Windows larger or smaller. In Summer Apartments, if the Windows are to the North, they should be made large every Way ; but if they are to the South Sun, it will be proper to make them low and small; such being best adapted for Reception of the Air, and least liable to be offended by the Sun's Rays; and there is no Danger such a Place should ever want Light, when the Sun lies in a Manner continually upon it; so that Shade and not Light is what is to be consulted there. On the contrary in Apartments for Winter, the Windows will be best contrived for admitting the Sun if they are made large, and yet we may avoid being troubled by the Winds at the same Time, if we place them high, so that the cold Air may not blow directly upon the People within. Lastly from whatever Side we take in the Light, we ought to make such an Opening for it, as may always give us a free Sight of the Sky, and the Top of that Opening ought never to be too low, because we are to see the Light with our Eyes; and not with our Heels; besides the Inconvenience, that if one Man gets between nother and the Window, the Light is intercepted, and all the rest of the Room is darken'd, which never happens when the Light comes from above. The Doors should imitate the Windows, that is, be larger or smaller, more or fewer, according to the Frequency or Necessity of the Place. But I observe, that

the

the Ancients in their Publick Buildings always left a great many of both the afore-mention'd Kinds of Apertures. This appears from their Theatres, which if we obferve are extremely full of Apertures, not only Stair-cafes, but Windows and Doors. And we ought fo to order the Proportions of thefe Openings, as not to make very little ones in great Walls, nor too large in fmall ones. In thefe Sorts of Apertures various Defigns have been commended; but the beft Architects have never made Ufe of any but Squares and ftrait Lines. However all have agreed in this, that let them be of what Shape they will, they fhould be acmodated to the Bignefs and Form of the Building. *The Doors, then they

Plate 2. fay fhould always be more high than broad; and the higheft be fuch as are capable of receiving two Circles [A] one upon t'other, and the loweft fhould be of the Heighth of the Diagonal of a Square [B] whereof the Groundfell is one of the Sides. It is alfo convenient to place the Doors in fuch a Manner, that they may lead to as many Parts of the Edifice as poffible: And in order to give Beauty to fuch Apertures, Care muft be taken that thofe of like Dimenfions correfpond with each other both on the Right and Left. It was ufual to leave the Windows and Doors in odd Numbers, but fo as for the Side ones to anfwer each other, and that in the Middle to be fomewhat larger than the reft. And particular Regard was always had to the Strength of the Building, for which Reafon they contrived to fet the Openings clear from the Corners and from the Columns, in the weakeft Parts of the Wall, but not fo weak as to be infufficient to fupport the Weight: It being their Cuftom to raife as many Parts of the Wall as they could plum, and as it were of one Piece without any Interruption from the Foundation quite up to the Covering. There is a certain Kind of an Aperture, which in Form and Pofition imitates the Doors and Windows, but which does not penetrate the whole Thicknefs of the Wall, and fo, as Niches leave very handfome and convenient Seats for Statues and Paintings. But in what Parts thefe are to be left, as alfo how frequent and large, will be fhewn more diftinctly when we come to treat of the Ornaments of Edifices. We fhall only obferve here, that they not only add to the Beauty of the Work, but alfo fave fome Expence, as they make lefs Stone and Lime to ferve for the Walling. This chiefly is to be taken Care of, that you make thefe Niches in convenient Numbers, not too big, and of a juft Form; and fo as in their Order to imitate the Windows. And let them be as you will, I have remark'd in the Structures of the Ancients, that they never ufed to fuffer them to take up above the feventh Part of the Front, nor lefs than the ninth. The Spaces between the Columns are to be reckoned among the principal Apertures, and are to be left varioufly according to the Variety of Buildings. But we fhall fpeak of thefe more clearly in their proper Place, and chiefly when we treat of Sacred Edifies. Let it be fufficient to premife here, that thofe Openings fhould be left in fuch a Manner, as to have particular Refpect to the Nature of the Columns, which are defign'd for the Support of the Covering; and firft, that thofe Columns be not too fmall, nor ftand too thin, fo as not to be duly able to bear the Weight, nor too big, or fet fo thick as not to leave open convenient Spaces for Paffage. Laftly, the Apertures muft be different, when the Columns are frequent from what they are when they ftand thin, becaufe over frequent Columns we lay an Architrave, and over the others we turn an Arch. But in all Openings over which we make Arches, we fhould contrive to have the Arch never lefs than a half Circle, with an Addition of the feventh Part of half its Diameter: The moft experienced Workmen having found that Arch to be by much the beft adapted for enduring in a Manner to Perpetuity; all other Arches being thought lefs ftrong for fupporting the Weight, and more liable to ruin. It is moreover imagined, that the half Circle is the only Arch which has no Occafion either for Chain or any other Fortification; and all others, if you don't either chain them or place fome Weight againft them for a Counterpoife, are found by their own Weight to burft out and fall to ruin. I will not omit here what I have taken Notice of among the Ancients, a Contrivance certainly very excellent and Praife-worthy: Their beft Architects placed thefe Apertures and the Arches of the Roofs of their Temples in fuch a Manner, that even tho you took away every Column from under them, yet they would ftill ftand firm and not fall down, the Arches on which the Roof was placed being drawn quite down to the Foundation with wonderful Art, known but to few: So that the Work upheld itfelf by being only fet upon Arches; for thofe Arches having the folid Earth for their Chain, no Wonder they ftood firm without any other Support.

Снар.

CHAP. XIII.

Of the Stair cafes, and their different Sorts, of the Steps of the Stairs which ought to be in odd Numbers, and how many. Of the refting Places, of the Tunnels for carrying away the Smoke. Of Pipes and Conduits for carrying off the Water, and of the proper Placing of Wells and Sinks.

THE placing of the Stairs is a Work of fuch Nicety, that without deliberate and mature Confideration you can never place them well: For in a Stair-cafe there meet three Apertures: One, the Door by which you enter upon the Stairs; another, the Window that fupplies you with Light to fee the Steps by, and the third, the Opening in the Ceiling which lets you into the *Area* above; and therefore it is faid to be no Wonder, that the Stairs fhould perplex the Defign of a Structure; but let him that is defirous to have the Stair not hinder him, take Care not to hinder the Stair, but allow it a determinate and juft Portion of the Platform, in order to give its free Courfe quite up to the Covering at the Top of all. And do not let us repine that the Stair-cafe fhould take up fo much of the *Area*, for it furnifhes us with very many Conveniencies, and is no Inconvenience to the other Parts of the Building. Add to this, that thofe little Vaults and Spaces under the Stairs are very ferviceable for a great many Purpofes. Our Stair-cafes therefore are of two Sorts (for as to thofe Steps or Ladders which belong to military Expeditions, I fhall not fpeak of them here.) The firft is that which has no Steps, but is mounted by a floping Afcent, and the other is that which is mounted by Steps. The Ancients ufed to make the floping one as eafy and as little fteep as poffible, and as I have obferved from their Works, thought it a convenient Afcent when the higheft Part of its Perpendicular was raifed one fixth Part of the Line at Bottom. In making of Stair-cafes with Steps, they recommend the making of the Steps in odd Numbers, and efpecially in their Temples: Becaufe they faid that by this Means we always fet our right Foot into the Temple firft; which was accounted a Point of Religion. And I have obferved, that the beft Architects never put above feven, or at moft nine Steps together in one Flight; imitating I fuppofe, the Number either of the Planets or of the Heavens; but at the End of

thefe feven or nine Steps, they very confiderately made a Plain, that fuch as were weak or tired with the Fatigue of the Afcent, might have Leifure to reft themfelves, and that if they fhould chance to ftumble, there might be a Place to break their Fall, and give them Means to recover themfelves. And I am thoroughly of Opinion, that the Stairs ought to be frequently interrupted by thefe landing Places, and that they fhould be well lighted, and be ample and fpacious according to the Dignity of the Place. The Steps they never made higher than nine Inches, nor lower than fix, and in Breadth never lefs than a Foot and a half, nor more than a Yard, The fewer Stair-cafes that are in a Houfe, and the lefs Room they take up, the more convenient they are efteem'd. The Iffues for Smoak and Water ought to be as direct as poffible, and fo built, that they may not lie and gather within, or foil, or offend, or endanger the Building For this Reafon too the Tunnels of the Chimnies fhould be carried quite clear from all Manner of Wood-work, for fear fome Spark, or their meer Heat fhould fet Fire to the Beams or Rafters that are near them. The Drains alfo for carrying off the Water fhould be fo contrived, as to convey away all Superfluities, and in their Paffage not to do any Harm to the Houfe, either by fapping or dirtying it. For if any of thefe Things do Mifchief, let it be ever fo little, yet by Length of Time and continuation, they will in the End be of the utmoft ill Confequence; and I have obferved, that the beft Architects have contrived either to throw off the Rain by Spouts, fo as not to wet any body that is going into the Houfe, or carried it thro Pipes into Cifterns to ferve for Ufe, or elfe brought it together to fome Place where it might wafh away all the Filth, fo that the Eyes and Nofes of the Inhabitants might not be offended with it. Indeed they feem to have been particularly careful to throw the Rain Water clear away from the Building, that it might not fap the Foundations, as well as for several other Reasons. In a Word, they were very observant to make all their Apertures in the most convenient Places, and where they might be most serviceable. I am particularly for having the Wells set in the most publick and open Part of the Structure, so that they do not take off from the Dignity of the Work, by being set in a Place improper for them; and the Naturalists affirm, that Water most exposed and open is best and most purified. But in whatever Part of the Building you make either Wells or Drains, or any other Conveyance for the Water, they ought to have such Apertures, as to admit a good Quantity of Air, that the Pavement may be kept dry from the damp Exhalations, which will be purged and carried off by the Passage of the Winds, and the Motion of the Air. We have now taken a sufficient Review of the Designs of Buildings, as far as they seem to relate to the Work in general, noting each Particular by itself that we intend to speak of. We are now to treat of the Work itself and of the Structure of Edifies. But first we will consider of the Materials, and of the Preparations necessary for the Materials.

End of the First Book.

THE
ARCHITECTURE
OF
Leone Batiſta Alberti.

BOOK II. CHAP. I.

Treating of the Materials. That no Man ought to begin a Building haſtily, but ſhould firſt take a good deal of Time to conſider, and revolve in his Mind all the Qualities and Requiſites of ſuch a Work: And that he ſhould carefully review and examine, with the Advice of proper Judges, the whole Structure in itſelf, and the Proportions and Meaſures of every diſtinct Part, not o in Draughts or Paintings, but in actual Models of Wood or ſome otheSu^n ly ſtance, that when he has finiſh'd his Building, he may not repent of his Labour.

Do not think the Labour and Expence of a Building to be enter'd upon in a hurry; as well for ſeveral other Reaſons, as alſo becauſe a Man's Honour and Reputation ſuffers by it. For as a Deſign well and compleatly finiſh'd brings Praiſe to him that has employ'd his Pains and Study in the Work; ſo if in any particular the Author ſeems to have been wanting, either of Art or Prudence, it detracts very much from that Praiſe, and from his Reputation. And indeed the Beauties or Faults of Edifices, eſpecially publick ones, are in a Manner clear and manifeſt to every body; and (I know not how it happens) any Thing amiſs ſooner draws Contempt, than any Thing handſome or well finiſh'd does Commendation. It is really wonderful, how, by a Kind of natural Inſtinct, all of us knowing or ignorant, immediately hit upon what is right or wrong in the Contrivance or Execution of Things, and what a ſhrewd Judgment the Eye has in Works of this Nature above all the other Senſes. Whence it happens, that if any Thing offers itſelf to us that is lame or too little, or unneceſſary, or ungraceful, we preſently find ourſelves moved and deſirous to have it handſomer. The Reaſons of thoſe Faults perhaps we may not all of us be acquainted with, and yet if we were to

G

be ask'd, there is none of us but would readily say, that such a Thing might be remedied and corrected. Indeed every one cannot propose the Remedy, but only such as are well practiced and experienced that Way. It is therefore the Part of a wise Man to weigh and review every particular thoroughly in his Mind: That he may not afterwards be forced to say, either in the Middle or at the End of this Work, I wish this, or I wish that were otherwise. And it is really surprizing, what a hearty Punishment a Man suffers for a Work ill managed: For in Process of Time, he himself at Length finds out the Mistakes he foolishly made in the Beginning for want of due Reflection: And then, unless he pulls it to pieces and reforms it, he is continually repenting and fretting at the Eye-sore; or if he pulls it down, he is blamed upon Account of the Loss and Expence, and accused of Levity and Instability of Mind. *Suetonius* tells us, that *Julius Cæsar* having begun a Structure at the Lake *Nemorensis* from the very Foundations, and compleated it at vast Expence, pull'd it all down again, because it was not exactly in all respects to his Mind. For which he is certainly very much to be blamed, even by us his Posterity, either for not sufficiently considering what was requisite at first, or else afterwards for disliking thro' Levity what might really not be amiss. I therefore always highly commend the ancient Custom of Builders, who not only in Draughts and Paintings, but in real Models of Wood or other Substance, examin'd and weigh'd over and over again, with the Advice of Men of the best Experience, the whole Work and the Admeasurements of all its Parts, before they put themselves to the Expence or Trouble. By making a Model you will have an Opportunity, thoroughly to weigh and consider the Form and Situation of your Platform with respect to the Region, what Extent is to be allow'd to it, the Number and Order of the Parts, how the Walls are to be made, and how strong and firm the Covering; and in a Word all those Particulars which we have spoken of in the preceding Book: And there you may easily and freely add, retrench, alter, renew, and in short change every Thing from one End to t'other, till all and every one of the Parts are just as you would have them, and without Fault. Add likewise, that you may then examine and compute (what is by no means to be neglected) the Particulars and Sum of your future Expence, the Size, Heighth, Thickness, Num-

ber, Extent, Form, Species and Quality of all the Parts, how they are to be made, and by what Artificers; because you will thereby have a clear and distinct Idea of the Numbers and Forms of your Columns, Capitals, Bases, Cornishes, Pediments, Incrustations, Pavements, Statues and the like, that relates either to the Strength or Ornament. I must not omit to observe, that the making of curious, polish'd Models, with the Delicacy of Painting, is not required from an Architect that only designs to shew the real Thing itself; but is rather the Part of a vain Architect, that makes it his Business by charming the Eye and striking the Fancy of the Beholder, to divert him from a rigorous Examination of the Parts which he ought to make, and to draw him into an Admiration of himself. For this Reason I would not have the Models too exactly finish'd, nor too delicate and neat, but plain and simple, more to be admired for the Contrivance of the Inventor, than the Hand of the Workman. Between the Design of the Painter and that of the Architect, there is this Difference, that the Painter by the Exactness of his Shades, Lines and Angles, endeavours to make the Parts seem to rise from the Canvass, whereas the Architect, without any Regard to the Shades, makes his Relieves from the Design of his Platform, as one that would have his Work valued, not by the apparent Perspective, but by the real Compartments founded upon Reason. In a Word, you ought to make such Models, and consider them by yourself, and with others so diligently, and examine them over and over so often, that there shall not be a single Part in your whole Structure, but what you are thoroughly acquainted with, and know what Place and how much Room it is to possess, and to what Use to be applied. But above all, nothing requires our Attention so much as the Covering, which seems in its Nature, if I mistake not, beyond any Thing else in Architecture to have been of the greatest and first Convenience to Mankind; so that indeed it must be own'd, that it was upon the Account of this Covering that they invented not only the Wall and those other Parts which are carried up with the Wall and necessarily accompany it, but also those Parts which are made under Ground, such as Conduits, Channels, Receptacles of Rain Water, Sewers and the like. For my Part, that have had no small Experience in Things of this Nature, I indeed know the Difficulty of performing

performing a Work, wherein the Parts are join'd with Dignity, Convenience and Beauty, having not only other Things praise-worthy, but also a Variety of Ornaments, such as Decency and Proportion requires; and this no Question is a very great Matter; but to cover all these with a proper, convenient and apt Covering, is the Work of none but a very great Master. To conclude, when the whole Model and the Contrivance of all the Parts greatly pleases both yourself and others of good Experience, so that you have not the least Doubt remaining within yourself, and do not know of any Thing that wants the least Re-examination; even then I would advise you not to run furiously to the Execution out of a Passion for Building, demolishing old Structures, or laying mighty Foundations of the whole Work, which rash and inconsiderate Men are apt to do; but if you will hearken to me, lay the Thoughts of it aside for some Time, till this favourite Invention grows old. Then take a fresh Review of every Thing, when not being guided by a Fondness for your Invention, but by the Truth and Reason of Things you will be capable of judging more clearly. Because in many Cases Time will discover a great many Things to you, worth Consideration and Reflection, which, be you ever so accurate, might before escape you.

C H A P. II.

That we ought to undertake nothing above our Abilities, nor strive against Nature, and that we ought also not only to consider what we can do, but what is fit for us to do, and in what Place it is that we are to build.

ON examining your Model, among other Points to be consider'd, you must take Care not to forget these. First, not to undertake a Thing, which is above the Power of Man to do, and not to pretend to strive directly contrary to the Nature of Things. For Nature, if you force or wrest her out of her Way, whatever Strength you may do it with, will yet in the End overcome and break thro' all Opposition and Hindrance; and the most obstinate Violence (to use such an Expression) will at last be forced to yield to her daily and continual Perseverence assisted by Length of Time. How many of the mighty Works of Men do we read of, and know ourselves to have been destroy'd by no other Cause than that they contended against Nature? Who does not laugh at him, that having made a Bridge upon Ships, intended to ride over the Sea? or rather, who does not hate him for his Folly and Insolence? The Haven of *Claudius* below *Ostia*, and that of *Hadrian* near *Terracina*, Works in all other Respects likely to last to Eternity, yet now having their Mouths stop'd with Sand, and their Beds quite choak'd up, they have been long since totally destroy'd by the continual Assaults of the Sea, which incessantly washing against it gains from it daily. What then think ye will happen in any Place, where you pretend to oppose or entirely repel the Violence of Water, or the enormous Weight of Rocks tumbling down on you in Ruins? This being consider'd, we ought never to undertake any Thing that is not exactly agreeable to Nature; and moreover we should take Care not to enter upon a Work in which we may be so much wanting to ourselves as to be forced to leave it imperfect. Who would not have blamed *Tarquin*, King of the *Romans*, if the Gods had not favoured the Greatness of the City, and if by the Enlargement of the Empire he had not received an Accession of Wealth sufficient to compleat the Magnificence of his Beginning, for throwing away the whole Expence of his future Work in laying the Foundations of his Temple. Besides it is not amiss to consider, and that not in the last Place, not only what you are able, but also what is decent for you to do. I do not commend *Rhodope* of *Thrace*, the famous Courtezan, and the Wonder of her Days, for building herself a Sepulcher of incredible Expence: For though she might possibly by her Whoredom have acquired the Riches of a Queen, yet she was by no means worthy of a Royal Sepulcher. But on the other Hand I do not blame *Artemisia*, Queen of *Caria*, for having built her beloved and worthy Consort a most stately

Mausoleum

Mausoleum: Though in Things of that Nature, I think Modesty is best. *Horace* blamed *Mæcenas* for having too furious a Passion for Building. I commend him, who according to *Cornelius Tacitus*, built *Otho*'s Sepulcher, modest, but extremely durable. And though it be true that private Monuments require Modesty and publick ones Magnificence; yet publick ones too are sometimes praised for being as modest as the others. We admire *Pompey*'s Theatre for the surprizing Greatness and Dignity of the Work: A Work truly worthy of *Pompey* and of *Rome* in the Midst of her Victories: but *Nero*'s unadvisedly Fondness for Building, and mad Passion for Undertaking immense Designs, is commended by nobody. And besides, who would not rather have wish'd, that he who employ'd so many thousand Men to bore through the Hill near *Pozzuolo*, had taken the same Pains, and bestowed the same Expence upon some Work of greater Use? Who will not detest the monstrous Folly and Vanity of *Heliogabalus*? who had Thoughts of erecting a huge Column with Stairs on the Inside of it to mount to the Top, whereon *Heliogabalus* himself was to be set as a God,

which he pretended to make himself. But not being able to find a Stone of that Bigness, tho' he sought for it quite to *Thebais*, he desisted from his wild Design. Hereunto we may add, that we ought not to begin a Thing, which though in some Respects worthy and useful, and not altogether so difficult of Execution, some particular Opportunity or Means favouring it at that Time, that yet is of a Nature to fall soon to decay, either thro' the Negligence of Successors, or Dislike of the Inhabitants. I therefore find Fault with the Canal which *Nero* made navigable for Gallies with five Rows of Oars from *Avernus* to *Ostia*, as well upon other Accounts, as because the Maintaining of it seem'd to require perpetual and eternal Felicity of the Empire, and a Succession of Princes all inclined to the same Works. These Considerations being granted, we ought to reflect duly upon all the Particulars beforemention'd, that is to say, what Work we undertake, the Place we are to build in, and what the Person is that is to build; and to contrive every Thing according to his Dignity and Necessities, is the Part of a discreet and prudent Architect.

CHAP. III.

That having consider'd the whole Disposition of the Building in all the Parts of the Model, we ought to take the Advice of prudent and understanding Men, and before we begin our Work, it will not only be proper to know how to raise Money for the Expence, but also long before hand to provide all the Materials for compleating such an Undertaking.

HAVING weigh'd and consider'd these Things you must proceed to the Examination of the Rest, whether each of them be perfectly contrived and conveniently disposed in its proper Place. And to do this effectually, it is necessary you should be full of this Persuasion, all the while you are meditating upon these Things, that it will be a Scandal to you, if as far as in you lies, you suffer any other Building with the same Expence or Advantages to gain more Praise and Approbation than your own. Nor is it sufficient in these Cases to be only not despised, unless you are highly and principally commended, and then imitated. Therefore we ought to be as severe and diligent as possible in our Scrutiny of every Particular, as well to suffer nothing but what

is excellent and elegant, as to have all Things mutually concur to make the whole Handsome and Beautiful, insomuch that whatever you attempted to add, or retrench, or alter, should be for the Worse and make a Defect. But herein, I repeat my Advice, let your Moderator be the Prudence and Counsel of the most experienced Judges, whose Approbation is founded upon Knowledge and Sincerity: Because by their Skill and Directions you will be much more likely, than by your own private Will and Opinion, to attain to Perfection or Something very near it. And besides, the Praise of good Judges is the highest Satisfaction; and as for others they praise you sufficiently, and indeed too much in not doing Something better themselves. So that you will be sure of

the

the Pleasure of having the Approbation of all that underſtand theſe Matters. And you may find your Advantage in hearkning to every Body; for ſometimes it happens, that Perſons of no Skill make Obſervations by no Means to be deſpiſed. When therefore you have well weigh'd, review'd, and examin'd all the Parts of your Model, and all the Proportions of the whole Building, ſo that there is not the leaſt Particular any where about it, which you have not conſider'd and reflected upon, and that you are fully reſolved to build in that Manner in every Reſpect, and can raiſe the Money conveniently for bearing the Expence; then prepare the other Things neceſſary for the Execution of your Work, that when you have begun, nothing may be wanting ſo as to prevent your finiſhing your Structure expeditiouſly. For as you will have Occaſion for a great Number of Things for carrying on the Buſineſs, and as if but one is unprovided, it may ſtop or ſpoil the whole Work, it is your Care to have every Thing at Hand that may be of Uſe to you, if provided, or a Detriment, if wanting. The Kings of *Judea, David* and *Solomon*, when they had undertaken to build the Temple of *Jeruſalem*, having amaſs'd great Quantities of Gold, Silver, Braſs, Timber, Stone and the like Materials, that they might want Nothing that could be ſerviceable in the eaſy and ſpeedy Execution of the Work (as *Euſebius Pamphilus* tells us) ſent to the neighbouring Kings for ſeveral Thouſands of Workmen and Architects. Which I highly commend: Becauſe it certainly adds Dignity to the Work, and encreaſes the Glory of the Author; and Structures that have been handſomely contrived and ſpeedily finiſh'd beſides, have been very much celebrated by ancient Writers. *Quintus Curtius* relates that *Alexander* the Great, in Building a City, and that no very ſmall one, near the *Tanais*, ſpent but ſeven Days; and *Joſephus* the Hiſtorian tells us, that *Nebuchadnezzer* built the Temple of *Belus* in fifteen, and in the ſame Space of Time girt the City of *Babylon* with three Circuits of Walls. That *Titus* made a Wall little leſs than five Miles long, and *Semiramis* near *Babylon* built the eighth Part of a Mile of a prodigious Wall every Day; and that ſhe erected another of above five and twenty Miles in Length, very High and Thick, to confine the Lake, and in no more than ſeven Days. But of theſe in another Place.

CHAP. IV.

What Materials are to be provided for the Building, what Workmen to be choſe, and in what Seaſons, according to the Opinions of the Ancients, to cut Timber.

THE Things to be prepared are theſe, Lime, Timber, Sand, Stone, as alſo Iron, Braſs, Lead, Glaſs and the like. But the Thing of greateſt Conſequence is to chuſe ſkilful Workmen, not light or inconſtant, whom you may truſt with the Care and Management of an Edifice well deſign'd, and who will compleat it with all Expedition. And in fixing upon all theſe, it will be of Uſe to you to be ſomewhat guided by the Conſideration of other Works already finiſh'd in your Neighbourhood, and by the Information you receive from them to determine what to do in your own Caſe. For by obſerving the Faults and Beauties in them, you will conſider that the ſame may happen in yours. *Nero* the Emperor having form'd a Deſign of dedicating a huge Statue of an hundred and twenty Foot high in Honour of the Sun at *Rome*, exceeding any Thing that had been done before in Greatneſs and Magnificence, as *Pliny* relates, before he gave final Orders for the Work to *Zenodarus*, a famous and excellent Sculptor in thoſe Days, would firſt ſee his Capacity for ſuch a Work by a *Coloſſus* of extraordinary Weight, which he had made in the Country of *Auvergne* in *France*. Theſe Things duly conſider'd, we proceed to the others. We intend, then, in treating of the Materials neceſſary for Building, to repeat thoſe Things which have been taught us by the moſt learned among the Ancients, and particularly *Theophraſtus, Ariſtotle, Cato, Varro, Pliny* and *Virgil,* becauſe they have learned more from long Obſervation than from any Quickneſs of Genius; ſo that they are beſt gathered from thoſe who have obſerved them with the greateſt Diligence. We ſhall there-

for

fore go on to collect those Rules which the most approved Ancients have left us in many and various Places, and to these, according to our Custom, we shall add whatever we ourselves have deduced from antique Works, or the Instructions of most experienced Artificers, if we happen to know any Thing that may be serviceable to our Purpose. And I believe it will be the best Method, following Nature herself, to begin with those Things which were first in Use among Men in their Buildings; which, if we mistake not, were Timber Trees which they fell'd in the Woods: Though among Authors, I find, some are divided upon this very Subject. Some will have it, that Men at first dwelt in Caves, and that they and their Cattle were both sheltered under the same Roof; and therefore they believe what *Pliny* tells us, that one *Gellius Texius* was the first, that, in Imitation of Nature built himself a House of Mud. *Diodorus* says that *Vesta*, the Daughter of *Saturn*, was the first that invented Houses. *Eusebius Pamphilus*, an excellent Searcher into Antiquity, tells us from the Testimony of the Ancients, that the Grandsons of *Protogenes* first taught Men the Building of Houses, which they patch'd up of Reeds and Bullrushes: But to return to our Subject. The Ancients, then, and particularly *Theophrastus*, inform us, that most Trees, and especially the Fir, the Pitch-tree and the Pine, ought to be cut immediately, when they begin to put forth their young Shoots, when through their abundance of Sap you most easily strip off the Bark. But that there are some Trees, as the Maple, the Elm, the Ash, and the Linden, which are best cut after Vintage. The Oak if cut in Summer, they observe is apt to breed Worms; but if in Winter, it will keep sound and not split. And it is not foreign to our Purpose what they remark, that Wood which is cut in Winter, in a North Wind, though it be green, will neverthelefs burn extremely well, and in a Manner without Smoak; which manifestly shews that their Juices are not crude, but well digested. *Vitruvius* is for cutting Timber from the beginning of Autumn, till such Time as the soft Westerly Winds begin to blow. And *Hefiod* says, that when the Sun darts his burning Rays directly upon our Heads, and turns Mens Complections to brown, then is the Time for Harvest, but that when the Trees drop their Leaves, then is the Season for cutting of Timber. *Cato* moderates the Matter thus; let the

Oak, says he, be felled during the Solstice, because in Winter it is always out of Season; other Woods that bear Seed may be cut when that is mature; those that bear none, when you please. Those that have their Seeds green and ripe at the same Time, should be cut when that is fallen, but the Elm when the Leaves drop. And they say it is of very great Importance, what Age the Moon is of when you fell your Timber: For they are all of Opinion, and especially *Varro*, that the Influence of the Moon is so powerful over Things of this Nature, that even they who cut their Heir in the Wane of the Moon, shall soon grow bald; and for this Reason, they tell us, *Tiberius* observed certain Days for cutting his Hair. The Astrologers affirm, that your Spirits will always be opprefsed with Melancholly, if you cut your Nails or Hair while the Moon is opprefsed or ill disposed. It is to our present Purpose what they say, that such Things as are designed in their Uses to be moveable, ought to be cut and wrought when the Moon is in *Libra* or *Cancer*; but such as are to be fixed and immoveable, when she is in *Leo*, *Taurus*, or the like. But that Timber ought to be cut in the Wane of the Moon, all the Learned are agreed, because they hold that the flegmatick Moisture, so very liable to immediate Putrefaction, is then almost quite dried up, and it is certain, that when it is cut in such a Moon, it is never apt to breed Worms. Hence they say you ought to reap the Corn which you intend to sell, at full Moon; because then the Ears are full; but that which you intend to keep in the Wane. It is also evident, that the Leaves of Trees cropt in the Wane of the Moon do not rot. *Columella* thinks it best to fell Timber from the twentieth to the thirtieth Day of the Moon's Age; *Vegetius*, from the fifteenth to the two and twentieth; and hence he supposes the religious Ceremony to arise, of celebrating all Mysteries relating to Eternity only on those Days, because Wood cut then lasted in a Manner for ever. They add, that we should likewise observe the Setting of the Moon. But *Pliny* thinks it a proper Time to fell Trees when the Dog-star reigns, and when the Moon is in Conjunction with the Sun, which Day is called an *Interlunium*, and says it is good to wait for the Night of that Day too, till the Moon is set. The Astronomers say, the Reason of this is, because the Action of the Moon puts the Fluids of all Bodies into Motion; and that therefore when those Fluids

are

are drawn down, or left by the Moon in the loweft Roots, the Reft of the Timber is clearer and founder. Moreover they think that the Tree will be much more ferviceable, if it is not cut quite down immediately, but chopt round about, and fo left ftanding upon the Stump to dry. And they fay, that if the Fir (which is not the moft unapt to fuffer by Moifture) be barked in the Wane of the Moon, it will never afterwards be liable to be rotted by Water. There are fome who affirm that if the Oak, which is fo heavy a Wood that naturally it finks in the Water, be chopt round the Bottom in the Beginning of Spring, and cut down when it has loft its Leaves, it will have fuch an Effect upon it, that it will float for the Space of ninety Days and not fink. Others advife to chop the Trees which you leave thus upon their Stumps, half way through, that the Corruption and bad Juices may diftil through, and be carried off. They add, that the Trees, which are defigned to be fawed or planed, fhould not be cut down till they have brought their Fruits and ripened their Seeds; and that Trees fo cut, efpecially Fruit-bearers, fhould be barked, becaufe while they are covered with the Bark, Corruption is very apt to gather between the Rind and the Tree.

C H A P. V.

Of preferving the Trees after they are cut, what to plaifter or anoint them with, of the Remedies againft their Infirmities, and of allotting them their proper Places in the Building.

AFTER the Timber is cut, it muft be laid where the fcorching Heat of the Sun or rude Blafts of Winds never come; and efpecially, that which falls of itfelf, ought to be very well protected with Shade. And for this Reafon, the ancient Architects ufed to plaifter it over with Ox-Dung; which *Theophraftus* fays they did, becaufe by that Means all the Pores being ftopped up, the fuperfluous Flegm and Humidity concreting within, diftils and vents itfelf by Degrees through the Heart, by which Means the Drynefs of the other Parts of the Wood is condenfed by its drying equally throughout. And they are of Opinion that Trees dry better, if fet with their Heads downward. Moreover, they prefcribe various Remedies againft their decaying and other Infirmities. *Theophraftus* thinks that burying of Timber hardens it extremely. *Cato* advifes to anoint it with Lees of Oil, to preferve it from all Manner of Worms; and we all know that Pitch is a Defence to it againft Water. They fay that Wood, which has been foaked in the Dregs of Oil, will burn without the Offence of Smoak. *Pliny* writes, that in the Labyrinth of *Egypt*, there are a great many Beams made of the *Egyptian* Thorn rubed over with Oil, and *Theophraftus* fays, that Timber dawbed over with Glue will not burn. Nor will I omit what we read in *Aulus Gellius*, taken out of the Annals of *Quintus Claudius*, that *Archelaus*, *Mithridates*'s Præ-fect, having thoroughly debawbed a wooden Tower in the Piræum with Allum, when *Sylla* befieged it, it would not take Fire. Several Woods are hardened and ftrengthened againft the Affaults of Storms in various Manners. They bury the Citron-wood under Ground, plaiftered over with Wax, for feven Days, and after an Intermiffion of as many more, lay it under Heaps of Corn for the fame Space of Time, whereby it becomes not only ftronger but eafier to be wrought, becaufe it takes away a very confiderable Part of its Weight; and they fay too, that the fame Wood thus dryed, being afterwards laid fome time in the Sea, acquires a Hardnefs incredibly folid and incorruptible. It is certain the Chefnut Tree is purged by the Sea-water. *Pliny* writes, the *Ægyptian* Fig-tree is laid under Water to dry and grow lighter, for at firft it will fink to the Bottom. We fee that our Workmen lay their Timber under Water or Dung for thirty Days, efpecially fuch as they defign for turning, by which Means they think it is better dried and more eafily worked for all Manner of Ufes. There are fome who affirm, that all Manner of Woods agree in this, that if you bury them in fome moift Place while they are green, they will endure for ever; but whether you preferve it in Woods, or bury, or anoint it, the Experienced are univerfally of this Opinion, that you muft not meddle with it under three Months: The Timber muft have

Time

Time to harden and to get a Kind of Maturity of Strength before it is applied to Use. After it is thus prepared, *Cato* directs, that it must not be brought out into the Air but in the Wane of the Moon, and after Mid-day, and even in the Wane of the Moon he condemns the four Days next after the fifteenth, and precautions us against bringing it out in a South Wind. And when we bring it out, we must take Care not to draw it through the Dew, nor to saw or cut it when it is covered with Dew or Frost, but only when it is perfectly dry in all Respects.

C H A P. VI.

What Woods are most proper for Building, their Natures and Uses, how they are to be employed, and what Part of the Edifice each Kind is most fit for.

THeophraſtus thinks that Timber is not dry enough for the making of Planks, especially for Doors, in less than three Years. The Trees of most Use for Building were reckoned to be these; the Holm, and all other Sorts of Oaks, the Beech, the Poplar, the Linden, the Willow, the Alder, the Ash, the Pine, the Cypress, the Olive, both Wild and Garden, the Chesnut, the Larch Tree, the Box, the Cedar, the Ebony, and even the Vine: But all these are various in their Natures, and therefore must be applied to various Uses. Some are better than others to be exposed without Doors, others must be used within; some delight in the open Air, others harden in the Water, and will endure almost for ever under Ground; some are good to make nice Boards, and for Sculptures, and all Manner of Joyner's Work; some for Beams and Rafters; others are stronger for supporting open Terrasses, and Coverings; and the Alder, for Piles to make a Foundation in a River or marshy Ground, exceeds all other Trees, and bears the Wet incomparably well, but will not last at all in the Air or Sun. On the contrary, the Beech will not endure the Wet at all. The Elm, set in the open Air, hardens extremely; but else it splits and will not last. The Pitch Tree and Pine, if buried under Ground, are wonderfully durable. But the Oak, being hard, close, and nervous, and of the smallest Pores, not admitting any Moisture, is the properest of any for all Manner of Works under Ground, capable of supporting the greatest Weights, and is the strongest of Columns. But though Nature has endued it with so much Hardness that it cannot be bored unless it be soaked, yet above Ground it is reckoned inconstant, and to warp and grow unmanageable, and in the Sea-water quickly rots; which does not happen to the Olive, nor Holm Oak, nor Wild Olive, though in other Things they agree with the Oak. The Mast-Holm never consumes with Age, because it's Inside is juicy, and as it were always green. The Beech likewise and the Chesnut do not rot in the Water, and are reckoned among the principal Trees for Works under Ground. The Cork Tree also, and the wild Pine, the Mulberry, the Maple, and the Elm are not amiss for Columns. *Theophraſtus* recommends the *Negropont* Nut Tree for Beams and Rafters, because before it breaks it gives Notice by a Crack, which formerly saved the Lives of a great many People, who, upon the falling of the publick Baths at *Andros*, by Means of that Warning had Time to make their Escape. But the Fir is much the Best for that Use; for as it is one of the Biggest and Thickest of Trees, so it is endued with a natural Stiffness, that will not easily give way to the Weight that is laid upon it, but stands firm and never yields. Add besides, that it is easy to work, and does not lie too heavy upon the Wall. In short, many Perfections, and Uses, and great Praises are ascribed to this single Wood; nevertheless we cannot disown that it has one Fault, which is, that it is too apt to catch Fire. Not inferior to this for Roofs, is the Cypress, a Tree, in many other Respects so useful, that it claims a principal Rank among the most excellent. The Ancients reckoned it as one of the Best, and not inferior to Cedar or Ebony. In *India* the Cypress is valued almost equal with the Spice Trees, and with good Reason; for whatever Praises may be bestowed upon the Ammony or Cirenaic Field Pine, which *Theophraſtus* says is everlasting, yet if you consult either Smell, Beauty, Strength, Bigness, Straitness, or Duration, or all these together, what Tree can you put in Competition with the Cypress? It is

affirmed

affirmed that the Cyprefs never fuffers either by Worms or Age, and never fplits of its own accord. For this Reafon *Plato* was of Opinion, that the publick Laws and Statutes fhould be carved in facred Tables of Cyprefs, believing they would be more lafting than Tables of Brafs. This Topick naturally leads me to give an Account of what I myfelf remember to have read and obferv'd of this Wood. It is related that the Gates of the Temple of *Diana*, at *Ephefus*, being of Cyprefs, lafted four hundred Years, and preferved their Beauty in fuch a Manner that they always feemed to be new. In the Church of St. *Peter* at *Rome*, upon the repairing of the Gates by Pope *Eugenius*, I found, that where they had not been injured by the Violence of the Enemy in ftripping away the Silver with which they were formerly covered, they had continued whole and found above five hundred and fifty Years; for if we examing the Annals of the *Roman* Pontiffs, fo long it is from the Time of *Hadrian* the Third, who fet them up, to *Eugene* the Fourth. Therefore, though the Fir is very much commended for making Rafters, yet the Cyprefs is preferred before it, perhaps only upon this one Account, namely, that it is more lafting; but then it is heavier than the Fir. The Pine and Pitch Trees alfo are valued, for the Pine is fuppofed to have the fame Quality as the Fir, of rifing againft the Weight that is laid upon it: But between the Fir and the Pine there is this Difference, among others, that the Firs is lefs injured by Worms, becaufe the Pine is of a fweeter Juice than the Fir. I do not know any Wood that is to be preferred to the Larch, or Turpentine Tree, which, within my Obfervation, has fupported Buildings perfectly ftrong, and to a very great Age, in many Places, and particularly in thofe very ancient Structures in the Market-place at *Venice*, and indeed this one Tree is reckoned to be furnifhed with the Conveniences of all the Reft; it is nervous, tenacious of its Strength, unmoveable in Storms, not molefted with Worms; and it is an ancient Opinion, that againft the Injuries of Fire it remains invincible, and in a Manner unhurt, infomuch that they advife us, on whatever Side we are apprehenfive of Fire, to place Beams of Larch by Way of Security. It is true I have feen it take Fire and burn, but yet in fuch a Manner that it feemed to difdain the Flames, and to threaten to drive them away. It has indeed one Defect, which is, that in Sea-water it is very apt to breed Worms. For Beams

the Oak and Olive are accounted improper, becaufe of their Heavinefs, and that they give Way beneath the Weight that is laid upon them, and are apt to warp even of themfelves; befides, all Trees that are more inclinable to break into Shivers than to fplit, are unfit for Beams; fuch are the Olive, the Fig, the Linden, the Sallow, and the like. It is a furprizing Property which they relate of the Palm Tree, that it rifes againft the Weight that is laid upon it, and bends upwards in fpite of all Refiftance. For Beams and Coverings expofed to the open Air, the Juniper is greatly commended; and *Pliny* fays it has the fame Properties as the Cedar, but is founder. The Olive too is reckoned extreamly durable, and the Box is efteemed as one of the Beft of all. Nor is the Chefnut, though apt to cleave and fplit, rejected for Works to the open Air. But the wild Olive they particularly efteem for the fame Reafon as the Cyprefs, becaufe it never breeds Worms, which is the Advantage of all Trees that have oily and gummy Juices, efpecially if thofe Juices are bitter. The Worm never enters into fuch Trees, and it is certain they exclude all Moifture from without. Contrary to thefe are fuppofed to be all Woods that have Juices of a fweet Tafte, and which eafily take Fire; out of which, neverthelefs, they except the fweet as well as the wild Olive. *Vitruvius* fays, that the Holm Oak and Beech are very weak in their Nature againft Storms, and do not endure to a great Age. *Pliny* fays, that the Maft-holm foon rots. But the Fir, and particularly that which grows in the *Alps*, for Ufes within Doors, as for Bedfteads, Tables, Doors, Benches, and the like, is excellent; becaufe it is, in its Nature, very dry, and very tenacious of the Glue. The Pitch-Tree and Cyprefs alfo are very good for fuch Ufes; the Beech for other Service is too brittle, but does mighty well for Coffers and Beds, and will faw into extreme thin Planks, as will likewife the Scarlet-Oak. The Chefnut, on the Contrary, the Elm, and the Afh are reckoned very unfit for Planks, becaufe they eafily fplit, and though they fplit flowly, they are very inclinable to it; though elfe the Afh is accounted very obedient in all Manner of Works. But I am furprized the Ancients have not celebrated the Nut Tree; which, as Experience fhews us, is extremely tractable, and good for moft Ufes, and efpecially for Boards or Planks, They commend the Mulberry-Tree, both for its Durablenefs, and becaufe by Length of

Time

it grows blacker and handfomer. *Theophraftus* tells us, that the Rich ufed to make their Doors of the Lote-Tree, the Scarlet-Oak, and of Box. The Elm, becaufe it firmly maintains its Strength, is faid to be very proper for Jambs of Doors, but it fhould be fet with its Head downwards. *Cato* fays, that Levers ought to be made of Holly, Laurel, and Elm: For Bars and Bolts, they recommend the Cornel-Tree; for Stairs, the wild Afh or the Maple. They hollowed the Pine, the Pitch-Tree and the Elm for Aqueducts, but they fay unlefs they are buried under Ground they prefently decay. Laftly, the Female Larch-Tree, which is almoft of the Colour of Honey, for the Ornaments of Edifices and for Tables for Painting, they found to be in a Manner eternal and never crack or fplit; and befides, as its Veins run fhort, not long, they ufed it for the Images of their Gods, as they did alfo the Lote, the Box, the Cedar, and the Cyprefs too, and the large Roots of the Olive, and the *Egyptian* Peach-Tree, which they fay is like the Lote-Tree.

IF they had Occafion to turn any Thing long and round, they ufed the Beech, the Mulberry, the Tree that yields the Turpentine, but efpecially the moft clofe bodied Box, moft excellent for Turning; and for very curious Works, the Ebony. Neither for Statues or Pictures did they defpife the Poplar, both white and black, the Sallow, the Hornbeam, the Service-Tree, the Elder, and the Fig; which Woods, by their Drynefs and Evennefs, are not only good for receiving and preferving the Gums and Colours of the Painter, but are wonderfully foft and eafy under the Carver's Tool for expreffing all Manner of Forms. Though it is certain that none of thefe for Tractablenefs can compare with the Linden. Some there are that for Statues chufe the Jubol-Tree. Contrary to thefe is the Oak, which will never join either with itfelf or any other Wood of the fame Nature, and defpifes all Manner of Glue: The fame Defect is fuppos'd to be in all Trees that are grained, and inclin'd to diftil. Wood that is eafily plain'd, and has a clofe Body, is never well to be faften'd with Glue; and thofe alfo that are of different Natures, as the Ivy, the Laurel and the Linden, which are hot, if glued to thofe that grow in moift Places, which are all in their Natures cold, never hold long together. The Elm, the Afh, the Mulberry, and the Cherry-Tree, being dry, do not agree with the Plane Tree or the Alder, which are Moift. Nay, the Ancients were fo far from joining together Woods different in their Natures, that they would not fo much as place them near one another. And for this Reafon *Vitruvius* advifes us againft joining Planks of Beech and Oak together.

CHAP. VII.

Of Trees more fummarily.

BUT to fpeak of all thefe more fummarily. All Authors are agreed that Trees which do not bear Fruit are ftronger and founder than thofe which do; and that the wild ones, which are not cultivated either with Hand or Steel, are harder than the Domeftick. *Theophraftus* fays, that the wild ones never fall into any Infirmities that kill them, whereas the Domeftick and Fruit-bearers are fubject to very confiderable Infirmities; and among the Fruit-bearers thofe which bear early are weaker than thofe which bear late, and the Sweet than the Tart; and among the tart ones, fuch are accounted the Firmeft, that have the Sharpeft and the leaft Fruit. Thofe that bear Fruit only once in two Years, and thofe which are entirely barren, have more Knots in them than thofe which bear every Year; the Shorteft likewife are the Hardeft, and the Barren grow fafter than the Fruitful. They fay likewife that fuch Trees as grow in an open Place, unfhelter'd either by Woods or Hills, but fhaken by frequent Storms and Winds, are ftronger and thicker, but at the fame Time fhorter and more knotty than fuch as grow down in a Valley, or in any other Place defended from the Winds. They alfo believe that Trees which grow in moift fhady Places are more tender than thofe which grow in a dry open Situation, and that thofe which ftand expofed to the North are more ferviceable than thofe which grow to the South. They reject, as abortive all Trees that grow in Places not agreeable to their Natures, and though fuch as ftand to the

South

South are very hard, yet they are apt to warp in their Sap, so that they are not strait and even enough for Service, Moreover, those which are in their Natures dry and slow growers, are stronger than those which are moist and fruitful; wherefore *Varro* suppos'd that the one were Male and the other Female, and that white Timber was less close and more tractable than that which has any other Colour in it. It is certain that heavy Wood is harder and closer than light; and the Lighter it is, the more Brittle; and the more Knotty the stronger. Trees likewise which Nature has endu'd with the longest Life, she has always endu'd with the Property of keeping longest from Decay when cut down, and the less Sap they have, so much they are the Stronger and more Hardy. The Parts nearest to the Sap are indeed harder and closer than the rest; but those next the Bark have more binding Nerves, for it is suppos'd, in Trees just as in Animals, the Bark is the Skin, the Parts next under the Bark are the Flesh, and that which encloses the Sap, the Bone; and *Aristotle* thought the Knots in Plants were in the Nature of Nerves. Of all the Parts of the Tree, the worst is the Alburnum, or Juice, that nourishes it, both because it is very apt to breed Worms, and upon several other Accounts. To these Observations we may add, that the Part of the Tree which, while it was standing, was towards the South, will be dryer than the rest, and thinner, and more extenuated, but it will be firmer and closer; and the Sap will be nearer to the Bark on that Side than on the other. Those Parts also which are nearest to the Ground and to the Roots, will be heavier than any of the rest; a Proof whereof is that they will hardly float upon the Water; and the Middle of all Trees is the most knotty. The Veins too, the nearer they are to the Roots, the more they are wreath'd and contorted; nevertheless the lower Parts are reckoned always stronger and more useful than the Upper. But I find in good Authors some very remarkable Things of some Trees; they say that the Vine exceeds even the Eternity of Time itself. In *Popolonia*, near *Piombino*, there was a Statue of *Jupiter* made of that Wood to be seen in *Cæsar*'s Days, which had lasted for a vast Number of Years without the least Decay; and indeed it is universally allow'd that there is no Wood whatsoever more durable. In *Ariana*, a Province of *India*, there are Vines so large, as *Strabo* informs us, that two Men can hardly embrace its Trunk. They tell us of a Roof of Cedar in *Utica* that lasted twelve Hundred and seventy eight Years. In a Temple of *Diana* in *Spain* they speak of Rafters of Juniper, that lasted from two Hundred Years before the Siege of *Troy* quite to the Days of *Hanibal*. The Cedar too is of a most wonderful Nature, if as they say it is the only Wood that will not retain the Nails. In the Mountains near the Lake *Benacus*, or the *Lago di Garda*, grows a Kind of Fir, which, if you make Vessels of it, will not hold the Wine, unless you first anoint them with Oil. Thus much for Trees.

CHAP. VIII.

Of Stones in general, when they are to be dug, and when used; which are the softest and which the hardest, and which best and most durable.

WE must likewise make Provision of the Stone which is to be used in our Walls, and this is of two Sorts; the one proper only for making the Lime and the Cement, the other for erecting the Building. Of this latter we shall treat first, omitting many Particulars, both for the Sake of Brevity, and because they are already sufficiently known. Neither shall we spend any Time here in philosophical Enquiries about the Principle and Origin of Stones; as, whether their first Particles, made viscous by a Mixture of Earth and Water, harden first into Slime, and afterwards into Stone; or what is said of Gems, that they are collected and concreted by the Heat and Power of the Rays of the Sun, or rather that there is in the Bosom of the Earth certain natural Seeds as of other Things, so also of Stones: And whether their Colour is owing to a certain proper blending of the Particles of Water with very minute ones of Earth; or to some innate Quality of its own Seed, or to an Impression receiv'd from the Sun's Rays. And though these Disquisitions might perhaps help

to

to adorn our Work, I shall omit them, and proceed to treat of the Method of Building as addressing myself to Artificers approv'd for Skill and Experience, with more Freedom than perhaps would be allow'd by those who are for more exact philosophising. *Cato* advises to dig the Stone in Summer, to let it lie in the open Air, and not to use it under two Years: In Summer, to the Intent that it may grow accustom'd by Degrees to Wind, Rain, and Frost, and other Inclemencies of the Weather, which it had not felt before. For if Stone, immediately upon its being dug out of the Quarry, while it is full of its native Juice and Humidity, is expos'd to severe Winds and sudden Frosts, it will split and break to Pieces. It should be kept in the open Air, in order to prove the Goodness of each particular Stone, and how well it is able to resist the Accidents that injure it, making Experiment by this small Trial, how long they are likely to hold against the Assaults of Time. They should not be used under two Years, to the Intent that you may have Time to find out such among them as are weak in their Nature, and likely to damage the Work, and to seperate them from the good ones; for it is certain, in one and the same Kind of Stones there is a Difference in Goodness of any Sort of Stone, and its Fitness for this or that particular Situation, is best learnt from Use and Experience; and you may much sooner come at their Values and Properties from old Buildings, than from the Writings and Precepts of Philosphers. However, to say something briefly of Stones in general, we will beg Leave to offer the following Observations.

ALL white Stone is softer than red, the clear is more easily wrought than the Cloudy, and the more like Salt it looks, the harder it is to work. Stone that looks as if it were strew'd over with a bright shining Sand, is harsh ; if little Sparks, as it were, of Gold are intermix'd, it will be stubborn; if it has a Kind of little black Points in it, it will be hard to get out of the Quarry: That which is spotted with angular Drops is stronger than that which has round ones, and the smaller those Drops are, the harder it will be ; and the finer and clearer the Colour is, the longer it will last. The Stone that has fewest Veins, will be most entire, and when the Veins come nearest in Colour to the adjoining Parts of the Stone, it will prove most equal throughout : The smaller the Veins, the handsomer ; the more winding they run, the more untoward ; and the more

knotty, the worse, Of these Veins that is most apt to split which has in the Middle a reddish Streak, or of the Colour of rotten Oker. Much of the same Nature is that which is stain'd here and there with the Colour of faded Grass, but the most difficult of all is such as looks like a cloudy Piece of Ice. A Multitude of Veins shews the Stone to be deceitful and apt to crack ; and the straiter they are, the more unfaithful. Upon breaking a Stone, the more fine and polish'd the Fragments appear, the closer bodied it is ; and that which when broken has its Outside the least rugged, will be more manageable than those which are rough. Of the Rough ones, those which are whitest will be worst for working ; whereas, on the Contrary, in brown Stones, those of the smallest and finest Grain are least obedient to the Tool. All mean ordinary Stones are the Harder for being spungy, and that which being sprinkled with Water is longest in drying, is the most crude.

ALL heavy Stones are more solid and easier to polish than light ones, which upon rubbing is much more apt to come off in Flakes than such as are heavy. That which upon being struck gives the best Sound, is closer made than that which sounds dull; and that which upon strong Friction smells of Sulphur, is stronger than that which yields no Smell at all. Lastly, that which makes the most Resistance against the Chizzel will be most firm and rigid against the Violence of Storms. They say, that those Stones which hold together in the largest Scantlings at the Mouth of the Quarry, are firmest against the Weather. All Stone too is softer when it is just dug up, than after it has been some Time in the Air, and when it is wetted, or softened with Water, is more yielding to the Tool than when it is dry. Also such Stones as are dug out of the moistest Part of the Quarry, will be the closest when they come to be dry ; and it is thought that Stones are easier wrought in a South-wind than in a North, and are more apt to split in a North-wind than in a South. But if you have a Mind to make an Experiment how your Stone will hold out against Time, you may judge from hence : If a Piece of it, which you soak in Water, increases much of its Weight, it will be apt to be rotted by Moisture ; and that which flies to Pieces in Fire, will bear neither Sun nor Heat. Neither do I think that we ought to omit here some Things worthy Memorial, which the Ancients relate of some Stones.

CHAP

CHAP. IX.

Some Things worthy Memorial, relating to Stones, left us by the Ancients.

IT will not be foreign to our Purpose to hear what a Variety there is in Stones, and what admirable Qualities some are endued with, that we may be able to apply each to its propereft Ufe. In the Territory of *Bolfena* and *Stratone*, they tell us there is a Stone extremely proper for all Manner of Buildings, which neither Fire nor any Injuries of Weather ever affects, and which preferves the Lineaments of Statues beyond any other. *Tacitus* writes, that when *Nero* repaired the City, which lay in Ruins by the Flames, he made use of the *Albanian* and *Gabinian* Stone for Beams, becaufe the Fire never hurts that Stone.

In the Territory of the *Genoefe* and of *Venice*, in the Dutchy of *Spoletto*, in the March of *Anconia*, and near *Burgundy*, they find a white Stone, which is eafily cut with a Saw and polifh'd, which if it were not for the Weaknefs and Brittlenefs of its Nature, would be ufed by every body ; but any thing of Froft or Wet rots and breaks it, and it is not ftrong enough to refift the Winds from the Sea. *Iftria* produces a Stone very like Marble, but if touch'd either by Flame or Vapour, it immediately flies in Pieces, which indeed is faid to be the Cafe of all Stones, efpecially of Flint both white and black, that they cannot endure Fire.

In the *Campagna di Roma* is a Stone of the Colour of black Afhes, in which there feems to be Coals mix'd and interfpers'd, which is beyond Imagination eafy to be wrought with Iron, thoroughly found, and not weak againft Fire or Weather ; but it is fo dry and thirfty, that it prefently drinks and burns up the Moifture of the Cement, and reduces it perfectly into Powder, fo that the Junctures opening, the Work prefently decays and falls to Ruins. But round Stones, and efpecially thofe which are found in Rivers, are of a Nature directly contrary ; for being always moift, they never bind with the Cement. But what a furprizing Difcovery is this which has been made, namely, that the Marble in the Quarry grows ! in thefe our Days they have found at *Rome* under Ground a Number of fmall Pieces of *Trevertine* Stone, very porous and fpungy, which by the Nourifhment (if we may fo call it) given it by the Earth and by Time, are grown together into one Piece.

In the Lake *di pie di Luco*, in that Part where the Water tumbles down a broken Precipice into the River *Nera*, you may perceive that the upper Edge of the Bank has grown continually, infomuch that fome have believ'd that this Encreafe and Growth of the Stone has in Length of Time clofed up the Mouth of the Valley and turn'd it into a Lake.

Below *la Bafilicata*, not far from the River *Silari*, on that Side where the Water flows from fome high Rocks towards the Eaft, there are daily feen to grow huge Pieces of hanging Stone, of fuch a Magnitude, that any one of them would be a Load for feveral Carts. This Stone while it is frefh and moift with its natural Juices, is very foft ; but when it is dry, it grows extremely hard, and very good for all Manner of Ufes. I have known the like happen in ancient Aqueducts, whofe Mouths, having contracted a Kind of Gumminefs, have feem'd incrufted all over with Stone. There are two very remarkable Things to be feen at this Day in *Romania* : In the Country of *Imola* is a very fteep Torrent, which daily throws out, fometimes in one Place and fometimes in another, a great Number of round Stones, generated within the Bowels of the Earth : In the Territory of *Faenza*, on the Banks of the River *Lamona*, there are found a great many Stones, naturally long and large, which continually throw out a confiderable Quantity of Salt, which in Procefs of Time is thought to grow into Stone too. In that of *Florence*, near the River *Chiane*, there is a Piece of Ground all ftrew'd over with hard Stones, which every feven Years diffolve into Clods of Earth.

Pliny relates, that near *Cizicus*, and about *Caffandra*, the Clods of Earth turn into Stone. In *Pozzuolo* there is a Duft which hardens into Stone, if mix'd with Sea-water. All the Way upon the Shore from *Oropus* to *Aulis*, every thing that is wafh'd by the Sea is petrified. *Diodorus* writes, that in *Arabia* the Clods dug out of the Ground have a fweet Smell, and

K   will

will melt in Fire like Metal, and run into Stone; and he adds, that this Stone is of such a Nature, that when the Rain falls upon it in any Building, the Cement all diffolves, and the Wall grows to be all of a Piece.

We are told, that they find in *Troas*, a Stone very apt to cleave, call'd the *Sarcophagus*, in which any dead Corpfe buried, is in-tirely confum'd in lefs than forty Days, all but the Teeth; and which is moft furprizing, all the Habits, and every Thing buryed with the Body, turns into Stone. Of a contrary Nature to this is the Stone called *Chernites*, in which *Darius* was buried, for that preferves the Body entire for a long Time. But of this Subject enough.

Chap. X.

Of the Origin of the Ufe of Bricks, in what Seafon they ought to be made, aud in what Shapes, their different Sorts, and the Usefulnefs of triangular Ones; and briefly, of all other Works made of baked Earth.

54

IT is certain the Ancients were very fond of ufing Bricks inftead of Stone. I confefs, I believe that at firft Men were put upon making Bricks to supply the Place of Stone in their Buildings, thro' Scarcity and Want of it; but afterwards finding how ready they were in working, how well adapted both to Ufe and Beauty, how ftrong and durable, they proceeded to make not only their ordinary Structures, but even their Palaces of Brick. At laft, either by Accident or Induftry, difcovering what Ufe Fire was of in hardening and ftrengthening them, they began in moft Places to bake the Bricks they built with. And from my own Obfervations upon the ancient Structures, I will be bold to fay, that there is not a better Material for any Sort of Edifice than Brick, not crude but baked; provided a right Method be ufed in baking them. But we will referve the Praifes of Works make of Bricks for another Place.

Our Bufinefs is to obferve here, that a whitifh chalky Earth is very much recommended for making them. The reddifh alfo is approved of, and that which is call'd male Sand. That which is abfolutely fandy and gravelly is to be avoided, and the ftony moft of all; becaufe in baking it is fubject to warp and crack, and if over baked will fret away of itfelf. We are advifed not to make our Bricks of Earth frefh dug, but to dig it in the Autumn, and leave it to digeft all Winter, and to make it into Brick early in the Spring; for if you make it in Winter, it is obvious that the Froft will crack it, and if you make it in the Middle of Summer, the exceffive Heat will make it fcale off in drying. But if Neceffity obliges you to make it in Winter, in extreme cold Weather, cover it immediately over with very dry Sand, and if in Summer, with wet Straw; for being fo kept, it will neither crack nor warp. Some are for having their Bricks glazed; if fo, you muft take Care not to make them of Earth that is either fandy, or too lean or dry; for thefe will fuck and eat away the Glazing: But you muft make them of a whitifh fat Clay, and you muft make them thin, for if they are too thick they will not bake thorowly, and it is a great Chance but they fplit; if you are oblig'd to have them thick, you may in a great Meafure prevent that Inconveniency, if you make one or more little Holes in them about half Way through, whereby the Damp and Vapour having proper Vents, they will both dry and bake the better.

The Potters rub their Veffels over with Chalk, by which Means, the Glazing, when it is melted over it, makes an even Surface; the fame Method may be ufed in making Bricks. I have obferv'd in the Works of the Ancients, that their Bricks have a Mixture of a certain Proportion of Sand, and efpecially of the red Sort, and I find they alfo mix'd them with red Earth, and even with Marble. I know by Experience that the very fame Earth will make harder and ftronger Brick, if we take the Pains to knead every Lump two or three Times over, as if we were making of Bread, till it grows like Wax, and is perfectly clear of the leaft Particle of Stone. Thefe, when they have pafs'd the Fire will attain the Hardnefs even of a Flint, and whether owing to the Heat in baking, or the Air in drying, will get a Sort of a ftrong Cruft, as Bread does. It will therefore be beft to make them thin, that they may have the more Cruft and the lefs Crum:

And

And we shall find, that if they are well rubb'd and polished, they will defy the Fury of the Weather. The same is true of Stones that are polished, which thereby escape being eaten with Rust. And it is thought that Bricks should be rubbed and ground either immediately upon their being taken out of the Kiln, before they are wetted; or when they have been wetted, before they are dry again; because when once they have been wetted and afterwards dryed, they grow so hard that they will turn and break the Edge of the Tool; but they are easier to grind when they are new, and hardly cold. There were three Sorts of Bricks among the Ancients; the First was a Foot and an Half Long, and a Foot Broad, the Second fifteen Inches every Way, the Third a Foot. We see in some of their Buildings, and especially in their Arches and *Mosaick* Works, Bricks two Foot every Way. We are told that the Ancients did not use the same Sort of Brick in their publick as in their private Edifices. I have observed in several of their Structures, and particularly in the *Appian* Way, several different Sorts of Bricks, some bigger, some smaller; so that I suppose they used them indifferently, and put in Practice not only what was absolutely necessary for Use, but any Thing that came into their Fancy, or which they thought would conduce to the Beauty of the Work. But, not to mention others, I have seen some not longer than six Inches, and not thicker than one, nor broader than three; but these they chiefly used in their Pavements, where they were laid edgeways. I am best pleased with their triangular ones, which they made in this Manner; they made one large Brick, a Foot Square, and an Inch and an Half Thick; and while it was fresh they cut it in two Lines crossways from one Angle to the other, which divided it into four equal Triangles. These Bricks had the following Advantages, they took up less Clay, they were easier to dispose in the Kiln and to take out again, they were more convenient for working, because the Bricklayer could hold four of them in one Hand, and with a small Stroke divide the one from the other; when placed in the Wall, with their Fronts foremost and their Angles inward, they appeared like compleat Bricks of a Foot Long: This made the Expence less, the Work more graceful, and the Wall stronger; for as there seemed to be none but entire Bricks in the Wall, the Angles being set like Teeth in the Rubbish that was laid in the Middle, made it extremely strong and durable. After the Bricks are moulded, they direct that they should not be put into the Kiln till they are perfectly dry, and they say they never are so under two Years; and they are reckoned to dry better in the Shade than in the Sun: But of these too enough, unless we will add that in all this Sort of Works, which are called Plastick, they reckon excellent, among others, the Earth that is called *Samian*, the *Aretinian*, and the *Modeneze*; in *Spain*, the *Saguntan*; and the *Pergamean* in *Asia*. Nor will I consult Brevity so much as to omit, that whatever I have here said of Bricks, will hold good of all Sorts of Tiles for Roofs of Houses or Gutters, and in a Word, of all Manner of Works made of baked Earth. We have treated of Stone, let us now proceed to speak of Lime.

CHAP. XI.

Of the Nature of Lime and Plaister of Paris, their Uses and Kinds, wherein they agree and wherein they differ, and of some Things not unworthy of Memory.

CATO the Censor, condemns Lime made of different Sorts of Stone, and takes that which is made of Flint to be good for no Manner of Work whatsoever; besides, in making of Lime all Stone is extremely improper that is dry and exhausted, or rotten, and which in burning has nothing in it for the Fire to consume, as all mouldering Stone, and the reddish and pale ones, which are found near *Rome* in the Country of the *Fidenates* and *Albanians*. The Lime commended by the best Judges, is that which loses a third Part of its Weight by burning; besides, Stone that is too moist in its Nature, is apt to vitrify in the Fire, so as to be of no Use for making of Lime. *Pliny* says, that the green, or *Serpentine*-stone mightily resists the Fire; but we know very well that the *Porphyry* will not only not burn itself, but will

will hinder the other Stones that are near it in the Kiln, from burning too. They also diſlike all earthy Stone, becauſe it makes the Lime foul. But the ancient Architects greatly praiſe the Lime made of very hard cloſe Stone, eſpecially white, which they ſay is not improper for any Sort of Work, and is extremely ſtrong in Arches. In the ſecond Place, they commend Lime made of Stone, not indeed light or rotten, but ſpungy; which they think for plaiſtering is better, and more tractable than any other, and gives the beſt Varniſh to the Work; and I have obſerved the Architects in *France*, to uſe no other Sort of Lime but what was made of the common Stones they found in Rivers or Torrents, blackiſh, and ſo very hard, that you would take them for Flints; and yet it is certain, both in Stone and Brickwork, it has preſerved an extraordinary Strength to a very great Age. We read in *Pliny*, that Lime made of the Stone of which they make Mill-ſtones, is excellent for all manner of Uſes; but I find upon Experience, that ſuch of them as ſeem ſpotted with Drops of Salt, being too rough and dry, will not do for this Uſe; but that which is not ſo ſpotted, but is cloſer, and when it is ground, makes a finer Duſt, ſucceeds extremely well. However, let the Nature of the Stone be what it will, that of the Quarry will be much better for making of Lime, than that which we pick up; and that dug out of a ſhady, moiſt Quarry, better than out of a dry one; and made of white Stone, more tractable than of black. In *France*, near the Sea-ſhore about *Vannes*, for Want of Stone, they make their Lime of Oyſter and Cockle-Shells. There is moreover a kind of Lime which we call Plaiſter of Paris, which too is made of burnt Stone; tho' we are told that in *Cyprus*, and about *Thebes*, this Sort of Plaiſter is dug out of the Surface of the Earth, ready baked by the Heat of the Sun. But the Stone that makes the Plaiſter of Paris, is different from that which makes the Lime; for it is very ſoft, and will eaſily rub to Pieces, except one found in *Syria*, which is very hard. It differs likewiſe in this, that the Plaiſter of Paris Stone requires but twenty Hours; and the Lime Stone takes threeſcore Hours in burning. I have obſerved, that in *Italy* there are four Sorts of Plaiſter of Paris, two of which are tranſparent, and two which are not: Of the tranſparent, one is like Lumps of Allum, or rather of Alabaſter, and they called it the

Scaly Sort, becauſe it conſiſts of extreme thin Scales, one over the other, like the Coats of an Onion. The other is ſealy too, but is more like a blackiſh Salt than Allum. The Sorts that are not tranſparent are both like a very cloſe Sort of Chalk, but one is pale and whitiſh, and the other with that Paleneſs has a Tincture of red; which laſt is firmer and cloſer than the firſt. Of the laſt, the reddeſt is the moſt tenacious. Of the firſt, that which is the cleareſt and whiteſt is uſed in Stuc Work for Figures and Corniſhes.

Near *Rimini* they find a Plaiſter of Paris ſo ſolid that you would take it for Marble or Alabaſter, which I had had cut with a Saw into large thin Pieces, extremely convenient for Incruſtations. That I may omit nothing that is neceſſary, all Plaiſter of Paris muſt be broken and pounded with wooden Mallets, till it is reduced to Powder, and ſo kept in Heaps in ſome very dry Place, and as ſoon as ever it is brought out, it muſt be watered and uſed immediately.

But Lime on the Contrary need not be pounded, but may be ſoak'd in the Lumps, and muſt be plentifully ſoak'd with Water a good while before you uſe it, eſpecially if it is for Plaiſtering; to the Intent that if there ſhould be any Lumps not enough burnt, it may be diſſolv'd and liquify'd by long lying in the Water: Becauſe, when it is uſed too ſoon, before it is duly ſoak'd, there will be ſome ſmall unconcocted Stones in it, which afterwards coming to rot, throw out little Puſtules, which ſpoil the Neatneſs of the Work. Add hereunto, that you need not give your Lime a Flood, as I may call it, of Water at once, but wet it by little and little, ſprinkling it ſeveral Times over, till it is in all Parts thoroughly impregnated with it; afterwards it muſt be kept in ſome ſhady Place, moderately moiſt, clear from all Mixture, and only cover'd over with a little Sand, till by Length of Time it is better fermented; and it has been found that Lime by this thorough Fermentation acquires inconceivable Virtue. I have known ſome found in an old neglected Ditch, that, as plainly appear'd by the ſtrongeſt Conjectures, was left there above five hundred Years; which when it was diſcover'd was ſo moiſt and liquid, and, to uſe the Expreſſion, ſo mature, that it far exceeded Honey or Marrow itſelf in Softneſs; and nothing in Nature can be imagin'd more ſerviceable for all Manner of Uſes. It requires double the Sand if prepared thus, than

than if you mix it immediately. In this, therefore, Lime and Plaister of Paris do not agree; but in other Things they do. Carry your Lime, therefore, immediately out of the Kiln into a shady, dry Place, and water it; for if you keep it either in the Kiln itself, or any where else in the Air, or expos'd to the Moon or Sun, especially in Summer, it would soon crumble to Powder, and be totally useless. But of this sufficient. They advise us not to put our Stone into the Kiln till we have broken it into Pieces, not smaller than the Clods; for, not to mention that they will burn the easier, it has been observed that in the middle of some Stones, and especially of round ones, there are sometimes certain Concavities, in which the Air being inclosed often does a great deal of Mischief: For when they come to feel the Fire in the Kiln, this Air is either compressed by the cold retiring inwards, or else when the Stone grows hot it turns to Vapour, which makes it swell till it bursts the Prison wherein it is confined, and breaks out with a dreadful Noise and irresistible Force, and blows up the whole Kiln. Some in the middle of such Stones have seen living Creatures, of various kinds, and particularly Worms with a hairy Back, and a great Number of Feet, which do a great deal of Harm to the Kiln. And I will here add some Things worthy to be recorded, which have been seen in our Days, since I do not write only for the Use of Workmen, but also for all such as are studious of curious Enquiries; for which Reason, I shall not scruple, now and then, to intermix any thing that is delightful, provided it is not absolutely foreign to my Purpose. THERE was brought to Pope *Martin* V. a Serpent found by the Miners in a Quarry in *la Romagna*, which lived pent up in the Hollow of a great Stone, without the least Crack or Hole in it for Admission of Air; in like Manner Toads too have been found and Crabs, but dead. I myself have been Witness to the finding of the Leaves of Trees in the Middle of a very white Piece of Marble. All the Summit of Mount *Vellino*, one of those which divide the Country of *Abruzzo* from *Marsi*, and is higher than any of the rest, is covered over with a white Stone, so that the very Mountain looks white with it, among which, especially on that Side, which looks towards *Abruzzo*, are a great many broken Pieces with Figures upon them, exactly like Sea-shells, not bigger than the Palm of a Man's Hand. But, what is more extraordinary, in the *Veroneze*, they daily find Stones upon the Ground marked with the Figure of the Cinquefoil, with every Line and Vein drawn so exactly and regularly, by the Hand of Nature, that the nicest Artist cannot pretend to come up to it; and which is most curious of all, every one of these Stones are found with the Impression turned downwards, and hid by the Stone, as if Nature had not been at the Pains of such fine Sculptures to gain the Approbation of Men, but for her own Diversion. But to return to our Subject.

I SHALL not spend Time here to shew how to make the Mouth of the Kiln, and its Covering, and the inward Seat of the Fire, and how to give Vent to the Flame when it grows hot, and to keep it, as it were, within its own Confines, so as to direct the whole united Strength and Power of the Fire to the burning of the Lime. Nor will I proceed to teach how the Fire is to be kindled by little and little, and never left till the Flame burns out at the Top of the Furnace perfectly clear, and without the least Smoke, and till the very uppermost Stones are red hot; and that the Stone is not burnt enough, till the Kiln, which had been swelled and cracked by the Fire, afterwards settles and closes itself again. It is a surprizing Thing to observe the Nature of this Element; for if you take away the Fire, the Kiln will grow cooler and cooler by Degrees at the Bottom, while it continues burning hot at Top. But as in Building, we have Occasion not only for Lime, but Sand, we will now say something about that.

CHAP. XII.

Of the three different Kinds of Sands, and of the various Materials in Building, in different Places.

THERE are three Sorts of Sand, Pitsand, River-sand, and Sea-sand; the best of all these is the Pit-sand; and this is of several Kinds; black, white, red, the carbuncly, and the gritty. But if any should ask what I take Sand to be, I might perhaps answer

swer, that it is nothing but a Composition of the smallest Stones, the large ones being all broken to Pieces; tho' it is *Vitruvius*'s Opinion, that Sand, especially that which in *Tuscany* they call the carbuncly Sort, is a Kind of Earth burnt by the Fire inclosed by Nature within the Hills, and made somewhat harder than Earth unburnt, but softer than any Stone. Of all these they most commend the carbuncly Sort. I have observed, that in the publick Buildings in *Rome*, they used the red as none of the worst. Of all the Pit-sand the white is the worst. The gritty is of Use in filling up of Foundations; but among the best, they give the second Place to the finest of the gritty, and especially to the sharp angular Sort, without the least Mixture of Earth in it, as is that which they find in the Territory of the *Vilumbrians*. Next to this they esteem the River Sand, which is dug after the uppermost Layer is taken off; and next to the River-sand that of the Torrent, especially of such Torrents as run between Hills, where the Water has the greatest Descent. In the last Place comes the Sea-sand, and of this Sort, the blackest and most glazed is not wholly to be despised. In the Country, near *Salerno*, they esteem their Sea-sand not inferior to Pit-sand, but they say it is not to be dug in all Parts of the Shore alike; for they find it worst of all where it is exposed to the South Wind; but it is not bad in those Places which look to the South-west. But of Sea-sands, it is certain the best is that which lies under Rocks, and which is of the coarsest Grain. There is a great deal of Difference in Sands, for that of the Sea is very slow in drying, and is continually moist and apt to dissolve, by Reason of its Salt, and is therefore very improper and unfaithful in supporting of great Weights. That of the River too is somewhat moister than the Pit-sand, and therefore is more tractable and better for Plaistering-work. The Pit-sand, by means of its Fatness, is most tenacious, but is apt to crack, for which Reason they use it in Vault-work, but not in plaistering. But of each Sort, that is always best, which being rubbed with the Hand creeks the most, and being laid upon a white Cloth, makes the least Soil, and leaves the least Earth behind it. On the contrary, that is the worst, which feels mealy instead of sharp, and which in Smell and

Colour resembles red Earth, and being mixed with Water makes it foul and muddy, and if left abroad in the Air, presently brings forth Grass. Neither will that be good, which after it is dug, is left for any Time exposed to the Sun, or Moon, or to Frosts; because it turns it in a Manner to Earth, and makes it very apt to rot; or when it is inclined to bring forth Shrubs, or wild Figs, it is extremly bad for cementing of Walls. We have now treated of Timber, Stone, Lime, and Sand, such as are approved of by the Ancients; but in all Places these Things are not to be found with all the Qualifications which we require. *Tully* says, that *Asia*, by means of its Abundance of Marble, always flourished in fine Buildings and Statues; but Marble is not to be got every where. In some Places there is either no Stone at all, or what there is, is good for no manner of Use. In all the Southern Parts of *Italy*, they say there is no Want of Sand-Pits, but on the other Side of the *Appenine* there are none. *Pliny* says, the *Babylonians* made Use of Slime, and the *Carthaginians* of Mud. In some Places, not having any Sort of Stone, they build with Hurdles and Potters Earth. *Herodotus* tells us, that the *Budini* make all their Structures, as well publick as private, of nothing but Wood, even to the Walls of their City, and the Statues of their Gods. *Mela* says, that the *Nervi* have no Wood at all; and that for Want of it they are obliged to make their Fires of Bones. In *Ægypt* their Fuel is the Dung of their Cattle. For this Reason, the Habitations of Men are different, according to the different Conveniencies of the Country. Among the *Ægyptians* there are Royal Palaces built of Rushes; and in *India*, of the Ribs of Whales. In *Carræ*, a Town in *Arabia*, they build with Lumps of Salt: But of these elsewhere. So that as we have already observed, there is not the same Plenty of Stone, Sand, and the like, every where, but in different Places there are different Accommodations and Conveniencies: Therefore we are to make Use of such as offer themselves; and out of those we should, in the first Place, make it our Business, always to select and provide the best and properest, and, secondly, in building with them, we should carefully allot to each its proper Place and Situation.

CHAP. XIII.

Whether the Observation of Times and Seasons is of any Use in beginning a Building; what Season is most convenient; as also, with what Auguries or Prayers we ought to set out upon our Work.

HAVING got ready the Materials before spoken of, it remains now that we proceed to treat of the Work itself. For as to the providing of Iron, Brass, Lead, Glass, and the like, it requires no Care, but merely the Buying, and having them in Readiness, that your Building may not stand still for them; tho' we shall in due Time lay down some Instructions about the Choice and Distribution of them, which is of Consequence to the compleating and adorning the Work. And we shall take and consider the Structure from the Foundation, in the same Manner as if we were actually about doing the Work ourselves. But here I must again admonish you to consider the Times, both with Relation to the Publick, and to yourself and Family, whether they are troublesome or peaceable, prosperous or calamitous, lest we expose ourselves to Envy, if we go on with our Undertaking, or to Loss if we give it over. We should also have a particular Regard to the Season of the Year; for we see that Buildings begun and prosecuted in Winter, especially in a cold Climate, are taken with the Frost, or in Summer, in a hot Climate, dry'd up with the Heat before ever they have fasten'd. For this Reason it was that *Frontinus*, the Architect, advis'd us never to undertake such a Work but in a proper Season of the Year, which is from the Beginning of *April* to the Beginning of *November*, resting, however, in the greatest Heat of Summer. But I am for hastening or delaying the Work just according to the Difference of the Climate and of the Weather; and therefore if you are prepar'd with all the Things before recited, and your Convenience suits, you have nothing to do but to mark out the Area of your Structure in the Ground, with all its Lines, Angles and Dimensions. But there are some who tell us that in Building we should observe and wait for happy Auspices, and that it is of the utmost Importance from what particular Point of Time the Structure is to date its Being. They relate, that *Lucius Tarutius* found out the exact Nativity of *Rome*, only

by the Observation of the Turns in its Fortune. The wisest Men among the Ancients had such an Opinion of the Consequence of the Moment of the Beginning a Thing might have as to its future Success, that *Julius Fermicus Maturnus* tells us of some Mathematicians that pretended to have discover'd the very instant when the World had its Beginning, and that wrote very accurately about it: For *Æsculapius*, and *Anubius*, and *Petosiris*, and *Necepso*, who only wrote from them, say that it begun just at the Rising of the *Crab*, when the Moon was fourteen Days old, the Sun being in *Leo*, Saturn in *Capricorn*, *Jupiter* in *Sagittary*, Mars in *Scorpio*, Venus in *Libra*, and *Mercury* in *Virgo*. And indeed, if we rightly consider them, the Times may have a great Influence in Things. For how is it else, that in the shortest Day of the Year, the Penny-royal, tho' quite dry, sprouts and flourishes; Bladders that are blown up burst; the Leaves of Willows, and the Kernels of Apples turn and change Sides; and that the small Fibres of a Shell-fish correspond, increase and decrease with the Increase and Decrease of the Moon. I must confess, though I have not so much Faith in the Professors of this Science, and the Observers of Times and Seasons, as to believe their Art can influence the Fortune of any Thing, yet I think they are not to be despised when they argue for the Happiness or Adversity of such stated Times as these from the Disposition of the Heavens. But let this be as it will, the following their Instructions may be of great Service, if true; and can do little harm, if false. I might here add some ridiculous Circumstances which the Ancients observed in the Beginning of their Undertakings; but I would not have them interpreted in a wrong Sense; and indeed they deserve only to be laughed at, who would perswade us that the very Marking out of the Platform ought to be done under proper Auspices. The Ancients were so governed by these Superstitions, that in making out the Lists of their Armies,

observed

they took great Care that the first Soldier had not an unlucky Name; which was a Rule they also observed in the Ceremony of purifying their Soldiers and their Colonies, wherein, the Person that was to lead the Beast to the Sacrifice must have a fortunate Name. And the Censors, in framing out the publick Revenues and Estates, always began with the Lake *Lucrinus,* because of the Lucrativenefs of its Name, So likewife, being terrified with the dismal Name of *Epidamnus,* that such as went thither might not be said to be gone a damnable Voyage, they changed its Name into *Dyrrachium*; so likewife they served *Beneventum,* which before was called *Maleventum.* Neither, on the other Hand, can I forbear laughing at their Conceit, that in beginning Undertakings of this Sort it was good to repeat certain favourable Words and Charms.

And there are some that affirm, that Men's Words are so powerful, that they are obey'd even by Beafts and Things inanimate. I omit *Cato*'s Fancy, that Oxen when fatigued may be refresh'd by certain Words. They tell us too, that they used with certain Prayers and Forms of Words to entreat and beseech their Mother Earth to give Nourishment to foreign Trees, and such as she was not accustom'd to bear; and that the Trees also were to be humbly pray'd to suffer themselves to be re-

mov'd, and to thrive in another Ground. And since we are got into this foolish Strain of recording the Follies of other Men, I will also mention, for Diversion Sake, what they tell us, that the Words of Mankind are of such Effect, that Turnips will grow incredibly, if when we sow them we at the same Time pray them to be gracious and lucky to us, our Families, and our Neighbourhood. But if these be so, I can't imagine why the Basilico-root should, as they say, grow the faster for being curst and abused when it is sown. But let us leave this idle Subject. It is undoubtedly proper, omitting all these uncertain Superstitions, to set about our Work with a holy and religious Preparation. 57

Ab Jove principium, Musæ ;----
Jovis omnia plena. 58

We ought therefore to begin our Undertaking with a clean Heart, and with devout Oblations, and with Prayers to Almighty God to implore his Assistance, and Blessing upon the Beginnings of our Labours, that it may have a happy and prosperous Ending, with Strength and Happiness to it and its Inhabitants, with Content of Mind, Encrease of Fortune, Success of Industry, Acquisition of Glory, and a Succession and Continuance of all good Things. So much for our Preparation.

The End of Book II.

THE

ARCHITECTURE

OF

Leone Batiſta Alberti.

BOOK III. CHAP. I.

Of the Work. Wherein lies the Buſineſs of the Work; the different Parts of the Wall, and what they require. That the Foundation is no Part of the Wall; what Soil makes the beſt Foundation.

THE whole Buſineſs of the working Part of Building is this; by a regular and artful Conjunction of different Things, whether ſquare Stone, or uneven Scantlings, or Timber, or any other ſtrong Material, to form them as well as poſſible into a ſolid, regular, and conſiſtent Structure. We call it regular and conſiſtent when the Parts are not incongruous and disjointed, but are diſpoſed in their proper Places, and are anſwerable one to the other, and conformable to a right Ordinance of Lines. We are therefore to conſider what are the principal eſſential Parts in the Wall, and what are only the Lines and Diſpoſition of thoſe Parts. Nor are the Parts of the Wall any Thing difficult to find out; for the Top, the Bottom, the right Side, the Left, the remote Parts, the Near, the Middle are obvious of themſelves; but the particular Nature of each of theſe, and wherein they differ, is not

ſo eaſily known. For the raiſing a Building is not, as the Ignorant imagine, merely laying Stone upon Stone, or Brick upon Brick; but as there is a great Diverſity of Parts, ſo there requires a great Diverſity of Materials and Contrivance. For one Thing is proper in the Foundation, another in the naked Wall and in the Corniſh, another for the Coins, and for the Lips of the Apertures, one for the outward Face of the Wall, another for the cramming and filling up the middle Parts: Our Buſineſs here is to ſhew what is requiſite in each of theſe. In doing this, therefore, we ſhall begin at the Foundation, imitating, as we ſaid before, thoſe that are actually going to raiſe the Structure. The Foundation, if I miſtake not, is not properly a Part of the Wall, but the Place and Seat on which the Wall is reared. For if we can find a Seat perfectly firm and ſolid, conſiſting perhaps of nothing but Stone, what Foundation are we obliged to make? None,

M   certain-

certainly, but to begin immediately from thence to erect our Wall. At *Siena* there are huge Towers raised immediately from the naked Earth, because the Hill is lined with a solid Rock. Making a Foundation, that is to say, digging up the Ground, and making a Trench, is necessary in those Places, where you cannot find firm Ground without digging; which, indeed, is the Case almost every where, as will appear hereafter. The Marks of a good Soil for a Foundation are these; if it does not produce any kind of Herb that usually grows in moist Places; if it bears either no Tree at all, or only such as delight in a very hard, close Earth; if every Thing round about is extremely dry, and, as it were, quite parched up; if the Place is stony, not with small round Pebbles, but large sharp Stones, and especially Flints; if there are no Springs nor Veins of Water running under it; because the Nature of all Streams is either to be perpetually carrying away, or bringing something along with them: And therefore it is that in all flat Grounds, lying near any River, you can never meet with any firm Soil, till you dig below the Level of the Channel. Before you begin to dig your Foundations, you should once again carefully review and consider all the Lines and Angles of your Platform, what Dimensions they are to be of, and how they are to disposed. In making these Angles we must

use a Square Rule, not of a small but of a very large Size, that our strait Lines may be the truer. The Ancients made their square Rule of three strait ones joined together in a Triangle, whereof one was of three Cubits, the other of four, and the third of five. The Ignorant do not know how to make these Angles till they have first cleared away every Thing that incumbers the Area, and have it all perfectly open, almost level before them: For which Reason, laying furiously hold of their Tools, they fall like so many Ravagers to demolishing and levelling every Thing before them; which would become them much better in the Country of an Enemy. But the Error of these Men ought to be corrected; for a Change of Fortune, or the Adversity of the Times, or some unforeseen Accident, or Necessity, may possibly oblige you to lay aside the Thoughts of the Undertaking you have begun. And it is certainly very unseemly, in the mean while, to have no Regard to the Labours of your Ancestors, or to the Conveniencies which your Fellow-Citizens find in these paternal Habitations, which they have been long accustomed to; and as for pulling down and demolishing, that is in your Power at any Time. I am therefore for preserving the old Structures untouched, till such Time as it is absolutely necessary to remove them to make Way for the new.   60

59

CHAP. II.

That the Foundation chiefly is to be marked out with Lines; and by what Tokens we may know the Goodness of the Ground.

IN marking out your Foundations, you are to remember, that the first Ground-work of your Wall, and the Soccles, which are called Foundations too, must be a determinate Proportion broader than the Wall that is to be erected upon it; in Imitation of those who walk over the Snow in the *Alps* of *Tuscany*, who wear upon their Feet Hurdles made of Twigs and small Ropes, plaited together for that very Purpose, the Broadness of which keeps them from sinking in the Snow. How to dispose the Angles, is not easy to teach clearly with Words alone; because the Method of drawing them, is borrowed from the Mathematicks, and stands in Need of the Example of Lines, a Thing foreign to our Design

here, and which we have treated of in another Place, in our Mathematical Commentaries. However, I will endeavour, as far as is necessary here, to speak of them in such a Manner, that if you have any Share of Ingenuity, you may easily comprehend many Things, by Means of which you may afterwards make yourself Master of all the rest. Whatever may chance to seem more obscure, if you have a Mind to understand it thoroughly, you may apply to those Commentaries. My Method, then, in describing the Foundations, is to draw some Lines, which I call radical ones, in this Manner *. From the Middle of the Fore-front of the Work, I draw a Line quite thro' to the Back-front, in the Middle

61

* Plate 4

of

of this Line I fix a Nail in the Ground, from which I raise, and let fall Perpendiculars, according to the Method of the Geometers; and to these two Lines I reduce every Thing that I have Occasion to measure; which succeeds perfectly well in all Respects; for the Parallel Lines are obvious; you see exactly where to make your Angles correspondent, and to dispose every Part consistently, and agreeably, with the others. But if it so happens, that any old Buildings obstruct your Sight from discovering and fixing upon the exact Seat of every Angle; your Business then is to draw Lines, at equal Distances, in those Places which are clear and free; then having marked the Point of Intersection, by the Assistance of the Diameter and Gnomon, and by drawing other Lines at equal Distances, fitted to the Square, we may compleatly effect our Purpose: And it will be of no small Convenience to terminate the Ray of Sight with a Line in those Places which lie higher than the rest; whence letting fall a Perpendicular, we may find the right Direction and Production of our Lines. Having marked out the Lines and Angles of our Trenches, we ought to have, if possible, as sharp and clear a Sight as a certain *Spaniard* in our Days was fabulously said to have, who they tell us, could see the lowest Veins of Water that run under Ground, as plainly as if they were above Ground. So the many Things happen under the Surface of Earth, which we know nothing of, as makes it unsafe to trust the Weight and Expence of a Building to it. And, certainly, as in all the rest of the Structure, so especially in the Foundations, we ought to neglect no Precaution which it becomes an accurate and diligent Architect to take; for an Error in any other Part does less Mischief, and is more easily remedied, or better borne, than in the Foundation; in which, a Mistake is inexcusable. But

the Ancients used to say, dig on, and good Fortune attend you, till you find a solid Bottom; for the Earth has several Strata, and those of different Natures; some sandy, others gravelly, some stony, and the like; under which, at certain Depths, is a hard, firm Bank, fit to support the heaviest Structure. This also is various, and hardly like any thing of its own kind in any Particular; in some Places it is excessively hard, and scarce penetrable with Iron; in others, fatter and softer; in some Places blacker, in others whiter; which last is reckoned the weakest of all; in some Places chalky, in others, stony; in others, a Kind of Potters Clay mixed with Gravel; of all which, no other certain Judgment can be made, but that the best is reckoned to be that which is hardest to the Pick-axe, and which when wetted does not dissolve. And for this Reason, none is thought firmer and stronger, or more durable, than that which serves as a Bottom to any Springs of Water in the Bowels of the Earth. But it is my Opinion, that the best Way is to take Counsel with discreet and experienced Men of the Country, and with the neighbouring Architects; who, both from the Example of old Structures, and from their daily Practice in actual Building, must be the best Judges of the Nature of the Soil, and what Weight it is able to bear. There are also Methods of proving the Firmness of the Soil. If you roll any great Weight along the Ground, or let it fall down from any Heighth, and it does not make the Earth shake, nor stir the Water set there on Purpose in a Bason; you may safely promise yourself a good, sound Foundation in that Place. But in some Countries there is no solid Bottom to be found any where; as near the *Adriatic*, and about *Venice*, where, generally, there is nothing to be met with but a loose, soft Mud.

C H A P. III.

That the Nature of Places is various, and therefore we ought not to trust any Place too hastily, till we have first dug Wells, or Reservoirs; but that in marshy Places, we must make our Foundation with Piles burnt at the Ends, and driven in with their Heads downward with light Beetles, and many repeated Blows, till they are driven quite into the Head.

YOU must therefore use different Methods for your Foundations, according to the Diversity of Places, whereof some are

lofty, some low, others between both, as the Sides of Hills: Some again are parcht and dry, as generally the Summits and Ridges of

Mountains; others damp and washy, as are those which lie near Seas or Lakes, or in Bottoms between Hills. Others are so situated as to be neither always dry nor always wet, which is the Nature of easy Ascents, where the Water does not lie and soak, but runs gently off. We must never trust too hastily to any Ground, tho' it does resist the Pick-axe, for it may be in a Plain, and be infirm, the Consequence of which might be the Ruin of the whole Work. I have seen a Tower at *Mestri*, a Place belonging to the *Venetians*, which in a few Years after it was built, made its Way thro' the Ground it stood upon, which, as the Fact evinced, was a loose weak Soil, and bury'd itself in Earth, up to the very Battlements. For this Reason they are very much to be blamed, who not being provided by Nature with a Soil fit to support the Weight of an Edifice, and Lightning upon the Ruins or Remains of some old Structure, do not take the Pains to examine the Goodness of its Foundation, but inconsiderately raise great Piles of Building upon it, and out of the Avarice of saving a little Expence, throw away all the Money they lay out in the Work. It is therefore excellent Advice, the first Thing you do to dig Wells, for several Reasons, and especially in order to get acquainted with the Strata of the Earth, whether found enough to bear the Superstructure, or likely to give way. Add, likewise, that the Water you find in them, and the Stuff you dig out, will be of great Service to you in several Parts of your Work; and moreover, that the Opening such Vents will be a great Security to the Firmness of the Building, and prevent its being injured by subterraneous Exhalations. Having therefore, either by digging a Well, or a Cistern, or a Shoar, or any other Hole of that Nature, made yourself thoroughly acquainted with the Veins or Layers of the Earth, you are to make Choice of that which you may most safely trust with your Superstructure. In Eminences, or wherever else the Water is running down washes away the Ground, the deeper you make your Trench, the better. And that the Hills are actually eaten and wash'd away, and wasted more and more daily by continual Rains, is evident from the Caverns and Rocks which every Day grow more visible, whereas at first they were so cover'd with Earth that we could hardly perceive them. Mount *Morello*, which is about *Florence*, in the Days of our Fathers was all over cover'd with Firs; and now it is

quite wild and naked; occasion'd, as I suppose, by the Washing of the Rain In Situations upon Slopes, *Columella* directs us to begin our Foundations at the lowest Part of the Slope first; which is certainly very right, for besides that whatever you lay there will always stand firm and unmoveable in its Place, it will also serve as a Prop or Buttress, to whatever you add to the upper Parts, if you afterwards think fit to enlarge your Structure. You will also thereby discover and provide against those Defects which sometimes happen in such Trenches by the cracking or falling in of the Earth. In marshy Grounds, you should make your Trench very wide, and fortify both Sides of it with Stakes, Hurdles, Planks, Sea-weeds, and Clay, so strongly that no Water may get in; then you must draw off every drop of Water that happens to be left within your Frame-work, and dig out the Sand, and clear away the Mud from the Bottom till you have firm dry Ground to set your Foot upon. The same you are to do in sandy Ground, as far as Necessity requires. Moreover, the Bottom of the Trench must be laid exactly level, not sloping on either Side, that the Materials laid upon it may be equally balanced. There is a natural instinct in all heavy Bodies to lean and press upon the lowest Parts. There are other Things which they direct us to do in marshy Situations, but they belong rather to the Walling than to the Foundations. They order us to drive into the Ground a great Number of Stakes and Piles burnt at the End, and set with their Heads downwards, so as to have a Surface of twice the Breadth that we intend for our Wall; that these Piles should never be less in length than the eighth Part of the Heighth of the Wall to be built upon them, and for their Thickness, it should be the twelfth Part of their Length, and no less. Lastly they should be drove in so close that their is not room for one more. The Instrument we use for driving in these Piles, whatever Sort it it is of, should do its Business by a great many repeated Strokes; for when it is too heavy, coming down with an immense and intolerable Force, it breaks and splits the Timber; but the continual Repetition of gentle Strokes wearies and overcomes the greatest Hardness and Obstinacy of the Ground. You have an Instance of this when you go to drive a small Nail into a hard Piece of Timber; if you use a great heavy Hammer, it won't do; but if you work with a manageable light one, it penetrates immediately

What has been said may suffice, with relation to our Trench, unless we would add, that sometimes, either to save Money, or to avoid an intermediate Piece of rotten Ground, it may not be amiss to make a Foundation not continued entire all the way, but with Intervals left between, as if we were only making Columns or Pilasters, then turning Arches * from one Pilaster to the other, to lay over them the rest of the Wall

In these we are to observe the same Directions as we gave before; but the greater Weight you are to raise upon them, the large. and stronger Pilasters and Bases you must make. But of these enough.

A. Plate 5.

CHAP. IV.

Of the Nature, Forms and Qualities of Stones, and of the Tempering of Mortar.

WE now come to begin our Wall; but as the Workman's Art and Manner of Building depends partly upon the Nature, Form and Quality of his Stone, and partly upon the Tempering of his Mortar, we are therefore first to treat briefly of these. Of Stones, some are living, juicy, and strong, such as Flint, Marble, and the like, which by Nature are heavy and sonorous; others are exhausted, light, and dead sounding, as are all Stones that are soft and sandy. Again, some have even Superficies, strait Lines, and equal Angles, which are call'd Squared Stones; others have uneven Superficies, of various Lines, and unequal Angles, which we call Rough. Of Stones also, some are big and unweildy, so that a Man's Hand cannot manage them at Pleasure, without the Assistance of Sleds, Leavers, Rowlers, Pullies, or the like Engines; others small, so as you may raise and manage them with one single Hand just as you please. The third Sort is between both, of a moderate Size and Weight, which are call'd sizeable. All Stone should be Entire, not Muddy, and well wash'd; you may know whether it is Entire or Crack'd, by the Sound it gives when you Strike upon it. You can wash them no where better than in a River; and it is certain that the Middling sizeable Sort are not soak'd enough under nine Days, and the large ones under more. That which is fresh dug out of the Quarry is better than that which has been long kept; and that which has been once cemented with Mortar will not cement well again a second Time. So much may suffice as to Stone. As for Lime, they condemn that which when it comes from the Kiln is not in entire Lumps, but in broken Pieces, and as it were in Powder, and they say it will never prove serviceable. They commend that which purges and grows white in the Fire, and which is light and sonorous, and when you water it, bursts, and throws out a strong thick Smoke high into the Air. The former, being weak, must of Course require less Sand; but this latter, being strong, requires more. *Cato* directs, that to every two Foot of Work, we should allow one Bushel of Lime and two of Sand: Others prescribe different Proportions. *Vitruvius* and *Pliny* are for mixing the Sand thus; namely to give to each Bushel of Lime three of Pit-sand, or two of River or Sea-sand. Lastly, when the Quality and Nature of your Stone requires your Mortar to be more liquid or tractable (which we shall speak of more clearly below) your Sand must be sifted through a Sieve; but when it is to be stiffer, then mix it with half Gravel and broken Fragments of Stone. All agree, that if you mix it with one third of broken Tile or Brick pounded, it will be much more tenacious. However, mix it as you will, you must stir it about often, till the smallest Pieces are incorporated; and some, for this Purpose, and that it may be well mingled together, stir it about and beat it a great while in a Mortar. But we shall say no more here of the Cement, only thus much, that Lime takes better hold with Stone of its own Kind, and especially out of the same Quarry, than with a Stranger.

N

Chap. V.

Of the lower Courses or Foundations, according to the Precepts and Example of the Ancients.

FOR making the lower Courses, that is to say, raising the Foundations up to the Level of the Ground, I do not find any Precepts among the Ancients, except this one, that all Stones which, after being in the Air two Years, discover any Defect, must be banish'd into the Foundation. For as in an Army, the sluggish and weak who cannot endure the Sun and Dust, are sent home with Marks of Infamy, so these soft enervated Stones ought to be rejected, and left to an inglorious Repose in their primitive Obscurity. Indeed I find by Historians, that the Ancients took as much Care of the Strength and Soundness of their Foundation in all its Parts as of any other Part of the Wall. *Asithis*, the Son of *Nicerinus*, King of *Ægypt*, (the Author of the Law, that whoever was sued for Debt should give the Corpse of his Father in Pawn) when he built a Pyramid of Bricks to make his Foundations, drove Piles into the Marsh, and laid his Bricks upon them. And we are inform'd that *Ctesipho*, the excellent Architect that built the famous Temple of *Diana* at *Ephesus*, having made Choice of a level Piece of Ground, thoroughly drain'd, and likely to be free from Earthquakes; that he might not lay the Foundations of such a huge Pile in so loose and unfaithful a Soil without due Precautions, first made a Bottom of Coals pounded to Dust; then drove in Piles with Fleeces and Coals wedged in between Pile and Pile; and over these a Course of Stone with very long Junctures.

We find that about *Jerusalem*, in the Foundations of their Publick Works, they sometimes used Stones thirty Feet long, and not less than fifteen high. But I have observed, that in other Places, the Ancients, who were wonderfully expert in managing of great Works, followed different Rules and Methods in filling up the Foundations. In the Sepulchre of the *Antonini* they filled them up with little Pieces of very hard Stone, each not bigger than a Handful, and which they perfectly drowned in Mortar. In the *Forum Argentarium*, with Fragments of all Sorts of broken Stones; in the *Comitia*, with Bits of the very worst Sort of soft Stuff. But I am mightily pleased with those who in the *Tarpeia* imitated Nature, in a Contrivance particularly well adapted to Hills; for as she, in the Formation of Mountains, mixes the softest Materials with the hardest Stone, so these Workmen first laid a Course of squared Stone, as strong as they could get, to the Heighth of two Feet; over these they made a Kind of Plaister of Mortar, and broken Fragments, then another Course of Stone, and with another of Plaister they finished their Foundation. I have known other Instances, where the Ancients have made much the same Sort of Foundations and Structures too, of coarse Pit-gravel, and common Stone that they have picked up by chance, which have lasted many Ages. Upon pulling down a very high and strong Tower at *Bologna*, they discovered that the Foundations were filled with nothing but round Stones and Chalk, to the Heighth of nine Feet; the other Parts were built with Mortar. We find therefore that very different Methods have been used, and which to approve most I confess myself at a Loss, all of them have so long endured firm and sound. So that I think we ought to chuse that which is least expensive, provided we do not throw in all manner of old Rubbish, and any thing apt to moulder. There are also other Sorts of Foundations; one belongs to Porticoes, and all other Places where Rows of Columns are to be set; the other to Maritime Places, where we cannot pick and chuse the Goodness of our Bottom as we could wish. Of the Maritime we will consider when we come to treat of making of Ports, and running Moles out into the Sea; because these do not relate to the general Work of all manner of Buildings, which is the Subject of our Discourse here, but only to one particular Part of the City, which we shall treat of together with other Things of the like Nature, when we give an Account of all Publick Works, Member by Member. In laying Foundations under Rows of Columns, there is no Occasion to draw an even continued Line of Work all the Way

without

without Interruption ; but only firft to ftrengthen the Places you intend for the Seats or Beds of your Columns, and then from one to the other draw Arches with their Backs downwards, fo that the Plane or Level of the Area will be the Chord of thofe Arches ; as you may fee by the Plate of the Page 41. let B. For ftanding thus, they will be lefs apt to force their Way into the Earth in any one Place, the Weight being counterpos'd and thrown equally on both Sides on the Props of the Arches. And how apt Columns are to drive into the Ground, by means of the great Preffure of the Weight laid upon them, is manifeft from that Corner of the noble Temple of *Vefpafian* that ftands to the North-Weft. For being defirous to leave the publick Way, which was interrupted by that Angle, a free and open Paffage underneath, they broke the Area of their Platform and turn'd an Arch againft the Wall, leaving that Corner as a Sort of Plaifter on the other Side of the Paffage, and fortifying it, as well as poffible, with ftout Work, and with the Affiftance of a Buttrefs. Yet this at laft, by the vaft Weight of fo great a Building, and the giving Way of the Earth, became ruinous. But let this fuffice upon this Head.

CHAP. VI.

That there ought to be Vents left open in thick Walls from the Bottom to the Top ; the Difference between the Wall and the Foundation ; the principal Parts of the Wall ; the three Methods of Walling ; the Materials and Form of the firft Courfe or Layer.

THE Foundations being laid, we come next to the Wall. But I will not omit here a Precaution which belongs as well to the Compleating of the Foundation as to the Structure of the Wall. In large Buildings, where the Wall is to be very thick, we ought to leave Vents and Tunnels in the Body of the Wall, at moderate Diftances one from the other, from the Foundation quite to the Top, through which any Vapour or Damp that may happen to engender or gather under Ground may have free Paffage without damaging the Work. The Ancients in fome of thefe Vents were ufed to make winding Stairs, as well for the Sake of the Beauty of the Contrivance itfelf, as for the Convenience of paffing up to the Top of the Edifice, and perhaps too for the Saving of fome Expence. But to return to our Subject ; between the Foundation and the naked Wall there is this Difference, that the former having the Support of the Sides of the Trench, may be made of nothing but Rubbifh, whereas the Latter confifts of Variety of Parts, as we fhall hereafter fhew. The principal Parts of the Wall are thefe ; firft, the bottom Part, which begins immediately from the Level of the Foundations ; this we call the firft Courfe laid upon the Level, or the Courfe rifing from the Ground : The middle Parts, which girt and furround the Wall, we fhall call the fecond Courfe : The higheft Parts, laftly, that is to fay, thofe which fupport the top Roof, we call Cornices. Some of the principal Parts or rather the principal Parts of all are the Corners of the Wall, and the Pilafters, or Columns, or any thing elfe in their ftead fet in the Wall to fupport the Beams and Arches of the Covering ; all which are comprized under the Name of Bones or Ribs. Likewife the Jambs on each Side of all Openings partake of the Nature both of Corners and of Columns. Moreover, the Coverings of Openings, that is to fay, the Lintels or Tranfoms, whether ftrait or arched, are alfo reckoned among the Bones. And indeed I take an Arch to be nothing more than a Beam bent, and the Beam or Tranfom to be only a Column laid croffways. Thofe Parts which interfere or lie between thefe principal Parts, are very properly called Fillers up. There are fome Things throughout the whole Wall which agree each with fome one of the Parts we have here fpoken of ; that is to fay, the filling up or cramming of the Middle of the Wall, and the two Barks or Shells of each Side, whereof that without is to bear the Sun and Weather, and that within is to give Shade and Shelter to the Infide of the Platform. The Rules for thefe Shells and for their ftuffing are various, according to the Variety of Structures. The different Sorts of Structures are thefe ; the ordinary Sort, the chequer Sort and the Irregular : And here it may not be amifs to take

Notice

Notice of what *Varro* says, that the *Tuscans* used to build their Country Houses of Stone, but the *Gauls* of baked Brick, the *Sabines* of Brick unbaked, the *Spaniards* of Mud and little Stones mixed together. But of these we shall speak elsewhere. The ordinary Sort of Structure, is that in which squared Stones, either the middling or rather the large Sort, are placed with their Fronts exactly answering to the square level and plumb Line; which is the strongest and most lasting Way of all. The chequered Way is when squared Stones, either the middle sized, or rather very small ones, are placed not on their Sides, but on their Corners, and lie with their Fronts answering to the square and plumb Line. The irregular Way is where ordinary rough Stones are placed with their Sides answering, as well as the Inequality of their Forms will permit, one to the other; and this is the Method used in the Pavement of the publick Ways. But these Methods must be used differently in different Places; for in the Bases, or first Course above the Ground, we must make our Shell of nothing but very large and very hard square Stones; for as we ought to make the whole Wall as firm and entire as possible, so there is no Part of it that requires more Strength and Soundness than this; insomuch that if it were possible for you to make it all of one single Stone you should do it, or at least make it only of such a Number as may come as near as may be to the Firmness and Durableness of one single Stone. How these great Stones are to be mov'd and manag'd, belonging properly to the Article of Ornaments, we shall consider of it in another Place.

Raise your Wall says *Cato*, of hard Stone and good Mortar to at least a Foot high above the Ground, and it matters not if you build the rest even of Brick unbak'd. His Reason for this Admonition is plainly because the Rain-Water falling from the Roof might not rot this Part of the Wall. But when we examine the Works of the Ancients, and find that not only in our own Country the lower Parts of all good Buildings are compos'd of the hardest Stone, but that even among those Nations which are under no Apprehensions from Rain, as in *Ægypt*, they used to make the Bases of their Pyramids of a black Stone of an extreme Hardness; we are obliged to look more nearly into this Matter. We should therefore consider that as Iron, Brass, and the like hard Metals, if bent several Times first this way and then that, will at last crack and break; so other Bodies, if wearied with a repeated Change of Injuries, will spoil and corrupt inconceivably; which is what I have observed in Bridges, especially of Wood: Those Parts of them which stand all the Changes of Weather, sometimes burnt with the Rays of the Sun, and sharp Blasts of Wind, at other Times soak'd with Night-dews or Rains, very soon decay and are quite eaten away by the Worms. The same holds good of those Parts of the Wall which are near to the Ground, which by the alternate Injuries of Dust and Wet are very apt to moulder and rot. I therefore lay it down as an indispensible Rule, that all the first Course of Work from the Level, should be compos'd of the hardest, soundest, and largest Stones, to secure it against the frequent Assaults of contrary Injuries: Which Stone is hardest and best, we have shewn sufficiently in the Second Book.

CHAP. VII.

Of the Generation of Stones; how they are to be dispos'd and join'd together, as also, which are the Strongest and which the Weakest.

IT is certainly of very great Consequence in what Manner we dispose and join our Stone in the Work, either in this or any other Part; for as in Wood so also in Stone, there are Veins and Knots, and other Parts, of which some are weaker than others, insomuch that Marble itself will warp and split. There is in Stones a Kind of Impostumes, or Collections of putrid Matter, which in Time swell and grow, by means, as I suppose of the Humidity of the Air, which they suck in and imbibe which breeds larger Pustules, and eats away the Building. For besides what we have already said of Stones in their proper Place, it is necessary to consider here that they are created by Nature, lying flat as we see them in the Ground, of a liquid and fluxible Substance, which, as we are told, when it is afterwards harden'd and grown, reserves in the Mass the original Figure of its Parts. Hence it it proceeds, that the lower Part of Stones is of a more folid and weighty Confiftence than the Upper, and that they interrupted with Veins, juft according as their Subftances happened to unite and conglutinate. That Matter which is found within the Veins, whether it be the Scum of the firft congealed Subftance mix'd with the Dregs of the adventitious Matter, or whatever elfe it be, as it is plainly of fo different a Confiftence, that Nature will not permit it to unite with the reft, it is no Wonder that it is the Part in Stone which is apt to crack. And indeed, as Experience teaches us, the Devaftations of Time too evidently demonftrate, without fearching into Caufes more remote, that all vegetative and compound Bodies confume and decay; fo in Stones, the Parts expos'd to the Weather are fooneft rotted. This being the Cafe, we are advifed in Placing our Stone to fet thofe Parts of it which are the ftrongeft, and leaft apt to putrify, againft the Violence of the alternate Injuries of the Weather, efpecially in thofe Parts of the Building where moft Strength is requir'd. For this Reafon we fhould not fet the Veins upright, left the Weather fhould make the Stone crack and fcale off; but they fhould be laid flat downwards that the Preffure of the incumbant Weight may hinder them from opening. The Side which in the Quarry lay moft hid, fhould be placed againft the Air; becaufe it is always the ftrongeft and moft unctious. But of all Stone, none will prove fo hardy as that which has its Veins not running in parellel Lines with thofe of the Quarry, but croffway and directly

transverfe. Moreover the Corners throughout the whole Building, as they require the greateft Degree of Strength, ought to be particularly well fortify'd; and, if I miftake not, each Corner is in effect the half of the whole Structure; for if one of them happens to fail, it occafions the Ruin of both the Sides to which it anfwers. And if you will take the Pains to examine, I dare fay you will find that hardly any Building ever begins to decay, but by the Fault of one of its Corners. It therefore fhew'd great Difcretion in the Ancients, to make their Corners much thicker than the reft of the Wall, and in Porticoes of Columns to ftrengthen their Angles in a particular Manner. This Strength in the Corners is not required upon Account of its Supporting the Covering (for that is rather the Bufinefs of the Columns) but only to keep the Wall up to its Duty, and hinder it from leaning any Way from its perpendicular. Let the Corners therefore be of the hardeft and longeft Stones, which may embrace both Sides of the Wall, as it were, like Arms; and let them be full as broad as the Wall, that there may be no need to ftuff the Middle with Rubbifh. It is alfo neceffary, that the Ribs in the Wall and the Jambs or Sides of the Apertures, fhould be fortify'd like the Corners, and made ftrong in proportion to the Weight they are defign'd to fupport. And above all we fhould leave Bits, that is to fay, Stones left every other Row jutting out at the Ends of the Wall, like Teeth, for the Stones of the other Front of the Wall to faften and catch into.

C H A P. VIII.

Of the Parts of the Finifhing; of the Shells, the Stuffing, and their different Sorts.

THE Parts of the Finifhing are thofe which, as we faid before, are common to the whole Wall; that is, the Shell and the Stuffing; but there are two Shells, one outward and the other inward; if you make the outward of the hardeft Stone you can get, the Building will be the more durable. And indeed in all Sorts of Finifhing, let it be of what Kind of Work you will, either chequer'd, or of rough Stones, it is indifferent, provided you fet againft the continual mifchievous Violence either of Sun, or Wind, or of Fire, or Froft,

fuch Stones as are in their Nature beft fitted for refifting either Force, Weight, or Injuries; and we fhould take Care to let our Materials be particularly Sound where-ever the Rain in its Fall from the Roof or Gutters is driven by the Wind againft the Wall; fince we often find in old Buildings, that fuch Sprinklings will rot and eat into Marble itfelf. Though all prudent Architects, to provide againft this Mifchief, have taken Care to bring all the Water on the Roof together into Gutters and Pipes, and fo carry it clear away. Moreover, the Ancients obſerv'd that in Autumn the Leaves of Trees always began to fall to the South-ſide firſt; and in Buildings ruinated by Time, I have taken Notice that they always began to decay firſt towards the South. The Reaſon of this may perhaps be that the Heat and Force of the Sun lying upon the Work while it was ſtill in Hand might exhauſt the Strength of the Cement; and the Stone itſelf being frequently moiſten'd by the South-wind, and then again dry'd and burnt by the Rays of the Sun, rots and moulders. Againſt theſe and the like Injuries therefore, we ſhould oppoſe our beſt and ſtouteſt Materials. What I think too is principally to be obſerv'd, is to let every Row or Courſe of Stone throughout the Wall be even and equally proportion'd, not patch'd up of great Stones on the right Hand and little ones on the left; becauſe we are told that the Wall by the Addition of any new Weight is ſqueezed cloſer together, and the Mortar in drying is hinder'd by this Preſſure from taking due hold, which muſt of Courſe make Cracks and Defects in the Work. But you may be ſafely allow'd to make the inward Shell, and all the Front of the Wall of that Side, of a ſofter and weaker Stone; but whatever Shell you make, whether inward or outward, it muſt be always perpendicular, and its Line exactly even. Its Line muſt always anſwer juſtly to the Line of the Platform, ſo as not in any Part to ſwell out or ſink in, or to be wavy, or not exactly plum, and perfectly well compacted and finiſhed. If you rough Caſt your Wall as you build it, or while it is freſh, whatever Plaiſtering or Whitening you do it over with afterwards will laſt, in a Manner, for ever. There are two Sorts of Stuffing; the one is that with which we fill the Hollow that is left between the two Shells, conſiſting of Mortar and broken Fragments of Stone thrown in together without any Order; the other conſiſting of ordinary rough Stone, with which we may be ſaid rather to wall than only to fill up. Both plainly appears to have been invented by good-husbandry, becauſe any ſmall Coarſe Stuff is uſed in this Kind of Work. But if there was Plenty of large ſquare Stone eaſily to be had, who I wonder, would chooſe to make Uſe of ſmall Fragments? And indeed herein alone the Ribs of the Wall differ from what we call the Finiſhing, that between the two Shells of this latter we ſtuff in coarſe Rubbiſh or broken Pieces that come to Hand;

whereas, in the Former we admit very few or no unequal Stones, but make thoſe Parts of the Wall quite through, of what we have call'd the *ordinary* Sort of Work. If I were to chooſe, I would have the Wall throughout made of nothing but regular Courſes of ſquared Stone, that it might be as laſting as poſſible; but whatever hollow you leave between the Shells to be filled up with Rubbiſh, you ſhould take Care to let the Courſes of each Side be as even as poſſible and it will be proper beſides to lay a good many large Stones, at convenient Diſtances, that may go quite through the Wall to both Shells in order to bind and gird them together, that the Rubbiſh you ſtuff them with may not burſt them out. The Ancients made it a Rule in ſtuffing their Walls, not to continue the Stuffing uninterrupted to the Heigth of above five Foot, and then they laid over it a Courſe of whole Stone. This faſten'd and bound the Wall, as it were, with Nerves and Ligaments; ſo that if any Part of the Stuffing, either through the Fault of the Workman, or by Accident, happen'd to ſink, it could not pull every Thing elſe along with it, but the Weight above had in a Manner a new Baſis to reſt upon. Laſtly, we are taught what I find conſtantly obſerved among the Ancients, never to admit any Stone among our Stuffing that weighs above a Pound, becauſe they ſuppoſe that ſmall ones unite more eaſily, and knit bettter with the Cement than large ones.

IT is not altogether foreign to our Purpoſe, what we read in *Plutarch* of King *Minos*, that he divided the Plebeans into ſeveral Claſſes, according to their ſeveral Profeſſions, upon this Principle, that the ſmaller the Parts are a Body is ſplit into, the more eaſily it may be governed and managed. It is alſo of no little Conſequence to have the Hollow completly fill'd up, and every the leaſt Crevice cloſe ſtopt, not only upon the Account of Strength, but likewiſe to hinder any Animals from getting in and making their Neſts there, and to prevent the Gathering of Dirt and Seeds, which might make Weeds grow in the Wall. It is almoſt incredible what huge Weights of Stone, and what vaſt Piles I have known moved and opened by the ſingle Root of one Plant. You muſt take Care therefore to let your whole Structure be girt and fill'd compleatly.

CHAP.

CHAP. IX.

Of the Girders of Stone, of the Ligament and Fortification of the Cornices, and how to unite several Stones for the strengthening of the Wall.

AMong the Girders we reckon those Courses of large Stone which tie the outward Shell to the Inward, and which bind the Ribs one into the other, such as are those which we said in the last Chapter ought to be made every five Foot. But there are other Girders besides, and those principal ones, which run the whole Length of the Wall to embrace the Corners and strengthen the whole Work : But these latter are not so frequent, and I do not remember ever to have seen above two, or at most three in one Wall. Their Place is the Summit of the Wall, to be as it were a Crown to the Whole, and to perform the same Service at the Top which the other more frequent Girders at the Distance of every five Foot do in the Middle, where smaller Stones are allow'd; but in these other Girders, which we call Cornices, as they are fewer and of more Importance, so much the larger and the stronger Stones they require. In both according to their different Offices, the best, the longest, and the thickest Stones are necessary. The smaller Girders are made to answer to the Rule and Plum-line with the rest of the Shell of the Wall : but these great ones, like a Crown, project somewhat forwards. These long, thick Stones must be laid exactly plum, and be well link'd with the under Courses, so as to make a Kind of Pavement at Top to shadow and protect the Substructure. The Way of placing these Stones one upon the other, is to let the Middle of the Stone above answer exactly to the Juncture of the two in the Course below, so that its Weight is equally pois'd upon them both; as (A.) Which way of Working, as it ought not indeed to be neglected in any Part of the Wall, ought to be particularly followed in the Girders. I have observed that the Ancients in their checquer'd Works used to make their Girders of five Courses of Bricks, or at least of three, and that all of them, or at least one Course was of Stone, not thicker than the rest, but longer and broader ; as (B.) But in their ordinary Sort of Brick-work, I find they were

content for Girders to make at every five Foot a Course of Bricks two Foot thick as (C)

I KNOW some too have interspers'd Plates or Cramps of Lead of a considerable Length, and as broad as the Wall was thick, in order to bind the Work. But when they built with very large Stone, I find they were contented with fewer Girders, or even only with the Cornices. In making the Cornices, which are to girt in the Wall with the strongest Ligature, we ought to neglect none of the Rules which we have laid down about the Girders ; namely, we should use in them none but the longest, thickest, and strongest Stones, which we should put together in the most exact and regular Order, each laid nicely even and level by the Square and Plum-line. And we ought to be more diligent and careful in this Part of the Work, because it is to gird in the Whole Wall, which is more apt to ruinate in this Part than in any other. The Covering too has its Office with relation to the Wall ; whence it is laid down as a Rule, that to a Wall of crude Bricks we are to make a Cornice of baked ones, to the Intent that if any Water should chance to fall from the End of the Covering, or from the Gutters, it may be it may do no Mischief, but that the Wall may be defended by the Projecting of the Cornice. For which Reason we ought to take Care that every Part of the Wall have a Cornice over it for a Covering to it, which ought to be firmly wrought and well stucco'd over to repel all the Injuries of the Weather. We are here again to consider in what Manner we are to unite and consolidate a Number of seperate Stones into one Body of Wall; and the principal Thing that offers itself to our Thoughts as necessary, is good Lime; though I do not take it to be the proper Cement for every Sort of Stone: Marble, for Instance, if touch'd with Lime, will not only loose its Whiteness, but will contract foul bloody Spots. But Marble, is so delicate and so coy of its Whiteness, that it will hardly bear the Touch of any Thing but itself; it disdains Smoke; smear'd
with

with Oil, it grows pale; wash'd with Red Wine, it turns of a dirty brown; with Water, kept some time in Chesnut-wood, it changes quite thro' to black, and is so totally stain'd, that no scraping will fetch out the Spots. For this Reason the Ancients used Marble in their Works naked, and if possible without the least Mortar: But of these hereafter.

CHAP. X.

Of the true Manner of Working the Wall, and of the Agreement there is between Stone and Sand.

NOW as it is the Business of an expert Workman, not so much to make Choice of the fittest Materials, as to put those which he is supplied with to the best and propereft Uses; we will proceed on our Subject in this Manner. Lime is well burnt, when after it has been water'd, and the Heat gone out of it, it rises up like the Froth of Milk, and swells all the Clods. Its not having been long enough soak'd you may know by the little Stones you will find in it when you mix the Sand with it. If you put too much Sand to it, it will be too sharp to cement well; if you put less than its Nature and Strength requires, it will be as stiff as Glue, and is not to be managed. Such as is not thoroughly soak'd, or that is weaker upon any other Account, may be used with less Danger in the Foundation than in the Wall, and in the Stuffing than in Shells. But the Corners, the Ribs, and the Band-stones must be entirely free from Mortar that has the least Defect; and Arches especially require the very best of all. The Corners, and Ribs, and the Band-stones, and Cornices require the finest, smallest and clearest Sand, particularly when they are built of polished Stone. The Stuffing may be done with coarser Stone.

STONE in its Nature dry and thirsty, agrees not ill with River-sand. Stone in its Nature moist and watery, delights in Pit-sand. I would not have Sea-sand used towards the South; it may perhaps do better against the Northern Winds. For small Stones, a thick lean Mortar is best; to a dry exhausted Stone, we should use a fat Sort; though the Ancients were of Opinion that in all Parts of the Walls the fattish Sort is more tenacious than the lean. Great Stones they always lay upon a very soft fluid Mortar, so that it rather seems design'd to lubricate and make the Bed they are laid upon slippery, to the Intent, that while they are fixing in their Places they may be easy to move with the Hand, then to cement and fasten them together. But it is certainly proper to lay a soft Stuff underneath in this Manner, like a Pillow, to prevent the Stones, which have a great Weight lying upon them, from breaking. There are some, who observing here and there in the Works of the Ancients, large Stones, which where they join seem dawb'd over with red Earth, imagine that the Ancients used that instead of Mortar. I do not think this probable, because we never find both Sides, but only one of them, smear'd with this Sort of Stuff. There are some other Rules concerning the Working of our Walls, not to be neglected. We ought never to fall upon our Work with a violent Haste, heaping one Stone upon another, in a Kind tumultuousHurry, without the least Respite: Neither ought we, after we have began to build, to delay it with a sluggish Heaviness, as if we had no Stomach to what we are about; but we ought to follow our Work with such a reasonable Dispatch, that Speed and Consideration may appear to go Hand in Hand together. Experienced Workmen forewarn us against raising the Structure too high, before what we have already done is thoroughly settled; because the Work, while it is fresh and soft, is too weak and pliable to bear a Superstructure. We may take Example from the Swallows, taught by Nature, which when they build their Nests, first dawb or glue over the Beams which are to be the Foundation and Basis of their Edifice, and then are not too hasty to lay the second dawbing over this, but intermit the Work till the first is sufficiently dry'd; after which they continue their Building reasonably and properly. They say the Mortar has taken sufficient hold when it puts forth a Kind of Moss or little Flower well known to Masons. At what Distances it is proper to respite the we may gather from the Thickness of the Wall itself, and from the Temperature of the

Place

Place and of the Climate. When you think it Time for a Respite, cover the Top of the Wall over with Straw, that the Wind and Sun may not exhaust the Strength of the Cement, and make it rather useless than dry and binding. When you resume your Work, pour a confiderable Quantity of clean Water upon it, till it is thoroughly soak'd and wash'd from all Manner of Dirt, that no Seeds may be left to engender Weeds. There is nothing that makes the Work stronger and more durable than moistening the Stone sufficiently with Water; and they say the Stone is never soak'd as it should be, if upon breaking, the Inside all through is not moist and turned black. Add to what has been said, that in erecting our Wall we ought, in such Places where it is possible new Openings may afterwards be wanting either for Conveniency or Pleasure, to turn Arches in the Wall, that if you afterwards take out any of the Work from beneath those Arches, for the aforesaid Purposes, the Wall may have a good Arch, built at the same Time with itself, to rest upon. It is hardly to be conceiv'd how much the Strength of a Building is impair'd only by taking out one single Stone, be it ever so little; and there is no such Thing as setting a new Structure upon an old one, but that they will open and part one from the other; and how much such a Crack must dispose the Wall to ruin, need not be mention'd. A very thick Wall has no need of Scaffolding, because it is broad enough for the Mason to stand upon the Wall itself.

CHAP. XI.

Of the Way of Working different Materials; of Plaistering; of Cramps, and how to preserve them; the most ancient Instructions of Architects; and some Methods to prevent the Mischiefs of Lightening.

WE have treated of the best Manner of Building, what Stone we are to choose, and how we are to prepare our Mortar: But as we shall sometimes be obliged to make use of other Sorts of Stone, whereof some are not cemented with Mortar, but only with Slime; and others which are join'd without any Cement at all: And there are also Buildings consisting only of Stuffing, or rough Work, and others again only of the Shells; of all these we shall say something as briefly as possible. Stones that are to be cemented with Slime, ought to be squared, and very arid; and nothing is more proper for this than Bricks, either burnt, or rather crude, but very well dried. A Building made of crude Bricks is extremely healthy to the Inhabitants, very secure against Fire, and but little affected by Earthquakes; But then if it is not of a good Thickness, it will not support the Roof; for which Reason *Cato* directs the Raising of Pilasters of Stone to perform that Office. Some tell us, that the Slime which is used for Cement ought to be like Pitch, and that the best is that which being steep'd in Water is slowest in dissolving, and will not easily rub off from one's Hand, and which condenses most in drying. Others commend the Sandy as best, because it is most tractable. This Sort of Work ought to be cloathed with a Crust of Mortar on the Outside, and within, if you think fit, with Plaister of *Paris*, or white Earth. And for the better Sticking these on, you must in Building your Wall, set little Pieces of Tile here and there in the Cracks of the Joining, jutting out like Teeth, for the Plaister to cleave to. When the Structure is to be composed of naked Stones, they ought to be squared and much bigger than the other, and very sound and strong; and in this Sort of Work we allow of no stuffing; the Courses must be regular and even, the Junctures contrived with frequent Ligatures of Cramps and Pins. Cramps are what fasten together two Stones sideways that lie even with one another, and unite them into a Row: Pins are fix'd into an upper Stone and an under one, to prevent the Row from being by any Violence driven out from the rest. Cramps and Pins of Iron are not reckoned amiss; but I have observed in the Works of the Ancients, that Iron rusts, and will not last; But Brass will almost endure for ever. Besides, I find that Marble is tainted by the Rust of the Iron, and breaks all round it. We likewise meet with Cramps made of Wood in very ancient Structures;

and

and indeed, I do not think them inferior to those of Iron. The Cramps of Brass and Iron are fastened in with Lead: But those of Wood are sufficiently secured by their Shape, which is made in such Manner, that for Resemblance, they are called Swallow, or Dove-tailed. The Cramps must be so placed that no Drops of Rain may penetrate to them; and it is Thought that the Brass ones are yet more strengthened against old Age, if in Casting they are mixed with one thirtieth Part of Tin: They will be less liable to rust if they are anointed with Pitch, or Oil. It is affirmed that Iron may be so tempered by White-lead, Plaister, and Liquid Pitch, as not to rust. Wooden Cramps done over with Maiden-wax and Lees of Oil, will never rot. I have known them pour so much Lead upon Cramps, and that so boyling Hot, that it has burst the Stones. In ancient Structures we often meet with very strong Walls made of nothing but Rubbish and broken Stuff; these are built like the Mud-Walls common in *Spain* and *Africa*, by fastening on each Side Planks or Hurdles, instead of Shells, to keep the Stuff together till it is dry and settled: But herein they differ, that the Ancients filled up their Work with Mortar liquid, and in a Manner floating; whereas, the other only took a clammy Sort of Earth which they trod and rammed with their Feet, and with Beetles, after having first made it tractable by thorough wetting and kneading. The Ancients also in those rough Works of theirs, at the Distance of every three Foot made a Kind of Band of Pieces of large Stone, especially of the ordinary Sort, or at least angular; because round Stones, though they are very hardy against all Sorts of Injuries, yet if they are not surrounded with strong Supports, are very unfaithful in any Wall. In these other Works, that is to say, in the *African* Buildings of Earth, they mixed with their Clay the *Spanish*-Broom, or Sea-Bullrush, which made a Stuff admirably good for Working, and which remained unhurt either by Wind or Weather. In *Pliny*'s Time there was to be seen upon the Ridges of Mountains several little Towers for viewing the Country built of Earth, which had endured quite from the Days of *Hanibal*. We make this Sort of Crust (which is a fitter Name for it than Shell) with Hurdles and Mats, made of Reeds not fresh gathered; a Work indeed not very magnificent, but generally used by the Old *Plebeian Romans*. They rough Cast the Hurdles over with Clay, beat up for three Days running with the Reeds, and then (as we said before) cloath it with Mortar, or Plaister of *Paris*, which they afterwards adorn with Painting and Statues. If you mix your Plaister up with a third Part of broken Tile, or Brick pounded, it will be the less injured by wet: If you mix it with Lime, it will be the Stronger: But in damp Places, or such as are exposed to Cold and Frost, Plaister of *Paris* is very unserviceable. I will now, by Way of Epilogue, give you a Law of very great Antiquity among Architects, which in my Opinion ought no less to be observed than the Answers of Oracles: And it is this. Make your Foundation as strong as possible: Let the Superstructure lie exactly plum to its Centre: Fortify the Corners and Ribs of the Wall from the Bottom to the Top with the largest and the strongest Stones: Soak your Lime well: Do not use your Stone till it is thoroughly watered: Set the hardest Sort to that Side which is most exposed to Injuries: Raise your Wall exactly by the Square, Level and Plum-line: Let the Middle of the upper Stone lie directly upon the Meeting of the two below it: Lay the entire Stones in the Courses, and fill up the Middle with the broken Pieces: Bind the inward and outside Shells to one another by frequent Cross or Band-stones. Let this suffice with Relation to the Wall; we come now to the Covering. But I will not pass over one Thing which I find the Ancients observed very religiously. There are some Things in Nature which are endued with Properties by no means to be neglected; particularly, that the Lawrel-tree, the Eagle, and the Sea-calf, are never to be touched by Lightening. There are some therefore who suppose that if these are inclosed in the Wall, the Lightening will never hurt it. This I take to be just as probable as another wonderful Thing which we are told, that the Land-toad, or Rudduck, if shut up in an earthen Pot, and burned in a Field, will drive away the Birds from devouring the Seeds; and that the Tree *Ostrys*, or *Ostrya* brought into a House, will obstruct a Woman's Delivery; and that the Leaves of the Lesbian Oemony kept but under the Roof, will give a Flux of the Belly and an Evacuation that will certainly prove Mortal. Let us now return to our Subject, for the better understanding of which, it will be proper to look back to what we have formerly said of the Lines of Building

CHAP.

CHAP. XII.

Of Coverings of ſtrait Lines ; of the Beams and Rafters, and of the uniting the Ribs.

OF Coverings, ſome are to the open Air, and ſome are within ; ſome conſiſt of ſtrait Lines, others of curve, and ſome of both : We may add, not improperly, that ſome are of Wood, and ſome of Stone. We will firſt, according to our Cuſtom, mention one Obſervation which relates in general to all Sorts of Coverings ; which is this : That all manner of Roofs, or Coverings have their Ribs, Nerves, Finiſhings, and Shells, or Cruſts, juſt the ſame as the Wall : Which will appear from the Conſideration of the Thing itſelf. To begin with thoſe of Wood, and conſiſting of ſtrait Lines ; it is neceſſary for ſupporting the Cover to lay very ſtrong Beams acroſs from one Wall to the other ; which, as we took Notice before, are Columns laid tranſverſe : Theſe Beams therefore, are a Sort of Ribs ; and if it were not for the Expences, who would not wiſh to have the whole Building conſiſt, if we may uſe the Expreſſion, of nothing but Ribs and ſolid Work ; that is to ſay, of continued Columns and Beams cloſe compacted ? but we here conſult Oeconomy, and ſuppoſe every Thing to be ſuperfluous, that without Prejudice to the Strength of the Work, may be poſſibly retrenched ; and for this Reaſon, we leave Spaces between the Beams. Between theſe we lay the Croſs-beams, Rafters, and the like ; which may not at all improperly be reckoned the Ligatures : To theſe we fit and joyn Boards and Planks of greater Breadth, which there is no Reaſon why we ſhould not call the Finiſhing ; and in the ſame Way of thinking, the Pavement and Tiling is the Outward Shell, and the Ceiling, or Roof, which is over our Head the Inward. If this be granted, let us conſider whether there is any Thing neceſſary to be obſerved with Relation to any of theſe Parts, that having duly examined it, we may the more eaſily underſtand what belongs to Coverings of Stone. We will ſpeak of them therefore as briefly as poſſible : Firſt, taking Notice of one Thing not foreign to our Purpoſe. There is a very vicious Practice among our modern Architects ; which is, that in order to make their Ceilings, they leave great Holes in the very Ribs of the Building to let the Heads of the Beams into after the Wall is finiſhed ; which not only weakens the Structure, but alſo makes it more expoſed to Fire ; becauſe by theſe Holes the Flames find a Paſſage from one Apartment to another. For which Reaſon, I like the Method uſed among the Ancients, of ſetting in the Wall ſtrong Tables of Stone called Corbels, upon which they laid the Heads of their Beams. If you 74 would bind the Wall, and the Beams together, you have Braſs Cramps, and Braces, and Catches or Notches in the Corbel itſelf, which will ſerve for that Purpoſe. The Beams ought to be perfectly ſound and clear ; and eſpecially about the Middle of its Length it ought to be free from the leaſt Defect, placing your Ear at one End of it while the other is ſtruck, if the Sound come to you dead, and flat, it is a Sign of ſome private Infirmity. Beams that have Knots in them are abſolutely to be rejected, eſpecially if there are many, or if they are crouded together in a Cluſter. The Side of the Timber that lies neareſt the Heart, muſt be planed, and laid uppermoſt in the Building ; but the Part that is to lie undermoſt, muſt be planed very ſuperficially, only the Bark, nay, and of that hardly any, or as little as poſſible. Which-ſoever Side has a Defect that runs croſſways of the Beam, lay uppermoſt ; if there is a Crak longways, never venture it of the Side, but lay it either uppermoſt, or rather undermoſt. If you happen to have Occaſion to bore a Hole in it, or any Opening, never meddle with the Middle of its length, nor its lower Superficies. If, as in Churches, the Beams are to be laid in Couples ; leave a Space of ſome Inches between them, that they may have Room to exhale, and not be ſpoyled by heating one another : And it will not be amiſs to lay the two Beams of the ſame Couple different Ways, that both their Heads may not lie upon the ſame Pillow ; but where one has its Head, the other may have its Foot : For by this Means the Strength of the one's Foot will aſſiſt the Weakneſs of the other's Head ; and ſo *vice verſa*. The

Beams

Beams ought alſo to be related to one another; that is, they ſhould be of the ſame Kind of Timber, and raiſed in the ſame Wood, expoſed if poſſible to the ſame Winds, and fell'd the ſame Day; that being endued with the ſame natural Strength, they may bear their Shares equally in the Service. Let the Beds for the Beams be exactly level, and perfectly firm and ſtrong; and in laying them take care that the Timber does not touch any Lime, and let it have clear and open Vents all about it, that it may not be tainted by the Contact of any other Materials, nor decay by being too cloſe ſhut up. For a Bed for the Beams, ſpread under them either Fern, a very dry Kind of Herb, or Aſhes, or rather Lees of Oil with the bruiſed Olives. But if your Timber is ſo ſhort, that you cannot make a Beam of one Piece, you muſt join two or more together, in ſuch a Manner as to give them the Strength of an Arch; that is to ſay, ſo that the upper Line of the compacted Beam, cannot poſſibly by any Preſſure become ſhorter; and on the contrary, that the lower Line cannot grow longer: And there muſt be a Sort of Cord to bind the two Beams together, which ſhove one another with their Heads, with a ſtrong Ligature. The Rafters, and all the reſt of the Wood-work, depend upon the Goodneſs and Soundneſs of the Beams; being nothing elſe but Beams ſplit. Boards or Planks are thought to be inconvenient if too thick, becauſe whenever they begin to warp they throw out the Nails; and thin Boards, eſpecially in Coverings expoſed to the Air, they ſay, muſt be faſtened with Nails in Pairs, ſo as to ſecure the Corners, the Sides and the Middle. They tell us, that ſuch Nails as are to bear any tranſverſe Weight, muſt be made thick; but as for others, it matters not if they are thinner; but then they muſt be longer, and have broader Heads.

BRASS Nails are moſt durable in the Air, or in wet; but I have found the Iron ones to be ſtronger under Cover. For faſtening of the Rafters together, wooden Pins are much uſed. Whatever we have here ſaid of Coverings of Wood, muſt be obſerved alſo with relation to thoſe of Stone; for ſuch Stones as have Veins, or Faults running croſſways, muſt be rejected for the making of Beams, and uſed in Columns; or if there are any ſmall inconſiderable Faults, the Side of the Stone in which it appears, when it is uſed, muſt be laid downwards, Veins running longways in Beams of any Sort, are more excuſable than tranſverſe ones. Tables, or Scantlings of Stones alſo, as well for other Reaſons, as upon Account of their Weight, muſt not be made too thick. Laſtly, the Beams, Rafters, and Planks that are uſed in Coverings, whether of Wood, or Stone, muſt be neither ſo thin, nor ſo few as not to be ſufficient for upholding themſelves, and their Burthens; nor ſo thick, or ſo crouded as to take from the Beauty, and Symmetry of the Work; but thoſe are things we ſhall ſpeak of elſewhere. And thus much for Coverings of ſtraight Lines; unleſs it may be proper to mention one Thing which is in my Opinion to be neglected in no Sort of Structure. The Philoſophers have obſerved, that Nature in forming the Bodies of Animals, always takes care to finiſh her Work in ſuch a Manner, that the Bones ſhould all communicate, and never be ſeperate one from the other: So we alſo ſhould connect the Ribs togther, and faſten them together well with Nerves and Ligatures; ſo that the Communication among the Ribs ſhould be ſo continued, that if all the reſt of the Structure failed, the Frame of the Work ſhould yet ſtand firm and ſtrong with all its Parts and Members.

75

C H A P. XIII.

Of Coverings, or Roofs of Curve Lines; of Arches, their Difference and Con-
ſtruction, and how to ſet the Stones in an Arch.

WE come now to ſpeak of Roofs made of Curve Lines, and we are firſt to conſider thoſe Particulars wherein they exactly agree with Coverings of ſtrait Lines. A curvilinear Roof is compoſed of Arches; and we have already ſaid that an Arch is nothing but a Beam bent. We might alſo here mention the

Ligatures, and thoſe Things which muſt be uſed for filling up the Vacuities; but I would be underſtood more clearly, by explaining what I take to be the Nature of an Arch, and of what Parts it conſiſts.

I SUPPOSE then, that Men learnt at firſt to turn Arches from this: They ſaw that two Beams

ſet

set with their Heads one against the other, and their Feet set wide, would, if fastened at Top, stand, very firm, by means of the Equalness of their Weight: They were pleased with this Invention, and began to make their Roofs in the same Manner, to throw off the Rain, both Ways. Afterwards, perhaps, not being able to cover a wider Space for want of Beams long enough, they put between the Heads of these two Beams another crossways at Top, so that they made a Figure much like that of the Greek Letter п, and this middle Beam they might call a Wedge; and as this succeeded very well, they multiplyed the Wedges, and thus made a Kind of Arch, whose Figure mightily delighted them. Then transferring the same Method to their Works of Stone, continuing to multiply the Wedges, they made an entire Arch, which must be allowed to be nothing else but a Conjunction of a Number of Wedges, whereof some standing with their Heads below the Arch, are called the Foot of the Arch, those in the Middle above, the Key of the Arch, and those on the Sides, the Turn, or Ribs of the Arch. It will not be improper here to repeat what we said in the first Book upon this Subject: There are different Sorts of Arches, the Entire, is the full half of a Circle, or that whose Chord runs through the Centre of the Circle; there is another which approaches more to the Nature of a Beam than of an Arch, which we call the Imperfect, or diminished Arch, because it is not a compleat Semi-circle; but a determinate Part less, having its Chord above the Centre, and at some Distance from it. There is also the Composite Arch, called by some the Angular, and by others an Arch compsed of two Arches less than Semi-circles; and its Chord has the two Centres of two Curve Lines, which mutually intersect each other. That the Entire Arch is the Strongest of all, appears not only from Experience but Reason; for I do not see how it can possibly disunite of itself, unless one Wedge shoves out another, which they are so far from doing, that they assist and support one another. And indeed, if they were to go about any such Violence, they would be prevented by the very Nature of Ponderosity, by which they are pressed downwards, either by some Superstructure, or by that which is in the Wedges themselves. This makes *Varro* say, that in Arches, the Work on the right Hand is kept up no less by that on the Left, than the Work on the Left is by that on the Right. And

if we look only into the Thing itself; how is it possible for the middle Wedge at Top, which is the Key-stone to the Whole, to thrust out either of the two next Side Wedges, or how can that be driven out of its Place by them? The next Wedges also in the Turn of the Arch, being justly counterpoised, will surely stand to their Duty; and lastly, how can the two Wedges under the two Feet of the Arch, ever be moved while the upper ones stand firm? Therefore we have no need of a Cord, or Bar in an entire Arch, because it supports itself by its own Strength; but in diminish'd Arches there is Occasion either for an Iron Chain or Bar, or for an Extension of Wall on both Sides, that may have the Effect of a Bar to supply the Want of Strength, that there is in the diminish'd Arch, and make it equal to the Entire. The ancient Architects always use these Precautions, and where-ever it was possible, constantly secured their diminish'd Arches, by setting them in a good Body of Wall. They also endeavour'd, if they had an Opportunity, to turn their imperfect Arches upon a strait Beam; and over these imperfect ones, they used to turn entire Arches, which protected the diminished ones which were within them, and took upon themselves the Burthen of the Superstructure. As for Composite Arches, we do not find any of them in the Buildings of the Ancients; some think them not amiss for the Apertures in Towers; because they suppose they will cleave the great Weight that is laid upon them, as the Prow of a Ship does the Water, and that they are rather strengthened than oppress'd by it.

THE Stones used in Building an Arch, should be every Way the biggest that can be got; because the Parts of any Body that are united and compacted by Nature, are more inseparable than those which are join'd and cemented by Art. The Stones also ought to be equal on both Sides, as if they were balanced with respect to their Fronts, Sizes, Weight, and the like. If you are to make a Portico, and to draw several Arches over continued Apertures, from the Capitals of Columns, never let the Seat from which two or more Arches are to rise, be made of two Pieces, or of as many as there are to be Arches, but only of one single Stone, and that as strong as may be, to hold together the Feet of all the Arches. The second Stones in the Arch, which rise next to these, if they are large Pieces, must be set

Q   with

with their Backs againſt each other, joining perpendicularly. The third Stone which is laid upon theſe ſecond ones, muſt be ſet by the Plum-lines, as we directed in raiſing the Wall, with even Joinings, ſo that they may ſerve both the Arches, and be a Binding to both their Wedges. Let the Lines of the Joinings of all the Stones in the Arch point exactly to the Centre of that Arch.

THE moſt skillful Workmen always make the Key-ſtone of one ſingle Piece, very large and ſtrong ; and if the Breadth of the Top is ſo great, that no one Stone will ſuffice, it will then be no longer only an Arch, but a vaulted Roof,

C H A P. XIV.

Of the ſeveral Sorts of Vaults, and wherein they differ ; of what Lines they are compoſed, and the Method of letting them ſettle.

THERE are ſeveral Sorts of Vaults ; ſo that it is our Buſineſs here to enquire wherein they differ, and of what Lines they are compoſed ; in doing of which, I ſhall be obliged to invent new Names, to make myſelf clear and perſpicuous, which is what I have principally ſtudied in theſe Books. I know *Ennius* the Poet calls the Arch of the Heavens the mighty Vaults ; and *Servius* calls all Vaults made like the Keel of a Ship, Caverns : But I claim this Liberty ; that whatever in this Work, is expreſſed aptly, clearly, and properly, ſhall be allowed to be expreſſed right. The different Sorts of Vaults are theſe, the plain Vault, the Camerated, or mixed Vault, and the hemiſpherical Vault, or Cupola ; beſides thoſe others which partake of the Kind of ſome of theſe. The Cupola in its Nature is never placed but upon Walls that riſe from a circular Platform : The Camerated are proper for a ſquare one ; the plain Vaults are made over any quadrangular Platform, whether long or ſhort, as we ſee in all ſubterraneous Porticoes. Thoſe Vaults too which are like a Hill bored through, we alſo call plain Vaults ; the plain Vault therefore, is like a Number of Arches join'd together Sideways ; or like a bent Beam extended out in Breadth, ſo as to make a Kind of a Wall turn'd with a Sweep over our Heads for a Covering. But if ſuch a Vault as this, running from North to South, happens to be croſs'd by another which runs from Eaſt to Weſt, and interſects it with equal Lines meeting at the Angles like crooked Horns, this will make a Vault of the Camerated Sort. But if a great Number of equal Arches meet at the Top exactly in the Centre, they conſtitute a Vault like the Sky, which therefore we call the Hemiſpherical, or compleat Cupola. The Vaults made of Part of theſe, are as follows : If Nature with an even and perpendicular Section, were to divide the Hemiſphere of the Heavens in two Parts, from Eaſt to Weſt, it would make two Vaults, which would be proper Coverings for any ſemi-circular Building. But if from the Angle at the Eaſt, to that at the South, and from the South to the Weſt, thence to the North, and ſo back again to the Eaſt, if Nature were to break and interrupt this Hemiſphere by ſo many Arches turn'd from Angle to Angle, ſhe would then leave a Vault in the Middle, which for its Reſemblance to a ſwelling Sail, we will venture to call a Velar Cupola. But that Vault which conſiſts of a Number of plain Vaults meeting in a Point at Top, we ſhall call an Angular Cupola.

IN the Conſtruction of Vaults, we muſt obſerve the ſame Rules as in that of the Walls, carrying on the Ribs of the Wall clear up to the Summit of the Vault ; and according to the Method preſcribed for the Former, obſerving the ſame Proportions and Diſtances : From Rib to Rib, we muſt draw Ligatures croſſways, and the Interſpaces we muſt fill up with Stuffing. But the Difference between the Working of a Vault and a Wall, lies in this ; that in the Wall the Courſes of Stone are laid even and perpendicular by the Square and Plumline ; whereas, in the Vault the Courſes are laid by a curve Line, and the Joints all point to the Centre of their Arch.

THE Ancients hardly ever made their Ribs of any but burnt Bricks, and thoſe generally about two Foot long, and adviſe to fill up the Interſpaces of our Vaults with the lighteſt Stone, that they might not oppreſs the Wall with too great a Weight. But I have obſerved that ſome have not always thought themſelves obliged to make continued ſolid Ribs, but in their ſtead, have at certain Diſtances, ſet Bricks lying Sideways, with their Heads jointing into each

each other, like the Teeth of a Comb ; as a Man locks his right Hand Fingers into his left ; and the Interſpaces they filled up with any common Stone, and eſpecially with Pumice Stone, which is univerſally agreed to be the propereſt of all, for the ſtuffing Work of Vaults. In building either Arches or Vaults, we muſt make uſe of Centres. Theſe are a Kind of Frames made with the Sweep of an Arch of any rough Boards juſt clapt together for a ſhort Service, and covered either with Hurdles, Ruſhes, or any ſuch common Stuff, in order to ſupport the Work till it is ſettled and hardened. Yet there is one ſort of Vault which ſtands in no Need of theſe Machines, and that is the *perfect Cupola* ; becauſe it is compoſed not only of Arches, but alſo, in a Manner, of Cornices. And who can conceive the innumerable Ligatures that there are in theſe, which all wedge together, and interſect one another both with equal and unequal Angles ? So that in whatſoever Part of the whole Cupola you lay a Stone, or a Brick, you may be ſaid at the ſame time to have laid a Key-ſtone to an infinite Number, both of Arches, and Cornices. And when theſe Cornices, or Arches are thus built one upon the other, if the Work were inclined to ruinate, where ſhould it begin, when the Joints of every Stone are directed to one Centre with equal Force and preſſure ? Some of the Ancients truſted ſo much to the Firmneſs of this Sort of Structure, that they only made plain Cornices of Brick at ſtated Diſtances, and filled up the Interſpaces with Rubble. But I think, thoſe acted much more prudently, who in raiſing this Sort of Cupola, uſed the ſame Methods as in Walling, to cramp and faſten the under Cornices to the next above, and the Arches too in ſeveral Places, eſpecially if they had not plenty of Pit Sand to make very good Cement, or if the Building was expoſed to South Winds, or Blaſts from the Sea. You may likewiſe turn the Angular Cupolas without a Centre, if you make a perfect one in the Middle of the Thickneſs of the Work. But here you will have particular Occaſion for Ligatures to faſten the weaker Parts of the outer one tightly to the ſtronger Parts of that within. Yet it will be neceſſary when you have laid one or two Rows of Stone to make little light Stays, or Catchers jutting out, on which, when thoſe Rows are ſettled, you may ſet juſt Frame-work enough to ſupport the next Courſes above, to the Height of a few Feet, till they are ſufficiently hardened ; and then you may remove theſe

Frames, or Supports, higher and higher to the other Courſes till you have finiſh'd the whole Work. The other Vaults, both plain and mixed, or camerated, muſt needs be turn'd upon Centres : But I would have the firſt Courſes, and the Heads of their Arches be placed upon very ſtrong Seats ; nor can I approve the Method of thoſe who carry the Wall clear up firſt, only leaving ſome Mouldings, or Corbels, upon which, after a Time, they turn their Arches ; which muſt be a very infirm and periſhable Sort of Work. The true Way is to turn the Arch immediately, and equally with the Courſes of the Wall which is to ſupport it, that the Work may have the ſtrongeſt Ligatures that is poſſible, and grow in a Manner all of one Piece. The Vacuities which are left between the Back of the Sweep of the Arch, and the Upright of the Wall it is turn'd from, call'd by Workmen, the *Hips* of the Arch, ſhould be fill'd up, not with Dirt, or old Rubbiſh, but rather with ſtrong ordinary Work, frequently knit and jointed into the Wall.

I AM pleaſed with thoſe who, to avoid overburthening the Arch, have ſtuffed up theſe Vacuities with earthen Pots, turn'd with their Mouths downwards, that they might not contain any wet, if it ſhould gather there, and over theſe thrown in Fragments of Stone not heavy, but perfectly ſound. Laſtly, in all Manner of Vaults, let them be of what Kind they will, we ought to imitate Nature, who, when ſhe has knit the Bones, faſtens the Fleſh with Nerves, interweaving it every where with Ligatures running in Breadth, Length, Height and circularly. This artful Contexture is what we ought to imitate in the joining of Stones in Vaults. Theſe Things being compleated, the next, and laſt Buſineſs is to cover them over ; a Work of the greateſt Conſequence in Building, and no leſs difficult than neceſſary ; in effecting, and compleating of which, the utmoſt Care and Study has been over and over employed. Of this we are to treat ; but firſt, it will be proper to mention ſomething neceſſary to be obſerved in working of Vaults ; for different Methods are to be taken in the Execution of different Sorts : Thoſe which are turn'd upon Centres muſt be finiſh'd out of hand, without Intermiſſion ; but thoſe which are wrought without Centres muſt be diſcontinued, and left to ſettle Courſe by Courſe, leſt new Work being added to the firſt before it is dry, ſhould ruin the Whole. As to thoſe

which

which are turned upon Centres, when they are clofed with their Key-ftones, it will be proper immediately to eafe the Props a little, that thofe Centres reft upon; not only to prevent the Stones frefh-laid from floating in the Beds of Mortar they are fet in, but that the whole Vault may fink and clofe by its own Weight epually, into its right Seat: Otherwife in drying, the Work would not compact itfelf as it ought, but would be apt to leave Cracks when it came afterwards to fettle. And therefore you muft not quite take away the Centre immediately, but let it down eafily Day afterDay, by little and little, for Fear, if you fhould take it away too foon, theBuilding fhould never duly cement. But after a certain Number of Days, according to the Greatnefs of theWork, eafe it a little, and fo go on gradually, till the Wedges all compact

themfelves in their Places, and are perfectly fettled. The beft Way of letting down the Frame is this: When you place your Centre upon the Pilafters, or whatever elfe it is to reft upon, put under each of its Feet two Wedges of Wood; aud when afterwards you want to let it down, you may with a Hammer fafely drive out thefe Wedges by little and little, as you fhall judge proper.

Lastly, it is my Opinion, that the Centres ought not to be taken away till after Winter, as well for other Reafons, as becaufe the Wafhing of the Rains may weaken and demolifh the whole Structure; though elfe we cannot do greater Service to a Vault than to give it Water enough, and to let it be thoroughly foak'd, that it may never feelThirft. But of this Subject we have faid enough.

Chap. XV.

Of the Shell of the Covering, and its Ufefulnefs; the different Sorts and Shapes of Tiles, and what to make them of.

I Now come to cover the Roof. And certainly, if we weigh the Matter duly, there is no Convenience in the whole Building greater than the having Shelter from the burning Sun, and the inclement Seafons; and this is a Benefit which you owe the Continuance of, not to the Wall, nor to Area, nor any of thefe; but principally to the outward Shell of the Roof; which all the Art and Induftry of Man, though they have tried all Means, has not yet been able to make fo ftrong and impenetrable againft the Weather as might be wifh'd: Nor do I think, it will be an eafy Matter to do it; for where, not only Rains, but Extremes of Heat and Cold, and above all, bluftering Storms of Wind, are continually affaulting the fame Place; what Materials are ftrong enough to refift fuch unwearied and powerful Adverfaries? Hence it happens, that fome Coverings prefently rot, others open, others opprefs the Wall, fome crack, or break, others are wafhed away; infomuch, that even Metals, which are fo hardy againft the Weather, in other Places, are not here able to hold out againft fuch frequent Affaults. But Men not defpifing fuch Materials as Nature furnifhed them with in their refpective Countries, have provided againft thefe Inconveniences as

well as they were able; and hence arofe various Methods of Covering in a Building. *Vitruvius* tells us, that the *Pyrgenfes* covered their Houfes with Reeds, and the People of *Marfeilles* with Clay kneaded, and mixed with Straw. The *Chelonophagi*, near the *Garamantes*, *Pliny* tells us, cover'd theirs with the Shells of Tortoifes. The greateft Part of *Germany* ufe Shingles. In *Flanders* and *Picardy*, they cut a white Sort of Stone which they have (which Saws eafier than Wood itfelf) into their Scantlings, which they ufe inftead of Tiles. The *Genoueze*, and *Florentines* ufe thin Pieces of a fcaly Sort of Stone. Others have tried the Pargets, which we fhall fpeak of by and by. But after having made Experiment of every Thing, the Wit and Invention of Man has found out nothing yet more convenient than Tiles of baked Clay. For all Sorts of Parget grow rugged in Frofts, and fo crack and break: Lead is melted by the Sun's Heat: Brafs, if laid in thick Plates, is very coftly; and if it is thin, it is apt to warp, and to be eaten and confumed with Ruft.

One *Grinias* of *Cyprus*, the Son of a Peafant, is faid to be the Inventer of Tiles, which are of two Sorts, the one broad and flat, one Foot broad, and a Foot and a half long, with

77

with Rims of each Side, a ninth Part of its Breadth, which is call'd a Gutter-tile; the other round, like Greaves, (a Piece of Armour for the Legs,) which is called a Ridge-tile; both broader in that Part which is to receive the Rain, and narrower in that from which they are to discharge it. But the Plain, or Gutter-tiles are the most Commodius, provided they are laid exactly even, so as not to lean of either Side, nor to make either Vallies or Hilocks to stop the Current of the Water, or to let it settle in, nor to leave any Cranny uncover'd. If the Superficies of the Roof is very large, it requires bigger Gutter-tiles, that the Rain may not overflow them for want of a sufficient Receptacle. To prevent the Fury of the Wind from ripping off the Tiles, I would have them all fastened with Mortar; especially in publick Buildings: But in private Ones, it will be enough if you secure only the Gutter-tiles from that Violence, because whatever Mischief is done, is easily repair'd. There is another very convenient Way of Tiling, in this Manner: If in Timber Roofs, instead of Planks, you lay along the Girders Squares of baked Clay, fasten'd with Plaister of *Paris*, and over these Squares lay your Tiles with Mortar, it will be a Covering very secure against Fire, and very commodious to the Inhabitants; and it will be less expensive, if, instead of Squares, you underlay it with Reeds, bound with Mortar. I would not have you use your Tiles, and especially those which you lay with Mortar, in publick Works, till they have supported the Frost and Sun two Years; because, if you happen to use any bad ones, there is no taking them out again without a good deal of Trouble and Expence. It may not be amiss here to mention what I have read in *Diodorus* the Historian, relating to the famous hanging Gardens in *Syria*, which were contrived with a new, and not unuseful Invention: For upon the Beams they laid Rushes dawb'd over with Pitch, and on these two Rows of baked Bricks, one above the other, cemented with Mortar; and in the third Place, they laid Plates of Lead so disposed, and fasten'd together, that not the least wet could penetrate to the Brick.

CHAP. XVI.

Of Pavements according to the Opinion of Pliny *and* Vitruvius, *and the Works of the Ancients; and of the proper Seasons for Beginning and Finishing the several Parts of Building.*

WE come now to treat of Pavements, which also partake somewhat of the Nature of Coverings. Of these, some are open to the Air; others are laid upon Rafters and Boards, others not: All require for their Foundation a solid, and even Superficies, laid exactly according to their proper Lines. Those which are open to the Air ought to be raised in such a Manner, that every ten Foot may have a Declivity of, at least, two Inches, to throw off the Water, which ought to be conveyed from thence either into Cisterns or Sinks. If from these Sinks you have not the Conveniency of a Drain, either into the Sea, or some River, dig Pits for the Soil in convenient Places, so deep as to come to some Spring of Water, and then fill up those Pits with round Pebbles.

Lastly, if you have no Opportunity to do this, make good large Sinks, and fling Coals into them, and then fill them up with Sand; which will suck up, and dry away the superfluous Moisture. If the Superficies that your Pavement is to be laid upon, is a soft loose Earth, ram it soundly, and lay it over with broken Fragments of Stone, well beat in with the Rammer also: But if the Pavement is to be upon Rafters, cover them over with Boards, and upon them lay your Rubbish or Fragments of Stone a Foot high, and beaten together, and consolidated with the Rammer. Some are of Opinion, that under these we ought to lay Fern, or Spart, to keep the Mortar from rotting the Timber. If your Rubbish is of new Stone, allow one Part of Mortar to three of Rubbish; if it is of old, you must allow two Parts in five; and when it is laid, the Way to stiffen it, is to pound it heartily with the Rammer. Over these you lay a Plaister six Inches high, made of broken Tiles, or Bricks pounded, mix'd with one fourth Part of Mortar; and upon this, lastly, you lay your Pavement, of whatsoever Sort it is, whether of Brick or Tile, exactly by Rule

R   and

78 and Level.   The Work will be more secure still, if between the Rubbish, and the Plaister you lay a Row of plain Tiles cemented with Mortar, mixed up with Oil.   As for Pavements which are not to be exposed to the open Air. *Varro* directs us to make them in the following Manner, which he tells us will be very serviceable by means of its extraordinary Dryness: Dig two Foot deep into the Ground, then ram the Bottom soundly, and lay a Pavement, either of Rubbish, or broken Brick, leaving Vent-holes for the Vapours to discharge themselves; over this lay Coals well levell'd, and ramm'd down, and over all a Crust made of Sand, Mortar, and Ashes.   These Things already mention'd, we have gathered from *Pliny* and *Vitruvius* especially: I will now set down what I have with great Pains and Labour discovered relating to Pavements from the actual Works of the Ancients; from whence, I confess, I have learnt much more than from their Writings.   We will begin with the Outward Shell, which it is very difficult to make, so as it shall not rot, or crack: For when once it has been thoroughly soak'd with wet, and comes to dry again, either by Sun, or Wind, it dries by Scales, and as we see in Mud left after Floods, the upper Coat shrinks, and leaves Cracks which cannot be filled up; for those Parts which are dried and hardened, cannot be made to cohere again by any Art whatsoever, and those which are still moist, yield and give Way to the least Violence.   I find the Ancients made their Shell either of baked Earth, or of Stone; and where Mens Feet were not to tread, they made their Tiles sometimes a Foot and a half every Way, cemented with Mortar mixed up with Oil; we also sometimes meet with small Bricks one Inch in Thickness, two in Breadth, and four in Length, join'd Sideways like a Fish's Backbone.   We often find Pavements of very large Slabs of Marble, and others again of smaller Pieces, and little Squares.   There are other Ancient Pavements made all of one Piece, which I suppose, was a Mixture of Lime, Sand, and pounded Brick, of each a third Part: which may be made more strong and lasting yet, by the Addition of one fourth Part of *Tyber*-Stone, beat to Powder.   Others in this Sort of Plaister mightily commend the Sand of *Pozzuolo*, which they call *Rapillo*.   Plaister that is designed for Pavements must be tried by continual beating, whereby it will daily acquire greater Stiffness and Hardness, till it comes to be

in a Manner firmer than Stone itself: And it is certain, that if this Plaister is sprinkled with Lime-water, and Linseed-oil, it will grow almost as hard as Glass, and defy all Manner of Weather.   Mortar worked up with Oil, is said in Pavements to keep out every Thing that is noxious.   Under the Shell I observe they made a Layer of Mortar, and small Pieces of broken Brick, of the Thickness of two or three Inches. Next to this we find a Course of Rubbish, of Bits of Bricks and Chippings of Stone, such as the Masons cut off with their Chizzel, and this is about a Foot in Thickness.   In some Places betwixt these two Courses, we find a regular one of baked Tile, or Brick, and at the Bottom of all a Layer of Stones, none bigger than a Man's Fist.   The Stones found in Rivers, which are called Male ones, as for Instance, those round ones which partake of the Nature of Flint, or Glass, grow dry immediately when they are taken out of the Water, whereas Brick and ordinary Stone retain Moisture a long Time; for which Reason, many affirm that the Damps which arise out of the Earth will never be able to penetrate to the Shell of the Pavement, if it is underlaid with those Stones.   We sometimes find that they made little square Pilasters a Foot and a half high next to the Ground, standing about two Foot distance one from the other, upon which they laid baked Tiles, and upon these the Pavement abovemention'd.   But this Kind of Pavement belongs chiefly to Baths; of which we shall treat in their proper Place.   Pavements delight in Damps, and a wet Air, while they are making, and endure best and longest in moist and shady Places; and their chief Enemies are the Looseness of the Earth, and sudden Droughts.   For as repeated Rains make the Ground close and firm, so Pavements being heartily wetted, grow compact, and hard as Iron.   That Part of the Pavement which is to receive the Water falling from the Gutters, ought to be made of the largest and soundest Stones, such as will not easily be worn away by the continual Malice (if we may so call it) of the Spouts that fall upon them.   In such Pavements as are laid upon Timber-work, or Roofing, you must take Care that the Ribs upon which it rests are sufficiently strong, and equal one to the other; for if it should be otherwise, or one Wall, or Rafter which it lies upon, should be stronger than another, the Pavement would decay and split in that Part; for as Timber-work will not always keep exactly in the same Condition,

but

but is affected and altered by the Variety of Weather, being fwell'd by wet, and dried and fhrunk by Heat, it is no Wonder that the weaker Parts fhould fink under the Weight, and fo crack the Pavement. But of this we have faid enough.

HOWEVER, I will not pafs over one Thing which is not at all foreign to our Purpofe; namely, that different Times and Seafons, and Difpofitions of the Air, are proper for digging the Foundations, filling them up, raifing the Wall, turning of Vaults, and finifhing the Shells. The Foundations are beft dug while the Sun is in *Leo*, and in *Autumn*, the Ground being then thoroughly dry, which will keep your Trench from being infefted with Water. The Spring is very convenient for filling them up, efpecially if they are pretty deep; becaufe they will be fufficiently defended from the Heat of the Summer, by means of the Ground which ftands about them as their Protector; though it will be ftill more convenient to fill them up in the Beginning of Winter, unlefs in Countries near the Pole, or in fuch cold Climates where they will be likely to freeze before they are dry. The Wall too abhors both exceffive Heat, exceffive Cold, and fudden Frofts, and efpecially Northerly Winds. Vaults, till they are dry and fettled, require an equal and temperate Seafon, more than any other Sort of Structure. The beft Time for laying on the Coat is about the rifing of the Stars, call'd the *Pleiadas*, (which is in Spring) and particularly fuch Days as have been fufficiently moiftened with foutherly Breezes; for if the Work which you are to plaifter over, or white-wafh, is not extreamly moift, nothing that you lay on will ftick to it, but it will part and crack, and always look rough and fcandalous. But of Plaiftering and Stuc-work we fhall treat more largely in its propet Place. Having now gone through the general Confideration of our Subject, it remains that we defcend to Particulars; and accordingly we defign to fhew firft the different Sorts of Buildings, and the Qualities requifite in each of them; then their Ornaments; and laftly, how to remedy fuch Defects in them as are owing either to the Fault of the Workman, or the Injury of Time.

The End of Book III.

THE

ARCHITECTURE

OF

Leone Batista Alberti.

BOOK IV. CHAP. I.

Of Works of a publick Nature. That all Buildings, whether contrived for Necessity, Conveniency or Pleasure, were intended for the Service of Mankind. Of the several Divisions of humane Conditions, whence arises the Diversity of Buildings.

 T is plain that Building was invented for the Service of Mankind; for if we consider the Matter ever so little, it is natural to suppose that their first Design was only to raise a Structure that might defend them and theirs from the ill Qualities of the Weather; afterwards they proceeded to make not only every Thing that was necessary to their Safety, but also every Thing that might be convenient or useful to them. At last, instructed and allured by the Opportunities that naturally offer'd themselves, they began to contrive how to make their Buildings subservient to their Pleasures and Recreations, and proceeded every Day further and further in so doing: So that if upon considering the various Sorts of Buildings, we should say, that some were contrived by Necessity, some by Convenience, and some by Pleasure, it might, perhaps, be no ill Definition of the Matter. Yet when we take a View of the great Plenty and Variety of Buildings all about us, we easily perceive that all were not erected merely upon those Accounts, or for one Occasion more than another, but that this great Variety and Difference among them, are owing principally to the Variety there is among Mankind. So that, if according to our Method we would make a careful Enquiry into their Sorts and Parts, it is here that we must begin our Disquisition, namely, from the Nature of Mankind, and wherein they differ from one another; since upon their Account it is that Buildings are erected, and for their Uses varied: So that having thoroughly considered these Things, we may treat of them more clearly. For this Purpose, it will not be amiss to recollect the Opinions of the wise Founders of ancient Republicks and Laws concerning

cerning

cerning the Division of the People into different Orders; in as much as they applied themselves to the Consideration of these Things with the greatest Care, Diligence and Application, and have received the highest Applauses for their Discoveries.

Plutarch tells us, that *Theseus* divided the Commonwealth into two Ranks, one that made and expounded the Laws, both Humane and Divine, and the other that follow'd manual Occupations. *Solon* distinguish'd his Citizens according to their Wealth, and such as did not raise from their Possessions three hundred Bushels of Grain every Year, he reckon'd scarce worthy to be esteem'd a Citizen. The *Athenians* gave the first Rank to Men of Learning and Wisdom; the second to the Orators, and the last to Artificers. *Romulus* separated the Knights and *Patricians* from the *Plebeians*; and *Numa* divided the *Plebeians* according to their respective Employments. In *France* the *Plebeians* were in a Manner Slaves; the rest, says *Cæsar*, were either Soldiers, or Professors of Religion, or the Study of Wisdom, whom they call'd *Druids*. Among the *Panchæi* the first were the Priests; the second, the Husbandmen, and the last, the Soldiers, with whom were reckon'd the Shepherds, and Tenders of Herds. The *Britons* were divided into four Orders; the first were those out of whose Number they chose their King; the second were the Priests; the third, the Soldiers, and the last the common People. The *Ægyptians* gave the first Rank to their Priests; the second to their King and Governours; the third to the Soldiers, and the rest of the People were subdivided into Husbandmen, Shepherds, and Artificers, and further, as *Herodotus* informs us, into Mercenaries, and Seamen. We are told, that *Hipodamus* divided his Republic into three Parts, Artificers, Husbandmen, and Soldiers. *Aristotle* seems not displeased with those who separated from the Multitude some Men of greatest Worth to manage their Counsels, and exercise their Office of Magistracy and Judicature, and divided the Remainder of the People into Husbandmen, Artificers, Merchants, Mercenaries, Horse, Foot and Seamen. Not much unlike this, according to *Diodorus* the Historian, was the Commonwealth of the *Indians*, who were distinguished into Priests, Husbandmen, Shepherds, Artificers, Soldiers, Ephori, or Super-intendants, and those who presided over the publick Counsels.

Plato observes that a Nation is sometimes peaceable and desirous of Quiet and Repose; and at other Times restless and warlike, according to the Temper of those at the Helm; and therefore he divides the Body of the Citizens according to the Parts of the Mind of Man; one to moderate every Thing with Reason and Counsel; another to resent and repel Injuries with Force; and a third to prepare and administer Nourishment to all the rest. These Things I have thus briefly recited out of numerous Writings of the Ancients; and the natural Result seems to be this, that all these which I have mentioned are every one of them different Parts of the Republick, and consequently that each requires a particular Kind of Building. But that according to our Custom we may be able to treat of this Subject more distinctly, it will not be amiss to reflect upon the following Considerations: If any one were to separate the whole Number of Mankind into different Parts, the first Thing that would offer itself to his Thoughts would be this; that it is not the same Thing to consider all the Inhabitants of any one Province all together collectively, and to consider them separately according to their respective Distinctions; and the next Thing would be, that by a Contemplation of Nature itself, he would take Notice in what Particular they differ'd most from one another, that from thence he might take Occasion to separate them into their proper Divisions. Now there is nothing wherein Men differ more one from the other, than in the very particular wherein they differ from Brutes; namely, in Reason, and the Knowledge of useful Arts, to which, if you please, you may add Prosperity of Fortune: In all which Gifts there are very few that excel at the same Time. This then opens to us our first Division, and instructs us to select from the Multitude, a small Number, whereof some are illustrious for their Wisdom, Experience and Capacity; others for their Progress, and Knowledge in useful Arts; and others, lastly, for their Riches, and Abundance in the Goods of Fortune. And who will deny that these are the most fit to be intrusted with the principal Offices in the Commonwealth? The most excellent Persons, therefore, who are endued with the greatest Share of Wisdom, ought to be intrusted with the chief Care and Power of moderating in all Affairs. Such

S

will

will order the facred Ceremonies with religious Minds, and frame Laws with Juftice and Equity, and themfelves fet the Example of Living orderly and happily. They will watch continually for the Defence and Enlargement of the Authority and Dignity of their Fellow-Citizens. And when they have determined upon any Thing convenient, ufeful, or necef-fary; being perhaps themfelves worn out with Years, and fitter for Contemplation than Action, they will commit the Execution of it to fuch as they know to be well experienced, and brisk and courageous to bring the Matter to effect, to whom they will give an Oppor-tunity of deferving well of their Country, by the Profecution of their Defign. Then thefe others, having taken the Bufinefs upon them-felves, will faithfully perform their Parts at home with Study and Application, and abroad with Diligence and Labour, giving Judgment, leading Armies, and exercifing their own In-duftry, and that of thofe who are under them. And laftly, as it is in vain to think of effecting any Thing without Means, the next in Place to thofe already mentioned are fuch as fupply thefe with their Wealth, either by Husbandry or Merchandize. All the other Orders of Men ought in Reafon to obey and be fub-fervient to thefe as chief. Now if any Thing is to be gather'd from all this to our Purpofe, it is certainly that of the different Kinds of Building, one Sort belongs to the Publick, another to the principal Citizens, and another to the Commonality.

AND again, among the principal Sort, one is proper for thofe who bear the Weight of the publick Counfels and Deliberations, an-other for thofe who are employ'd in the Exe-cution, and another for fuch as apply them-81 felves to the amaffing of Wealth. Of all which one Part, as we obferved before, having Relation to Neceffity, and another to Con-venience; it will be no Prefumption in us who are treating of Buildings to allow another Part to Pleafure, while inftead of claiming any Merit upon this Account to ourfelves, we confefs that the Principles of this Divifion are to be drawn from the firft Rudiments of the Philofophers.

OF this, therefore, we are now to treat, what belongs to a publick Building, what to thofe of the principal Citizens, and what to thofe of the common Sort. But where fhall we begin fuch great Matters? Shall we follow the gradual Courfe of Mankind in their pro-curing of all thefe, and fo beginning with the mean Huts of poor People, go on by degrees to thofe vaft Structures which we fee of Thea-tres, Baths, and Temples. It is certain it was a great while before Mankind enclofed their Cities with Walls. Hiftorians tell us that when *Bacchus* made his Progrefs thro' *India*, he did not meet with one walled Town; and *Thucydides* writes, that formerly there were none in *Greece* itfelf: And in *Burgundy*, a Province of *Gaul*, even in *Cæfar*'s Time, there were no Towns encompafs'd with Walls, but the People dwelt up and down in Villages. The firft City I find any Mention of is *Biblus*, belonging to the *Phænicians*, which *Saturn* girt in with a Wall drawn round all their Houfes: Whatever *Pomponius Mela* may fay of *Joppa* built even before the Flood. *Hero-dotus* informs us, that while the *Æthiopians* had Poffeffion of *Ægypt*, they never punifh'd any Criminal with Death, but obliged him to raife the Earth all round the Village he lived in; and this, they fay, was the firft Beginning of Cities in *Ægypt*. But we fhall fpeak of them in another Place. And though it muft be confefs'd that all humane Inventions take their Rife from very fmall Beginnings, yet I intend here to begin with the Works of the greateft Perfection.

C H A P. II.

Of the Region, Place, and Conveniencies and Inconveniencies of a Situation for a City, according to the Opinion of the Ancients, and that of the Author.

ALL the Citizens are concerned in every Thing of a publick Nature that makes Part of the City: And if we are convinced of what the Philofophers teach, that the Occafion and Reafon of Building Cities is that the In-habitants may dwell in them in Peace, and, as far as poffibly may be, free from all Incon-veniencies and Moleftations, then certainly it

requires

requires the moſt deliberate Conſideration in what Place or Situation, and with what Circuit of Lines it ought to be fix'd. Concerning theſe Things there have been various Opinions.

Cæſar writes, that the _Germans_ accounted it the greateſt Glory to have vaſt uninhabited Deſarts for their Confines: Becauſe they thought theſe Deſarts ſecured them againſt ſudden Irruptions from their Enemies. The Hiſtorians ſuppoſe that the only Thing which deterr'd _Seſoſtris_, King of _Ægypt_, from leading his Army into _Æthiopia_ was the Want of Proviſions, and the Difficulty of the Places through which he muſt march. The _Aſſyrians_ being defended by their Deſarts and Marſhes, never fell under the Dominion of any foreign Prince. They ſay, that the _Arabians_ too wanting both Water and Fruits, never felt the Aſſaults, or Injuries of any Enemies. _Pliny_ ſays that _Italy_ has been ſo often infeſted with Armies of Barbarians only for the Sake of her Wines and Figs: We may add that the too great Plenty of ſuch Things as ſerve only to Luxury, are very prejudicial, as _Crates_ teaches, both to Young and Old; becauſe it is apt to make the Latter cruel, and the Former effeminate.

Livy tells us, that among the _Æmerici_ there is a Region wonderfully fruitful, which as it generally happens in rich Soils, engenders a very cowardly weak Race of Men; whereas on the contrary the _Ligii_, who dwelt in a ſtony Country, being forced to conſtant Labour, and to live with great Frugality, were extremely robuſt and induſtrious. The State of Things being ſo, it is probable ſome may not diſlike theſe barren difficult Places for fixing a City in; tho' others again may be of a contrary Opinion, deſiring to enjoy all the Benefits and Gifts of Nature, and to want nothing that may contribute either to Neceſſity or Pleaſure; and for the right uſing of theſe Benefits, the Fathers may provide by Laws and Statutes. And they think the Conveniencies of Life are much more pleaſing when they may be had at home, than when they are obliged to fetch them from abroad: for which Reaſon, they deſire ſuch a Soil as _Varro_ tells us is to be found near _Memphis_, which enjoys ſo favourable a Climate, that all the Trees even the Vines themſelves, never drop their Leaves the whole Year round: or ſuch a one as is under Mount _Taurus_ in thoſe Parts which look to the North, where _Strabo_ ſays the Bunches of Grapes are three Foot long, and that every ſingle Vine Tree yields half a Barrel of Wine, and one Fig Tree an hundred and forty Pound Weight of Figs; or ſuch a one as is in _India_, or the _Hyperborean_ Iſland in the Ocean, where _Herodotus_ tells us they gather their Fruits twice every Year; or like that of _Portugal_, where the Seeds that fall by chance yields ſeveral Harveſts, or rather like _Talge_, in the _Caſpian_ Mountains, where the Earth brings forth Corn without Tillage. But theſe Things are uncommon, and rather to be wiſh'd for than had. And therefore the wiſe Ancients who have written upon this Subject, either from their own Obſervations, or the Books of others, are of Opinion, that a City ought to be ſo placed as to have all ſufficient Neceſſaries within its own Territory (as far as the Condition of human Affairs will permit) without being obliged to ſeek them abroad; and that the Circuit of its Confines ought to be fortified, that no Enemy can eaſily make an Irruption upon them, though at the ſame time they may ſend out Armies into the Countries of their Neighbours, whatever the Enemy can do to prevent it; which is a Situation that they tell us will enable a City not only to defend its Liberty, but alſo to enlarge the Bounds of its Dominion. But after all, what ſhall we ſay? No Place ever had thoſe Advantages more than _Ægypt_, which was ſo ſtrongly fortified in all its Parts, as to be in a Manner inacceſſible, having on one Side, the Sea, and on the other a vaſt Deſart; on the right Hand ſteep Mountains; and on the Left, huge Marſhes; beſides, the Fruitfulneſs of the Soil is ſo great, that the Ancients uſed to call _Egypt_ the Granary of the World, and fabled that the Gods made it their common Retreat either for Safety or Pleaſure; and yet even this Country, though ſo ſtrong, and ſo abounding in all Manner of Plenty, that it could boaſt of feeding the Univerſe, and of entertaining and harbouring the Gods themſelves, could not, as _Joſephus_ informs us, always preſerve its Liberty.

THOSE therefore are entirely in the Right, who teach us, though in Fables, that human Affairs are never perfectly ſecure though laid in the Lap of _Jupiter_ himſelf. Upon which Occaſion we may not improperly make uſe of the ſame Anſwer that _Plato_ made when he was ask'd where that perfect Commonwealth was to be found, which he had made ſo fine a Deſcription of; that, ſays he, was not the Thing

Thing I troubled myself about; all I studied was how to frame the best that possibly could be, and that which deviates least from a Resemblance of this, ought to be preferred above all the rest. So our Design is to describe and illustrate by Examples such a City as the wisest Men judge to be in all Respects the most convenient; and in other Respects accommodating ourselves to Time and Necessity, we shall follow the Opinion of *Socrates*, that whatever cannot be alter'd but for the worse, is really best. I lay it down therefore for granted, that our City ought to be contrived as to suffer none of the Inconveniencies spoken of in the first Book, nor to want any of the Necessaries of Life. Its Territory shall be healthy, wide, pleasant, various, fruitful, secure, and abounding with Plenty of Fruits, and great Quantities of Water. It must not want Rivers, Lakes, and an open Passage to the Sea for the convenient bringing in of such Things as are wanted, and carrying out such as may be spared. All Things, in a Word, must contribute to the establishing and improving all Affairs both civil and military, whereby the Commonwealth may be a Defence to its Subjects, an Ornament to itself, a Pleasure to its Friends, and a Terror to its Enemies. I take it to be a great Happiness to any City, to be able to cultivate a good handsome Part of its Territory, in Spite of any Enemy whatsoever. Moreover your City ought to stand in the Middle of its Territory, in a Place from whence it can have a View all round its Country, and watch its Opportunities, and be ready where-ever Necessity calls, which may lie convenient for the Farmer, and Ploughman to go out to his daily Labour, and return with Ease laden with Grain and Fruits. But the Situation is one of the Things of greatest Importance, whether it should be upon an open Plain, or upon the Shore, or on a Hill: because each of these have some particular Qualities that are useful, and others on the contrary that are not so agreeable.

When *Bacchus* led his Army through *India*, the excessive Heat bred Distempers among them; whereupon he carried them up to the Hills, where the Wholesomness of the Air immediately cured them. Those that first built Cites upon Hills, seem to have done it upon Account of the Security of such a Situation; but then they generally want Water. The Plains afford great Conveniencies of Water, and of Rivers; but the Air is more gross, which

makes the Summer excessively hot, and the Winter as cold; besides, being less defended against any Violence.

The Sea-shore is mighty convenient for the Importation of Merchandizes; but all Sea-towns are reckoned too fond and greedy of Novelties, and to suffer perpetual Commotions from the too great Concourse, and the Broils of Strangers, and are exposed to very dangerous Insults and Revolutions from foreign Fleets. In which soever of these Situations therefore you build your City, you should endeavour to contrive that it may partake of all the Advantages, and be liable to none of the Disadvantages. Upon a Hill I would make the Ground level, and upon a Plain I would raise it to an Eminence in that Part where my City was to be placed. And if we cannot effect this just according to our Wish, by reason of the great Variety of Places, let us make use of the following Methods to obtain at least every Thing that is necessary: On a maritime Coast, if it is a Plain, do not let the City stand too near the Sea; nor too far from it, if it is hilly. We are told that the Shores of the Sea are liable to Alteration; and that several Towns, and particularly *Baiæ* in *Italy*, have been swallow'd up by the Waves.

Pharos in *Ægypt*, which anciently was surrounded by the Sea, is now become a *Chersonesus*, or Neck of Land. *Strabo* writes, that *Tyre* and *Clazomene* underwent the same Change: Nay they tell us, that the Temple of *Jupiter Hammon* stood once upon the Sea-shore, though now the Sea has left it, and it stands far within the Land. They advise us to build our City either close to the Shore, or else at a pretty good Distance from the Sea: for we find that the Winds from the Sea are heavy and sharp, by reason of their Saltness: And therefore, when they arrive at some Place at a middling Distance from the Sea, especially if it is a Plain, you will find the Air there extremely moist through the dissolving of the Salt which it took from the Sea, which makes it thick and heavy, and perfectly ropy; so that in such Places you shall sometimes see a Sort of Strings flying about in the Air like Cobwebs; And they tell us, that a Mixture of Salt has the same Effect upon the Air as it has upon Water, which it will corrupt to such a Degree as to make it stink very offensively. The Ancients, and chiefly *Plato*, are for having a City stand at ten Miles Distance from

from the Sea; but if you cannot place it so far off, let it be at least in some Situation where the above-mention'd Winds cannot reach it, otherwise than broken, tired and purified; placing it so, that between it and the Sea there may stand some Hill to interrupt any noxious Vapour from thence. A Prospect of the Sea from the Shore is wonderfully pleasant, and is generally attended with a wholesome Air; and *Ariſtotle* thinks those Countries are most healthy where the Winds keep the Atmosphere in continual Motion: but then the Sea there must not be weedy, with a low Beach scarce covered with Water; but deep, with a high bold Shore of a living craggy Rock. The placing a City upon the proud Shoulders of a Mountain (if we may be allowed so florid an Expreſſion) contributes greatly not only to Dignity and Pleasure, but yet more to Health. In those Places where the Hills overshadow the Sea, the Water is always deep; besides that if any grofs Vapours do arise from the Sea, they spend themselves before they reach so high; and if any sudden Attack is made upon you from an Enemy, you lie leſs liable to be surprized, and more advantageously for defending yourself. The Ancients commend a Situation upon the East Side of a Hill, and in hot Countries, that Side which lies open to Northern Winds. Others perhaps may rather chuse the West Side, from this Inducement, that manured Ground lying to that Aſpect is the most fruitful: And indeed it is certain Historians tell us, that under Mount *Taurus*, the Side which looks to the North, is much more healthy than the others, for the very same Reason that it is also more fruitful. Lastly, if we build our City upon a Hill, we should take particular Care that we are not exposed to one great Inconvenience which generally happens in such a Situation, especially if there are other Hills near, which raise their Heads above us; namely, that there is not a settled heavy Body of Clouds to darken and eclipse the Day and infect the Air. We ought, besides, to have a Care that this Situation is not exposed to the raging Fury and Violence of Winds, and especially of the North-wind; which, as *Heſiod* tells us, shrinks up and bends every Body, and particularly old People. It will make the Situation very bad if there is any neighbouring Rock standing above the City, so as to throw upon it the Vapours raised by the Sun, or any very deep Valley reaking with unwholesome Steams. Others advise that the Circuit of the Town should ter-

minate in Clifts and Precipices; but that these are not always safe against Earthquakes, or Storms, is sufficiently evident from very many Towns, and particularly *Voltera* in *Tuſcany*; for the very Ground itself falls away in such Places, and brings down after it whatsoever is built upon it.

You ought also to take particular Care that such a Situation has no Hill near that rises above it, which falling into the Hands of an Enemy, may enable him to give you continual Trouble; nor any Plain laying under it big enough to conceal an Army in Safety, and give it Time to make Lodgments and open Trenches, or to range its Forces in Order of Battle to attack you. We read that *Dedalus* built the Town of *Agrigentum*, now called *Gergento*, upon a very steep Rock, with a very difficult Paſſage to it, insomuch that only three Men were sufficient to defend it; a Fortreſs certainly very convenient, provided your Paſſage out cannot be stopt by the same Number of Men that can secure the Paſſage in. Men of Experience in military Affairs greatly commend the Town of *Cingoli*, built by *Labienus* in the Mark of *Ancona*; because, besides several other Advantages that it has, it will not allow of one Thing common in mountainous Situations, which is that when once you have climbed up to the Top, you then can fight upon an equal Foot; for here you are repulsed by a very high steep Precipice: Neither can the Enemy here waste and destroy the Country round with one single Excursion, nor secure all the Ways at one Time, nor make a secure Retreat to their Camp, nor send out to Forage, or to get Wood or Water without Danger; whereas those in the Town enjoy all the contrary Advantages; for by Means of the Hills that lie beneath them all running one into another with a great Number of little Vallies between, they can at any Time issue out of a sudden to attack the Enemy unawares, and surprize them whenever any immediate Opportunity offers itself. Nor are they leſs pleased with *Biſſeium*, a Town of the *Marſians*, prodigiously secured by the three Rivers which meet there from different Quarters, and very difficult of Access thro' the narrow Paſſes of the Vallies guarded all round with steep and unpaſſable Mountains: so that the Enemy can find no Place to fix a Camp for a Siege, and can never guard all the Paſſes, which are vastly convenient to those in the Place for bringing in Provisions and Succours,

T　　　　　　　　　and

and making Sallies: But let this fuffice as to mountainous Situations. But if you build your City in a Plain, and according to the general Practice on the Banks of a River, fo perhaps as to have the Stream run through the Middle of the Town, you muft have a Care that this River does not come from the South, nor run towards that Point: Becaufe on one Side the Damps, and on the other the Cold being encreafed by the Vapours of the Water, will come to you with double Violence and Unwholefomefs. But if the River flows without the Compafs of the Walls, you muft take a View of the Country round about, and confider on which Side the Winds have the freeft Paffage, that you may there erect a fufficient Wall to reftrain the River within its Limits. As for other Precautions, it may not be amifs to confider what the Mariners tell us; to wit, that the Winds are naturally inclined to follow the Sun and the Eaftern Breezes, when the Phyficians obferve, that thofe of the Morning are the pureft, and thofe of the Evening the moft damp: Whereas on the Contrary when they blow from the Weft they are heavieft at Sun-rife, and lighteft at Sun-fet. For thefe Reafons the beft Pofition for a City will be to have the River come in from the Eaft, and go out towards the Weft; becaufe then that Breeze or gentle Wind which rifes with the Sun, will carry the Vapours out of the City, if any noxious ones fhould arife, or at leaft it will not encreafe them itfelf. However, I would rather have a River, Lake, or any other Water extend to the North than to the South, provided the Town do not ftand under the Sha-

dow of a Mountain, which is the worft Situation in the World. I will not repeat what we have faid before, and we know that the South Wind is very heavy and flow in its Nature, infomuch that when the Sails of a Ship are filled with it, the Veffel feems oppreffed with its Weight, and draws more Water; whereas, the North Wind on the contrary feems to lighten the Ship and the Sea too: however, it is better to keep both thefe at a Diftance, than to have them continually beating againft the Wall. Nothing is more condemned than a River flowing under high fteep Banks, with a very deep ftony Channel, and always fhaded; becaufe its Water is unwholfome to drink, and the Air upon it dangerous: And to avoid fettling near Bogs and Marfhes, or ftanding muddy Waters is the Part of every prudent confiderate Builder. I need not mention here the Difeafes occafion'd by fuch Neighbourhoods: We need only obferve of thefe Places, that befides the common Nuifances in Summer of ill Smells, Fleas and other nafty Vermin, they are liable to one great Inconvenience befides, when you imagine the Air to be wholefomeft and cleareft (which we alfo took Notice of in relation to all Plains) that they are Subject to exceffive Colds in Winter and exceffive Heats in Summer. Laftly, we muft be very fure that none of thefe, whether Hill, Rock, Lake, Bog, River or Well, or the like, may be fo difpofed as to be likely to ftrengthen or fupport an Enemy, or to bring any Manner of Inconveniencies upon your own Citizens. And this is as much as is neceffary with Regard to the Region and Situation. 83

CHAP. III.

Of the Compaſs, Space and Bigneſs of the City, of the Form and Diſpoſition of the Walls and Fortifications, and of the Cuſtoms and Ceremonies obſerved by the Ancients in marking them out.

IT is certain the Form of the City and the Diftribution of its Parts muft be various according to the Variety of Places; fince we fee it is impoffible upon a Hill to lay out an Area whether round or fquare, or of any other regular Form, with that Eafe, that you may upon an open Plain. The ancient Architects in encompaffing their Towns with Walls, condemn'd all Angles jutting out from the naked of the Wall, as thinking they help the Enemy

more in their Affault than the Inhabitants in their Defence; and that they were very weak againft the Shocks of military Engines; and indeed for Treacheries, and for the fafer throwing their Darts they are of fome Advantage to the Enemy, efpecially where they can run up to the Walls, and withdraw again immediately to their Camp; but yet they are fometimes of very great Service in Towns feated upon Hills, if they are fet juft anfwering

to

84
85

to the Streets. At the famous City *Perusia*, which has several little Towers placed here and there upon the Hills, like the Fingers of a Man's Hand extending out, if the Enemy offers to attack one of the Angles with a good Number of Men, he can find no Place to begin his Assault, and being obliged to march under those Towers, is not able to withstand the Weapons that will be cast, and the Sallies made upon him. So that the same Method for walling of Towns will not serve in all Places. Moreover the Ancients lay it down for a Rule, that Cities and Ships should by no means be either so big as to look empty, nor so little as to be crowded. Others are for having their Towns full and close, believing that it adds to their Safety: Others, feeding themselves with great Hopes of Times to come, delight in having a vast deal of Room: Others, perhaps, have an Eye to the Fame and Honour of Posterity. The City of the *Sun*, built by *Busiris*, and call'd *Thebes*, as Histories inform us, was twenty Miles in Circuit; *Memphis*, eighteen Miles, six Furlongs; *Babylon*, three and forty Miles, six Furlong; *Nineveh*, threescore Miles; and some Towns enclosed so much Ground, that even within the Walls they could raise Provisions for the whole Year. But, I think, there is a great deal of Wisdom in the old Proverb, which tells us, that we ought in all Things to avoid excess; though if I were to commit an Error of either Side, I should rather chuse that Proportion which would allow of an Encrease of Citizens, than that which is hardly sufficient to contain the present Inhabitants. Add to this, that a City is not built wholly for the Sake of Shelter, but ought to be so contrived, that besides their civil Conveniencies there may be handsome Spaces left for Squares, Courses for Chariots, Gardens, Places to take the Air in, for Swimming, and the like, both for Ornament and Recreation.

We read in the Ancients *Varro*, *Plutarch* and others, that their Forefathers us'd to design the Walls of their Town with abundance of religious Rites and Ceremonies. After the repeated taking of Auspices they yoked a Bull and a Cow together to draw a brazen Plough, with which they traced out the Line that was to be the Circuit of the Wall, the Cow being placed on the Inside, and the Bull without. The Fathers and Elders that were to dwell in the Town followed the Plough, laying all the Clods of Earth into the Furrow again inward, so that none might lie scattering outward, and when they came to those Places where the Gates were to be, they lifted up the Plough and carried it in their Hands, that the Groundsell of the Gates might remain untouch'd; and for this Reason they esteem'd the whole Circle of the Wall to be sacred, all except the Gates, which were by no means to be called so.

In the Days of *Romulus*, *Dionysius* of *Halicarnassus*, tells us, that the Fathers in Beginning their Towns, used, after performing a Sacrifice, to kindle Fires before their Tents, and to make the People pass through them, believing that they were purged and purified by the Flame; and they held it unlawful to admit any Body to this Ceremony that was polluted or unclean. This is what we find to have been the Custom of those Nations. In other Places they used to mark out the Foundation of their Walls by strowing all the Way a Dust made of white Earth, which they called *pure*; and *Alexander*, upon laying out the Town of *Pharos*, for want of this Earth made use of Meal. From these Ceremonies the Diviners took Occasion to foretell what should happen in Times to come; for noting the Nativity, as we may call it, of the City, and some Events that seemed to have some Connection with it, they imagined they might thence draw Predictions of its future Successes. The *Hetrurians* too in the Books of their Ceremonies taught this Art of foretelling the Fortune of Towns from the Day of their Nativities; and this not from the Observation of the Heavens, which we mentioned in the Second Book, but from Principles and Conjectures founded upon present Circumstances. *Censorinus* informs us, that the Method they taught was this: Such Men as happened to be born the very same Day that the City was begun, and lived the Longest of any one born on that Day, were reckoned by their Death to put a Period to the first Age of that City; next, the longest Liver of those that dwelt in the City; at that Time, when they died concluded the second Age; and so for the other Ages. Then they supposed that the Gods generally sent Omens to point out the Conclusion of each particular Age. These were the Superstitions which they taught; and they add that the *Hetrurians* by these Prognosticks could certainly fix every Age of their City, which they determined to to be as follows; their first four Ages they made an hundred Years each; the Fifth, an hundred and Twenty-three; the Sixth, an hundred and Twenty, and as many the Seventh;

Seventh; the Eighth was the Time they then lived in under the Emperors, and the Ninth was to come; and by thefe Prognofticks they thought it no hard Matter to difcover even the Events of future Ages. They conjectured that *Rome* fhould come to be Miftrefs of the World, from this Symptom, namely, becaufe a Man born on the Day of her Foundation became in Time her Mafter. And this Man, I find, was *Numa* : for *Plutarch* informs us, that on the Nineteenth of *April, Rome* was begun, and *Numa* born. But the *Spartans* gloried in having no Walls at all about their City; for confiding in the Valour and Fortitude of their Citizens, they thought there was no Occafion for any Fortification befides good Laws. The *Ægyptians* and *Perfians*, on the contrary, enclofed their Cities with the ftrongeft Walls; for not to mention others, *Nineveh* and *Semiramis* made the Walls of their Towns fo thick, that two Chariots might pafs upon the Top abreaft, and fo high, that they were above an hundred Cubits. *Arrian* relates that the Walls of *Tyre* were an hundred and Fifty Foot high. Some again have not been fatisfied with one Wall: The *Carthaginians* enclofed their City with Three; and *Herodotus* writes that *Deioces* fortified his Town of *Ecbatana*, though it was feated upon an Hill with Seven. Now as it is certain that Walls are a very powerful Defence both of our Perfons and Liberties, when the Enemy happens to be fuperior either in Number or Fortune, I cannot join in with thofe who are for having their City quite naked without any Wall, neither with fuch as feem to place all their Hopes of Defence in their Wall alone. I agree with what *Plato* obferves, that every City ftands continually expofed to the Danger of being brought under Subjection; fince, whether it be owing to Nature or Cuftom, neither publick Bodies nor private Perfons can ever fet Bounds to their infatiable Defire of getting and poffeffing ftill more and more; from which one Source arifes all the Mifchiefs of War. So that what is there to be faid againft adding Security to Security, and Fortification to Fortification? From what has been already faid, we may conclude that of all Cities, the moft Capacious is the round One; and the moft Secure, that which is encompaffed with Walls broken here and there into Angles or Baftions jutting out at certain Diftances, as *Tacitus* informs us *Jerufalem* was: Becaufe it is certain, the Enemy cannot come up to the Wall between two

Angles jutting out, without expofing themfelves to very great Danger; nor can their military Engines attack the Heads of thofe Angles with any Hopes of Succefs. But, however, we fhould be fure to make ufe of all the natural Advantages that offer themfelves for the Security of our Town or Fortification; as we may obferve the Ancients did, according to the Opportunity or Neceffity of the Situation. Thus *Antium*, an ancient City of 86 the *Latins*, in order to embrace the Winding of the Shore, appears from the old Ruins which are left, to have been built of a very great Length. *Cairo*, upon the *Nile*, is faid alfo to be a very long City. *Palimbrota*, a City of *India*, belonging to the *Grafii*, as *Metafthenes* informs us, was fixteen Miles long, and three broad, running along the Side of the River. We read that the Walls of *Babylon* were fquare; and thofe of *Memphis* built in Shape of a D. But whatever Shape is chofen for the Walls, *Vegetius* thinks it fufficient for Service, if they are fo broad, that two armed Soldiers pofted there for Defence, may eafily pafs without being in one anothers Way; and fo high, that they cannot be fcaled with Ladders; and built fo firm and ftrong, as not to yield to the battering Rams and other Engines. The military Engines are of two Sorts; one Sort are thofe which break and demolifh the Wall by Battery; the other are fuch as attack and undermine the Foundation, and fo bring down the Superftructure. Now the greateft Security againft both thefe, is not fo much a Wall as a good Ditch. The Wall is of no Ufe in the laft Cafe, unlefs its Foundation lies under Water, or upon a folid Rock. The Ditch ought to be very broad and very deep; for then it will hinder the moveable Tortoifefhell, Towers, or other fuch Machines from approaching the Wall; and when the Foundation is under Water, or on a Rock, it will be in vain to think of undermining it. It is a Difpute among the military Men, whether it is beft for the Ditch to be full of Water, or to be kept dry; but it is allow'd, that the firft Thing to be confulted is, which is moft for the Health of the Inhabitants; and then fome fay thofe Ditches are certainly beft which are fo contrived, that if by the Force of Battery any Part of the Wall is beaten into them, it may be foon removed, and the Ditch kept clear, that it may not be filled up, and fo make a Path for the Enemy.

C H A P.

C H A P. IV.

Of the Walls, Battlements, Towers, Cornishes and Gates, and the Timber-work belonging to them.

BUT to return to the Walls. The Ancients advise us to build them after this Manner. Raise two Walls one within the other, leaving between them a Space of twenty Foot, which Space is to be fill'd up with the Earth dug out of the Ditch, and well ramm'd in; and let these Walls be built in such a Manner, that you may mount from the Level of the City quite to the Top of the Battlements, by an easy Ascent, as it were by Steps. Others say, that the Earth which is dug out of the Ditch, ought to be thrown without the Wall, on the other Side of the Ditch, and there cast up into a Rampart, and from the Bottom of the Ditch a Wall should be run up, thick and strong enough to support the Weight of the aforesaid Earth which bears upon it. At a Distance from this another Wall should be raised in the Town, higher than the other, and as far from it, as to leave Space enough for the Soldiers to be drawn up, and to have Room to fight in. Besides this, you should between the principal Walls, and those within, erect other Walls crossways from one to the other, by the Help whereof, the principal Walls may unite with those behind, and more easily support the Weight of the Earth cast in between them. But indeed for my Part, I am best pleased with those Walls which are so situated, that if they happen to be at length demolished by the Force of Battery, they have somewhat of a Plain at the Foot of them, where they may lie and form a Kind of Rampart, and so be kept from filling up the Ditch with their Ruins. In other Respects I am very well pleased with *Vitruvius*, who says the Wall ought to be built thus: Within the Body of the Wall we should lay a good many Timbers of Olive-wood burnt, to the Intent that the two Sides of the Walls being fastened together by these wooden Bracers, the Work may be the more durable. Such a Wall as this, we are told by *Thucydides*, was made by the *Plataeans*, to defend themselves against the People of the *Morea*, by whom they were besieged; inasmuch as they mixed Timbers among their Brick-work, and made a very stout

Fortification of it. And *Caesar* informs us, that in *France* most of their Walls were built in this Manner: They laid Beams within the Wall, and braced them together at equal Distances, filling up the Vacancies with huge Stones, so that one Beam never touched the other; and so proceeded with several Courses of Work in the same Method, till they raised a Wall of a good considerable Height. This Kind of Work was not unhandsome to the Sight, and was a very strong Fortification, because the Stones secured it against Fire, and the Timbers against the Battering Rams. But this mix'd Work others disapprove of; because they say the Lime and the Wood will not long agree together, for Timber is eaten and burnt up both by the Saltness and Heat of the Lime. Besides that, if the Wall should happen to be demolish'd by Battery, they say, that as it is thus made in a Manner all of one Piece, the whole Wall will be apt to go all together at once. In my Opinion one very good Way of Building a strong Wall, capable to stand the Shocks of Engines, is this: make triangular Projections out from the naked of the Wall, with one Angle facing the Enemy, at the Distance of every ten Cubits, and turn Arches from one Projection to the other; then fill up the Vacancies between them with Straw and Earth, well rammed down together. By this Means the Force and Violence of the Shocks of the Engines, will be deadened by the Softness of the Earth, and the Wall will not be weakned by the Battery, only here and there, and those small Breaches, or rather Holes, that are made in it, will presently be stopt up again. In *Sicily*, their Pumice-stones, which they have in great Plenty, will do extreamly well for this Kind of Work: But in other Places, for want of Pumice-stones and Earth, any soft Stone may be made use of; nor is Terrass amiss for this Purpose. Lastly, if any Part of such a Structure stands exposed to the most southerly Winds, or nocturnal Vapours, cloath and face it with a Shell of Stone. And particularly it will be of great Service to let the outer Bank of the Ditch have a good Slope, and lie a pretty deal higher than the Ground beyond it: For this will baulk the Aim of the military Engines, and make them throw over the Wall. And some think no Wall is so safe against Battery, as those which are built in uneven Lines, like the Teeth of a Saw.

I am very well pleased with those Walls in *Rome*, which at about half Way up to the Top have a Walk with little private Holes, out of which, the Archers may privately annoy the Enemy, as he moves about the Field in Security; and at the Distance of every fifty Cubits are Towers, adjoining to the Wall like Buttresses, projecting out in a round Figure forwards, and somewhat higher than the Wall itself; so that whoever offers to approach between these Towers, is exposed to be taken in Flank and slain; and thus the Wall is defended by these Towers, and the Towers mutually by one another. The Back of the Towers, which look into the Town, ought to have no Wall, but should be left quite open and naked; that if the Enemy should get Possession of them, they may not be safe in them from the Assaults of the Inhabitants.

The Cornishes of the Towers and Walls, besides that they add to their Beauty, and are a Ligature to strengthen their Work, do also by their Projection hinder the getting into the Town from scaling Ladders. Some are for leaving Precipices of deep Holes here and there along the Side of the Wall, and especially near the Towers, fortified with wooden Bridges which may be presently raised or let down, as Occasion requires.

The Ancients used on each Side of their Gates to erect two Towers, larger than the rest, and strongly fortified on all Sides, to secure and protect the Entrance into the Town. There ought to be no Rooms with vaulted Roofs in the Towers, but only wooden Floors, that upon any Emergency may easily be removed or burnt; and those Floors should not be fastened with Nails, that if the Enemy gets the better, they may be taken away without Difficulty. All that is necessary is to have a Covering to shelter the Centinels from the Storms and Injuries of the Weather. The Battlements over the Gate should have Holes through the Bottom of them, through which, Stones and Firebrands may be thrown down upon the Enemy's Heads, or even Water, if they have set Fire to the Gate; which for its Security against such a Misfortune, they tell us ought to be covered over with Leather and Plates of Iron. But of this, enough.

C h a p. V.

Of the Proportion, Fashion and Construction of great Ways, and private Ones.

IN making our Gates we should observe, that they ought to be just as many in Number as the Highways, or Streets; for some we shall call High Streets, and others, private ones. Not that I intend to trouble my self about the Distinction of the Lawyers, who say that the Road for Beasts, and the Way for Men, ought to be called by different Names: But by the Name of Way, I shall understand them all. The Highways are properly those by which we go into the Provinces, with our Armies and all their Baggage; for which Reason the Highways ought to be much broader than others, and I find the Ancients seldom used to make them less than eight Cubits in any Part. By a Law in the twelve Tables it was ordained, that the Ways which ran strait should be twelve Foot broad, and those which were crooked or winding, not less than sixteen. The private Ways are those which leaving the publick ones, lead us to some Town or Castle, or else into some other Highway, as Lanes in Cities, and cross Roads in the Country. There are another Kind of publick Ways, which may not improperly be called High Streets, as are such which are designed for some certain Purpose, especially any publick one; as for Instance, those which lead to some Temple, or to the Course for Races, or to a Place of Justice. The Ways are not to be made in the same Manner in the Country, that they are in the City. In the Country they ought to be spacious and open, so as a Man may see all about him; free and clear from all Manner of Impediments, either of Water or Ruins; without lurking Places or Retreats of any Sort for Rogues to hide themselves in, nor too many cross Roads to favour their Villanies: Lastly, they ought to be as strait, and as short as possible: I do not reckon the shortest Way to be always

always that which is the ftraiteft, but that which is the fafeft: I would rather chufe to have it fomewhat the longer, than to have it inconvenient. Some think the Country of *Piperno* the moft fecure of any, becaufe it is cut through with deep Roads almoft like Pits, doubtful at the Entrance, uncertain in their Paffage, and unfafe upon Account of the Ground which lies above them, from whence any Enemy may be prodigioufly infefted.

The Men of beft Experience think that Way the moft fecure, which is carried over the Backs of fmall Hills, made level. Next to this are fuch as are made through the Fields upon a high raifed Bank, according to the Manner of the Ancients, who indeed upon that Account gave them the Name of *Aggeres*, or *Highways*. And it is certain fuch raifed Caufeys have a vaft many Conveniences: It relieves the Traveller from the Fatigue and Vexation of his Journey, to enjoy a fine Profpect from the Heighth of the Caufey all the Way as he travels; befides that, it is a great Convenience to be able to perceive an Enemy at a good Diftance, and to have fuch an Advantage as either to be able to repel them with a fmall Force, or to retire without Lofs, if you find they are the ftronger. There is a great Convenience, not at all foreign to our Purpofe, which I have obferved in the Road that goes to the Port of *Oftia*. As there is a vaft Concourfe of People, and great Quantities of Merchandize brought thither from *Ægypt*, *Africa*, *Lybia*, *Spain*, *Germany*, and the Iflands, the Road is made double, and in the Middle of it is a Row of Stones, ftanding up a Foot high like Terms to direct the Paffengers to go on one Side, and return on the other, fo to avoid the Inconvenience of meeting one another.

To conclude, fuch fhould be the Ways out of the City; fhort, ftrait, and fecure. When they come to the Town, if the City is noble and powerful, the Streets fhould be ftrait and broad, which carries an Air of Greatnefs and Majefty; but if it is only a fmall Town or a Fortification, it will be better, and as fafe, not for the Streets to run ftrait to the Gates; but to have them wind about fometimes to the Right, fometimes to the Left, near the Wall, and efpecially under the Towers upon the Wall; and within the Heart of the Town, it will be handfomer not to have them ftrait, but winding about feveral Ways, backwards

and forwards, like the Courfe of a River. For thus, befides that by appearing fo much the longer, they will add to the Idea of the Greatnefs of the Town, they will likewife conduce very much to Beauty and Convenience, and be a greater Security againft all Accidents and Emergencies. Moreover, this winding of the Streets will make the Paffenger at every Step difcover a new Structure, and the Front and Door of every Houfe will directly face the Middle of the Street; and whereas in larger Towns even too much Breadth is unhandfome and unhealthy, in a fmall one it will be both healthy and pleafant, to have fuch an open View from every Houfe by Means of the Turn of the Street.

Cornelius Tacitus writes, that *Nero* having widened the Streets of *Rome*, thereby made the City hotter, and therefore lefs healthy; but in other Places, where the Streets are narrow, the Air is crude and raw, and there is a continual Shade even in Summer. But further; in our winding Streets there will be no Houfe but what, in fome Part of the Day, will enjoy fome Sun; nor will they ever be without gentle Breezes, which whatever Corner they come from, will never want a free and clear Paffage; and yet they will not be molefted by ftormy Blafts, becaufe fuch will be broken by the turning of the Streets. Add to all thefe Advantages, that if the Enemy gets into the Town, he will be in Danger on every Side, in Front, in Flank, and in Rear, from Affaults from the Houfes. So much for the publick Streets. The private ones fhould be like the publick; unlefs there be this Difference, that they be built exactly in ftrait Lines, which will anfwer better to the Corners of the Building, and the Divifions and Parts of the Houfes. The Ancients in all Towns were for having fome intricate Ways and turn-again Streets, without any Paffage through them, that if an Enemy comes into them, he may be at a Lofs, and be in Confufion and Sufpence; or if he pufhes on daringly, may be eafily deftroyed. It is alfo proper to have fmaller fhort Streets, running crofs from one great Street to another; not to be as a direct publick Way, but only as a Paffage to fome Houfe that fronts it; which will both give Light to the Houfes, and make it more difficult for an Enemy to overrun all Parts of the Town.

Q. Curtius writes that *Babylon* was divided into a great Number of feparate Quarters, and that

that the Buildings there did not joyn one to ano her. *Plato*, on the contrary, is fo far from approving of thofe Separations, that he would have the Houfes all clofe contiguous, and that the joyning together of their Walls fhould make a Wall to the City.

CHAP. VI.

Of Bridges both of Wood and Stone, their proper Situation, their Peers, Arches, Angles, Feet, Key-ftones, Cramps, Pavements, and Slopes.

THE Bridge, no doubt, is a main Part of the Street ; nor is every Part of the City proper for a Bridge ; for befides that it is inconvenient to place it in a remote Corner of the Town, where it can be of Ufe but to few, and that it ought to be in the very Heart of the City, to lie at hand for every body ; it ought certainly to be contrived in a Place where it may eafily be erected, and without too great an Expence, and where it is likely to be the moft durable. We fhould therefore chufe a Ford where the Water is not too deep ; where the Shore is not too fteep ; which is not uncertain and moveable, but conftant and lafting. We fhould avoid all Whirl-pools, Eddies, Gulphs, and the like Inconveniences common in bad Rivers. We fhould alfo moft carefully avoid all Elbows, where the Water takes a Turn ; for very many Reafons ; the Banks in fuch Places being very liable to be broken, as we fee by Experience, and becaufe Pieces of Timber, Trunks of Trees, and the like, brought down from the Country by Storms and Floods, cannot fwim down fuch Elbows in a ftrait Line, but turn aflant, meet and hinder one another, and lodging againft the Piles grow into a great Heap, which ftops up the Arches, and with the additional Weight of the Water at length quite breaks them down.

Of Bridges, fome are of Stone, others of Wood. We fhall fpeak firft of thofe which are of Wood, as the moft eafy of Execution ; next we fhall treat of thofe which are built of Stone. Both ought to be as ftrong as poffible ; that therefore which is built of Wood, muft be fortified with a good Quantity of the ftrongeft Timbers. We cannot give a better Example of this Sort of Bridges than that built by *Julius Cæfar*, which he gives us a Defcription of himfelf, as follows : He faftened together two Timbers, leaving a Diftance between them of two Foot ; their Length was proportioned to the Depth of the River, and they were a Foot and an half thick, and cut fharp at the Ends. Thefe he let down into the River with Cranes, and drove them well in with a Sort of Rammers, not perpendicularly down like Piles, but flanting upwards, and giving Way according to the Current of the River. Then, oppofite to thefe, he drove in two others, faftened together in the fame Manner, with a Diftance between them at Bottom of forty Foot, flanting contrary to the Force and Current of the Stream. When thefe were thus fixed, he laid acrofs from one to the other, Beams of the Thicknefs of two Foot, which was the Diftance left between the Timbers drove down ; and faftened thefe Beams at the End, each with two Braces, which being bound round and faftened of oppofite Sides, the Strength of the whole Work was fo great and of fuch a Nature, that the greater the Force of Water was which bore againft it, the clofer and firmer the Beams united. Over thefe other Beams were laid acrofs and faftened to them, and a Floor, as we may call it, made over them with Poles and Hurdles. At the fame Time, in the lower Part of the River, below the Bridge, other Timbers, or floping Piles, were driven down, which being faftened to the reft of the Structure, fhould be a Kind of Buttrefs to refift the Force of the Stream ; and other Piles were alfo driven in at a fmall Diftance above the Bridge, and ftanding fomewhat above the Water, that if the Enemy fhould fend Trunks of Trees, or Veffels, down the Stream, in order to break the Bridge, thofe Piles might receive and intercept their Violence, and prevent their doing any Prejudice to the Work. All this we learn from *Cæfar*. Nor is it foreign to our Purpofe to take Notice of what is practiced at *Verona*, where they pave their wooden Bridges with Bars of Iron, efpecially where the Wheels of Carts and Waggons are to pafs. It remains now that we

treat

treat of the Stone-Bridge, the Parts whereof are these: The Banks of the Shore, the Piers, the Arches, and the Pavement. Between the Banks of the Shore and the Piers, is this Difference, that the Banks ought to be by much the strongest, inasmuch as they are not only to support the Weight of the Arches like the Piers, but are also to bear the Foot of the Bridge, and to bear against the Weight of the Arches, to keep them from opening in any Part. We ought therefore to be very careful in the Choice of our Shore, and to find out, if possible, a Rock of solid Stone, since nothing can be too strong that we are to intrust with the Feet of the Bridge; and as to the Piers, they must be more or less numerous in Proportion to the Breadth of the River. An odd Number of Arches is both most pleasant to the Sight, and conduces also to Strength; for the farther the Current of the River lies from the Shore, the freer it is from Impediment, and the freer it is the swifter and easier it flows away; for this therefore we ought to leave a Passage perfectly free and open, that it may not shake and prejudice the Piers by struggling with the Resistance which it meets with from them. The Piers ought to be placed in those Parts of the River, where the Water flows the most slowly, and (to use such an Expression) the most lazily: And those Parts you may easily find out by means of the Tides: Otherwise you may discover them in the following Manner: Imitate those who threw Nuts into a River, whereby the Inhabitants of a Town besieged, gathering them up, were preserved from starving; strew the whole Breadth of the River, about fifteen hundred Paces above the Place which you intend for your Bridge, and especially when the River is fullest, with some such light Stuff that will easily float: And in those Places where the Things you have thrown in Clusters thickest together, you may be sure the Current is strongest. In the Situation of your Piers therefore avoid those Places, and chuse those others to which the Things you throw in come the slowest and thinnest.

KING *Mina*, when he intended to build the Bridge of *Memphis*, turned the *Nile* out of its Channel, and carried it another Way among some Hills, and when he had finished his Building brought it back again into its old Bed. *Nicore* Queen of the *Assyrians*, having prepared all the Materials for building a Bridge, dug a great Lake, and into that turned the River; and as the Channel grew dry as the Lake filled, she took that Time to build her

Piers. These mighty Things were done by those great Princes: As for us, we are to proceed in the following Manner: Make the Foundations of your Piers in Autumn, when the Water is lowest, having first raised an Inclosure to keep off the Water, which you may do in this Manner: Drive in a double Row of Stakes, very close and thick set, with their Heads above the Top of the Water, like a Trench; then put Hurdles within this double Row of Stakes, close to that Side of the Row which is next the intended Pier, and fill up the Hollow between the two Rows with Rushes and Mud, ramming them together so hard that no Water can possibly get through. Then whatever you find within this Inclosure, Water, Mud, Sand, and whatever else is a Hindrance to you, throw out. For the rest of your Work, you must observe the Rules we have laid down in the preceding Book. Dig till you come to a solid Foundation, or rather make one of Piles burnt at the End, and driven in as close together as ever they can stick. And here I have observed that the best Architects used to make a continued Foundation of the whole Length of the Bridge, and not only under each Pier; and this they did, not by shutting out the whole River at once by one single Inclosure, but by first making one Part, then another, and so joyning the whole together by degrees; for it would be impossible to withstand and repulse the whole Force of the Water at once; we must therefore, while we are at work with one Part, leave another Part open, for a Passage for the Stream.

You may leave these Passages either in the Channel itself, or if you think it more convenient, you may frame wooden Dams, or hanging Channels, by which the superfluous Water may run off. But if you find the Expence of a continued Foundation for the whole Bridge too great, you may only make a separate Foundation for every particular Pier, in the Form of a Ship with one Angle in the Stern, and another in the Head, lying directly even with the Current of the Water, that the Force of the Water may be broken by the Angle. We are to remember that the Water is much more dangerous to the Stern, than to the Head of the Piers, which appears from this, that at the Stern the Water is in a more violent Motion than at the Head, and forms Eddies, which turn up the Ground at the Bottom; while the Head stands firm and safe, being guarded and defended by the Banks of Sand thrown up before it by the Channel. Now

X

this

this being so, this Part ought of the whole Structure to be best fortified against the Violence of the Waters; and nothing will conduce more to this, than to make the Pile-work deep and broad every Way, and especially at the Stern, that if any Accidents should carry away any of the Piles, there may be enow left to sustain the Weight of the Pier. It will be also extremely proper to begin your Foundation at the upper Part of the Channel, and to make it with an easy Descent, that the Water which runs over it may not fall upon it violently as into a Precipice, but glide over gently, with an easy Slope; because the Water that rushes down precipitately, routs up the Bottom, and so being made still rougher carries away every Thing that it can loosen, and is every Moment undermining the Work.

Build the Piers of the biggest and longest Stones, and of such as in their Nature are best adapted for supporting of Frosts, and as do not decay in Water, nor are easily softened by any Accident, and will not crack and split under a great Weight; and build them exactly according to the Square, Level and Plumb-line, omitting no Sort of Ligature Length-ways, and placing the Stones Breadth-ways in alternate Order, so as to be a Binding one to another; absolutely rejecting any Stuffing with small Pieces of Stone. You must also fasten your Work with a good Number of Brass Cramps and Pins, so well fitted in, that the Joynts of the Structure may not separate, but be kept tight and firm. Raise both the Fronts of the Building angular, both Head and Stern, and let the Top of the Pier be sure to be higher than the fullest Tide; and let the Thickness of the Pier be one fourth of the Heighth of the Bridge. There have been some that have not terminated the Head and Stern of their Piers with an Angle, but with an half Circle; induced thereto, I suppose, by the Beautifulness of that Figure. But though I have said elsewhere, that the Circle has the same Strength as an Angle, yet here I approve better of an Angle, provided it be not so sharp as to be broken and defaced by every little Accident: Nor am I altogether displeased with those which end in a Curve, provided it be very much lengthened out, and not left so obtuse as to resist the Force and Weight of the Water. The Angle of the Pier is of a good Sharpness, if it is three Quarters of a Right Angle, or if you like it better, you may make it two thirds. And thus much may suffice as to the Piers. If

the Nature of your Situation is such, that the Sides or Banks of the Shore are not as you could wish; make them good in the some Manner as you build your Piers, and indeed make other Piers upon the Shore, and turn some Arches even upon the dry Ground; to the Intent, that if in Process of Time, by the continual washing of the Water, and the Force of the Tides, any Part of the Bank should be carried away, your Passage may still be preserved safe, by the Production of the Bridge into the Land. The Arches ought upon all Accounts, and particularly because of the continual violent shaking and Concussion of Carts and other Carriages, to be extreamly stout and strong. Besides, as sometimes you may be obliged to draw immense Weights over them, such as a Colossus, an Obelisk or the like; you should provide against the Inconvenience which happened to *Scaurus*, who when he was removing that great Boundary Stone, alarmed all the publick Officers, upon Account of the Mischief that might ensue. For these Reasons, a Bridge both in its Design, and in its whole Execution, should be well fitted to bear the continual and violent Jars which it is to receive from Carriages. That Bridges ought to be built of very large and stout Stones, is very manifest by the Example of an Anvil, which, if is large and heavy, stands the Blows of the Hammer unmoved; but if it is light, rebounds and trembles at every Stroke. We have already said, that all vaulted Work consists of Arches and Stuffing, and that the strongest of all Arches is the Semi-circle. But if by the Disposition of the Piers, the Semi-circle should rise so high as to be inconvenient, we may make use of the Scheme Arch, only taking Care to make the last Piers on the Shore the stronger and thicker. But whatever Sort of Arch you vault your Bridge with, it must be built of the hardest and largest Stones, such as you use in your Piers; and there should not be a single Stone in the Arch but what is in Thickness at least one tenth Part of the Chord of that Arch; nor should the Chord itself be longer than six Times the Thickness of the Pier, nor shorter than four Times. The Stones also should be strongly fastened together with Pins and Cramps of Brass. And the last Wedge, which is called the Key-stone, should be cut according to the Lines of the other Wedges, but left a small Matter bigger at the Top, so that it may not be got into its Place without some Strokes of a light Beetle; which will
drive

drive the lower Wedges clofer together, and fo keep them tight to their Duty. The filling up, or ftuffing between the Arches fhould be wrought with the ftrongeft Stone, and with the clofeft Joynts that can poffibly be made, But if you have not a fufficient Plenty of ftrong Stone to make your Stuffing of it, you may in Cafe of Neceffity make ufe of a weaker Sort; ftill provided that the whole Turn of the Arch, and the Courfe of Work behind both the Sides of it, be built entirely of ftrong Stone.

THE next Work it to pave the Bridge; and here we fhould obferve, that we ought to make the Ground upon a Bridge as firm and folid as the moft durable Roads; we fhould raife it with Gravel or coarfe Sand, to the Heighth of a Cubit, and then pave it with Stone, filling up the Joints either with River or Sea-fand. Bnt the Subftrature or Layer under the Pavement of a Bridge ought firft to be levelled and raifed quite to the Top of the Arches; with regular Mafonry, and then the Pavement itfelf fhould be cemented with Mortar. In all other Refpects we fhould obferve the fame Rules in paving a Bridge, as in paving a Road. The Sides fhould be made firm with the ftrongeft Work, and the reft paved with Stones, neither fo fmall as to be eafily raifed and thrown out upon the leaft Strain; nor fo large, that the Beafts of Burden fhould flide upon them as upon Ice, and fall before they meet with any Catch for their Foot. And certainly we muft own it to be of very great Importance what Kind of Stone we ufe in our Pavements, if we confider how much they muft be worn by the continual grinding of the Wheels, and the Hoofs of all Manner of Cattle, when we fee that even fuch fmall Animals as Ants, with conftant paffing up and down, will wear Traces even in Flints.

I HAVE obferved that the Ancients in many Places, and particularly in the Way to *Tivoli*, paved the Middle of the Road with Flints, and only covered the Sides with fmall Gravel. This they did, that the Wheels might make the lefs Impreffion, and that the Horfes Hoofs might not want fufficient Hold. In other Places, and efpecially over Bridges, there was a raifed Way on each Side, with Stone Steps, for Foot Paffengers; and the Middle of the Way was left for Beafts and Carriages. Laftly, the Ancients, for this Sort of Work greatly commend Flints, and efpecially thofe which are fulleft of Holes; not becaufe fuch are the ftrongeft, but becaufe they are the leaft flippery. But we may make ufe of any Sort of Stone, according to what we have in greateft Plenty, provided we only ufe the ftrongeft we can get, and with thofe pave at leaft that Part of the Way which is moft beaten by Cattle; and the Part moft beaten by them is always moft level, becaufe they always avoid all floping Ground as much as they can. Let the Middle and higheft Part of the Way be laid with Flints, or whatever other Stone you ufe, of the Thicknefs of a Foot and an half, and the Breadth of at leaft a Foot, with the upper Face even, and fo clofe compacted together that there are no Crevices left in order to throw off the Rain. There are three different Slopes for all Streets; either towards the Middle, which is proper for a broad Street; or to the Sides, which is leaft Hindrance to a narrow one; or elfe Lengthways. But in this we are to govern ourfelves according to the Conveniences and Advantages of our Drains and Currents, whether into the Sea, Lake or River. A very good Rife for a Slope is half an Inch in every three Foot. I have obferved that the Rife with which the Ancients ufed to build their Bridges, was one Foot in every thirty; and in fome Parts, as particularly at the Summit of the Bridge, four Inches in every Cubit or Foot and an half; but this was only for fo little a Way, that a Beaft heavy loaden could get over it at one Strain.

CHAP. VII.

Of Drains or Sewers, their different Sorts and Ufes; and of Rivers and Canals for Ships.

DRAINS or Sewers are look'd upon as a Part of the Street, inafmuch as they are to be made under the Street, thro' the Middle of it; and are of great Service, as well in the paving and levelling, as in cleaning the Streets; for which Reafon they are by no means to be neglected here. And indeed, may we not very properly fay that a Drain is a

Bridge,

Bridge, or rather a very long Arch; so that in the Construction of it we ought to observe all the same Rules that we have just now been laying down concerning Bridges. The Ancients had so high a Notion of the Serviceableness of Drains and Sewers, that they bestowed no greater Care and Expence upon any Structure whatsoever, than they did upon them; and among all the wonderful Buildings in the City of *Rome,* the Drains are accounted the noblest. I shall not spend Time to shew how many Conveniences arise from good Drains; how clean they keep the City, and how neat all Buildings both publick and private, or how much they conduce to the Clearness and Healthiness of the Air.

The City of *Smyrna,* where *Trebonius* was besieged and relieved by *Dolabella,* is said to have been extremely beautiful, both for the Straitness of the Streets, and its many noble Structures; but not having Drains to receive and carry away its own Filth, it offended the Inhabitants abominable with ill Smells. *Siena,* a City in *Tuscany,* not having Drains wants a very great Help to Cleanliness; by which Means the Town not only stinks every Night and Morning, when People throw their Nastiness out of the Windows, but even in the Day Time it is seen lying about the Streets. Drains are of two Sorts; one carries away the Filth into some River, Lake or Sea; the other is a deep Hole dug in the Ground, where the Nastiness lies till it is consumed in the Bowels of the Earth. That which carries it away, ought to have a smooth sloping Pavement, strong compacted, that the Ordure may run off freely, and that the Structure itself may not be rotted by the Moisture lying continually soaking upon it. It should also lie so high above the River, that no Floods or Tides may fill it with Mud and choak it up. A Drain that is to lie open and uncover'd to the Air, need have no other Pavement but the Ground itself; for the Poets call the Earth *Cerberus,* and the Philosophers, the *Woolf of the Gods,* because it devours and consumes every Thing. So that whatever Filth and Nastiness is brought into it, the Earth rots and destroys it, and prevents its emitting ill Steams. Sinks for the Reception of Urine, should be as far from the House as possible; because the Heat of the Sun makes it rot and smell intolerably. Moreover, I cannot help thinking that Rivers and Canals, especially such as are for the Passage of Ships, ought to be included under the Denomination of Roads; since many are of Opinion, that Ships are nothing but a Sort of Carriages, and the Sea itself no more than a huge Road. But there is no Necessity to say any thing more of these in this Place. And if it happens that the Conveniences we have here treated of, are not found sufficient, our Business is to study how to mend the Faults, and make whatever other Additions are needful: The Method of doing which, we shall speak of in due Time. 88

CHAP. VIII.

Of the proper Structure for a Haven, and of making convenient Squares in the City.

NOW if there is any other Part of the City that falls in properly with the Subject of this Book, it is certainly the Haven, which may be defined a Goal or proper Place from whence you may begin a Voyage, or where having performed it you may put an End to the Fatigue of it, and take Repose. Others perhaps would say that a Haven is a Stable for Ships; but let it be what you will, either a Goal, a Stable, or a Receptacle, it is certain that if the Business of a Haven is to give a Reception to Ships out of the Violence of Storms, it ought to be made in such a Manner as to be a sufficient Shelter for that Purpose: Let its Sides be strong and high, and let there be Room enough for large Vessels heavy laden to come in and lie quiet in it. Which Conveniences, if they are offered to you by the natural Situation of the Place, you have nothing more to wish for; unless, as at *Athens* where *Thucidides* says there were three Havens made by Nature, it should happen that you are doubtful among such a Number, which to chuse. But it is evident from what we have already said in the first Book, that there are some Places where all the Winds cannot be, and others where some actually are continually troublesome and dangerous. Let us therefore make

make Choice of that Haven into whose Mouth none blow but the moſt gentle and temperate Winds, and where you may enter or go out, with the moſt eaſy Breezes, without being forced to wait too long for them.

THEY ſay, that of all Winds the North is the gentleſt; and that when the Sea is diſturbed by this Wind, as ſoon as ever the Wind ceaſes, it is calm again : But if a Southwind raiſes a Storm, the Sea continues turbulent a long while. But as Places are various, our Buſineſs is to chuſe ſuch a one as is beſt provided with all Conveniencies for Shipping : we muſt be ſure to have ſuch a Depth, in the Mouth, Boſcm and Sides of the Haven, as will nor refuſe Ships of Burthen, though ever ſo deep laden; the Bottom too ought to be clear, and not full of any Sort of Weeds : Though, ſometimes, thick entangled Weeds are of a good deal of Uſe in faſtening the Anchor. Yet I ſhould rather chuſe an Haven that does not produce any thing which can contaminate the Purity of the Air, or prejudice the Ships, as Ruſhes and Weeds which grow in the Water really do ; for they engender a great many Kinds of Worms which get into the Timbers of the Veſſel, and the rotting of the Weeds raiſes unwholeſome Vapours. There is another Thing which makes an Haven noiſome and unhealthy, and that is a Mixture of freſh Water; eſpecially Rainwater that runs down from Hills : Though I would be ſure to have Streams and Springs in the Neighbourhood, from whence, freſh Water that will keep may be brought for the Uſe of the Veſſels. A Port alſo ought to have a clear, ſtrait and ſafe Paſſage outwards, with a Bottom not often ſhifting, free from all Impediments, and ſecure from the Ambuſhes of Enemies and Pirates. Moreover, I would have it covered with ſome high ſteep Hill, that may be ſeen a great Way off, and ſerve as a Landmark for the Sailors to ſteer their Courſe by. Within the Port we ſhould make a Key and a Bridge for the more eaſy unlading of the Shipping. Theſe Works the Ancients raiſed in different Ways, which it is not yet our Time to ſpeak of; and we ſhall come to it

more properly when we ſpeak of the Method of improving a Haven and running up a Pier. Beſides all this, a good Haven ſhould have Places to walk in, and a Portico and Temple, for the Reception of Perſons that are juſt landed ; nor ſhould it want Pillars, Bars and Rings to faſten Ships to ; and there ſhould alſo be a good Number of Warehouſes or Vaults for the laying up of Goods. We ſhould alſo at the Mouth erect high and ſtrong Towers, from the Lanterns of which we may ſpy what Sails approach, and by Fires give Directions to the Mariners, and which by their Fortifications may defend the Veſſels of our Friends, and lay Chains acroſs the Port to keep out an Enemy. And from the Port ſtrait thro' the Heart of the City ought to run a large Street, in which ſeveral other Quarters of the Town ſhould center, that the Inhabitants may preſently run thither from all Parts to repulſe any Inſult from an Enemy. Within the Boſom of the Haven likewiſe, ſhould be ſeveral ſmaller Docks, where battered Veſſels may refit. But there is one Thing which we ought not to omit, ſince it relates entirely to the Haven ; which is, that there have been, and now are, many famous Cities, whoſe greateſt Security has lain in the unſafe and uncertain Entrance of their Harbours, and from the Variety of its Channels made almoſt hourly for the continual Alteration of the Bottom. Thus much we thought proper to ſay of publick Works in the univerſal Acceptation ; and I cannot tell whether there is any Occaſion to add what ſome inſiſt upon, that there ought to be ſeveral Squares laid out in different Parts of the City, ſome for the expoſing of Merchandizes to ſale in Time of Peace ; others for the Exerciſes proper for Youth ; and others for laying up Stores in Time of War, of Timber, Forage, and the like Proviſions neceſſary for the ſuſtaining of a Siege. As for Temples, Chapels, Halls for the Adminiſtration of Juſtice, and Places for Shows, they are Buildings that, tho' for publick Uſe, are yet the Property of only a few Perſons ; which are the Prieſts and Magiſtrates ; and therefore we ſhall treat of them in their proper Places.

The End of Book IV.

THE
ARCHITECTURE
OF
Leone Batista Alberti.

BOOK V. CHAP. I.

Of Buildings for particular Persons. Of the Castles or Habitations of a King or a Tyrant; their different Properties and Parts.

E shewed in the last Book, that Buildings ought to be variously accommodated, both in City and Country, according to the Necessities of the Citizens and Inhabitants; and that some belong'd to the Citizens in common, others to those of greater Quality, and others to the meaner Sort; and finish'd our Account of those of the first Kind. The Design of this fifth Book is to consider of the supplying the Necessaries and Conveniencies for particular Persons. And in this copious and difficult Subject we shall make it our Study, to the utmost of our Ability and Industry, to omit nothing really material or instructive, and not to say any thing more for the Embellishment of our Discourse than for the necessary Explanation of our Subject. Let us begin therefore with the noblest. The noblest are certainly those who are entrusted with the supreme Authority and Moderation in publick Affairs. This is sometimes a single Person, and sometimes Many. If it is a single Person, that Person ought certainly to be him that has the greatest Merit. We shall therefore first consider what is necessary to be done for one that has the sole Power in himself. But we must previously enquire into one very material Difference; what Kind of a Governour this is;

whether one that with Justice and Integrity rules over willing Subjects; one not guided so much by his own Interest, as the Good and Welfare of his People: or such a one as would have Things so contrived with Relation to his Subjects, that he may be able to continue his Dominion over them, let them be ever so uneasy under it. For the Generality of particular Buildings, and the City itself ought to be laid out differently for a Tyrant, from what they are for those who enjoy and protect a Government as if it were a Magistracy voluntarily put into their Hands. A good King takes Care to have his City strongly fortified in those Parts, which are most liable to be assaulted by a foreign Enemy: a Tyrant, having no less Danger to fear from his Subjects than from Strangers, must fortify his City no less against his own People, than against Foreigners: and his Fortifications must be so contrived, that upon Occasion he may employ the Assistance of Strangers against his own People, and of one Part of his People against the other. In the preceding Book, we shewed how a City ought to be fortified against foreign Enemies: Let us here consider how it is to be provided against the Inhabitants themselves.

Euripides thinks the Multitude is naturally a very powerful Enemy, and that if they added
Cunning

Cunning and Fraud to their Strength, they would be irrefiftible. The politick Kings of *Cairo* in *Ægypt*, a City fo populous that they thought it was extremely healthy and flourifh-ing, when no more than a thoufand People died in a Day, divided it by fo many Cuts and Chan-nels, that it feemed not to be one fingle City, but a great Number of fmall Towns lying toge-ther. This I fuppofe they did, not fo much that the Conveniencies of the River might be equally diftributed, as to fecure themfelves againft the popular Commotions of a great Multitude, and that if any fuch fhould happen, they might the more eafily fupprefs them : juft as if a Man out of one huge Coloffus, fhould make two or more Statues, that he might be better able to manage or remove them. The *Romans* never ufed to fend a Senator into *Ægypt*, with Proconfular Authority, to govern the whole Province ; but only fome Knights, with Com-miffion to govern feparate Parts of it And this they did, as we are informed by *Arrian*, to Intent that a Province fo inclined to Tumults and Innovations, might not be under the Care of a fingle Perfon : and they obferved that no City was more exempt from Difcord, than thofe which were divided by Nature, either by a Ri-ver flowing thro' the Middle of it, or by a Num-ber of little feparate Hills ; or by being built one Part upon a Hill, and the other upon a Plain, with a Wall between them. And this Wall or Divifion, I think, ought not to be drawn like a Diameter clear thro' the Area, but ought rather to be made to enclofe one Circle within another : for the richer Sort, defiring a more open Space and more Room, will eafily confent to be fhut out of the inner Circle, and will be very willing to leave the Middle of the Town, to Cooks, Victuallers and other fuch Trades ; and all the fcoundrel Rabble belonging to *Te-rence*'s Parafite, Cooks, Bakers, Butchers and the like, will be lefs dangerous there than if they were not to live feparate from the nobler Citizens. Nor is it foreign to our Purpofe what we read in *Feftus*, that *Servius Tullius* commanded the *Patricians* to dwell in a cer-tain Part of the Town, where if they offered at any Difturbance, he was immediately ready to quell them from a fuperior Situation. This Wall within the City ought to run thro' every Diftrict of the Town ; and it fhould be built fo ftrong and thick in all Refpects, and be raifed fo high (as indeed fo ought all the other City

Walls) that it may overlook all the private Houfes. It fhould alfo be fortified with Bat-tlements and Towers ; and a good Ditch on both Sides would not be amifs ; that your Men may the more eafily defend it on any Side. The Towers upon this Wall ought not to be open on the Infide, but walled up quite round ; and they fhould be fo feated as not only to re-pulfe the Affaults of a foreign Enemy, but of Domeftick one too upon Occafion ; and particu-larly they ought to command the great Streets, and the Tops of all high Temples. I would have no Paffage into thefe Towers but from off the Wall itfelf ; nor any Way up to the Wall but what is entirely in the Power of the Prince. There fhould be no Arches nor Tow-ers in the Streets that lead from the Fortrefs into the City ; nor Leads or Terraffes from whence the Soldiers may be molefted with Stones or Darts as they pafs to their Duty. In a Word, the whole fhould be fo contrived that every Place, which any Way commands the Town, fhould be in the Hands of the Prince ; and that it fhould not be in the Power of any Perfon whatfoever, to prevent his Men from over-running the whole City as he pleafes. And herein the City of a Tyrant differs from that of a King ; and perhaps they differ too in this, that a Town in a Plain is moft conveni-ent for a free People ; but one upon a Hill the fafeft for a Tyrant. The other Edifices for the Habitation both for King and Tyrant, are not only the fame in moft refpects, but alfo differ very little from the Houfes of private Perfons : And in fome Particulars they differ both from one another, and from thefe latter too. We fhall fpeak firft of thofe Things wherein they agree ; and of their Peculiarities afterwards. This Sort of Buildings is faid to have been invented only for Neceffity : Yet there are fome Parts of them which ferve be-fides to Conveniency, that by Ufe and Habit feem to be grown as neceffary as any : Such as Porticoes, Places for taking the Air in, and the like : Which, though Method may feem to re-quire it, I fhall not diftinguifh fo nicely, as to divide what is convenient from what is necef-fary : But fhall only fay, that as in the City it-felf, fo in thefe Particular Structures, fome Parts belong to the whole Houfhold, fome to the Ufes of a few, and others to that of a fingle Perfon.

CHAP.

CHAP. II.

Of the Portico, Vestibule, Court-yard, Hall, Stairs, Lobbies, Apertures, Back-doors, concealed Passages and private Apartments; and wherein the Houses of Princes differ from those of private Men; as also of the separate and common Apartments for the Prince and his Spouse.

I Do not think the Portico and Vestibule were made only for the Conveniency of Servants, as *Diodorus* says; but rather for the common Use of the Citizens: But Places for walking in within the House, the inner Court-yard, the Hall (which I believe took its Name from Dancing, because Nuptials and Feasts are celebrated in it) do not belong at all to the Publick, but entirely to the Inhabitants. Parlours for eating in are of two Sorts, some for the Master, and others for the Servants: Bed-chambers are for the Matrons, Virgins, Guests, and are to be separate for each. Of the universal Division of these, we have already treated in our first Book of Designs, as far as was necessary under a general Title: We shall now proceed to shew the Number of all these, their Proportions, and proper Situations for the greatest Convenience of the Inhabitants. The Portico and Vestibule are adorned by the Nobleness of Entrance; the Entrance is adorned by the View which it has before it, and by the Magnificence of its Workmanship. Then the inner Rooms for eating, laying up all Manner of Necessaries, and the like, ought to be so contrived and situated, that the Things preserved in them may be well kept, that there be no want of Sun or Air, and that they have all Manner of proper Conveniencies, and be kept distinct, so that too great Familarity may not lessen the Dignity, Conveniency or Pleasure of Guests, nor encourage the Impertinence of Persons that pay their Attendance to you. And indeed Vestibules, Halls, and the like Places of publick Reception in Houses, ought to be like Squares and other open Places in Cities; not in a remote private Corner, but in the Center and the most publick Place, where all the other Members may readily meet: For here all Lobbies and Stair-cases are to terminate; here you meet and receive your Guests. Moreover, the House should not have above one Entrance, to the Intent that nobody may come in, nor any thing be carried out, without the Knowledge of the Porter. Take Care too,

that the Windows and Doors do not lie handy for Thieves, nor be so open to the Neighbours that they can interrupt, or see or hear what is said or done in the House. The *Ægyptians* built their private Houses without any Windows outwards. Some perhaps may be for having a Back-gate to which the Fruits of the Harvest may be brought home, either in Carts or on Horses, and not make a Nastiness before the principal Entrance; as also a smaller private Door, at which the Master of the House, without the Knowledge of any of his Family, may receive any private Messages or Advices, and go out himself, as his Occasions call him. I have nothing to say against these: And I am entirely for having concealed Passages and private and hidden Apartments, barely known to the Master himself; where, upon any Misfortune, he may hide his Plate and other Wealth, or by which, if need be, he may escape himself. In *David*'s Sepulchre there were several private Places made for concealing the King's Hereditary Treasures; and they were contrived so cunningly, that it was hardly possible to find them out. Out of one of these Places, *Josephus* informs us, that *Hircanus*, the High Priest, thirteen hundred Years afterwards. took three thousand Talents of Gold (which makes eighteen hundred thousand *Italian* Crowns) to free the City from *Antiochus*'s Siege: And out of another of them, *Herod*, a long Time after that, got a vast Quantity of Gold. In these Things therefore the Houses of Princes agree with those of private Persons. The chief Difference between private Houses and Palaces is, that there is a particular Air suitable to each: In the Latter the Rooms designed for the Reception of Company should be more numerous and spacious; those which are intended only for the Use of a Few, or only of one Person, should be rather neat than large: But here again a Palace should differ from the House of a private Person, and even these private Apartments should be made more spacious and large, because all Parts of a Prince's Palace are

generally

generally crowded. In private Houses, those Parts which are for the Reception of many, should not be made at all different from those of a Prince; and the Apartments should be kept distinct for the Wife, for the Husband, and for the Servants; and every thing is not to be contrived merely for Conveniency, but for Grandeur too, and so, that the Number of Servants may not breed any Confusion. All this indeed is very difficult, and hardly possible to be done under a single Roof: therefore every Member of the House must have its particular Area and Platform, and have a distinct Covering and Wall of its own: but then all the Members should be so joined together by the Roof and by Lobbies, that the Servants, when they are wanted about their Business, may not be called, as it were, out of another House, but be always ready at Hand. Children and Maids, among whom there is an eternal Chattering, should be entirely separated from the Master's Apartment, and so should the Dirtiness of the Servants. The Apartments where Princes are to eat should be in the no-blest Part of the Palace; it should stand high, and command a fine Prospect of Sea, Hills, and wide Views, which gives it an Air of Greatness. The House for his Spouse should be entirely separated from that of the Prince her Husband, except only in the last Apartment or Bed-chamber, which should be in common between both; but then a single Gate, under the Care of the same Porter, should serve both their Houses. The other Particulars wherein the Houses of Princes differ from those of private Persons, are such as are in a Manner peculiar to these latter; and therefore we shall speak of them in their Place. The Houses of Princes agree with one another in another Respect; which is, that besides those Conveniencies which they ought to have for their private Use, they should have an Entrance from the Master Way, and especially from the Sea or River; and instead of a Vestibule, they should have a large open Area, big enough to receive the Train of an Ambassador, or any other Great Man, whether they come in Coaches, in Barks, or on Horseback.

92

CHAP. III.

Of the Properties of the Portico, Lobby, Halls, both for Summer and Winter, Watch-Towers, and the Difference between the Castle for a Tyrant, and the Palace for a King.

I Would have the Portico be not only a convenient Covering for Men, but for Beasts also, to shelter them from Sun or Rain. Just before the Vestibule nothing can be nobler than a handsome Portico, where the Youth, waiting till their old Gentlemen return from transacting Business with the Prince, may employ themselves in all Manner of Exercise, Leaping, Tennis, Throwing of Stones, or Wrestling. Next within should be a handsome Lobby, or a large Hall; where the Clients waiting for their Patrons, may converse together; and where the Prince's Seat may be prepared for his giving his Decrees. Wherein this there must be another Hall, where the principal Men in the State may assemble themselves together in order to salute their Prince, and to give their Thoughts concerning whatsoever he questions them about: Perhaps it may not be amiss to have two of those, one for Summer and another for Winter; and in the Contrivance of them, particular Regard must be had to the great Age of the Fathers that are to meet in them, that there be no Inconveniencies in them which may any way endanger their Health, and that they may stay in them as long as their Business requires, with Safety and Pleasure. We are told by *Seneca*, that *Gracchus* first, and afterwards *Drusus*, contrived not to give Audience to every body in the same Place, but to make proper Distinctions among the Crowd, and to receive some in private, others in select Numbers, and the Rest in publick, to shew which had the first, and which only the second Share in their Friendship. If you are in the same high Rank of Fortune, and this Manner of Proceeding either becomes or pleases you, the best Way will be to have several Doors to receive your Friends at, by which you may dismiss those that have had Audience, and keep out such as you don't care to grant it to, without giving them too much Offence. At the Top of the House there should be a high Watch-Tower, from whence you may at any

Z

Time

Time fee any Commotion in the City. In thefe Particulars the Palace of a King and of a Tyrant agree; but then they differ in thefe other. The Palace of a King fhould ftand in the Heart of a City, it fhould be eafy of Accefs, beautifully adorned, and rather delicate and polite than proud or ftately: But a Tyrant fhould have rather a Caftle than a Palace, and it fhould ftand in a Manner out of the City and in it at the fame Time. It looks noble to have the Palace of a King be near adjoyning to the Theatre, the Temple, and fome Noblemens handfome Houfes: The Tyrant muft have his Caftle entirely feparated from all other Buildings. Both fhould be built in a handfome and noble Manner, but yet fo that the Palace may not be fo large and rambling as to be not eafily defended againft any Infult; nor the Caftle fo clofe and fo crampt up, as to look more like a Jail than the Refidence of a great Prince. We fhould not omit one Contrivance very convenient for a Tyrant, which is to have fome private Pipes concealed within the Body of the Wall, by which he may fecretly hear every Thing that is faid either by Strangers or Servants. But as a Royal Houfe is different from a Fortrefs in almoft all Refpects, and efpecially in the main Ones, the beft Way is to let the Palace join to the Fortrefs. The Ancients ufed to build their Fortrefs in the City, that to they or their King might have a Place to fly to in any Time of Adverfity, and where the Virtue of their Virgins and Matrons might be protected by the Holinefs of a Sanctuary: For

Feftus tells us, that the Ancients ufed to confecrate their Fortreffes to Religion, upon which Account they were called *Auguriales*, and that in them a certain Sacrifice ufed to be performed by Virgins, which was extremely fecret and entirely remote from the Knowledge of the Vulgar. Accordingly you feldom meet with an ancient Fortrefs without its Temple. But Tyrants afterwards ufurped the Fortrefs to themfelves, and overthrew the Piety and Religion of the Place, converting it to their cruel and wicked Purpofes, and fo made what was defigned as a Refuge to the Miferable, a Source of Miferies. But, to return. The Fortrefs belonging to the Temple of *Jupiter Hammon* was encompaffed with three Walls; the firft Fortification was for the Prince, the fecond for his Spoufe and her Children, and the laft was the Poft of the Soldiers. A Stucture very well contrived, only that it was much better adapted for Defence than Offence. I muft confefs that as I cannot fay much for the Valour of a Soldier that only knows how to repulfe an Enemy that affaults him, fo I cannot much commend a Fort that, befides being able to defend itfelf, is not alfo well difpofed for offending its Enemies. But yet you fhould contrive the Matter fo, that though you have both thofe Advantages, you fhould feem to have had an Eye only to one of them, namely, your own Defence; that it may be thought the other happened only from the Situation and Nature of the Building.

C H A P. IV.

Of the proper Situation, Structure and Fortification of a Fortrefs, whether in a Plain, or upon a Hill, its Inclofure, Area, Walls, Ditches, Bridges, and Towers.

I Find that even Men of good Experience in military Affairs, are in Doubt which is the beft and ftrongeft Manner of building a Fortrefs, either upon a Hill or Plain. There is fcarce any Hill but what may be either attacked or undermined; nor any Plain but what may be fo well fortified that it fhall be impoffible to affault it without great Danger. But I fhall not difpute about this Queftion. Our Bufinefs is to contrive every Thing fuitably to the Nature of the Place; and indeed all the Rules which we have laid down for the

building a City, fhould be obferved in the building a Fortrefs. The Fortrefs particularly fhould be fure to have even and direct Streets, by which the Garrifon may march to attack an Enemy, or in Cafe of Sedition or Treachery, their own Citizens and Inhabitants, and bring in Succours, either out of their own Country or from Abroad, without Impediment, by Land, River, Lake, or Sea. One very good Form for the Area of a Fortrefs, is that of a C joining to all the City Walls as to a round O with bending Horns, but not encomcompassing them quite round; as is also that which is shaped like a Star with Rays running out to the Circumference; and thus the Fortress will be, as we before observed it ought, neither within nor without the City. If we were to give a brief Description of the Fortress, or Citadel, it might perhaps be not amiss to say that it is the Back-door to the City strongly fortified on all Sides. But let it be what it will, whether the Crown of the Wall, or the Key to the City, it ought to look fierce, terrible, rugged, dangerous, and unconquerable; and the less it is, the stronger it will be. A small one will require the Fidelity only of a few, but a large one that of a great many: And, as *Euripides* says, there never was a Multitude without a great many dangerous Spirits in it; so that in the Case before us, the Fewer we have occasion to trust, the Safer we shall be. The outward Wall, or Inclosure of the Fortress should be built very strong, of large Stone, with a good Slope on the Outside, that the Ladders set against it may be weakened by their standing too oblique; and that the Enemy who Assaults it and endeavours to scale it, may lie entirely open to the Stones thrown down upon him; and that Things cast at the Wall by the military Engines may not strike it full, but be thrown off aslant. The Ground or Area on the Inside should be all paved with two or even three Layers of very large Stones, that the Besiegers may not get in upon you by Mines run under the Wall. All the Rest of the Walls should be made very high, and very strong and thick quite to the uppermost Cornish, that they may stoutly resist all Manner of Battery, and not easily be mounted by Ladders, nor commanded by Intrenchments cast up on the Outside. In other Respects the same Rules are to be observed that we have given for the Walls of the City. The greatest Defence to the Walls either of a City or Fortress is to be so provided, that the Enemy cannot approach you on any Side without being exposed to imminent Danger. This is done both by making very broad and deep Ditches, as we said before; and also by leaving private Loop-Holes almost at the very Bottom of the Wall, by which, while the Enemy is covering himself with his Shield from the Besieged above, he may be taken in his Flank which lies unguarded. And indeed, there is no Kind of Defence so serviceable as this. You gaul the

Enemy from these Loop-Holes with the greatest Safety to yourself, you have a nearer Aim at him, and you are sure to do most Execution, since it is impossible he should defend all Parts of his Body at the same Time: And if your Weapon passes by the first Man without hurting him, it meets another, and sometimes wounds two or three at a Time. On the Contrary, when the besieged throws Things down from the Top of the Wall, they must stand exposed to a good Deal of Danger, and it is a great Chance whether they hit so much as one Man, who may easily see what is coming upon him, and avoid it, or turn it aside with his Buckler. If the Fortress stands upon the Sea-side, you should fix Piles and Heaps of Stone scattered up and down about the Coast to make it unsafe, and prevent any Batteries in Shipping from coming too near. If it is upon a Plain it should be surrounded with a Ditch filled with Water; but then to prevent its stinking and infecting the Air, you should dig for it till you come to a living Spring. If it is upon a Hill, it should be encompassed with broken Precipices; and where we have an Opportunity we should make use of all these Advantages together. Those Parts which are exposed to battery, should be made Semi-circular, or rather with a sharp Angle like the Head of a Ship. I am not to learn that some People of good Experience in military Matters, are of Opinion that very high Walls are dangerous in Case of Battery; because their Ruins fill up the Ditch, and make a Way in it for the Enemy to approach and assault the Place. But we shall avoid this Inconvenience, if we observe all the Rules before laid down. But to return. Within the Fortress ought to be one principal Tower, built in the stoutest Manner, and fortified as strongly as possible, higher than any other Part of the Castle, and not accessible by more than one Way, to which there should be no other Entrance but by a Draw-bridge. Draw-bridges are of two Sorts; one which is lifted up and stops up the Entrance; the other, which slides out and in, as you have occasion for it. In a Place exposed to boisterous Winds, this last is the most Convenient. Any Tower that may possibly infest this principal One, ought to be left quite open and naked on that Side which stands towards it, or faced only with a very thin weak Wall.

93

CHAP.

CHAP. V.

Of those Parts of the Fortress where the Soldiers are to stand either to keep centinel, or to fight. Of the Covering or Roof of the Fortress, and in what Manner it is to be made strong, and of the other Conveniencies necessary in the Castle, either of a King or a Tyrant.

THE Place where the Soldiers are to stand to keep centinel, and to defend the Wall, should be so laid out, that some may guard the lower Parts of the Fortress, others the upper, thus being all distributed into various Posts and Employments. In a Word, the Entrance in, and Passage out, and every separate Part should be so contrived and secured, that it may be exposed neither to the Treachery of Friends, nor the Force or Fraud of Enemies. The Roofs in a Fortress should be built with an acute Angle, and very strong, that they may not easily be demolished by the Weight of what is thrown from the military Engines; the Rafters in them must stand very close together, and a Covering over them, and then lay the Gutters for carrying off the Rain, but entirely without Lime or Mortar. Then make a Covering over the Whole of Pieces of Tile, or rather of Pumice-stones, to the Heighth of three Foot: Thus it will neither be in Danger from any Weight falling upon it, nor from Fire. In short, a Fortress is to be built like a little Town: It should be fortified with the same Care and Art, and if possible, provided with all the Conveniencies that a Town should be. It must not want Water, nor sufficient room for lodging the Soldiers, and laying up Stores of Arms, Corn, Salted-meat, Vinegar, and particularly Wood. And within this Fortress too, that which we called the principal Tower, ought to be a little Fortress within itself, and should want none of the Conveniencies required in a great one. It should have its own Cisterns, and Store-rooms for all Provisions necessary, either for its Maintenance or Defence. It should have Passages, by which it may upon Occasion attack even its own Friends, and for the Admission of Succours. I will not omit one Circumstance, which is, that Castles have sometimes been defended by Means of their private Passages for Water, and Towns taken by Means of their Drains. Both these may be of Use for sending out private Messengers. But you should be sure to contrive them so, that they may do you more Service than Prejudice. Let them therefore be made but just big enough; let them run winding several Ways, and let them end in some very deep Place, that there may not be room enough for a Man with his Arms, and that even one unarmed may not get into the Castle without being permitted or called. The Mouths of them may end very conveniently in some common Drain, or rather in some unknown desart Place, or in a private Chapel, or a Tomb in some Church. We should likewise never be unprovided against human Accidents and Calamities; and therefore it will be very proper to have some Passage into the very Heart of the Fortress, known to nobody but yourself; by which if you should ever happen to be shut out, you may immediately get in with an armed Force: And perhaps one good Way to do this may be to have some very private Part of the Wall built only of Earth or Chalk, and not of Stone and Mortar. Thus much may suffice for what is necessary to be done for a single Person that is possessed of the Government, whether King or Tyrant.

CHAP. VI.

Of the several Parts of which the Republick consists. The proper Situation and Building for the Houses of those that govern the Republick, and of the Priests. Of Temples, as well large as small, Chapels and Oratories.

WE are now to treat of those Things which are proper to such as are at the Head not of a Monarchy but of a Commonwealth; and here the Power is lodged either in the Hands of some one single Magistrate, or else is divided among a certain Number.

The

The Republick confifts of Things facred, which appertain to the publick Worfhip: The Care of which is in the Priefts; and of Things profane, which regard the Welfare and good of the Society; the Care of which is in the Senators and Judges at Home, and in the Generals of Armies and Fleets Abroad. To each of thefe belong two Kinds of Building, one upon account of the Perfon's Office, the other for the Ufe of his own private Family. Every Man's Houfe fhould certainly be fuited to the Condition of Life which he is in, whether he is a King, a Tyrant, or a private Perfon. There are fome Circumftances which in a particular Manner become Men in high Stations. *Virgil* very judicioufly makes *Anchifes* have his Houfe in a private Part of the City, and fhaded with Trees; knowing very well that the Habitations of great Men, for the Dignity and Quiet both of themfelves and Families, fhould be remote from the Concourfe of the Vulgar, and from the Noife of Trades; and this not only for the Pleafure and Conveniency of having Room for Gardens, Groves, or the like, but alfo that fo large a Family, confifting of different Sorts of People, may not lie in the Way to be corrupted and debauched by an ill Neighbourhood, fince (as is rightly obferved) more Mifchief is done by Wine Abroad than at Home: And moreover, in order to avoid the eternal Torment of numerous Vifitors and Attendants. I have indeed obferved that wife Princes have not only placed themfelves out of the Way of the Crowd, but even out of the City itfelf, that the common People might not be troublefome to them, but when they were in fome particular Want of their Protection: And, in Reality, what fignifies all their Wealth and Greatnefs, if they can never enjoy a few Hours of Repofe and Leifure? However, their Houfes, let them ftand where they will, ought to have large fpacious Apartments to receive thofe that come to attend them, and the Street which leads from them to the Places where the publick Affairs are tranfacted, fhould be of a good Breadth, that their Servants, Clients, Suitors and Followers crowding to attend their Patron, may not ftop up the Way, and breed Confufion. The different Places where the Magiftrates are to exercife their Offices, are known to every Body: The Bufinefs of the Senator, is in the Senate-houfe; of the Judge, in the Tribunal, or Court of Juftice; of the General in the Army; of the Admiral on board the Fleet. But what fhall we fay of the Priefts? to whom belongs not only the Temple, but alfo the Cloyfter, which might be called a Lodgement, or Camp for Soldiers, fince the chief Priefts, and all his inferior Minifters, are employed in a ftubborn and laborious Warfare, (as we have fhewed in the Book called *The Prieft*) namely, that of Virtue againft Vice. Of Temples, fome are principal, as is that wherein the chief Prieft upon ftated Seafons celebrates fome folemn Rites and Sacrifices: Others are under the Guardianfhip of inferior Priefts, as all Chapels in Town, and Oratories in the Country. Perhaps the moft convenient Situation for the principal Temple may be in the Middle of the City; but it is more Decent to have it fomewhat remote from the Crowd: A Hill gives it an Air of Dignity, but it is more fecure from Earthquakes in a Plain. In a Word, the Temple is to be placed where it may appear with moft Majefty and Reverence: For which Reafon it fhould lie entirely out of the Way of all Filth and Indecency, to the Intent that Fathers, Matrons and Virgins, who come to offer up their Prayers, may not be fhocked and offended, or perverted from their intended Devotions. *Nigrigeneus* the Architect, who wrote about the *Termini*, informs us, that the ancient Architects were for having the Fronts of their Temples facing the Weft: But this Cuftom was afterwards quite altered, and it was thought better to have the Temples and the *Termini* look to the Eaft, that they might have a View of the rifing Sun. But I have obferved myfelf that the Ancients in the fituating of their fmaller Temples or Chapels, generally turned their Fronts fo as they might be feen from the Sea, or fome River or great Road. To conclude, a Structure of this Kind ought to be fo built as to entice thofe who are abfent to come and fee it, and to charm and detain thofe that are prefent by the Beauty and Curiofity of its Workmanfhip. An arched Roof will fecure it moft againft Fire, and a flat one againft Earthquakes; but the former will be the leaft liable to Decay by the Injury of Time. And this may fuffice as to the Temples, becaufe many Things which feem neceffary to be faid here, belong more properly to their Ornament than to their real Ufe: And therefore of thofe we fhall treat elfewhere. Smaller Temples and Chaples muft imitate the Greater, according to the Dignity of their Situation and Ufes.

94

95

96

CHAP. VII.

That the Priest's Camp is the Cloyster; the Duty of the Priest; the various Sorts of Cloysters and their proper Situations.

THE Priest's Camp is the Cloyster, in which a certain Number of Persons shut themselves up together in order to devote themselves either to Religion or Virtue; such are those who have dedicated themselves to the sacred Functions, or who have taken upon themselves a Vow of Chastity. Besides this Cloyster is a Place where Persons of studious Dispositions employ themselves about the Knowledge of Things as well Divine as Human; for as the Priest's Duty is as far as in him lies to lead Mankind into a Course of Life as near to Perfection as possible, this can never be done more effectually than by Philosophy. For as there are two Things in the Nature of Man to which this must be owing, Virtue and Truth; when the former has taught us to calm and govern our Passions, and the latter to know the Principles and Secrets of Nature, which will purge the Mind from Ignorance and the Contagion of the Body; we may then be qualified to enter into a happy Course of Life, and to have some Resemblance with the divine Nature itself. Add to this, that it is the Duty of all good Men, as the Priests ought and would be thought to be, to exercise themselves in all those Offices of Humanity which are due from every Man to his Neighbour, namely, to assist and relieve the Poor, the Distressed and the Infirm, to the utmost of their Power. These are the Things in which the Priest is to employ himself and all those under his Direction. Of the Structures proper for these Purposes, whether belonging to the superior or inferior Rank of Priests, we are now to treat; and first we shall begin with the Cloyster. Cloysters are of several Sorts, either for such Persons as are to be so strictly confined that they must never appear in publick at all, unless at Church or in Processions; or for those who are to be allowed a little more Liberty. Of these again some are for Men, others for Women. Those for Women should, in my Opinion, be neither too much in the City, nor too much out of it: For though in a Solitude they may not be so much frequented, yet any one that has a Design may have more Opportunity to execute any villanous Enterprize where there are so few Witnesses, than where there are a great many both to shame and disswade him from such an Attempt. It is our Business in both to take Care not that they have no Inclinations to be unchaste, but no means. For this Purpose every Entrance must be so secured, that nobody can possibly get in; and so well watched, that nobody may loyter about in order to attempt it without instant Suspicion and Shame. No Camp for an Army should be so well guarded by Intrenchments and Palisadoes, as a Monastery ought to be by high Walls, without either Doors or Windows in them, or the least Hole by which not only no Violator of Chastity, but not so much as the least Temptation either by the Eye or Ear, may possibly get in to disorder, or pollute the Minds of the Recluse. Let them receive their Light from an open Court on the Inside. Round this Court the Portico, Cells, Refectory, Chapter-house and the like Conveniencies should be disposed according to their various Uses, in the same Manner as in private Houses. Nor should Space be wanting for Gardens and Meadows, for the moderate Recreation of the Mind, but not for administring to Pleasure. If all these Precautions are taken, it will be best to have them out of the Way of a Concourse of People. The Cloysters for both Sexes therefore cannot be better placed than without the City; that the Attention of their Thoughts which are entirely dedicated to Holiness, and the calm and settled Religion of their Minds may not be disturbed by too many Visitors. But then I would have their Houses, whether they are for Men or Women, situated in the most healthy Air that can be found out; that the Recluse, while they are wholly intent upon the Care of their Souls, may not have their Bodies, already impared, by constant fasting and watching, oppressed likewise with Weakness and Diseases. Those who are without the City should be placed in a Situation naturally strong, that neither Robbers nor any plundering Enemy with a small Force, may be able at every turn to sack it; and I would have it moreover fortified with a Trench and a Wall,

Wall, nor would it be amifs to add a Tower, which is not at all inconfiftent with a religious Edifice.   The Monaftery for thofe Recluse who to Religion join the Study of the liberal Arts, that they may be the more ready to promote the Good of Mankind, according to the Obligation of their Character, ought to be neither within the Noife and Hurry of Tradefmen, nor too far remote from the Accefs of the Citizens.   And as they are a great many in Family, and there is generally a great Concourfe of People to hear them Preach and Difpute concerning facred Things; they require a very large Houfe. They can be placed no where better than among fome publick Buildings, fuch as Theatres, Circuffes, or Squares, where the Multitude going for their Pleafure may more eafily by the Exhortations, Example and Admonition of the Religious, be drawn from Vice to Virtue, and from Ignorance to Knowledge.

C H A P.   VIII.

Of Places for Exercife, publick Schools, and Hofpitals both for Men and Women.

THE Ancients, and efpecially the *Greeks*, ufed in the very Middle of their Cities to erect thofe Edifices which they called 97 *Palæftræ*, where thofe who applied themfelves to Philofophy, attended publick Difputations. They were large fpacious Places full of Windows, with a free Profpect on all Sides, and raifed Seats, and Porticoes running round fome green flowery Meadow.   Such a Structure is extremely proper for thefe Perfons, who may be reckoned a Kind of Religious; and I would have thofe who delight in the Study of Learning, be provided with every Thing that may induce them to ftay with their Tutors with Pleafure, and without Uneafinefs or Satiety. For this Reafon, I would have the Meadow, the Portico, and every Thing elfe fo laid out, that nothing whatfoever could be better contrived for Recreation.   In Winter let them receive the kindly Beams of the Sun, and in Summer be fhady and open to gentle refrefhing Breezes.   But of the Delicacies of this Kind of Structures we fhall fpeak more particularly in 98 another Place. Only if you do refolve to erect publick Schools, where the Learned may meet and converfe, place them in that Situation which may be moft convenient and pleafant for them. Let there be no Noifes of working Trades, no noifome ill Smells; and do not let it be a Place for idle People to loyter in; but let it have more the Air of a Solitude, fuch as becomes Men of Gravity employed about the nobleft and moft curious Enquiries: In a Word, it fhould have more of Majefty than Nicety. As for Hofpitals where the Prieft is to exercife his Charity towards the Poor and Diftreffed,

they are to be built with much Thought, and a good Deal of Variety; for one Place is proper for harbouring the Diftreffed, and another for curing and foftering the Sick and Infirm: Among thefe laft too we fhould take Care to make a good Deal of Diftinction, that while we are providing for a few ufelefs People, we do not neglect more that might really be of Service. There have been fome Princes in *Italy* that would never fuffer any tattered Cripples to go about their Cities begging Charity from Door to Door; but as foon as ever they came, an Order was brought to them not to be feen in that City without working at fome Trade above three Days: For there is hardly any fo maimed but what may do fome Work or other; and even a blind Man may turn a Ropemaker's Wheel, if he can do nothing elfe. As for thofe who are entirely oppreffed and difabled by fome heavier Infirmity, they were taken care of by Magiftrates appointed on purpofe to provide for fick Strangers, and diftributed regularly to inferior Hofpitlers, to be looked after.   And by this Means thefe poor Wretches did not wander about begging Relief, perhaps in vain; and the City was not offended by miferable and filthy Objects.   In *Tufcany*, always famous for Religion and Piety, there are noble Hofpitals, built at a vaft Expence; where as well Strangers as Natives, are furnifhed plentifully with all Manner of Neceffaries for their Cure.   But as the Sick are of various Sorts, fome afflicted with Leprofy or Plague, with which they might infect thofe who are in Health, and others, if fuch an Expreffion may be allowed, with more wholfome Diftempers:

Diftempers: They ought to have Places entirely feperate. The Ancients dedicated their Buildings of this Nature to *Æculapius, Apollo,* and *Health,* Gods among them to whom they afcribed the Cure of Sicknefs and Prefervation Health, and fituated them in the beft Air they could find out, and near Plenty of the cleareft Water, where the Sick might recover their Health, not fo much by the Affiftanc of thofe Gods, as the natural Healthinefs of the Place: And certainly nothing can be more reafonable than to carry the Sick, whether under a private or a publick Cure, into the moft healthy Places; and perhaps none are more fo, than thofe which are very dry and ftony, fanned with continual Breezes, not burnt up by the Sun, but cool and temperate: Since we find that all Moifture is the Mother of Corruption. We fee that Nature in every Thing loves a Medium; and even Health itfelf is nothing but a due Moderation of the Qualities of the Body; and indeed nothing that is in Extreams can pleafe. For the Reft, thofe who are feized with Difeafes which are contagious, fhould be taken Care of not on-ly without the City, but remote even from any high Road; the others may be kept in the City. The Apartments for all thefe fhould be fo laid out and diftributed, that there may be diftinct Places for thofe who are curable, and thofe whom you take in rather to maintain them for the Remainder of their unhappy Days, than to cure them: Of this Sort are the Superannuated, and thofe who want their Senfes. Add further, that the Men and Women, as well the Patients, as the Perfons that attend them, fhould have Apartments feparate from one another; and as fome Parts of the Building fhould be for Particulars, others fhould be in common, according as it fhall be found neceffary for the Management of the Patients, and the more eafy cohabiting together: Of which there is no Occafion to fay more in this Place. We fhall only obferve that all thefe Conveniencies are to be contrived according to the Rules hereafter to be laid down for the Houfes of private Perfons. We fhall therefore now proceed according to the Method which we have prefcribed to ourfelves.

C H A P. IX.

Of the Senate-houfe, the Temple, and the Tribunals for the Adminiftration of Juftice.

HAVING already obferved that the Republick confifts of two Parts, the Sacred and the Profane, and having treated of the Sacred as much as was requifite, and in a good Meafure too of the Profane, where we took Notice of the Place in the Palace of the Prince where the Senate was to meet, and where Caufes were to be heard; we fhall now very briefly fpeak of thofe Things which feem neceffary to be further added, then proceed to Incampments and Fleets, and laftly treat of Things relating to the Ufes of private Perfons. The Ancients ufed to call their Senates together in Temples, and afterwards it grew a Cuftom for them to meet fomewhere out of the City. But at length, both for greater Dignity and Conveniency in tranfacting the publick Affairs, it was found neceffary to raife Structures for this Purpofe only; where neither the Length of the Way, nor any Inconveniency in the Place itfelf, might deter the aged Fathers from meeting often, and continuing a good while together; and for this Reafon they placed the Senate-houfe in the Middle of the City, with the Place for the Adminiftration of Juftice and the Temple near adjoining, that not only thofe who made Intereft for Offices, or were obliged to attend Law-fuits, might with greater Convenience, and without lofing their Time or Opportunity, look after their Affairs of both Natures; but alfo that the Fathers (as Men are generally moft devoted to Religion in their old Age) might firft pay their Devotions in the Temple, and afterwards repair immediately to the Tranfaction of the publick Bufinefs. Add to all this, that when any Ambaffador or foreign Prince defires Audience of the Senate, it becomes the Republick to have a Place fuitable to the Dignity both of the Stranger and of the City, to receive them in, while they wait for Introduction. Laftly, in publick Buildings of this Sort, you muft neglect none of thofe Rules which belong to the convenient and honourable Reception of a Multitude of Citizens, and their eafy Difmiffion: And above all you muft take particular Care, that there is not the leaft

Want

Want of sufficient Paffages, Lights, open Areas, and the like. But in the Hall for the Adminiftration of Juftice, where Numbers of People refort about various Contentions, the Apertures muft be more and larger, and more direct than either in the Temple or Senate-houfe. The Entrance into the Senate-houfe ought to be made no lefs ftrong than handfome, for very many Reafons, and particularly to the Intent that no foolifh headftrong Rabble, at the Inftigation of any feditious Ringleader, may be able at any Time to attack and infult the Senators: For which Reafon, more than for any other, there ought to be Porticoes, Veftibules, and the like, where Servants, Clients and Attendants, waiting for their Patrons, may be ready at Hand to defend them in Cafe of any fudden Commotion. I will not omit one Obfervation, namely, that no Place where we are to hear the Voices of Perfons either fpeaking, finging, or difputing, fhould ever be vaulted becaufe fuch Roofs confound the Voice with Ecchoes: Whereas a flat Ceiling made of Timbers renders the Sound more clear and diftinct.

C H A P. X.

That Incampments, or Lodgments for Soldiers by Land are of three Sorts; in what Manner they are to be fortified; and the various Methods ufed by different Nations.

IN laying down a Camp we ought to review and re-confider all thofe Rules which we gave in the laft Book for the Situation of a City; for, indeed, Camps are as it were the Seeds of Cities, and you will find that not a few Cities have been built in thofe very Places, where excellent Generals had before incamped with their Armies. In making a Camp, the chief Matter is to know to what Intent it is defigned. There would not be the leaft Occafion for a Camp if it were not for unforefeen Accidents in War, and for the Apprehenfion of Affaults from a fuperior Force: And therefore we are to confider the Nature of the Enemy. Of Enemies fome are inferior as to Valour and Number; fome equal, fome fuperior. For this Reafon we fhall determine the different Sorts of Incampments to be three; the Firft is that which is made only for a Time, and is moveable every Moment, which is proper for withftanding and managing an Enemy equal to yourfelf, and is defigned partly for keeping the Soldier fafe from fudden Attacks, and partly for watching and obtaining Opportunities of effecting your Defigns. The fecond Sort of Incampment is ftationary, in which you wait to opprefs and fubdue an Enemy, who, diftrufting his own Forces, fhuts himfelf up in fome ftrong Hold. The third Sort is that in which you fhut up yourfelf, to receive and repulfe the Attacks of a fuperior Force, fo as to be able to fend the Enemy away weary of the Fatigues and Lofs in befieging you. In all thefe you muft take great Care that every Thing be fo ordered, that not the leaft Particular be wanting which can be of Service to your own Security and Welfare, and to the fuftaining, repulfing and breaking the Enemy; and on the Contrary, that the Enemy, as far as lies in your Power, may have no Conveniency whatfoever, by means of which he may either hurt you, or fecure himfelf. For this Reafon, the firft Thing to be confulted, is the Nature of the Situation, that it be in a Country well furnifhed with all Manner of Provifions, and lie convenient for the eafy bringing in either of Convoys or Supplies upon all Occafions. Let Water by no means be wanting, and let Wood and Pafture be not far off. Take care to have a free Communication with your own Territory, and an open Paffage at pleafure into the Enemy's. Let the Enemy on the Contrary, have nothing but Difficulties and Obftacles. I am for having a Camp placed on a Situation fo high, as to have an open View of the Enemy's Country all round; fo that they may not begin or attempt any Thing whatfoever, without your being immediately aware of it. Let it be fecured all round with fteep Slopes, difficult Afcents, and broken Precipices; that the Enemy may not be able to furround you with Multitudes, nor to attack you on any Side, without expofing himfelf to imminent Danger; or that if he fhould come clofe up to you, he may not conveniently ufe his Engines, or make any fecure Lodgments for himfelf near you.

If

If the Situation offers all thefe Advantages, be fure to be the Firft to lay hold of them; if not, we muft then confider what Sort of Camp, and what Kind of Situation will beft anfwer your Purpofe. A ftationary Camp ought to be much better fortified than a Flying one: And a Plain requires more Art and Diligence to ftrengthen it, than a Hill. We fhall begin with the moveable, or flying Camp, becaufe it is much more frequently ufed than a ftationary one: And indeed, the frequent moving the Camp, has very often conduced extremely to the Health of the Army. In placing a Camp, it is a Queftion that naturally arifes in the Mind, whether it is beft to fix it upon our own Territory, or upon that of the Enemy. *Xenophon* fays, that by frequent changing our Camp, our Enemy is oppreffed, but our Friends eafed. Without doubt, it is honourable and brave to lie upon the Enemy's Country; but it is convenient and fafe to be upon our own. But indeed a Camp is, with regard to all the Territory which is fubject to it, what a Citadel is to a City; which ought to have a fhort and eafy Retreat towards its Friends, and an open and ready Paffage upon its Enemies. Laftly, in the fortifying of Camps various Methods have been ufed. The *Britains* ufed to make a Fence round their Camps with Stakes ten foot long, fharpened and burnt at the Ends, with one End fixed in the Ground, and the other

ftanding up to keep off the Enemy. *Cæfar* tells us, that the *Gauls* ufed to make a Rampart of their Waggons, as he fays the *Thracians* alfo did againft *Alexander*. The *Nervii* (or People of *Tournay*) ufed to cut down young Trees, and binding and interlacing the Boughs together made them into a ftrong Hedge, which ferved chiefly for keeping off the Horfe. *Arrian* relates that when *Nearchus*, *Alexander's* Admiral, failed along the *Indian* Sea, having Occafion to land, he furrounded his Camp with a Wall to fecure himfelf againft the *Barbarians*. The *Romans* were always fo well provided, and had fo much Forefight, that whatever happened they took care it fhould never be by their own Fault; and they ufed to exercife their Soldiers no lefs in making Incampments, than in the other Parts of the Military Duty. Nor did they think there was fo much Merit in offending their Enemies, as in fecuring their own Men; and they accounted it no fmall Part of the Victory, to be able to withftand the Enemy, and to repulfe him fo ftoutly as to make him Defpair of Succefs. For which Reafon they never neglected any Means of Defence that they could learn or invent for their own Safety: And if high Hills or Precipices were not to be had, they imitated them as well as they could with very deep Ditches and high Ramparts, emcompaffed with ftrong Fences of Stakes and Hurdles.

Chap. XI.

The moft convenient Situation for a Camp, and its Size, Form and various Parts; together with the different Methods of attacking and defending a Camp or other Fortification.

WE fhall here proceed further upon this Subject of Camps according to the Methods of the aforementioned Ancients. We muft take Care to pitch upon a Place not only convenient, but fo well adapted for whatever Purpofe we have in Hand, that none could be found more fuitable. And befides the other Advantages before recited, let the Soil be dry, not muddy nor liable at any Time to be overflowed; but let the Situation be fuch that it may be always clear and free for your own Men, and unfafe for the Enemy. Let there be no foul Puddle in the Neighbourhood, and let there be good Water at an eafy Diftance. Contrive, if poffible, to have fome clear Springs

within the Camp itfelf, or to have the Fofs filled with fome River or running Stream. The Camp ought not to be fo large, out of Proportion to the Number of your Soldiers, that they cannot be able to keep fufficient Centry about it, fo as to give the Watch-word round one to another; or to relieve one another fo often as may be requifite in defending the Ramparts: Nor, on the Contrary, ought it to be fo crampt up and confined, as not to afford fufficient room for all proper Conveniencies. *Lycurgus* was of Opinion that Angles were ufelefs in a Camp, and therefore he always laid out his in a Circle, unlefs he had fome Hill, River or Fortification at his Back. Others commend a

square

square Area for Incampments: But indeed in situating a Camp we must accommodate ourselves to the Necessity of the Time, and the Nature of the Place, according to the Purpose which we have in Hand, whether it be to oppress the Enemy or to resist him. Let us make our Foss so big, that it may not be filled up without great Labour, and a long Space of Time; or rather let us have two Fosses, with some intermediate Space between them. The Ancients, in Works of this Nature also, held it a Point of Religion to make use of odd Numbers; for which Reason it was their Custom to make their Ditches fifteen Foot wide, and nine deep. Let the Sides of the Ditch be Perpendicular, so that it may be as broad at the Bottom as the Top; but where the Soil is loose, you may allow a small Slope, running somewhat narrower towards the Bottom. In a Plain, or a low Situation, fill your Ditch with Water brought from some River, Lake, or Sea: But if this cannot be effected strew all the Bottom with sharp Points of Steel and Caltrops, and fix up and down a good Number of Stakes with their Ends smoothed and sharpened, to keep off the Enemy. Having compleated your Ditch, make your Rampart so thick, that it may not be to be shaken by every little military Engine, and so high as to be above the Reach of the grappling Hooks, and even of Darts thrown by the Hand. The Earth dug out of the Foss lies very convenient and ready at Hand for making up the Rampart. The Ancients for that Work very much commended Turfs dug out of the Meadows with the Grass upon them, the Roots whereof fasten them very strongly together. Others intermix them with Twigs of green Oziers, which strike their Roots into the Rampart, and by the Contexture of their Fibres strengthen the whole Work. Along the inward Edge of the Foss and the Outside of the Rampart set Thorns, Spikes, Tenter-hooks and the like, to retard the Enemy in his Ascent. Let the Top of the Rampart be girt with a strong Frame of Timbers joyned to one another crossways like a Cornish, with Hurdles and Earth well rammed in together between them; and upon these raise your Battlements, and stick in forked Palisadoes like Stag's Horns. In a Word, let every Thing be so contrived in this Kind of Structure, as to make it difficult to be either undermined, thrown down, or mounted; and to protect the Soldier who is to defend it. Upon the Edge of this Rampart erect Towers

at the Distance of every hundred Feet, and especially in such Parts as are most likely to be attacked, where they ought to stand closer and be built higher that they may the more effectually annoy the Enemy, when he attempts to make his Way into the Camp. Let the *Prætorium*, or General's Tent, and the Gate looking towards the Enemy, as also that in the Back of the Camp, which two Gates used formerly to be called the *porta Quintana*, and the *porta Decumana*, be placed in the strongest Parts of the Camp, and lie convenient for making any sudden Sally with the Army, or bringing in of Provisions, or giving a ready Retreat to your own Men. All these Conveniencies belong more particularly to a stationary Camp, than to a flying one: But as we ought to be provided against all Accidents that either Fortune or the Calamity of the Times can produce, we should not, even in a flying Camp, neglect any of those Particulars which we have spoken of, as far as may be necessary. Those Things which belong to a stationary Camp, especially one that is to expect a Siege, are very nearly the same with those which we spoke of with Relation to the Citadel of a Tyrant. A Citadel is a Structure purposely designed for the Sustaining a Siege, since the Citizens always look upon it with an irreconcileable Hatred: And it is indeed the most cruel Kind of Siege that can be imagined, to be continually watching it, and to be always upon the Catch for an Opportunity that may offer, by Means of which you may satisfy the strong Desire you have to destroy it: And for this Reason, as we observed before, we should take the greatest Care to make it strong, stout, durable, well provided for its own Defence, and for weakening and repulsing the Enemy, and able to defy the most obstinate and violent Attacks. On the other Hand in those Camps, where you are to be shut up and molest an Enemy, all the same Things are to be observed with the same Care: For it is indeed a just Observation, that the Nature of War is such, that he who besieges is in a great Measure besieged himself. For this Reason you are to consider not only how you may take the Place, but also how you may keep yourself from being oppressed, either by the Boldness or Diligence of the Enemy, or by the Carelessness of your own Men. In order to take the Place, you must proceed either by Siege or by Assault: And to keep yourself from being oppressed, there are also two Methods, which are, being stoutly fortified,

and

and making a brave Defence. The whole Purpose of an Assault is to break in either upon a Town or a Fortification. I shall not speak here either of Scaling-ladders, by Means whereof you mount the Wall in spite of the Enemy; nor of Mines, moveable Towers, Engines for Battery, nor of any other Methods of Offence either by Fire, Water, or any other Force: Inasmuch as we intend to treat of these military Engines more clearly in another Place. Thus much it may be proper here to mention, that against the Violence of Battery we should oppose Beams, Planks, Parapets of strong Timber, Hurdles, Ropes, Fascines, Sacks stuffed with Wool, Rushes, or Earth; and they should be so contrived as to hang loose and pliable. Against Fire these Things ought to be wetted, and especially with Vinegar, or Mud, and covered with Brick unbaked; against Water, to prevent the Bricks from being washed away, they should be covered over with the Hides of Beasts; and lastly, against Battery, that the Hides may not be broken through or torn away, add any coarse Cloths or Tarpawlins thoroughly wetted and soaked. Circumvallations or Trenches round the Place besieged, ought for several Reasons to be drawn pretty near it; for by that Means their Circuit will be less, they will require fewer Hands, Expence and Materials, to finish them, and when finished, the fewer Men will be necessary to defend them: But they must not run so close under the Wall, that the Besieged may annoy your Men within their Trenches by Engines upon the Wall. If the Circumvallation be only intended to cut off from the Besieged all Manner of Supplies, either of Men or Provisions from without; you may do this by stopping up all the Ways and Passages, either by barracading the Bridges, and Fords, and blocking up the Roads with strong Fences of Wood or Stones; or by running up a continued Rampart to joyn together the Lakes, Bogs,

Marshes, Rivers and Hills; or if you can any Ways lay the Country under Water. To these Precautions we should add those which relate to the Defence of our own Camp: For the Trenches, Ramparts, Towers and the like ought to be so well fortified both towards the Place besieged, and on the Side of any Country that might throw in Succours, that the former may not be able to annoy you by Sallies, nor the Latter by Incursions. Moreover, in convenient Places erect Watch-towers and Forts, that your Men may go out to forage for Wood, Water and Provisions with Safety and Freedom. But do not let your Troops be dispersed up and down in Places so remote from one another, that they cannot obey the Orders of a single General, nor fight with united Forces, nor be ready at Hand to assist one another upon any sudden Emergency. It will not be foreign to our Purpose to set down here an Account of a Fortification out of *Appian*, well worthy to be remembered. He tells us, that when *Octavianus Augustus* besieged *Lucius Antonius* in *Perusia*, he made a Trench quite to the *Tyber*, seven Miles long, thirty Foot broad, and as many deep: Which he fortified with a high Wall, and with a thousand and fifty wooden Towers standing up, each threescore Foot above the Wall, and made the Whole so strong, that the Besieged were not more straitened in by it, than they were excluded from annoying the Enemy in any Part. And thus much may suffice for Incampments or Stations by Land, unless it may be thought necessary to add, that we ought to chuse out a Place of the greatest Dignity and Honour, wherein to plant the Standard of the Commonwealth with befitting Majesty, where the Rites of Religion may be performed with all due Reverence, and where the Generals and other chief Officers may meet either in Council or for the Administration of Justice.

C H A P. XII.

Of Incampments or Stations at Sea, which are Fleets; of Ships and their Parts; as also of Havens and their proper Fortification.

SOME perhaps will not allow that Fleets are Sea Incampments; but will be rather for saying, that we use Ships like a Kind of Water Elephant, which we direct as we please

by its Bridle; and that the Haven is much more like a Sea Incampment, than the Fleet. Others on the Contrary, will say, that a Ship is no other than a travelling Fortress. We shall

pass

pass by these Disputes, and proceed to shew that there are two Things by Means of which the Art of Building may contribute to the Safety and Victory of Generals of Fleets and their Forces: The First consists in the right Construction and Rigging of the Vessels, and the Second in the proper fortifying the Haven; whether you are to go to attack the Enemy, or to stay to defend yourself. The primary Use of Shipping is to convey you and yours: The Second, is to fight without Danger. The Danger must arise either from the Ships themselves, in which Case it seems to be innate and incorporate with them; or else must happen to them from without. That from without, is from the Force and Violence of Winds and Waves, from Rocks and Shelves; all which are to be avoided by Experience in Sea-affairs, and a thorough Knowledge of Places and Winds: But the Danger incorporate and innate with the Vessel itself, arises either from the Design, or the Timbers; against which Defects it falls under our Province to provide. We should reject all Timber that is brittle, or apt to split, too heavy or liable to rot soon. Nails and Pins of Brass or Copper, are reckoned better than those of Iron. I have observed by Means of *Trajan*'s Ship, which while I was writing this Treatise was dug up out of the *lago di Nemi*, where it had lain under Water above thirteen hundred Years, that the Pine and Cypress Wood which was in it had remained surprizingly found. It was covered on the Outside with double Planks, done over with *Greek* Pitch, to which stuck a Coat of Linen Cloth, and that again was plated over with Sheets of Lead fastened on with brass Nails. The ancient Architects took the Model of their Ships from the Shape of a Fish; that Part which was the Back of the Fish, in the Ship was the Keel; that which in the Fish was the Head, in the Ship was the Prow; the Tail was the Helm, and instead of Fins and Gills, they made Oars. Ships are of two Sorts, and are built either for Burthen or for Speed: A long Vessel cuts its Way quickest through the Water, especially when it Sails before the Wind; but a short one is most obedient to the Helm. I would not have the Length of a Vessel of Burthen less than three Times its Breadth; nor that of a Vessel for Speed, more than nine Times. We have treated more particularly of every Thing relating to a Vessel in a Book intended wholly for that Purpose, called the Ship; and therefore shall have Occasion to say

no more of it here, than what is just necessary. The Parts of a Ship are these, the Keel, the Poop, the Prow, the two Sides, to which you may, if you please, add the Sail, the Helm, and the Rest of the Parts that belong to the Course of the Ship. The Hollow of the Vessel will bear any Weight that is equal to the Weight of Water that would fill it quite up to the Top. The Keel must be straight, but all the other Parts made with curve Lines. The broader the Keel is, the greater Weight the Vessel will carry, but then it will be the slower; the narrower the Keel is, the Swifter will be the Ship, but then it will be unsteady, unless you fill it with Ballast. The broad Keel is most convenient in shallow Water; but in deep Seas the narrow one will be more secure. The Sides and Prow built high will make the stoutest Resistance against the Waves, but then they are more exposed to Danger from the Winds; the Sharper the Head is, the Swifter the Ship will make its Way; and the Thinner the Stern, the more Steady will be the Vessel in its Course. The Sides of the Ship towards the Head ought to be very stout, and a little Swelling outwards to throw off the Waves when it ploughs through the Water both with Sails and Oars; but towards the Stern they should grow narrower, in order to slip through the Waves with the more Ease. A Number of Helms adds Firmness to the Vessel, but takes off from its Swiftness. The Mast should be as long as the whole Ship. We shall not here descend to other minute Particulars necessary both to the Way and Defence of the Vessel, such as Oars, Ropes, sharp Beaks, Towers, Bridges and the like; but shall only observe, that the Planks and Timbers which hang down by the Sides and stick out by the Beak of the Vessel, will serve instead of a Fortification against the Attacks of the Enemy as will Poles stuck upright, instead of Towers, and the Boom, or the Skiff laid over the Boom, instead of Bridges. The Ancients used in the Prow of their Ships to place a military Engine, which they called a *Corvus*: But our Mariners now in the Head and Stem of their Vessels near the Masts have learnt to set up Towers, which they fence 'round with old coarse Cloths, Ropes, Sacks, and the like, to deaden the Force of any Violence that might attack them; and to keep off any Enemy that should attempt to board them, they set up a Fence of Net-work. I have in another Place contrived and shewn how the Floor of the Ship

may

may in a Moment, in the midſt of an Engagement, be filled with ſharp Points ſticking up
cloſe to one another, ſo that an Enemy can
never ſet his Foot any where without a Wound;
and on the other Hand when there is Occaſion,
how all theſe may in leſs Space of Time be all
removed and cleared away; but this is not a
proper Place for repeating it again, and it is
ſufficient to have given the Hint to an ingenious Mind. Moreover I have found a Way how,
with a ſlight Stroke of a Hammer, to throw
down the whole Floor, with all the Men that
have boarded the Veſſel and ſtand upon it, and
then again with very little Labour to replace
it as it was before, whenever it is thought neceſſary ſo to do. Neither is this a proper Place
to relate the Methods which I have invented
to ſink and burn the Enemy's Ships and deſtroy their Crews by miſerable Deaths. We
may perhaps ſpeak of them elſewhere. One
Thing muſt not be omitted, namely, that Veſſels of different Heights and Sizes are requiſite in different Places. In the *Mare Mag-*
103 *giore,* in the Narrows among the Iſlands, a
large Ship, that cannot be managed without a great Number of Hands, is very unſafe when the Winds are any thing boiſterous:
On the Contrary out of the Strait's Mouth, in
the wide Ocean, a little Veſſel will not be able
to live. To this Head of maritime Affairs alſo
belong the Defending and Blocking up a Haven. This may be done by ſinking any great

Body, or by Moles, Piers, Chains and the like,
whereof we have treated in the preceding
Book. Drive in Piles, block the Port up with
huge Stones, and ſink large hollow Frames
made either of Planks or Oziers and filled
with any heavy Stuff. But if the Nature of
the Place, or the Greatneſs of the Expence will
not allow of this, as for Inſtance, if the Bottom be a Sand or Mud continually moving, or
the Water be of too great a Depth, you may
then block up the Haven in the following
Manner. Make a Float of great Barrels faſtened together, with Planks and Timbers joyned
croſs-ways to one another, and with large
Spikes and ſharp Beaks ſticking out from the
Float, and Piles with Points of Iron, ſuch as
are called ſhod Piles, to the Intent that none
of the Enemy's light Ships may dare to drive
againſt the Float with full Sails, in order to
endeavour to break or paſs it. Dawb the Float
over with Mud to ſecure it againſt Fire, and
fortify it with a Paliſado of Hurdles or ſtrong
Boards, and in convenient Places with wooden
Towers, faſtening the whole Work againſt the
Fury of the Waves with a good Number of
Anchors concealed from the Enemy. It would
not be amiſs to make ſuch a Work ſinuous or
wavy, with the Backs of the Arches turned
againſt the Streſs of the Weather, that the
Float may bear the leſs upon its Anchors.
But upon this Subject, thus much may ſuffice.

C H A P.   XIII.

Of the Commiſſaries, Chamberlains, publick Receivers and the like Magiſtrates,
whoſe Buſineſs is to ſupply and prefide over the publick Granaries, Chambers
of Accompts, Arſenals, Marts, Docks and Stables; as alſo of the three Sorts
of Priſons, their Structures, Situations and Compartitions.

NOW as the Execution of all theſe
Things requires good Store of Proviſions, and of Treaſures to ſupply the Expence;
it will be neceſſary to ſay ſomething of the Magiſtrates who have the Care of this Part of the
Buſineſs; as for Inſtance, Commiſſaries, Chamberlains, publick Receivers, and the like, for
whom the following Structures muſt be erected: The Granary, the Chamber for keeping
the Treaſures, the Arſenal, the Mart or Place
for the tranſacting Commerce, the Dock and
the publick Stables for Horſes. We ſhall have

but little to ſay here upon theſe Heads, but
that little muſt not be neglected. It is evident
to every Man's Reaſon, that the Granary, the
Chamber of Accompts, and the Arſenal or
Magazine for Arms ought to be placed in the
Heart of the City, and in the Place of greateſt Honour, for the greater Security and Conveniency. The Docks or Arſenals for Shipping ſhould be placed at a Diſtance from the
Houſes of the Citizens, for fear of Fire. We
ſhould alſo be ſure, in this laſt Sort of Structure, to raiſe a good many entire Party-walls
in

in different Places, running from the Ground quite up above the Roof, to confine the Flame, if any fhould happen, and prevent it catching from one Roof to another. Marts ought to be fixed by the Sea-fide, upon the Mouths of Rivers, and the Meeting of feveral great Roads. The Docks or Arfenals for Shipping fhould have large Bafons or Canals of Water, wherein to receive fuch Veffels as want refitting, and from which they may be conveniently launched out again to Sea; but we fhould take Care that this Water be not a ftanding one, but be kept in conftant Motion. Shipping is very much rotted by foutherly Winds, and cracked by the mid-day Heat; but the Afpect of the rifing Sun preferves it. All Granaries, or other Structures built for the laying up of Stores, abfolutely require a Drinefs both of Air and Situation. But we fhall fpeak more fully of the Particulars, when we come to the Conveniencies belonging to private Perfons, to whofe use they are indeed referred; only we fhall fay fomething here of the Places for laying up Salt. A Storehoufe for Salt ought to be made in the following Manner. Make up the Ground with a Layer of Coal to the Height of one Cubit or Foot and an half, and ftamp it down very tight; then ftrew it with Sand pounded together with clean Chalk, to the Height of three Hands breadths, and lay it exactly level; and then pave it with fquare Bricks baked till they are quite black. The Face of the Walls on the Infide ought to be made of the fame Sort of Bricks; but if you have not a fufficient Quantity of them, you may build it with fquare Stone, not either with foft Stone or Flint, but with fome Stone of a middle Nature between thofe two, only very hard; and let this Sort of Work go the Thicknefs of a Cubit into the Wall; and then let the whole Infide be lined with Planks of Wood, faftened with brafs Nails, or rather joynted together without any Nails at all, and fill up the intermediate Space between the Lining and the Wall, with Reeds. It would alfo have a mighty good Effect to dawb over the Planks with Chalk fteeped in Lees of Oil, and mixed with Spart and Rufhes fhred fmall. Laftly, all publick Buildings of this Nature ought to be well fortified with ftout Walls, Towers, and Ammunition, againft all Manner of Force, Malice, or Fraud either of Robbers, Enemies or feditious Citizens. I think I have now faid enough of publick Structures, unlefs it may be thought neceffary to confider of one Particular more which con-

cerns the Magiftrate, and that not a little; namely, that it is neceffary he fhould have Places for the Confinement of fuch as he has condemned either for Contumacy, Treachery or Villany. I obferve that the Ancients had three Sorts of Prifons. The firft was that wherein they kept the Diforderly and the Ignorant, to the Intent that every Night they might be doctored and inftructed by learned and able Profeffors of the beft Arts, in thofe Points which related to good Manners and an honeft Life. The Second was for the Confinement of Debtors, and for the Reformation of fuch as were got into a licentious Way of Living. The laft was for the moft wicked Wretches and horrid Profligates, unworthy of the Light of the Sun or the Society of Mankind, and foon to be delivered over to capital Punifhment or perpetual Imprifonment and Mifery. If any Man is of Opinion that this laft Sort of Prifon ought to be made like fome fubterraneous Cavern, or frightful Sepulchre, he has certainly a greater Regard to the Punifhment of the Criminal than is agreeable either to the Defign of the Law or to Humanity; and though wicked Men do by their Crimes deferve the higheft Punifhment, yet the Prince or Commonwealth ought never to forget Mercy in the Midft of Juftice. Therefore let it be fufficient to make this Sort of Buildings very ftrong and fecure, with ftout Walls, Roofs and Apertures, that the Perfon confined may have no Means of making his Efcape; which may in a great Meafure be obtained, by the Thicknefs, Depth and Height of the Walls, and their being built with very hard and large Stones, joyned together with Pins of Iron or Brafs. To this you may, if you pleafe, add Windows grated with ftrong Bars of Iron or Wood; though in reality nothing of this Sort whatfoever can fully fecure a Prifoner always thoughtful of his Liberty and Safety, nor prevent his making his Efcape, if you let him ufe the Strength which Nature and Cunning have beftowed upon him, and on which Account there is an excellent Admonition contained in this Saying, that the vigilant Eye of a Goaler is a Prifon of Adamant. But in other Refpects, let us follow the Method and Cuftoms of the Ancients. We muft remember that in a Prifon there muft be Privies and Hearths for Fire, which ought to be contrived to be without either Smoake or ill Smells. the following Plan of an entire Prifon may anfwer all the aforementioned Purpofes. Enclofe with very high and ftrong Walls, without any Apertures,

　　　　　　　　　　　　　　　a Space

a Space of Ground in fome fecure and not un-frequented Part of the City, and fortify it with Towers and Galleries. From this Wall inwards the Apartments where the Prifoners are to be confined, let there be an open Walk about four Foot and an half wide, where the Keepers may take their Rounds every Night to prevent any Efcapes by Confpiracy among the Prifoners. The Space remaining in the Middle of this Circuit divide in the following Manner. Inftead of a Veftibule make a good pleafant Hall, where thofe may be inftructed who are fent thither in order to be forced to learn how to demean themfelves. Next to this Hall,

make Habitations for the Goalers and Places for them to keep guard in, within an Enclofure of Lattices and Crofs-bars. Next let there be an open Court, with Porticoes on each Side of it, with Windows in them, through which you may fee into all the Cells within; in which Cells Bankrupts and Debtors are to be confined, not all together, but in different Apartments. In the Front of this Court there muft be a clofer Prifon, for fuch as are guilty of fmall Offences, and beyond that a Place where Prifoners for capital Crimes may be confined with yet greater Strictnefs and Privacy.

C H A P. XIV.

Of private Houfes and their Differences; as alfo of the Country Houfe, and the Rules to be obferved in its Situation and Structure.

I Now come to treat of private Edifices. I have already obferved elfewhere, that a House is a little City. We are therefore in the building of it, to have an Eye almoft to every Thing that relates to the Building of a City; that it be healthy, furnifhed with all Manner of Neceffaries, not defficient in any of the Conveniencies that conduce to the Repofe, Tranquility or Delicacy of Life. What thofe are and how they are to be obtained, I think I have already, in a great Meafure, fhewn in the preceding Books. However, as the Occafion here is different, we fhall confider them over again in the following Manner. A private Houfe is manifeftly defigned for the Ufe of a Family, to which it ought to be a ufeful and convenient Abode. It will not be fo convenient as it ought, if it has not every Thing within itfelf that the Family has Occafion for. There is a great Number of Perfons and Things in a Family, which you cannot diftribute as you would in a City fo well as you can in the Country. In building a Houfe in Town, your Neighbour's Wall, a common Gutter, a publick Square or Street, and the like, fhall all hinder you from contriving it juft to your own Mind; which is not fo in the Country, where you have as much Freedom as you have Obftruction in Town. For this, and other Reafons, therefore, I fhall diftinguifh the Matter thus: That the Habitation for a private Perfon muft be different in Town from what it is in the Country. In both thefe there muft again be a Dif-

ference between thofe which are for the meaner Sort of Citizens, and thofe which are for the Rich. The meaner Sort build only for Neceffity; but the Rich for Pleafure and Delight. I fhall fet down fuch Rules as the Modefty of the wifeft Men may approve of in all Sorts of Buildings, and for that Purpofe fhall begin with thofe which are moft eafy. Habitations in the Country are the freeft from all Obftructions, and therefore People are more inclined to beftow their Expence in the Country than in Town. We fhall therefore firft take a Review of fome Obfervations which we have already made, and which are very material with Relation to the chief Ufes of a Country Houfe. They are as follows: We fhould carefully avoid a bad Air and an ill Soil. We fhould build in the Middle of an open Champian, under the Shelter of fome Hill, where there is Plenty of Water, and pleafant Profpects, and in the healthieft Part of a healthy Country. A heavy unhealthy Air is faid to be occafioned not only by thofe Inconveniencies which we mentioned in the firft Book, but alfo by thick Woods, efpecially if they are full of Trees with bitter Leaves; becaufe the Air in fuch Places being not kept in Motion either by Sun or Winds, wants its due Concoction; it is alfo occafioned by a barren and unwholfome Soil, which will never produce any Thing but Woods. A Country Houfe ought to ftand in fuch a Place as may lie moft convenient for the Owner's Houfe in Town. *Xenophon* would have a Man

go

go to his Country Houſe on Foot, for the Sake of Exerciſe, and return on Horſeback. It ought not therefore to lie far from the City, and the Way to it ſhould be both good and clear, ſo as he may go it either in Summer or Winter, either in a Coach, or on Foot, and if poſſible by Water. It will be alſo very convenient to have your Way to it lie through a Gate of the City that is not far from your Town Houſe, but as near it as may be, that you may go backwards and forwards from Town to Country, and from Country to Town, with your Wife and Family, as often as you pleaſe, without being too much obſerved by the People, or being obliged in the leaſt to conſult your Dreſs. It is not amiſs to have a Villa ſo placed, that when you go to it in a Morning the Rays of the riſing Sun may not be troubleſome to your Eyes, nor thoſe of the ſetting Sun in the Evening when you return to the City. Neither ſhould a Country Houſe ſtand in a remote, deſart, mean Corner, diſtant from a reaſonable Neighbourhood; but in a Situation where you may have People to converſe with, drawn to the ſame Place by the Fruitfulneſs of the Soil, the Pleaſantneſs of the Air, the Plentifulneſs of the Country, the Sweetneſs of the Fields, and the Security of the Neighbourhood. Nor ſhould a Villa be ſeated in a Place of too much Reſort, near ad-

joyning either to the City, or any great Road, or to a Port where great Numbers of Veſſels and Boats are continually putting in; but in ſuch a Situation, as though none of thoſe Pleaſures may be wanting, yet your Family may not be eternally moleſted with the Viſits of Strangers and Paſſengers. The Ancients ſay that in windy Places Things are never ſpoilt by Ruſt or Mildew; but in moiſt Places, and low Vallies, where the Winds have not a free Courſe, they are very much expoſed to them. I cannot approve of one general Rule which is laid down for all Places, namely, that a Country Houſe ought to be built ſo as to look towards the riſing of the Sun when it is in the Equinox: For nothing can be ſaid relating to the Sun and Winds but what muſt alter according to the Difference of the Climate, ſince the North Wind is not light and the South unhealthy in all Places. *Celſus*, the Phyſician, very well obſerved that all Winds which blow from the Sea, are groſſer than thoſe which blow over Land, which are always lighter. Upon this Account of the Winds we ought to avoid the Mouths of all Vallies, becauſe in ſuch Places the Winds are too cold if they come in the Night, or too hot, if in the Day, being over-heated by the too great Reflection of the Sun's Rays.　　　107

C H A P. XV.

That Country Houſes are of two Sorts; the proper Diſpoſition of all their Members whether for the Lodging of Men, Animals, or Tools of Agriculture and other neceſſary Inſtruments.

BUT as of Habitations in the Country ſome are deſigned for Gentlemen, others for Huſbandmen, ſome invented for Uſe, others perhaps for Pleaſure; we ſhall begin with thoſe which belong to Husbandmen. The Habitations of theſe ought not to be far from their Maſter's Houſe, that he may be at Hand to over-look them every now and then, to ſee what they are doing, and what Orders it is neceſſary for him to give. The peculiar Buſineſs of theſe Structures is for the getting in, ordering and preſerving the Fruits of the Earth: Unleſs you will ſay that this laſt Office, namely, of preſerving the Grain, belongs rather to the Houſe of the Maſter, and even rather to his Houſe in the City than to that in the Country. This Buſineſs is to be done by a Number of

Hands and a good Quantity of Tools, but moſt of all by the Diligence and Induſtry of the Farmer or Overſeer. The Ancients computed the neceſſary Family of a Farmer to be about fifteen Perſons; for theſe therefore you muſt have convenient Places where they may warm themſelves when they are cold, or retire for Shelter when they are driven from their Labour by foul Weather, where they may eat their Meals, reſt themſelves and prepare the Things they will want in their Buſineſs. Make therefore a large Kitchen, not obſcure, nor liable to Danger from Fire, with an Oven, Stove, Pump and Sink. Beyond the Kitchen let there be a Room where the better Sort among your People may lie, and a Larder for preſerving all Sorts of Proviſions for daily Uſe. Let all the

　　　other

other People be so distributed, that every one may be near those Things which are under his particular Care. Let the Overseer lie near the principal Gate, that nobody may pass and re-pass or carry any Thing out in the Night without his Knowledge. Let those who have the Care of the Cattle, lie near the Stable, that they may be always at Hand to keep every Thing in good Order. And this may be sufficient with Relation to your People. Of Tools or Instruments, some are animate, as Cattle; and some inanimate, as Carts, all Sorts of iron Tools, and the like; for these erect on one Side of the Kitchen a large Shed under which you may set your Cart, Plough, Harrow, Yoke, Hay-baskets, and the like Utensils; and let this Shed have a South Aspect, that in Winter Time the Family may divert themselves under it on Holydays. Make a very large and neat Place for your Presses both of Wine and Oil. Let there be also a Store-house for the laying up and preserving your Measures, Hampers, Baskets, Cordage, Houghs, Pitch-forks and so forth. Over the Rafters that run across within the Shed, you may spread Hurdles, and upon them you may lay up Poles, Rods, Staves, Boughs, Leaves and Fodder for your Oxen, Hemp and Flax unwrought, and such like Stores. Cattle is of two Sorts; one, for Labour; as Oxen and Horses; the other, for Profit, as Hogs, Sheep, Goats, and all Sorts of Herds. We shall speak first of the labouring Sort, because they seem to come under the Head of Instruments; and afterwards we shall say something of those which are for Profit, which belong properly to the Industry of your Overseer or Farmer. Let the Stables for Horses, and for Oxen, and all other black Cattle, be warm in Winter, and let their Racks be strong and well fenced, that they may not scatter their Meat. Let the Hay for the Horses be above them, that they may not reach it without some Pains, and that they may be forced to raise their Heads high for it, which makes their Heads drier and their Shoulders lighter. On the Contrary, let their Oats and other Grain lie so as they may be forced to stoop low for it; which will prevent their taking too large Mouthfuls, and swallowing too much whole; besides that it will strengthen their Breast and Muscles. But above all you must take particular Care that the Wall behind the Manger, against which the Horse's Head is to stand, be not damp. The Bone which covers the Horse's Brain is so thin, that it will bear neither Damp nor Cold; and therefore take Care also that the Moon's Beams do not come in at the Windows; which are very apt to make him Wall-eyed and to give him grievous Coughs; and indeed the Moon's Beams are as bad as a Pestilence to any Cattle that are infirm. Let the Oxe's Manger be set lower, that he may eat as he lyes. If Horses see the Fire, they are prodigiously frightened and will grow rugged. Oxen are pleased with the Sight of Men. If a Mule is set up in a hot or dark Place, she runs Mad. Some think the Mule does not want so much as the least Shelter for any other Part but her Head, and that it is not at all the Worse if her other Parts are exposed to Dews and Colds. Let the Ground under the Oxen be paved with Stone, that the Filth and Dung may not rot their Hoofs. Under Horses, make a Trench in the Pavement, and cover it with Planks of Holm or Oak, that their Urine may not settle under them, and that by their pawing they may not spoil both their Hoofs and the Pavement.

C H A P. XVI.

That the Industry of the Farmer or Overseer ought to be employed as well about all Sorts of Animals, as about the Fruits of the Earth; as also of the Construction of the Threshing-floor.

WE shall just briefly mention that the Industry of the Overseer, is not only to be employed about gathering in the Fruits of the Earth, but also about the Management and Improvement of Cattle, Fowls, Fish and other Animals. Set the Stalls for Cattle in a dry Place, and never in a Damp one; clear away every little Stone from under them, and make them with a Slope, that you may easily sweep and clean them; let one Part of them be covered, and the other open, and take Care that no southerly or other moist Wind can affect the Cattle in the Night, and that they be sheltered from all other troublesome Blasts. For

For a Place to keep Rabbits in, build a Wall of square Stone, with its Foundations dug so low as to be in Water; within the Space enclosed make a Floor of male Sand, with little Hillocks here and there of Fuller's Earth. Let your Poultry have a Shed in the Yard facing the South, and thick strewed with Ashes, and over this Places for them to lay their Eggs, and Perches to roost upon in the Night. Some are for keeping their Poultry in large Coops in some handsome inclosed Area facing the East; but those that are designed for laying and hatching of Eggs, as they are more cheerful, having their Liberty, so too they are more fruitful; whereas, those which are kept in a dark confined Place, seldom bring their Eggs to any Thing. Place your Dove-house so as to be in View of Water, and do not make it too lofty, but of such an easy Heigth, that the Pidgeons wearied with flying, or after sporting about in the Air with one another, may gently glide down upon it with Ease and Pleasure. Some there are who say that when the Pidgeon has found her Meat in the Field, the farther she has it to carry to her Young, the Fatter she makes them with it; and the Reason they give is, because the Meat which they carry Home to feed their Young in their Crop, by staying there a good While is half concocted; and upon this Account, they are for placing the Dove-house on some very high steep Situation. They think too, that it is best for the Dove-house to be at a pretty good Distance from its Water, that the Pidgeons may not chill their Eggs by coming to them with their Feet wet. If in one Corner of the Tower you enclose a Kastrel, it will secure your Dove-house from Birds of Prey. If under the Door you bury the Head of a Wolf strewed over with Cummin-seed, in an earthen Vessel full of Holes for the Smell to get out, it will bring you an infinite Number of Pidgeons. If you make your Dove-house Floor of Chalk, and wet it thoroughly with Man's Urine, you will bring Multitudes of Pidgeons from the Seats of their Ancestors, to take up their Abode with you. Before the Windows let there be Cornices of Stone, or of Olive-wood, projecting out a Cubit, for the Pidgeons to light upon at their coming Home, and to take their Flight from at their going Abroad. If the Young ones which are confined have a View of Trees and the Sky before they can fly, it will make them Droop and Pine away. Other smaller Birds which you have a Desire to breed, ought to have their Nests and Apartments made for them in some warm Place. Those which walk more than they fly, should have them low, and upon the Ground itself; for others they should be made higher. Each should have a separate Apartment, divided by Partitions on each Side to keep their Eggs or Young from falling out of the Nest. Clay is better to make the Nests of than Lime, and Lime than Terrass. All Sort of old Stone new cut is bad; Bricks are better than Turf, if not too much baked. The Wood either of Poplar or Fir is very useful. All the Apartments for Birds ought to be smooth, clean and sweet, and especially for Pidgeons. Even four footed Beasts, if kept nasty, will grow Scabby. Let every Part, therefore, be well done over with Rough-cast, and plaistered and white washed, not leaving the least Cranny unstopped, that Pole-cats, Weezels, Newts, or the like Vermin may not destroy the Eggs, or the Young, or prejudice the Wall; and be sure to make convenient Places to keep their Meat and Water in. It will be very Convenient for this Purpose to have a Moat quite round your House, wherein your Geese, Ducks, Hogs and Cows may water and wash themselves, and near which, in all Weathers, they may have as much Meat lying ready for them as they will eat. Let the Water and Meat for your smaller Fowls be kept in Tunnels along the Wall, so that they may not scatter or dirty it with their Feet; and you may have Pipes into these Tunnels from without, through which you may convey their Food into them. In the Middle, let there be a Place for them to wash in, with a constant supply of clean Water. Make your Fish-pond in a chalky Soil, and dig it so deep that the Water may neither be over heated by the Rays of the Sun, nor too easily frozen up by the Cold. Moreover, make some Caverns in the Sides, for the Fish to run into upon any sudden Disturbance of the Water, that they may not be wasted and worn away by continual Alarms. Fish are nourished by the Juices of the Earth; great Heat torments them, and extreme Frost kills them; but they are very much pleased and delighted by the Mid-day Sun. It is thought not amiss to have the turbid Floods after Rains flow into the Pond sometimes; but never upon the first Rain after the Dog-days; because they then have a strong Tincture of Lime, and will kill the Fish; and afterwards too they should be admitted but rarely, because their stinking Slime is apt to prejudice both the Fish and Water too; but still

still there ought to be a continual Flux and Reflux of Water, either from some Spring, River, Lake or Sea. But concerning Fish-ponds which are to be supplied by the Sea-water, the Ancients have given us fuller Instructions, in the following Manner. A muddy Soil affords the best Nourishment for flat Fish, such as Soals and the like, and a sandy is best for shell Fish. The Sea itself is best for others, as the Dory and Shark; and the Sea-thrust and Whiting feed best among the Rocks where they are naturally bred Lastly, they say that there can be no better Pond for keeping Fish in, than one so situated that the Waves of the Sea which flow into it are continually removing those which were in it before, not suffering the Water ever to stagnate, and that the flower the Water is in renewing, the less wholesome it is. And thus much may suffice as to the Care and Industry of the Farmer or Overseer, in the Affairs abovementioned. But we must not here omit the chief Thing needful with Re-lation to the gathering together and storing up the Fruits of the Harvest, and that is the Threshing-floor which ought to lie open to the Sun and Air, and not far from the Shed mentioned before, that upon any sudden Rain you may immediately remove both your Grain and Workmen into Shelter. In order to make your Floor, you need not give yourself the Trouble to lay the Ground exactly level; but only plain it pretty even, and then dig it up and throw a good Quantity of Lees of Oil upon it, and let it soak in thoroughly; then break the Clods very small and lay them down even, either with a Roller or a Harrow, and beat it down close with a Rammer; then pour some more Lees of Oil upon it, and when this is dried into it, neither Mice, nor Ants will come a-near it, neither will it ever grow poachy or produce Grass or Weeds. Chalk likewise adds a good Deal of Firmness to a Work of this Nature. And thus much for the Habitation of the Labourers.

Chap. XVII.

Of the Country House for a Gentleman; its various Parts, and the proper Disposition of each of those Parts.

SOME are of Opinion that a Gentleman's Country House should have quite different Conveniencies for Summer and for Winter; and the Rules they give for this Purpose are these: The Bed-chambers for the Winter should look towards the Point at which the Sun rises in Winter, and the Parlour, towards the Equinoctial Sun-setting; whereas the Bed-chambers for Summer should look to the South, the Parlours, to the Winter Sun-rising, and the Portico or Place for walking in, to the South. But, in my Opinion, all these Conveniencies ought to be varied according to the Difference of the Country and Climate, so as to temper Heat by Cold and Dry by Moist. I do not think it necessary for the Gentleman's House to stand in the most fruitful Part of his whole Estate, but rather in the most Honourable, where he can uncontrolled enjoy all the Pleasures and Conveniencies of Air, Sun, and fine Prospects, go down easily at any Time into his Estate, receive Strangers handsomely and spaciously, be seen by Passengers for a good Way round, and have a View of some City, Towns, the Sea, an open Plain, and the Tops of some known Hills and Mountains. Let him have the Delights of Gardens, and the Diversions of Fishing and Hunting close under his Eye. We have in another Place observed, that of the different Members of a House, some belong to the whole Family in general, other to a certain Number of Persons in it, and others again only to one or more Persons separately. In our Country House, with Regard to those Members which belong to the whole Family in general, let us imitate the Prince's Palace. Before the Door let there be a large open Space, for the Exercises either of Chariot or Horse Racing, much longer than a Youth can either draw a Bow or throw a Dart. Within the House, with Regard to those Conveniencies necessary for a Number of Persons in the Family, let there not be wanting open Places for Walking, Swimming, and other Diversions, Court-yards, Grass-plots and Porticoes, where the old Men may chat together in the kindly Warmth of the Sun in Winter, and where the Family may divert themselves and enjoy the Shade in Summer. It is manifest some Parts of the House are for the Family themselves, and others for the

the Things neceffary and ufeful to the Family. The Family confifts of the following Perfons: The Husband, the Wife, their Children and Relations, and all the different Sorts of Servants attendant upon thefe; befides which, Guefts too are to be reckoned as Part of the Family. The Things ufeful to the Family are Provifions and all Manner of Neceffaries, fuch as Cloths, Arms, Books, and Horfes alfo. The principal Member of the whole Building, is that which (whatever Names others may give it) I fhall call the Court-yard with its Portico; next to this is the Parlour, within this the Bedchambers, and laftly, the private Rooms for the particular Ufes of each Perfon in the Family. The other Members of the Houfe are fufficiently known by their Ufes. The Courtyard therefore is the principal Member, to which all the other fmaller Members muft correfpond, as being in a Manner a publick Market-place to the whole Houfe, which from this Court-yard derives all the Advantages of Communication and Light. For this Reafon every one defires to have his Court-yard as fpacious, large, open, handfome and convenient as poffible. Some content themfelves with one Courtyard, others are for having more, and for enclofing them all with very high Walls, or fome with higher and fome with lower; and they are for having them fome covered and others open, and others again half covered and half uncovered; in fome they would have a Portico only on one Side, in others on two or more, and in others all round; and thefe Porticoes, laftly, fome would build with flat, others with arched Roofs. Upon thefe Heads I have nothing more to fay, but that Regard muft be had to the Climate and Seafon, and to Neceffity and Convenience; fo as in cold Countries to ward againft the bleak North-wind, and the Severity of the Air and Soil; and in hot Climates, to avoid the troublefome and fcorching Rays of the Sun. Admit the pleafanteft Breezes on all Sides, and fuch a grateful Quantity of Light as is neceffary; but do not let your Court-yard be expofed to any noxious Vapours exhaled from any damp Place, nor to frequent hafty Showers from fome overlooking Hill in the Neighbourhood. Exactly anfwering the Middle of your Court-yard place your Entrance, with a handfome Veftibule, neither narrow, difficult or obfcure. Let the firft Room that offers itfelf be a Chapel dedicated to God, with its Altar, where Strangers and Guefts may offer their Devotions, beginning their Friend-

fhip by Religion; and where the Father of the Family may put up his Prayers for the Peace of his Houfe and the Welfare of his Relations. Here let him embrace thofe who come to vifit him, and if any Caufe be referred to him by his Friends, or he has any other ferious Bufinefs of that Nature to tranfact, let him do it in this Place. Nothing is handfomer in the Middle of the Portico, than Windows of Glafs, through which you may receive the Pleafure either of Sun or Air, according to the Seafon. *Martial* fays, that Windows looking to the South, receive a pure Sun and a clear Light; and the Ancients thought it beft to place their Porticoes fronting the South, becaufe the Sun in Summer running his Courfe higher, did not throw in his Rays, where they would enter in Winter. The Profpect of Hills to the South, when thofe Hills, on the Side which you have a View of, are continually covered with Clouds and Vapours, is not very pleafant, if they are at a great Diftance; and if they are near, and in a Manner juft over your Head, they will incommode you with chill Shadows and cold Rimes; but if they are at a convenient Diftance, they are both pleafant and convenient, becaufe they defend you from the fouthern Winds. Hills towards the North reverberating the Rays of the Sun, encreafe the Heat; but at a pretty good Diftance, they are very delightful, becaufe the Clearnefs of the Air, which is always ferene in fuch a Situation, and the Brightnefs of the Sun, which it always enjoys, is extremely chearful to the Sight. Hills to the Eaft and fo likewife to the Weft, will make your Mornings cold and the Dews plentiful, if they are near you; but both, if at fome tolerable Diftance, are wonderfully Pleafant. So too, Rivers and Lakes are inconvenient if too near, and afford no Delight, if too far off: Whereas, on the Contrary, the Sea, if it is at a large Diftance, makes both your Air and Sun unhealthy; but when it is clofe to you, it does you lefs Harm, becaufe then you have always an Equality in your Air. Indeed there is this to be faid, that when it is at a great Diftance, it encreafes the Defire we have to fee it. There is a good Deal too in the Point to which we lie open to it: For if you are expofed to the Sea towards the South, it fcorches you; if towards the Eaft, it infefts you with Damps; if to the Weft, it makes your Air cloudy and full of Vapours; and if to the North, it chills you with exceffive Cold. From the Court-yard we proceed to the Parlours, which muft be contrived for different Seasons, some to be used in Summer, others in Winter; and others as we may say in the middle Seasons. Parlours for Summer require Water and the Verdure of Gardens; those for Winter, must be warm and have good Fire-places. Both should be large, pleasant and delicate. There are many Arguments to convince us that Chimnies were in Use among the Ancients; but not such as ours are now. One of the Ancients says, the Tops of the Houses smoke, *Et fumant culmina tecti:* And we find it continues the same all over *Italy* to this Day, except in *Lombardy* and *Tuscany,* and that the Mouths of none of the Chimnies rise higher than the Tops of the Houses. *Vitruvius* says, that in Winter Parlours it is ridiculous to adorn the Ceiling with handsome Painting, because it will be presently spoilt by the constant Smoke and continual Fires; for which Reason the Ancients used to paint those Ceilings with Black, that it might seem to be done by the Smoke itself. I find too, that they made Use of a purified Sort of Wood, that was quite clear of Smoke, like our Charcoal, upon which Account it was a Dispute among the Lawyers, whether or no Coal was to come under the Denomination of Wood; and therefore it is probable they generally used moveable Hearths or Chafing-pans either of Brass or Iron, which they carried from Place to Place where-ever they had Occasion to make a Fire. And perhaps that warlike Race of Men, hardened by continual Incampments, did not make so much Use of Fire as we do now; and Physicians will not allow it wholesome, to be too much by the Fire-side. *Aristotle* says, that the Flesh of Animals gains its Firmness and Solidity from Cold; and those whose Business it is to take Notice of Things of this Nature have observed, that those working Men who are continually employed about the Furnace have generally dry wrinkled Skins; the Reason of which they say is, because the Juices, of which the Flesh is formed, are exhausted by the Fire, and evaporate in Steam. In *Germany, Colchos,* and other Places, where Fire is absolutely necessary against the extreme Cold, they make Use of Stoves; of which we shall speak elsewhere. Let us return to the Chimney, which may be best made serviceable in the following Manner. It must be as direct as possible, capacious, not too far from the Light, it must not draw the Wind too much, but enough however to carry up the Smoke, which else would not go up the Tunnel. For

these Reasons do not make it just in a Corner, nor too far within the Wall, nor let it take up the best Part of the Room where your chief Guests ought to sit. Do not let it be incommoded by the Air either of Doors or Windows, nor should it project too far out into the Room. Let its Tunnel be very wide and carried up perpendicular, and let the Top of it rise above the highest Part of the whole Building; and this not only upon Account of the Danger of Fire, but also to prevent the Smoke from being driven down the Chimney again by any Eddy of Wind on the Top of the House. Smoke being hot naturally mounts, and the Heat of the Flame quickens its Ascent: When it comes therefore into the Tunnel of the Chimney, it is compressed and straitened as in a Channel, and being pushed on by the Heat of the Fire, is thrust out in the same Manner as the Sound is out of a Trumpet. And as a Trumpet, if it is too big, does not give a clear Sound, because the Air has Room to rowl about in it; the same will hold good with Relation to the Smoke in a Chimney. Let the Top of the Chimney be covered to keep out Rain, and all round the Sides let there be wide Holes for the Passage of the Smoke, with Breaks projecting out between each Hole to keep off the Violence of the Wind. Where this is not so convenient, erect an upright Pin, and on it hang a brass Cover broad enough to take in the whole Mouth of the Chimney, and let this Cover have a Vane at the Top like a Sort of Crest, which like a Helm may turn it round according to the Wind. Another very good Method also is to set on the Chimney Top some Spire like a Hunter's Horn, either of Brass or baked Earth, broader at one End than the other, with the broad End turned downwards to the Mouth of the Chimney; by which means the Smoke being received in at the broad End, will force its Way out at the Narrow, in Spite of the Wind. To the Parlours we must accommodate the Kitchen, and the Pantry for setting by what is left after Meals, together with all Manner of Vessels and Linen. The Kitchen ought to be neither just under the Noses of the Guests, nor at too great a Distance; but so that the Victuals may be brought in neither too hot nor too cold, and that the Noise of the Scullions, with the Clatter of their Pans, Dishes and other Utensils, may not be troublesome. The Passage through which the Victuals are to be carried, should be handsome and convenient, not open to the Weather, nor

nor difhonoured by any Filth that may offend the Stomachs of the Guefts. From the Parlour the next Step is to the Bed-chamber; and for a Man of Figure and Elegance, there fhould be different ones of thefe latter, as well as of the former, for Summer and for Winter. This puts me in Mind of *Lucullus*'s Saying, that it is not fit a great Man fhould be worfe lodged than a Swallow or a Crane. However I fhall only fet down fuch Rules, with Relation to thefe Apartments, as are compatible with the greateft Modefty and Moderation. I remember to have read in *Æmilius Probus* the Hiftorian, that among the *Greeks* it was never ufual for the Wife to appear at Table, if any body was there befides Relations; and that the Apartments for the Women, were Parts of the Houfe where no Men ever fet his Foot except the neareft Kindred. And indeed I muft own I think the Apartments for the Ladies, ought to be facred like Places dedicated to Religion and Chaftity. I am befides for having the Rooms particularly defigned for Virgins and young Ladies, fitted up in the neateft and moft delicate Manner, that their tender Minds may pafs their Time in them with lefs Regret and be as little weary of themfelves as poffible. The Miftrefs of the Family fhould have an Apartment, in which fhe may eafily hear every Thing that is done in the Houfe. However, in thefe Particulars, the Cuftoms of every Country are always to be principally obferved. The Husband and the Wife fhould each have a feparate Chamber, not only that the Wife, either when fhe lies in, or in Cafe of any other Indifpofition, may not be troublefome to her Husband; but alfo that in Summer Time, either of them may lie alone whenever they think fit. Each of thefe Chambers fhould have its feparate Door, befides which there fhould be a common Paffage between them both, that one may go to the other without being obferved by any body. The Wife's Chamber fhould go into the Wardrobe; the Husband's into the Library. Their ancient Mother, who requires Tranquility and Repofe, fhould have a warm Chamber, well fecured againft the Cold, and out of the Way of all Noifes either from within or without. Be fure particularly to let it have a good Fire-place, and all other Conveniencies neceffary for an infirm Perfon, to comfort and cheer both the Body and Mind. Out of this Chamber let there be a Paffage to the Place where you keep your Treafure. Here place the Boys; and by the Wardrobe the

Girls, and near them the Lodgings for the Nurfes. Strangers and Guefts fhould be lodged in Chambers near the Veftibule or Fore-gate; that they may have full Freedom both in their own Actions, and in receiving Vifits from their Friends, without difturbing the Reft of the Family. The Sons of fixteen or feventeen Years old, fhould have Apartments oppofite to the Guefts, or at leaft not far from them, that they may have an Opportunity to converfe and grow familiar with them. The Strangers too fhould have fome Place to themfelves, where they may lock up any Thing private or valuable, and take it out again whenever they think fit. Next to the Lodgings of the young Gentlemen, fhould be the Place where the Arms are kept. Stewards, Officers and Servants fhould be fo lodged afunder from the Gentlemen, that each may have a convenient Place, fuitable to his refpective Bufinefs. The Maid-fervants and Valets fhould always be within eafy Call, to be ready upon any Occafion that they are wanted for. The Butler's Lodging fhould be near both to the Vault and Pantry. The Grooms fhould lie near the Stable. The Saddle-horfes ought not to be kept in the fame Place with thofe of Draught or Burthen; and they fhould be placed where they cannot offend the Houfe with any Smells, nor prejudice it by their Kicking, and out of all Danger of Fire. Corn and all Manner of Grain is fpoilt by Moifture, tarnifhed and turned pale by Heat, fhrunk by Wind, and rotted by the Touch of Lime. Where-ever therefore you intend to lay it, whether in a Cave, Pit, Vault, or on an open Area, be fure that the Place be thoroughly dry and perfectly clean and new made. *Jofephus* affirms, that there was Corn dug up near *Siboli* perfectly good and found, though it had lain hid above an hundred Years. Some fay, that Barley laid in a warm Place, will not fpoil; but it will keep very little above a Year. The Philofophers tell us, that Bodies are prepared for Corruption by Moifture, but are afterwards actually corrupted by Heat. If you make a Floor in your Granary of Lees of Oil mixed with Potter's Clay and Spart or Straw chopt fmall, and beat well together, your Grain will keep found upon it a great While, and be neither fpoilt by Weevil nor ftolen by the Ant. Granaries defigned only for Seeds are beft built of unbaked Bricks. The North-wind is lefs prejudicial than the South to all Stores of Seeds and Fruits; but any Wind whatfoever blowing from damp

Places

Places will fill them with Maggots and Worms; and any constant impetuous Wind will make them shrivelled and withered. For Pulse and especially Beans make a Floor of Ashes mixed with Lees and Oil. Keep Apples in some very close, but cool boarded Room. *Aristotle* is of Opinion, that they will keep the whole Year round in Bladders blown up and tied close. The Inconstancy of the Air is what spoils every Thing; and therefore keep every Breath of it from your Apples, if possible; and particularly the North-wind, which is thought to shrivel them up. We are told that Vaults for Wine should lie deep under Ground, and be very close stopt up; and yet there are some Wines which decay in the Shade. Wine is spoilt by the Eastern, Southern and Western Winds, and especially in the Winter or the Spring. If it is touched even by the North-wind in the Dog-days, it will receive Injury. The Rays of the Sun make it heady; those of the Moon, thick. If it is in the least stirred, it loses its Spirit and grows weak. Wine will take any Smell that is near it, and will grow dead near a Stink. When it is kept in a dry cool Place, always equally tempered, it will remain good for many Years. Wine, says *Columella*, so long as it is kept cool, so long it will keep good. Make your Vault for Wine therefore in a steady Place, never shaken by any Sort of Carriages; and its Sides and Lights should be towards the North. All Manner of Filth and ill Smells, Damps, Vapours, Smoke, the Stinks of all Sorts of rotten Garden-stuff, Onions, Cabbage, wild or domestick Figs, should by all Means be quite shut out. Let the Floor of your Vault be pargetted, and in the Middle make a little Trench, to save any Wine that may be spilt by the Fault of the Vessels. Some make their Vessels themselves of Stuc or Stone. The big-

ger the Vessel is, the more Spirit and Strength will be in the Wine. Oil delights in a warm Shade, and cannot endure any cold Wind; and is spoilt by Smoke or any other Steam. We shall not dwell upon coarser Matters; namely, how there ought to be two Places for keeping Dung in, one for the Old, and another for the New; that it loves the Sun and Moisture, and is dried up and exhausted by the Wind; but shall only give this general Rule, that those Places which are most liable to Danger by Fire, as Hay-lofts and the like, and those which are unpleasant either to the Sight or Smell, ought to be set out of the Way and separated by themselves. It may not be amiss just to mention here, that the Dung of Oxen will not breed Serpents. But there is one filthy Practise which I cannot help taking Notice of. We take Care in the Country to set the Dunghill out of the Way in some remote Corner, that the Smell may not offend our Ploughmen; and yet in our own Houses, in our best Chambers (where we ourselves are to rest) and as it were at our very Bolsters, we are so unpolite as to make secret Privies, or rather Store-rooms of Stink. If a Man is Sick, let him make use of a Close-stool; but when he is in Health, surely such Nastiness cannot be too far off. It is worth observing how careful Birds are, and particularly Swallows, to keep their Nests clean and neat for their young ones. The Example Nature herein sets us is wonderful. Even the young Swallows, as soon as ever Time has strengthened their Limbs will never Mute, but out of the Nest; and the old ones, to keep the Filth at a still greater Distance, will catch it in their Bills as it is falling, to carry it further off from their own Nest. Since Nature has given us this excellent Instruction, I think we ought by no means to neglect it.   112

Chap. XVIII.

The Difference between the Country House and Town House for the Rich. The Habitations of the middling Sort ought to resemble those of the Rich; at least in Proportion to their Circumstances. Buildings should be contrived more for Summer, than for Winter.

THE Country House and Town House for the Rich differ in this Circumstance; that they use their Country House chiefly for a Habitation in the Summer, and

their Town House as a convenient Place of Shelter in the Winter. In their Country House therefore they enjoy the Pleasures of Light, Air, spacious Walks and fine Prospects; in
Town,

Town, there are but few Pleasures, but those of Luxury and the Night. It is sufficient therefore if in Town they can have an Abode that does not want any Conveniencies for living with Health, Dignity and Politeness: But yet, as far as the Want of Room and Prospect will admit, our Habitation in Town should not be without any of the Delicacies of that in the Country. We should be sure to have a good Court-yard, Portico, Places for Exercise, and some Garden. If you are crampt for Room, and cannot make all your Conveniencies upon one Floor, make several Stories, by which means you may make the Members of your House as large as is necessary; and if the Nature of your Foundation will allow it, dig Places under Ground for your Wines, Oil, Wood, and even some Part of your Family, and such a Basement will add Majesty to your whole Structure. Thus you may build as many Stories as you please, till you have fully provided for all the Occasions of your Family. The principal Parts may be allotted to the principal Occasions; and the most Honourable, to the most Honourable. No Store-rooms should be wanting for laying up Corn, Fruits, and all Manner of Tools, Implements and Houshold-stuff; nor Places for divine Worship; nor Wardrobes for the Women. Nor must you be without convenient Store-rooms for laying up Cloaths designed for your Family to wear only on Holidays, and Arms both defensive and offensive, Implements for all Sorts of Works in Wool, Preparations for the Entertainment of Guests, and all Manner of Necessaries for any extraordinary Occasions. There should be different Places for those Things that are not wanted above once a Month, or perhaps once a Year, and for those that are in Use every Day. Every one of which, though they cannot be always kept lockt up in Store-rooms, ought however to be kept in some Place where they may be constantly in Sight; and especially such Things as are seldomest in Use; because those Things which are most in Sight, are least in Danger of Thieves. The Habitations of middling People ought to resemble the Delicacy of those of the richer Sort, in Proportion to their Circumstances; still imitating them with such Moderation, as not to run into a greater Expence than they can well support. The Country Houses for these, therefore, should be contrived with little less Regard to their Flocks and Herds, than to their Wives. Their Dove-house, Fish-ponds, and the like should be less for Pleasure, than for Profit: But yet their Country House should be built in such a Manner, that the Wife may like the Abode, and look after her Business in it with Pleasure; nor should we have our Eye so entirely upon Profit, as to neglect the Health of the Inhabitants. Whenever we have Occasion for Change of Air, *Celsus* advises us to take it in Winter; for our Bodies will grow accustomed to Winter Colds, with less Danger of our Health than to Summer Heats. But we, on the Contrary, are fond of going to our Country Houses chiefly in Summer; we ought therefore to take Care to have that the most Healthy. As for the Town House for a Tradesman, more Regard must be had to the Conveniency of his Shop, from whence his Gain and Livelihood is to arise than to the Beauty of his Parlour; the best Situation for this is, in Cross-ways, at a Corner; in a Market-place or Square, in the Middle of the Place; in a High-street, some remarkable jutting out; inasmuch as his chief Design is to draw the Eyes of Customers. In the middle Parts of his House he need have no Partitions but of unbaked Bricks and common Plaister; but in the Front and Sides, as he cannot always be sure of having honest Neighbours, he must make his Walls stronger against the Assaults both of Men and Weather. He should also build his House either at such a proper Distance from his next Neighbour's, that there may be room for the Air to dry the Walls after any Rain; or so close, that the Water may run off from both in the same Gutter; and let the Top of the House, and the Gutters particularly, have a very good Slope, that the Rain may neither lie soaking too long, nor dash back into the House; but be carried away as quick and as clear as possible. There remains nothing now but to recollect some few Rules laid down in the first Book, and which seem to belong to this Head. Let those Parts of the Building which are to be particularly secure against Fire, and the Injuries of the Weather, or which are to be closer or freer from Noise, be all vaulted; so likewise should all Places under Ground: But for Rooms above Ground, flat Ceilings are wholesomer. Those which require the clearest Light, such as the common Parlour, the Portico, and especially the Library, should be situated full East? Those Things which are injured by Moths, Rust or Milldew, such as Cloaths, Books, Arms, and all Manner

        of

of Provifions, fhould be kept towards the South or Weft. If there be Occafion for an equal conftant Light, fuch as is neceffary for Painters, Writers, Sculptors and the like, let them have it from the North. Laftly, let all Summer Apartments ftand open to the Northern Winds, all Winter ones to the South, and all thofe for Spring and Autumn to the Eaft. Baths and fupper Parlours for the Spring Seafon fhould be towards the Weft. And if you cannot poffibly have all thefe exactly according to your Wifh, at leaft chufe out the moft convenient Places for your Summer Apartments: For in-deed, in my Opinion, a wife Man fhould build rather for Summer than for Winter. We may eafily arm ourfelves againft the Cold by making all clofe, and keeping good Fires; but many more Things are requifite againft Heat, and even all will fometimes be no great Relief. Let Winter Rooms therefore be fmall, low and little Windows, and Summer ones, on the Contrary, large, fpacious, and open to cool Breezes, but not to the Sun or the hot Air that comes from it. A great Quantity of Air inclofed in a large Room, is like a great Quantity of Water, not eafily heated.

The End of Book V.

THE

THE
ARCHITECTURE
OF
Leone Batiſta Alberti.

BOOK VI. CHAP. I.

Of the Reaſon and Difficulty of the Author's Undertaking, whereby it appears how much Pains, Study and Application he has employed in writing upon theſe Matters.

N the five preceding Books we have treated of the Deſigns, of the Materials for the Work, of the Workmen, and of every Thing elſe that appeared neceſſary to the Conſtruction of an Edifice, whether publick or private, ſacred or profane, ſo far as related to its being made ſtrong againſt all Injuries of Weather, and convenient for its reſpective Uſe, as to Times Places, Men and Things: With how much Care we have treated of all theſe Matters, you may ſee by the Books themſelves, from whence you may judge whether it was poſſible to do it with much greater. The Labour indeed was much more than I could have foreſeen at the Beginning of this Undertaking. Continual Difficulties every Moment aroſe either in explaining the Matter, or inventing Names, or methodizing the Subject, which perfectly confounded me, and diſheartened me from my Undertaking. On the other Hand, the ſame Reaſons which induced me to begin this Work, preſſed and encouraged me to proceed. It grieved me that ſo many great and noble Inſtructions of ancient Authors ſhould be loſt by the Injury of Time, ſo that ſcarce any but *Vitruvius* has eſcaped this general Wreck: A Writer indeed of univerſal Knowledge, but ſo maimed by Age, that in many Places there are great Chaſms, and many Things imperfect in others. Beſides this, his Style is abſolutely void of all Ornaments, and he wrote in ſuch a Manner, that to the *Latins* he ſeems to write *Greek*, and to the *Greeks*, *Latin*: But indeed it is plain from the Book itſelf, that he wrote neither *Greek* nor *Latin*, and he might almoſt as well have never wrote at all, at leaſt with Regard to us, ſince we cannot underſtand him. There remained many Examples of the ancient Works, Temples and Theatres, from whence, as from the moſt ſkilful Maſters, a great deal was to be learned; but theſe I ſaw, and with Tears I ſaw it, mouldering away daily. I obſerved too that thoſe who in theſe Days happen to undertake any new Structure, generally ran after the Whims of the Moderns, inſtead of being delighted and directed by the Juſtneſs of more noble Works. By this Means it was plain, that this Part of Knowledge, and in a Manner of Life itſelf, was likely in a ſhort Time to be wholly loſt. In this unhappy State of Things, I could not help having it long, and often, in my Thoughts to write upon this Subject myſelf. At the ſame Time I conſidered that in the Examination of ſo many noble and uſeful

Matters,

Matters, and so necessary to Mankind; it would be a Shame to neglect any of those Observations which voluntarily offered themselves to me; and I thought it the Duty of an honest and studious Mind, to endeavour to free this Science, for which the most Learned among the Ancients had always a very great Esteem, from its present Ruin and Oppression. Thus I stood doubtful, and knew not how to resolve, whether I should drop my Design, or go on. At length my Love and Inclination for these Studies prevailed; and what I wanted in Capacity, I made up in Diligence and Application. There was not the least Remain of any ancient Structure, that had any Merit in it, but what I went and examined, to see if any Thing was to be learned from it. Thus I was continually searching, considering, measuring and making Draughts of every Thing I could hear of, till such Time as I had made myself perfect Master of every Contrivance or Invention that had been used in those ancient Remains; and thus I alleviated the Fatigue of writing, by the Thirst and Pleasure of gaining Information. And indeed the Collecting together, rehearsing without Meanness, reducing into a just Method,

writing in an accurate Style, and explaining perspicuously so many various Matters, so unequal, so dispersed, and so remote from the common Use and Knowledge of Mankind, certainly required a greater Genius, and more Learning than I can pretend to. But still I shall not repent of my Labour, if I have only effected what I chiefly proposed to myself, namely, to be clear and intelligible to the Reader, rather than Eloquent. How difficult a Thing this is, in handling Subjects of this Nature, is better known to those who have attempted it, then believed by those who never tried it. And I flatter myself, it will at least be allowed me, that I have wrote according to the Rules of this Language, and in no obscure Style. We shall endeavour to do the same in the remaining Parts of this Work. Of the three Properties required in all Manner of Buildings, namely, that they be accommodated to their respective Purposes, stout and strong for Duration, and pleasant and delightful to the Sight, we have dispatched the two first, and are now to treat of the third, which is by much the most Noble of all, and very necessary besides.

C H A P. II.

Of Beauty and Ornament, their Effects and Difference, that they are owing to Art and Exactness of Proportion; as also of the Birth and Progress of Arts.

IT is generally allowed, that the Pleasure and Delight which we feel on the View of any Building, arise from nothing else but Beauty and Ornament, since there is hardly any Man so melancholy or stupid, so rough or unpolished, but what is very much pleased with what is beautiful, and pursues those Things which are most adorned, and rejects the unadorned and neglected; and if in any Thing that he Views he perceives any Ornament is wanting, he declares that there is something deficient which would make the Work more delightful and noble. We should therefore consult Beauty as one of the main and principal Requisites in any Thing which we have a Mind should please others. How necessary our Forefathers, Men remarkable for their Wisdom, looked upon this to be, appears, as indeed from almost every thing they did, so particularly from their Laws, their Militia, their sacred and all other pub-

lick Ceremonies; which it is almost incredible what Pains they took to adorn; insomuch that one would almost imagine they had a Mind to have it thought, that all these Things (so absolutely necessary to the Life of Mankind) if stript of their Pomp and Ornament, would be somewhat stupid and insipid. When we lift up our Eyes to Heaven, and view the wonderful Works of God, we admire him more for the Beauties which we see, than for the Conveniencies which we feel and derive from them. But what Occasion is there to insist upon this? When we see that Nature consults Beauty in a Manner to excess, in every Thing she does, even in painting the Flowers of the Field. If Beauty therefore is necessary in any Thing, it is so particularly in Building, which can never be without it, without giving Offence both to the Skilful and the Ignorant. How are we moved by a huge shapeless ill-contrived Pile
of

of Stones? the greater it is, the more we blame the Folly of the Expence, and condemn the Builder's inconsiderate Lust of heaping up Stone upon Stone without Contrivance. The having satisfied Necessity is a very small Matter, and the having provided for Conveniency affords no Manner of Pleasure, where you are shocked by the Deformity of the Work. Add to this, that the very Thing we speak of is itself no small help to Conveniency and Duration: For who will deny that it is much more convenient to be lodged in a neat handsome Structure, than in a nasty ill-contrived Hole? or can any Building be made so strong by all the Contrivance of Art, as to be safe from Violence and Force? But Beauty will have such an Effect even upon an enraged Enemy, that it will disarm his Anger, and prevent him from offering it any Injury: Insomuch that I will be bold to say, there can be no greater Security to any Work against Violence and Injury, than Beauty and Dignity. Your whole Care, Diligence and Expence, therefore should all tend to this, that whatever you build may be not only useful and convenient, but also handsomely adorned, and by that means delightful to the Sight, that whoever views it may own the Expence could never have been better bestowed. But what Beauty and Ornament are in themselves, and what Difference there is between them, may perhaps be easier for the Reader to conceive in his Mind, than for me to explain by Words. In order therefore to be as brief as possible, I shall define Beauty to be a Harmony of all the Parts, in whatsoever Subject it appears, fitted together with such Proportion and Connection, that nothing could be added, diminished or altered, but for the Worse. A Quality so Noble and Divine, that the whole Force of Wit and Art has been spent to procure it; and it is but very rarely granted to any one, or even to Nature herself, to produce any Thing every Way perfect and compleat. How extraordinary a Thing (says the Person introduced in *Tully*) is a handsome Youth in *Athens!* This Critick in Beauty found that there was something deficient or superfluous, in the Persons he disliked, which was not compatible with the Perfection of Beauty, which I imagine

might have been obtained by Means of Ornament, by painting and concealing any Thing that was deformed, and trimming and polishing what was handsome; so that the unsightly Parts might have given less Offence, and the more lovely more Delight. If this be granted we may define Ornament to be a Kind of an auxiliary Brightness and Improvement to Beauty. So that then Beauty is somewhat lovely which is proper and innate, and diffused over the whole Body, and Ornament somewhat added or fastened on, rather than proper and innate. To return therefore where we left off. Whoever would build so as to have their Building commended, which every reasonable Man would desire, must build according to a Justness of Proportion, and this Justness of Proportion must be owing to Art. Who therefore will affirm, that a handsome and just Structure can be raised any otherwise than by the Means of Art? and consequently this Part of Building, which relates to Beauty and Ornament, being the Chief of all the Rest, must without doubt be directed by some sure Rules of Art and Proportion, which whoever neglects will make himself ridiculous. But there are some who will by no means allow of this, and say that Men are guided by a Variety of Opinions in their Judgment of Beauty and of Buildings; and that the Forms of Structures must vary according to every Man's particular Taste and Fancy, and not be tied down to any Rules of Art. A common Thing with the Ignorant, to despise what they do not understand! It may not therefore be amiss to confute this Error; not that I think it necessary to enter into a long Discussion about the Origin of Arts, from what Principles they were deduced, and by what Methods improved. I shall only take Notice that all Arts were begot by Chance and Observation, and nursed by Use and Experience, and improved and perfected by Reason and Study. Thus we are told that Physick was invented in a thousand Years by a thousand thousand Men; and so too the Art of Navigation; as, indeed, all other Arts have grown up by Degrees from the smallest Beginnings.

G g

CHAP. III.

That Architecture began in Asia, *flourished in* Greece, *and was brought to Perfection in* Italy.

THE Art of Building, as far as I can gather from the Works of the Ancients, spent the first Vigour of its Youth (if I may be allowed that Expreſſion) in *Aſia:* It afterwards flouriſhed among the *Greeks*; and at laſt came to its full Maturity in *Italy.* And this Account ſeems very probable; for the Kings of *Aſia* abounding in Wealth and Leiſure, when they came to conſider themſelves, their own Riches, and the Greatneſs and Majeſty of their Empire, and found that they had Occaſion for larger and nobler Habitations, they began to ſearch out and collect every Thing that might ſerve to this Purpoſe; and in order to make their Buildings larger and handſomer, began perhaps with building their Roofs of larger Timbers, and their Walls of a better Sort of Stone. This ſhewed noble and great, and not unhandſome. Then finding that ſuch Works were admired for being very large, and imagining that a King was obliged to do ſomething which private Men could not effect, theſe great Monarchs began to be delighted with huge Works, which they fell to raiſing with a Kind of Emulation of one another, till they came to erecting thoſe wild immenſe Moles, the Pyramids. Hereupon I imagine that by frequent Building they began to find out the Difference that there was between a Structure built in one Manner, and one built in another, and ſo getting ſome Notion of Beauty and Proportion, began to neglect thoſe Things which wanted thoſe Qualities. *Greece* came next; which flouriſhing in excellent Geniuſſes and Men of Learning, paſſionately deſirous of adorning their Country, began to erect Temples and other publick Structures. They then thought fit to look abroad and take a more careful View of the Works of the *Aſſyrians* and *Ægyptians*, till at laſt they came to underſtand that in all Things of this Nature the Skill of the Workman was more admired than the Wealth of the Prince: For any one that is rich may raiſe a great Pile of Building; but to raiſe ſuch a one as may be commended by the Skilful, is the Part only of a ſuperior Genius. Hereupon *Greece* finding that in theſe

Works ſhe could not equal thoſe Nations in Expence, reſolved to try if ſhe could not out-do them in Ingenuity. She began therefore to trace and deduce this Art of Building, as indeed ſhe did all others, from the very Lap of Nature itſelf, examining, weighing and conſidering it in all its Parts with the greateſt Diligence and Exactneſs: enquiring with the greateſt Strictneſs into the Difference between thoſe Buildings which were highly praiſed, and thoſe which were diſliked, without neglecting the leaſt Particular. She tried all Manner of Experiments, ſtill tracing and keeping cloſe to the Footſteps of Nature, mingling uneven Numbers with even, ſtrait Lines with Curves, Light with Shade, hoping that as it happens from the Conjunction of Male and Female, ſhe ſhould by the Mixture of theſe Oppoſites hit upon ſome third Thing that would anſwer her Purpoſe: Nor even in the moſt minute Particulars did ſhe neglect to weigh and conſider all the Parts over and over again, how thoſe on the right Hand agreed with thoſe on the left, the Upright with the Platform, the nearer with the more remote, adding, diminiſhing, proportioning the great Parts to the Small, the Similar to the Diſſimilar, the Laſt to the Firſt, till ſhe had clearly demonſtrated that different Rules were to be obſerved in thoſe Edifices which were intended for Duration, to ſtand as it were Monuments to Eternity, and thoſe which were deſigned chiefly for Beauty. Theſe were the Methods purſued by the *Greeks.* *Italy*, in her firſt Beginnings, having Regard wholly to Parſimony, concluded that the Members in Buildings ought to be contrived in the ſame Manner as in Animals; as, for Inſtance, in a Horſe, whoſe Limbs are generally moſt beautiful when they are moſt uſeful for Service: from whence they inferred that Beauty was never ſeparate and diſtinct from Conveniency. But afterwards when they had obtained the Empire of the World, being then no leſs inflamed than the *Greeks* with the Deſire of adorning their City and themſelves, in leſs than thirty Years that which before was the fineſt Houſe in the whole City of *Rome*, could not then

then be reckoned so by a hundred; and they abounded in such an incredible Number of ingenious Men who exercise their Talent this Way, that we are told there was at one Time no less than seven hundred Architects at *Rome*, whose Works were so noble that the extraordinary Praise which is bestowed upon them, is hardly equal to their Merit. And as the Wealth of the Empire was sufficient to bear the Expence of the most stately Structures, so we are told that a private Man, by Name *Tatius*, at his own proper Charges built Baths for the People of *Ostia* with an hundred Columns of *Numidian* Marble. But still though the Condition of their State was thus flourishing, they thought it most laudable to join the Magnificence of the most profuse Monarchs, to the ancient Parsimony and frugal Contrivance of their own Country: But still in such a Manner, that their Frugality should not prejudice Conveniency, nor Conveniency be too cautious and fearful of Expence; but that both should be embellished by every thing that was delicate or beautiful. In a Word, being to the greatest Degree careful and exact in all their Buildings, they became at last so excellent in this Art, that there was nothing in it so hiden or secret but what they traced out, discovered and brought to light, by the Favour of Heaven, and the Art itself not frowning upon their Endeavours: For the Art of Building having had her ancient Seat in *Italy*, and especially among the *Hetrurians*, who besides those miraculous Structures which we read to have been erected by their Kings, of Labyrinths and Sepulchres, had among them some excellent ancient Writings, which taught the Manner of building Temples, according to the Practice of the Ancient *Tuscans*: I say, this Art having had her ancient Seat in *Italy*, and knowing with how much Fervour she was courted there, she seems to have resolved, that this Empire of the World, which was already adorned with all other Virtues, should be made still more admirable by her Embellishments. For this Reason she gave herself to them to be throughly known and understood; thinking it a Shame that the Head of the Universe and the Glory of all Nations should be equalled in Magnificence by those whom she had excelled in all Virtues and Sciences. Why should I insist here upon their Porticoes, Temples, Gates, Theatres, Baths, and other gigantick Structures; Works so amazing, that though they were actually executed, some very great foreign Architects thought them impracticable. In short, I need say no more than that they could not bear to have even their common Drains void of Beauty, and were so delighted with Magnificence and Ornament, that they thought it no Profusion to spend the Wealth of the State in Buildings that were hardly designed for any thing else. By the Examples therefore of the Ancients, and the Precepts of great Masters, and constant Practice, a thorough Knowledge is to be gained of the Method of raising such magnificent Structures; from this Knowledge sound Rules are to be drawn, which are by no means to be neglected by those who have not a Mind to make themselves ridiculous by building, as I suppose nobody has. These Rules it is our Business here to collect and explain, according to the best of our Capacity. Of these some regard the universal Beauty and Ornament of the whole Edifice; other the particular Parts and Members taken separately. The former are taken immediately from Philosophy and are intended to direct and regulate the Operations of this Art; the others from Experience, as we have shewn above, only filed and perfected by the Principles of Philosophy. I shall speak first of those wherein this particular Art is most concerned; and as for the others, which relate to the Universality, they shall serve by Way of Epilogue.

118

Chap. IV.

That Beauty and Ornament in every Thing arise from Contrivance, or the Hand of the Artificer, or from Nature; and that though the Region indeed can hardly be improved by the Wit or Labour of Man, yet many other Things may be done highly worthy of Admiration, and scarcely credible.

THAT which delights us in Things that are either beautiful or finely adorned, must proceed either from the Contrivance and Invention of the Mind, or the Hand of the Artificer, or from somewhat derived immediately from Nature herself. To the Mind belong

long the Election, Distribution, Disposition, and other Things of the like Nature which give Dignity to the Work: To the Hand, the amassing, adding, diminishing, chipping, polishing, and the like, which make the Work delicate: The Qualities derived from Nature are Heaviness, Lightness, Thickness, Clearness, Durability, &c. which make the Work wonderful. These three Operations are to be adapted to the several Parts according to their various Uses and Offices. There are several Ways of dividing and considering the different Parts: But at present we shall divide all Buildings either according to the Parts in which they generally agree, or to those in which they generally differ. In the first Book we saw that all Edifices must have Region, Situation, Compartition, Walling, Covering, and Apertures; in these Particulars therefore they agree. But then in these others they differ, namely, that some are Sacred, others Profane, some Publick, others Private, some designed for Necessity, others for Pleasure, and so on. Let us begin with those Particulars wherein they agree. What the Hand or Wit of Man can add to the Region, either of Beauty or Dignity, is hardly discoverable; unless we would give into those miraculous and superstitious Accounts which we read of some Works. Nor are the Undertakers of such Works blamed by prudent Men, if their Designs answer any great Conveniency; but if they take Pains to do what there was no Necessity for, they are justly denied the Praise they hunt after. For who would be so daring as to undertake, like *Staficrates*, (according to *Plutarch*) or *Dinocrates* (according to *Vitruvius*) to make Mount *Athos* into a Statue of *Alexander*, and in one of the Hands to build a City big enough to contain ten thousand Men? Indeed I should not discommend Queen *Nitocris* for having forced the River *Euphrates*, by making vast Cuts, to flow three Times round the City of the *Assyrians*, if she made the Region strong and secure by those Trenches, and fruitful by the overflowing of the Water. But let us leave it to mighty Kings to be delighted with such Undertakings: Let them join Sea to Sea by cutting the Land between them: Let them level Hills: Let them make new Islands, or join old ones to the Continent: Let them put it out of the Power of any others to imitate them, and so make their Names memorable to Posterity: Still all their vast Works will be commended not so much in Proportion to their Greatness as their Use. The Ancients sometimes added Dignity not only to particular Groves, but even to the whole Region, by Means of Religion. We read that all *Sicily* was consecrated to *Ceres*; but these are Things not now to be insisted upon. It will be of great and real Advantages, if the Region be possessed of some rare Quality, no less useful than extraordinary: As for Instance, if the Air be more temperate than in any other Place, and always equal and uniform, as we are told it is at *Moroe*, where Men live in a Manner as long as they please; or if the Region produces something not to be found elsewhere and very desirable and wholesome to Man, as that which produces Amber, Cinnamon, and Balsam; or if it has some divine Influence in it, as there is in the Soil of the Island *Eubœa*, where we are told nothing noxious is produced. The Situation, being a certain determinate Part of the Region, is adorned by all the same Particulars as beautify the Region itself. But Nature generally offers more Conveniencies, and those more ready at Hand, for adorning the Situation than the Region; for we very frequently meet with Circumstances extreamly noble and surprising, such as Promontories, Rocks, broken Hills vastly high and sharp, Grottoes, Caverns, Springs and the like; near which, if we would have our Situation strike the Beholders with Surprize, we may build to our Hearts desire. Nor should their be wanting in the Prospect Remains of Antiquity, on which we cannot turn our Eyes without considering the various Revolutions of Men and Things, and being filled with Wonder and Admiration. I need not mention the Place where *Troy* once stood, or the Plains of *Leuctra* stained with Blood, nor the Fields near *Trasumenus*, and a thousand other Places memorable for some great Event. How the Hand and Wit of Man may add to the Beauty of the Situation, is not so easily shewn. I pass over Things commonly done; such as Plane-trees brought by Sea to the Island of *Tremeti* to adorn the Situation, or Columns, Obelisks and Trees left by great Men in order to strike Posterity with Veneration; as for Instance, the Olive-tree planted by *Neptune* and *Minerva*, which flourished for so many Ages in the Citadel of *Athens*: I likewise pass over ancient Traditions handed down from Age to Age, as that of the Turpentine-tree near *Hebron*, which was reported to have stood from the Creation of the World to the Days of *Josephus* the Historian. Nothing can give

119
120
121

give a greater Air of Dignity and Awfulnefs to a Place than fome artful Laws made by the Ancients; fuch as thefe: That nothing Male fhould prefume to fet Foot in the Temple of the *Bona Dea*, nor in that of *Diana* in the Patrician Portico; and at *Tanagra*, that no Woman fhould enter the facred Grove, nor the inner Parts of the Temple of *Jerufalem*; and that no Perfon whatfoever, befides the Prieft, and he only in order to purify himfelf for Sacrifice, fhould wafh in the Fountain near *Panthos*; and that nobody fhould prefume to fpit in the Place called *Doliola* near the great Drain at *Rome*, where the Bones of *Numa Pompilius* were depofited; and upon fome Chapels there have been Infcriptions, ftrictly forbidding any common Proftitute to enter; in the Temple of *Diana* at *Crete*, none were admitted, except they were bare-footed; it was unlawful to bring a Bond-woman into the Temple of the Goddefs *Matuta*; and all common Cryers were excluded from the Temple of *Orodio* at *Rhodes*, and all Fiddlers from that of *Tewnius* at *Tenedos*. So again, it was unlawful to go out of the Temple of *Jupiter Alfiftius* without facrificing, and to carry any Ivy into the Temple of *Minerva* at *Athens*, or into that of *Venus* at *Thebes*. In the Temple of *Fauna*, it was not lawful fo much as to mention the Name of Wine. In the fame Manner it was decreed, that the Gate *Janualis* at *Rome* fhould never be fhut, but in Time of War, nor the Temple of *Janus* ever opened in Time of Peace; and that the Temple of the Goddefs *Hora* fhould ftand always open. If we were to imitate any of thefe Cuftoms, perhaps it might not be amifs to make it criminal for Women to enter the Temples of Martyrs; or Men, thofe dedicated to Virgin Saints. Moreover there are fome Advantages very defirable, faid to be procured by Art, which when we read of, we could fcarcely believe, unlefs we faw fomething like it in fome particular Places even at this Day. We are told that it was brought about by human Art, that in *Conftantinople* Serpents will never hurt any body, and that no Daws will fly within the Walls; and that no Grafshoppers are ever heard in *Naples*, nor any Owls in *Candy*. In the Temple of *Achilles*, in the Ifland of *Boriftbenes* no Bird whatfoever will enter, nor any Dog or Fly of any Sort in the Temple of *Hercules* near the *Forum Boarium* at *Rome*. But what fhall we fay of this furprizing Particularity, that at *Venice*, even at this Day, no Kind of Fly ever enters the pub-

lick Palace of the *Cenfors*? And even in the Flefh-market at *Toledo*, there is never more than one Fly feen throughout the Year, and that a remarkable one for its Whitenefs. Thefe ftrange Accounts which we find in Authors, are too numerous to be all inferted here, and whether they are owing to Nature or Art, I fhall not now pretend to decide. But then, again, how can we, either by Nature or Art, account for what they tell us of a Laurel-tree growing in the Sepulchre of *Bibrias* King of *Pontus*, from which if the leaft Twig is broken, and put aboard a Ship, that Ship fhall never be free from Mutinies and Tumults till the Twig is thrown out of it: Or for its never raining upon the *Altar* in *Venus*'s Temple at *Paphos*: Or for this, that whatever Part of the Sacrifice is left at *Minerva*'s Shrine in *Phrygia minor*, will never corrupt: Or this, if you break off any Part of *Anteus*'s Sepulchre, it immediately begins to rain, and never leaves off till it is made whole again? Some indeed affirm, that all thefe Things may be done by an Art, now loft, by means of little conftellated Images, which Aftronomers pretend are not unknown to them. I remember to have read in the Author of the Life of *Apollonius Tyaneus*, that in the chief Apartments of the Royal Palace at *Babylon*, fome Magicians faftened to the Cieling four golden Birds, which they called the Tongues of the Gods, and that thefe were endued with the Virtue of conciliating the Affection of the Multitude towards their King: And *Jofephus*, a very grave Author, fays that he himfelf faw a certain Man named *Eleazer*, who in the Prefence of the Emperor *Vefpafian* and his Sons, immediately cured a Man that was poffeffed, by faftening a Ring to his Nofe; and the fame Author writes that *Solomon* compofed certain Verfes, which would give Eafe in Diftempers; and *Eufebius Pamphilus* fays, that the *Ægyptian* God *Serapis*, whom we call *Pluto*, invented certain Charms which would drive away evil Spirits, and taught the Methods by which *Dæmons* affumed the Shapes of brute Beafts to do mifchief. *Servius* too fays, that there were Men who ufed to carry Charms about them, by which they were fecured againft all unhappy Turns of Fortune; and that thofe Charms were fo powerful, that the Perfons who wore them could never die till they were taken from them. If thefe Things could be true, I fhould eafily believe what we read in *Plutarch*, that among the *Pelenei* there was an Image, which if it were brought out of the

Temple

Temple by the Priest, filled every Creature with Terror and Dread on whatever Side it was turned; and that no Eye durst look towards it, for Fear. These miraculous Accounts we have inserted only by way of Amusement. As to other Particulars which may help to make the Situation beautiful, considered in a general View, such as the Circumference, the Space round about it, its Elevation, Levelling, Strengthening, and the like, I have nothing more to say here, but to refer you for Instructions to the first and third Books. The chief Qualities requisite in a Situation or Platform (as we have there observed) are to be perfectly dry, even, and solid, as also convenient and suitable to the Purpose of the Building; and it will be a very great Help to it, to strengthen it with a good Bottom made of baked Earth, in the Manner which we shall teach when we come to treat of the Wall. We must not here omit an Observation made by *Plato*, that it will be a great Addition to the Dignity of the Place, if you give it some great Name; and this we find the Emperor *Adrian* was very fond of doing, when he gave the Names of *Lycus*, *Canopeis*, *Academia*, *Tempe* and other great Titles to the several Parts of his *Villa* at *Tivoli*.

C H A P. V.

A short Recapitulation of the Compartition, and of the just Composition and adorning the Wall and Covering.

THOUGH we have already said almost as much as was necessary of the Compartition in the first Book, yet we shall take a brief Review of it again here. The chief and first Ornament of any Thing is to be free from all Improprieties. It will therefore be a just and proper Compartition, if it is neither confused nor interrupted, neither too rambling nor composed of unsuitable Parts, and if the Members be neither too many nor too few, neither too small nor too large, not mis-matcht nor unsightly, nor as it were separate and divided from the Rest of the Body: But every Thing so disposed according to Nature and Convenience, and the Uses for which the Structure is intended, with such Order, Number, Size, Situation and Form, that we may be satisfied there is nothing throughout the whole Fabrick, but what was contrived for some Use or Convenience, and with the handsomest Compactness of all the Parts. If the Compartition answers in all these Respects, the Beauty and Richness of any Ornaments will sit well upon it; if not, it is impossible it should have any Air of Dignity at all. The whole Composition of the Members therefore should seem to be made and directed entirely by Necessity and Conveniency; so that you may not be so much pleased that there are such or such Parts in the Building, as that they are disposed and laid out in such a Situation, Order and Connection. In adorning the Wall and Covering, you will have sufficient Room to display the finest Materials produced by Nature, and the most curious Contrivance and Skill of the Artificer. If it were in your Power to imitate the ancient *Osiris*, who, we are told, built two Temples of Gold, one to the Heavenly, the other to the Royal *Jupiter*; or if you could raise some vast Stone, almost beyond humane Belief, like that which *Semiramis* brought from the Mountains of *Arabia*, which was twenty Cubits broad every Way, and an hundred and fifty long; or if you had such large Stone, that you could make some Part of the Work all of one Piece, like a Chapel in *Latona*'s Temple in *Ægypt*, forty Cubits wide in Front, and hollowed in one single Stone, and so also covered with another: This no doubt would create a vast deal of Admiration in the Beholders, and especially if the Stone was a foreign one, and brought through difficult Ways, like that which *Herodotus* relates to have been brought from the City of *Elephantis*, which was about twenty Cubits broad, and fifteen high, and was carried as far as *Susa* in twenty Days. It will also add greatly to the Ornament and Wonder of the Work, if such an extraordinary Stone be set in a remarkable and honourable Place. Thus the little Temple at *Chemmis*, an Island in *Ægypt*, is not so surprizing upon Account of being covered with one single Stone, as upon Account of such a huge Stone's being raised to so great a Height. The Rarity and Beauty of the Stone itself will also add greatly to the Ornament; as for Instance, if it is that sort of Marble, with which

which we are told *Nero* built a Temple to *Fortune* in his golden Palace, which was so white, so clear and transparent, that even when all the Doors were shut the Light seemed to be enclose within the Temple. All these Things are very Noble in themselves; but they will make no Figure if there is not Care and Art used in their Composition or putting together: For every Thing must be reduced to exact Measure, so that all the Parts may correspond with one another, the Right with the Left, the lower Parts with the Upper, with nothing interfering that may blemish either the Order or the Materials, but every Thing squared to exact Angles and similar Lines. We may often observe that base Materials managed with Art, make a handsomer Shew than the Noblest heaped together in Confusion. Who can imagine that the Wall of *Athens*, which *Thucydides* informs us was built so tumultuously that they even threw into it some of the Statues of their Sepulchres, could have any Beauty in it, or be any ways adorned by being full of broken Statues? On the Contrary, we are very much pleased with the Walls of some old Country-Houses, though they are built of any Stone that the People could pick up; because they are disposed in even Rows, with an alternate Checquer of Black and White: so that considering the Meanness of the Structure, nothing can be desired handsomer. But perhaps this Consideration belongs rather to that Part of the Wall which is called the outward Coat, than to the Body of the Wall itself. To conclude, all your Materials should be so distributed that nothing should be begun, but according to some judicious Plan; nothing carried on but in pursuance of the same; and no Part of it left imperfect, but finished and compleated with the utmost Care and Diligence. But the principal Ornament both of the Wall and Covering, and especially of all vaulted Roofs (always excepted Columns) is the outward Coat: And this may be of several Sorts; either all white, or adorned with Figures and Stuc-work, or with Painting, or Pictures set in Pannels, or with *Mosaic* Work, or else a Mixture of all these together.

Chap. VI.

In what Manner great Weights and large Stones are moved from one Place to another or raised to any great Height.

OF those Ornaments last mentioned we are to treat; and to shew what they are and how they are to be made; but having in the last Chapter mentioned the moving of vast Stones, it seems necessary here to give some Account in what Manner such huge Bodies are moved, and how they are raised to such high and difficult Places. *Plutarch* relates that *Archimedes*, the great Mathematician of *Syracuse*, drew a Ship of Burthen with all its lading through the Middle of the Market Place, with his Hand, as if he had been only leading along a Horse by the Bridle: But we shall here consider only those Things that are necessary in Practice; and then take Notice of some Points, by which Men of Learning and good Apprehensions may fully and clearly understand the whole Business of themselves. *Pliny* says, that the Obelisk brought from *Phœnicia* to *Thebes*, was brought down a Canal cut from the *Nile*, in Ships full of Bricks, so that by taking out some of the Bricks they could at any Time lighten the Vessel of its Lading. We find in *Ammianus Marcellinus* the Historian, that an Obelisk was brought from the *Nile*, in a Vessel of three hundred Oars, and laid upon Rollers at three Miles distance from *Rome*, and so drawn into the great *Circus* through the Gate that leads to *Ostia*: And that several thousand Men laboured hard at the erecting it, though the whole *Circus* was full of nothing but vast Engines and Ropes of a prodigious Thickness. We read in *Vitruvius* that *Ctesiphon* and his Son *Metagenes* brought his Columns and Architraves to *Ephesus* by a Method which they borrowed from those Cylinders with which the Ancients used to level the Ground: For in each End of the Stone they fixed a Pin of Iron which they fastened in with Lead, which Pin stood out and served as an Axis, and at each End was let into a Wheel so large as for the Stone to hang upon its Pins above the Ground; and so by the Motion of the Wheels the Stones were carried along with a great deal of Ease. We are told that *Chemminus* the *Ægyptian*, when he built that vast
Pyramid 125

Pyramid of above six Furlongs high, raised a Mound of Earth all the Way up along with the Building, by which he carried up those huge Stones into their Places. *Herodotus* writes that *Cheops*, the Son of *Rhampsinites*, in the building of that Pyramid which employed an hundred thousand Men for many Years, left Steps on the Outside of it, by means of which the largest Stones might by proper Engines, be raised up into their Places without having Occasion for very long Timbers. We read too of Architraves of vast Stones being laid upon huge Columns in the following Manner: Under the Middle of the Architrave they set two Bearers across, pretty near each other. Then they loaded one End of the Architraves with a great Number of Baskets full of Sand, the Weight of which raised up the other End, on which there were no Baskets, and one of the Bearers was left without any Weight upon it: Then removing the Baskets to the other End so raised up, and putting under some higher Bearers in the Room of that which was left without Weight, the Stone by little and little rose up as it were of its own accord. These Things which we have here briefly collected together, we leave to be more clearly learnt from the Authors themselves. But the Method of this Treatise requires, that we should speak succinctly of some few Things that make to our Purpose. I shall not waste Time in explaining any such curious Principles, as that it is the Nature of all heavy Bodies to press continually downwards, and obstinately to seek the lowest Place; that they make the greatest Resistance they are able against being raised aloft, and never change their Place, but after the stoutest Conflict, being either overcome by some greater Weight or some more powerful contrary Force. Nor shall I stand to observe that Motions are various, from high to low or from low to high, directly, or about a Curve; and that some Things are carried, some drawn, some pushed on, and the like; of which Enquiries we shall treat more copiously in another Place. This we may lay down for certain, that a Weight is never moved with so much Ease as it is downwards; because it then moves itself, nor ever with more Difficulty, than upwards; because it naturally resists that Direction; and that there is a Kind of middle Motion between these two, which perhaps partakes somewhat of the Nature of both the others, inasmuch as it neither moves of itself, nor of itself resists, as when a Weight is drawn

126

upon an even Plain, free from all Rubs. All other Motions are easy or difficult in Proportion as they approach to either of the preceding. And indeed Nature herself seems in a good Measure to have shewn us in what Manner great Weights are to be moved: for we may observe, that if any considerable Weight is laid upon a Column standing upright, the least Shove will push it off, and when once it begins to fall, hardly any Force is sufficient to stop it. We may also observe, that any round Column, or Wheel, or any other Body that turns about, is very easily moved, and very hard to stop when once it is set on going; and if it is draged along without rowling, it does not move with half the Ease. We further see, that the vast Weight of a Ship may be moved upon a standing Water with a very small Force, if you keep pulling continually; but if you strike it with ever so great a Blow suddenly, it will not stir an Inch: On the Contrary, some Things will move with a sudden Blow or a furious Push, which could not otherwise be stirred without a mighty Force or huge Engines. Upon Ice too the greatest Weights make but a small Resistance, against one that tries to draw them. We likewise see that any Weight which hangs upon a long Rope, is very easily moved as far as a certain Point; but not so easily, further. The Consideration of the Reasons of these Things, and the Imitation of them, may be very useful to our Purpose; and therefore we shall briefly treat of them here. The Keel or Bottom of any Weight, that is to be drawn along, should be even and solid; and the Broader it is, the less it will plough up the Ground all the Way under it, but then the Thinner it is, it will slip along the Quicker, only it will make the deeper Furrows, and be apter to stick: If there are any Angles or Inequalities in the Bottom of the Weight, it will use them as Claws to fasten itself in the Plain, and to resist its own Motion. If the Plain be smooth, sound, even, hard, not rising or sinking on any Side, the Weight will have nothing to hinder its Motion, or to make it refuse to obey, but its own natural Love of Rest, which makes it lazy and unwilling to be moved. Perhaps it was from a Consideration of these Things, and from a deeper Examination of the Particulars we have here mentioned, and *Archimedes* was induced to say, that if he had only a Basis for so immense a Weight, he would not doubt to turn the World itself about. The Preparation of the Bottom of the Weight and the

the Plain upon which it is to be drawn, which is what we are here to confider, may be effected in the following Manner. Let such a Number of Poles be laid along, and of such a Strength and Thickness as may be sufficient for the Weight; let them be found, even, smooth, and close joined to one another: Between the Bottom of the Weight and this Plain which it is to slide upon, there should be something to make the Way more slippery; and this may be either Soap, or Tallow, or Lees of Oil, or perhaps Slime. There is another Way of making the Weight slip along, which is by underlaying it cross-ways with Rollers: But these, though you have a sufficient Number of them, are very hard to be kept even to their proper Lines and exact Direction; which it is absolutely necessary they should be, and that they should all do Duty equally and at once,

or else they will run together in Confusion, and carry the Weight to one Side. And if you have but few of them, being continually loaded, they will either be split or flatted, and so be rendered useless; or else that single Line with which they touch the Plain underneath, or that other with which they touch the Weight that is laid upon them, will stick fast with their sharp Points and be immoveable. A Cylinder or Roller is a Body consisting of a Number of Circles joined together; and the Mathematicians say that a Circle can never touch a right Line in more than one Point; for which Reason I call the single Line which is pressed by the Weight, the Point of the Roller. The only Way to provide against this Inconvenience, is to have the Roller made of the strongest and soundest Stuff, and exactly according to Rule and Proportion.

CHAP. VII.

Of Wheels, Pins, Leavers, Pullies, their Parts, Sizes and Figures.

BUT as there are several other Things, besides those already mentioned, which are necessary for our Purpose, such as Wheels, Pullies, Skrews and Leavers, we shall here treat of them more distinctly. Wheels in a great Measure are the same as Rollers, as they always press down perpendicularly upon one Point: But there is this Difference between them, namely, that Rollers are more expeditious, Wheels being hindered by the Friction of their Pins or Axis. The Parts of a Wheel are three: The large outer Circle, the Pin or Axis in the Middle, and the Hole or Circle into which the Pin is let. This Circle some perhaps would rather call the Pole; but because in some Machines it stands still, and in others moves about, we rather desire Leave to call it the Axicle. If the Wheel turns upon a very thick Axis, it will go very hard; if upon too thin a one, it will not support its Load; if the outer Circle of the Wheel be too small, the same Inconvenience will happen that we observed of the Roller, that is, it will stick in the Plain; if it be too large, it will go along tottering from Side to Side, and it will never be ready or handy at turning one way or the other. If the Axicle or Circle in which the Axis turns, be too large, it will grind its Way out; if it be too narrow, it will hardly be able to turn. Be-

tween the Axis and the Circle in which it turns, there should be somewhat to lubricate: Because one of these is to be considered as the Plain, and the other as the Bottom or Keel of the Weights. Rollers and Wheels should be made of Elm or Holm-Oak: The Axis of Holly or the Cornel-tree, or indeed rather of Iron: The Circle for the Wheel to turn in, is made best of Brass with one third of Tin. Pullies are little Wheels. Leavers are of the Nature of the Radii or Spokes of a Wheel. But every Thing of this Sort, whether large Wheels which Men turn about by walking within them, or Cranes or Skrews, or any other Engine, working either by Leavers or Pullies; the Principles, I say, of all these are deduced from the Balance. They tell us, that *Mercury* was believed to be a God chiefly upon this Account, that without the least Gesture with his Hand, he could make his Meaning perfectly clear and plain by his Words. This, though I am a little fearful of succeeding in it, I shall here endeavour to do to the utmost of my Power: For my Design is to speak of these Things not like a Mathematician, but like a Workman; and to say no more than is absolutely necessary. For the clearer understanding therefore of this Matter, I will suppose that you have in your Hand, a Dart. In this Dart I

I i   would

would have you confider three Places, which I call Points; the two Ends, that is the Steel and the Feathers, and the third is the Loop in the Middle for throwing the Dart by; and the two Spaces between the two Ends and the Loop, I fhall call the Radii. I fhall not difpute about the Reafons of thefe Names, which will appear better from the Confideration of the Thing itfelf. If the Loop be placed exactly in the Middle of the Dart, and the Feather End be juft equal in Weight to the Steel, both Ends of the Dart will certainly hang even and be equally poifed; if the fteel End be the Heavieft, the Feather will be thrown up, but yet there will be a certain Point in the Dart further towards the heavy End, to which if you flip the Loop, the Weight will be immediately brought to an equal Poife again; and this will be the Point by which the larger Radius exceeds the fmaller juft as much as the fmaller Weight is exceeded by the larger. For thofe who apply themfelves to the Study of thefe Matters, tell us, that unequal Radii may be made equal to unequal Weights, provided the Number of the Parts of the Radius and Weight of the right Side, multiplied together, be equal to the Number of thofe Parts on the oppofite left Side: Thus if the Steel be three Parts, and the Feather two, the Radius between the Loop and the Steel muft be two, and the other Radius between the Loop and the Feather muft be three. By which Means, as this Number five will anfwer to the five on the oppofite Side, the Radii and the Weights anfwering equally to one another, they will hang even and be equally poifed. If the Number on each Side do not anfwer to one another, that Side will overcome on which that Inequality of Numbers lies. I will not omit one Obfervation, namely, that if equal Radii run out from both Sides of the Loop, and you give the Ends a twirl round in the Air they will defcribe equal Circles; but if the Radii be unequal, the Circles which they defcribe, will be unequal alfo. We have already faid that a Wheel is made up of a Number of Circles: Whence it is evident, that if two Wheels let into the fame Axis be turned by one and the fame Motion, fo as when one moves the other cannot ftand ftill, or when one ftands

ftill the other cannot move; from the Length of the Radii or Spokes in each Wheel we may come at the Knowledge of the Force which is in that Wheel, remembring always to take the Length of the Radius from the very Center of the Axis. If thefe Principles are fufficiently underftood, the whole Secret of all thefe Engines of which we are here treating, will be manifeft; efpecially with Relation to Wheels and Leavers. In Pullies indeed we may confider fome further Particulars: For both the Rope which runs in the Pully and the little Wheel in the Pully are as the Plain, whereon the Weight is to be carried with the middle Motion, which we obferved in the laft Chapter was between the moft Eafy and the moft Difficult, inafmuch as it is neither to be raifed up nor let down, but to be drawn along upon the Plain keeping always to one Center. But that you may underftand the Reafon of the Thing more clearly, take a Statue of a thoufand Weight; if you hang this to the Trunk of a Tree by one fingle Rope, it is evident this Rope muft bear the whole thoufand Weight. Faften a Pully to the Statue, and into this Pully let the Rope by which the Statue hangs, and bring this Rope up again to the Trunk of the Tree, fo as the Statue may hang upon the double Rope, it is plain the Weight of the Statue is then divided between two Ropes, and that the Pully in the Middle divides the Weight equally between them. Let us go on yet further, and to the Trunk of the Tree faften another Pully and bring the Rope up through this likewife. I ask you what Weight this Part of the Rope thus brought up and put through the Pully will take upon itfelf: You will fay five hundred; do you not perceive from hence that no greater Weight can be thrown upon this fecond Pully by the Rope, than what the Rope has itfelf; and that is five hundred. I fhall therefore go no farther, having, I think, demonftrated that a Weight is divided by Pullies, by which means a greater Weight may be moved by a fmaller; and the more Pullies there are, the more ftill the Weight is divided; from whence it follows that the more Wheels there are in them, fo many more Parts the Weight is fplit into and may fo much the more eafily be managed.

CHAP. VIII.

Of the Skrew and its Circles or Worm, and in what Manner great Weights are either drawn, carried or pushed along.

WE have already treated of Wheels, Pullies and Leavers; we are now to proceed to the Skrew. A Skrew consists of a Number of Circles like Rings, which take upon themselves the Burthen of the Weight. If these Rings were entire, and not broken in such a Manner, that the End of one of them is the Beginning of the other; it is certain the Weight which they support, though it might be moved about, would neither go upwards nor downwards, but evenly round upon an equal Plain according to the Direction of the Rings: The Weight therefore is forced to slide either upwards or downwards along the Slope of the Rings, which act herein after the Manner of the Leaver. Again, if these Rings or this Worm be of a small Circumference, or be cut in too near to the Center of the Skrew, the Weight will then be moved by shorter Leavers and with a smaller Force. I will not here omit one Thing which I did not think to have mentioned in this Place: Namely, that if you could so order it that the Bottom or Keel of any Weight which you would move might (as far as could be done by the Art and Skill of the Workman) be made no broader than a Point, and be moved in such a Manner upon a firm and solid Plain as not in the least to cut into it, I would engage you should move *Archimedes*'s Ship, or effect any thing else of this Nature whatsoever. But of these Matters we shall treat in another Place. Each of these Forces in particular, of which we have already spoken, are of great Power for the moving of any Weight; but when they are all joined together, they are vastly stronger. In *Germany* you every where see the Youth sporting upon the Ice with a sort of wooden Pattens with a very fine thin Bottom of Steel, in which with a very small Strain they slip over the Ice with so much Swiftness, that the quickest flying Bird can hardly out-go them. But as all Weights are either drawn, or pushed along, or carried, we may distinguish them thus: That they are drawn by Ropes; pushed along by Leavers; and carried by Wheels, Rollers and the like: And how all these Powers may be made use of at the same Time, is manifest. But in all these Methods, there must of Necessity be some one Thing, which standing firm and immoveable itself, may serve to move the Weight in Question. If this Weight is to be drawn, there must be some greater Weight, to which you may fasten the Instruments you are to employ; and if no such Weight can be had, fix a strong iron Stake of the Length of three Cubits, deep into the Ground which must be rammed down tight all about it, or well strengthened with Piles laid cross-ways: And then fasten the Ropes of your Pullies or Cranes to the Head of the Stake which stands up out of the Ground. If the Ground be sandy, lay long Poles all the Way for the Weight to slide upon, and at the Head of these Poles fasten your Instruments to a good strong Stake. I will take Notice of one Thing which the Unexperienced will never allow, till they understand the Matter thoroughly; which is, that along a Plain it is more convenient to draw two Weights than one; and this is done in the following Manner: Having moved the first Weight to the End of the Timbers laid for it to slide upon, fix it there with Wedges in such a Manner that nothing can stir it, and then fasten or tie to it the Engines, or Instruments with which you are to draw your other Weight; and thus the moveable Weight will be overcome and drawn along the same Plain by the other Weight, which is no more than equal to it, but only that it is fixed. If the Weight is to be drawn up on high, we may very conveniently make use of one single Pole, or rather of the Mast of a Ship; but it must be very stout and strong. This Mast we must set upright, fastening the Foot of it to a Stake, or fixing it strong in any other Manner that you please. To the upper End of it we must fasten no less than three Ropes, one on the right Side, another on the left, and the other running down directly even with the Mast. Then at some Distance from the Foot of the Mast fix your Capstern and Pullies in the Ground, and putting this last Rope through the Pullies, let it run through them so as to draw the Head of the Mast a little downwards,

and

and we may guide it which way we think proper by means of the two side Ropes, as with two Reins, making it either stand upright whenever we find it necessary, or stoop whichsoever way we Please to set down the Weight in the proper place. As to these two side Ropes, if you have no greater Weight to fasten them to, you may fix them in the following Manner: Dig a square Pit in the Ground, and in it lay the Trunk of a Tree, to which fasten one or more Loops that may stand up out of the Ground; then lay some cross Timbers over the Trunk, and fill up the Pit with Earth, ramming it down very close, and if you wet it, it will be the heavier. In all the other Particulars, you may observe the Rules we have laid down as to the Plain on which the Weight is to slide: For you must fasten Pullies both to the Head of the Mast and to the Weight which is to be raised, and near the Foot of the Mast you must fix your Capstern, or whatever other Instrument you use that acts with the Power of the Leaver. In all Engines of this Nature designed for the moving of great Weights, we should take Care that none of the Parts of the Machine which are to have any Stress upon them, be too small, and that none of our Ropes, Spokes, or any other Medium which we use in the Movement be weak by means of their Length; for indeed long and thin are in a Manner synonimous Terms, and so, on the Contrary, are short and thick. If the Ropes are small let them run double in the Pullies; if they are very thick, you must get larger Pullies, that the Rope may not be cut by the Edges of the Pully-wheel. The Axis of the Pully should be Iron, and not less in Thickness than the sixth Part of the Semidiameter of the Pully itself, nor more than the eighth Part of the whole Diameter. If the Rope be wetted, it will be the more secure from taking Fire, which sometimes happens by means of its Motion and Friction in the Pully; it will also turn the Pully round the better, and keep better within the Wheel. It is better to wet the Rope with Vinegar than with Water; but if you do it with Water, Sea-water is best. If you wet with fresh Water, and it is exposed to the Heat of the Sun, it will rot presently. Twisting the Ropes together is much safer than tying them; and especially you must take Care that one Rope does not cut the other. The Ancients used a Bar or Rule of Iron, to which they fastened the first Knots of their Ropes, and their Pullies, and for taking up any Weight,

and especially of Stone, they had a Kind of Pincers or Forceps of Iron. The Shape of these Pincers or Forceps was taken from the Letter X, the lower Limbs of it being turned inwards like a Crab's Claw, by which means it fastened itself to the Weight. The two upper Limbs had Holes at the Top, through which they put a Rope, which being tied, and strained tight by the moving Force, made the Teeth of the Pincers keep closer to the Weight -A- In very large Stones, and especially in the Middle of Columns, though perfectly smooth in all other Parts, I have seen little Knobs left jutting out, like Handles, against which the Ropes were hitched, to prevent their slipping. It is also common, especially in Cornices, to make a Hole in the Stone like a Mortise, after this Manner; you make a Hole in the Stone like an empty Purse, of a Bigness answerable to the Size of the Stone, narrower at the Mouth than at the Bottom. I have seen some of these Holes a Foot deep. You then fill it with iron Wedges, -B- the two side Wedges being shaped like the letter D, which are put in first to fill up the Sides of the Hole, and the middle Wedge is put in last between these two. All these three Wedges have their Ears which project out beyond the Mortise, and these Ears have a Hole drilled in them, through which you put an iron Pin, which fastens on a strong Handle or Ring; and to this Ring you fasten the Rope which runs through the Pully that is to draw up the Weight. My way of fastening my Ropes about Columns, Jambs of Doors, and other such Stones which are to be set upright, is as follows. I make a Cincture or Hoop of Wood or Iron of a due Strength for bearing the Weight which I am to move, and with this Hoop I surround the Column or other Stone in some convenient Part, making it tight to the Stone with long thin Wedges drove in gently with a Hammer, then I fasten my Ligatures to this Hoop, and by this Means I neither spoil the Beauty of the Stone by making Mortises in it, nor break the Edges of the Jambs by the Rubbing of the Ropes against them: Besides that it is the most expeditious, convenient and safest Way of fastening the Ropes that has been thought of. In another Place I shall enlarge more particularly upon many Things relating to this Subject. All I shall observe further here is, that all Engines may be looked upon to be a Sort of Animals, with prodigious strong Hands; and that they move Weights just in the same Manner as we

Men

Men do with our Arms. For this Reason, the same Diftention and Contraction of the Members and Nerves which we ufe in pulling, thrufting or lifting, we are to imitate in our Engines. I fhall only add one Piece of Advice more, which is, that whenever you are to move any great Weight, in any Manner whatfoever, you would go about it carefully, cautioufly and deliberately, remembering the many uncertain and irrecoverable Accidents and Dangers which fometimes happen in Attempts of this Nature, even to the moft experienced: For you will never get fo much Honour and Reputation if what you undertake, fucceeds, as you will incur Blame and the Imputation of Rafhnefs, if it fails. We fhall now leave this Subject, to proceed to the outward Coat of the Wall.

CHAP. IX.

That the Incruftations which are made upon the Wall with Mortar, muft be three in Number: How they are to be made, and to what Purpofes they are to ferve. Of the feveral Sorts of Mortar, and in what Manner the Lime is to be prepared for making them: Of Bafs-relieves in Stuc-work and Paintings, with which the Wall may be adorned.   130

IN all Incruftations there muft be at leaft three Coats of Mortar; the firft is called Rough-cafting, and its Office is to ftick as clofe as poffible to the Wall and to bind on the two outer Coats; the Office of the outer Coat, is to make the Work fhew neat, fmooth, and polifhed; that of the middle Coat, which we call Plaiftering, is to prevent any Faults or Defects in either of the other two. The Defects are thefe: If the two laft, that is to fay, the Plaiftering and the outer Coat are fharp, and to ufe fuch an Expreffion, tenacious of the Wall, as the Rough-caft ought to be, their Acrimony will occafion an infinite Number of Cracks in them in drying. And if the Rough-caft be foft, as the outer Coat fhould be, it will not take hold of the Wall as it ought, but will fall off in Pieces. The oftener we plaifter the Wall over, the better we may polifh it, and the longer it will endure the Injuries of Time. Among the ancient Buildings I have feen fome which have been done over no lefs than nine Times. The firft of thefe fhould be very fharp, and made of Pit-Sand and Brick beaten not too fine, but about the Size of fmall Gravel, and laid on about the Thicknefs of three Inches. For the Plaiftering, or middle Coat, River-Sand is better, and is lefs apt to crack. This Coat too fhould be fomewhat rough, becaufe to a fmooth Surface nothing will ftick that you lay on. The laft of all fhould be as white as Marble; for which Reafon, inftead of Sand you fhould ufe the whiteft Stone that can be got pounded fmall; and it will be fufficient if this Coat be laid on about half an Inch thick, for when it is much more, it will not eafily dry. I know fome that, out of good Hufbandry, make it no thicker than a Piece of Shoe-leather. The fecond Coat, or Plaiftering, ought to be ordered according to its Proximity to either of the other two. In Mountains where there are Stone-pits, you meet with certain Veins extremely like a tranfparent Alabafter, which are neither Marble nor Tarres, but of a Kind of middle Nature between both, and very friable. If this be beat fmall and mixed up inftead of Sand, it will fhew full of little Sparks that will fhine like a fine Sort of Marble. In many Places we fee Nails ftuck into the Wall to keep on the Plaiftering, and Time has proved to us that it is better to have them of Brafs than of Iron. I am very much pleafed with thofe who, inftead of Nails, ftick little Pieces of Flint in between the Joints of the Stone; which they drive in gently with a wooden Hammer. The frefher and rougher the Wall itfelf is, the fafter all your plaiftering Work will cleave to it: For which Reafon, if, as you build the Wall, and while the Work is Green, you rough-caft it, though but flightly, the Plaiftering and outer Coat will ftick to it fo faft, as hardly ever to peel off. After foutherly Winds, it is very proper to do any of this Sort of Work; but if when a north Wind blows, or in any great Cold or Heat, you offer at any Sort of Plaiftering, efpecially at laying on the outer Coat, it will fcale off prefently. Laftly, all Incruftations are of two Sorts; either

K k   fpread spread on, or fastened to the Work. Stuc and Plaister are spread on; but Stuc is never good but in very dry Places. The Moisture trickling down from old Walls is extremely prejudicial to all Sorts of Incrustations. These Incrustations which are fastened to the Work are Stone, Glass and the like. The different Sorts of Incrustations which are spread on are either flat White, Bass-relieve, or painted in Fresco. Those which are fastened on, are either plain, pannelled or tesselated. We shall speak first of those which are spread on, for which the Lime must be prepared in the following Manner: Quench it in a covered Pit with clear Water, and let there be much more Water than Lime; then with an Axe chop and cut it as if you were chopping of Wood, and you will know when it is sufficiently soaked and dissolved by the Axes not being offended by the least Stone or Grit. It is thought not to be sufficiently soaked under three Months. It is never good unless it be very glutinous and clammy; for if the Axe comes out of it dry, it is a Sign it has not had a sufficient Quantity of Water to quench its Thirst. When you mix it up with the Sand, or any other pounded Materials, beat it over and over again very heartily, till it perfectly foams again. That which was designed for the outer Coat the Ancients used to pound in a Mortar, and they tempered their Mixture so well, that it never stuck to the Trowel when they came to lay it on. Upon this first Coat, while it is still wet and fresh, lay on the second, and be sure to let all the three be laid on so fast as to dry together, beating them even and smooth while they are wet. The outer Coat of flat White, if you rub and smooth it well, will shine like a Looking-glass; and if when it is almost dry, you anoint it with Wax and Gum Mastix dissolved in a little Oil, and heat the Wall thus anointed with a Pan of Charcoal, so that it may imbibe that Ointment, it will out-do any Marble in Whiteness. I have found by Experience that this Coat will never scale off, if while you are working it, upon the first Appearance of any Crack, you make it good with a few Twigs of white Mallows or wild Spart. But if you are obliged to plaister in the Dog-days, or in any very hot Place, cut and beat some old Ropes very small, and mix

them with the Plaister. You may also give it a very fine Polish, by throwing in a little white Soap dissolved in warm Water; but if you use too much of this, it will make your Work look pale. Figures in Stuc-work are easily made from a Mold; and the Mold itself is taken off from any Relieve, by pouring some liquid Plaister over it; and as it is drying, if it is anointed with the Composition above mentioned, it will get a Surface like Marble. These Figures are of two Sorts, one alto Relieve and the other basso Relieve. In an upright Wall, the alto Relieve do extremely well: But on an arched Cieling the basso Relieve are better; because those of the high Relieve being to hang down from the Cieling, are very apt to break off by their own Weight, which may endanger the Persons in the Room. It is a very good Admonition, that where there is likely to be much Dust, we should never make Ornaments of high Relieve; but flat and low, that they may be easily cleaned. Of painted Surfaces some are done while the Work is fresh, and others when it is dry. All natural Colours which proceed from the Earth, from Mines or the like, are proper for Paintings in Fresco: But all artificial Colours, and especially those which are altered by Means of Fire, require a very dry Surface, and abhor Lime, the Rays of the Moon, and southern Winds. It has been newly found out that Colours mixed up with Linseed Oil, will stand a vast While against all the Injuries of the Air and Seasons, provided the Wall on which they are laid be perfectly dry, and quite clear of all Moisture; though I have observed that the antient Painters, in painting the Poops of their Ships, make use of liquid Wax, instead of Size. I have also seen in the Works of the Ancients, some Colours of Gems laid on the Wall, if I judge rightly, with Wax, or perhaps with a white Sort of Terrass, which was so hardened by Time, that it could not be got off either by Fire or Water, and you would have taken it for a hard Sort of Glass. I have known some too, that with the white milky Flower of Lime, have laid Colours upon the Wall, while it was still fresh, that have looked as much like Glass as possible. But of this Subject, we need say no more.

CHAP. X.

*Of the Method of cutting Marble into thin Scantlings, and what Sand is best
for that Purpose; as also of the Difference and Agreement between* Mosaic
Work in Relieve, and Flat, and of the Cement to be used in that Sort of Work.

AS to those Incrustations which are fastened on to the Work, whether flat Facings,
or pannelled Work, the same Method is to be
used in both. It is very surprizing to consider
the Diligence which the Antients used in sawing and polishing their Scantlings of Marble.
I myself have seen some Pieces of Marble above
six Foot long and three broad, and yet scarce
half an Inch thick, and these have been joined
together with a curve Line, that the Spectators
might not easily find out where the Junctures
were. *Pliny* tells us, that the Ancients commended the Sand of *Æthiopia* as the Best for
sawing of Marble, and that the *Indian* came up
the nearest to it: But that the *Ægyptian* was
rather too soft, though even that was better than
ours. They tell us that there is a Sort found
in a certain Flat in the *Adriatic* Sea, which
was much used by the Ancients. We dig a
Sand about the Shore of *Pozzuolo,* which is not
improper for this Purpose. The sharp Sand
found in any Sort of Torrent is good, but the
larger it is, the wider it cuts and the more it
eats into the Stone; whereas the softer it goes
through, the Smoother it leaves the Surface,
and the more easily to be polished. The Polishing must be begun with chizzelling, but
ended with the softest and smoothest rubbing.
The *Theban* Sand is much commended for rubbing and polishing of Marble; so is the Whet-
stone, and the Emeril, whose Dust nothing can
exceed for this Purpose. The Pumice-stone
too, for giving the last Polish, is very useful.
The Scum of calcined Tin, which we call Put-
ty, white Lead burnt, the *Tripoli* Chalk in
particular, and the like, if they are beat into the finest Dust that possibly can be, still retaining their Sharpness, are very good for this
Work. For fastening on the Scantlings, if
they are thick, fix into the Wall either Pins of
Iron, or little Spars of Marble sticking out from
the Wall, to which you may fasten your Scant-
ling without any Thing of Cement. But if the
Scantlings are thin, after the second Plaistering, instead of Mortar, take Wax, Pitch, Ro-
sin, Gum Mastic, and a good Quantity of any

other Sort of Gum whatsoever, all melted and
mixed together, and warm your Piece of Marble by degrees, lest if you put it to the Fire at
once of a Sudden, the Heat should make it
crack. In fixing up your Scantlings, it will be
very laudable if the Juncture and Order in
which you place them, produce a beautiful Effect, by means of the Veins and Colours answering and setting off one another. I am
mightily pleased with the Policy of the Ancients, who used to make those Parts which lay
nearest to the Eye as neat and as exactly polished
as was possible, but did not take so much Pains
about those which stood at any Distance, or
Heighth, and in some Places put them up without any polishing at all, where they knew the
Eye of the most curious Examiner could not
reach them. *Mosaic* Work in Relieve, and
that which is flat, agree in this Particular,
that both are designed to imitate Painting, by
means of an artful Composition of various Colours of Stones, Glass, and Shells. *Nero* is said
to have been the First that had Mother of
Pearl cut and mixed in *Mosaic* Work. But
herein they differ, that in *Mosaic* Work in Relieve we use the largest Pieces of Marble, &c.
that we can get; whereas in the flat *Mosaic,*
we put none but little square Pieces, no bigger than a Bean; and the smaller these Pieces
are, the more Bright and Sparkling they make
the Work, the Light by so many different Faces
being broke into the more various Parts. They
differ too in this, that in fastening on the former, Cement made of Gums is the Best; but
in the flat Work, we should use Mortar made
of Lime, with a Mixture of *Tyburtine* Stone,
beat as small as Dust. There are some that, in
flat Work *Mosaic* Work, are for steeping the
Lime often in hot Water, in order to get out
its Saltness and make it softer and more gluey.
I have known some of the hardest Stone polished upon a Grind-stone, in order to be used in
the *Mosaic* in Relieve. In the flat *Mosaic* Work
you may fasten Gold to Glass with a Cement
of Lead or Litharge, which may be made more
liquid than any Sort of Glass whatsoever. All
that

that we have here said of the outer Coat, or Surface of the Wall may likewise serve as to Pavements, of which we promised to speak, only that on Pavements we never bestow fine Painting nor such good *Mosaic* Work, unless you will grant the Name of Painting to a Parget of various Colours poured into hollow little Spaces separated from each other by thin Partitions of Marble in Imitation of Painting. This Parget may be made of red Oker burnt, with Brick, Stone and the Dross of Iron; and when it is laid on and is thoroughly dry, it must be cleared and ground down smooth, which is done in the following Manner: Take a hard Stone, or rather a Piece of Lead of threescore Pound Weight, with its lower Surface perfectly smooth; to each End of this fasten a Rope, by which you must draw it backwards and forwards over your Pavement, still keeping it supplied with

Sand and Water, till it is rubbed exactly smooth, and is polished as it ought, which it never is unless all the Lines and Angles of the Dies answer and fit one another to the greatest Niceness. If this Parget be rubbed over with Oil, especially that of Linseed, it will get a Coat like Glass. It also does very well to anoint it with Lees of Oil, as also with Water in which Lime has been quenched, with which you should rub it over often. In all our *Mosaic* Works we should avoid using the same Colours too often in the same Places, as also too frequent Repetitions of the same Figures and Irregularity in the Composition of them. We should likewise take Care that the Junctures are not too wide, but that every Thing be fitted together with the utmost Exactness, that equal Care may appear to have been used in all Parts of the Work. 131

CHAP. XI.

Of the Ornaments of the Covering, which consist in the Richness and Beauty of the Rafters, Vaults and open Terrasses.

THE Coverings too have their Beauty and Gratefulness from the Contrivance of the Rafters, Vaults and open Terrasses. There are Roofs yet to be seen in *Agrippa*'s Portico with Rafters of Brass, forty Foot long; a Work wherein we know not which to admire most, the Greatness of the Expence, or the Skill of the Workmen. In the Temple of *Diana* at *Ephesus*, as we have taken Notice elsewhere, was a Roof of Cedar, which lasted a vast While. *Pliny* relates that *Salauces* King of *Colchos*, after he had overcome *Sesostris* King of *Ægypt*, made his Rafters of Gold and Silver. There are still to be seen Temples covered with Slabs of Marble, as, we are told, was the Temple of *Jerusalem* with prodigious large ones of such wonderful Whiteness and Splendor, that at a Distance the whole Roof appeared like a Mountain of Snow. *Catulus* was the first that gilt the Brass Tiles on the Capitol with Gold. I find too that the *Pantheon*, or *Rotonda* at *Rome*, was covered with Plates of Brass gilt; and Pope *Honorius*, he in whose Time *Mahomet* taught *Ægypt* and *Africa* a new Religion and Worship, covered the Church of St. *Peter* all over with Plates of Brass. *Germany* shines with Tiles glazed over. In many Places we cover our Roofs with Lead, which

will endure a great While, shews very handsome, and is not very expensive; but it is attended with this Inconvenience, that if it is laid upon a Stone Roof, not having room for Air under it, when the Stones come to be heated by the Rays of the Sun, it will melt. There is an Experiment which may convince us of the Truth of this. If you set a leaden Vessel full of Water upon the Fire, it will not melt; but if you throw the least Stone into it, where that touches it will immediately melt into a Hole. Besides this, if it is not well cramped and pinned down in all Parts, it is easily ripped off by the Wind. Moreover it is presently eat into and spoilt by the Saltness of Lime; so that it does much the best upon Timbers, if you are not afraid of Fire: But here again, there is a great Inconvenience arising from the Nails, especially if they are of Iron, inasmuch as they are more apt to grow hoter than Stone, and, besides, eat away the Lead all about them with Rust. For this Reason the Cramps and Pins ought also to be all of Lead, and must be fastened into the Sheets with hot Sodder. Under this Covering you should make a thin Bed of Ashes of Willow, washed and mixed with Chalk. Brass Nails are not so apt to grow hot or to rust, as

Iron

132

133

Iron ones. If Lead is daubed with any Sort. of Filth, it quickly fpoils; and for this Reafon we fhould take Care that our Roof be not a convenient Harbour for Birds; or if it is a likely Place for them to get together in, we fhould make our Stuff thick where their Dung is to fall. *Eufebius* tells us, that all round the Top of *Solomon*'s Temple there was a great Number of Chains, to which hung four hundred little Bells continually vibrating, the Noife of which drove away the Birds. In the Covering we alfo adorn the Ridge, Gutters and Angles, by fetting up Vafes, Balls, Statues, Chariots and the like, each of which we fhall fpeak of in particular in its due Place. At prefent I do not call to Mind any thing further relating to this Sort of Ornaments in general, except that each be adapted to the Place to which it is moft fuitable.

C H A P.　XII.

That the Ornaments of the Apertures are very pleafing, but are attended with many and various Difficulties and Inconveniences; that the falfe Apertures are of two Sorts, and what is required in each.

THE Ornaments of the Aperture give no fmall Beauty and Dignity to the Work, but they are attended with many great Difficulties, which cannot be provided againft without a good deal of Skill in the Artificer, and a confiderable Expence. They require very large Stones, found, equal, handfome and rare, which are Things not eafily to be got, and when got not eafily removed, polifhed, or fet up according to your Intention. *Cicero* fays, that the Architects owned they could not fet up a Column exactly perpendicular, which in all Apertures is abfolutely neceffary both with Refpect to Duration and Beauty. There are other Inconveniencies befides; which, as far as lies in our Power, we fhall endeavour to provide againft. An Aperture naturally implies an Opening; but fometimes behind this Opening we run up a Wall which makes a Kind of falfe Opening which is not pervious but clofed up; which for this Reafon we fhall accordingly call a falfe Aperture. This Sort of Ornaments, as indeed were moft of thofe which ferve either to ftrengthen the Work or to fave Expence, was firft invented by the Carpenters, and afterwards imitated by the Mafons, who thereby gave no fmall Beauty to their Structures. Any of thefe Apertures would be more beautiful if their Ribs were all of one Piece, made of one entire Stone; and next to this, is the having the Parts fo nicely joined that the Joints cannot be feen. The Ancients ufed to erect their Columns and other Stones which ferved as Ribs to thefe falfe Apertures, and fix them firm on their Bafes, before they carried up the Wall; and herein they did very wifely; for by this Means they had more Room to ufe their Engines, and could take the Perpendicular more exactly. You may plant your Column perpendicular upon its Bafe in the following Manner: In the Bafe and at the Top and Bottom of the Column mark the exact Center of each Circle. Into the Center of the Bafe faften an iron Pin, foddering it in with Lead, and make a Hole in the Center of the Bottom of the Column, juft big enough to receive the Pin which fticks up in the Center of the Bafe. In the Top of your Engine, or Scaffolding, make a Mark exactly perpendicular over the Pin which fticks up in the Center of the Bafe, which you may find by letting fall Line from thence to that Pin. When you have thus prepared every Thing, it will be no hard Matter to move the Head of the Shaft till its Center anfwers exactly to the Mark which you have made above and is perpendicular to the Center of its Bafe. I have obferved from the Works of the Ancients that the fofter Sort of Marble may be fmoothed with the very fame Inftruments with which we plane Wood. The Ancients alfo ufed to fet up their Stones quite rough, only fmoothing the Heads and Sides of them which were to join to other Stones, and afterwards when the Building was raifed, they polifhed the Faces of the Stones, which they had left rough before; and this I believe they did that they might leave the leaft Expence that was poffible to the Hazards of their Engines: For it would have been a much greater Lofs to them, if by Accident any Stone that was quite fmoothed and polifhed had been let fall and broke, than if

　　　　　　　　　　　　　　　they

they broke one that was only half wrought. Befides that by this means they had the Advantage of doing their Work at different Times, according to the different Seafons which are requifite for building the Wall, and for cloathing and polifhing it.   There are two Sorts of falfe Apertures : One is that where the Columns or Pilafters are fo joined to the Wall, that one Part of them is hid within it, and only Part of them appears ; the other is that wherein the whole Columns ftand out of the Wall, fomewhat imitating a Portico. The former therefore we may call the low Relieve, and the latter the whole Relieve. In the low Relieve we may ufe either half Columns or Pilafters.   The half Columns muft never ftand more nor lefs out of the Wall than one half of their Diameter. Pilafter, never more than one fourth Part of its Breadth, nor lefs than a fixth.   In the whole Relieve the Columns muft never ftand out from the Naked of the Wall more than with their whole Bafe and one fourth Part of the Breadth of their Bafe ; and never lefs than with

their whole Bafe and Shaft ftanding out clear from the Wall.   But thofe which ftand out from the Wall with their whole Bafe and one fourth Part more muft have their Pilafters of the low Relieve, fixed againft the Wall to anfwer to them.   In the whole Relieve the Entablature muft not run all along the Wall but be broke and project over the Head of each Column, as you may fee in Plate 19. No. 4. But in the half Relieve you may do as you think fit, either carrying on your Entablature entire all the Length of the Wall, or breaking it over each Pilafter with a Sweep, after the Manner of the whole Relieve.   We have now treated of thofe Ornaments wherein all Buildings agree : But of thofe wherein they differ, we fhall fpeak in the following Book, this being already long enough.   But as in this we undertook to treat of every Thing relating to Ornaments in general, we fhall not pafs by any Thing that may be ferviceable under this Head.

A. *Plan of the Inter-fpace of the two half Columns, called* Baffo Relievo.

C H A P.   XIII.

Of Columns and their Ornaments, their Plans, Axes, Out-lines, Sweeps, Diminutions, Swells, Aftragals and Fillets.

THE principal Ornament in all Architecture certainly lies in Columns ; for many of them fet together embellifh Porticoes, Walls and all Manner of Apertures, and even a fingle one is handfome, and adorns the Meeting of feveral Streets, a Theatre, an open Square, ferves for fetting up Trophies, and preferving the Memory of great Events, and is fo Beautiful and Noble that it is almoft incredible what Expence the Ancients ufed to beftow in fingle Pillars, which they looked upon as a very ftately Ornament : For oftentimes, not being content with making them of *Parian, Numidian* or other fine Marbles, they would alfo have them carved with Figures and Hiftories by the moft excellent Sculptors ; and of fuch Columns as thefe we are told there were above an Hundred and Twenty in the Temple of *Diana* at *Ephefus.* Others made their Capitals and Bafes of gilt Brafs, as we may fee in the double Portico at *Rome,* which was built in the Confulfhip of that *Octavius* who triumphed over *Perfeus.* Some made their whole Columns of Brafs, and others plated them all over with Silver ; but we fhall not dwell upon fuch Things as thofe.   Columns muft be ex-

actly round and perfectly fmooth.   We read that one *Theodorus* and one *Tholus,* Architects of *Lemnos,* contrived certain Wheels in their Workhoufes, wherein they hung their Columns with fo nice a Poife, that they could be turned about by a little Boy, and fo polifhed fmooth. But this is a *Greek* Story.   We fhall proceed to fomething more material.   In all Columns we may confider two long Lines in the Shaft ; one we may call the Axis of the Shaft, and the other the Out-lines ; the fhort Lines that we are to confider are the feveral Diamcters of thofe Circles which in different Places gird the Column about ; and of thofe Circles, the principal are the two Superficies ; one at the Top and the other at the Bottom of the Shaft. The Axis of the Shaft is a Line drawn through the very Center of the Column from the Center of the Circle which forms the flat Superficies at the Top, to the Center of the Circle which is the flat Superficies at the Bottom, and this Line may be alfo called the Perpendicular in the Middle of the Column. In this Line meet the Centers of all the Circles. But the out Line is one drawn from the Sweep of the Fillet at the Top along the Surface of the Column to the

the Sweep of the Fillet at Bottom; and in this terminate all the Diameters that are in the Thickneſs of the Shaft, and it does not run ſtrait like the Axis, but is compoſed of a great Number of Lines, ſome ſtrait and ſome curve; as we ſhall ſhew hereafter. The ſeveral Diameters of Circles which we are to conſider in different Parts of the Column, are five; the Sweeps, the Diminutions, and the Swell or Belly of the Shaft. The Sweeps are two, one at the Top and the other at the Bottom of the Column, and are called Sweeps upon account of their running out a little beyond the Reſt of the Shaft, The Diminutions are likewiſe two, cloſe by the Sweeps at the Bottom and Top, and are ſo called becauſe in thoſe Parts the Shaft diminiſhes inwards. The Diameter of the Swell or Belly of the Column is to be obſerved about the Middle of the Shaft, and is called the Belly, becauſe the Column ſeems to ſwell out juſt in that Part. Again, the Sweeps differ from one another, for that which is at the Bottom is formed by the Fillet and a ſmall Curve running from the Fillet to the Body of the Shaft; but the Sweep at the Top of the Shaft, beſides this Curve and its Fillet has likewiſe the Aſtragal. Laſtly, the Out-lines muſt be formed in the following Manner: On the Pavement, or upon the flat Side of a Wall, which is proper for the Drawing your Deſign, draw a ſtrait Line, of the Length which you intend to give the Column, which perhaps is as yet in the Quarry. This Line we call the Axis of the Shaft. Then divide this Axis into a certain Number of determinate Parts, according to the Nature of the Building, and of the various Sorts of Columns which you are to erect, of which Variety we ſhall ſpeak in due Time; and according to a due Proportion of theſe Parts you muſt make the Diameter of the Bottom of your Shaft, with a little Line drawn acroſs the Axis. The Diameter you divide into four-and-twenty Parts, one of which you give to the Height of the Fillet, which Height we mark upon the Wall with a ſmall Stroke; then take three more of thoſe Parts, and at that Height make a Mark in the Axis of the Shaft, which is to be the Center of the next Diminution, and through this Center draw a Line exactly parallel with the Diameter of the Bottom of the Shaft, which Line muſt be the Diameter of the lower Diminution, and be one ſeventh Part ſhorter than the Diameter of the Bottom of the Shaft. Having marked theſe two Lines, that is to ſay, the Diameter of the Diminution, and the Fillet, draw from the

Point of the End of the Fillet to the Point of that Diameter in the Shaft of the Column a curve Line, as eaſy and neat as poſſible; the Beginning of this curve Line muſt be one Quarter of a little Circle, the Semi-diameter of which muſt be the Height of the Fillet. Then divide the whole Length of the Shaft into ſeven equal Parts, and mark thoſe Diviſions with little Dots. At the fourth Dot, counting from the Bottom, make the Center of the Belly of the Shaft, acroſs which draw its Diameter, whoſe Length muſt be equal to the Diameter of the Diminution at the Bottom. The Diminution and Sweep at the Top muſt be made as follows: According to the Species of the Column, of which we ſhall treat elſewhere, take the Diameter of the upper Superficies from the Diameter of the Bottom of the Shaft, and draw it at the Top of the Column in your Deſign; which Diameter ſo drawn muſt be divided into twelve Parts, one of which Parts muſt be allowed to the Projecture of the Fillet and Aſtragal, giving two thirds of it to the latter, and one third to the former. Then make the Center of your Diminution, at the Diſtance of one and a half of thoſe Parts from the Center of the upper Surface of the Shaft, and the Diameter of this Diminution a ninth Part leſs than the largeſt Diameter of that Surface. You muſt afterwards draw the Curve or Sweep in the ſame Manner as I taught you to draw that below. Laſtly, having thus marked in your Deſign the Sweeps, Diminutions, and all the other Particulars which we have here mentioned, draw a ſtrait Line from the Diminution at the Top, and another from the Diminution at the Bottom to the Diameter of the Belly or Swell of the Column, and this will make in your Deſign what we called the Outline of the Column, and by this Line you may make a Model of Wood by which your Maſons may ſhape and finiſh the Column itſelf. The Superficies of the Bottom of the Shaft, if the Column be exactly rounded, muſt make equal Angles on all Sides with the Axis in the Middle, and with the like Superficies at the Top of the Shaft. Theſe Things I do not find committed to writing by any of the Ancients, but I have gathered them by my own Induſtry and Application from the Works of the beſt Maſters. All that is to follow may be for the moſt Part referred to the Proportions of the Lines already treated of, and will be very delightful and of great Uſe, eſpecially to the Improvement of Painters.

The End of Book VI.

THE

ARCHITECTURE

OF

Leone Batista Alberti.

BOOK VII. CHAP. I.

Of the ORNAMENTS of Sacred EDIFICES.

*That the Walls of Cities, the Temples, and Courts of Justice, used to be con-
secrated to the Gods; of the proper Region for the City, its Situation and
principal Ornaments.*

E have already observed that all
Buildings consist of several Parts,
and that of these Parts some are
those wherein all Manner of Buildings in general agree; such as Situation, Covering, and the like; and others,
those wherein they differ. We have already
treated of the Ornaments which belong to the
former; we are now to speak of those which
are proper to the latter. And this Discourse
will be of so useful a Nature, that even Painters,
those most accurate Searchers after every Thing
that is beautiful, will confess, that they themselves have absolute Occasion for it. As for
the Pleasantness of it, I shall only say, that I believe nobody will repent his having read it.
But I must now desire not to be blamed, if,
having proposed new Ends to myself, I begin
to handle my Subject upon fresh Principles.
The Principles and Steps to any Subject are
found by the Division, Intent and Consideration of the Parts whereof that Subject consists.
For as in a Statue made of Brass, Gold and
Silver melted together, the Workman considers

the Parts with regard to their Weight, the
Statuary with regard to their Out-lines, and
others perhaps as to other Respects; so, as we
have observed before, the Parts of Architecture
ought to be divided in such a Manner, that our
Considerations upon each of them may be as
clear and distinct as possible. We shall now
therefore proceed upon that Division which
regards the Beauty and Ornament of Buildings,
more than either their Conveniency or Strength.
Though indeed all these Qualifications have
such a mutual Agreement with one another,
that where any one of them is wanting, the
others also lose their Commendation. All
Buildings therefore are either publick or private; and both publick and private, are either
sacred or profane. We shall first treat of publick Edifices. The Ancients used to found the
Walls of their Cities with the greatest Religion,
dedicating them to some God who was to be
their Guardian: Nor did they think that it
was possible for the publick Weal to be so perfectly secured by the Prudence of any Man
whatsoever, but that it might be endangered

by

by the Infults and Treachery of thofe who were concerned with it ; and they were of Opinion that a City, either through the Negligence of its own People, or the Envy of its Neighbours, was continually expofed to Dangers and Accidents ; juft as a Ship is which is toffed on the Sea. And upon this Account I fuppofe, they fabled that *Saturn*, out of his Care of human Affairs, appointed Semi-Gods and Heroes to be Guardians over Cities and to protect them by their Wifdom ; fince indeed we are not to truft wholly to Walls for our Defence, but ftand in need befides of the Favour of Heaven. And the Reafon they gave for *Saturn*'s fo doing was this, that as we do not fet one of the Beafts themfelves to take Care of a Flock or Herd, but a Shepherd; fo it was reafonable that the Guardians appointed over Men, fhould be fome other Kind of Beings of fuperior Wifdom and greater Virtue than common Men ; and therefore they dedicated their Walls to the Gods. Others fay, that it is fo ordered by the Providence of the great and good God, that as the Minds of Men have their fatal *Genii*, fo have Cities alfo. It is no Wonder therefore that the Walls within which the Citizens were to be affociated and defended, were accounted holy ; and that the Ancients, whenever they were about to lay Siege to any Town, left they fhould feem to offer any Infult to Religion, ufed to invoke, and with facred Hymns endeavoured to appeafe the Gods that were Guardians of the Place, befeeching them to pafs willingly over to them. As for the Temple, who can doubt that to be facred, as well for other Reafons, as chiefly becaufe we there pay the due Reverence and Honour to God for thofe infinite Obligations which Mankind has towards him ? Piety is one of the Principal Parts of Juftice, and who can doubt that Juftice is a Prefent from Heaven ? Another Part of Juftice which has a very near Relation to the preceding, and is of the greateft Excellence and Dignity, and extremely grateful to the divine Being, and confequently highly facred, it is that which is difpenfed between Man and Man for the Maintenance of Peace and Tranquillity, and giving to every one his due Deferts : For this Reafon the Places fet apart for the Adminiftration of Juftice, fhould always be looked upon as facred to Religion. What fhall we fay of the Monuments of great Actions and Events which are dedicated to Eternity, and left to future Ages ? Surely we may venture to affirm, that all thefe have fome

Relation to Juftice and Religion. We are now therefore to treat of the Walls, Temples, Places for the Adminiftration of Juftice, and Monuments of great Events ; unlefs it may be firft thought neceffary to fet down fome Obfervations concerning Cities in general, which ought not to be omitted. A large Number of Edifices well diftributed, and difpofed in their proper Places, cannot fail of giving a City a great Air of Magnificence. *Plato* was for dividing the whole Area of a City into twelve Parts, allotting to each its particular Temples and Chapels, To thefe I would add particular Courts of Judicature for each Diftrict, together with Places for other inferior Magiftrates, Fortreffes, Spaces for publick Races, Exercifes and Games, and every Thing elfe of this Nature, provided there be a fufficient Number of Houfes to be allotted to every Diftrict : For of Cities, fome are large, others fmall ; fuch as are generally fortified Towns, and Places defigned chiefly for Strength. The ancient Writers were of Opinion that the Cities which ftood in Plains were not very ancient, and therefore could not pretend to much Authority ; believing that fuch could not be built till long after the Deluge. But, indeed, Cities in large open Plains, and Caftles in Places of fteep and difficult Accefs, are beft fituated both for Pleafure and Convenience : But ftill in each of thefe I would always have this Difference, that the Town which ftands in a Plain fhould rife upon a gentle Slope, for the Removal of Dirt and Filth ; and that which is on a Hill, fhould be built upon a level and even Area, for the greater Beauty of the Streets and Buildings. *Cicero* was of Opinion, that *Capua* was preferable to *Rome*, becaufe it neither hung upon Hills, nor was broken by Vallies, but lay open and level. *Alexander* defifted from compleating the Town he had begun to build in the Ifland of *Pharos*, though otherwife a Place of great Strength and many Conveniences, becaufe he found it would not have Room enough to enlarge itfelf, as in all Probability it would have Occafion to do. Nor fhould we omit to take Notice here, that the greateft Ornament of a City is the Multitude of her Citizens. We read that *Tigranes*, when he built the City of *Tigranocerta*, conftrained a vaft Number of the Richeft and moft Honourable of his Subjects, to remove thither with all their Wealth to inhabit it, publifhing an Edict, that whatever Effects they did not carry with them, but left elfewhere, fhould be forfeited to the publick

M m   Treafury.

Treasury. But this is no more than what the Neighbours all around, and other Strangers, will do willingly and of their own Accord, to a Place where they know they can live with Health, Pleasure and Plenty, and among a People of a fair and regular Behaviour. But the principal Ornament of the City will arise from the Disposition of the Streets, Squares and publick Edifices, and their being all laid out and contrived beautifully and conveniently, according to their several Uses; for without Order, there can be nothing Handsome, Convenient or Pleasing. In a well regulated City, *Plato* is of Opinion that the Laws should prevent the introducing of any foreign Delicacies or Corruptions; and, in order thereto should suffer no Citizen to travel till full forty Years of Age; and that such Strangers as should be admitted into the City, in order to prosecute their Studies, when they had sufficiently improved themselves, should be sent Home again to their own Country. And this is necessary, because the Citizens, from the Contagion of Foreigners, are apt to fall off daily more and more from that Parsimony wherein they were educated by their Ancestors, and to despise their own old Customs and Usages; which is the chief Reason that Cities grow so universally corrupted. *Plutarch* tells us, that the People of *Epidaurus* observing that their Citizens grew vicious by their Intercourse with the *Illyrians*, and knowing that a Depravity of Manners is always the Occasion of continual Innovations; in order to prevent it, elected one Citizen yearly out of their Number, who was always to be a Man of Gravity and Circumspection, who should go among the *Illyrians*, and provide and bring them all such Things as any of these Citizens gave him Commission to procure them. In a Word, all the wisest Men are agreed in this, that the greatest Care and Precaution ought to be used to keep the City from being corrupted by the Intercourse of Strangers who come to it. Not that I am for imitating those who are against granting Admission to any Strangers whatsoever. Among the *Greeks* it was the ancient Custom never to receive any People that were not in League with them, though not in Enmity neither, if they had Occasion to pass through their Country in Arms: Neither would they drive them away; but

they used to appoint a Market for all Necessaries at some little Distance without the Walls, where the Strangers might refresh themselves with whatever Conveniencies they wanted, and the Citizens might not be exposed to any Danger. But I, for my Part, am best pleased with the *Carthaginians*, who, though they permitted Strangers to come among them, would not suffer them to have every Thing in common with their own Citizens. The Streets which led to the Market or publick Place were open to all Strangers; but the more private Parts of the City, such as the Arsenal, and the like, they were not allowed so much as to see. Instructed therefore by these Examples, let us lay out the Platform of our City in such a Manner, that not only Strangers may have their Habitations separate, convenient for them, and not inconvenient to the Citizens; but also that the Citizens themselves may converse, negociate and dwell together commodiously and honourably, according to their several Ranks and Occasions. It will add much to the Beauty of the City, if the Shops for particular Trades stand in particular Streets and Districts in the most convenient Parts of the Town. Goldsmiths, Silversmiths and Painters may have their Shops in the publick Place, and so may the Sellers of Drugs, of Habits, and other creditable Trades; but all nasty, stinking Occupations should be removed out of the Way, especially the offensive Smells of Tanners, which should be set by themselves and towards the North, because the Winds seldom blow into the City from that Corner; or, if they do, they blow so strong that they rather fly than pass over it. There may perhaps be some who would like better to have the Habitations of the Gentry separate by themselves, quite clear and free from all Mixture with the meaner Sort of People. Others are for having every District of the City so laid out, that each Part might be supplied at Hand with every Thing that it could have Occasion for, and for this Reason they are not against having the meanest Trades in the Neighbourhood of the most honourable Citizens. But of this Subject we have said enough. Conveniency is one Thing, and Dignity another. Let us now return.

Chap. II.

Of how large and what Kind of Stone the Walls ought to be built, and who were the first that erected Temples.

THE Ancients, and particularly the *Hetrurians*, built their Walls of square Stones, and the Largest that could be got. The *Athenians*, as we are informed by *Themistocles*, did the same in their *Pireum*. There are some very ancient Castles still to be seen in *Tuscany*, and in the Territory of *Spoleto*, and near *Piperno* in *Campania*, built of huge unwrought Stone; which Sort of Work pleases me extremely, because it gives the Building a rugged Air of the antique Severity, which is a very great Ornament to a Town. I would have the Walls of a City built in such a Manner, that the Enemy at the bare Sight of them may be struck with Terror, and be sent away with a Distrust of his own Forces. There is a good deal of Majesty too in very broad deep Ditches close to the Foot of the Wall, with very steep Sides, like those which we are told were at *Babylon*, which were fifty royal Cubits broad and above an hundred deep. There is also much Majesty in the Height and Thickness of the Walls themselves, such as we are told were built by *Ninus, Semiramis* and *Tigranes*, and most of those whose Minds were inclined to Magnificence. In the Towers and Corridors of the Walls of *Rome*, I have seen Pavements of *Mosaic* Work, and Walls incrustated with the handsomest Materials; but all Ornaments are not suitable to all Cities, alike. Delicate Cornices and Incrustations are not so proper for the Walls of a Town; but instead of a Cornice let there be a projecting Row of long Stones, somewhat more regularly wrought than the Rest, and set by the Level and Plum-line; and instead of Incrustations, tho' I would have the Front preserve its rugged and threatning Aspect, yet I would have the Stones so well fitted to one another, that there may be no Cracks in the Building. The best Way to fit such Stones together is by Means of the *Doric* Rule; like which *Aristotle* used to say, the Laws ought to be made; for it was of Lead and pliable; because having very hard Stones and difficult to be wrought, for the saving of Expence and Labour, they did not take the Pains to square them, but set them in the Wall without any certain Order and where-ever they would fit in; and finding it an endless Task to remove them from Place to Place till they could fit them in exactly, they invented this Rule which would bend any Way, which they moulded to the Sides and Corners of the Stone which they had already set, and to which they were to fit the next, and made use of the Rule thus moulded for chusing out such Stones as would fit the Vacancies they were to fill up, and answer best to the Stones which they had already set in the Wall. Moreover, for a still greater Addition of Reverence and Dignity, I would have a very handsome open Space left both within and without the Walls, and dedicated to the publick Liberty; which should not be cumbered up by any Person whatsoever, either with Trench, Wall, Hedge, or Shrub, under very great Penalties. Let us now proceed to the Temple. The first Builders of Temples I find to have been in *Italy*, Father *Janus*, and for that Reason the Ancients, in their Sacrifices, used always to begin with a Prayer to *Janus*. Some were of Opinion that *Jupiter* in *Crete* was the first that built Temples, and upon that Account thought him the first God to be adored. They say that in *Phenicia, Uso* was the first that erected Altars, and built Temples to Fire and Wind. Others tell us that *Dionysius*, another Name for *Bacchus*, in his Passage through *India*, finding no Cities in all that Region, after he had built Towns there, also erected Temples and established religious Rites. Others say that in *Achaia, Cecrops* was the first that built a Temple to the Goddess *Ops*, and the *Arcadians* the first that built one to *Jupiter*. Some write that *Isis*, who was also called the Law-giver, because she was the first Deity that commanded Men to live according to her Laws, was also the first that raised a Temple to *Jupiter* and *Juno* her Progenitors, and appointed Priests to attend their Worship. But what Manner of Temples any of these were, is not so well known. I am very much inclined to believe they were like that which was in the Citadel of *Athens*, or that in the Capitol at *Rome*; which, even when the

the City flourished, was covered with Straw and Reeds, the *Romans* still adhering to the ancient Parsimony of their Forefathers. But when the great Wealth of their Kings and of many of their Citizens brought them to think of honouring themselves and their City by the Statelinefs of their Edifices, they looked upon it to be a Shame that the Habitations of the Gods should not be made handfomer than the Houfes of Men; and this Humour in a short Time made fo great a Progrefs, that only in the Foundation of one fingle Temple, while the City was yet extremely frugal, King *Numa* laid out four thousand Pounds Weight of Silver: And I highly commend that Prince for this Act of Generofity, as it was done out of Regard to the Dignity of the City, and to the Reverence which is due to the Gods, to whom we owe all Things: Though it has been the Opinion of fome, who have had the Reputation of Wifdom, that it is very improper to dedicate or build any Temples at all to the Gods, and we are told, that it was in this Perfuafion that *Xerxes* burnt down the Temples in *Greece*, thinking it an impious Thing to shut up the Gods between Walls, to whom all Things ought to be open, and to whom the whole World ought to ferve as a Temple. But let us return to our Subject.

C H A P. III.

With how much Thought, Care and Diligence we ought to lay out and adorn our Temples; to what Gods and in what Places we should build them, and of the various Kinds of Sacrifices.

IN the whole Compafs of the Art of Building, there is nothing in which we ought to employ more Thought, Care and Diligence than in the laying out and adorning a Temple; becaufe, not to mention that a Temple well built and handfomely adorned is the greateft and nobleft Ornament a City can have; it is moreover the Habitation of the Gods: And if we adorn and beautify the Houfe where a King or any great Man is to dwell, with all the Art we are Mafters of, what ought we to do to thofe of the immortal Gods? Whom we expect, when invoked, to be prefent at our Sacrifices, and to give Ear to our Prayers. And though the Gods may defpife thofe perifhable Things which we moft highly value; yet Men are moved by the Purity of beautiful Materials, and raifed by them to Reverence and Devotion for the Deity to which they are facred. It is certain that Temples may be of great Ufe for ftirring up Men to Piety, by filling their Minds with Delight, and Entertaining them with Admiration of their Beauty. The Ancients were wont to fay, that Piety was honoured when the Temples were frequented. For this Reafon I would have the Temple made fo beautiful, that the Imagination fhould not be able to form an Idea of any Place more fo; and I would have every Part fo contrived and adorned, as to fill the Beholders with Awe and Amazement, at the Confideration of fo many noble and excellent Things, and almoft force them to cry out with Aftonifhment: This Place is certainly worthy of God! *Strabo* fays, that the *Milefians* built their Temple fo large, that they were not able to make a Roof to cover it; which I do not approve. The *Samians* boafted of having the biggeft Temple in the World. I am not againft building them fuch, that it fhould be very hard to make any Addition to them. Ornaments are in a Manner infinite, and even in fmall Temples there is always fomething which we imagine might and ought to be added. I would have the Temple as large as the Bignefs of the City requires, but not unmeafurably huge. What I fhould chiefly defire in a Temple, would be this, that every Thing which you behold fhould be fuch; that you fhould be at a Stand which moft to commend, the Genius and Skill of the Workmen, or the Zeal and Generofity of the Citizens in procuring and dedicating fuch rare and beautiful Materials to this Service; and be doubtful whether thofe very Materials conduce moft to Beauty and Statelinefs, or to Duration, which, as in all other Buildings both publick and private, fo chiefly in the Structure of Temples, ought to be very carefully confulted; in as much as it is in the higheft Degree reafonable that fuch a great Expence fhould be well fecured from being loft by means of any Accidents, befides that Antiquity gives

no

no lefs Awfulnefs, than Ornaments do Beauty, to any Structure of this Nature. The Ancients, who had their Inftructions from the *Etrurians*, thought the fame Kind of Situation not proper for the Temples of different Gods: The Temples to the Gods that prefided over Peace, Modefty and good Arts, they judged fit to be placed within the Compafs of the Walls; but thofe Deities that were the Guardians of Pleafures, Feuds and Combuftions, fuch as *Venus*, *Mars* and *Vulcan*, they placed fomewhere without the City. *Vefta*, *Jupiter* and *Minerva*, whom *Plato* calls the Protectors of Cities, they feated in the Heart of the Town, or in the Citadel; *Pallas*, the Goddefs of working Trades, and *Mercury*, to whom the Merchants facrificed in the Month of *May*, and *Ifis*, they fet in the publick Market-place; *Neptune*, upon the Sea-fhore, and *Janus* on the Summit of the higheft Hills; the Temple of *Æfculapius* they built in the Ifland of the *Tiber*, being of Opinion, that the chief Thing neceffary to the Sick, was Water. In other Countries *Plutarch* tells us, that they ufed to place the Temple of this God out of the City, for the Sake of the Goodnefs of the Air. Further, they imagined that the Temples of various Gods ought to be built in various Forms. The Temple of the *Sun* and of *Bacchus* they thought fhould be round; and *Varro* fays, that of *Jupiter* fhould be partly uncovered at the Top, becaufe it was that God who opened the Seeds of all Things. The Temple of the Goddefs *Vefta*, fuppofing her to be the Earth, they built as round as a Ball: Thofe of the other celeftial Gods they raifed fomewhat above the Ground; thofe of the infernal Gods they built under Ground, and thofe of the terreftrial they fet upon the Level. If I am not miftaken too, their various Sorts of Sacrifices made them invent different Sorts of Temples: For fome wafhed their Altars with Blood, others facrificed with Wine and a Cake; others were daily practifing new Rites. *Pofthumius* enacted a Law among the *Romans*, that no Wine fhould be fprinkled upon a funeral Pile; for which Reafon the Ancients ufed to perform their Libations not with Wine but Milk. In the *Hy*-

perborean Ifland in the Ocean, where *Latona* was fabled to be born, the Metropolis was confecrated to *Apollo*; the Citizens of which, being ufed conftantly every Day to fing the Praifes of their Gods, were all good Mafters of Mufick. I find in *Theophraftus* the Sophift, that the People of the Ifthmus, or the *Morea*, ufed to facrifice an Ant to the Sun and to *Neptune*. It was not lawful for the *Ægyptians* to appeafe their Gods by any Thing but Prayers within their City; wherefore, that they might facrifice Sheep to *Saturn* and *Serapis*, they built their Temples out of the Town. But our Countrymen by Degrees got into a Way of making ufe of Bafiliques or Palaces for their Places of Worfhip; which was occafioned by their being accuftomed from the Beginning to meet and get together in the Palaces of private Perfons; befides, that the Altar had a very great Air of Dignity when fet in the Place of the Tribunal, as had alfo the Choir when difpofed about the Altar. The other Parts of the Structure, fuch as the Nave and the Portico, ferved the People either to walk about in, or to attend the religious Ceremonies. Add to this, that the Voice of the Pontiff, when he preached, might be more diftinctly heard in a Bafilique cieled with a Timber, than in a Temple with a vaulted Roof: But of thefe Things we fhall treat in another Place. It may not be amifs to take Notice here of what the Ancients tell us, that the Temples dedicated to *Venus*, *Diana*, the *Mufes*, the Nymphs and the more tender Goddeffes, ought in their Structure to imitate that Virgin's Delicacy and fmiling Gaiety of Youth, which is proper to them; but that *Hercules*, *Mars*, and the other greater Deities fhould have Temples which fhould rather fill the Beholders with Awe by their Gravity, than with Pleafure by their Beauty. Laftly, the Place where you intend to fix a Temple, ought to be noted, famous, and indeed ftately, clear from all Contagion of fecular Things, and, in order thereunto, it fhould have a fpacious handfome Area in its Front, and be furrounded on every Side with great Streets, or rather with noble Squares, that you may have a beautiful View of it on every Side.

N n   C H A P.

C H A P. IV.

Of the Parts, Forms and Figures of Temples and their Chapels, and how these
latter should be distributed.

143

THE Parts of the Temple are two ; the
Portico and the Inside : But they differ
very much from one another in both these Respects ; for some Temples are round, some
square, and others, lastly, have many Sides. It
is manifest that Nature delights principally in
round Figures, since we find that most Things
which are generated, made or directed by Nature, are round.   Why need I instance in the
Stars, Trees, Animals, the Nests of Birds, or
the like Parts of the Creation, which she has
chosen to make generally round ? We find too
that Nature is sometimes delighted with Figures
of six Sides ; for Bees, Hornets, and all other
Kinds of Wasps have learnt no other Figure
for building their Cells in their Hives, but the
Hexagon.   The Area for a round Temple
should be marked out exactly circular.   The
Ancients, in almost all their quadrangular
Temples made the Platform half as long again
as it was broad.   Some made it only a third
Part of the Breadth longer ; and others would
have it full thrice the Breadth long.   But in
all these quadrangular Platforms the greatest
Blemish is for the Corners to be not exactly
rectangular.   The Polygons used by the Ancients were either of six, eight, or sometimes
ten Sides.   The Angles of such Platforms
should all terminate within a Circle, and indeed
from a Circle is the best Way of deducing
them ; for the Semidiameter of the Circle will
make one of the six Sides which can be contained in that Circle.   And if from the Center you draw Right-lines to cut each of those
six Sides exactly in the Middle, you will plainly
see what Method you are to take to draw a
Platform of twelve Sides, and from that of
twelve Sides you may make one of four, or
eight, as in Fig. *B. C.*   However here is another easier Way of drawing a Platform of eight
Sides. Having drawn an equilateral and right-
angled Square together with its Diagonals from
Corner to Corner; from the Point where those
Diagonals intersect each other in the Middle, I
turn a Circle, opening the Compasses so wide
as to take in all the Sides of the Square; then
I divide one of those Sides into two equal Parts,

and through the Point of that Division draw a
Line from the Center to the Circumference of
the Circle *D*, and thus from the Point where
that Line touches the Circumference to the
Angle of the Square, will be exactly one of the
eight Sides which that Circle will contain.
We may also draw a Platform of ten Sides by
means of a Circle, in the following Manner :
Draw two Diameters in the Circle, intersecting
each other at Right-angles, and then divide
the Half of either of those Diameters into two
equal Parts, and from that Division draw a
straight Line upwards aslant to the Head of
the other Diameter ; and if from this slant
Line you take off the Quantity of the fourth
Part of one of the Diameters, the Remainder of
that Line will be one of the ten Sides which
can be contained in that Circle, as you may
see in Letter *E*.   To Temples it is usual to
joyn Chapels ; to some, more ; to others fewer.
In quadrangular Temples it is very unusual to
make above one, and that is placed at the
Head, so as to be seen immediately by those
that come in at the Door. If you have a Mind
to make more Chapels on the Sides, they will
not be amiss in those quadrangular Temples
which are twice as long as broad ; and there
we should not make more than one in each
Side : Though if you do make more, it will
be better to make an odd Number on each Side
than an even one.   In round Platforms, and
also in those of many Faces (if we may venture so to call them) we may very conveniently
make a greater Number of Chapels, according
to the Number of those Faces, one to each, or one
with and one without alternately, answering to
each other.   In round Platforms six Chapels,
or even eight will do extremely well.   In Platforms of several Faces you must be sure to let
the Corners be exactly answering and suiting
to one another. The Chapels themselves must
be made either Parts of a rectangled Square, or
of a Circle. For the single Chapel at the Head
of a Temple, the semicircular Form is much
the handsomest ; and next to that is the rectangular.   But if you are to make a good Number of Chapels, it will certainly be much more
pleasing

pleafing to the Eye, to make Part of them fquare and Part round alternately, and anfwering one to the other. For the Aperture of thefe Chapels obferve the following Rule. When you are to make a fingle Chapel in a quadrangular Temple, divide the Breadth of the Temple into four Parts, and give two of thofe Parts to the Breadth of the Chapel. If you have a Mind to have it more fpacious, divide that Breadth into fix Parts, and give four of them to the Breadth of your Chapel. And thus the Ornaments and Columns which you are to add to them, the Windows, and the like, may be handfomely fitted in their proper Places. If you are to make a Number of Chapels about a round Platform, you may, if you pleafe, make them all of the fame Size with the principal one; but to give that the greater Air of Dignity, I fhould rather chufe to have it a twelfth Part bigger than the reft. There is alfo this other Difference in quadrangular Temples, that if the principal Chapel is made of equal Lines, that is to fay, in an exact Square, it may not be amifs; but the other Chapels ought to be twice as broad as they are deep. The Solid of the Walls, or thofe Ribs of the Building which in Temples feparate one Chapel from the other, fhould never have lefs Thicknefs than the fifth Part of the Break which is left between them, nor more than the third; or, if you would have them extremely ftrong, the half. But in round Platforms, if the Chapels are in Number fix, let the Solid or Rib which is left between each Chapel, be one half of the Break; and if there be eight of thofe Chapels, let the folid Wall between them, efpecially in great Temples, be as thick as the whole Break for the Chapel: But if the Platform confift of a great Number of Angles, let the Solid always be one third of the Break. In fome Temples, according to the Cuftom of the ancient *Hetrurians*, it has been ufual to adorn the Sides not with Chapels, but with a fmall Sort of Ifles, in the following Manner: They chofe a Platform, which was one fixth Part longer than it was broad: Of this Length they affigned two of thofe fix Parts to the Depth of the Portico, which was to ferve as a Veftibule to the Temple; the reft they divided into three Parts, which they gave to the three Breadths of the fide Ifles. Again, they divided the Breadth of the Temple into ten Parts, three of which they affigned to the little Ifles on the right Hand, and as many to thofe on the left, and the other four they gave to the Area in the Middle. At the Head of the Temple, and fo fronting the Middle of each fide Ifle, they placed Chapels, and the Walls which feparated the feveral Ifles they made in Thicknefs one fifth Part of the Interfpace.   144

Chap. V.

Of the Porticoes and Entrance to the Temple, its Afcent, and the Apertures and Interfpaces of the Portico.

HITHERTO we have fpoken of the Platform for the Infide. The Portico to a quadrangular Temple may be either only in Front, or on the Back of the Structure, or elfe both in the Front and the back Part at the fame Time, or, laftly, it may run quite round the Fabrick. Where-ever any Chapel projects out, there fhould be no Portico. The Portico fhould never be fhorter, in quadrangular Temples, than the full Breadth of the Temple; and never broader than the third Part of its Length. In thofe Porticoes which run along the Sides of the Temple, let the Columns be fet as far from the Wall as they ftand from one another. The back Portico may imitate which you pleafe of the afore-mentioned. Circular Temples have either a Portico quite round them, or elfe have only one Portico, which muft be in Front. In both, the fame Proportions muft be obferved as in thofe to quadrangular Platforms; nor indeed muft fuch Porticoes be ever made other than quadrangular. As to their Length, it muft either be equal to the whole Breadth of the Infide of the Platform, or an eighth Part lefs, or at the moft a fourth Part, which is the fhorteft that is ever allowed. The *Hebrews*, according to the ancient Laws of their Forefathers, were to have one facred and chief City in a fit and convenient Place, and therein one fingle Temple and one Altar built of Stones, not hewn by Men's Hands, but juft fuch as they could find, provided they were white and clean; and there was to be no Steps to afcend to this Temple;   145

inafmuch

inafmuch as they were to be one People joyning in the Worfhip of one God, by whom alone they were defended and preferved. Now I cannot approve of either of thefe Particulars: For as to the Firft, it muft be extremely inconvenient to the People, and efpecially to thofe who frequent the Temples moft, as the old Folks and the Infirm; and the Second muft take very much from the Majefty of the Structure. As to what I have obferved in fome facred Edifices, built not long before our Time, to which you afcend by a few Steps on the Outfide, and afterwards have as many to go down again within, I will not abfolutely call it ridiculous; but why they fhould contrive it in this Manner, I cannot imagine. Indeed I would have the Plain of the Portico, and fo of the whole Temple, fomewhat raifed above the Level of the reft of the Town, which gives the Fabrick a great Air of Dignity. But as in an Animal, the Head, the Feet, and every particular Member, fhould be exactly proportioned to all the other Members, and to all the reft of the Body; fo in a Building, and efpecially in a Temple, all the Parts fhould be made to correfpond fo exactly, that let us confider which of them we pleafe, it may bear its juft Proportion to all the Reft. Thus I find that moft of the beft ancient Architects ufed to take their Elevation of the Plain of their Temple, from the Breadth of the Temple itfelf, which they divided into fix Parts, giving one of thofe Parts to the Height of the Plain or Mound of the Structure. Others, in larger Temples, raifed it only a feventh Part, and in the Biggeft of all, only a ninth. The Portico, by its Nature, fhould have a continued Wall but of one Side, and all the other Sides fhould be full of large Apertures for Paffage. Your Bufinefs therefore is to confider what Kind of Apertures you would make ufe of; for Colonades are of two Sorts; one where the Columns ftand wide and at a great Diftance from each other; and the other, where they ftand clofe and thick. And neither of thefe Sorts is without its Inconveniencies; for in the wide Sort, the Apertures are fo large, that if you would make ufe of an Architrave, it is apt to break in the Middle, and if you would carry Arches over it, it is no eafy Matter to turn them upon the Heads of the Columns. Where the Columns ftand clofe and thick, they intercept the View, the Light and the Paffage, and upon this Account, a third Manner has been found out, in a Medium between the other two, which is called Elegant,

and avoids the Defects of the others; is more convenient and much more approved. And with thefe three Sorts we might have been contented; but the Diligence of Architects have added two other Sorts, which I fuppofe may be accounted for as follows: Not having a fufficient Number of Columns for the Extenfivenefs of their Area, they deviated fomewhat from the laudable Medium, and imitated the wider Apertures; and when they happen to have Plenty of Columns, they were fond of fetting them clofer together; whence arofe five Sorts of Intercolumniations, which we may call by the Names of Wide, Clofe, Elegant, Lefswide, Lefs-clofe. I further fuppofe it to have happened, that the Architects being fometimes deftitute of long Stones, were obliged to make their Columns fhorter, knowing that this would take much from the Beauty of the Structure, they fet a Plinth under their Columns, in order to give them their juft Height; for they found by a careful View and Examination of other Buildings, that Columns had no Grace in a Portico, unlefs a right Proportion was obferved both in their Height and Thicknefs. This induced them to lay down the following Rules for this Purpofe. The Intercolumniation may be unequal; but the Columns themfelves muft always be exactly equal. Let the Apertures that anfwers to the Door be fomewhat wider than the reft. Where the Intercolumniation is clofe, make ufe of thinner Columns; where it is wide, make ufe of thicker; thus always proportioning the Thicknefs of the Colums to the Interfpaces, and the Interfpaces to the Thicknefs of the Columns, which you may do by the following Rules. In the clofeft Sort of Colonades, let the Intercolumniation be never narrower than one Diameter and a Half of the Column; and in the wideft, let it be never broader than three Diameters and three eighths. In the elegant Sort of Colonades you may allow two Diameters and a Quarter, in the Lefs-clofe, two; in the Lefs-wide, three. The middle Interfpace in the Colonade fhould be fomewhat wider than the reft, and the Ancients direct us to give it an Addition of one fourth Part: But by an Examination of old Buildings, I find that this middle Interfpace was not always made according to this Rule; for in the wide Colonades, no good Architect ever made it a fourth Part wider, but only about a twelfth; and herein they acted very prudently, left an unfaithful Architrave fhould not be able to bear even the Weight of its own Length, but

but crack in the Middle. Others indeed, in other Colonades, have allowed a sixth Part; but most have made it only a twelfth, especially in those Colonades which we have called Elegant.

149

Chap. VI.

Of Columns, and the different Sorts of Capitals.

WHEN we have resolved upon our Intercolumniation, we are to erect our Columns which are to support the Roof or Covering. But we are to make a great Difference between a Work that consists of Pilasters, and one that consists of Columns, and between covering them with Arches, or with Architraves. Arches and Pilasters are very proper in Theatres, and Arches are not amiss in Basiliques; but in the nobler Temples, we 150 never see any Porticoes without Architraves. Of these Things we are now to treat. The Parts of the Column are these: The lower Plinth, upon that the Base, upon the Base the Column, then the Capital, next to that the Architrave, after which comes the Freeze, where the Ends of the Rafters either terminate or are concealed, and over all is the Cornice. I think it will be proper to begin with the Capitals, by which chiefly Columns are dis- 151 tinguished from one another. And here I entreat those who shall hereafter copy this Book, that they would take the Pains to write the Numbers which I set down, with Letters at length, in this Manner, twelve, twenty, forty, and not with numeral Characters, as XII. XX. XL. Necessity first taught Men to set Capitals upon their Columns, for the Heads of the Timbers of their Architraves to meet and rest upon; but this being at first nothing but a square Block of Wood, looked very mean and unhandsome. Some Artists therefore among the *Dorians* (if we may thus allow the *Greeks* the Honour of all Inventions) were the first that endeavoured to improve it by making it round, so as to look like a Cup covered with a square Tile; and because it seemed somewhat too squat, they raised it higher by lengthening the Neck. The *Ionians*, seeing the Invention of the *Dorians*, commended this Introduction of the Cup into the Capital; but they did not like to see it so naked, nor with so long a Neck, and therefore they added to it the Imitation of the Bark of a Tree hanging down on each Side, which by its Convolution inwards,

or Volute, embraced the Sides of the Cup. Next came the *Corinthians*, among whom a certain Artist, named *Callimachus*, disliking the squat Cup, made use of a high Vase covered with Leaves, in Imitation of one which he had seen on the Tomb of a young Maiden, all over-grown with the Leaves of an Acanthus, which had sprung up quite round it, and which he thought looked very beautiful. Thus three 152 Sorts of Capitals were now invented and received into Practice by the best Workmen in those Days: The *Doric* (though I am convinced that this was in use before among the ancient *Etrurians*) the *Doric*, I say, the *Ionic* and the *Corinthian*. And what think you, was the Occasion of that infinite Number of other Capitals which we see quite different the one from the other, but the Diligence and Application with which Men have been continually studying to find out something new? But yet there is none that deserves to be preferred before those already mentioned, except one which, that we may not own ourselves obliged to Strangers for every thing, I call the *Italian*; for this Order to the Richness of the *Corinthian*, has added the Delicacy of the *Ionic*, and instead of those Ears, has substituted Volutes, which are extremely admired and commended. But to return to the Ordonnance of Co- 153 lumns; the ancient Architects have left us the following Rules for their Proportions. They tell us that the *Doric* Capital requires a Shaft seven Times as long as its Diameter at Bottom; the *Ionic* must have eight, and the *Corinthian* ten of its own Diameters. The Bases of all these Columns they made of the same Height; but they made them of different Lineaments and Designs: And indeed they differed as to 154 the Lineaments of almost every particular Part, though they in a great Measure agreed as to the Proportions of Columns in general, and particularly as to those Lineaments of Columns, whereof we treated in the last Book, all were of one accord, as well the *Dorians* and *Ionians*, as the *Corinthians*. In this Point too they

O o   they

they agreed, from an Imitation of Nature, namely, that the Tops of the Shafts of all Columns ought to be thinner than they were at Bottom. Some laid it down as a Rule, that they should be a fourth Part thicker at Bottom than at the Top. Others considering that Things always seem to lose of their Bigness in Proportion to the Distance from which they are viewed, very prudently advise that such Columns as were to be of a great Length, should be made somewhat thicker at the Top than those that were shorter; and for this Purpose they gave the following Directions. The Diameter of the Bottom of a Column of fifteen Foot high, should be divided into six Parts, whereof five should be given to the Diameter at the Top. Of all Columns from fifteen to twenty Foot high, the lower Diameter should be divided into thirteen Parts, eleven whereof are to be allowed to the Thickness at the Top; all Columns from twenty to thirty Foot high, must have seven Parts at the Bottom, and six at the Top; those from thirty to forty Foot, must have fifteen Parts Thickness below and thirteen above: Lastly, those amounting to fifty Foot height, must have eight Parts at the Bottom, and seven at the Top. According to the same Rule and Proportion, as the Column grows still longer, the larger Diameter we must allow to the Top of its Shaft: So that in these Points all Columns agree. Not that I can say, upon those Measurements which I have taken of ancient Structures, that these Rules were always strictly observed among the *Romans*. 155

C H A P. VII.

A necessary Rehearsal of the several Members of Columns, the Base, Torus, Scotia, Lists, Die, and of the smaller Parts of those Members, the Platband, Corona, Ovolo, small Ogee, Cima-inversa, and Cymatium, both upright and reversed.

WE shall here take a second Review of the same Things relating to Columns, which we considered in the last Book; not indeed in the same Method, but in another no less useful. For this Purpose, out of those Columns which the Ancients made use of in their publick Buildings, I shall take one of a middle Proportion between the Biggest and the Least, which I suppose to be of about thirty Foot. The biggest Diameter of the Shaft of this Column, I shall divide into nine equal Parts, eight of which I shall assign to the biggest Diameter of its Cincture at the Top: Thus its Proportion will be as eight to nine, which the *Latins* call a Sesquioctave. In the same Proportion I shall make the Diameter of the Diminution at Bottom, to the largest Diameter of the Shaft, making the latter nine and the former eight. Again I shall make the Diameter of the Cincture at the Top to that of the upper Diminution, as seven to eight, or in the Proportion which the *Latins* call Sesquiseptimal. I now proceed to the Description of those Members wherein they differ. Bases consist of these following; the Die, the Torus and the Scotia. The Die is that square Member which is at the Bottom of all, and I call it by this Name, because it is square on every Side, like a flat Die; the Torusses are those Cushions, upon one of which the Column rests, and the other stands upon the Die; the Scotia is that circular Hollow which lies between two Torusses, like the Hollow in the Wheel of a Pully. All the Measures of these Members are taken from the Diameter of the Bottom of the Shaft; and first the *Dorians* gave the following Proportions for them. They made the Height of the Base to be half the Diameter of the Bottom of the Shaft, and the Plinth or Die, as broad at most every Way as one Diameter and a Half of the Column, and as one Diameter and a Third at least. They then divided the Height of the whole Base into three Parts, one of which they assigned to the Height of the Die. Thus the Height of the whole Base was three Times that of the Die, and the Breadth of the Die was three times the Height of the Base. Then exclusive of the Die they divided the Rest of the Height of the Base into four Parts, the uppermost of which they gave to the upper Torus. Again, what remained between the upper Torus and the Die at Bottom, they divided into two Parts, one of which they allowed to the lower Torus, and the other they hollowed

156

hollowed into a Scotia which lay between the two Toruffes. A Scotia confifts of a hollow Channel edged on each Side with an Annulet; to each of thofe Annulets they allowed one feventh Part of the Scotia, and the reft they hollowed. We have formerly laid it down as a Rule, that in all Building particular Care muft be taken that all the Work be fet upon a perfeft Solid. Now it would not be fo, if a Perpendicular falling from the Edge of the upper Stone were to meet with any void Space or Hollow. For this Reafon in cutting their Scotias, they took Care not to go in fo far as to come within the Perpendicular of the Work above. The Toruffes muft projeft one Half and an Eighth of their Thicknefs, and the extremeft Edge of the Circle of the biggeft Torus muft be exaftly Perpendicular to the Die. This was the Method of the *Dorians*. The *Ionians* approved of the *Doric* Height, but they made two Scotias, and placed two Fillets between them. Thus their Bafe was the Height of half the Diameter of the Bottom of the Shaft; and this Height they divided into four Parts, one of which they affigned to the Height of the Plinth, giving eleven of thofe fourth Parts to its Breadth : So that the whole Height of the Bafe was as four, and the Breadth as eleven. Having thus defigned their Plinth, they divided the reft of the Height into feven Parts, two of which they gave to the Thicknefs of the lower Torus, and what remained befides this Torus and the Plinth, they divided into three Parts, one of which they hollowed to the upper Torus, and the two middle Parts they gave to the two Scotias with their two Fillets, which feemed to be fqueezed between the two Toruffes. The Proportions of thefe Scotias and Fillets were as follows : They divided the Space between the two Toruffes into feven Parts, one of which they gave to each Fillet, dividing the reft equally between the two Scotias. As to the Projefture of the Toruffes they obferved the fame Rules as the *Dorians*, and in hollowing their Scotias had regard to the Perpendicular Solid of the Stone that was to be laid over them; but they made their Annulets only an eighth Part of the Scotia. Others were of Opinion, that exclufive of the Plinth, the Bafe ought to be divided into fixteen Parts, which we call Minutes; and of thefe they gave four to the lower Torus, and three to the upper, three and a half to the lower Scotia, and three and a half to the upper, and the other two they affigned to the Fillets between them.

Thefe were the *Ionic* Proportions. The *Corinthians* liked both the *Ionic* and the *Doric* Bafe too, and made ufe indifferently of them both ; fo that indeed they added nothing to the Column, but a Capital. We are told that the *Etrurians* under their Columns (which we call the *Italian*) ufed to put not a fquare but a round Plinth; but I never met with fuch a Bafe among the Works of the Ancients. Indeed I have taken Notice, that in Porticoes which ufed to go clear round their circular Temples, the Ancients carved one continued Plinth quite round, which ferved for all the Columns, and of the due Height which the Plinth of the Bafe ought to be of. This I doubt not they did, becaufe they were convinced that fquare Members did not fuit with a circular Structure. I have obferved, that fome have made even the Sides of the Abacus of their Capitals point to the Center of the Temple, which, if it were to be done in the Bafes, might not be altogether amifs, though it would fcarce be much commended. And here it may not be improper to fay fomething of the feveral Members of the Ornaments made ufe of in Architecture ; and they are thefe ; the Plat-band, the Corona, the Ovolo, or Quarter-round, the fmall Ovolo, or Ogee, the Cima-inverfa, and the Cymatium, or Doucine, both upright and reverfed. All thefe particular Members have each a Projeêture, but with different Lines. The Plat-band projeéts in a Square like the Letter L, and is indeed the fame as a Lift or Fillet, but fomewhat broader. The Corona has a much greater Projeéture than the Plat-band ; the Ovolo, or Quarter-round, I was almoft tempted to call the Ivy, becaufe it runs along and cleaves to another Member, and its Projeéture is like a C placed under the Letter L, thus $\frac{L}{C}$ and the fmall Ovolo, or Ogee is only fomewhat lefs. But if you place this Letter C reverfed under the Letter L, thus $\frac{L}{\supset}$ it forms the Cima-inverfa. Again, if under the fame Letter L you place an S in this Manner $\frac{L}{S}$ it is called the Cymatium, or Gola from its Refemblance to a Man's Throat; but if you place it inverted thus $\frac{L}{\infty}$ it is called Cima-inverfa, or by fome from the Similitude of its Curve, the Onda, or Undula. Again, thefe Members are either plain, or elfe have fome other Ornaments inferted into them. In the Plat-band or Fafcia it is common to carve Cockle-fhells, Birds, or Infcriptions. In the Corona we frequently have Dentils, which are made in the following Proportions: Their

Breadth

Breadth is one half of their Height, and the Interspace between them is two thirds of their Breadth. The Ovolo, or Quarter-round, is sometimes adorned with Eggs and sometimes with Leaves, and these Eggs are sometimes carved entire, and sometimes sheared off at the Top. The Ogee, or Baguette is make like a Row of Beads, strung upon a Thread. The Cymatiums are never carved with any thing but Leaves. The Annulets are always left plain on every Side. In the putting these Members together, we must always keep to this Rule, that the upper ones have always

more Projecture than those below them. The Annulets are what separate one Member from the other, and serve as a Kind of Cymaize to each Member; the Cymaize being any Lift that is at the Top of any Member whatsoever. These Cymaizes, or Annulets being always smooth and polished, are also of Use in distinguishing the rough carved Members from each other, and their Breadth is a sixth Part of the Member over which they are set, whether it be the Corona or Ovolo; but in the Cymatium their Breadth is one whole third.

C H A P. VIII.

Of the Doric, Ionic, Corinthian and Composite Capitals.

LET us now return to the Capitals. The *Dorians* made their Capital of the same Height as their Base, and divided that Height into three Parts: The First they gave to the Abacus, the Second to the Ovolo which is under the Abacus, and the Third they allowed to the Gorgerin or Neck of the Capital which is under the Ovolo. The Breadth of the Abacus every Way was equal to one whole Diameter, and a twelfth of the Bottom of the Shaft. This Abacus is divided into two Members, an upright Cymatium and a Plinth, and the Cymatium is two fifth Parts of the whole Abacus. The upper Edge of the Ovolo joyned close to the Bottom of the Abacus. At the Bottom of the Ovolo some made three little Annulets, and others a Cymatium as an Ornament, but these never took up above a third Part of the Ovolo. The Diameter of the Neck of the Capital, which was the lowest Part of it, never exceeded the Thickness of the Top of the Shaft, which is to be observed in all Sorts of Capitals. Others, according to the Observations which I have made upon ancient Buildings, used to make the Height of the *Doric* Capital three Quarters of the Diameter of the Bottom of the Shaft, and divided this whole Height of the Capital into eleven Parts, of which they allowed four to the Abacus, four to the Ovolo, and three to the Neck of the Capital. Then they divided the Abacus into two Parts, the uppermost of which they gave to the Cymatium and the lowermost to the Plinth. The Ovolo also they divided into two Parts, assigning the lowermost either to the Annulets or to a Cymatium, which served as an Edging to the

Ovolo, and in the Neck of the Capital some cut Roses, and others Leaves with a high Projecture. This was the Practice of the *Dorians.* Our Rules for the *Ionic* Capital are as follows. Let the whole Height of the Capital be one half the Diameter of the Bottom of the Column. Let us divide this Height into nineteen Parts, or Minutes, three of which we must give to the Abacus, four to the Thickness of the Volute, six to the Ovolo, and the other six below we must leave for the Turn of the Volutes on each Side. The Breadth of the Abacus every Way must be equal to the Diameter of the Top of the Shafts; the Breadth of the Rind which is to terminate in the Scroll must both in the Front and Back of the Capital be equal to the Abacus. This Rind must fall down on each Side winding round like a Snail-shell. The Center of the Volute on the right Side must be distant from that on the Left two-and-thirty Minutes, and from the highest Point of the Abacus twelve Minutes. The Method of turning this Volute is as follows: About the Center of the Volute describe a little Circle, the Semi-diameter of which must be one of the afore-mentioned Minutes. This is the Eye of the Volute. In the Circumference of this little Circle make two Points opposite to each other, one above and the other below. Then fix one Foot of your Compasses into the uppermost Point, and extend the other to the Line that divides the Abacus from the Rind, and turn it outwards from the Capital till you have made a perfect Semi-circle ending Perpendicular under the lowest Point or Dot in the Eye of the Volute. Then contract your Compasses,

Compasses, and fixing one Foot in the Point below the Eye, let the other reach to the End of the Line which you have already turned, that is to say, to the End of your Semi-circle, and turn it upwards till you touch the upper Edge of the Ovolo. Thus with two unequal Semi-circles, you will have made one entire Compass about the Eye of your Volute. Then go on with your Sweep in the same Manner, till you have turned it quite to the Eye of the Volute, or that little Circle in the Middle. The Top of the Ovolo in the Front must have a Projecture of two Minutes beyond the Rind, and the lower Part of it must be even with the Top of the Shaft. The Sides of the Volutes where the hindmost joins to the foremost on each Side of the Capital, must be contracted to the same Width as the Ovolo, with the Addition only of one half Minute. The Abacus must be adorned with an upright Cymatium of one Minute. The Back of the Volute must be adorned with a little Channel half a Minute deep, and the Annulets on the Side of this Channel must be one Fourth of its Breadth, and the Spaces on each Side the Channel must be filled with Leaves or Fruits. That Part of the Ovolo which appears forward in the Front of the Capital must be carved with Eggs, and under them with Berries. In the Void left on each Side by the Sweep of the Volute, carve Leaves or Scales. And thus much for the *Ionic*

163 Capital. The *Corinthian* Capital is in Height one whole Diameter of the Bottom of the Shaft. This Height must be divided into seven Parts or Minutes, of which the Abacus must be allowed one. The rest is entirely taken up by the Bell or Vase, the Breadth of which at the Bottom must be exactly equal to that of the Top of the Shaft, without any of its Projectures, and the Breadth of the Top of the Vase must be equal to the largest Diameter of the Bottom of the Shaft. The Length of the Abacus on every Side must be equal to ten of the afore-mentioned Parts; but the Corners of it must be cut away to the Breadth of one half of those Parts. The Abacus of the other Capitals consists entirely of straight Lines, but that of the *Corinthian* must go with a Sweep inwards to the Thickness of the Bottom of the Vase. The Thickness of the Abacus is divided into three Parts, the Uppermost of which must be made exactly as we adorn the Top of the Shaft, that is to say, with a Fillet and small Baguette. The Vase must be covered with

two Rows of Leaves standing upright, each Row consisting of eight Leaves. Each Row must be in Height two of the afore-mentioned Parts, and the remaining Parts must be given to several little Shoots rising out of the Leaves to the Top of the Vase. These Shoots are in Number sixteen, of which four are tied in each Front of the Capital, two on the left Hand in one Knot, and two on the right in another, spreading away from each Knot in such a Manner, that the Tops of the two outward ones make a Sort of a Volute exactly under the Horns of the Abacus. The two Middle ones in each Front join together, winding also like Volutes, and exactly over the Middle of them is carved a beautiful Flower rising out of the Vase, which must not exceed the Abacus in Breadth. The Breadth of those Parts of the Lips of the Vase which those Shoots do not conceal from us, is only one of the afore-men- 164 tioned seventh Parts. The Leaves must be divided into five Plumes, and never more than into seven. The Tops of the Leaves must project half a Minute. It looks handsome in the Leaves of this Capital, and all other Carving of the same Nature, to have all the Lines cut in deep and bold. This was the Capital of the *Corinthians*. The *Italians* brought into 165 their Capital all the Ornaments that they found in the others, and observed the same Method in making the Vase, Abacus, Leaves, and the Flower in the Abacus, as the *Corinthians*. But instead of Shoots they made use of a Sort of Volutes, under the four Horns of the Abacus, projecting two whole Minutes. The Front of the Capital, being otherwise naked, borrowed its Ornaments from the *Ionic*; for instead of Shoots it has Volutes, and the Lips of its Vase are carved full of Eggs with Berries underneath them, like an Ovolo. Besides the Capitals here 166 described, we up and down see a great many other Sorts made up of the Members of these, with either Additions or Diminutions: But I do not find that they are much approved. 167 And thus much may suffice of Capitals, unless it be necessary just to mention one Practice; which is, that it is common over the Abacus to lay a very thick square Piece of Stone, or Plinth, which seems as it were to give the Capital-Breadth, and to prevent its being oppressed by the Architrave, and at the same Time is of Use to keep the nicest and most delicate Parts of the Work from being injured in laying the Superstructure.

C H A P. IX.

Of the Entablature, the Architrave, Triglyphs, Dentils, Mutules, Cavetto, and Drip or Crona, as also of Flutings and some other Ornaments belonging to Columns.

HAVING fixed our Capitals, we upon them raise our Architraves, upon the Architrave the Freze, Cornice and other Members of the Covering. In most of these Members the *Ionians* and all others differ very much from the *Dorians*; though in some Particulars they agree. For Instance, it is a general Rule, that the Thickness of the Bottom of the Architrave should be never greater than the Solid of the Top of the Shaft of the Column, nor should the Breadth of the Top of the same Architrave be greater than the Diameter of the Bottom of the Shaft. The Cornice is that Member which lies upon the Freze, and projects over it. • In this too they observed the Rule which we have already given, that the Projecture of all Members that stood out from the Naked of the Wall ought to be equal to their Height. It was also usual with them to make their Cornice lean forwards about a twelfth Part of its Width, knowing that this Member would seem to be falling backwards, if it were set up at right Angles. I here again entreat those who shall hereafter transcribe this Book, and I do it in the most earnest Manner, that they would write the Numbers which I set down with Letters at Length, and not with numeral Characters, for the avoiding of more numerous Errors. The *Dorians* then never made the Height of their Architrave less than half the Diameter of the Bottom of their Column, and this Architrave they divided into three Fascias, under the uppermost of which ran some short Mouldings, in each whereof stuck six Nails, which were fixed in those Mouldings with their Heads downwards, and might at first be intended to keep the Freze from retiring backward. The whole Height of this Architrave they divided into twelve Parts or Minutes, by which we shall measure all the following Members. Four of these Minutes they gave to the lower Fascia, six to the Middle one which is above it, and the other two they left for the upper Fascia; and of the six Minutes given to the middle Fascia, one was allowed to the Reglet or Moulding under

the Tænia, and another to the Nails which stuck in that Moulding. The Length of these Reglets was twelves Minutes, and the Spaces from one Reglet to the other were eighteen. Over the Architrave for an Ornament they set the Triglyphs, the Front of which, being raised High and Perpendicular, projected over the Architrave half a Minute. The Breadth of the Triglyphs must be equal to the Thickness of the Architrave, and their Height or Length half as much more, so that this will be eighteen Minutes. Lengthways in the Face of these Triglyphs we cut three Furrows at equal Distance from each other, and hollowed at right Angles, allowing the Breadth of the opening one Minute. The Corners of these Furrows or Channels must be cut away to the Breadth of half a Minute. The Spaces or Metopes between the Triglyphs, where the Proportions are elegant, are flat Tables exactly square, and the Triglyphs themselves must be set perpendicularly over the Solid of their Columns. The Face of the Triglyphs project half a Minute out from the Metopes; but the Perpendicular of the Metopes must fall exactly upon the lower Fascia of the Architrave. In these Metopes it is usual to carve the Skulls of Oxen, Pateras, Wheels, and the like. Over each of these Triglyphs and Metopes, instead of a Cymatium, must run a Fillet of the Breadth of two Minutes, over these a Cima-inversa of the Breadth of two Minutes, and above that a Platband of the Breadth of three Minutes, which is adorned with little Eggs, in Imitation, perhaps, of the small Stones which sometimes burst out between the Joints of a Pavement through the too great Abundance of Mortar. In these we fix the Mutules of the same Breadth as the Triglyphs, and of the same Height as the Platband, placed directly over the Heads of the Triglyphs and projecting twelve Minutes. The Heads of the Mutules are cut Perpendicular, with a Cymaise over them. Over the Mutules runs a small Cima of three Quarters of a Minute. In the Plat-fond of the Entablature between the Mutules we carve a Rose or a Flower of of the Branca Urſina. Upon the Mutules lies the Corona, which is allowed four Minutes, and this Corona conſiſts of a Plat-band or Drip and a Cima Recta, which laſt takes up one Minute and a Half. If you are to have a Pediment over your Building, all the Members of the Cornice muſt be transferred to that, and every Member in the Pediment muſt correſpond with the ſame in the Cornice, and anſwer to the ſame Perpendiculars and Proportions. There is only this Difference between Pediments and the firſt Cornices, that in Pediments the higheſt Member of the Cornice is always the Drip, which in the *Doric* Order is a Cima-reverſa, four Minutes in Height, whereas this Drip or Cima has never Place in a Cornice that is to have a Pediment over it; but in thoſe which are to have no Pediment it is conſtantly uſed. But of Pediments we ſhall ſpeak by and by. This was the Entablature of the *Dorians*. The *Ionians* were of Opinion, and not without Reaſon, that the Proportion of the Architrave ought to encreaſe according to the Bigneſs of the Column; which muſt certainly have a good Effect both here and in the *Doric* Order too. The Rules they gave for enlarging this Proportion were as follows: When the Column was twenty Foot high the Architrave ought to be the thirteenth Part of that Length; but when the Column was to be five-and-twenty Foot, the Architrave ſhould be the twelfth Part of the Length of the Column. Laſtly, if the Column was to be thirty Foot high, the Architrave was to be the eleventh Part, and for higher Columns in the ſame Gradation. The *Ionic* Architrave, beſides its Cymaiſe, conſiſted of three Faſcias, and the Whole was divided into nine Parts, two of which were allowed to the Cymaiſe, which was an upright one. The Remainder below the Cymaiſe they divided into twelve Parts, three of which went to the lower, four to the middle, and five to the upper Faſcia, which lies juſt below the Cymaiſe. Some made theſe Faſcias without any Sort of Mouldings between them, but others made them with Mouldings, and theſe were ſometimes a ſmall Cima-inverſa, taking up a fifth Part of the Faſcia, and ſometimes a Baguette taking up a ſeventh Part. We may obſerve in the Works of the Ancients, that the Lineaments or Members of the ſeveral Orders were often mixed, one borrowing from another, and often with a very good Effect. But they ſeemed chiefly pleaſed with an Architrave of only two Faſcias, which I take to be entirely *Doric*

without its Reglets and Drops. Their Manner of deſigning this Architrave was thus. They divided the whole Height into nine Parts, aſſigning one Part and two Thirds to the Cymaiſe. The upper Faſcia had four Parts and one Third, and the lower Faſcia the other three. Half the upper Part of this Cymaiſe was taken up with a Cima-inverſa and a Fillet, and the other half with a ſmall Quarter-round. The upper Faſcia for its Cymaiſe had a Baguette, which took up an eighth Part of the Faſcia, and the lower Faſcia had a Cima-recta of the third Part of its whole Breadth. Upon the Architrave lay the Rafters; but their Heads did not appear out, as in the *Doric* Order, but were cut away Perpendicular to the Architrave, and were covered with a flat Pannel which I call the Freze, the Breadth of which was the ſame as the Height of the Architrave which is under it. Upon this they uſed to carve Vaſes and other Utenſils belonging to their Sacrifices, or Skulls of Oxen at certain ſtated Diſtances, with Feſtoons of Flowers and Fruits hanging between their Horns. This Freze had over it a Cima-recta, which was never higher than four Parts of the Freze, nor lower than three. Over this ran the Denticle, four Parts high, ſometimes carved and ſometimes left quite plain. Above this was the Ovolo, out of which came the Mutules, three Parts in Height, and carved with Eggs, and from hence came the Mutules ſupporting the Drip, which was four Parts high and ſix Parts and a half Broad in its Soffit, or that Face underneath which lay over the Mutules. Over this Drip was a ſmall Cima-recta, or elſe a Baguette two Parts in Height, and at the Top of all was a Cymaiſe or Cima-inverſa of three Parts, or if you pleaſe of four. In this Cymaiſe both the *Ionians* and the *Dorians* uſed to carve the Mouths of Lyons, which ſerved for Spouts to throw out the Water; but they took Care that they ſhould neither ſprinkle any Body that was going into the Temple, nor beat back into any Part of the Temple itſelf; and for this Reaſon they ſtopt up thoſe Mouths that were over the Doors and Windows. The *Corinthians* added nothing either to the Architrave, Freze or Cornice, that I can call to Mind, except only that they did not make their Mutules ſquare like the *Dorians*, but with a Sort of Sweep like a Cymaiſe, and made the Diſtances between them equal to their Projecture from the Naked of the Building. In all other Reſpects they followed the *Ionians*. Thus much may

173 may fuffice for thofe Colonades which are to be covered with Architraves; of thofe which are to fupport Arches we fhall fpeak by and by, when we come to treat of the Bafilique. There are only fome few Particulars more relating to Colonades of this Sort, which ought by no Means to be omitted. It is certain that a Column which ftands in the open Air, always feems fmaller than one that is under Cover, and the more Flutings there are in its Shaft, the Thicker it will appear. For this Reafon we are advifed either to make thofe fluted Columns that ftand in the open Air fomewhat thicker, or elfe to encreafe the Number of the

174 Channels. Thefe Channels are made either direct along the Shaft, or elfe run fpiral about it. The *Dorians* made them direct along the Shaft. Thefe Channels are called by Architects Striæ, and among the *Dorians* they were in Number Twenty. Others made Twenty-four. Others feparated thefe Channels by fmall Lifts, which were never more than a third, nor lefs than a fourth Part of the Groove of the Fluting, and thefe Flutings were a femi-circular Concave. In the *Doric* Order the Flutings are plain without any Lift, with very little hollow, or at moft but the Quarter of a Circle, terminating the Channels in an Angle. For the lower third Part of the Shaft of the Column, they generally filled their Flutings with a Cable, to make the Column ftronger, and lefs liable to Injuries. Thofe Flutings which run direct along the Shaft, make the Column appear to the Eye of the Beholder thicker than it really is. Thofe Channels that run fpiral about the Shaft, vary it too; but the lefs they fwerve from the Perpendicular of the Column, the Thicker the Column will appear. They muft round clear round the Column never more than three Times, nor ever make lefs than

175 one compleat Revolution. Whatever Flutings you make, they muft always run from the Bottom to the Top of the Shaft in even and con-tinued Lines, with an equal Hollow all the Way. The Sides of the Builder's Square will ferve us as a Guide for making our Channels. There is a mathematical Line, which being drawn from any certain Point of the Circumference of a Semi-circle to the End of its Diameter is called a right Angle, which is the fame as the Builder's Square. Having then marked out the Sides of your Flutings, fink them fo deep in the Middle, that the Angle of your Square may touch the Bottom and its two Sides of the Lips of them at the fame Time. At each End of the Shaft of a fluted Column, you muft leave a proper Diftance plain between the Channels and the Cincture at one End, and the Aftragal at the other. We are told, that all round the Temple of *Memphis*, inftead of Columns, they made ufe of Coloffal Statues eighteen Foot high. In other Places they had wreathed Columns twifted round with Tendrils and Vine-leaves carved in Relief, and with the Figures of little Birds here and there interfperfed. But the plain Column is much more agreeable to the Majefty of a Temple. There are certain Dimentions which are great Helps to the Workmen in the placing of their Columns, and thefe are taken from the Number of the Columns themfelves that are to be ufed in the Structure. Thus, for Inftance, to begin with the *Dorians*; when they had four Columns for the Front of their Building, they divided the Front of the Platform into feven-and-twenty Parts. If they had fix Columns, they divided it into one-and-forty, and if eight into fix-and-fifty, and of thefe Parts they allowed two for the Thicknefs of each Column 176 But in *Ionic* Structures where four Columns are to be ufed, the Front of the Platform muft be divided into eleven Parts and a half; where thefe are to be fix, into eighteen, and where eight, into four-and-twenty and a half; whereof only one Part muft be given to the Thicknefs of each Column. 17

C H A P. X.

Of the Pavement of the Temple and its inner Area, of the Place for the Altar, and of the Walls and their Ornaments.

IT is the moft approved Tafte to afcend to the Floor of the Temple and to the inner Area by fome Number of Steps, and to have the Place where the Altar is to be fixed, raifed higher than the Reft. The Apertures and Entrance to the Chapels on the Sides were fometimes left quite open without any Inclofure whatfoever, and fometimes fhut in with two Columns, 17

Columns, over which ſan an Architrave, Freze and Cornice, according to the Rules juſt now laid down for Porticoes; and the reſt of the Void above the Cornice was left quite open for ſetting of Statues or large Candleſticks. Others incloſed the Entrance into ſuch Chapels with a Walls brought half Way on each Side. Thoſe who imagine that the great Thickneſs of the Walls adds Dignity to a Temple, are greatly miſtaken; for who is there that does not diſlike a Body compoſed of gouty Limbs? beſides that when the Walls are too thick, they always intercept the Light. In the *Rotonda* at *Rome*, the excellent Architect who had the Care of that great Work having in it Occaſion for thick Walls, built the Ribs entirely of ſolid Work, without any Stuffing, and thoſe Inter-ſpaces which a leſs skilful Artiſt would have ſtuffed, he employed in Niches and other A-pertures, whereby he ſaved Expence, and made the Structure leſs heavy, and more beautiful. The Thickneſs of the Walls muſt be proporti-oned after the Manner of Columns; that is to ſay, their Thickneſs muſt correſpond to their Height, as in thoſe. I have obſerved that the Ancients, in building their Temples, uſed to divide the Front of their Platform into twelve Parts; or, when they would make them parti-cularly ſtrong, into nine, and one of thoſe Parts was the Thickneſs of the Wall. In cir-cular Temples the Wall was never leſs high than half the Diameter of its inner Area; many made it two Thirds of that Diameter, and ſome three Fourths, which was the Height to which they carried the Wall before they be-gan the Sweep of the Cupola. But the more diſcreet Workmen divided the Circumference of this circular Platform into four Parts; and one of thoſe fourth Parts being extended to a Line was equal to the inward Height of the Wall, which is as four to eleven: And this Practice has been alſo imitated in ſquare Tem-ples as well as round ones, and in many other Kinds of Structures that were to be covered with Arches. But where there were to be Chapels on each Side in the Wall, to make the Aperture ſeem the Larger they ſometimes raiſed their Wall equal in Height to the whole Breadth of the Area. In round Temples the inward Height of the Wall will not be the ſame as the outward: Becauſe within the Wall ends exact-ly where the Sweep of the Arch begins; but without, it is carried up ſtraight to the Top of the Cornice. If the Cupola have a Cover on the Outſide made with Degrees like Steps, the outward Wall will take up a third Part of it; but if the Cover be made with ſtraight Lines and a common Slope, then the outward Wall will take up half. Nothing is more conveni-ent for building the Walls of a Temple, than Brick; but then it muſt be eaſed with ſome-thing handſomer. There have been many dif-ferent Opinions with Relation to the Adorning of the Walls of Temples. At *Cyzicus* a Town in *Bythinia* there was a Temple which had its Walls adorned with a very beautiful Stone, and all the Joints pointed with maſſy Gold. In the Tem-ple of *Minerva* at *Elis*, the Brother of *Phidias*, the celebrated Carver, made an Incruſtation of Stuc tempered with Saffron and Milk. The Kings of *Ægypt* encompaſſed the Monument of *Simandes*, which was the Sepulchre for the Concubines of *Jupiter*, with a Circle of Gold no leſs than a Cubit or Foot and half broad, and three hundred ſixty-five Cubits round, with a Day of the Year inſcribed upon every Cubit. Others condemned this Exceſs of Or-nament in Temples. *Cicero*, being guided by *Plato*'s Opinion, thought it neceſſary that the People ſhould be admoniſhed by the Laws to lay aſide all Manner of Delicacy in the Adorn-ing their Temples, and take Care only to have them perfectly clean and white. However, ſays he, let the Structure of them be beautiful: I confeſs, for my own Part, I am very ready to believe, that Purity and Simplicity of Colour, as of Life, muſt be moſt pleaſing to the Divine Being; and that it is not proper to have any Thing in a Church that may be likely to draw off Men's Thoughts from Devotion and fix them upon the Pleaſure and Delight of the Senſes: But ſtill I am of Opinion, that he is highly to be commended, who, as in other publick Structures, ſo alſo in Temples, without departing from the Gravity requiſite in ſuch Works, endeavours to have all the Parts, the Walls, Roof, and Pavement, as handſome and elegant as poſſible, ſtill chiefly having it in his Eye to make all his Ornaments the moſt dura-ble that may be. Thus nothing can be more proper for the Ornament of the Roof on the Inſide than all Sorts of *Moſaic* Work made of Marble, Glaſs, and other laſting Materials. Stuc-work with Figures, according to the Prac-tice of the Ancients, may be a very handſome Coat for the Outſide. In both you muſt take the greateſt Care to chuſe proper Places as well for your Pictures as Figures. The Por-tico, for Inſtance, is the fitteſt Place for the Repreſentation of great Actions in Pictures.

Q q   Indeed,

Indeed, within the Temple I think detached Pictures do much better than painting upon the Wall itself, and in my Mind Statues are handsomer than Pictures. unless they be such excellent ones as those two, for which *Cæsar* the Dictator gave ninety Talents, or fourteen hundred of our Crowns, in order to adorn the Temple of *Venus* his Progenitor; and I look upon a Picture with no less Pleasure (I mean a good one, for ill Painting is a Disgrace to the Wall) than I read a good History. They both indeed are Pictures, only the Historian paints with Words, and the Painter with his Pencil. All other Qualifications are common to them both, and they both require the greatest Genius and Application. But I would have nothing either on the Wall or Pavement of the Temple but what favours entirely of Philosophy. We read that in the Capitol there were Tables of Brass whereon were inscribed the Laws by which the Empire was to be governed; which, when the Temple was destroyed by Fire, were restored by the Emperor *Vespasian*, to the Number of three Thousand. We are told that at the Entrance of the Temple of *Apollo* at *Delos*, there were Verses engraved, containing several Compositions of Herbs proper to be used as Remedies against all Sorts of Poison. Thus I should think it would be proper among us, by Way of Inscription, to have such Precepts as may make us more just, more modest, more useful, more adorned with all Virtues, and more acceptable in the Sight of God; such as these, *Be what you would be thought*; *Love if you would be beloved*, and the like. And I would have the Composition of the Lines of the Pavement full of musical and geometrical Proportions; to the Intent that which-soever Way we may turn our Eyes, we may be sure to find Employment for our Minds. One Method which the Ancients took to adorn their Temples, was to fill them with Things that were

uncommon and excellent; as in the Temple of *Hercules*, where were to be seen some Horns of Emmets brought from *India*; or like those Crowns made of Cinnamon which *Vespasian* gave to the Capitol; or like that great Root of Cinnamon which *Augusta* placed in the principal Temple of Mount *Palatine*, in a Cup of Gold. At *Thermus*, a Town in *Ætolia* plundered by *Philip*, we are told, that in the Porticoes of the Temple there were above fifteen thousand Suits of Armour, and to adorn the Temple itself above two thousand Statues; all which, according to *Polybius*'s Relation, were destroyed and broken by *Philip*, except those which were inscribed with the Name, or bore the Representation of some God; and perhaps Variety is more to be consulted in such Collections than Number. *Solinus* informs us, that in *Sicily* there were some Artificers who had the Secret of making Statues of Salt; and *Pliny* tells us, that there was one made of Glass. There is no Question but such Things must be exceeding rare, and very worthy to raise our Admiration of the Work both of Nature and Art. But of Statues we shall speak in another Place. The Walls and Apertures must be adorned with Columns; but not like a Portico. There is one Thing which I have observed in the Covering of some of the biggest Temples, which is, that not having Columns of Height sufficient to reach to the Spring of their Arches, they heightened the Sides of the Arches themselves in such a Manner that their Sagitta was a third Part longer than their Semi-diameter, which added not a little to the Clearness and Beauty of the Work itself. And here I must not omit one Precept, namely, that the Spring of the Arch should have at least so much Perpendicular, as to prevent the Projecture of the Cornices from taking away any Part of the Arch from the Sight of those that staid below in the Middle of the Temple.

C H A P. XI.

Why the Roofs of Temples ought to be arched.

I Am entirely for having the Roofs of Temples arched, as well because it gives them the greater Dignity, as because it makes them more durable. And indeed I know not how it happens that we shall hardly meet any one Temple whatsoever that has not fallen into the Calamity of Fire. We read that *Cambyses* burnt

all the Temples in *Ægypt* in general, and removed the Treasure and Ornaments belonging to them to *Persepolis*. *Eusebius* relates, that the Oracle of *Delphos* was burnt three Times by the *Thracians*, and another Time it took Fire of itself, and was rebuilt by *Amasis*, as we are informed by *Herodotus*. We read too that it
was

was once burnt by *Phlegyas*, about the Time that *Phœnice* invented some Characters for the Use of his Citizens.   It was also consumed by Fire in the Reign of *Cyrus*, a few Years before the Death of *Servius Tullus*, the King of *Rome*; and it is certain, that it was again burnt about the Time of the Birth of those three great Luminaries of Learning, *Catullus, Sallus* and *Varro*.   The Temple of *Ephesus* was burnt by the *Amazons*, in the Reign of *Sylvius Posthumus*, as it was also about the Time that *Socrates* was condemned to drink Poison at *Athens*: and the Temple of the *Argives* was destroyed by Fire the same Year that *Plato* was born at *Athens*, at which Time *Tarquin* reigned at *Rome*. Why should I mention the sacred Porticoes of *Jerusalem?* Or the Temple of *Minerva* at *Miletus?* Or that of *Serapis* at *Alexandria?* Or at *Rome*, the *Pantheon?* And the Temple of the Goddess *Vesta?* And that of *Apollo?* In which last we are told the Sibyls Verses were destroyed.   We indeed find, that scarce any Temple escaped the same Calamity. *Diadorus* writes, that there was none besides that dedicated to *Venus*, in the City of *Eryx* in *Sicily*, that had escaped to his Time unhurt by the Flames. *Cæsar* owned that *Alexandria* escaped being burnt, when he himself took it, because its Roofs were vaulted.   Nor are vaulted Roofs destituted of their Ornaments.   The Ancients transferred all the same Ornaments to their Cupolas, as the Goldsmiths used about the Pateras or Cups for the Sacrifices; and the same Sort of Work as was used in the Quilts of their Beds, they imitated in their vaulted Roofs, whether plain or camerated.   Thus we see them divided into four, eight, or more Pannels, or crossed different Ways with equal Angles and with Circles, in the most beautiful Manner that can be imagined.   And here it may be proper to observe, that the Ornaments of vaulted Roofs, which consist in the Forms of their Pannels or Excavations, are in many Places exceeding handsome, and particularly at the *Rotonda* at *Rome*; yet we have no where any Instruction left us in Writing how to make them.   My Method of doing it, which is very

easy and cheap, is as follows: I describe the Lineaments of the future Pannels or Excavations upon the Boards of the Scaffolding itself, whether they are to be Quadrangular, Sexangular, or Octangular.   Then those Parts which I intended to excavate in my Roof, I raise to the stated Height with unbaked Bricks set in Clay instead of Mortar.   Upon this Kind of Mount thus raised on the Back of the Scaffolding, I build my vaulted Roof of Brick and Mortar, taking great Care that the thinner Parts cohere firmly with the Thicker and Stronger. When the Vault is compleated and settled and the Scaffolding is taken away from under it, I clear the solid Building from those Mounts of Clay which I had raised at first; and thus the Shape of my Evcavations or Pannels are formed according to my original Design.   But to return to our Subject.   I am extremely delighted with an Ornament mentioned by *Varro*, who tells us of a Roof on which was painted a Sky with a moving Star in it, which by a Kind of Hand shewed at once the Hour of the Day and what Wind blew abroad.   I should be wonderfully pleased with such a Contrivance.   The Ancients were of Opinion that raising the Roof high and ending it with a Pedient gave such an Air of Greatness to a Building, that they used to say the House of *Jove* himself, though they never supposed it rained in Heaven, could not look handsome without it.   The Rule for these Pediments is as follows.   Take not more than the Fourth nor less than the Fifth of the Breadth of your Front along the Cornice, and let this be the Summit or upper Angle of your Pediment.   Upon this Summit, as also at each End, you set Acroteria, or little Pedestals for Statues.   The Height of the Acroteria or Pedestals at the Ends should be equal to that of the Freze and Cornice; but that which stands on the Summit, should be an eighth Part higher than the others.   We are told that *Buccides* was the first that adorned his Pediments with Statues, which he made of Earth coloured red; but afterwards they came to be made of Marble, and the whole Covering too.

181

182

183

C H A P. XII.

Of the Apertures proper to Temples, namely, the Windows, Doors, and Valves; together with their Members, Proportions and Ornaments.

THE Windows in the Temple ought to be small and high, so that nothing but the Sky may be seen through them; to the

Intent that both the Priests that are employed in the Performance of divine Offices, and those that assist upon Account of Devotion, may
                                                               not

not have their Minds any Ways diverted by foreign Objects. That Horror with which a solemn Gloom is apt to fill the Mind naturally raises our Veneration, and there is always somewhat of an Austerity in Majesty: Besides that those Lights which should be always burning in Temples, and than which nothing is more awful for the Honour and Ornament of Religion, look faint and languish, unless favoured by some Obscurity. For this Reason the Ancients were very often contented without any other Aperture besides the Gate. For my own Part, I am for having the Entrance into the Temple thoroughly well lighted, and those Parts within, where People are to walk, not melancholy; but the Place where the Altar is to be seated, I think should have more of Majesty than Beauty. But to return to the Apertures themselves. Let us here remember what has formerly been said, namely, that Apertures consist of three Parts, the Void, the Jambs and the Lintel, which two last we may call the Frame of the Door or Window. The Ancients never used to make either Doors or Windows otherwise than square. We shall treat first of Doors. All the best Architects, whether *Dorians, Ionians* or *Corinthians*, always made their Doors narrower at the Top than at the Bottom by one fourteenth Part. To the Lintel they gave the same Thickness as they found at the Top of the Jamb, making the Lines of their Ornaments answer exactly to one another, and meet together in just Angles: And they raised the Cornice over the Door equal in Height to the Capital of the Columns in the Portico. Thus far they all agreed, but in other Particulars they differed very much. And first the *Dorians* divided this whole Height, that is to say, from the Level of the Pavement up to the Roof, into sixteen Parts, whereof they gave ten to the Height of the Void, which the Ancients used to call the Light; five to its Breadth, and one to the Breadth of the Frame. This was the *Doric* Division; but the *Ionians* divided the whole Height to the Top of the Columns, as aforementioned, into nineteen Parts, whereof they gave twelve to the Height of the Light, six to its Breadth, and one to the Frame. The *Corinthians* divided it into one-and-twenty Parts, assigning seven to the Breadth of the Light, and doubling that Breadth for its Length, and allowing for the Breadth of the Frame one seventh Part of the Breadth of the Light. In all these Doors the Frame was an Architrave.

And, unless I am much mistaken, the *Ionians* made use of their own Architrave, adorned with three Fascias, as did the *Dorians* too of theirs, only leaving out the Reglets and Drops; and all adorned their Lintels with most of the Delicacies of their Cornice; only the *Dorians* left out their Triglyphs, and instead of them made use of a Freze as broad as the Jamb or Frame of the Door. Over the Freze they added an upright Cymatium; and over that a plain Dentil, and next an Ovolo; above that ran the Mutules with their Cymaise, and over them an inverted Cymatium; observing in all these Members the same Proportions as we have already set down for the *Doric* Entablature. The *Ionians*, on the contrary, did not make use of a plain Freze, as in their common Entablature; but instead of it made a swelling Freze, one third Part of the Breadth of the Architrave, adorned with Leaves bound about with a Kind of Swathes. Over this they made their Cymase, Dentil, Ovolo, Mutules, with their Cymaise, and above all the Drip and inverted Cymatium. Besides this, at each End of the Entablature, on the Outside of the Jamb, under the Drip, they made a Sort of Ears, as we may call them, from their Resemblance to the handsome Ears of a fine Spaniel, by Architects called, *Consoles*. These Consoles were turned like a great S. The Ends winding round in this Manner, ∽, and the Thickness of the Console at the Top was equal to the Breadth of the swelling Freze, and one fourth Part less at Bottom. The Length reached down to the Top of the Void or Light. The *Corinthians* applied to their Doors all the Embellishments of a Collonade. And to avoid further Repetitions, we adorn a Door, especially when it is to stand under the open Air with a Sort of little Portico, attached against the Wall, in this Manner. Having made the Frame of the Door, we place on each Side an entire Column, or if you will only an half Column, with their Bases at such a Distance from each other, as to leave the Jambs, or whole Antipagment clear. The Length of the whole Columns with their Capitals, must be equal to the Distance between the outward Edge of the left Base to the outward Edge of the Right. Over these Columns you make a regular Architrave, Freze, Cornice and Pediment, according to all the same Proportions as as we have above laid down for a Portico. Some on each Side of the Door, instead of a plain Jamb, made use of all the Ornaments of a

Cornice,

Cornice, so allowing the Open a greater Width; but this is a Delicacy much more suitable to the House of a private Person, and especially about Windows, than to the Door of a Temple. In very large Temples, and especially in such as have no other Apertures but the Door, the Height of the Open of that Door is divided into three Parts, the uppermost of which is left by Way of Window, and grated, the Remainder serves for the Door. The Door itself too, or Valve, consists of different Members and Proportions. Of these Members the Chief is the Hinge, which is contrived after two Manners; either by an iron Staple fixed in the Door-case; or else by Pins coming out from the Top and Bottom of the Door itself, upon which it balances and turns, and so shuts and opens. The Doors of Temples, which for the Sake of Duration, are generally made of Brass, and consequently must be very heavy, are better trusted to Axles, in the later Manner, than to hang upon any Staples. I shall not here spend Time in giving an Account of those Doors which we read of in Historians and Poets, enriched with Gold, Ivory, and Statues, and so heavy that they could never be opened without a Multitude of Hands, and such a Noise as terrified the Hearers, I own Facility in opening and shutting them is more to my Mind. Under the Bottom therefore of the lower Pin or Axle, make a Box of Brass mixed with Tin, and in this Box sink a deep hollow Concave at the Bottom; let the Bottom of the Axle have also a Concavity in it, so that the Box and the Axle may contain between them a round Ball of Steel, perfectly smooth and well polished. The upper Pin or Axle must also be let into a brass Box made in the Lintel, and besides must turn in a moveable iron Circle as smooth as it can be made; and by this Means the Door will never make the least Resistance in turning, but swing which Way you please with all the Ease imaginable. Every Door should have two Valves or Leaves, one opening to one Side, and the other to the other. The Thickness of these Leaves should be one twelfth Part of their Breadth. Their Ornament are Pannels or square Mouldings applied lengthways down the Leaf, and you may have as many of them as you will, either two or three. one above the other, or only one. If you have two, they must lie like the Steps of a Stair, one above the other, and both must take up no more of the Breadth of the Leaf than a fourth, nor less than a sixth Part; and let the last, which lies above the other, be one fifth Part broader than the under one. If you have three of these Mouldings, observe the same Proportions in them as in the Faces of the *Ionic* Architrave: But if you have only one Moulding, let it be not more than a fifth, nor less than a seventh Part of the Breadth of the Leaf. These Mouldings must all fall inward to the Leaf with a Cimarecta. The Length of the Leaf should also be divided by other Mouldings crosways, giving the upper Pannel two fifth Parts of the whole Height of the Door. In Temples the Windows must be adorned in the same Manner as the Doors; but their Apertures, being near the highest Part of the Wall, and their Angles terminating near the Vault of the Roof, they are therefore made with an Arch, contrary to the Practice in Doors. Their Breadth is twice their Height; and this Breadth is divided by two little Columns, placed according to the same Rules as in a Portico; only that these Columns are generally square. The Designs for Niches, Statues or other Representations, are borrowed from those of Doors; and their Height must take up one third Part of their Wall. The Ancients in the Windows of their Temples, instead of Panes of Glass, made use of thin transparent Scantlings of Alabaster, to keep out Wind and Weather; or else made a Grate of Brass or Marble, and filled up the Interspaces of this Grate not with brittle Glass, but with a transparent Sort of Stone brought from *Segovia*, a Town in *Spain*, or from *Boulogne* in *Picardy*. The Scantlings are seldom above a Foot broad, and are of a bright transparent Sort of Plaister or Talk, endued by Nature with a particular Property, namely, that it never decays.

185

Chap. XIII.

Of the Altar, Communion, Lights, Candlesticks, Holy Vessels, and some other noble Ornaments of Temples.

THE next chief Point to be considered in the Temple, is fixing the Altar, where Divine Office is to be performed, which should be in the most honourable Place, and this seems to be exactly in the Middle of the Tribune. The Ancients used to make their

186 Altar fix Foot high and twelve Broad; and on it placed the Statue of their Deity. Whether or no it be proper to have more Altars for Sacrifice in a Temple, than one, I fhall leave to the Judgment of others. Among our Forefathers, in the primitive Times of our Religion, the devout Chriftians ufed to meet together at the Holy Supper, not to fill their Bodies with Food, but in order to foften and humanize their Manners by frequent Converfation and Communion with each other; and having filled their Minds with good Inftructions, they returned every Man to his own Home, warmed and inflamed with the Love of Virtue. For having rather tafted than eat the moderate Portion that was fet before them, they read and reafoned upon all Sort of divine Subjects. Every one burnt with Charity towards his Neighbour, for their common Salvation, and for the Divine Worfhip. Laftly, every Man, according to his Power, paid a Kind of Tax due to Piety, for the Maintenance of fuch as truly deferved it, and the Bifhop diftributed thefe Contributions among fuch as wanted. Thus all Things were common among them, as among loving Brethren. Afterwards when Princes confented that thefe Duties fhould be performed publickly, they did not indeed deviate much from the Inftitution of their Forefathers; but as greater Numbers came in than before, the Supper was ftill more moderate. The Sermons preached in thofe Times by the learned Bifhops, are ftill extant in the Writings of the Fathers. Thus in thofe Ages they had but one Altar, where they ufed to meet to celebrate only one Sacrifice in a Day. Next fucceeded thefe our Times, which I wifh to God fome worthy Man might arife to reform, and be this faid without Offence to our Popes, who, though to keep up their own Dignity, they hardly fuffer themfelves to be feen by the People once in a Year, yet have fo crowded every Place with Altars, and perhaps too with

187 - - - - - - -But I fhall venture to fay no more. This I may venture to affirm, that as there is nothing in Nature can be imagined more Holy or Noble than our Sacrifice, fo I believe no Man of Senfe can be for having it debafed by being made too common. There are other Sorts of Ornaments alfo, not fixed, which ferve to adorn and grace the Sacrifice; and others of the fame Nature that embellifh the Temple itfelf, the Direction of which belongs likewife to the Architect. It has been a Queftion which is the moft beautiful Sight: A large

Square full of Youth employed about their feveral Sports; or a Sea full of Ships; or a Field with a victorious Army drawn out in it; or a Senate-houfe full of venerable Magiftrates; or a Temple illuminated with a great Number of chearful Lights? I would defire that the Lights in a Temple fhould have fomewhat of a Majefty in them which is not to be found in the blinking Tapers that we ufe now-a-days. They might, indeed, have a good Effect enough if they were fet in Rows with any thing of a pretty Regularity, or ftuck all along the Edge of the Cornice. But I am much better pleafed with the Ancients, who on the Top of their Candlefticks fixed large Shells in which they lighted an odoriferous Flame. They divided the whole Length of the Candlefticks into feven Parts, two of which they gave to the Bafe, which was triangular, and longer than it was broad   , and broader at Botton than at Top   . The Shaft of the Candle- 188 ftick was divided by feveral little Pans placed one above the other, to catch the Drops that fell from the upper Shell; and at the Top of all was that Shell, full of Gums and odoriferous Woods. We have an Account how much fweet Balm ufed to be burnt on every Holyday in the principal Churches by the Emperor's Order in *Rome*, at the publick Charge; and it was no lefs than five hundred and four fcore Pounds Weight. And this may fuffice as to Lamps: Let us now juft mention fome other Things, which are very noble Ornaments in Temples. We read that *Gyges* gave to the Temple of the *Pythian Apollo*, fix great Cups of maffy Gold, which weighed thirty thoufand Pound Weight; and that at *Delphos* there were Veffels of folid Gold and Silver, each of which would contain fix Amphoras, or about four-and-fifty of our Gallons, among which there were fome that were more valued for the Invention and Workmanfhip than for the Metal. We are told that in the Temple of *Juno* at *Samos*, there was a Veffel, carved all about with Figures in Steel, fent by the *Spartans* as a Prefent to *Crœfus*, fo large, that it would hold three hundred Amphoras, or two thoufand feven hundred Gallons. We read too that the *Samians* fent as a Prefent to *Delphos* an iron Cauldron with the Heads of feveral Animals finely wrought upon it, and fupported feveral kneeling coloffal Statues ten Foot and a half high. It was a wonderful Contrivance of *Sanniticus* the *Ægyptian*, in the Temple of the God *Apis*, which was extremely rich in different
rent

rent Columns and Statues, in making an Image of that God which was continually turning round to face the Sun. And there was somewhat yet more wonderful than this in the Temple of *Diana* at *Ephesus*; which was, *Cupid*'s Dart hanging upon nothing. For such kind of Ornaments no other certain Rule can be given, but that they be set in decent Places, where they may be viewed with Wonder and Reverence.

CHAP. XIV.

Of the first Original of Basiliques, their Porticoes and different Members, and wherein they differ from Temples.

IT is certain that at first Basiliques were nothing but Places where the Magistrates used to meet to administer Justice under Shelter, and the Tribunal was added to give the greater Air of Majesty to the Structure. Afterwards in order to enlarge them, the principal Roof being found not sufficient, Porticoes were added on each Side, first a single, and in Time a double one. Others across the Tribunal made a Nave, which we shall call the Justiciary Nave, as being the Place for the Concourse of the Notaries, Sollicitors and Advocates, and joined this Nave to the other Isles after the Manner of the Letter T. The Porticoes without were supposed to be added afterwards for the Convenience of Servants: So that the Basilique consists of Naves or Isles, and of Porticoes: But as the Basilique seems to partake of the Nature of the Temple, it has claimed most of the Ornaments belonging to the Temple, but still in such a Manner as to seem rather to imitate than to pretend to equal it in Embellishments. It is raised above the Level of the Ground, like the Temple, but an eighth Part less; that so it may yield to the Temple, as to the more honourable Structure: And indeed none of its other Ornaments must be allowed the same Solemnity as those used in a Temple. Moreover there is this further Difference between the Basilique and the Temple, that the Isles in the former must be clear and open, and its Windows perfectly lightsome, upon account of the sometimes tumultuous Crowd of Litigants, and for the Conveniency of examining and subscribing to Writings; and it would be very proper, if it could be so contrived, that such as came to seek either their Clients or their Patrons, might immediately find them out; For which Reason the Columns ought to be set at a greater Distance from each other; and therefore those that support Arches are the most proper, though such as bear Architraves are

not to be wholly rejected. Thus we may define the Basilique to be a clear spacious Walk covered with a Roof, with Porticoes or Isles on the Inside; because that which is without Isles seems to me to have more in it of the Court of Justice or Senate-house, whereof we shall speak in due Time, than of the Basilique. The Platform of the Basilique should be twice as long as broad; and the chief Isle, which is that in the Middle, and the cross one, which we have called the Justiciary, should be entirely clear and free for Walkers. If it is to have only one single Isle on each Side, without the Justiciary Nave, you may order your Proportions as follows: Divide the Breadth of the Platform into nine Parts, whereof five of them must be allowed to the middle Isle, and two to each Portico or side Isle. The Length too must be divided into nine Parts, one of which must be given to the Sweep of the Tribunal, and two to the Breadth or Entrance into that Tribunal. But if besides the side Isle you would have a Justiciary Nave, then divide the Breadth of the Platform only into four Parts, giving two to the middle Isle, and one to each side Isle; and divide the Length as follows: Give one twelfth Part of it to the Sweep of the Tribunal, two twelfths and an half to the Breadth of its Entrance, and let the Breadth of the Justiciary Nave be the sixth Part of the Length of the whole Platform. But if you are to have not only the Justiciary Nave, but double Isles besides; then divide the Breadth of the Platform into ten Parts, giving four to the middle Isle, and three on each Side to be divided equally for the side Isles, and divide the Length into twenty Parts, giving one and a half to the Sweep of the Tribunal, and three and one third to its Entrance, and allowing only three Parts to the Breadth of the Justiciary Nave. The Walls of the Basilique need not be so thick as those of the Temple; because they

they are not defigned to fupport the Weight of a vaulted Roof, but only a flat one of Summers and Rafters. Let their Thicknefs therefore be only one twentieth Part of their Height, and let their Height be only once the Breadth of the Front and an Half, and never more. At the Angles of the Ifles come out Pilafters from the Naked of the Wall, running parallel with, and on a Line with, the Columns, not lefs than twice, nor more than three Times the Thicknefs of the Wall. Others, ftill more to ftrengthen the Building, make fuch a Pilafter in the Middle of the Row of Columns, in Breadth

three of the Diameters of one the Columns, or at moft four. The Columns themfelves too muft never have the fame Solidity as thofe ufed in Temples; and therefore, if we make our Colonades with an Architrave over it, we may obferve the following Rules. If the Columns are to be *Corinthian*, fubftract a twelfth Part from their Diameter; if *Ionic*, a tenth; if *Doric*, a ninth. As for the Compofition of the other Members, the Capitals, Architrave, Freze, Cornice, and the like, you may proceed in the fame Manner as in Temples.

191

CHAP. XV.

Of Colonades both with Architraves and with Arches; what Sort of Columns are to be ufed in Bafiliques, and what Cornices, and where they are to be placed; of the Height and Wedth of Windows and their Gratings; of the Roofs and Doors of Bafiliques, and their Ornaments.

COLUMNS that are to have Arches over them, ought by rights to be fquare; for if they were round, the Work would not be true, becaufe the Heads of the Arches would not lie plum upon the Solid of the Column underneath; but as much as their Squares exceeded a Circle, fo much of them would hang over the Void. To remedy this Defect, the beft ancient Mafters placed over the Capitals of their Columns another Abacus or Plinth, in Thicknefs fometimes one fourth and fometimes one fifth Part of the Diameter of the Column; the upper Part of this Plinth, which went off with a Cima-recta, was equal to the greateft Breadth of the Top of the Capital, and its Projecture was equal to its Height, fo that by this means the Heads and Angles of the Arches had a fuller and firmer Seat. Colonades with Arches, as well as thofe with Architraves, are various, fome being thinner fet, others clofer, and fo on. In the clofer Sort the Height of the Void muft be three Times and an half the Breadth of the Aperture; in the thin Set, the Height muft be once the Breadth and two thirds; in the lefs thin, the Height muft be twice the Breadth; in the clofeft of all, the Breadth muft be one third of the Height. We have formerly obferved, that an Arch is nothing elfe but a Beam bent. We may therefore give the fame Ornaments to Arches as to Architraves, according to the different Sorts of Columns over which they are turned; befides

192

193

which, if we would have our Structure very rich, over the Heads of our Arches we may run an Architrave, Freze, and Cornice in a ftraight Line, with the fame Proportions as we fhould make them over Columns that fhould reach to that Height. But as the Bafilique is fometimes encompaffed only with one fingle Ifle, and at other Times with two, the Place of the Cornice over the Columns and Arches muft vary accordingly. In thofe which are encompaffed only with one fingle Portico, having divided the Height of your Wall into nine Parts, the Cornice muft go only to five; or if you divide it into feven, to four. But in thofe which are to have double Ifles, the Cornice muft be placed at one third of the Height of the Wall at leaft, and at never more than three eighths. We may alfo over the firft Cornice, as well for the greater Ornament as for real Ufe, place other Columns, and efpecially Pilafters, directly plum over the Centers of the Columns which are below them. And this indeed is of great Service, as it maintains the Strength and Firmnefs of the Ribs of the Work, and adds Majefty to it, and at the fame Time takes off much from the Weight and Expence of the Wall; and over this upper Colonade too we make a regular Entablature, according to the Order of the Columns. In Bafiliques with double Side Ifles, we may raife three Rows of Columns in this Manner one above another; but in others we fhould make but two. Where

you

you have three Rows of Columns, divide the
Space that is between the firſt Row and the
Roof into two Parts, and in that Diviſion end
the ſecond Cornice. Between the firſt and ſecond Cornices, let the Wall be preſerved entire, and adorn it with ſome beautiful Sorts of
Stuc-work ; but in the Wall between the ſecond and the third Cornices, you muſt make
your Windows for lighting the whole Structure.
The Windows in Baſiliques muſt be ſet exactly
over the Intercolumnations, and anſwer regularly to one another. The Breadth of theſe
Windows muſt not be leſs than three Fourths
of the Intercolumnation, and their Height
may very conveniently be twice their Breadth.
Their Head-piece may be upon a Line with
the Top of the Columns, excluſive of the Capitals, if theſe Windows be made ſquare ; but
if they are round, their Arch may come almoſt even with the Architrave, and ſo lower
as you think fit to diminiſh the Arch ; but
they muſt never riſe above the Tops of the
Columns. At the Bottom of the Window
muſt be a Plat-band for a Reſt or Leaning
Place, with a Cima-recta and an Ovolo. The
Open of the Window muſt be grated, tho' not
paned with ſcantling Tale like thoſe of the
Temple ; but ſtill they muſt have ſomething
to keep out Wind and Weather. On the other
Hand, it is neceſſary to have a free Vent for
the Air, that the Duſt which is raiſed by the
Peoples Feet may not injure their Eyes and
Lungs ; and therefore I think nothing does
better here, than thoſe fine Grates, either of
Braſs or Lead, with an infinite Number of
ſmall Holes diſpoſed in a regular Order, almoſt like a Picture, which admit both Light
and Air to refreſh the Spirits. The Roof or Ceiling will be extreamly handſome, if it is compoſed of different Pannels nicely jointed together,
with large Circles, in handſome Proportions,
mixed with other Compartments and Angles,
and if thoſe Pannels are ſeparated from each

other with flying Cornices, with all their due
Members, and with their Coffits adorned with
carved Work of Gems in Relief, intermixed
with beautiful Flowers, either of the Acanthus
or any other, the Pannels being enriched with
lively Colours, by the Hand of ſome ingenious Painter, which will add a ſingular Grace
to the whole Work. *Pliny* tells us of an extraordinary Cement for laying Gold upon
Wood-work ; which may be made as follows.
Mix together ſix Pounds of Sinoper, or Terra
Pontica, and ten Pounds of red Oker, mixed
with two Pounds of Terra Melina or White
Lead, which muſt be all ground together, and
the paſt kept full ten Days before it is uſed.
Maſtic ſteept in Linſeed Oil, and mixed with
Helbic Sinoper or Ruddle well burnt, makes
a Cement or Glue that will hardly ever come
off. The Height of the Door of the Baſilique
muſt be anſwerable to that of the Iſles. If
there be a Portico on the Outſide, by Way of
Veſtibule, it muſt be of the ſame Height and
Breadth as the Iſle within. The Void Cham-
branle, and other Members of the Door muſt
be made after the ſame Rules as the Door of
the Temple ; but in a Baſilique the Leaf
ſhould never be of the Braſs. But you may
make it of Cypreſs, Cedar, or any other fine
Wood, and enrich it with Boſſes of Braſs, contriving the Whole rather for Strength than
Delicacy : Or if you would have it beautiful
or noble, do not embeliſh it with any minute
Ornaments in Imitation of Painting, but adorn
it with ſome Relieve, not too high raiſed,
that may make the Work look handſome, and
not to be too liable to be injured. Some have
of late begun to build Baſiliques circular. In
theſe the Height in the Middle muſt be equal
to the Breadth of the whole Structure ; but
the Porticoes, Colonades, Doors and Windows
muſt be in the ſame Proportions as in the
ſquare Baſilique. Of this Subject ſufficient has
been ſaid.

194

C H A P. XVI.

Of Monuments raiſed for preſerving the Memory of publick Actions and
Events.

I Come now to ſpeak of Monuments erected
for preſerving the Memory of great Events ;
and here by Way of Relief I ſhall take the
Liberty to unbend myſelf a little from that In-

tenſeneſs and Dryneſs which is neceſſary in
thoſe Parts of this Work which turn altogether
upon Numbers and Proportions : However,
I ſhall take Care not to be too prolix. Our

Anceſtors,

Anceftors, when, having overcome their Ene-, mies, they were endeavouring with all their Power to enlarge the Confines of their Empire, ufed to fet up Statues and Terms to mark the Courfe of their Victories, and to diftinguifh the Limits of their Conquefts. This was the Origin of Pyramids, Obelisks, and the like Monuments for the Diftinction of Limits. Afterwards being willing to make fome Acknowledgment to the Gods for the Victories which they had gained, they dedicated Part of their Plunder to Heaven, and confecrated the publick Rejoycings to Religion. This gave Rife to Altars, Chapels, and other Monuments neceffary for their Purpofes. They were alfo defirous of eternizing their Memory to Pofterity, and of making even their Perfons, as well as Virtues known to future Ages. This produced Trophies, Spoils, Statues, Infcriptions, and the like Inventions for propagating the Fame of great Exploits. People of lower Rank too, tho' not eminent for any particular Service done their Country, but only for their Wealth or Profperity, were fond of imitating the fame Practice, in which many different Methods have been taken. The Terms erected by *Bacchus*, at the End of his Progrefs thro' *India*, were Stones fet up at certain Diftances, and great Trees with their Trunks encompaffed with Ivy. At *Lyfimachia* was a very large Altar, which was fet up by the *Argonauts*, when they paffed by that Place in their Voyage. *Paufanias*, on the Banks of the River *Hippanis*, near the Black Sea, fixed a huge Vafe of Brafs, fix Inches thick, which would contain fix hundred * Amphoras. *Alexander*, near the River *Alceftes*, which falls into the Ocean, erected twelve Altars of prodigious large fquare Stones, and near the *Tanais* furrounded all the Space of Ground which his Army took up in its Encampment, with a Wall which was feven Miles and an half in Compafs. *Darius*, having fet down his Camp near *Othryfia*, upon the River *Artefroe*, commanded his Soldiers to throw each of them one Stone in different Heaps, which being very large and numerous, might fill Pofterity with Aftonifhment. *Sefoftris*, in his Wars, erected an Obelisk with handfome Infcriptions, in Honour of thofe who made a brave Refiftance againft him; but thofe who fubmitted bafely he branded with Infamy, by fetting up Obelisks and Columns with the Pudenda of a Woman carved upon them. *Jafon*, in all the

* An Amphora was about nine Gallons of our Meafure.

Countries thro' which he paffed, erected Temples in his own Honour, which we are told were all demolifhed by *Parmenio*, to the Intent, that no Memorial might any where remain but that of *Alexander*. Thefe were Monuments erected during the Expeditions themfelves; others, fuch as follow, were raifed after the Victory obtained, and the Conqueft compleated. In the Temple of *Pallas, the Diligent* hung the Shackles with which the *Lacedemonians* had been fettered. The *Evians* not only preferved in their Temple the Stone with which the *Phymian* King flew the King of *Machienfes*, but even worfhiped it as a God. The *Ægineta* dedicated to their Temple the Beaks of the Ships which they took from their Enemies. In Imitation of them *Auguftus*, having overcome the *Ægyptians*, erected four Trophies of the Beaks of their Ships; which were afterwards removed to the Capitol by the Emperor *Domitian*. *Julius Cæfar* had before raifed two of the fame Sort, one upon the Roftrum, and the other before the Senate, upon defeating the *Carthaginians* in a naval Engagement. Why need I mention that infinite Number of Towers, Temples, Obelisks, Pyramids, Labyrinths, and the like Works which we read of in Hiftorians? I fhall only obferve, that this Defire of perpetuating their Names by fuch Structures, rofe to fuch a Pitch among the Heroes of old, that they even built Towns for no other Purpofe, calling them by their own Names to deliver them down to Pofterity. *Alexander*, not to mention many others, befides thofe Cities which he built in Honour of his own Name, went fo far as to build one after the Name of his Horfe *Bucephalus*. But in my Opinion, what *Pompey* did was much more decent; when having defeated *Mithridates* in the lower *Armenia*, he built the City *Nicopolis* (or of Victory) in the very Place where he had been Conqueror. But *Seleucus* feems to have far outftript all thefe; for he built three Cities in Honour of his Wife, and called them *Apamia*; five in Honour of his Mother, by the Name of *Laodicea*; nine called *Seleucia*, in Honour of his own Name; and ten in Memory of his Father, which were called *Antiocha*. Others have made themfelves famous to Pofterity, not fo much by Magnificence and Expence, as by fome particular new Invention. *Cæfar*, with the Berries of the Laurel which he had worn in Triumph, planted a Grove which he confecrated to future Triumphers. Near *Afcalon* in *Syria*, was

a famous

a famous Temple, in which ftood the Statue of *Dercetis* (the fame that is called in Scripture *Dagon*) with his upper Parts like a Man, and his lower like a Fifh ; who was thus honoured, becaufe from that Place he threw himfelf into the Lake : And if any *Sytian* tafted of the Fifh that was in it, he was looked upon as excommunicate.   The *Mutinii*, or ancient *Modeneze*, near the Lake *Fucinus*, reprefented *Medea* the Serpent-killer, under the Shape of a Serpent, becaufe by her Means they fancied themfelves freed from thofe Animals.   Of the fame Nature was *Hercules*'s *Lernæan Hydra*, *Io* changed into a Cow, and the other Fables related in the Verfes of the ancient Poets ; with which Inventions I am very much delighted, provided fome virtuous Precept be contained in them ; as in that Symbol which was carved upon *Symandes*'s Sepulchre, in which was a Judge furrounded by fome other chief Magiftrates cloathed in the Habits of Priefts, and from their Necks hung down upon their Breafts the Image of Truth with her Eyes clos'd, and feeming to nod her Head towards them.   In the Middle was a Heap of Books, with this Infcription upon it : This is the true Phyfick of the Mind.

But the Invention of Statues was the moft excellent of all, as they are a noble Ornament for all Sorts of Structures, whether facred or profane, publick or private, and preferve a wonderful Reprefentation both of Perfons and Actions.   Whatever great Genius it was that invented Statues, it is thought they owe their Beginning to the fame Nation as the Religion of the ancient *Romans* ; the firft Statue being by fome faid to be made by the *Etrurians*. Others are of Opinion, that the *Telchines* of *Rhodes*, were the firft that made Statues of the Gods, which being formed according to certain magical Rules, had Power to bring up Clouds and Rain, and other Meteors, and to change themfelves into the Shapes of different Animals.   Among the *Greeks*, *Cadmus*, the Son of *Agenor*, was the firft that confecrated Statues of the Gods to the Temple.   We are informed by *Ariftotle*, that the firft Statues that were placed in the publick Forum of *Athens*, were thofe of *Harmodius* and *Ariftogiton*, who were the firft Deliverers of the City from Tyranny ; and *Arrian* the Hiftorian tells us, that thefe very Statues were fent back again to *Athens* by *Alexander* from *Sufa*, whither *Xerxes* had removed them.   The Number of Statues was fo great at *Rome*, that they were call-

ed a Marble People.   *Rhapfinates*, a very ancient *Ægyptian* King, erected a Statue of Stone to *Vulcan* above feven-and-thirty Foot high. *Sefoftris* made Statues of himfelf and his Wife of the Height of eight-and-forty Foot.   *Amafis* fet up a Statue near *Memphis*, in a leaning Pofture, which was forty-feven Foot long, and in its Pedeftal were two others, each twenty Foot high.   In the Sepulchre of *Simandes* were three Statues of *Jupiter*, made by *Memnon*, of wonderful Workmanfhip, being all cut out of one fingle Stone, whereof one, which was in a fitting Pofture, was fo large, that only its Foot was above feven Foot and an Half long ; and what was extremely furprizing in it, befides the Skill of the Artift, in all that huge Stone there was not the leaft Spot or Flaw.   Others afterwards, when they could not find Stones large enough to make Statues of the Size which they defired, made ufe of Brafs, and formed fome of no lefs than an hundred Cubits, or an hundred and fifty Foot high.   But the greateft Work we read of in this Kind, was that of *Semiramis*, who not being able to find any Stone large enough for her Purpofe, and being refolved to make fomething much bigger than was poffible to be done with Brafs, contrived near a Mountain in *Media* called *Bagiftan*, to have her own Image carved out of a Rock of two Miles and a furlong in Length, with the Figures of an hundred Men offering Sacrifice to her, hewn out of the fame Stone.   There is one Particular relating to this Article of Statues, mentioned by *Diodorus*, by no means to be omitted ; which is, that the *Ægyptian* Statuaries were arrived at fuch a Pitch of Skill in their Art, that they would out of feveral Stones in feveral different Places make one Statue, which when put together fhould feem to be all the Work of one Hand ; in which furprizing Manner we are told the Statue of the *Pythian Apollo* at *Samos* was made, one half of it being wrought by *Thelefius*, and the other half by *Theodorus* at *Ephefus*.   Thefe Things I thought it not amifs 195 to write here by way of Recreation, which, though very ufeful in themfelves, are here inferted only as an Introduction to the following Book, where we fhall treat of the Monuments raifed by private Perfons ; to which they properly belong.   For as private Men have fcarce fuffered even Princes to outdo them in Greatnefs of Expence for perpetuating their Memories, but being equally fired with the Defire of making their Names famous, have fpared for no Coft which their Fortunes would

bear,

bear, to get the Assistance and Skill of the best Artists for their Purpose; they have accordingly rivalled the greatest Kings in fine Designs and noble Compositions, so as, in my Opinion, to be very little, if at all, inferior to them. But

those Works are reserved for the next Book, in which I dare promise the Reader he shall find some Entertainment worth his Pains. But first we are here to speak of some few Particulars necessary to our present Subject.

CHAP. XVII.

Whether Statues ought to be placed in Temples, and what Materials are the most proper for making them.

SOME are against placing any Statues in Temples; and we are told that *Numa*, being a Disciple of *Pythagoras*, would allow of none: And *Seneca* rallies himself and his Countrymen upon this Account; we play with Babies, says he, like Children. The Ancients, who were of this Opinion, used to argue concerning the Gods in the following Manner: Who can be so weak as not to know, that every Thing relating to the Gods is to be considered with the Mind, and not with the Eyes, since it is impossible to give them any Form that can be in the least Degree answerable to the Excellence of their Nature? And indeed they thought that the having no visible Representations of them made by Hands, must have a very good Effect, as it would put every Man upon forming such an Idea of the first Mover, and of the supreme Intelligence, as best suited his own Capacity and Way of Thinking: By which he would be the more induced to revere the Majesty of the Divine Name. Others thought quite differently, holding, that the Gods were represented under human Forms to a very wise End, and that they had a very good Influence upon the Minds and Morals of the Vulgar, who when they approached those Statues, imagined they were in the Presence of the Gods themselves. Others especially were for setting up to publick View in consecrated Places, the Effigies of such as had deserved well of Mankind, and were therefore supposed to be admitted among the Gods, believing it must inspire Posterity, when they came to worship them, with a Love of Glory, and an Emulation of their Virtue. It is certainly a Point of great Importance what Statues we set up, especially in Temples, as also whereabouts, in what Number, and of what Materials: For no ridiculous Figures are to be admitted here, as of the God *Priapus*, that is usually set up in Gardens to scare away the Birds; nor of fight-

ing Soldiers, as in Porticoes, or the like; neither do I think they should be placed in close Nooks and mean Corners. But first let us treat of the Materials with which they should be made, and then proceed to the other Points. Of old, says *Plutarch*, they used to make their Images of Wood; as was that of *Apollo* at *Delos*; and at *Popolonia*, near *Piombino*, was one of *Jupiter* of Vine-tree, which many affirmed to have remained perfectly clear of the least Corruption. Of the same Sort was that of the *Ephesian Diana*, which some said was of Ebony, but *Musianus* tells us it was of Vine-tree. *Peras*, who built the Temple of *Juno* the *Argive*, and dedicated his Daughter to be Priestess of it, made a *Jupiter* out of the Trunk of a Peartree. Some would not allow the Statues of the Gods to be made of Stone, as thinking that Material had something in it too rugged and cruel. They also disapproved of Gold and Silver for this Use, because those Metals are produced of a barren ungrateful Soil, and have a wan sickly Hue. The Poet says:

Great Jove *stood crampt beneath the lowly Roof,*
Scarce full erect; and in his mighty Hand
Brandish'd aloft a Thunderbolt of Clay.

SOME among the *Ægyptians* were of Opinion, that the Substance of God was Fire, and that he dwelt in the elemental Flame, and could not be conceived by the Senses of Mankind: For which Reason they made their Gods of Christal. Others thought the Gods ought to be made of black Stone, in the Supposition of that Colour being incomprehensible; and others lastly of Gold, in Conformity with the Colour of the Stars. I own for my Part, I have been very much in Suspense what Materials was most proper for making Images that are to be the Objects of Worship. You will say, no doubt, that whatever is to be made

into

into the Reprefentation of God, ought to be the nobleft Material that can be had. Next to the nobleft is the rareft; and yet I would not be for making them of Salt, as *Solinus* informs us the *Sicilians* ufed to do; nor of Glafs, like fome mentioned by *Pliny*; neither would I have them of maffy Gold or Silver, not that I diflike thofe Materials for being produced of a barren Soil, or for their fickly Hue; but for other Reafons: Among which one is, that I think it fhould be a Point of Religion with us that thofe Reprefentations which we fet up to be adored as Gods, fhould bear as much Refemblance to the Divine Nature as poffible. For this Reafon, I would have them made immortal in Duration, as far as it is in the Power of mortal Men to effect it. And here I cannot help enquiring, what fhould be the Reafon of a very whimfical, though very old Perfuafion, which is firmly rooted in the Minds of the Vulgar, that a Picture of God, or of fome Saint in one Place fhall hear the Prayers of Votaries, when in another Place the Statue of the very fame God or Saint fhall be utterly deaf to them? Nay, and what is ftill more nonfenfical, if you do but remove the very fame Statue, for which the People ufed to have the higheft Veneration, to fome other Station, they feem to look upon it as a Bankrupt, and will neither truft it with their Prayers, nor take the leaft Notice of it. Such Statues fhould therefore have Seats that are fixed, eminent and peculiar to themfelves. It is faid, that there never was any beautiful Piece of Workmanfhip known in the Memory of Man to be made of Gold, as if that Prince of Metals difdained to owe any thing to the Skill of an Artificer. If this be true, we fhould never ufe it in the Statues of our Gods, which we fhould defire to make fuitable to the Subject. Befides that, the Thirft of the Gold might tempt fome not only to rob our Statue

of his Beard, but to melt him quite down. I fhould chufe Brafs, if the lovely Purity of fine white Marble did not oblige me to give that the Preference. Yet there is one Confideration which weighs very much in Favour of Brafs, and that is its Duration, provided we make our Statue not fo maffy, but that the Odium and Deteftation of fpoiling it may be much greater than the Profit to be made by melting it down for other Purpofes: I would have it indeed no more than if it were beat out with a Hammer, or run into a thin Plate, fo as to feem no more than a Skin. We read of a Statue made of Ivory, fo large that it would hardly ftand under the Roof of the Temple. But that I diflike, for there ought to be a due Proportion obferved as well in Size, as in Form and Compofition: Upon which Accounts too the Figures of the greater Deities, with their gruff Beards, and ftern Countenances, do not fuit well in the fame Place with the foft Features of Virgins. I am likewife of Opinion, that the having but few Statues of Gods, may help to increafe the People's Veneration and Reverence to them. Two, or at moft three, may be placed properly enough upon the Altar. All the reft may be difpofed in Niches in other convenient Places. In all fuch Reprefentations of Gods and Heroes, the Sculptor fhould endeavour as much as poffible, to exprefs both by the Habit and Action of the Figure, the Character and Life of the Perfon. Not that I approve of thofe extravagant Attitudes which make a Statue look like the Hero of a Droll, or a Prize-fighter; but I would have fomewhat of a Dignity and Majefty both in the Countenance, and all the reft of the Body, that fhould fpeak the God, fo that he may feem both by his Look and Pofture to be ready to hear and receive his Adorers. Such fhould be the Statues in Temples. Let others be left to Theatres, and other profane Edifices.

196

THE
ARCHITECTURE
OF
Leone Batiſta Alberti.

BOOK VIII. CHAP. I.

Of the Ornaments of the great Ways either within or without the City, and of the proper Places for interring or burning the Bodies of the Dead.

WE have formerly obſerved, that the Ornaments annexed to all Sorts of Buildings make an eſſential Part of Architecture, and it is manifeſt that every Kind of Ornament is not proper for every Kind of Structure. Thus we are to endeavour, to the utmoſt of our Power, to make our ſacred Works, eſpecially if they are of a publick Nature, as compleatly adorned as poſſible, as being intended for the Honour of the Gods; whereas profane Structures are deſigned entirely for Men. The meaner therefore ought to yield to the more honourable; but yet they too may be embelliſhed with ſuch Ornaments as are ſuitable to them. In what Manner ſacred Buildings of a publick Nature are to be adorned, we have ſhewn in the laſt Book: We now come to profane Structures, and to give an Account what Ornaments are proper to each diſtinct Sort of them. And firſt I ſhall take Notice, that all Ways are publick Works, as being contrived for the Uſe of the Citizens, and the Convenience of Strangers: But as there are Travellers by Water as well as by Land, we ſhall ſay ſomething of both. And here it will be proper to call to Mind what has been ſaid elſewhere, that of Ways ſome are properly Highways, others in a Manner but private ones; as alſo, that there muſt be a Difference between the Ways within the City, and thoſe in the Country. Highways in the Country receive their greateſt Beauty from the Country itſelf through which they lie, from its being rich, well cultivated, full of Houſes and Villages, affording delightful Proſpects, now of the Sea, now of a fine Hill, now a River, now a Spring, now a barren Spot and a Rock, now a fine Plain, Wood, or Valley; nor will it be a ſmall Addition to its Beauty, that it be not ſteep, broken by Precipices, or deep with Dirt; but clear, ſmooth, ſpacious and open on all Sides: and what Pains were not the Ancients at to obtain theſe Advantages? I ſhall not waſte the Reader's Time to relate how they paved their Highways for above an hundred Miles round their Capital with extreme hard Stones, raiſing ſolid Cauſeways under them with huge Stones all the Way. The *Appian* Way was paved from *Rome* quite to *Brunduſium.* In many Places along their Highways we ſee Rocks demoliſhed, Mountains levelled, Vallies raiſed, Hills cut through, with incredible Expence and miraculous Labour; Works of great Uſe and Glory. Another great Embelliſhment to a Highway, is its furniſhing Travellers with frequent Occaſion of Diſcourſe, eſpecially upon notable Subjects. A Friend or Companion that is not ſparing of his Speech, ſays *Laberius*, upon a Journey is as good as a Vehicle; and there is no doubt but Diſcourſe takes of much

from

197

from the Fatigue of Travelling. For which Reaſon, as I had always the higheſt Eſteem for the Prudence of our Anceſtors in all their Inſtitutions, ſo I particularly commend them for that Cuſtom of theirs, whereof we ſhall ſpeak immediately, by which, though in it they aimed at much greater Ends, they afforded ſo much Recreation to Travellers. It was a Law of the twelve Tables, that no dead Body ſhould be interred or burnt within the City, and it was a very ancient Law of the Senate that no Corpſe ſhould be interred within the Walls, except the Veſtal Virgins, and the Emperors, who were not included within this Prohibition. *Plutarch* tell us, that the *Valeri* and the *Fabricii*, as a Mark of Honour, had a Privilege to be buried in the Forum; but their Deſcendants, having only ſet their dead down in it, and juſt clapt a Torch to the Body, uſed immediately to take it up again to bury it elſewhere; thereby ſhewing that they had ſuch a Privilege, but that they did not think it decent to make uſe of it. The Ancients therefore choſe their Sepulchres in convenient and conſpicuous Places by the Side of Highways, and embelliſhed them, as far as their Abilities and the Skill of the Architect would reach, with a perfect Profuſion of Ornaments. They were built after the nobleſt Deſigns; no Columns or Pilaſters were ſpared for, nor did they want the richeſt Incruſtations, nor any Delicacies that Sculpture or Painting could afford; and they were generally adorned with Buſts of Braſs or marble finiſhed after the moſt exquiſite Taſte: By which Cuſtom how much that prudent People promoted the Service of the Commonwealth and good Manners, would be tedious now to recapitulate. I ſhall only juſt touch upon thoſe Points which make to our preſent Purpoſe. And how, think ye, muſt it delight Travellers as they paſſed along the *Appian* Way, or any other great Road, to find them full of a vaſt Number of Tombs of the moſt excellent Workmanſhip, and to be every Moment picking out ſome more beautiful than the reſt, and obſerving the Epitaphs and Effigies of their greateſt Men? Do you not think that from ſo many Monuments of ancient Story, they muſt of Neceſſity take continual Occaſion to diſcourſe of the noble Exploits performed by thoſe Heroes of old, thereby ſweetning the Tediouſneſs of their Journey, and exalting the Honour of *Rome*, their native City? But this was the leaſt of the good Effects which they produced; and it was of much more Importance that they conduced not a little the Preſervation of the Commonwealth, and of the Fortunes of private Perſons. One of the chief Cauſes why the Rich rejected the *Agrarian* Law, as we are informed by the Hiſtorian *Appian*, was becauſe they looked upon it to be an Impiety to ſuffer the Property of the Tombs of their Forefathers to be transferred to others. How many great Inheritances may we therefore ſuppoſe them to have left untouched to their Poſterity, merely upon this Principle of Duty, Piety or Religion, which elſe would have been prodigally waſted in Riot and Gaming? Beſides that thoſe Monuments were a very great Honour to the Name of the City itſelf, and of a great Number of private Families, and was a conſtant Incitement to Poſterity to imitate the Virtues of thoſe whom they ſaw ſo highly revered. Then again, with what Eyes think you, whenever ſuch a Misfortune happened, muſt they behold a furious and inſolent Enemy ranſacking among the Sepulchres of their Anceſtors? And what Man could be ſo baſe and cowardly, as not to be immediately inflamed with Rage and Deſire of revenging ſuch an Inſult upon his Country and his Honour? And what Boldneſs and Courage muſt Shame, Piety and Grief ſtir up in the Hearts of Men upon ſuch an Occaſion? The Ancients therefore are greatly to be praiſed; not that I preſume to blame the preſent Practice of burying our Dead within the City, and in holy Places, provided we do not lay them in our Temples, where our Magiſtrates and great Men are to meet for the Celebration of holy Rites, ſo as to pollute the moſt ſacred Offices with the noiſome Vapours of a rotting Corpſe. The Cuſtom of burning the Dead was much more convenient.

Chap. II.

Of Sepulchres, and the various Manner of Burial.

I Shall here take an Opportunity to inſert ſome Things, which in my Opinion, are by no means to be omitted, concerning the Structure of Sepulchres, ſince they ſeem to partake of the Nature of publick Works, as being dedicated to Religion. Let the Place where you
inter

inter a dead Body, says the old Law, be sacred; and we still profess the same Belief, namely, that Sepulchres belong to Religion. As Religion therefore ought to be preferred before all Things, I shall treat of these, though intended for the Use of private Persons, before I proceed to profane Works of a publick Nature. There scarce ever was a People so barbarous, as to be without the Use of Sepulchres, except, perhaps, those wild *Ichthyophagi* in the remote Parts of *India*, who are said to throw the Bodies of their Dead into the Sea, affirming that it mattered little whether they were consumed by Fire, Earth, or Water. The *Albani* of *Scythia* too thought it to be a Crime to take any Care of the Dead. The *Sabæans* looked upon a Corpse to be no better than so much Dung, and accordingly they cast the Bodies, even of their Kings, upon the Dunghill. The *Troglodytes* used to tie the Head and Feet of their Dead together, and so hurried them away, with Scoffs and Flouts, to the first convenient Spot of Ground they could find, without more Regard to one Place than to another, where they threw them in, setting up a Goat's Horn at their Head. But no Man who has the least Tincture of Humanity, will approve of these barbarous Customs. Others, as well among the *Ægyptians* as the *Greeks*, used to erect Sepulchres not only to the Bodies, but even to the Names of their Friends; which Piety must be universally commended. It was a very laudable Notion among the *Indians*, that the best Monument was to live in the Memory of Posterity; and therefore they celebrated the Funerals of their greatest Men no otherwise than by singing their Praises. However, it is my Opinion, that Care ought to be taken of the dead Body, for the Sake of the Living; and for the Preservation of the Name to Posterity, there can be no Means more effectual than Sepulchres. Our Ancestors used to erect Statues and Sepulchres, at the publick Expence, in Honour of those that had spilt their Blood and lost their Lives for the Commonwealth, as a Reward of their Services, and an Incitement to others to emulate their Virtue: But perhaps they set up Statues to a great many, but Sepulchres to few, because they knew that the former were defaced and consumed by Age; whereas the Sanctity of Sepulchres, says *Cicero*, is so annexed to the very Ground itself, that nothing can either efface or remove it: For whereas other Things are destroyed, Tombs grow more sacred by Age. And they dedicated these Se-

pulchres to Religion, as I imagine, with this View, that the Memory of the Person, which they trusted to the Protection of such a Structure, and to the Stability of the Ground, might be defended by the Reverence and Fear of the Gods, from all Violence from the Hand of Man. Hence proceeded the Law of the twelve Tables, that the Vestibule or Entrance of a Sepulchre should not be employed to any Man's private Use, and there was moreover a Law which ordained the heaviest Punishment upon any Man that should violate an Urn, or throw down or break any of the Columns of a Tomb. In a Word, the Use of Sepulchres has been received by all the politest Nations, and the Care and Respect of them was so great among the *Athenians*, that if any of their Generals neglected to give honourable Burial to one of those that were slain in War, he was liable to capital Punishment for it. There was a Law among the *Hebrews*, which injoined them to give Burial even to their Enemies. Many and various are the Methods of Burial and Sepulture which we read of; but they are entirely foreign to our Design: As for Instance, that which is related of the *Scythians*, who thought the greatest Honour they could do their Dead, was to eat them at their Meals; and others kept Dogs to devour them when they died: But of this we need say no more. Most of the wisest Legislators have been careful to prevent Excess in the Expence and Magnificence of Funerals and Tombs. *Pittacus* ordained, that the greatest Ornament that should be erected over any Person's Grave, should be three little Columns, one single Cubit high; for it was the Opinion, that it was ridiculous to make any Difference in a Thing that was common to the Nature of every Man, and therefore in this Point the Richest and the Poorest were set upon the same Foot, and all were covered with common Earth, according to the old Custom; in doing which it was the received Notion, that as Man was originally formed of Earth, such a Burial was only laying him once more in his Mother's Lap. We also find an ancient Regulation, that no Man should have a more magnificent Tomb, than could be built by ten Men in the Space of three Days. The *Ægyptians*, on the contrary, were more curious about their Sepulchres than any other Nation whatsoever; and they used to say, that it was very ridiculous in Men to take so much Pains in the building of Houses where they were to dwell but a very short Space of Time, and to neglect the Structure of a Habitation where they
were

were to dwell for ever. The most probable Account I can find of the first Original of these Structures, is as follows: The *Getæ*, in the most remote Antiquity, used at first, in the Place where they interred a dead Body, to set up a Stone for a Mark, or perhaps (as *Plato* in his Laws more approves) a Tree, and afterwards they used to raise something of a Fence about it to keep off the Beasts from routing it up, or moving it out of its Place; and when the same Season of the Year came round again, and they saw that Field either chequered with Flowers, or laden with Grain as it was when the Person died, it was no wonder if it awakened in them the Love of their dear Friends whom they had lost, and prompted them to go together to the Place where they lay, relating and singing their Actions and Sayings, and dressing up their Monuments with whatever they thought would embellish them. Hence perhaps arose the Custom among several different Nations, and particularly among the *Greeks*, of adorning and offering Sacrifices upon the Tombs of those to whom they were much obliged. They met, says *Thucydides*, upon the Place, in Habits suitable to the Occasion, bringing with them the first Fruits of their Harvest, thinking the publick Performance of these Rites to be an Act of the greatest Piety and Devotion. From whence I proceed to conjecture, that besides raising the Ground over the Place of Burial, and erecting little Columns for Marks, they used also to raise little Alars whereon to celebrate those Sacrifices with the greatest Decency, and consequently they took care to make them as convenient and beautiful as was possible. The Places where these Tombs were erected, were various amongst the Ancients. According to the Pontificial Law, it was not permitted to erect a Tomb in any publick Square. *Plato* was of Opinion, that a Man ought not to be in the least offensive to human Society either alive or dead; and for this Reason he ordained that the Dead should be interred without the City, in some barren Place. In Imitation of this, others set apart a certain determined Place of Burial, under the open Air, and out of the Way of all Resort; which I highly approve: Others, on the contrary, preserved the Bodies of their Dead in their Houses, inclosed either in Salt or Terrass. *Mycerinus*, King of *Ægypt*, inclosed the dead Body of his Daughter within a wooden Figure of a Bull, and commanded the Sacrificers to perform Obsequies in her Honour every Day. *Servius* relates, that the Ancients used to place the Sepulchres of their Sons, that had the greatest Stock of Merit and Nobility, upon the Top of very high Hills. The *Alexandrians*, in the Time of *Strabo* the Historian, had Gardens and Inclosures consecrated wholly to the Burial of the Dead. Our more modern Ancestors used to build little Chapels, along the Sides of their great Churches, on purpose for Tombs. All through the Country, which was once the ancient *Latium*, we find the Burial-places of whole Families, made under Ground, with Urns standing in Rows along the Walls full of the Ashes of the Deceased, with short Inscriptions, and the Names of the Baker, Barber, Cook, Surgeon, and other Officers and Servants that were reckoned Part of the Family; in those Urns which inclosed the Ashes of little Children, once the Joy of their Mothers, they made their Effigies in Stuc; but those of grown Men, especially if they were noble, were made of Marble. These were the Customs of the Ancients: Nor do I blame the making use of any Place indifferently for burying the Body, provided some distinguished Place be chosen for setting up an Inscription in the Person's Honour. Now what chiefly delights us in all Tombs, is the Design of the Structure, and the Epitaph. What Sort of Design the Ancients approved most in these Works, I cannot so easily affirm. *Augustus*'s Sepulchre in *Rome* was built of square Blocks of Marble, shaded with Ever-greens, and at the Top stood his Statue. In the Island of *Tyrina*, not far from *Carmania*, the Sepulchre of *Erythræa* was a great Mound of Earth planted with wild Palm-trees. The Sepulchre of *Zarina*, Queen of the *Saces*, was a Pyramid of three Sides, with a Statue of Gold on the Top. *Archatheus*, one of *Xerxes*'s Lieutenants, had a Tomb of Earth erected for him by the whole Army. But the main Point which all seem to have aimed at, was to have something different from all others, not as to condemn the Sepulchres of others, but to draw the Eyes of Men to take the greater Notice of them: And from this general Use of Sepulchres, and these constant Endeavours to invent something new in that Way, the Consequence at last was, that it was impossible to think of any thing which had not already been put in Practice to a very great Perfection, and all were extremely beautiful in their several Kinds. From the Observation I have made of the numberless Works of this Nature, I find that some had nothing in their Eye, but adorning that which was to contain the Body, while others

198

others went farther, and raised such a Super-structure as was proper for placing Epitaphs and Inscriptions of the Person's Exploits. The former were contented with a plain Case for the Body, or with adding somewhat of a little Chapel about it, according to the Religion of the Place. But the others erected either a Column, or a Pyramid, an Obelisk, or some other great Superstructure, not principally for con-taining the Body, but rather for delivering down the Name with Glory to Posterity. We have already taken Notice, that there is a Stone called *Sarcophagus*, found at *Ason*, a Town of *Troas*, which consumes a dead Body im-mediately; and in any made Ground, con-sisting chiefly of old Rubbish, the Moisture is presently dried up. But I shall insist no longer upon these minute Particulars.

CHAP. III.

Of little Chapels, by way of Sepulchres, Pyramids, Columns, Alars and Moles.

NOW since the Sepulchres of the An-cients are generally approved, and we find them in different Places built sometimes after the Manner of little Chapels, sometimes in Pyramids, sometimes Columns, and in se-veral other Forms, as Moles and the like, we shall say something of each of these: And first of Chapels. These little Chapels should be like so many little Models of Temples; nor is it at all improper to add the Ornaments and Designs of any other Sort of Building, provi-ded they be equally well adapted both for Beauty and Duration. Whether it be most adviseable to build a Sepulchre which we would have, if possible, endure to Eternity, of noble or mean Materials, is not thoroughly deter-mined, upon Account of the Danger of their being removed for their Value: But the Beau-ty of its Ornaments, as we have observed else-where, is extremely effectual to its Preserva-tion, and to securing the Monument to Pos-terity. Of the Sepulchres of those great Prin-ces *Caius Caligula*, and *Claudius Cæsar*, which no doubt must have been very noble, nothing now remains but some few small square Stones of two Cubits broad, on which their Names are inscribed; and if those Inscriptions had been cut upon larger Stones, I doubt not they too would e'er now have been carried away with the other Ornaments. In other Places we see Sepulchres of very great Antiquity, which have never been injured by any body, because they were built of common Chequer-work, or of Stone that would not adorn any other Building, so that they were never any Temptation to Greediness. From whence I draw this Admonition to those who would have their Sepulchres remain to Perpetuity, that they build not indeed with a base Sort of Stone, but not with such excellent, as to be a Temptation to every Man that beholds it, and to be in perpetual Danger of being stolen away. Besides, in all Works of this Nature, a decent Modesty should be observed according to every Man's Quality and Degree; so that, I con-demn a Profusion of Expence in the Tombs even of Monarchs themselves, nor can I help blaming those huge Piles, built by the *Ægyp-tian* Kings for their Sepulchres, which seem to have been displeasing to the Gods themselves, since none of them were buried in those proud Monuments. Others perhaps may praise our *Etrurians* for not coming short even of the *Ægyptians* in the Magnificence of their Tombs, and particularly *Porsena*, who built himself a Sepulchre below the Town of *Clusium*, all of square Stone, in the Base whereof, which was fifty Foot high, was a Labyrinth which no Man could find his Way thro', and over this Base five Pyramids, one in the Middle, and one at each Corner, the Breadth of each whereof, at the Bottom was seventy-five Foot; at the Top of each hung a brazen Globe, to which several little Bells were fastened by Chains, which being shaken by the Wind might be heard at a considerable Distance: Over all this were four other Pyramids, an hundred Foot high, and others again over these, aston-ishing no less for their Workmanship than for their Greatness. I cannot be pleased with these enormous Structures, serving to no good Pur-pose whatsoever. There is something much more commendable in the Tomb of *Cyrus*, King of the *Persians*, and there is more true Greatness in his Modesty, than in the vain Glory of all those haughtier Piles. Near the Town of *Pasargardæ*, in a little vaulted Temple built of square Stone, with a Door scarce two Foot high, lay the Body of *Cyrus*, inclosed in a golden Urn, as the Royal Dignity required; round

round this little Chapel was a Grove of all Sorts of Fruit-trees, and a large green Meadow, full of Roses and other Flowers and Herbs of grateful Scent, and of every Thing that could make the Place delightful and agreeable.   The Epitaph was adapted to the Structure:

Cyrus *am I that founded* Persia's *State,*
Then envy not this little Place of Rest.

But to return to Pyramids. Some few perhaps may have built their Pyramids with three Sides, but they have generally been made with four, and their Height has most commonly been made equal to their Breadth. Some have been particularly commended for making the Joints of the Stones in their Pyramids so close, that the Shadow which they cast was perfectly straight without the least Interruption. Pyramids have for the most Part been made of square Stone, but some few have been built with Brick.   As for these Columns which have been erected as Monuments; some have been such as are used in other Structures; others have been so large as to be fit for no Edifice; but merely to serve as a Monument to Posterity.

Of this last Sort we are now to treat, and its Members are as follows: Instead of a Basement there are several Steps rising above the Level of the Platform, over these a square Plinth, and above that another not less than the first.   In the third Place came the Base of the Column, then the Column with its Capital, and last of all the Statue standing upon a Plinth.   Some between the first and second Plinths under the Base placed a Sort of Die to raise the Work higher, and give it the greater Air of Majesty. The Proportions of all these Members are taken from the Diameter of the Bottom of the Shaft, as we observed with Relation to the Columns of the Temples; but the Base, in this Case where the Superstructure is to be so very large, must have but one Torus, and not several like common Columns. The whole Thickness of the Base therefore must be divided into five Parts, two of which must be given to the Torus, and three to the Plinth. The Measure of the Plinth every Way must be one Diameter and a Quarter of the Shaft of the Column. The Pedestal on which this Base lies must have the following Parts. The uppermost Member in this, and indeed all other Ornaments, must be a Cymatium, and the lowermost a Plinth, which, whether it be in the Nature of Steps, or of a Cyma either upright or reversed, is properly the

Base of each Member.   But we have some few Things relating to Pedestals to take Notice of, which we purposely omitted in the last Book, in order to consider them here.   We observed that it was usual to run up a continued low Wall under all the Columns, in order to support them; but then to make the Passage more clear and open, it was common to remove that Part of this Wall which lay between the Columns, and to leave only that Part which was really necessary to the Support of the Column. This Part of the Wall thus left I call the Pedestal.   The Ornament of this Pedestal at the Top was a Cymatium, either upright or reversed, or something of the same Nature, which was answerd at the Bottom by a Plinth. These two Ornaments went clear round the Pedestal. The Cymatium was the fifth Part of the Height of the whole Pedestal, or else the sixth; and the Body of the Pedestal was never less in Thickness than the Diameter of the Bottom of the Shaft, that the Plinth of the Base might not lie upon a Void. Some, in order to strengthen the Work yet more, made the Pedestal broader than the Plinth of the Base, by an eighth Part of that Plinth. Lastly, the Height of the Pedestal, besides its Cymatium and Plinth, was either equal to its Breadth, or a fifth Part more: And this I find to have been the Ordonnance of the Pedestal under the Columns used by the most excellent Workmen.   But to return to the Column.   Under the Base of the Column we are to place the Pedestal, answering duly to the Proportions of the Base in the Manner just now mentioned.   This Pedestal must be crowned with an entire Cornice, which is most usually of the *Ionic* Order; the Members of which you may remember to be as follows: The first and lowest Member is a Cymatium, then a Denticle, next an Ovolo, with a small Baguette and a Fillet.   Under this Pedestal is placed another answerable to the former in every Member, and of such a Proportion that no Part of the Superstructure may lie over a Void; but to this Pedestal we must ascend from the Level of the Ground by three or five Steps, unequal both in their Height and Breadth; and these Stepts all together must not be higher than a fourth, nor lower than a sixth Part of the Height of the Pedestal which stands upon them. In this lower Pedestal we make a Door dressed after the Manner of the *Doric* or *Ionic* Order, according to the Rules already laid down for the Doors of Temples.   In the upper Pedestal we place our Inscriptions or carve Trophies. If we make

any

any Thing of a Plinth between these two Pedestals, the Height of that Plinth must be a third Part of the Height of the Pedestal itself; and this Interspace must be filled up with the Figures of chearful Deities, such as Victory, Glory, Fame, Plenty, and the like. Some covered the upper Pedestal with Plates of Brass, gilt. The Pedestals and the Base being compleated, the next Work is to erect the Column upon them, and its Height is usually seven Times its Diameter. If the Column be very high, let its upper Diameter be no more than one tenth Part less than its lower; but in smaller Columns, observe the Rules given in the last Book. Some have erected Columns an hundred Foot high, and enriched all the Body of the Shaft with Figures and Stories in Relieve, leaving a Hollow within for a winding Stair to ascend to the Top of the Column. On such Columns they set a *Doric* Capital, but without any Gorgerine. Over the upper Cymaise of the Capital in smaller Columns they made a regular Architrave, Freze and Cornice, full of Ornaments on every Side; but in these great Columns those Members were omitted, it being no easy Matter to find Stones sufficiently large for such a Work, nor to set them in their Places when found. But at the Top of the Capital both of great and small, there was always something to serve as a Pedestal for the Statue to stand upon. If this Pedestal was a square Plinth, then none of its Angles ever exceeded the Solid of the Column: But if it was round, its Diameter was not to be more than one of the Sides of such a Square. The Height of the Statue was one third of the Column; and for this Sort of Columns thus much may suffice. The Structure of Moles among the Ancients was as follows: First they raised a square Basement as they did for the Platforms of their Temples. Then they carried up a Wall not less high than a sixth, nor higher than a fourth of the Length of the Platform. The whole Ornament of this Wall was either at the Top and Bottom, and sometimes at the Angles, or else consisted in a Kind of Colonade all along the Wall. If there were no Columns but only at the Angles, then the whole Height of the Wall, above the Basement, was divided into four Parts, three of which were given to the Column with its Base and Capital, and one to the other Ornaments

at the Top, to wit, the Architrave, Freze and Cornice; and this last Part was again divided into sixteen Minutes, five of which were given to the Architrave, five to the Freze, and six to the Cornice and its Cymaise. The Space between the Architrave and the Basement was divided into five-and-twenty Parts; three whereof were given to the Height of the Capital, and two to the Height of the Base, and the Remainder to the Height of the Column, and there were always square Pilasters at the Angles according to this Proportion: The Base consisted of a single Torus, which was just half the Height of the Base itself. The Pilaster at the Bottom, instead of a Fillet, had just the same Projecture as at the Top of the Shaft. The Breadth of the Pilaster, in this Sort of Structure, was one fourth of its Height; but when the rest of the Wall was adorned with an Order of Columns, then the Pilasters at the Angles were in Breadth only a sixth Part of their Length, and the other Columns along the Wall borrowed all their Ornaments and Proportions from the Design of those used in Temples. There is only this Difference between this Sort of Colonades and the former; that in the first, as the Base is continued on from one Angle of the Wall to the other, at the Bottom, so also are the Fillet and Astragal at the Top of the Column under the Architrave, which is not practiced where there are a Number of Columns set against the Wall; though some are for carrying on the Base quite round the Structure here as well as in Temples. Over this square Structure which served for a Basement, rose a round one of excellent Workmanship, exceeding the Basement in Height not less than half its Diameter, nor more than two thirds, and the Breadth of this Rotunda was never less than half one of the Sides of the Basement, nor more than five sixths. Many took five thirds, and over this round Building raised another square one, with a second round over that, after the same Manner as the former, till the Edifice rose to four Stories, adorning them according to the foregoing Description. Neither within the Mole itself wanted there Stairs, or little Chapels for Devotion, or Columns rising from the Basement to the upper Stories, with Statues between them, and Inscriptions disposed in convenient Places.

CHAP. IV.

Of the Inscriptions and Symbols carved on Sepulchres

LET us now proceed to the Inscriptions themselves, the Use whereof was various, and almost infinite among the Ancients, being by them not only used in their Sepulchres, but also in their Temples, and even in their private Houses. *Symmachus* tells us, that on the Pediments of their Temples they used to cut the Name of the God to whom they dedicated, and it is the Practice, with our Countrymen to inscribe upon their Churches the Name of the Saints, and the Year when they were consecrated to them; which I highly approve. Nor is it foreign to our Subject to take Notice, that when *Crates* the Philosopher came to *Cyzicus*, finding these Verses wrote over the Door of almost every private House:

The mighty Hercules, *the Son of* Jove,
The Scourge of Monsters, dwells within these Walls.
Let nothing ill dare to approach the Place.

HE could not help laughing, and advised them rather to write over their Doors: *Here dwells Poverty*; thinking that would drive away all Sorts of Monsters must faster than *Hercules* himself, though he were to live again. Epitaphs on Sepulchres are either written, which are properly Epigrams, or represented by Figures and Symbols. *Plato* would not have an Epitaph consist of more than four Lines; and accordingly *Ovid* says:

On the rear'd Column be my Story wrote,
But brief, that every Passenger may read.

AND it is certain that Prolixity, though it is to be condemned every where, is worse in this Case than any other: Or if the Inscription be of any Length, it ought to be extremely elegant, and apt to raise Compassion, and so pleasing that you may not regret the Trouble of reading it, but be fond of getting it by Heart, and repeating it often. That of *Omenea* has been much commended.

If cruel Fate allow'd the sad Exchange
Of Life for Life, how chearfully for thee,
My best-lov'd Omenea *had I died!*
But since it must not be, these weeping Eyes

The hated Sun and painful Light shall fly;
To seek thee in the gloomy Realms below.

So this other:

Behold, O Citizens, the Bust and Urn
Of ancient Ennius, *your old Bard, who sung*
In lofty Notes your Fathers brave Exploits.
Let none with Tears or solemn funeral Pomp
Bewail my Death, for Ennius *still survives;*
Still honour'd lives upon the Tongue of Fame.

ON the Tombs of those that were slain at *Thermopylæ*, was this Inscription: *O Passenger, tell the* Spartans *that we lie here, obeying their Commands.* Nor is there any thing amiss in throwing in a Stroke of Pleasantry upon such an Occasion.

Thy Journey, Traveller, a Moment stay
To view a Wonder strange and seldom seen:
A Man and Wife that lie for once at Peace.
Thou ask'st our Name. Ne'er shalt thou know
    from me.
Mind not my stutt'ring Husband; come to me:
His Name is Balbus, Bebbra *mine. Ah Wife!*
Will nothing stop that drunken Tongue of thine!

I AM extremely delighted with such Inscriptions. The Ancients used to gild the Letters which they used in their Inscriptions. The *Ægyptians* employed Symbols in the following Manner: They carved an Eye, by which they understood God; a Vulture for Nature; a Bee for King; a Circle for Time; an Ox for Peace, and the like. And their Reason for expressing their Sense by these Symbols was, that Words were understood only by the respective Nations that talked the Language, and therefore Inscriptions in common Characters must in a short Time be lost: As it has actually happened to our *Etrurian* Characters: For among the Ruins of several Towns, Castles and Burial-places, I have seen Tomb-stones dug up with Inscriptions on them, as is generally believed, in *Etrurian* Characters, which are like both those of the *Greeks* and *Latins*; but no body can understand them: And the same, the *Ægyptians* supposed, must be the Case with all Sorts of

    Writing

Writing whatſoever; but the Manner of expreſſing their Senſe which they uſed upon theſe Occaſions, by Symbols, they thought muſt always be underſtood by ingenious Men of all Nations, to whom alone they were of Opinion, that Things of Moment were fit to be communicated. In Imitation of this Practice, various Symbols have been uſed upon Sepulchres. Over the Grave of *Diogenes* the *Cynic*, was a Column with a Dog upon the Top of it, cut in *Parian* Marble. *Cicero* glories, that he who was of *Arpinum*, was the Diſcoverer at *Syracuſe* of *Archimedes*'s Tomb, which was quite decayed and neglected, and all over-grown with Brambles, and not known, even to the Inhabitants of the Place, and which he found out by a Cylinder and ſmall Sphere which he ſaw cut upon a high Column that ſtood over it. On the Sepulchre of *Symandes*, King of *Ægypt*, the Figure of his Mother was cut out of a Piece of Marble twenty Cubits high, with three Royal Diadems upon her Head, denoting her to be the Daughter, Wife and Mother of a King.

On the Tomb of *Sardanapalus*, King of the *Aſſyrians*, was a Statue which ſeemed to clap its Hands together by Way of Applauſe, with an Epitaph to this Effect: *In one ſingle Day I built* Tarſus *and* Archileum; *but do you, Friend, eat, drink and be merry; for there is nothing elſe among Men that is worthy of this Applauſe.* Such were the Inſcriptions and Symbols uſed in thoſe Nations. But our *Romans* recorded the Exploits of their great Men, by carving their Story in Marble. This gave riſe to Columns, Triumphal Arches, Porticoes enriched with memorable Events, preſerved both in Painting and Sculpture. But no Monument of this Nature ſhould be made, except for Actions that truly deſerve to be perpetuated. But we have now dwelt long enough upon this Subject. We have ſpoken of the publick Ways by Land; and the ſame Ornaments will ſerve thoſe by Water: But as high Watch-towers belong to both, it is neceſſary here to ſay ſomething of them.

CHAP. V.

Of Towers and their Ornaments.

THE greateſt Ornaments are lofty Towers placed in proper Situations, and built after handſome Deſigns: And when there are a good Number of them ſtrewed up and down the Country, they afford a moſt beautiful Proſpect: Not that I commend the Age about two hundred Years ago, when People ſeemed to be ſeized with a Kind of general Infection of building high Watch-towers, even in the meaneſt Villages, inſomuch that ſcarce a common Houſe-keeper thought he could not be without his Turret: By which means there aroſe a perfect Grove of Spires. Some are of Opinion, that the Minds of Men take particular Turns, at certain Seaſons, by the Influence of ſome Planet. Between three and four hundred Years ſince the Zeal for Religion was ſo warm, that Men ſeemed born for no other Employment but to build Churches and Chapels; for, to omit other Inſtances, in the ſingle City of *Rome* at this Day, though above half thoſe ſacred Structures are now ruinate, we ſee above two thouſand five hundred Churches ſtill remaining. And now again, what can be the Reaſon, that juſt at this Time all *Italy* ſhould be fired with a Kind of Emulation to put on

quite a new Face? How many Towns, which when we were Children, were built of nothing but Wood, are now lately ſtarted up all of Marble? But to return to the Subject of Towers. I ſhall not here ſtay to repeat what we read in *Herodotus*, that in the Middle of the Temple at *Babylon* there was a Tower, the Baſe whereof was a whole Furlong, or the eighth Part of a Mile, on every Side, and which conſiſted of eight Stories built one above another; a Way of Building which I extremely commend in Towers, becauſe each Story growing leſs and leſs all the Way up, conduces both to Strength and Beauty, and by being well knit one into another, makes the whole Structure firm. Towers are either ſquare or round, and in both theſe the Height muſt anſwer in a certain Proportion to the Breadth. When they are deſigned to be very taper, ſquare ones ſhould be ſix Times as high as they are broad, and round ones ſhould have four Times the Height of their Diameter. Thoſe which are intended to be very thick, ſhould have in Height, if ſquare, but four Times their Breadth, and if round, but three Diameters. The Thickneſs of the Walls, if they are forty Cubits high, muſt

muſt never be leſs than four Foot; if fifty Cubits, five Foot; if ſixty Cubits, ſix Foot, and ſo on in the ſame Proportion. Theſe Rules relate to Towers that are plain and ſimple: But ſome Architects, about half Way of the Height of the Tower, have adorned it with a Kind of Portico with inſulate Columns, others have made theſe Porticoes ſpiral all the Way up, others have ſurrounded it with ſeveral Porticoes like ſo many Coronets, and ſome have covered the whole Tower with Figures of Animals. The Rules for theſe Colonades are not different from thoſe for publick Edifices; only that we may be allowed to be rather more ſlender in all the Members, upon Account of the Weight of the Building. But whoever would erect a Tower beſt fitted for reſiſting the Injuries of Age, and at the ſame Time extremely delightful to behold, let him upon a ſquare Baſis, raiſe a round Superſtructure, and over that another ſquare one, and ſo on, making the Work leſs and leſs by Degrees, according to the Proportions obſerved in Columns. I will here deſcribe one which I think well worthy Imitation. Firſt from a ſquare Platform riſes a Baſement in Height one tenth Part of the whole Structure, and in Breadth one fourth Part of that whole Height. Againſt this Baſement, in the Middle of each Front ſtand two Columns, and one at each Angle, diſtinguiſhed by their ſeveral Ornaments, in the ſame Manner as we juſt now appointed for Sepulchres. Over this Baſement we raiſe a ſquare Superſtructure like a little Chapel, in Breadth twice the Height of the Baſement, and as high as broad, againſt which, we may ſet three, four or five Orders of Columns, in the ſame Manner as in Temples. Over this, we make our Rotondas, which may even be three in Number, and which from the Similitude of the ſeveral Shoots in a Cane or Ruſh, we ſhall call the Joints. The Height of each of theſe Joints ſhall be equal to its Breadth, with the Addition of one twelfth Part of that Breadth, which twelfth Part ſhall ſerve as a Baſement to each Joint. The Breadth ſhall be taken from that ſquare Chapel which we placed upon the firſt Baſement, in the following Manner: Dividing the Front of that ſquare Chapel into twelve Parts, give eleven of thoſe Parts to the firſt Joint; then dividing the Diameter of this firſt Joint into twelve Parts, give eleven of

them to the ſecond Joint, and ſo make the third Joint a twelfth Part narrower than the ſecond, and thus the ſeveral Joints will have the Beauty which the beſt ancient Architects highly commended in Columns, namely, that the lower Part of the Shaft ſhould be one fourth Part thicker than the upper. Round theſe Joints we muſt raiſe Columns with their proper Ornaments, in Number not leſs than eight, nor more than ſix: Moreover, in each Joint, as alſo in the ſquare Chapel, we muſt open Lights in convenient Places, and Niches with the Ornaments ſuitable to them. The Lights muſt not take up above half the Aperture between Column and Column. The ſixth Story in this Tower, which riſes from the third Rotonda muſt be a ſquare Structure, and its Breadth and Height muſt not be allowed above two third Parts of that third Rotonda. Its Ornament muſt be only ſquare Pilaſters ſet againſt the Wall, with Arches turned over them, with their proper Dreſs of Capitals, Architraves and the like, and between Pilaſter and Pilaſter, half the Break may be left open for Paſſage. The ſeventh and laſt Story ſhall be a circular Portico of inſulate Columns, open for Paſſage every Way; the Length of theſe Columns, with their Intablature, ſhall be equal to the Diameter of this Portico itſelf, and that Diameter ſhall be three fourths of the ſquare Building, on which it ſtands. This circular Portico ſhall be covered with a Cupola. Upon the Angles of the ſquare Stories in theſe Towers we ſhould ſet Acroteria equal in Height to the Architrave, Freze and Cornice which are beneath them. In the lowermoſt ſquare Story, placed juſt above the Baſement, the open Area within may be five eighths of the outward Breadth. Among the ancient Works of this Nature, I am extremely well pleaſed with *Ptolomey*'s Tower in the Iſland of *Pharos*, on the Top of which, for the Direction of Mariners, he placed large Fires, which were hung in a continual Vibration, and kept always moving about from Place to Place, leſt at a Diſtance thoſe Fires ſhould be miſtaken for Stars; to which he added moveable Images, to ſhew from what Corner the Wind blew with others, to ſhew in what Part of the Heavens the Sun was at that Time, and the Hour of the Day: Inventions extremely proper in ſuch a Structure.

CHAP. VI.

Of the principle Ways belonging to the City, and the Methods of adorning the Haven, Gates, Bridges, Arches, Cross-ways and Squares.

IT is now Time to make our Entrance into the City; but as there are some Ways both within and without the Town which are much more eminent than the common Sort, as those which lead to the Temple, the Basilique, or the Place for publick Spectacles, we shall first say something of these. We read that *Heliogabalus* paved these broader and nobler Ways with *Macedonian* Marble and Porphiry. Historians say much in Praise of a noble Street in *Bubaftus,* a City of *Ægypt,* which led to the Temple; for it ran thro' the Market-place, and was paved with very fine Stone, was four Jugera, or four hundred and eighty Foot broad, and bordered on each Side with stately Trees. *Arifteas* tells us, that in *Jerusalem* there were some very beautiful Streets, tho' narrow, thro' which the Magistrates and Nobles only were allowed to pass, to the Intent chiefly that the sacred Things which they carried, might not be polluted by the Touch of any Thing profane. *Plato* highly celebrates a Way all planted with Cypress Trees which led from *Gnossus* to the Cave and Temple of *Jupiter.* I find that the *Romans* had two Streets of this Sort, extremely noble and beautiful, one from the Gate to the Church of St. *Paul,* fifteen Stadia, or a Mile and seven Furlongs in Length, and the other from the Bridge to the Church of St. *Peter,* two thousand five hundred Foot long, and all covered with a Portico of Columns of Marble, with a Roof of Lead. Such Ornaments are extremely proper for Ways of this Nature. But let us now return to the more common Highways. The principal Head and Boundary of all Highways, whether within or without the City, unless I am mistaken, is the Gate for those by Land, and the Haven for those by Sea; Unless we will take notice of subterraneous Ways, of the Nature of those which we are told were at *Thebes* in *Ægypt,* thro' which their Kings could lead an Army unknown to any of the Citizens, or those which I find to have been pretty numerous near *Prenefte,* in the ancient *Latium,* dug under Ground from the Top of the Hill to the Level of the Plain, with wonderful Art; in one of which

we are told, that *Marius* perished when close pressed by the Siege. We are told by the Author of the Life of *Apollonius,* of a very wonderful Passage made by a Lady of *Media* at *Babylon,* under the River, and arched with Stone and Bitumen, thro' which she could go dryshod from the Palace to a Country House, on the other Side of the River. But we are not obliged to believe all that the *Greek* Writers tell us. To return to our Subject. The Gates are adorned in the same Manner as triumphal Arches, of which anon. The Haven is adorned by broad Porticoes, raised somewhat above the Level of the Ground, by a stately Temple, lofty and beautiful, with spacious Squares before it, and the Mouth of the Haven itself by huge Statues, such as were formerly to be seen in several Places, and particularly at *Rhodes,* where *Herod* is said to have erected three. Historians very much celebrate the Mole at *Samos,* which they say was an hundred and twenty Foot high, and ran out two Furlongs into the Sea. Doubtless such Works must greatly adorn the Haven, especially if they are masterly wrought, and not of base Materials. The Streets within the City, besides being handsomely paved and cleanly kept, will be rendered much more noble, if the Doors are built all after the same Model, and the Houses on each Side stand in an even Line, and none higher than another. The Parts of the Street which are principally to be adorned, are these: The Bridge, the Cross-ways, and the Place for publick Spectacles, which last is nothing else but an open Place, with Seats built about it. We will begin with the Bridge, as being one of the chief Parts of the Street. The Parts of the Bridge are the Piers, the Arches and the Pavement, and also the Street in the Middle for the Passage of Cattle, and the raised Causeways on each Side for the better Sort of Citizens, and the Sides or Rail, and in some Places Houses too, as in that most noble Bridge called *Adrian's Mole,* a Work never to be forgotten, the very Skeleton whereof, if I may so call it, I can never behold without a Sort of Reverence and Awe. It

was

was covered with a Roof supported by two-and-forty Columns of Marble, with their Architrave, Freze and Cornice, the Roof plated with Brass, and richly adorned. The Bridge must be made as broad as the Street which leads to it. The Piers must be equal to one another on each Side both in Number and Size, and be one third of the Aperture in Thickness. The Angles or Heads of the Piers that lie against the Stream must project in Length half the Breadth of the Bridge, and be built higher than the Water ever rises. The Heads of the Piers that lie along with the Stream must have the same Projecture, but then it will not look amiss to have them less acute, and as it were blunted. From the Heads of the Piers on each Side, it will be very proper to raise Butresses for the Support of the Bridge, in Thickness not less than two thirds of the Pier itself. The Crowns of all the Arches must stand quite clear above the Water: Their Dress may be taken from the *Ionic* or rather the *Doric* Architrave, and in large Bridges it must not be less in Breadth than the fifteenth Part of the whole Aperture of the Arch. To make the Rail or Side-wall of the Bridge the stronger, erect Pedestals at certain Distances by the Square and Plum-line, on which, if you please, you may raise Columns to support a Roof or Portico. The Height of this Side-wall with its Zocle and Cornice must be four Foot. The Spaces between the Pedestals may be filled up with a slight Breast-wall. The Crown both of the Pedestals and Breast-wall may be an upright Cymatium, or rather a reversed one, continued the whole Length of the Bridge, and the Plinth at Bottom must answer this Cymatium. The Causeway on each Side for Women and Foot Passengers must be raised a Foot or two higher than the Middle of the Bridge, which being intended chiefly for Beasts of Carriage, may be paved only with Flints. The Height of the Columns, with their Intablature, must be equal to the Breadth of the Bridge. The Crossways and Squares differ only in their Bigness, the Crossway being indeed nothing else but a small Square. *Plato* ordained that in all Crossways there should be Spaces left for Nurses to meet in with their Children. His Design in this Regulation was, I suppose, not only that the Children might grow strong by being in the Air, but also that the Nurses themselves, by seeing one another, might grow neater and more delicate, and be less liable to Negligence among so many careful Observers in the same

Business. It is certain, one of the greatest Ornaments either of a Square, or of a Crossway, is a handsome Portico, under which the old Men may spend the Heat of the Day, or be mutually serviceable to each other; besides that the Presence of the Fathers may deter and restrain the Youth, who are sporting and diverting themselves in the other Part of the Place, from the Mischievousness and Folly natural to their Age. The Squares must be so many different Markets, one for Gold and Silver, another for Herbs, another for Cattle, another for Wood, and so on; each whereof ought to have its particular Place in the City, and its distinct Ornaments; but that where the Traffick of Gold and Silver is to be carried on, ought to be much the Noblest? The *Greeks* made their Forums or Markets exactly square, and encompassed them with large double Porticoes, which they adorned with Columns and their Intablatures, all of Stone, with noble Terrasses at the Top, for taking the Air upon. Among our Countrymen the *Italians*, the Forums used to be a third Part longer than they were broad: And because in ancient Times they were the Places where the Shows of the *Gladiators* were exhibited, the Columns in the Porticoes were set at a greater Distance from each other, that they might not obstruct the Sight of those Diversions. In the Porticoes were the Shows for the Goldsmiths, and over the first Story were Galleries projecting out for seeing the Shows in, and the publick Magazines. This was the Method among the Ancients. For my Part I would have a Square twice as long as broad, and that the Porticoes and other Buildings about it should answer in some Proportion to the open Area in the Middle, that it may not seem too large, by means of the Lowness of the Buildings, nor too small, from their being too high. A proper Height for the Buildings about a Square is one third of the Breadth of the open Area, or one sixth at the least. I would also have the Porticoes raised above the Level of the Ground, one fifth Part of their Breadth, and that their Breadth should be equal to half the Height of their Columns, including the Intablature. The Proportions of the Columns should be taken from those of the Basilique, only with this Difference, that here the Architrave, Freze and Cornice together should be one fifth of the Column in Height. If you would make a second Row of Columns over this first, those Columns should be one fourth Part thinner and shorter than those below, and

for

Y y

for a Bafement to them you muft make a Plinth half the Height of the Bafement at the Bottom. But nothing can be a greater Ornament either to Squares or the Meeting of feveral Streets, than Arches at the Entrance of the Streets; an Arch being indeed nothing elfe but a Gate ftanding continually open. I am of Opinion, that the Invention of Arches were owing to thofe that firft enlarged the Bounds of the Empire: For it was the ancient Cuftom with fuch, as we are informed by *Tacitus*, to enlarge the Pomoerium, or vaçant Space left next the City Walls, as we find particularly that *Claudius* did. Now though they extended the Limits of the City, yet they thought it proper to preferve the old Gates, for feveral Reafons, and particularly becaufe they might fome Time or other happen to be a Safeguard againft the Irruption of an Enemy. Afterwards as thefe Gates ftood in the moft confpicuous Places, they adorned them with the Spoils which they had won from their Enemies, and the Enfigns of their Victories. To thefe Beginnings it was that Arches owed their Trophies, Infcriptions, Statues and Relieves. A very proper Situation for an Arch is where a Street joins into a Square, and efpecially in the Royal Street, by which Name I underftand the moft eminent in the City. An Arch, like a Bridge, fhould have no lefs than three open Paffages: That in the Middle for the Soldiers to return through in Triumph to pay their Devotions to their paternal Gods, and the two Side ones for the Matrons and Citizens to go out to meet and welcome them Home. When you build one of thefe Triumphal Arches, let the Line of the Platform which runs lengthways with the Street be the Half of the Line that goes crofs the Street from Right to Left, and the Length of this Crofs-line fhould never be lefs than fifty Cubits. This Kind of Structures is very like that of a Bridge, only it never confifts of more than four Piers and three Arches. Of the fhorteft Line of the Platform which runs lengthways with the Street, leaves one eighth Part towards the Square, and as much behind on the other Side, for the Platforms of Columns to be erected againft the Piers. The other longer Line which croffes the Street muft alfo be divided into eight Parts, two whereof muft be given to the Aperture in the Middle, and one to each Pier and to each Side opening. The perpendicular Upright of the Piers that fupport the middle Arch, to the Spring of that Arch, muft be two of the afore-

faid Parts and a Third; and the Piers of the two Side Arches muft bear the fame Proportion to their refpective Aperture. The Soffit of the Arches muft be perfect Vaults. The Crowns of the Piers beneath the Spring of the Arch, may be made in Imitation of the *Doric* Capital, only inftead of the Ovolo and Abacus they may have a projecting Cornice either *Corinthian* or *Ionic*, and beneath the Cornice by Way of Gorgerine, a plain Freze, and below that an Aftragal and a Fillet like thofe at the Top of the Shaft of a Column. All thefe Ornaments togther fhould take up the ninth Part of the Height of the Pier. This ninth Part muft be again fubdivided into nine fmaller Parts, five whereof muft be given to the Cornice, three to the Freze, and one to the Aftragal and Fillet. The Architrave or Face of the Arch that turns from Pier to Pier muft never be broader than the tenth Part of its Aperture, nor narrower than the twelfth. The Columns that are placed in Front againft the Piers muft be regular and infulate; they muft be fo raifed that the Top of their Shafts may be equal to the Top of the Arch, and their Length muft be equal to the Breadth of the middle Aperture. Thefe Columns muft have their Bafes, Plinths and Pedeftals as alfo their Capitals, either *Corinthian* or *Compofite* together with Architrave, Freze and Cornice, either *Ionic* or *Corinthian*, according to the Proportions already prefcribed for thofe feveral Members. Above thefe Columns muft be a plain Wall, half as high as the whole Subftructure from the loweft Bafement to the Top of the Cornice, and the Height of this additional Wall muft be divided into eleven Parts, one of which muft be given to a plain Cornice at the Top, without either Freze or Architrave, and one and an Half to a Bafement with a reverfed Cymatium which muft take up one third of the Height of that Bafement. The Statues muft be placed directly over the Intablature of the Columns, upon little Pedeftals whofe Height muft be equal to the Thicknefs of the Top of the Shaft of the Columns. The Height of the Statues with their Pedeftals muft be eight of the eleven Parts to which we divided the upper Wall. At the Top of the whole Structure, efpecially towards the Square, muft be placed larger Statues, triumphal Cars, Animals and other Trophies. The Bafe for thefe to ftand upon, muft be a Plinth three Times as high as the Cornice, which is immediately below it. Thefe larger Statues which we thus place uppermoft,

must

21

muſt in Height exceed thoſe which ſtand below them over the Columns, not leſs than a ſixth Part, nor more than two ninths. In convenient Places in the Front of the upper Wall we may cut Inſcriptions or Stories in Relieve, in ſquare or round Pannels. Beneath the Vault of the Arch the upper half of the Wall, upon which the Arch turns, is extremely proper for Stories in Relieve, but the lower Half being expoſed to be ſpattered with Dirt, is very unfit for ſuch Ornaments. For a Baſement to the Piers we may make a Plinth not more than a Cubit and an Half high, and that its Angle may not be broke by the Bruſh of Wheels, we may carry it off into a Cima-reverſa, which muſt take up one fourth of the Height of the Baſement itſelf.

C H A P.   VII.

Of the adorning Theatres and other Places for publick Shows, and of their Uſefulneſs.

WE come now to Places for publick Shows. We are told that *Epimenides*, the ſame that ſlept fifty-ſeven Years in a Cave; when the *Athenians* were building a Place for publick Shows reproved them, telling them, you know not how much Miſchief this Place ſhall occaſion; if you did, you would pull it to Pieces with your Teeth. Neither dare I preſume to find Fault with our Pontiffs, and thoſe whoſe Buſineſs it is to ſet good Examples to others, for having, with good Cauſe no doubt, aboliſhed the Uſe of publick Shows. Yet *Moſes* was commended for ordaining, that all his People ſhould upon certain ſolemn Days meet together in one Temple, and celebrate publick Feſtivals at ſtated Seaſons. What may we ſuppoſe his View to have been in this Inſtitution? Doubtleſs he hoped the People, by thus meeting frequently together at publick Feaſts, might grow more humane, and be the cloſer linked in Friendſhip one with another. So I imagine our Anceſtors inſtituted publick Shows in the City, not ſo much for the Sake of the Diverſions themſelves, as for their Uſefulneſs. And indeed if we examine the Matter thoroughly, we ſhall find many Reaſons to grieve that ſo excellent and ſo uſeful an Entertainment ſhould have been ſo long diſuſed: For as of theſe publick Diverſions ſome were contrived for the Delight and Amuſement of Peace and Leiſure, others for an Exerciſe of War and Buſineſs; the one ſerved wonderfully to revive and keep up the Vigour and Fire of the Mind, and the other to improve the Strength and Intrepidity of the Heart. It is indeed true that ſome certain and conſtant Medium ſhould be obſerved, in order to make theſe Entertainments uſeful and ornamental to a Country. The *Arcadi-*ans, we are told, were the firſt that invented publick Games, to civilize and poliſh the Minds of their People, who had been too much accuſtomed to a hard and ſevere Way of Life; and *Polybius* writes, that thoſe who afterwards left off thoſe Entertainments, grew ſo barbarous and cruel, that they became execrable to all *Greece*. But indeed the Memory of publick Games is extremely ancient, and the Invention of them is aſcribed to various Perſons. *Dionyſius* is ſaid to have been the firſt Inventor of Dances and Sports, as *Hercules* was of the Diverſion of the Combate. We read that the Olympick Games were invented by the *Æto-lians* and the *Eleans*, after their return from the Siege of *Troy*. We are told, that *Dionyſius* of *Lemnos*, who was the Inventor of the Chorus in Tragedies, was alſo the firſt that built a Place on purpoſe for publick Shows. In *Italy*, *Lucius Mummius*, upon Occaſion of his Triumph, firſt introduced theatrical Entertainments two hundred Years before the Emperor *Nero*'s Time, and the Actors were brought to *Rome* from *Etruria*. Horſe-Races were brought from the *Tyrians*, and almoſt the whole Variety of publick Diverſions came to *Italy* from *Aſia*. I am inclined to believe that the ancient Race of Men, that firſt began to cut the Figure of *Janus* upon their brazen Coins, were content to ſtand to ſee theſe Sort of Games under ſome Beech or Elm, according to thoſe Verſes of *Ovid*, ſpeaking of *Romulus*'s Show.

His Play-houſe, not of Parian *Marble made,*
Nor was it ſpread with purple Sails for ſhade.
The Stage with Ruſhes or with Leaves they ſtrew'd:
No Scenes in Proſpect, no machining God.

On

On Rows of homely Turf they sat to see,
Crown'd with the Wreaths of every common Tree.
                            DRYDEN's Translation.

HOWEVER, we read that *Jolaus*, the Son of *Iphiclus*, first contrived Seats for the Spectators in *Sardinia*, which he received the Thefpiad from *Hercules*. But at first Theatres were built only of Wood; and we find that *Pompey* was blamed for having made the Seats fixed and not moveable, as they used to be anciently: But Diversions of this Nature were afterwards carried to such a Height, that there were no less than three vast Theatres within the City of *Rome*, besides several Amphitheatres, one of which was so large that it would hold above two hundred thousand Persons, besides the *Circus Maximus*: All which were built of square Stone and adorned with Columns of Marble. Nay, not content with all these, they erected Theatres, only for temporary Entertainments, prodigiously enriched with Marble, Glass, and great Numbers of Statues. The noblest Structure in those Days, and the most capacious, which was at *Placentia*, a Town in *Lombardy*, was burnt in the Time of *Octavianus*'s War. But we shall dwell no longer upon this ancient Magnificence. Of publick Shows, some are proper to Peace and Leisure, others to War and Business. Those proper to Leisure, belong to the Poets, Musicians and Actors: Those proper to War, are Wrestling, Boxing, Fencing, Shooting, Running, and every Thing else relating to the Exercise of Arms. *Plato* ordained that Shows of this last Nature should be exhibited every Year, as highly tending to the Welfare and Ornament of a City. These Diversions required various Buildings, which therefore have been called by various Names. Those designed for the Use of the Poets, Comick, Tragick and the like, are called Theatres by way of Excellence. The Place where the noble Youth exercised themselves in driving Races in Chariots with two or four Horses, was called the *Circus*. That lastly, where wild Beast were enclosed and baited, was called an Amphitheatre. Almost all the Structures for these different Sorts of Shows were built in Imitation of the Figure of an Army drawn up in Order of Battle, with its two Horns or Wings protending forwards, and consisted of an Area wherein the Actors, or Combatants, or Chariots are to exhibit the Spectacle, and of Rows of Seats around for the Spectators to sit on: But then they differ as to the Form of the aforesaid Area; for those which have this Area in the Shape of a Moon in its Decrease are called Theatres, but when the Horns are protracted a great Way forwards, they are called *Circusses*, because in them the Chariots make a Circle about the Goal. Some tell us, that the Ancients used to celebrate Games of this Kind in Rings between Rivers and Swords (*interenses & flumina*) and that therefore they were called *Circenses*, and that the Inventor of these Diversions was one *Monagus* at *Elis* in *Asia*. The Area inclosed between the Fronts of two Theatres joined together was called *Cavea*, or the Pit, and the whole Edifice an Amphitheatre. The Situation of a Building for publick Shows ought particularly to be chosen in a good Air, that the Spectators may not be incommoded either by Wind, Sun, or any of the other Inconveniences mentioned in the first Book, and the Theatre ought in an especial Manner to be sheltered from the Sun, because it is in the Month of *August* chiefly, as *Horace* observes, that the People are fond of the Recitals of the Poets, and the lighter Recreations: And if the Rays of the Sun beat in, and were confined within any Part of the Theatre, the excessive Heat might be apt to throw the Spectators into Distempers. The Place ought also to be proper for Sound, and it is very convenient to have Porticoes, either adjoining to the Theatre, or at an easy Distance from it, for People to shelter themselves under from sudden Rains and Storms. *Plato* was for having the Theatre within the City, and the *Circus* somewhere out of it. The Parts of the ancient Theatres were as follows: The Area or open Space in the Middle, which was quite uncovered; about this Area, the Rows of Seats for the Spectators, and opposite to them the raised Floor or Stage for the Actors, and the Decorations proper to the Representation, and at the Top of all, Colonades and Arches to receive the Actor's Voice, and make it more sonorous. But the *Greek* Theatres differed from those of the *Romans* in this Particular, that the *Greeks* brought their Choruses and Actors within the Area, and by that Means had Occasion for a smaller Stage, whereas the *Romans* having the whole Performance upon the *Pulpitum*, or Stage, beyond the Semicircle of the Seats, were obliged to make their Stage much larger. In this they all agreed, that at first in marking out the Platform for the Theatre, they made use of a Semicircle, only drawing out the Horns somewhat farther than to be exactly semicircular, with

with a Line which some made strait, others curve. Those who extended them with Strait-lines, drew them out beyond the Semicircle, parallel to each other, to the Addition of one fourth Part of the Diameter: But those who extended them with Curve-lines, first mark'd out a compleat Circle, and then taking off one fourth Part of its Circumference, the Remainder was left for the Platform of the Theatre. The Limits of the Area being marked out and fixed, the next Work was to raise the Seats; and the first Thing to be done in order to this, was to resolve how high the Seats should be, and from their Height to calculate how much of the Platform they must take up. Most Architects made the Height of the Theatre equal to the Area in the Middle, knowing that in low Theatres the Voice was sunk and lost, but made stronger and clearer in high ones. Some of the best Artists made the Height of the Building to be four fifths of the Breadth of the Area. Of this whole Height the Seats never took up less than half, nor more than two thirds, and their Breadth was sometimes equal to their Height, and sometimes only two fifths of it. I shall here describe one of these Structures which I think the most compleat and perfect of any. The outermost Foundations of the Seats, or rather of the Wall against which the highest Seat must terminate, must be laid distant from the Center of the Semicircle one whole Semidiameter of the Area, with the Addition of a third. The first or lowest Seat must not be upon the very Level of the Area, but be raised upon a Wall, which in the larger Theatres must be in Height the ninth Part of the Semidiameter of the middle Area, from the Top of which Wall the Seats must take their first Flight: And in the smallest Theatres, this Wall must never be less than seven Foot high. The Benches themselves must be a Foot and an half high, and two and an half broad. Among these Seats, Spaces must be left at certain Distances for Passages into the middle Area, and for Stairs to go up from thence to those Seats, which Stair-cases and Passages should be with vaulted Roofs, and in Number proportionable to the Bigness of the Theatre. Of these Passages there should be seven principal ones, all directed exactly to the Center of the Area, and perfectly clear and open, at equal Distances from each other; and of these seven, one should be larger than the rest, answering to the middle of the Semicircle, which I call the Master Entrance, be-

cause it must answer to the high Street. Another Passage must be made at the Head of the Semicircle on the Right Hand, and so another on the Left to answer it; and between these and the Master Entrance four others, two on each Side. There may be as many other Openings and Passages as the Compass of the Theatre requires, and will admit of. The Ancients in their great Theatres divided the Rows of Seats into three Parts; and each of these Divisions was distinguished from the other by a Seat twice as broad as the others, which was a Kind of Landing-place, separating the higher Seats from the lower; and at these Landing-places, the Stairs for coming up to the several Seats terminated. I have observed, that the best Architects, and the most ingenious Contrivers used at each great Entrance to make two different Stairs, one more upright and direct, for the Young and the Nimble, and another broader and easier, with more frequent Rests, for the Matrons and old People. This may suffice as to the Seats. Opposite to the Front of the Theatre was raised the Stage for the Actors, and every thing belonging to the Representation, and here sate the Nobles in peculiar and honourable Seats, separate from the common People, or perhaps in the middle Area in handsome Places erected for that Purpose. The *Pulpitum* or Stage, was made so large as to be fully sufficient for every thing that was to be acted upon it. It came forward equal to the Center of the Semicircle, and was raised in Height not above five Foot, that the Nobles who sate in the Area might from thence easily see every Gesture of the Actors. But when the middle Area was not reserved for the Nobles to sit in, but was allowed to the Actors and Musicians: Then the Stage was made less, but raised higher, sometimes to the Height of six Cubits. In both Kinds the Stage was adorned with Rows of Colonades one over another, in Imitation of Houses, with their proper Doors and Windows, and in Front was one principal Door with all the Dress of the Door of a Temple, to represent a Royal Palace, with other Doors on each Side for the Actors to make their Entrances and Exits at, according to the Nature of the Drama. And as there are three Sorts of Poets concerned in theatrical Performances, the Tragick, who describe the Misfortunes and Distresses of Princes; the Comick who represent the Lives and Manners of private Persons, and the Pastoral, who sing the Delights of the Country, and the Loves of

Shepherds:

Shepherds: There was a **Contrivance** upon the Stage of a Machine which turning upon a Pin, in an Inftant changed the Scene to a Palace for Tragedy, an ordinary Houfe for Comedy, or a Grove for Paftoral, as the Nature of the Fable required. Such was the Manner of the Middle, Area, Seats and Stage, Paffages and the like. I have already faid in this Chapter, that one of the principal Parts of the Theatre was the Portico, which was defigned for rendering the Sound of the Voice ftronger and clearer. This was placed upon the higheft Seat, and the Front of its Colonade looked to the middle Area of the Theatre. Of this we are now to give fome Account.

216

The Ancients had learnt from ɯe Philofophers, that the Air, by the Percuffion of the Voice, and the Force of Sound, was put into a circular Motion, in the fame Manner as Water is when any thing is fuddenly plunged into it, and that, as for Inftance, in a Lute, or in a Valley, between two Hills, efpecially if the Place be woody, the Sound and Voice are rendered much more clear and ftrong, becaufe the fwelling Circles of the Air meet with fomething which beats back the Rays of the Voice that iffue from the Center, in the fame Manner as a Ball is beat back from a Wall againft which it is thrown, by which means thofe Circles are made clofer and ftronger: For this Reafon the Ancients built their Theatres circular; and that the Voice might meet with no Obftacle to ftop its free Afcent to the very higheft Part of the Theatre, they placed their Seats in fuch a Manner, that all the Angles of them lay in one exact Line, and upon the higheft Seat, which was no fmall Help, they raifed Porticoes facing the middle Area of the Theatre, the Front of which Porticoes were as open and free as poffible, but the Back of them was entirely fhut up with a continued Wall. Under this Portico they raifed a low Wall, which not only ferved for a Pedeftal to the Columns, but alfo helped to collect the fwelling Orbs of the Voice, and to throw it gently into the Portico itfelf, where being received into a thicker Air, it was not reverberated from thence too violently, but returned clear and a little more ftrengthened. And over all this, as a Cieling to the Theatre, both to keep off the Weather, and to retain the Voice, they fpread a Sail all ftrewed over with Stars, which they could remove at Pleafure, and which fhaded the middle Area, the Seats, and all the Spectators. The upper Portico was built with a

217

great deal of Art; for in order to fupport it, there were other Porticoes and Colonades at the Back of the Theatre, out to the Street, and in the larger Theatres, thefe Porticoes were made double, that if any violent Rain or Storm obliged the Spectators to fly for Shelter, it might not drive in upon them. Thefe Porticoes and Colonades, thus placed under the upper Portico, were not like thofe which we have defcribed for Temples or Bafiliques, but built of ftrong Pilafters, and in Imitation of triumphal Arches. We fhall firft therefore treat of thefe under Porticoes, as being built for the Sake of that above. The Rule for the Apertures of thefe Porticoes is, that to every Paffage into the middle Area of the Theatre, there ought to be one of them, and each of thefe Apertures fhould be accompanied with others in certain Proportions, anfwering exactly one to the other in Height, Breadth, Defign and Ornaments. The Breadth of the Area for walking in thefe Porticoes, fhould be equal to the Aperture between Pilafter and Pilafter, and the Breadth of each Pilafter fhould be equal to half that Aperture: All which Rules muft be obferved with the greateft Care and Exactnefs. Laftly, againft thefe Pilafters we muft not fet Columns entirely infulate, as in triumphal Arches, but only three quarter Columns with Pedeftals under them, in Height one fixth of the Column itfelf. The other Ornaments muft be the fame as thofe in Temples. The Height of thefe three quarter Columns, with their whole Entablature, muft be equal to half the perpendicular Height of the Seats within, fo that on the Outfide there muft be two Orders of Columns one over the other, the fecond of which muft be juft even with the Top of thofe Seats, and over this we muft lay the Pavement for the upper Portico, which as we fhewed before, muft look into the middle Area of the Theatre, in Shape refembling a Horfe-fhoe. This Subftructure being laid, we are to raife our upper Portico, the Front and Colonade whereof is not to receive its Light from without, like thofe before defcribed, but is to be open to the Middle of the Theatre, as we have already obferved. This Work being raifed in order to prevent the Voice from being loft and difperfed, may be called the Circumvallation. Its Height fhould be the whole Height of the outer Portico, with the Addition of one half, and its Parts are thefe. The low Wall under the Columns, which we may call a continued Pedeftal. This Wall of the whole Height of

218

the

the Circumvallation, from the upper Seat to the Top of the Entablature, muſt in great Theatres be allowed never more than a Third, and in ſmall ones, not leſs than a Fourth. Upon this continued Pedeſtal ſtand the Columns which with their Baſes and Capitals muſt be equal to half the Height of the whole Circumvallation. Over theſe Columns lies their Entablature, and over all a Plain Wall, ſuch as we deſcribed in Baſiliques, which Wall muſt be allowed the ſixth remaining Part of the Height of the Circumvallation. The Columns in this Circumvallation ſhall be inſulate; raiſed after the ſame Proportions as thoſe in the Baſiliques, and in Number juſt anſwering to thoſe of the three quarter Columns ſet againſt the Pilaſters of the outward Portico, and they ſhall be placed exactly in the ſame Rays, by which Name I underſtand Lines drawn from the Center of the Theatre to the outward Columns. In the low Wall, or continued Pedeſtal, ſet under the Columns of the inner Portico, muſt be certain Openings, juſt over the Paſſages below into the Theatre, which Openings muſt be in the Nature of Niches, wherein, if you think fit, you may place a Sort of Vaſes of Braſs, hung with their Mouths downwards, that the Voice reverberating in them, may be returned more ſonorous. I ſhall not here waſte Time in conſidering thoſe Inſtructions in *Vitruvius*, which he borrows from the Precepts of Compoſition in Muſick, according to the Rules of which he is for placing the juſt mentioned Vaſes in Theatres, ſo as to correſpond with the differerent Pitches of the ſeveral Voices: A Curioſity eaſily talked of, but how it is to be executed, let thoſe inform us, who know. Thus much I muſt readily aſſent to, and *Ariſtotle* himſelf is of the Opinion, that hollow Veſſels of any Sort, and Wells too, are of Service in ſtrengthening the Sound of the Voice. But to return to the Portico on the Inſide of the Theatre. The back Wall of this

Portico muſt be quite cloſe and entire, and ſo ſhut in the whole Circumvallation, that the Voice arriving there, may not be loſt. On the Outſide of the Wall to the Street, we may apply Columns as Ornaments, in Number, Height, Proportions and Members, exactly anſwering to thoſe in the Porticoes under them, in the outward Front of the Theatre. From what has been ſaid, it is eaſy to collect in what Particulars the greater Theatres differ from the ſmaller. In the greater, the outward Portico below is double, in the ſmaller ſingle: In the former, there may be three Orders of Columns, one over the other; in the latter, not more than two. They alſo differ in this, that ſome ſmall Theatres have no Portico at all on the Inſide, but for their Circumvallation, have only a plain Wall and a Cornice, which is intended for the ſame Purpoſe of returning the Voice, as the Portico in great Theatres, and in ſome of the largeſt Theatres, even this inward Portico is double. Laſtly, the outward Covering of the Theatre muſt be well plaiſtered or coated, and made ſo ſloping that the Water may run into Pipes placed in the Angles of the Building, which muſt carry it off privately into proper Drains. Upon the upper Cornice on the Outſide of the Theatre, Mutules and Stays muſt be contrived to ſupport Poles, like the Maſts of Ships to which to faſten the Ropes for ſpreading the Vela or Covering of the Theatre upon any extraordinary Repreſentation. And as we are to raiſe ſo great a Pile of Building to a juſt Height, the Wall ought to be allowed a due Thickneſs for the ſupporting ſuch a Weight. Let the Thickneſs therefore of the outward Wall of the firſt Colonade be a fifteenth Part of the Height of the whole Structure. The middle Wall between the two Porticoes, when theſe are double, muſt want one fourth Part of the Thickneſs of the outward one. The next Story raiſed above this may be a twelfth Part thinner than the lower one.　221

CHAP. VIII.

Of the Ornaments of the Amphitheatre, Circus, publick Walks, and Halls, and Courts for petty Judges.

HAVING ſaid thus much of Theatres, it is neceſſary to give ſome Account of the Circus and Amphitheatre which all owe their Original to the Theatre, for the Circus is indeed nothing elſe but a Theatre with its Horns ſtretched further on in Lines equi-diſtant one from the other, only that the Nature of this Building does not require Portices; and

the

the Amphitheatre is formed of two Theatres with their Horns joined together, and the Rows of Seats continued quite round; and the chief Difference between them is, that a Theatre is properly an half Amphitheatre, with this further Variation too, that the Amphitheatre has its middle Area quite clear from any Thing of a Stage or Scenes; but in all other respects, and particularly in the Seats, Porticoes, Entrances and the like, they exactly agree. I am inclined to believe, that the Amphitheatre was at first contrived chiefly for Hunting, and that for this Reason it was made round, to the Intent that the wild Beasts which were enclosed and baited in it, not having any Nook or Corner to fly to, might be the sooner obliged to defend themselves against their Assailants, who were extremely bold and dextrous at engaging with the fiercest wild Beasts. Some armed only with a Javelin, would with the Help of that leap over a wild Bull that was making at him full Speed, and so elude his Blow. Others having put on a Kind of Armour, composed of nothing but thick Thorns and Prickles, would suffer themselves to be rowled about and mumbled by a Bear. Others enclosed in a Kind of wooden Cage, teazed and provoked a Lion, and some with nothing but a Cloak about their left Arm, and a small Ax or Mallet in their right Hand would attack him openly. In a Word, if any Man had either Dexterity to deceive, or Courage and Strength to cope with wild Beasts, he offered himself as a Champion, either merely for the Sake of Honour, or for Reward. We read too, that both in the Theatres and Amphitheatres, the great Men used to throw Apples, or let fly little Birds among the Mob, for the Pleasure of seeing them scramble for them. The middle Area of the Amphitheatre, though it is surrounded by two Theatres joined together, yet must not be made so long as two compleat Theatres would make it, if their Horns both protended to meet each other: But its Length must bear a certain Proportion to its Breadth. Some among the Ancients made the Length eight, and the Breadth seven Parts, and some made the Breadth three fourths of the Length. In other Particulars it agrees with the Theatre: It must have Porticoes on the Outside, and one at the Top within, over the highest Seat, which we have called the Circumvallation. We are next to treat of the Circus. Some tell us, that this was built in Imitation of the heavenly Bodies;

222

for as the Heavens have twelve Houses, so the Circus has twelve Gates for Entrance; and as there are seven Planets, so this has seven Goals, lying from East to West at a good Distance one from the other, that through them the contending Chariots may hold their Course, as the Sun and Moon do through the Zodiac; which they did four-and-twenty Times, in Imitation of the four-and-twenty Hours. The Concurrents were also divided into four Squadrons, each of which was distinguished by its particular Colour; the one was cloathed in Green, in Representation of the verdant Spring; another to denote the flaming Summer in Red; the third in White, in Imitation of the pale Autumn; and the fourth in dusky Brown for the gloomy Winter. The middle Area of the Circus was neither clear nor open like the Amphitheatre, nor taken up with a Stage like the Theatre, but it was divided Lengthways into two Courses by the Goals or Terms which were set up at proper Distances, about which the Horses or Men performed their Races. Of these Goals there were three principal ones, whereof the Middlemost was the chief of all, and this was a Pile of Stone tapering up to the Top, upon account of which regular Diminution, it was called an Obelisk. The other two principal Goals were either colossal Statues, or lofty Piles of Stones in the Nature of Trophies, designed after the Workman's Fancy, so as they were only great and beautiful. Between these principal Goals were two others on each Side, either Columns or Obelisks less than the former, which made up the Number of Seven. We read in Historians, that the Circus Maximus at *Rome* was three Furlongs in Length, and one in Breadth. Now indeed it is entirely destroyed, and there are not the least Footsteps remaining by which we can form a Judgment of its ancient Structure: But by an actual Survey of other Works of this Nature I find the Manner of them was as follows: The Ancients used to make the middle Area of the Circus in Breadth at least threescore Cubits, or ninety Foot, and in Length seven Times that Breadth. The Breadth was divided into two equal Parts or Courses by a Line drawn the Length of the Circus, on which Line the Goals or Terms were placed according to the following Method: The whole Length being divided into seven Parts, one of those Parts was given to a Sweep at each End for the Concurrents to turn out of the right Course into the left, and the Remainder was allowed for the Goals, which standing

22

standing at equal Diftances from each other, took up the other five fevenths of the whole Length of the Circus. One Goal was joined to the other by a Kind of Breaft-wall which was never lefs than fix Foot high, to keep the Horfes that were running from croffing out of one Courfe into the other. On each Side of the Circus were Seats raifed to the Height of never more than the fifth, nor lefs than the fixth of the whole Breadth of the middle Area; and thefe Seats began from a Bafement, as in Amphitheatres, that the Spectators might not be within reach of any Hurt from the Beafts. Among publick Works we may reckon thofe publick Walks, in which the Youth exercife themfelves at Tennis, Leaping, or the Ufe of Arms, and where the old Men walk to take the Air, or if they are infirm, are carried about for the Recovery of their Health. *Celfus*, the Phyfician, fays, that Exercife is much better in the open Air, than under Cover; but that they might exercife themfelves more commodioufly even in the Shade, they added Porticoes which enclofed the whole Square. The Square itfelf was fometimes paved with Marble and Mofaick Work, and fometimes turfed with Grafs, and planted with Myrtles, Juniper, Cyprefs and Cedar Trees. The Porticoes on three Sides were fingle, and fo large, that their Proportion was two ninth Parts greater than that of the Forum before treated of in this Book; but on the fourth Side, which fronted the South, the Portico was yet more fpacious, and double. In Front it had *Doric* Columns, whofe Height was equal to the Breadth of the Portico; the Columns behind, which divided the inner Portico from the outward, were higher than the former one fifth Part, for fupporting the Cover, and giving a Slope to the Roof; and for this Reafon they made them of the *Ionic* Order, *Ionic* Columns being in their very Nature taller than the *Doric:* Though I cannot fee why the Cieling of thefe Porticoes fhould not have been exactly level, which certainly muft have been more beautiful to the Eye. In both thefe Colonades, the Diameters of the Columns were as follows: In the *Doric*, the lower Diameter of the Shaft was two fifteenths of the whole Height, including the Bafe and Capital; but in the *Ionic* and *Corinthian*, the lower Diameter of the Shaft was three fixteenths of the Length of only the Shaft of the Column. In other Refpects they were the fame as thofe ufed in Temples. To the back Walls of thefe Porticoes, they added hand-

fome Walls or Rooms, where Philofophers and Men of Knowledge might converfe and difpute upon the noblest Subjects; and of thefe Rooms, fome were proper for Winter, and others for Summer. Thofe which lay any thing to the North, were for Summer, as 224 thofe to the South, and which were not expofed to any fharp Winds, were for Winter; befides that thofe for Winter were fhut in with entire Walls, whereas thofe for Summer were full of Windows, or rather were feparated only by a Colonade, and had an open View towards the North, with Profpects of Sea, Hills, Lakes, or fome other agreeable Landskip, and admitted as much Light as poffible. The Porticoes on the Right and Left of thefe Squares, had the fame Sort of back Rooms, fhut in from Winds, but open to the Morning and to the Evening Sun, which fhone in upon them from the middle Area. The Plan of thefe retiring Rooms was various, fometimes they were femicircular, fometimes rectangular, but always in a due Proportion to the Square itfelf, and to the Porticoes which encompaffed it it. The Breadth of the whole Square with its Porticoes, was half its Length, and this Breadth was divided into eight Parts, fix whereof were given to the open Square, and one to each Portico. When the back retiring Rooms were femicircular, their Diameter was two fifths of the open Area. In the back Wall of the Porticoes, were the Apertures for Entrance, and for Light into thofe Rooms. The Height of the femicircular Retirements, in the greateft Proportion, was only equal to their Breadth; but in fmaller Works, it was one fifth Part more. Over the Top of the Roof of the Portico, Openings were broke for the Admiffion of a ftronger and more chearful Light into the Room. If thefe Withdrawing-rooms were fquare, then their Breadth was twice the Breadth of the Porticoes, and their Length twice their own Breadth. That I call Length which runs along with the Portico, fo that upon entering into thofe Rooms from the Right, their Length lies to the Left, and entering them from the Left, to the Right. Among publick Works, we are alfo to include the Portico for the inferior Judges, which 225 the Ancients ufed to build after the following Manner: Their Bignefs was according to the Dignity of the City, but rather too large than too fmall, and along them was a Row of Chambers, contiguous to each other, where petty Contefts were heard and determined. Thofe Works which I have hitherto defcribed

feem

seem to be truly publick, as they are defigned for the Ufe of all the People in general, both noble and vulgar: But there are ftill fome other Works of a publick Nature, which are for the Ufe only of the principal Citizens, and of the Magiftrates; as for Inftance, the Senate-houfe and Council-chambers, whereof we are now to give fome Account.

CHAP. IX.

Of the proper Ornaments for the Senate-houfe and Council-chambers, as alfo of the adorning the City with Groves, Lakes for Swimming, Libraries, Schools, publick Stables, Arfenals and Mathematical Inftruments.

PLATO appointed the Council to be held in a Temple, and the *Romans* had a determined Place for that Purpofe, which they called their Comitium. At *Ceraunia* there was a thick Grove, confecrated to *Jupiter*, in which the *Greeks* ufed to meet to confult about the Affairs of their State, and many other Cities ufed to hold their Councils in the Middle of the publick Forum. It was not lawful for the *Roman* Senate to meet in any Place that was not appointed by Augury, and they commonly chofe fome Temple. Afterwards they erected *Curiæ*, or Courts for that particular Purpofe, and *Varro* tells us, that thefe were of two Sorts: One in which the Priefts confulted about religious Matters; the other where the Senate regulated fecular Affairs. Of the peculiar Properties of each of thefe I can find nothing certain; unlefs we may be allowed to conjecture, that the former had fome Refemblance to a Temple, the latter to a Bafilique. The Priefts Court therefore may have a vaulted Roof, and that of the Senators a flat one. In both, the Members of the Council are to declare their Opinion, by fpeaking; and therefore Regard is to be had in thefe Edifices to the Sound of the Voice. For this Reafon there ought to be fomething to prevent the Voice from afcending too high and being loft, and efpecially in vaulted Roofs to prevent it from thundering in the Top of the Vault and deafening the Hearers: Upon which Account, as well for Beauty as for this neceffary Ufe, the Wall ought to be crowned with a Cornice. I find from Obfervation of the Structures of this Sort left by the Ancients, that they ufed to make their Courts fquare. The Height of their vaulted Courts was fix fevenths of the Breadth of the Front, and the Roof was a plain Arch. Juft oppofite to the Door the Beholder's Eye was ftruck with the Tribunal, the Sagitta whereof was the Third of its Chord: The Breadth of the Aperture of the Door, was one feventh of the whole Front. At half the Height of the Wall, and one eighth Part of that half, projected an Architrave, Freze and Cornice upon an Order of Columns, either clofe or thin fet, as the Architect liked beft, according to the Rules of the Colonades and Porticoes of a Temple. Over the Cornice on the right and left Sides, in certain Niches opened in the Wall, were Statues and other Figures of religious Veneration, but in the Front at the fame Height with thofe Niches, was a Window twice as broad as high, with two little Columns in the Middle of it, to fupport the Tranfom. This was the Structure of the Priefts Court. The Court for the Senators may be as follows: The Breadth of the Platform muft be two thirds of its Length. The Height to the Rafters of the Roof muft be equal to the Breadth of the Platform, with the Addition of one fourth Part of that Breadth: The Wall muft be crowned with a Cornice, according to the following Rule. Having divided the whole clear Height into nine Parts, one of thofe Parts muft be given to the folid Bafement, or continued Pedeftal of the Columns, and againft this Bafement muft be the Seats for the Senators. The Remainder muft afterwards be divided into feven Parts; whereof four muft be given to the firft Row of Columns, over which you muft raife another, both with their proper Bafes, Capitals, Architraves, Frezes and Cornices, in the Manner before prefcribed for a Bafilique. The Intervals between the Columns on each Side, muft always be in an odd Number, and all equal to each other; but in Front, thofe Intervals muft be no more than three, the Middlemoft whereof muft be one fourth Part broader than the other two. In every Interval in the upper Row of Columns muft be a Window, this Sort of Courts requiring as much Light as poffible, and under each Window muft be

226

be a Reſt, according to the Rules already given for the Baſilique, and no Part of the Dreſs of theſe Windows muſt riſe higher than the Shaft of the Columns between which they ſtand, excluſive of their Capitals. The Height of the Aperture of the Window being divided into eleven Parts, ſeven muſt be given to its Breadth. If you would have no upper Row of Columns at all, then you may ſupport the upper Cornice with Conſoles, inſtead of Capitals, according to the Method already given in the Deſcription of the *Ionic* Door. Then each Window will ſtand between two Conſoles made after the following Proportions. The Breadth of the Conſole muſt be the ſame as the Top of the naked Shaft of a Column in the ſame Place ought to be, excluſive of the Aſtragal and Fillet, and its Length equal to the Height of the *Corinthian* Capital without its Abacus. The Projecture of the Conſole muſt not exceed that of the Freze of its Entablature. The Ancients in a great many Places had ſeveral other Kinds of Structures and Inventions which admitted of Ornaments, and rendered the City more magnificent. We are told, that near the Academy of *Athens* there was a very fine Grove conſecrated to the Gods, which was cut down by *Sylla* in order for the caſting up an Intrenchment againſt *Athens*. *Alexander Severus* adorned his own Thermes, or Baths, with a pleaſant Grove, and added to thoſe of *Antoninus* ſeveral fine Lakes for Swimming in. The *Agrigentines*, upon *Zelo*'s Victory againſt the *Chalcedonians* made ſuch a Lake ſeven Furlongs long and twenty Cubits deep, from which they raiſed a conſiderable Income. We read, that at *Tivoli* there was a very famous publick Library. *Piſiſtratus* was the firſt that erected ſuch a Library at *Athens*, conſiſting of a great Number of Books, which were carried away by *Xerxes* into *Perſia*, and afterwards brought back again to *Athens* by *Seleucus*. The *Ptolomeys* King of *Ægypt* had a Library conſiſting of ſeven hundred thouſand Volumns; but why ſhould we wonder at ſuch a Number of Books in a publick Collection, when there was no leſs than ſixty-two thouſand Volumns in the particular Library of the *Gordians?* In the Country of *Laodicea*, beſides the Temple of *Nemeſis*, there was a noble Phyſick School, erected by *Zeuxis*, which was highly celebrated. *Appian* tells us, that at *Carthage* there was a Stable of three hundred Elephants, and another of hundred Horſes, an Arſenal for two hundred and twenty Ships, together with other

Magazines both of Arms and Proviſions ſufficient to ſupply a whole Army. At *Thebes*, which was anciently called the City of the Sun, we read, that there were no leſs than an hundred publick Stables, each big enough to hold two hundred Horſes. In *Cizycus*, an Iſland of the *Propontis*, there were two Ports, and between them an Arſenal, the Roofs of which would give Shelter to two hundred Veſſels. Upon the *Pireum*, or Port of *Athens*, was a noble Station for no leſs than four hundred Ships, which was the celebrated Work of *Philo*. *Dionyſius*, at the Haven of *Syracuſe*, made an Arſenal divided into an hundred and ſixty Partitions, each whereof would contain two Veſſels, together with a Magazine, which in a few Days would furniſh above an hundred and twenty thouſand Shields, and an incredible Number of Swords. At *Sithicus* the *Spartans* had an Arſenal of above an hundred and ſixty Furlongs long. Thus we find Variety of Structures among various Nations: But as to their particular Forms, Deſigns and Contrivances, I have nothing certain to preſcribe, except that thoſe Parts of them which are for Uſe, muſt be borrowed from the Rules of private Edifices, and thoſe which are for Ornament and Magnificence, from thoſe of publick ones. I ſhall only obſerve, that the principal Ornament of a Library, is the Number and Variety of the Books contained in it, and chiefly their being collected from among the learned Remains of Antiquity. Another great Ornament, are curious mathematical Inſtruments of all Sorts, eſpecially if they are like that made by *Poſdonius*, in which all the ſeven Planets performed their proper Revolutions by their own Motion; or that of *Ariſtarchus*, who we are told deſcribed a Plan of the whole World, with all its ſeveral Provinces, upon a Table of Iron, to a moſt curious Exactneſs, and the Buſts of the ancient Poets, which *Tiberius* placed in his Library, were certainly a very proper and beautiful Ornament. I think I have now gone through with all the Ornaments that relate to publick Edifices. I have treated both of the Sacred and of the Profane, of Temples, Baſiliques, Porticoes, Sepulchres, Highways, Havens, Squares, Bridges, Triumphal Arches, Theatres, Circuſſes, Courts, Council-chambers, publick Places for Exerciſe, and the like, ſo that there ſeems nothing of this Nature now left for me to ſpeak of, except it be Thermes or publick Baths.

CHAP. X.

Of Thermes or publick Baths ; their Conveniencies and Ornaments.

SOME have condemned Baths, imagining they made Men effeminate, while others have had fo great an Opinion of them, that they have wafhed in them feven Times a Day. The ancient Phyficians, in order for the Cure of various Diftempers by means of Bathing, erected a great Number of Thermes or publick Baths in the City of *Rome* at an incredible Expence. *Heliogabalus* particularly built *Thermæ* in a great many Places, but having wafhed once in each, he immediately ordered it to be demolifhed, fcorning ever to wafh twice in the fame Bath.   I am not thoroughly determined whether this Kind of Structure be of a publick or private Nature : And indeed I cannot help thinking that it partakes fomewhat of both, fince in many Particulars, it borrows from the Defigns of private Edifices, and in many others from thofe of publick ones.   A publick Bath or Thermæ requiring a very large Area of Ground to ftand upon, it is not proper to build it in the principal and moft frequented Part of the City, neither fhould it be placed too far out of the Way, becaufe both the chief Citizens and the Women muft refort thither to wafh themfelves. The Thermæ itfelf muft have a large open Space clear round it, which muft be encompaffed with a high Wall, with proper Entrances at convenient Places.   In the Middle of the Therme muft be a large ftately Hall, which muft be as it were the Center of the whole Edifice, with Cells all round it after the Manner of the *Etrurian* Temple, which we have already defcribed.   Into this Hall we are to enter through a handfome Veftibule, fronting to the South, from which we pafs into another fmaller Veftibule or Lobby, and fo into the great Hall.   From the Hall is a large Gate fronting to the North, which opens into a large open Square, on the Right and Left of which are fpacious Porticoes, and immediately behind thofe Porticoes are the cold Baths. Let us once more go back into the great Hall.   On the right Side of this Hall, which lies to the Eaft, is a broad fpacious Lobby, with three Cells on each Side of it, lying oppofite to each other. This Lobby carries us into another open Square, which I call the Xyftus, which is encompaffed

227

with Porticoes on every Side.   Of thefe Porticoes, that which fronts you as you come into the Square, has a handfome Withdrawing-room behind it.   The Portico whofe Front lies to the South has cold Baths behind it, in the fame Manner as in the other Square, with convenient Dreffing-rooms adjoining to them : And in the oppofite Portico are the warm Baths, which receive the fouth Sun by Windows broke out behind the Portico.   In convenient Angles in the Porticoes of the Xyftus are the other fmaller Veftibules, for Paffages out into the open Space which encompaffes the whole Thermæ.   Thefe are the feveral Members of the Thermæ which lie on the right Side of the great Hall, and there muft be juft the fame on the left which lies to the Weft, anfwering to the former :   The Lobby with three Cells on each Side, the open Square or Xyftus with its Porticoes and Withdrawing-rooms, and the fmaller Veftibules in the Angles of the Xyftus.   Let us return once more to that principal Veftibule of the whole Structure, which I faid fronted the South ; on the right Hand of which, upon the Line which runs to the Eaft are three Rooms, and as many on that which runs to the Weft ; the one for the Women, and the other for the Men.   In the firft Room they undreffed ; in the fecond they anointed themfelves, and in the third they wafhed : And fome for the greater Magnificence, added a fourth, for the Friends and Servants of thofe that were bathing to wait for them in.   Thefe Bathing-rooms received the Noon-day Sun at very large Windows.   Between thefe Rooms and thofe Cells which I told you lay along the Side of the inner Lobbies, which lead out of the great Hall into the open Square on the Side or Xyftus, another open Area was left, which threw Light into the fouth Side of thofe inner Cells that lie along thofe Lobbies from the great Hall.   The whole Edifice of the Thermæ, as I before obferved, was encompaffed clear round with a broad open Space, which was even fpacious enough for Races, nor were Goals wanting in proper Places of it for that Purpofe.   In the open Space on the fouth Side in which is the principal Veftibule of the whole Edifice,

was

was a large femicircular Area verging to the South, in which feveral Rows of Seats were raifed like thofe in the Theatre, and the Wall was raifed very high on that Side to keep off the fouth Sun. All this open Space quite round the whole Thermæ was enclofed, like a Caftle, with a continued Wall, and in this outward Wall were feveral handfome Rooms, either quadrangular or femicircular, which looked towards the Thermæ itfelf. In thefe Rooms the Citizens at Morning or Evening, or any Hour they liked beft, enjoyed either Sun or Shade. Befides all thefe, and efpecially towards the North, behind the inclofing Wall were open Piazzas, of moderate Height, longer than broad, and drawn upon a curve Platform. Thefe Piazzas were furrounded by circular Porticoes, with a clofe Wall at their Back, fo that very little Sky was to be feen in thefe Piazzas, and between thefe Porticoes and the main Inclofure was a very good Refuge from the Heat in Summer, becaufe by means of the Narrownefs of the Piazza itfelf, and the Height of the main Wall, the Sun, even in the Summer Solftice could hardly ftrike in upon it. In the Angles of the main Inclofure were Veftibules and little Temples in which the Matrons, having cleanfed and purified themfelves, offered Oblations to their Gods. This is a brief Account of the feveral Members and Parts of the ancient Thermæ or Baths, and the Defigns of the feveral Members were taken either from the Structures which we have already defcribed, or from thofe which we are ftill to treat of, according as they had the greateft Relation either to publick or to private Edifices; and the Platform of moft of the ancient Edifices of this Sort contained above ten thoufand Foot fquare.

228

The End of Book VIII.

THE

THE
ARCHITECTURE
OF
Leone Batiſta Alberti.
BOOK IX. CHAP. I.

That particular Regard muſt be had to Frugality and Parſimony, and of the adorning the Palaces or Houſes of the King and principal Magiſtrates.

WE are here to remember, that there are two Sorts of Houſes for private Men; ſome for the Town and others for the Country; and of theſe again ſome are intended for Citizens of meaner Rank, and others for thoſe of the higheſt Quality. We are now to treat of the proper Ornaments for each of theſe; but firſt I would premiſe ſome few neceſſary Precautions. We find that among the Ancients the Men of the greateſt Prudence and Modeſty were always beſt pleaſed with Temperance and Parſimony in all Things, both publick and private, and particularly in the Affair of Building, judging it neceſſary to prevent and reſtrain all Extravagance and Profuſion in their Citizens in theſe Points, which they did to the utmoſt of their Power both by Admonitions and Laws. For this Reaſon *Plato* commends thoſe who, as we have before obſerved, made a Decree, that no Man ſhould have in his Houſe any Picture that was finer than thoſe which had been ſet up in the Temples of their Gods by their Forefathers, and that even the Temple itſelf ſhould be adorned with no other Painting but ſuch a ſingle Picture as one Painter could draw in one ſingle Day. He alſo ordained, that the Statues of the Gods themſelves ſhould be made only of Wood or Stone, and that Iron and Braſs ſhould be left for the Uſes of War, whereof they were the proper Inſtru-

ments. *Demoſthenes* cried up the Manners of the ancient *Athenians*, much beyond thoſe of his Cotemporaries; for he tells us, they left an infinite Number of publick Edifices, and eſpecially of Temples, ſo magnificent and richly adorned that nothing could exceed them; but they were ſo modeſt in their private Buildings, that the Houſes of the very nobleſt Citizens differed very little from thoſe of the meaneſt; by which means they effected, what is very rarely known among Men, to overcome Envy by Glory. But the *Spartans* condemned even theſe, for having embelliſhed their City more with the Builder's Skill, than with the Splendor of their own Exploits, while they themſelves gloried, that they had adorned their own City more by their Virtue than by their fine Buildings. Among them it was one of *Lycurgus*'s Laws, that their Roofs ſhould be wrought with no nicer Tool than the Ax, and their Doors with the Saw. *Ageſilaus*, when he beheld ſquare Rafters in the Houſes in *Aſia*, laughed at them; and asked the People, whether if they had grown naturally ſquare, they would not have made them round? And doubtleſs he was in the Right; becauſe, according to the ancient Modeſty of his Nation, he was of Opinion, that the Houſes of private Perſons ought to be built only for Convenience, and not for Beauty or Magnificence. It was a Law in
Germany

Germany, in *Cæsar*'s Time, that no Man should build too delicately, and especially in the Country, to prevent Diffention among the People from a Desire of usurping each other's Possessions. *Valerious Poplicola* having built a stately House on that which is now the *Monte Cavallo* at *Rome*, pulled it down to avoid Envy, and built himself another in the Plain; and the same Modesty appeared in every Thing both Publick and Private in those ancient Times, while the Manners of the *Romans* continued uncorrupted: But afterwards, when the Empire was enlarged, the Luxury of Building ran so high in almost every Body (except in *Octavianus*, who had so great a Dislike to sumptuous Buildings, that he pulled down a Country-house only for its being too magnificent) I say, the Extravagance of Building ran so high in the City of *Rome*, that some of the *Gordian* Family, among others, built a House on the Road to *Preneste*, with two hundred Columns all of the same Bigness, and upon one Row, whereof fifty were of *Numidian*, fifty of *Claudian*, fifty of *Samian*, and fifty of *Titian* Marble, as I remember to have read. What a Piece of Magnificence was that which we read of in *Lucretius*, that in some Houses there were Statues of young Men all of Gold, holding lighted Torches in their right Hands, to light up their Feasts at Night? My Design in mentioning these Things is to confirm by the Comparison, what I said before, that the Magnificence of the Building should be adapted to the Dignity of the Owner; and if I may offer my Opinion, I should rather, in private Edifices, that the greatest Men fell rather a little short in Ornament, than they should be condemned for Luxury and Profusion by the more Discreet and Frugal. But since all agree, that we should endeavour to leave a Reputation behind us, not only for our Wisdom but our Power too; for this Reason, as *Thucydides* observes, we erect great Structures, that our Posterity may suppose us to have been great Persons. When therefore we adorn our Habitations not more for Delicacy than to procure Honour to our Country and our Families, who can deny this to be a Work well becoming the wisest Men? Accordingly I would have those Parts of the House which are chiefly in the publick View, and which are in a Manner to give the first Welcome to every Guest, as the Front, the Vestibule, and the like, be made as handsome as possible. And, though indeed I think those ought to be very much blamed that are guilty

of too much Excess; yet I think those are much more to be condemned that lay out a great Expence upon a Building capable of no Ornament, than those that turn both their Thoughts and Money upon Ornament principally: Tho' I believe, I may venture to say, that whoever considers the true Nature of Ornament in Building will be convinced, that it is not Expence so much that is requisite, as Taste and Contrivance. I think no prudent Man in building his private House should willingly differ too much from his Neighbours, or raise their Envy by his too great Expence and Ostentation; neither, on the other Hand, should he suffer himself to be out-done by any one whatsoever in the Ingenuity of Contrivance, or Elegance of Taste, to which the whole Beauty of the Composition, and Harmony of the several Members must be owing, which is indeed the highest and principal Ornament in all Building. But to return to our Subject.

The Royal Palace, or in a free City, the House of the Senator or chief Magistrate ought to be the first in Beauty and Magnificence. Of the Ornaments of those Parts of this Palace or House which bear any Relation to a publick Edifice, I have treated already. We are now to adorn those Parts which are intended only for private Use. I would have the Vestibule adorned in the most handsome and splendid Manner, according to the Quality of the Owner; besides which there should be stately Porticoes, and handsome Courts, with every Thing else in Imitation of a publick Edifice, that tends either to Dignity or Ornament, as far as the Nature of the Structure itself will bear, only using so much Moderation as to seem rather to aim at Beauty and Gracefulness, than at any Thing sumptuous: And as we observed in the last Book, with relation to Works of a publick Nature, that secular Buildings ought to yield in Dignity to the sacred, so here the Edifices of private Persons ought to give Way in Excellence and Number of Ornaments to those of the publick. A private House ought not to have Doors of Brass or Ivory, which was objected to *Camillus* as a Crime, nor Roofs fretted with great Quantities of Gold, or inlaid with Glass, nor should every Part be incrusted with *Hymettian* or *Parian* Marble; such Materials being proper only in Temples: But the Builder's chief Commendation in a private Structure, is to use moderate Materials elegantly, and elegant ones moderately. Let him be contented with Cypress, Larch and Box Wood;

Wood; let his Incruſtations or outward Coat be adorned with plain Figures in Stuc, or with ſome ſlight Painting, and his Cornices at moſt of common Marble. Not that he muſt abſolutely rejeċt the moſt precious Materials; but he ſhould place them only in the moſt honourable Parts, like Gems in a Crown. But to give my Opinion of the whole Matter in one Word, I think that a ſacred Edifice ſhould be adorned in ſuch a Manner, that it ſhould be impoſſible to add any Thing that can conduce either to Majeſty, Beauty or Wonder: Whereas a private Structure ſhould be ſo contrived, that it ſhall be impoſſible to take any Thing from it, without leſſening its Dignity. Other Buildings, that is to ſay, the Profane of a publick Nature, ſhould obſerve the Medium between theſe two Extremes. Buildings of a private Sort ſhould keep ſtriċtly to the Ornaments proper to them, only they may be made uſe of here with ſomewhat more Freedom. For Inſtance, if the Columns be of rather a ſmaller Diameter, or elſe more turgid, or if the Diminution of the Top of the Shaft be greater than the exaċt Proportions for publick Structures, they ought not here to be condemned, provided they do not look deformed or unſightly. And whereas in publick Works not the leaſt Deviation is allowed from the exaċteſt Laws of Proportion, in private Works ſuch a Deviation is often handſome and commendable. Thus we may obſerve with what a beautiful Effeċt ſome of the more lively Architeċts uſed in the Doors of Halls, inſtead of Jambs to place huge Statues of Slaves, which ſupported the Lintel on their

Heads; and to make Columns, eſpecially in the Porticoes of their Gardens, with Knots in the Shafts, in Imitation of Trees that had their Branches cut off, or girded round with a Cincture of Boughs, or with their whole Shaft wreathed and enriched with Leaves, Birds, and Channels: or where they would make the Work extremely ſtrong, we find them erecting ſquare Columns, fortified with a half Column on each Side; which inſtead of Capitals had either Baskets full of Vine Branches laden with Fruit, or the Head of a Palm-tree riſing up and full of Leaves, or a Knot of Serpents wreathed together, or an Eagle with its Wings expanded in Token of Pleaſure, or a *Meduſa*'s Head with the Snakes hiſſing at each other, or any other Fancy of the ſame Kind; to enumerate all which, would be endleſs. But in all theſe Liberties the Architeċt muſt be as careful as poſſible to keep the ſeveral Parts within the Terms of the regular Lines and Angles, and not ſuffer his Work to want a due Proportion in its ſeveral Members: So that the Beholder may immediately find, that his Deſign was to be wanton in theſe Particulars, and to indulge a Freedom of Invention. And as of the Parlours, Paſſages and Apartments, ſome are more publick, ſome more concealed, and as it were hidden; the former may be allowed ſomewhat more of the Splendor of a publick Structure, but yet ſo as not to create Envy; and in the latter we may allow ourſelves more Liberty in departing out of the common Road, and contriving ſomething new.

Chap. II.

Of the Adorning of private Houſes, both in City and Country.

BUT as of the Houſes of private Perſons, ſome are in the City, and ſome in the Country, we muſt ſay ſomething of the Ornaments proper to each of theſe. Between a Houſe in Town and a Houſe in the Country, there is this further Difference, beſides what we took notice of in the laſt Book, that the Ornaments, for that in Town ought to be much more grave than thoſe for a Houſe in the Country, where all the gayeſt and moſt licentious Embelliſhments are allowable. There is another Difference too between them, which is, that in Town you are obliged to moderate

yourſelves in ſeveral Reſpeċts according to the Privileges of your Neighbour; whereas you have much more Liberty in the Country. In Town you muſt not raiſe your Platform or Baſement too high above your Neighbours, nor let your Portico projeċt too far forwards from the Line of the adjacent Buildings. The Thickneſs and Height of the Walls at *Rome* anciently were not ſuffered to be according to every Man's particular Fancy, but by an old Law were all to be made according to a certain Standard; and *Julius Cæſar*, upon account of the Miſchiefs that might happen from bad Foundations,

ons, ordained that no House should be more than one Story high: To which Regulations a
232 Country-house is not subject. It was reckoned one of the Glories of *Babylon*, that their Houses had Inhabitants in the fourth Story. *Ælius Aristides*, the Orator, praising *Rome* in a publick Oration, cried it up as a miraculous Work of the *Romans* to have built upon great Houses other Houses as great: a handsome Piece of Flattery; but it shewed the Numerousness of the People much more than the Magnificence of the Buildings themselves. We are told that in Height of Houses the City of *Rome* was outdone by *Tyre*, which by that means was formerly very near being wholly destroyed by Earthquakes. It is one very great Beauty and Convenience in a Building to have no more Ascents and Descents in it than are absolutely necessary; and it is certainly a very true Saying, that Stairs are nothing but Incumbrances to a House, from which Incumbrances I find the Ancients were very studious to keep clear. But in the Country there is no Manner of Necessity for setting one House thus upon another: For only taking a larger Platform we may make whatever Conveniencies we think fit upon the same Floor; which I should like extremely well in Town too, if it could be had. There is another Sort of private Houses, in which the Dignity of the Town-house, and the Delights and Pleasures of the Country-house are both required; of which we said nothing in the former Books, reserving it purposely for this very Place: And these are the Pleasure-houses just without the Town, or the Villa's which are by no means to be passed by without some Observations, though I shall be as brief in them as possible. Accordingly I shall here lay together all that I have to say of each of these three Sorts of Structures, and first of the Villa close to the Town. The Saying among the Ancients, Let him that buys a Country-house sell his House in Town, and let him that has Business in Town, never think of a House in the Country, seems to imply, that a Villa near Town is extremely convenient. The Physicians advise us to dwell in the clearest and openest Air that we can find; and there is no room to doubt but a Country-house seated upon an Eminence, must of Course be the Best: But then on the other Hand, the Master of a Family, upon account of his private Business, or the publick Affairs, may be obliged to be often in the City; for which Purpose a House in Town seems necessary: But then as the former

is inconvenient for Business, so the latter is prejudicial to the Health. It is a common Thing for the Generals of Armies to remove their Camps often, to avoid being incommoded by ill Smells: What can we think then of a great City, where such vast Quantities of Filth, and so long kept, are continually exhaling their offensive Steams? To reconcile this Dilemma therefore, I do not think that of all the Structures which are raised for the Conveniency of Mankind, there is any so commodious or so healthy as the Villa; which at the same Time as it lies in the Way for Business, is not wholly destitute of pure Air. *Cicero* desired his Friend *Atticus* to build him a Villa in a Place of eminent Note: But I, for my Part, am not for having it in a Place of such Resort, that I must never venture to appear at my Door without being compleatly dressed. I would have it afford me the Pleasure which the old Gentleman in *Terence* boasts he enjoyed, *of being never tired either with the Town or Country. Martial* too gives a very just Description of his Way of Living in such a Villa.

You tell me, Friend, you much desire to know,
What in my Villa I can find to do?
I eat, drink, sing, play, bathe, sleep, eat again,
Or read, or wanton in the Muses Train.

There is certainly a vast deal of Satisfaction in a convenient Retreat near the Town, where a Man is at Liberty to do just what he pleases. The great Beauties of such a Retreat, are being near the City, upon an open airy Road, and on a pleasant Spot of Ground. The greatest Commendation of the House itself is its making a chearful Appearance to those that go a little Way out of Town to take the Air; as if it seemed to invite every Beholder: And for this Reason I would have it stand pretty high, but upon so easy an Ascent, that it should hardly be perceptible to those that go to it, till they find themselves at the Top, and a large Prospect opens itself to their View. Nor should there be any Want of pleasant Landskips, flowery Meads, open Champains, shady Groves, or limpid Brooks, or clear Streams and Lakes for swimming, with all other Delights of the same Sort, which we before observed to be necessary in a Country Retreat, both for Convenience and Pleasure. Lastly, what I have already said conduces extremely to the Pleasantness of all Buildings, I would have the Front and whole Body of the House perfectly well

lighted,

lighted, and that it be open to receive a great deal of Light and Sun, and a sufficient Quantity of wholfome Air. Let nothing be within View that can offend the Eye with a melancholy Shade. Let all Things fmile and feem to welcome the Arrival of your Guefts. Let thofe who are already entered be in Doubt whether they fhall for Pleafure continue where they are, or pafs on further to thofe other Beauties which tempt them on. Let them be led from fquare Rooms into round ones, and again from round into fquare, and fo into others of mixed Lines, neither all round nor all fquare; and let the Paffage into the very innermoft Apartments be, if poffible, without the leaft Afcent or Defcent, but all be upon one even Floor, or at leaft let the Afcents be as eafy as may be.

C H A P.   III.

That the Parts and Members of a Houfe are different both in Nature and Species, and that they are to be adorned in various Manners.

BUT as the Members or Parts of a Houfe are very different one from the other both in Nature and Species, it may now be proper to fay fomething of each, having indeed purpofely referved them for this very Place: For there are many Parts which it matters very little whether you make round or fquare, provided they are fit for the Purpofes to which they are intended; but it is not equally indifferent what Number they are in, and how they are difpofed; and it is neceffary that fome fhould be larger, as the inner Courts, while fome require a fmaller Area, as the Chambers and all the private Apartments. Some others muft be in a Medium between the others, as Eating-parlours and the Veftibule. We have already in another Place given our Thoughts of the apt Difpofition of each Member of a Houfe, and as to the refpective Difference of their Areas, there is no Occafion to fpeak here, becaufe they are infinite both from the different Humours of Men, and the different Ways of Living in different Places. The Ancients, before their Houfes made either a Portico, or at leaft a Porch, not always with ftraight Lines, but fometimes with curve, after the Manner of the Theatre. Next to the Portico lay the Veftibule, which was almoft conftantly circular; behind that was the Paffage into the inner Court, and thofe other Parts of the Houfe which we have already fpoken of in their proper Places, whereof to enter upon a frefh Defcription would make us too prolix. The Things that we ought not to omit are thefe. Where the Area is round it muft be proportioned according to the Defign of the Temple; unlefs there be this Difference, that here the Height of the Walls muft be greater than in the Temple, for

233
234

Reafons which you fhall know fhortly. If it be quadrangular, then in fome Particulars it will differ from thofe Inftructions which we have given for facred Edifices, as alfo for profane ones of a publick Nature; but yet in fome others it will agree with the Council-chambers and Courts. According to the general Cuftom of the Ancients, the Breadth of the Porch was either two thirds of its Length, or elfe the Length was one whole Breadth and two thirds more, or elfe the Length was one whole Breadth with the Addition of two fifths. To each of thefe Proportions the Ancients feem always to have allowed the Height of the Wall to be equal to its wholeLength, and one third more. By taking the actual Dimenfion of a great many Structures, I find that fquare Platforms require a different Height of Wall where they are to be covered with vaulted Roofs, from what they do when their Roof is to be flat: As alfo that fome Difference is to be made between the Proportions of a large Building and thofe of a fmall one: Which arifes from the different Interval that there is from the Beholder's Eye, which muft in this Cafe be confidered as the Center, to the extreme Height which it furveys: But of thofe Things we fhall treat elfewhere. We muft Proportion the Areas of our Apartments to our Roof, and our Roof to the Length of the Rafters with which it is to be covered in. I call that a moderate Roof which may be fupported by a Piece of Timber of a moderate Length. But befides the Proportions which I have already treated of, there are feveral other proper Dimenfions and Agreements of Lines which I fhall here endeavour to explain as clearly and fuccinctly as poffible. If the Length of the Platform be twice its Breadth; then,

235
236

then, where the Roof is to be flat, the Height muſt be equal to the Breadth; where the Roof is to be vaulted, a third Part of that Breadth more muſt be added. This may ſerve for middling Buildings. In very large ones, if they are to have a vaulted Roof, the whole Height muſt be one whole Breadth, with the Addition of one fourth Part; but if the Roof is to be flat it muſt be one whole Breadth and two fifths. If the Length of the Platform be three Times its Breadth, and the Roof is to be flat, let the Height be one whole Breath and three quarters, if the Roof is to be vaulted, let the Height be one whole Breadth and an half. If the Length of the Platform be four Times its Breadth, and the Roof is to be vaulted, let the Height be half its Length; and if the Roof is to be flat, divide the Breadth into four Parts, and give one and three quarters of thoſe Parts to the Height. If the Length be five Times the Breadth, make the Height the ſame as where it is four Times, only with the Addition of one ſixth Part of that Height; and if it is ſix Times the Breadth, make it as before, adding not a ſixth as in the former, but a fifth. If the Platform be an exact Square with equal Sides, and the Roof is to be vaulted, let the Height exceed the Breadth as in the Platform of three Breadths; but if the Roof is to be flat, it muſt not exceed ſo much, and in the larger Platforms, it muſt not exceed this Breadth above one fourth Part. In thoſe Platforms where the Length exceeds the Breadth only one ninth Part, let the Height be exceeded by the Breadth one ninth Part too; but this muſt be only in a flat Roof. When the Length is to be one whole Breadth and a third, let the Height be one whole Breadth and a ſixth in flat Roofs; but in vaulted ones, let the Height be one whole Breadth and a ſixth of the Length. When the Length is one Breadth and an Half, let the Height be one Breadth and a ſeventh of that Breadth, in a flat Roof; but in a vaulted one, let the Height be one Breadth, and a ſeventh of the Length of the Platform. If the Platform conſiſt of Lines whereof one is as ſeven, and the other as five, or the Length be as five and the Breadth as three, or the like, according as the Neceſſity of the Place, or Variety of Invention, or the Nature of the Ornaments requires; add thoſe two Lines together, and allow one half of the Amount to the Height. I muſt not here omit one Precaution, namely, that the Veſtibule ought never to be above twice as long as broad, and the Apartments never leſs broad than two thirds of their

Length. The Platforms which are in Length three or four Times their Breadth or more, belong only to Porticoes, and even they ought never to be above ſix Times their Breadth. In the Wall Apertures are to be left both for Windows and Doors. If the Window is broke in the Wall of the Breadth-line of the Platform, which in its very Nature is ſhorter than that of the Length, then there muſt be only a ſingle one; and this Window itſelf muſt either be higher than it is broad, or elſe on the contrary broader than it is high, which laſt Sort is called a reclining Window. If the Breadth is to be like that of the Door, ſomewhat leſs than the Length; then let the Breadth of the clear Opening be not more than a third, nor leſs than a fourth Part of the Inſide of the Wall in which it is made; and let the Reſt or Bottom of the Window be in Height from the Floor not more than four ninths of the whole Height, nor leſs than two. The Height of the clear Open of the Window muſt be one third more than its Breadth; and this is the Proportion, if the Window is to be higher than broad; but if the Window is to be broader then high, than of the whole inſide Length of the Wall in which it is made, you muſt not allow the Open of the Window leſs than one half, nor more than two thirds. In the ſame Manner its Height too muſt be made either half its Breadth, or two thirds, only it muſt have two little Columns to ſupport the Tranſom. If you are to make Windows in the longer Side, there muſt be more of them, and they ſhould be in an odd Number. I find the Ancients were beſt pleaſed with three, which were made in the following Manner: The whole longeſt Side of the Wall muſt be divided into never more than ſeven, nor leſs than five Parts, of which taking three, in each of them make a Window, making the Height of the Open one whole Breadth and three quarters, or one Breadth and four fifths. If you would make your Windows more numerous; as they will then partake of the Nature of a Portico, you may borrow the Dimenſions of your Openings from the Rules of the Portico itſelf, and eſpecially from that of the Theatre, as we laid them down in their proper Place. The Doors muſt be made after the Manner of thoſe which we deſcribed for the Court and Council-chamber. Let the Dreſs of the Windows be *Corinthian*; of the principal Door, *Ionic*; of the Doors of the Halls and Chambers, *Doric*. And thus much of the Lines, as far as they relate to this preſent Purpoſe.

237

CHAP. IV.

With what Paintings, Plants, and Statues, it is proper to adorn the Pavements, Porticoes, Apartments and Gardens of a private House.

THERE are some other Ornaments extremely proper for a private House, by no means to be omitted in this Place. The Ancients stained the Pavements of their Porticoes with Labyrinths, both square and circular, in which the Boys used to exercise themselves. I have myself seen Pavements stained in Imitation of the Bell-flower-weed, with its Branches twining about very beautifully. Other have paved their Chambers with a Sort of *Mosaic* Work of Marble, in Imitation of Carpets, others in Imitation of Garlands and Branches of Trees. It was a very ingenious Invention of *Osis*, who strewed the Pavement at *Pergamus* with inlaid Work, in Imitation of the Fragments that lie scattered about after Meals; an Ornament not ill suited to a Parlour. *Agrippa* was very right in making his Floors of common baked Earth. I, for my Part, hate every Thing that savours of Luxury or Profusion, and am best pleased with those Ornaments which arise principally from the Ingenuity and Beauty of the Contrivance. Upon side Walls no Sort of Painting shews handsomer than the Representation of Columns in Architecture. *Titius Cæsar* adorned the Walls of the Portico in which he used to walk, with a Sort of *Phœnician* Stone so finely polished, that it returned the Reflection of all the Objects like a Looking-glass. *Antoninus Caracalla*, the Emperor, painted his Portico with the memorable Exploits and Triumphs of his Father. *Severus* did the same; but *Agathocles* painted not his Father's Actions, but his own. Among the *Persians*, according to their ancient Laws, it was not permitted to paint or carve any other Story, but of the wild Beasts slain by their Kings. It is certain, the brave and memorable Actions of one's Countrymen, and their Effigies, are Ornaments extremely suitable both to Porticoes and Halls. *Caius Cæsar* embellished his Portico with the Statues of all those that had enlarged the Confines of the Republick, and he gained a general Approbation by so doing. I am as much pleased as any body with this Kind of Ornaments; but yet I would not have the Wall too much crowded with Statues or History Pieces. We

may find by Gems, and especially by Pearls, that if they are set too thick together, they lose their Beauty. For this Reason, in some of the most convenient and most conspicuous Parts of the Wall, I am for making handsome Pannels of Stone, in which we may place either Statues, or Pictures; such as *Pompey* had carried along in his Triumph, Representing his Exploits both by Sea and Land in Picture. Or rather, I am for having Pictures of such Fictions of the Poets, as tend to the Promotion of good Manners; such as that of *Dædalus*, who painted the Gates of *Cumæ* with the Representation of *Icarus* flying. And as the Subjects both of Poetry and Painting are various, some expressing the memorable Actions of great Men; others Representing the Manners of private Persons; others describing the Life of Rusticks: The former, as the most Majestick, should be applied to publick Works, and the Buildings of Princes; and the latter, as the more chearful, should be set apart for Pleasurehouses and Gardens. Our Minds are delighted in a particular Manner with the Pictures of pleasant Landskips, of Havens, of Fishing, Hunting, Swimming, Country Sports, of flowery Fields and thick Groves. Neither is it foreign to our present Purpose just to mention, that *Octavianus*, the Emperor, adorned his Palace with the huge Bones of some extraordinary Animals. The Ancients used to dress the Walls of their Grottoes and Caverns with all Manner of rough Work, with little Chips of Pumice, or soft *Tyburtine* Stone, which *Ovid* calls the living Pumice; and some I have known dawb them over with green Wax, in Imitation of the mossy Slime which we always see in moist Grottoes. I was extremely pleased with an artificial Grotto which I have seen of this Sort, with a clear Spring of Water falling from it; the Walls were composed of various Sorts of Sea-shells, lying roughly together, some reversed, some with their Mouths outwards, their Colours being so artfully blended as to form a very beautiful Variety. In that Apartment which is peculiar to the Master of the Family and his Wife, we should take Care that nothing

be

be painted but the moft comely and beautiful Faces; which we are told may be of no fmall Confequence to the Conception of the Lady, and the Beauty of the Children. Such as are tormented with a Fever are not a little refrefhed by the Sight of Pictures of Springs, Cafcades and Streams of Water, which any one may eafily experience; for if at any Time you find it difficult to compofe yourfelf to reft in the Night, only turn your Imagination upon fuch clear Waters as you can remember any where to have feen, either of Springs, Lakes or Streams, and that burning Drowth of the Mind, which kept you waking, fhall prefently be moiftened, and a pleafant Forgetfulnefs fhall creep upon you, till you fall into a fine Sleep. To thefe Delicacies we muft add thofe of well-difpofed Gardens and beautiful Trees, together with Porticoes in the Garden, where you may enjoy either Sun or Shade. To thefe add fome little pleafant Meadow, with fine Springs of Water burfting out in different Places where leaft expected. Let the Walks be terminated by Trees that enjoy a perpetual Verdure, and particularly on that Side which is beft fheltered from Winds, let them be enclofed with Box, which is prefently injured and rotted by ftrong Winds, and efpecially by the leaft Spray from the Sea. In open Places, moft expofed to the Sun, fome fet Myrtles, which will flourifh extremely in the Summer: But *Theophraftus* affirms, that the Myrtle, the Laurel, and the Ivy rejoyce in the Shade, and therefore directs us to plant them thick, that they may mutually fhelter one another from the Sun by their own Shade: Nor let there be wanting Cyprefstrees cloathed with Ivy. Let the Ground alfo be here and there thrown into thofe Figures that are moft commended in the Platforms of Houfes, Circles, Semicircles, and the like, and furrounded with Laurels, Cedars, Junipers with their Branches intermixed, and twining one into the other. *Phiteon* of *Agrigentum*, though but a private Man, had in his Houfe three hundred Vafes of Stone, each whereof would hold an hundred Amphoras, or about fifteen of our Hogfheads. Such Vafes are very fine Ornaments for Fountains in Gardens. The Ancients ufed to make their Walks into a Kind of Arbours by Means of Vines fupported by Columns of Marble of the *Corinthian* Order, which were ten of their own Diameters in Height. The Trees ought to be planted in Rows exactly even, and anfwering to one another exactly upon ftraight Lines; and the

Gardens fhould be enriched with rare Plants, and fuch as are in moft Efteem among the Phyficians. It was a good agreeable Piece of Flattery among the ancient Gardeners, to trace their Mafters Names in Box, or in fweet-fmelling Herbs, in Parterres. Rofe-trees, intermixed with Pomegranates and Cornels, are very beautiful in a Hedge: But the Poet fays,

Your Hedge of Oak with Plums and Cornel made,
To yield the Cattle Food, the Mafter Shade.

But perhaps this may fuit better with a Farm intended for Profit, than with a Villa calculated chiefly for taking the Air in: And indeed what we are told *Democritus* very much condemned, namely, the inclofing a Garden with any Sort of Wall, I fhould not blame in the Cafe before us, but am rather of Opinion, that it is a very proper Defence againft Malice or Rapine. Nor am I difpleafed with the placing ridiculous Statues in Gardens, provided they have nothing in them obfcene. Such fhould be the Difpofition of the Villa. In Houfes in Town, the inner Apartments and Parlours fhould not in the leaft give way, either in Chearfulnefs or Beauty, to the Villa; but in the more publick Rooms, fuch as the Hall and Veftibule, you fhould not aim fo much at Delicacy, as to forget a decent Gravity. The Porticoes of the Houfes of the principal Citizens may have a compleat regular Entablature over the Columns; but thofe of lower Degree, fhould have only Arches. Vaulted Roofs are proper in both. The whole Entablature muft be in Height one fourth Part of the Shaft. If there is to be a fecond Order of Columns over the firft, let that fecond Order be one fourth Part fhorter than the lower one; and if there is to be a third Order over this, let it be one fifth Part fhorter than that below it. In each of thefe the Pedeftal or Plinth under each Order of Columns, muft be in Height one fourth Part of the Column which it fupports; but where there is to be only one fingle Row of Columns, the Proportions may be taken from thofe of profane Works of a publick Nature. A private Houfe fhould never have fuch a Pediment as may feem to rival the Majefty of a Temple. However, the Front of the Veftibule may be raifed fomewhat above the reft of the Building, and be adorned with a fmaller Pediment. The reft of the Front on each Side this Pediment may be adorned with a fmall Plinth, which may rife fomewhat higher at the princi-

238

pal

pal Angles I cannot be pleafed with thofe who make Towers and Battlements to a private Houfe, which belong of right entirely to a Fortification, or to the Caftle of a Tyrant, and are altogether inconfiftent with the peaceable Afpect of a well-governed City or Commonwealth, as they fhew either a Diftruft of our Countrymen, or a Defign to ufe Violence againft them. Balconies in the Front of a Houfe are beautiful enough, provided they are not too large, heavy, and out of Proportion.

Chap. V.

That the Beauty of all Edifices arifes principally from three Things, namely, the Number, Figure and Collocation of the feveral Members.

I Now come once more to thofe Points which I before promifed to enquire into, namely, wherein it is that Beauty and Ornament, univerfally confidered, confift, or rather whence they arife. An Enquiry of the utmoft Difficulty; for whatever that Property be which is fo gathered and collected from the whole Number and Nature of the feveral Parts, or to be imparted to each of them according to a certain and regular Order, or which muft be contrived in fuch a Manner as to join and unite a certain Number of Parts into one Body or Whole, by an orderly and fure Coherence and Agreement of all thofe Parts: Which Property is what we are here to difcover; it is certain, fuch a Property muft have in itfelf fomething of the Force and Spirit of all the Parts with which it is either united or mixed, otherwife they muft jar and difagree with each other, and by fuch Difcord deftroy the Uniformity or Beauty of the Whole: The Difcovery of which, as it is far from being eafy or obvious in any other Cafe, fo it is particularly difficult and uncertain here; the Art of Architecture confifting of fo many various Parts, and each of thofe Parts requiring fo many various Ornaments as you have already feen. However, as it is neceffary in the Profecution of our Defign, we fhall ufe the utmoft of our Abilities in clearing this obfcure Point, not going fo far about as to fhew how a compleat Knowledge of a Whole is to be gained by examining the feveral Parts diftinct; but beginning immediately upon what is to our prefent Purpofe, by enquiring what that Property is which in its Nature makes a Thing beautiful. The moft expert Artifts among the Ancients, as we have obferved elfewhere, were of Opinion, that an Edifice was like an Animal, fo that in the Formation of it we ought to imitate Nature. Let us therefore enquire how it happens that in the Bodies produced by Nature herfelf fome are accounted more, others lefs beautiful, or even deformed. It is manifeft, that in thofe which are efteemed beautiful, the Parts or Members are not conftantly all the fame, fo as not to differ in any Refpect: But we find, that even in thofe Parts wherein they vary moft, there is fomething inherent and implanted which though they differ extremely from each other, makes each of them beautiful. I will make ufe of an Example to illuftrate my Meaning. Some admire a Woman for being extremely flender and fine fhaped; the young Gentleman in *Terence* prefered a Girl that was plump and flefhy: You perhaps are for a Medium between thefe two Extremes, and would neither have her fo thin as to feem wafted with Sicknefs, nor fo ftrong and robuft as if fhe were a Ploughman in Difguife, and were fit for Boxing: In fhort, you would have her fuch a Beauty as might be formed by taking from the firft what the fecond might fpare. But then becaufe, one of thefe pleafes you more than the other, would you therefore affirm the other to be not at all handfome or graceful? By no means; but there may be fome hidden Caufe why one fhould pleafe you more than the other, into which I will not now pretend to enquire. But the Judgment which you make that a Thing is beautiful, does not proceed from mere Opinion, but from a fecret Argument and Difcourfe implanted in the Mind itfelf; which plainly appears to be fo from this, that no Man beholds any Thing ugly or deformed, without an immediate Hatred and Abhorrence. Whence this Senfation of the Mind arifes, and how it is formed, would be a Queftion too fubtle for this Place: However, let us confider and examine it from thofe Things which are obvious, and make more immediately to the Subject in Hand: For without Queftion there is a certain Excellence and

natural

natural Beauty in the Figures and Forms of Buildings, which immediately ftrike the Mind with Pleafure and Admiration. It is my Opinion, that Beauty, Majefty, Gracefulnefs, and the like Charms, confift in thofe Particulars which if you alter or take away, the Whole would be made homely and difagreeable. If we are convinced of this, it can be no very tedious Enquiry to confider thofe Things which may be taken away, encreafed or altered, efpecially in Figures and Forms: For every Body confifts of certain peculiar Parts, of which if you take away any one, or leffen, or enlarge it, or remove it to an improper Place; that which before gave the Beauty and Grace to this Body will at once be lamed and fpoild. From hence we may conclude, to avoid Prolixity in this Refearch, that there are three Things principally in which the Whole of what we are looking into confifts: The Number, and that which I have called the Finifhing, and the Collocation. But there is ftill fomething elfe befides, which arifes from the Conjunction and Connection of thefe other Parts, and gives the Beauty and Grace to the Whole: Which we will call Congruity, which we may confider as the Original of all that is graceful and handfome. The Bufinefs and Office of Congruity is to put together Members differing from each other in their Natures, in fuch a Manner, that they may confpire to form a beautiful Whole: So that whenever fuch a Compofition offers itfelf to the Mind, either by the Conveyance of the Sight, Hearing, or any of the other Senfes, we immediately perceive this Congruity: For by Nature we defire Things perfect, and adhere to them with Pleafure when they are offered to us; nor does this Congruity arife fo much from the Body in which it is found, or any of its Members, as from itfelf, and from Nature, fo that its true Seat is in the Mind and in Reafon; and accordingly it has a very large Field to exercife itfelf and flourifh in, and runs through every Part and Action of Man's Life, and every Production of Nature herfelf, which are all directed by the Law of Congruity, nor does Nature ftudy any Thing more than to make all her Works abfolute and perfect, which they could never be without this Congruity, fince they would want that Confent of Parts which is fo neceffary to Perfection. But we need not fay more upon this Point, and if what we have here laid down appears to be true, we may conclude Beauty to be fuch a Confent and Agreement of the Parts of a Whole in which it

is found, as to Number, Finifhing and Collocation, as Congruity, that is to fay, the principal Law of Nature requires. This is what Architecture chiefly aims at, and by this fhe obtains her Beauty, Dignity and Value. The Ancients knowing from the Nature of Things, that the Matter was in Fact as I have here ftated it, and being convinced, that if they neglected this main Point they fhould never produce any Thing great or commendable, did in their Works propofe to themfelves chiefly the Imitation of Nature, as the greateft Artift at all Manner of Compofitions; and for this Purpofe they laboured, as far as the Induftry of Man could reach, to difcover the Laws upon which fhe herfelf acted in the Production of her Works, in order to transfer them to the Bufinefs of Architecture. Reflecting therefore upon the Practice of Nature as well with Relation to an entire Body, as to its feveral Parts, they found from the very firft Principles of Things, that Bodies were not always compofed of equal Parts or Members; whence it happens, that of the Bodies produced by Nature, fome are fmaller, fome larger, and fome middling: And confidering that one Building differed from another, upon account of the End for which it was raifed, and the Purpofe which it was to ferve, as we have fhewn in the foregoing Books, they found it neceffary to make them of various Kinds. Thus from an Imitation of Nature they invented three Manners of adorning a Building, and gave them Names drawn from their firft Inventors. One was better contrived for Strength and Duration: This they called *Doric*; another was more taper and beautiful, this they named *Corinthian*; another was a Kind of Medium compofed from the other two, and this they called *Ionic*. Thus much related to the whole Body in general. Then obferving, that thofe three Things which we have already mentioned, namely, the Number, Finifhing and Collocation, were what chiefly conduced to make the whole beautiful, they found how they were to make ufe of this from a thorough Examination of the Works of Nature, and, as I imagine, upon the following Principles. The firft Thing they obferved, as to Number, was that is was of two Sorts, even and uneven, and they made ufe of both, but in different Occafions: For, from the Imitation of Nature, they never made the Ribs of their Structure, that is to fay, the Columns, Angles and the like, in uneven Numbers; as you fhall not find any Animal that ftands or

moves

241

242

moves upon an odd Number of Feet. On the contrary, they made their Apertures always in uneven Numbers, as Nature herself has done in some Instances, for tho' in Animals she has placed an Ear, an Eye, and a Nostril on each Side, yet the great Aperture, the Mouth, she has set singly in the Middle. But among these Numbers, whether even or uneven, there are some which seem to be greater Favourites with Nature than others, and more celebrated among learned Men; which Architects have borrowed for the Composition of the Members of their Edifices, upon Account of their being endued with some Qualities which make them more valuable than any others.

Thus all the Philosophers affirm, that Nature herself consists in a ternary Principle; and so the Number five, when we consider the many Things, and those so admirable and various, which either follow this Number in themselves, or are derived from those Things which do, must be allowed to be divine in its Nature, and worthily dedicated to the Gods of the Arts, and particularly to *Mercury*. It is certain, that Almighty God himself, the Creator of all Things, takes particular Delight in the Number Seven, having placed seven Planets in the Skies, and having been pleased to ordain with Regard to Man, the Glory of his Creation, that Conception, Growth, Maturity and the like, should all be reduceable to this Number Seven. *Aristotle* says, that the Ancients never used to give a Child a Name, till it was seven Days old, as not thinking it was destined to Life before; because both the Seed in the Womb, and the Child after its Birth, is liable to very dangerous Accidents till the seventh Day is over. Among odd Numbers, that of Nine is highly celebrated, in which Number that great Artist, Nature, made the Spheres of Heaven; and the Philosophers say, that Nature in many, and those the greatest Things, is contented with making use of the ninth Part of a Whole. Thus forty is about the Ninth Part of all the Days of the Year, according to the Revolution of the Sun, and *Hippocrates* tells us, that in forty Days the *Foetus* is formed in the Womb. Moreover we find, that in the Generality of acute Distempers, the Patient recovers at the End of forty Days. At the End of the same Time Women that are with Child of a Male, cease their Purgations, which, if they are delivered of a Boy, after the same Term of forty Days, begin

afresh. They say further, that the Child itself for forty Days is never seen either to laugh or shed Tears while it is awake; tho' in its Sleep it will do both. And thus much of odd Numbers.

As to even Numbers, some Philosophers teach, that the Number four is dedicated to the Deity, and for this Reason it was used in the Taking the most solemn Oaths, which were repeated four Times; and they tell us, that even among the most excellent Numbers, that of six is the most perfect, or consisting of all its own entire Parts, for Example:

$$\underbrace{1.1.1.1.1.1.}_{6.} \quad \underbrace{1.2.3.}_{6.} \quad \underbrace{1.5.}_{6.} \quad \underbrace{2.2.2.}_{6.}$$

$$\underbrace{2.4.}_{6.} \quad \underbrace{3.3.}_{6.}$$

And it is certain, that the Number eight has an extraordinary Power in the Nature of Things. Except in *Ægypt*, we never find, that any Child born in the eighth Month, lives long; nay, and even the Mother herself who is is so delivered in the eighth Month, when the Child is dead, will certainly, we are told, die soon afterwards. If the Father touches his Wife in the eighth Month, the Child will be full of foul Humours, and its Skin will be leprous and Scurfy, and nauseous to the Sight. *Aristotle* was of Opinion, that the Number ten was the most perfect of all, which was probably because its square is composed of four continued Cubes put together. Upon these Accounts the Architects have most frequently made use of the foregoing Numbers; but in their Apertures they seldom have exceeded that of ten for an even, or nine for an odd Number, especially in Temples. We are now to treat of the Finishing.

By the Finishing I understand a certain mutual Correspondence of those several Lines, by which the Proportions are measured, whereof one is the Length, the other the Breadth, and the other the Height.

The Rule of these Proportions is best gathered from those Things in which we find Nature herself to be most compleat and admirable; and indeed I am every Day more and more convinced of the Truth of *Pythagoras*'s Saying, that Nature is sure to act consistently, and with a constant Analogy in all her Operations: From whence I conclude, that

243

that the same Numbers, by means of which the Agreement of Sounds affects our Ears with Delight, are the very same which please our Eyes and our Mind. We shall therefore borrow all our Rules for the finishing our Proportions, from the Musicians, who are the greatest Masters of this Sort of Numbers, and from those particular Things wherein Nature shews herself most excellent and compleat: Not that I shall look any further into these Matters than is necessary for the Purpose of the Architect. We shall not therefore pretend to say any thing of Modulation, or the particular Rules of any Instrument; but only speak of those Points which are immediately to our Subject, which are these. We have already observed, that Harmony is an Agreement of several Tones, delightful to the Ears. Of Tones, some are deep, some more acute. The deeper Tones proceed from a longer String; and the more acute, from a shorter: And from the mutual Connection of these Tones arises all the Variety of Harmony. This Harmony the Ancients gathered from interchangeable Concords of the Tones, by means of certain determinate Numbers; the Names of which Concords are as follows: *Diapente*, or the Fifth, which is also called *Sesquialtera: Diatessaron*, or the Fourth, called also, *Sesquitertia: Diapason*, or the Eighth, also called the double Tone; *Diapason Diapente*, the twelfth or triple Tone, and *Disdiapason*, the fifteenth or *Quadruple*. To these was added the *Tonus*, which was also called the *Sesquioctave*. These several Concords, compared with the Strings themselves, bore the following Proportions. The *Sesquialtera* was so called, because the String which produced it bore the same Proportion to that to which it is compared, as one and an half does to one; which was the Meaning of the Word *Sesqui*, among the Ancients. In the *Sesquialtera* therefore the longer String must be allowed three, and the shorter, two.

$$\left.\begin{array}{l} 3\ 000 \\ 2\ 00 \end{array}\right\} \textit{Sesquialtera.}$$

THE *Sesquitertia* is where the longer String contains the shorter one and one third more: The longer therefore must be as four, and the shorter as three.

$$\left.\begin{array}{l} 4\ 0000 \\ 3\ 000 \end{array}\right\} \textit{Sesquitertia}$$

BUT in that Concord which was called *Diapason*, the Numbers answer to one another in a double Proportion, as two to one, or the Whole to the Half: And in the *Triple*, they answer as three to one, or as the Whole to one third of itself.

$$\left.\begin{array}{l} 2\ 00 \\ 1\ 0 \end{array}\right\} \textit{Diapason, or double} \qquad \left.\begin{array}{l} 3\ 000 \\ 1\ 0 \end{array}\right\} \textit{Triple}$$

IN the *Quadruple* the Proportions are as four to one, or as the Whole to its fourth Part.

$$\left.\begin{array}{l} 4\ 0000 \\ 1\ 0 \end{array}\right\} \textit{Quadruple}$$

LASTLY, all these musical Numbers are as follows: One, two, three, four, and the Tone before-mentioned, wherein the long String compared to the shorter, exceeds it one eighth Part of that shorter String.

$$\left.\begin{array}{l} 1.\ 2.\ 3.\ 4. \\ \text{Musical Numbers} \end{array}\right. \left.\begin{array}{l} 8\ 00000000 \\ 9\ 000000000,0 \end{array}\right\} \textit{Tone}$$

OF all these Numbers the Architects made very convenient Use, taking them sometimes two by two, as in planning out their Squares and open Areas, wherein only two Proportions were to be considered, namely, Length and Breadth; and sometimes taking them three by three, as in publick Halls, Council-chambers, and the like; wherein as the Length was to bear a Proportion to the Breadth, so they made the Height in a certain harmonious Proportion to them both.

244

CHAP. VI.

Of the Proportions of Numbers in the Measuring of Areas, and the Rules for some other Proportions drawn neither from natural Bodies, nor from Harmony.

OF these Proportions we are now to treat more particularly, and first we shall say something of those Areas where only two are used. Of Areas, some are short, some long, and some between both. The shortest of all is the perfect Square, every Side whereof is of

245

equal

E e e

equal Length, all corresponding with one another at Right Angles. The neareft to this is the *Sefquialtera*, and the *Sefquitertian* alfo may be reckoned among the fhorter Areas. Thefe three Proportions therefore, which we may alfo call fimple, are proper for the fmaller Platforms. There are likewife three others, which are proper for middling Platforms: The beft of all is the Double, and the next beft is that which is formed of the *Sefquialtera* doubled, which is produced as follows: Having fet down the leaft Number of the Area, as, for Inftance, four, lengthen it to the firft *Sefquialtera*, which will make fix, and then add the *Sefquialtera* of this fix, which will produce nine. Thus the Length will exceed the Breadth in a double Proportion, and one Tone more.

4 oooo   } *Sefquialtera*
6 oooooo }
9 ooooooooo *Sefquialtera* doubled

FOR moderate Platforms alfo, we may ufe that Proportion which arifes from the *Sefquitertian* doubled in the fame Manner as the former; wherein the Length and Breadth will be as nine and fixteen.

9 ooooooooo   } *Sefquitertia*
12 oooooooooooo }
16 oooooooooooooooo *Sefquitertia* doubled

HERE the longer Line contains the fhorter twice, excluding one Tone of that fhorter Line. In the longeft Areas we either add the *Duple* to the *Sefquialtera*, which will produce the *Triple*; or add the *Sefquitertia* to the *Duple*, which will make the Proportion as three to eight; or laftly make the Lines correfpond to each other in a *Quadruple* Proportion. We have now fpoke of the fhorter Platforms, wherein the Numbers anfwer to each other equally, as two to three, or three to four, and of the Middling, wherein they correfpond as two to four, or as four to nine, or as nine to fixteen: And laftly of the longeft, wherein the Numbers anfwer in a *Triple* or *Quadruple* Proportion, or as three to eight. We may join together or compound all the three Lines of any Body whatfoever, by Means of thefe feveral Number, which are either innate with Harmony itfelf, or produced from other Proportions in a certain and regular Method. We find in Harmony thofe Numbers from whofe mutual Relations we may form their feveral Proporions, as in the *Duple*, the *Triple* and the *Quadruple*. For In-

ftance, the *Duple* is formed of the fimple *Sefquialtera*, with the Addition of the *Sefquitertia*, in the following Method. Let the leaft Number of the *Duple* be two; the *Sefquialtera* of this is three, and the *Sefquitertia* of this Number three is four, which is juft the Double of two before-mentioned.

oo
ooo   The *Sefquialtera*
oooo   The *Sefquitertia* or *Duple*

OR elfe the fame is done in the following Manner: Let the fmaller Number be, for Inftance, three; I add one to make it a *Sefquitertia*, and it becomes four, to which adding a *Sefquialtera*, it makes it fix, which, compared to three, is juft in a double Proportion.

The *Duple* { ooo
{ oooo   *Sefquitertia*
{ oooooo   *Sefquialtera*

THE *Triple* is likewife made of the *Duple*, and of the *Sefquialtera* joined together: For Inftance, let the fmaller Number here be two; this being doubled, makes four; to which adding a *Sefquialtera*, it becomes fix, which is the *Triple* of two.

The *Triple* { oo
{ oooo   doubled
{ oooooo   *Sefquialtera*

OR the fame Thing is done as follows; placing the fame Number of two for the fmaller Number, take the *Sefquialtera*, and you will have three, which being doubled, gives fix, and fo we fhall have the *Triple* of two.

The *Triple* { oo
{ ooo   *Sefquialtera*
{ oooooo   doubled

BY Means of the fame Extenfions we may produce the *Quadruple*, by compounding one *Duple* with another, fince it is indeed nothing more than the *Duple* doubled, which is alfo called *Difdiapafon*, and is performed as follows: Let the fmaller Number here, for Inftance, be two; double this, and it makes the *Diapafon*, that is to fay four, which is the *Duple* of two, and doubling this four, it makes the *Difdiapafon*, which is as eight to two.

The *Quadruple*. { oo
{ oooo   *Diapafon*.
{ oooooooo   *Difdiapafon*.

THIS

246

THIS *Quadruple* may be also formed by adding a *Sesquialtera* and a *Sesquitertia* to the *Duple*; and how this is done, is manifest by what we have said above: But for its clearer Explanation, we shall give a further Instance of it here. The Number two, for Example, by Means of a *Sesquialtera* is made three, which by a *Sesquitertia* becomes four, which four being doubled makes eight.

The *Quadruple*.
$$\begin{cases} \text{oo} & \\ \text{ooo} & \textit{Sesquialtera} \\ \text{oooo} & \textit{Sesquitertia} \\ \text{oooooooo} & \text{doubled} \end{cases}$$

OR rather in the following Manner. Let us take the Number three; this being doubled makes six, to which adding another three, we have nine, and adding to this a third of itself, it produces twelve, which answers to three in a *Quadruple* Proportion.

The *Quadruple*
$$\begin{cases} \text{ooo} & \\ \text{oooooo} & \text{doubled} \\ \text{ooooooooo} & \text{a third added} \\ \text{oooooooooooo} & \text{a third added} \end{cases}$$

THE Architects make use of all the several Proportions here set down, not confusedly and indistinctly, but in such Manner as to be constantly and every way agreeable to Harmony: As, for Instance, in the Elevation of a Room which is twice as long as broad, they make use, not of those Numbers which compose the Triple, but of those only which form the Duple; and the same in a Room whose Length is three Times its Breadth, employing only its own proper Proportions, and no foreign ones, that is to say, taking such of the triple Progressions above set down, as is most agreeable to the Circumstances of their Structure. There are some other natural Proportions for the Use of Structures, which are not borrowed from Numbers, but from the Roots and Powers of Squares. The Roots are the Sides of square Numbers: The Powers are the Areas of those Squares: The Multiplication of the Areas produce the Cubes. The first of all Cubes, whose Root is one, is consecrated to the Deity, because, as it is derived from One, So it is One every Way; to which we may add, that it is the most stable and constant of all Figures, and the very Basis of all the rest. But if, as some affirm, the Unite be no Number, but only the Source of all others, we may then suppose the first Number to be the Number two. Taking this Number two for the Root, the Areas will be four, which being raised up to a Height equal to its Root, will produce a

Cube of eight; and from this Cube we may gather the Rules for our Proportions; for here in the first Place, we may consider the Side of the Cube, which is called the Cube Root, whose Area will in Numbers be four, and the compleat or entire Cube be as eight. In the next Place we may consider the Line drawn from one Angle of the Cube to that which is directly opposite to it, so as to divide the Area of the Square into two equal Parts, and this is called the Diagonal. What this amounts to in Numbers is not known: Only it appears to be the Root of an Area, which is as Eight on every Side; besides which it is the Diagonal of a Cube which is on every Side, as twelve, *Fig.* 1.

LASTLY, In a Triangle whose two shortest Sides form a Right Angle, and one of them the Root of an Area, which is every Way as four, and the other of one, which is as twelve, the longest Side subtended opposite to that Right Angle, will be the Root of an Area, will be the Root of an Area, which is as sixteen *Fig.* 2.

THESE several Rules which we have here set down for the determining of Proportions, are the natural and proper Relations of Numbers and Quantities, and the general Method for the Practice of them all is, that the shortest Line be taken for the Breadth of the Area, the longest for the Length, and the middle Line for the Height, tho' sometimes for the Convenience of the Structure, they are interchanged. We are now to say something of the Rules of those Proportions, which are not derived from Harmony or the natural Proportions of Bodies, but are borrowed elsewhere for determining the three Relations of an Apartment; and in order to this we are to observe, that there are very useful Considerations in Practice to be drawn from the Musicians, Geometers, and even the Arithmeticians, of each of which we are now to speak. These the Philosophers call *Mediocrates*, or *Means*, and the Rules for them are many and various; but there are three particularly which are the most esteemed; of all which the Purpose is, that the two Extreams being given, the middle Mean or Number may correspond with them in a certain detemined Manner, or to use such an Expression, with a regular Affinity. Our Business, in this Enquiry, is to consider three Terms, whereof the two most remote are one the greatest, and the other the least; the third or mean Number must answer to

these

thefe other two in a juft Relation or proportionate Interval, which Interval is the equal relative Diftance which this Number ftands from the other two. Of the three Methods moft approved by the Philofophers for finding this Mean, that which is called the arithmetical is the moft eafy, and is as follows. Taking the two extreme Numbers, as for Inftance, eight for the greateft, and four for the leaft, you add them together, which produce twelve, which twelve being divided in two equal Parts, gives us fix.

$$8 \qquad 4$$
$$12$$
$$6$$

248

THIS Number fix the Arithmeticians fay, is the Mean, which ftanding between four and eight, is at an equal Diftance from each of them.

$$8. \quad 6. \quad 4.$$

THE next Mean is that which is called the Geometrical, and is taken thus. Let the fmalleft Number, for Example, four, be multiplied by the greateft, which we fhall fuppofe to be nine; the Multiplication will produce 36: The Root of which Sum as it is called, or the Number of its Side being multiplied by itfelf muft alfo produce 36. The Root therefore will be fix, which multiplied by itfelf is 36, and this Number fix, is the Mean.

$$4 \text{ Times } 9 \quad 36$$
$$6 \text{ Times } 6 \quad 36$$

249   THIS geometrical Mean is very difficult to find by Numbers, but it is very clear by Lines; but of thofe it is not my Bufinefs to fpeak here. The third Mean, which is called the Mufical, is fomewhat more difficult to work

than the Arithmetical; but, however, may be very well performed by Numbers. In this the Proportion between the leaft Term and the greateft, muft be the fame as the Diftance between the leaft and the Mean, and between the Mean and the greateft, as in the following Example. Of the two given Numbers, let the leaft be thirty, and the greateft fixty, which is juft the Double of the other. I take fuch Numbers as cannot be lefs to be double, and thefe are one, for the leaft, and two, for the greateft, which added together make three. I then divide the whole Interval which was between the greateft Number, which was fixty, and the leaft, which was thirty, into three Parts, each of which Parts therefore will be ten, and one of thefe three Parts I add to the leaft Number, which will make it forty; and this will be the mufical Mean defired.

$$30 \qquad 60$$
$$1 \qquad 2$$
$$3$$
$$3 \qquad 30$$
$$10$$
$$30$$
$$10$$
$$30 \qquad 40 \qquad 60$$

AND this mean Number forty will be diftant from the greateft Number juft double the Interval which the Number of the Mean is diftant from the leaft Number; and the Condition was, that the greateft Number fhould bear that Portion to the leaft. By the Help of thefe Mediocrites the Architects have difcovered many excellent Things, as well with Relation to the whole Structure, as to its feveral Parts; which we have not Time here to particularize. But the moft common Ufe they have made of thefe Mediocrities, has been however for their Elevations.

CHAP. VII.

Of the Invention of Columns, their Dimenfions and Collocation.

IT will not be unpleafant to confider fome further Particulars relating to the three Sorts of Columns which the Ancients invented, in three different Points of Time: And it is not at all improbable, that they borrowed the Proportions of their Columns from that of the Members of the human Body. Thus they found that from one Side of a Man to the other was a fixth Part of his Height, and that

from the Navel to the Reins was a tenth. From this Obfervation the Interpreters of our facred Books, are of Opinion, that *Noah*'s Ark for the Flood was built according to the Proportions of the human Body. By the fame Proportions we may reafonably conjecture, that the Ancients erected their Columns, making the Height in fome fix Times, and in others ten Times, the Diameter of the Bottom of the Shaft.

Shaft. But from that natural Inſtinct or Senſe in the Mind by which, as we have already obſerved, we judge of Beauty and Gracefulneſs, they found, that one of theſe was too thick and the other too ſlight; for which Reaſon they altered them both, rightly ſuppoſing that the Truth muſt lie in ſome Medium between theſe two vitious Extremes. Accordingly, with the Help of the Rules of the Arithmeticians, they joined their two Numbers together, and divided the Total in half, and then they found that the mean Number between ſix and ten was eight: Whereupon they made the Height of their Column eight Times the Diameter of the Bottom of the Shaft; and this they called the *Ionic*. They alſo formed their *Doric* Column, which is proper for Buildings of greater Solidity, by the ſame Rules. For Example, they joined the ſmaller Number before-mentioned, which was ſix, with the *Ionic* mean, which was eight, whereof the Total was fourteen; this Total they divided into two equal Parts, and this gave them the Number ſeven, which they took for their *Doric* Column, making its Length ſeven Times the Diameter of the Bottom of the Shaft. Laſtly, they made their thinneſt Order, which they called the *Corinthian*, from the *Ionic* mean Number joined to the greateſt of the former Numbers, and ſo taking the Half as before; for the *Ionic* mean Number was eight, and the greateſt Number was ten, which added together made eighteen, the Half whereof was nine, whence they made the Height of their *Corinthian* Column nine Times the Diameter of the Bottom of its Shaft, as they did the *Ionic* eight, and the *Doric* ſeven: Of which we need ſay no more in this Place. We are now to ſay ſomething of the Collocation, which relates to the Situation of the ſeveral Parts; and this is much eaſier to conceive where it is ill done, than it is to lay down exact Rules for the doing it: Becauſe indeed it is chiefly to be referred to the natural Judgment which we have formerly obſerved to be innate in the Mind of Man, though it may in ſome Meaſure be derived from the foregoing Rules for the Finiſhing. However, we ſhall juſt mention a few general Remarks upon this Head. The very ſmalleſt Parts or Members of the

Work, if they are ſet in their right Places, add to the Beauty of the whole; if they are placed in mean or improper Situations, though excellent in themſelves, they become mean. We ſee the very ſame Thing in the Works of Nature: As for Inſtance, if a Dog had one Ear like that of an Aſs, or if a Man had one Foot bigger than the other, or one Hand very large, and the other very ſmall, we ſhould immediately pronounce ſuch a one deformed; or to ſee even an Horſe with one Eye grey, and the other black, is very offenſive: So agreeable it is to Nature, that the Members on the right Side ſhould exactly anſwer the left: Wherefore the very firſt Thing we are to take Care of muſt be, that every Part, even the moſt Inconſiderable, lie duly to the Level and Plum-line, and be diſpoſed with an exact Correſpondence as to the Number, Form and Appearance; ſo that the Right may anſwer to the Left, the High to the Low, the Similar to the Similar, ſo as to form a correſpondent Ornament in that Body whereof they are Parts. Even Statues, Pictures, or any other Ornaments of that ſort with which we embelliſh our Work, muſt be ſo diſpoſed as to ſeem to have ſprung up naturally in their propereſt Places, and to be Twins. The Ancients were ſo punctual in this mutual Correſpondence of the Parts, that even in fixing up their Scantlings of Marble, they uſed to make them anſwer each other exactly to a Size, Quality, Angles, Situation and Colour: And eſpecially in thoſe moſt beautiful Ornaments, Statues, wherein the Ancients were ſuch great Maſters, and in which I ſo much admire the Excellence of Art, they were careful in fixing them up, as well on Pediments of their Temples, as elſewhere, that thoſe on one Side ſhould not differ from thoſe on the other, in the ſmalleſt Particular either of Deſign or Material. We ſee Statues of two or four Horſes, and of their Drivers and Lookers on ſo exactly like to each other, that Art in them may be ſaid to have exceeded Nature, in whoſe Works we hardly ever ſee one Feature ſo exactly like the other. Thus we have ſhewn what is Beauty, and wherein it conſiſts, and with what Numbers and Finiſhing the Ancients uſed to erect their Structures.

CHAP. VIII.

Some short, but general Observations which may be looked upon as Laws in the Business of Building and Ornament.

I Shall here put together some short and general Admonitions, which are absolutely
necessary to be observed as so many Laws, as
well in Point of Ornament or Embellishment,
as in all the other Parts of Architecture. And
this may serve to acquit us of the Promise
which we made of taking a short Review of
the whole Work by Way of Epilogue. First
therefore, as we laid it down for a Rule at the
Beginning, that all Errors which any Ways de-
form the Structure were to be avoided principally: We will now speak in the first Place of
such Errors, and especially of the greatest. Errors arise either from the Judgement, and lie
either in the Design or Election; or from the
Hand, and lie in the Workmen's Execution:
The Errors of the Judgment are both in Time
and in their Nature of much the greatest Importance, and when committed, less capable of
being remedied. With these therefore we shall
begin.   The first Error is to chuse for your
Structure a Region which is unhealthy, not
peaceable, barren, unfortunate, melancholy, or
afflicted with Calamities, either apparent or
concealed.   The next Errors to this are chusing a Platform not proper or convenient; adding one Member to another, without constant
Regard to the Accommodation of the Inhabitants, and not providing fit and suitable Conveniencies for every Rank and Degree of them,
as well Masters as Servants, Citizens as Rusticks, Inmates as Visitants: Making your Building either too large and spacious, or too small
and narrow; too open and naked, or too much
shut in and confined; too much crowded, or
too rambling with too many Apartments, or
too few: If there be a Want of Rooms where
you may secure yourself against excessive Heats,
or excessive Colds, of Places where you may
exercise and divert yourself when you are in
Health, and of others where you may be sufficiently sheltered against any Inclemency of
Air when you are sick: To which add the
Structures not being sufficiently strong, and as
we may say, fortified to be safe against any sudden Attack: If the Wall be either so slight as
not to be sufficiently strong to support itself

and the Roof, or much thicker than Necessity
requires, if the different Roofs bespatter each
other with their Waters, or throw them against
any Part of the Wall, or near the Entrances:
If they be either too low, or too high: If your
Windows be too wide, and admit unwholesome Winds, noxious Dews, or too much burning Sun; or, on the other Hand, if they be so
narrow as to occasion a melancholy Gloom:
If they break into any of the Ribs of the Building: If the Passages are any Ways obstructed,
or lead us to any Object that is offensive: Or,
in short, if any of those other Instructions are
neglected, which we have given in the preceding Books.   Among the Errors in Ornament,
the Principal, in Architecture as in Nature, is
making any Thing preposterous, maimed, excessive, or any other Ways unsightly: For if
these Things are reckoned defective and monstrous in Nature herself, what must we say of
an Architect that throws the Parts of his Structures into such improper Forms? And as the
Parts whereof those Forms consist, are Lines,
Angles, Extension, and the like, it is certainly
true, that there can be no Error or Deformity
more absurd and shocking, than the mixing
together either Angles or Lines, or Superficies
which are not in Number, Size and Situation
equal to each other, and which are not blended
together with the greatest Care and Accuracy.   254
And indeed who can avoid blaming a Man extremely, that without being forced to it by any
Manner of Necessity, draws his Wall crooked
and askew, winding this way and that like a
Worm crawling upon the Ground, without
any Rule or Method, with one Side long, and
another short, without any Equality of Angles,
or the least Connection with Regard to each
other; making his Platform with an obtuse
Angle on one Side, and an acute one on the
other, and doing every Thing with Confusion,
Absurdity and at a Venture: It is another
great Error to have raised your Structure in
such a Manner, that, though indeed with Relation to its Platform, it is not amiss, yet, not-
withstanding it may be in very great Want of
Ornament, it may be utterly incapable of any
Sort

Sort of Embellishment as if all you consulted in raising your Wall, was to sustain the Roof, not leaving any Space where you can afterwards conveniently or distinctly add either the Dignity of Columns, the Embellishment of Statues, the Majesty of Picture, or the Delicacy of any Incrustation. An Error of much the same Nature as this is, the Building with so little Consideration, that though the same Expence might make our Structure beautiful and graceful, yet we neglect the Pains and Contrivance of effecting it: For it is undeniable that there may be in the mere Form or Figure of a Building, an innate Excellence and Beauty, which strikes and delights the Mind, and is immediately perceived where it is, as much as it is missed where it is not; for, indeed, the Eye is naturally a Judge and Lover of Beauty and Gracefulness, and is very critical and hard to please in it; neither can I give any Account why it should always happen, that we should be much more offended at what is wanting, than ready to commend what is done well; for still we are continually thinking what further might be added to make the Object still more splendid, and are naturally displeased if any thing is omitted, which the most accurate, ingenious, and diligent Artist might possibly have procured: So that indeed we are often at a Loss to say what it is offends us, unless it be that there is not wherewithal fully to satisfy our immoderate Desire of Perfection. This being the true State of the Case, we should certainly endeavour, as much as in us lies, by the greatest Study and Care, to make whatever Structure we raise as handsome, and as compleatly adorned as possibly, especially if it be such a one as every body expects to see in the utmost Perfection, as, for Instance, a publick Structure, and particularly a sacred one, which no Man can bear to see naked of Ornament. It is another Error to apply the Ornaments peculiar to a publick Structure, to a private one; or, on the other Hand, those peculiar to private Edifices to one of a publick Nature: Especially if such Ornaments are any thing petty, or not durable, as, for Instance, to dish up a publick Structure with slight or paultry Painting; for every Thing used about a publick Edifice ought, if possible, to be eternal. It is another gross Error, which we see some ridiculous People run into, who e'er they have well begun their Building, fall to painting it, and decking it with

Statues and other Embellishments without Number; all which are sure to be spoiled and demolished before the Building is finished. We should erect our Building naked, and let it be quite compleated before we begin to dress it with Ornaments, which should always be our last Work, being best done at leasure, when we can do it without any Impediment, and can take the Advantage of such Opportunities as may offer for that Purpose. I would have the Ornaments which you affix to your Structure, to be the Work of various Hands, and those moderate Masters; but if you can procure any rare Pieces of greater Excellence and Perfection, Statues and Pictuaes like those of a *Phidias* or a *Zeuxis*, let them be fixed only in Places of peculiar Dignity and Honour. I cannot commend *Dejoces* the King of *Media*, who encompassed his City of *Ecbatana* with seven Walls, and made each of them of different Colours, one Purple, another Blue, another gilt with Silver, and one even with Gold; nor can I help blaming *Caligula*, who made his Stable of Marble, and the Manger of Ivory. All that *Nero* built was covered with Gold and enriched with Gems. *Heliogabalus* was still more extravagantly profuse, for he paved his Apartments with Gold, and grieved that he could not do it with Amber. Contempt is the best Reward for these wild Prodigals who are ostentatious of such Vain-glories, or rather Follies, and who are thus profuse of the Labours and Sweat of Mankind, about Things which are of no Manner of Use or Advantage to the main Structure, nor capable of raising the least Admiration either for Ingenuity or Contrivance.

I THEREFORE over and over again advise you to avoid these Errors; and before you begin your Work, thoroughly consider the whole Design your self, and take the Advice of Men of Skill upon it; be sure to have a compleat Model of the Whole, by which examine every minute Part of your future Structure eight, nine, ten Times over, and again, after different Intermissions of Times; till there be not the least Member from the Foundation to the Roof of your whole Building, within or without, great or small, but what you have throughly and long weighed and considered, and determined of what Materials it shall be made, where placed, in what Order and Proportions, and to what it shall answer and bear Relation.

CHAP. IX.

The Bufineſs and Duty of a good Architect, and wherein the Excellence of the Ornaments conſiſts.

A Prudent Architect will proceed in the Method which we have been juſt laying down. He will never ſet about his Work without proper Caution and Advice. He will ſtudy the Nature and Strength of the Soil where he is to build, and obſerve, as well from a Survey of Structures in the Neighbourhood, as from the Practice and Uſe of the Inhabitants, what Materials, what Sort of Stone, Sand, Lime or Timber, whether found on the Place, or brought from other Parts, will beſt ſtand againſt the Injuries of the Weather. He will ſet out the exact Breadth and Depth of the Foundations, and of the Baſement of the whole Wall, and take an Account of every Thing that is neceſſary for the Building, whether for the outward Coat or the filling up, for the Ligatures, the Ribs, or the Apertures, the Roof, the Incruſtation, for Pavements abroad, or Floors within; he will direct which Way, and by what Method every thing ſuperfluous, noxious or offenſive ſhall be carried off by Drains for conveying away the rain Water, and keeping the Foundations dry, and by proper Defences againſt any moiſt Vapours, or even againſt any unexpected Floods or Violence from Winds or Storms. In a Word, he will give Directions for every ſingle Part, and not ſuffer any thing to eſcape his Notice and Decree. And tho' all theſe Particulars ſeem chiefly to relate to Convenience and Stability, yet they carry this along with them, that if neglected they deſtroy all the Beauty and Ornament of the Edifice. Now the Rules which give the Ornaments themſelves their main Excellence, are as follows. Firſt all your Ornaments muſt be exactly regular, and perfectly diſtinct, and without Confuſion: Your Embelliſhments muſt not be too much crowded together or ſcattered as it were under Foot, or thrown on in Heaps, but ſo aptly and neatly diſtributed, that whoever ſhould go about to alter their Situation, ſhould be ſenſible that he deſtroyed the whole Beauty and Delicacy of the Work. There is no Part whatſoever but what the Artiſt ought to adorn; but there is no Occaſion that all ſhould be adorned equally, or that every thing ſhould be enriched with equal Expence; for indeed I would not have the Merit of the Work conſiſt ſo much in Plenty as in Variety. Let the Builder fix his richeſt Ornaments in the principal Places; thoſe of a middling Sort, in Places of leſs Note, and the meaneſt in the meaneſt. And here he ſhould be particularly careful, not to mix what is rich with any thing trifling, nothing little with what is great, nor to ſet any thing too large or high in narrow or cloſe Places; tho' things which are not equal to each other in Dignity, nor alike even in Species, may very well be placed together, ſo it be done artfully and ingeniouſly, and in ſuch a Manner, that as the one appears ſolemn and majeſtick, the other may ſhew chearful and pleaſant, and that they may not only unite their different Beauties for the Embelliſhment of the Structure, but alſo ſeem as if the one without the other had been imperfect; nor may it be amiſs in ſome certain Places to intermix ſomewhat even of a coarſe Sort, that what is noble may receive a yet further Addition from the Compariſon: Always be ſure never to make a Confuſion of the Orders, which will happen if you mix the *Doric* Members with the *Corinthian,* as I obſerved before, or the *Corinthian* with the *Ionic,* or the like. Let every Order have its own regular Members, and thoſe all in their proper Places, that nothing may appear perplexed or broken. Let ſuch Ornaments as are proper to the Middle be placed in the Middle, and let thoſe which are at equal Diſtances on each Side, be proportioned exactly alike. In ſhort, let every thing be meaſured, and put together with the greateſt Exactneſs of Lines and Angles, that the Beholder's Eye may have a clear and diſtinct View along the Cornices, between the Columns on the Inſide and without, receiving every Moment freſh Delight from the Variety he meets with, inſomuch, that after the moſt careful and even repeated Views, he ſhall not be able to depart without once more turning back to take another Look, nor, upon the moſt critical Examination, be able in any Part of the whole Structure to find one Thing unequal,

equal, incongruous, out of Proportion, or not conducive to the general Beauty of the Whole. All these Particulars you must provide for by means of your Model; and from thence too you should before-hand consider not only what the Building is that you are to erect, but also get together all the Materials you shall want for the Execution, that when you have begun your Work you may not be at a Loss, or change or supersede your Design: but having before-hand made Provision of every Thing that you shall want, you may be able to keep your Workmen constantly supplied with all their Materials. These are the Things which the Archi-tect is to take care of with the greatest Diligence and Judgement. The Errors which may happen in the manual Execution of the Work, need not be repeated here; but only the Workmen should be well looked after, to see that they work exactly by their Square, Level and Plumb-line; that they do their Business at the proper Seasons, take proper Seasons to let their Work rest, and at proper Seasons go to it again; that they use good Stuff, sound, unmixed, solid, strong, and suitable to the Work, and that they use it in proper Places, and finish every Thing according to their Model.

CHAP. X.

What it is that an Architect ought principally to consider, and what Sciences he ought to be acquainted with.

BUT to the Intent that the Architect may come off worthily and honourably in preparing, ordering and accomplishing all these Things, there are some necessary Admonitions, which he should by no means neglect. And first he ought to consider well what Weight he is going to take upon his Shoulders, what it is that he professes, what Manner of Man he would be thought, how great a Business he undertakes, how much Applause, Profit, Favour and Fame among Posterity he will gain when he executes his Work as he ought, and on the contrary, if he goes about any thing ignorantly, unadvisedly, or inconsiderately, to how much Disgrace, to how much Indignation he exposes himself, what a clear, manifest and everlasting Testimony he gives Mankind of his Folly and Indiscretion. Doubtless Architecture is a very noble Science, not fit for every Head. He ought to be a Man of a fine Genius, of a great Application, of the best Education, of thorough Experience, and especially of strong Sense and sound Judgement, that presumes to declare himself an Architect. It is the Business of Architecture, and indeed its highest Praise, to judge rightly what is fit and decent: For though Building is a Matter of Necessity, yet convenient Building is both of Necessity and Utility too: But to build in such a Manner, that the Generous shall commend you, and the Frugal not blame you, is the Work only of a prudent, wise and learned Architect. To run up any thing that is immediately necessary for any particular Purpose, and about which there is no doubt of what Sort it should be, or of the Ability of the Owner to afford it, is not so much the Business of an Architect, as of a common Workman: But to raise an Edifice which is to be compleat in every Part, and to consider and provide before-hand every Thing necessary for such a Work, is the Business only of that extensive Genius which I have described above: For indeed his Invention must be owing to his Wit, his Knowledge, to Experience, his Choice to Judgment, his Composition to Study, and the Completion of his Work to his Perfection in his Art; of all which Qualifications I take the Foundation to be Prudence and mature Deliberation. As to the other Virtues, Humanity, Benevolence, Modesty, Probity; I do not require them more in the Architect, than I do in every other Man, let him profess what Art he will: For indeed without them I do not think any one worthy to be deemed a Man: But above all Things he should avoid Levity, Obstinacy, Ostentation, Intemperance, and all those other Vices which may lose him the good Will of his Fellow-Citizens, and make him odious to the World. Lastly, in the Study of his Art I would have him follow the Example of those that apply themselves to Letters: For no Man thinks himself sufficiently learned in any Science, unless he has read and examined all the Authors, as well bad as good that have wrote in that Science which he is pursuing. In the same Manner I would have the Architect diligently consider all the Buildings that have any tolerable Reputation; and not only so, but take them down in Lines and Numbers, nay, make Designs and Models of them, and by means of those, consider and examine the Order, Situation, Sort and Number of every Part which others have employed, especially such as have done any thing very great and excellent, whom we may reasonably suppose to have been Men of very great Note, when they were intrusted with the Direction of so great an Expence. Not that I would have him admire a Structure merely for being huge, and imagine that to be a sufficient Beauty; but let him principally enquire in every Building what there is particularly artful and excellent for Contrivance or Invention, and gain a Habit of being pleased with nothing but what is really elegant and praise-worthy for the Design: And where-ever he finds any thing noble, let him make use of it, or imitate it in his own Performances; and when he sees any thing well done, that is capable of being still further improved and made delicate, let him study to bring it to Perfection in his own Works; and when he meets with any Design that is only not absolutely bad, let him try in his own Things to work it if possible into something excellent. Thus by a continued and nice Examination of the best Productions, still considering what Improvements might be made in every thing that he sees, he may so exercise and sharpen his own Invention, as to collect into his own Works not only all the Beauties which are dispersed up and down in those of other Men, but even those which lie in a Manner concealed in the most hidden Recesses of Nature, to his own immortal Reputation. Not satisfied with this, he should also have an Ambition to produce something admirable, which may be entirely of his own Invention; like him, for Instance, who built a Temple without using one iron Tool in it; or him that brought the *Colossus* to *Rome*, suspended all the Way upright, in which Work we may just mention that he employed no less than four-and-twenty Elephants; or like an Artist that in only seemingly working a common Quarry of Stone, should cut it out into a Labyrinth, a Temple, or some other useful Structure, to the Surprise of all Mankind. We are told that *Nero* used to employ miraculous Architects, who never thought of any Invention, but what it was almost impossible for the Skill of Man to reduce

to practice. Such Geniusses I can by no means approve of; for, indeed, I would have the Architect always appear to have consulted Necessity and Convenience in the first Place, even tho' at the very same Time his principal Care has been Ornament. If he can make a handsome Mixture of the noble Orders of the Ancients, with any of the new Inventions of the Moderns, he may deserve Commendation. In this Manner he should be continually improving his Genius by Use and Exercise in such Things as may conduce to make him Excellent in this Science; and indeed, he should think it becomes him to have not only that Knowledge, without which he would not really be what he professed himself; but he should also adorn his Mind with such a Tincture of all the liberal Arts, as may be of Service to make him more ready and ingenious at his own, and that he may never be at a Loss for any Helps in it which Learning can furnish him with. In short, he ought still to be persevering in his Study and Application, till he finds himself equal to those great Men, whose Praises are capable of no further Addition: Nor let him ever be satisfied with himself, if there is that Thing any where that can possibly be of Use to him, and that can be obtained either by Diligence or Thought, which he is not thoroughly Master of, till he is arrived at the Summit of Perfection in the Art which he professes. The Arts which are useful, and indeed absolutely necessary to the Architect, are Painting and Mathematicks. I do not require him to be deeply learned in the rest; for I think it ridiculous, like a certain Author, to expect that an Architect should be a profound Lawyer, in order to know the Right of conveying Water or placing Limits between Neighbours, and to avoid falling into Controversies and Lawsuits as in Building is often the Case: Nor need he be a perfect Astronomer, to know that Libraries ought to be situated to the North, and Stoves to the South; nor a very great Musician, to place the Vases of Copper or Brass in a Theatre for assisting the Voice: Neither do I require that he should be an Orator, in order to be able to display to any Person that would employ him, the Services which he is capable of doing him; for Knowledge, Experience and perfect Mastery in what he is to speak of, will never fail to help him to Words to explain his Sense sufficiently, which indeed is the first and main End of Eloquence. Not that I would have him Tongue-tied, or so

deficient

255

deficient in his Ears, as to have no Taste for Harmony: It may suffice if he does not build a private Man's House upon the publick Ground, or upon another Man's: If he does not annoy the Neighbours, either by his Lights, his Spouts, his Gutters, his Drains, or by obstructing their Passage contrary to Law: If he knows the several Winds that blows from the different Points of the Compass, and their Names; in all which Sciences there is no Harm indeed in his being more expert; but Painting and Mathematicks are what he can no more be without, than a Poet can be without the Knowledge of Feet and Syllables; neither do I know whether it be enough for him to be only moderately tinctured with them. This I can say of myself, that I have often started in my Mind Ideas of Buildings, which have given me wonderful Delight: Wherein when I have come to reduce them into Lines, I have found in those very Parts which most pleased me, many gross Errors that required great Correction; and up-

on a second Review of such a Draught, and measuring every Part by Numbers, I have been sensible and ashamed of my own Inaccuracy. Lastly, when I have made my Draught into a Model, and then proceeded to examine the several Parts over again, I have sometimes found myself mistaken, even in my Numbers. Not that I expected my Architect to be a *Zeuxis* in Painting, nor a *Nicomachus* at Numbers, nor an *Archimedes* in the Knowledge of Lines and Angles: It may serve his Purpose if he is a thorough Master of those Elements of Painting which I have wrote; and if he is skilled in so   256 much practical Mathematicks, and in such a Knowledge of mixed Lines, Angles and Numbers, as is necessary for the Measuring of Weights, Superficies and Solids, which Part of Geometry the *Greeks* call *Podismata* and *Emboda*. With these Arts, joined to Study and Application, the Architect may be sure to obtain Favour and Riches, and to deliver his Name with Reputation down to Posterity.

CHAP. XI.

To what Sort of Persons the Architect ought to offer his Service.

THERE is one Thing that I must not omit here, which relates personally to the Architect. It is, that you should not immediately run and offer your Service to every Man that gives out he is going to build; a Fault which the inconsiderate and vain-glorious are too apt to be guilty of. I know not whether you ought not to wait till you are more than once importuned to be concerned. Certainly they ought to repose a free and voluntary Confidence in you, that want to make use of your Labours and Advice. Why should I offer those Inventions which have cost me so much Study and Pains, to gain perhaps no other Recompence, but the Confidence of a few Persons of no Taste or Skill? If by my Advice in the Execution of your intended Work, I either save you from an unnecessary Expence, or procure you some great Convenience or Pleasure; surely such a Service deserves a suitable Recompence. For this Reason a prudent Man should take care to maintain his Reputation; and certainly it is enough if you give honest Advice, and correct Draughts to such as apply themselves to you. If afterwards you undertake to supervise and compleat the Work, you will find it very difficult

to avoid being made answerable for all the Faults and Mistakes committed either by the Ignorance or Negligence of other Men: Upon which Account you must take care to have the Assistance of honest, diligent, and severe Overseers to look after the Workmen under you. I would also have you, if possible, con-   257 cern yourself for none but Persons of the highest Rank and Quality, and those too such as are truly Lovers of these Arts: Because your Work   258 loses of its Dignity by being done for mean Persons. Do you not see what Weight the Authority of great Men is to advance the Reputation of those who are employed by them? And, indeed, I insist the more upon this Piece of Advice, not only because the World has generally a higher Opinion of the Taste and Judgment of great Men, than for the most Part they deserve, but also because I would have the Architect always readily and plentifully supplied with every thing that is necessary for compleating his Edifice; which those of lower Degree are commonly not so able, and therefore not so willing to do: to which add, what we find very frequent Instances of, that where the Design and Invention has been perfectly equal in two different Works,

one

one has been much more efteemed than the other, for the Sake of the Superiority of the Materials. Laftly, I advife you not to be fo far carried away by the Defire of Glory, as rafhly to attempt any thing entirely new and unufual: Therefore be fure to examine and confider thoroughly what you are going to undertake, even in its minuteft Parts; and remember how difficult it is to find Workmen that fhall exactly execute any extraordinary Idea which you may form, and with how much Grudging and Unwillingnefs People will fpend their Money in making Trial of your Fancies. Laftly, beware of that very common Fault, by means of which there are fo few great Structures but what have fome unpardonable Blemifhes. We always find People very ready to criticize, and fond of being thought Counfellors and Directors. Now as, by reafon of the Shortnefs of Man's Life, few great Works are compleated by the firft Undertaker, we that fucceed him, either out of Envy or Officioufnefs, are vain of making fome Alteration in his original Defign. By this means what was well begun is fpoiled in the finifhing. For this Reafon I think we fhould adhere to the original Defign of the Inventor, who we are to fuppofe had maturely weighed and confidered it. It is poffible he might have fome wife Inducement to do what he did, which upon a more diligent and attentive Examination, you may at length difcover yourfelf. If however you do make any Alteration, never do it without the Advice, or rather abfolute Direction of the moft approved and experienced Mafters: By which means you will both provide for the Neceffities of the Structure, and fecure yourfelf againft the Malice of envious Tongues. We have now treated of publick Buildings, and of private; of facred, and of profane; of thofe which relate to Dignity, and thofe of Pleafure. What remains is to fhew how any Defects in an Edifice, which have arifen either from Ignorance or Negligence, from the Violence of Men or Times, or from unfortunate and unforefeen Accidents, may be repaired and amended: Still hoping that thefe Arts will meet with the Favour and Protection of the Learned.

The End of Book IX.

THE
ARCHITECTURE
OF
Leone Batista Alberti.

BOOK X. CHAP. I.

*Of the Defects in Buildings, whence they proceed, and their different Sorts;
which of them can be corrected by the Architect, and which cannot; and the
various Causes of a bad Air.*

SINCE in the Remainder of this Work we are to treat of the correcting the several Defects in Building, it is necessary first to consider what those Defects are which are capable of Emendation by the Hand of Man: As the Physicians think that the Knowledge of the Patient's Distemper, is the greatest Step towards his Cure. Of the Defects in Buildings, as well publick as private, some are innate and owing to the Architect, and others proceed from foreign Causes: And again, of these some are capable of being repaired by Art and Contrivance, and others will not possibly admit of any Remedy. What those are which are owing to the Architect, we have pointed out so plainly in the last Book, that a Repetition of them here is not necessary, having there shewn that some are the Errors of the Mind, some of the Hand; that those of the Mind are an injudicious Election, an inconvenient Compartition, an improper Distribution, or confused Proportions; whereas those of the Hand are an inaccurate or inconsiderate Preparation, Collection, Working, and putting together the Materials: Faults which the Negligent and Unadvised easily fall into. But the Defects which proceed from foreign Causes are scarcely to be numbered for their Multiplicity and Variety: Of which Causes the first is that which is said to overcome all Things, Time, whose Violence is no less deceitful than it is powerful, nor can any Sort of Bodies elude that great Law of Nature, of Feeling the Decays of old Age; insomuch that some are of Opinion, the very Heavens themselves are corruptible only for this Reason, because they are Bodies. We all know the Power of the Sun, of Damps, of Frosts and of Storms. Battered by these Engines, we see the hardest Flints shiver and fall to Pieces, and huge Pieces of Rock broken down from the Mountains, with Parts of the Hill itself along with them. To these add the Violence or Negligence of Men. I call Heaven to Witness, that I am often filled with the highest Indignation when I see Buildings demolished and going to Ruin by the Carelessness, not to say abominable Avarice of the Owners, Buildings whose Majesty has saved them from the Fury of the most barbarous and enraged Enemies, and which Time himself, that perverse and obstinate Destroyer, seems to have destined to Eternity. To these again add the sudden Accidents of Fire, Lightening, Earthquakes, Inundations, and those many surprizing, unheard of and incredible Phænomena which the miraculous Power of Nature so frequently produces, and which are capable of

over-

over-turning the beft finifhed Structure of the wifeft Architect. *Plato* fays, that the whole *Atlantick* Ifland, which was not lefs than *Epirus*, vanifhed away at once into Smoke. Hiftory informs us, that the Cities of *Helice* and *Bura* were both fwallowed up, one by the Sea and the other by an Earthquake: That the Lake *Tritonis* difappeared in an Inftant, and on the contrary, that of *Stymphalis* in *Argos*, appeared as fuddenly: That at *Teramene* an Ifland ftarted up at once, with hot Springs in it; and that between the two Iflands of *Therafia* and *Thera* a Flame burft out of the Sea, which made it foam and boil four whole Days fucceffively, and at laft appeared an Ifland twelve Furlongs in Length, wherein the *Rhodians* built a Temple to *Neptune* their Protector. In other Places we are told of fuch numerous Swarms of Mice, that they bred an Infection, and that the *Spaniards* fent Ambaffadors to the *Roman* Senate to implore their Affiftance againft infinite Numbers of Hares which eat up their Country; and many other wonderful Accidents of the fame Nature, whereof we have made a Collection in our little Treatife, entitled *Theogenius*. But all the Defects which proceed from foreign Caufes are not uncapable of being corrected: Neither will thofe which are owing to the Architect, always admit of Amendment; for where every thing is wrong and out of Order, no Improvement is practicable. Where the Building cannot be any ways altered for the better, but by changing almoft every Line and Angle, it is much better to pull the Whole quite down, and begin upon a new Foundation. But that is not our Bufinefs now: We are here to fhew what may be amended or improved by Art. And firft we fhall fpeak of Buildings of a publick Nature. Of thefe the greateft and moft important is the City, or rather, if we may fo call it, the Region of the City. The Region wherein an inconfiderable Architect has placed his City, may perhaps have thofe Defects which will admit of Amendment. Either it may be unfecure againft fudden Incurfions of Enemies, or it may ftand in a bad unhealthy Air, or it may not be well fupplied with all Neceffaries. Of thefe therefore we fhall now treat. The Way from *Lydia* into *Cilicia* lies through a narrow Pafs cut by Nature among the Hills, in fuch a Manner that you would think fhe defigned it as a Gate to that Province. At *Thermopylæ*, now called the *Bocca de Lupo*, is a Pafs which three armed Men may

defend, being a broken Way interrupted by numberlefs Rills of Water on every Side, which rife from the very Root of the Mountain. Much like this are the broken Rocks in the Mark of *Ancona*, called by the Vulgar *Foffo ombrone*, and many others in other Places. But fuch Paffes, fo fortified by Nature, are not to be found every where: However, they feem in a great Meafure, to be capable of being imitated by Art; and accordingly we find it to have been very often prudently done by the Ancients, who in order to fecure their Country from the Inroads of their Enemies, ufed the following Methods, which we fhall briefly gather from as many of the great Works of the old Heroes, as may ferve to illuftrate our prefent Subject. *Artaxerxes* near the River *Euphrates*, cut a Trench between himfelf and the Enemy, threefcore Foot broad, and ten Miles long. The *Cæfars* (and particularly *Adrian*) built a Wall acrofs *Britain* forefcore Miles in Length, by which they divided the Lands of the *Barbarians* from thofe of the *Romans*. *Antoninus Pius* made another of Turf acrofs the fame Ifland. After him *Severus* threw up a Trench an hundred and twenty-two Miles long, which divided the Ifland clear from Sea to Sea. *Antiochus Soter* encompaffed *Margiana* a Province of *India*, where he built *Antiochia*, with a Wall fifteen hundred Furlongs in Length; and *Seofofis* carried a Wall of the fame Length from the Borders of *Ægypt* towards *Arabia*, thro' a Defart quite from the City of the Sun, which was called *Thebes*. The *Neritones*, whofe Country formerly joined to *Leucadia*, cutting away the Neck of Land, and letting in the Sea, made it an Ifland: On the contrary, the *Chalcidians* and the *Boeotians* raifed a Dike over the Straits, called the *Euripus*, to join *Euboia* to *Boeotia*, that they might be able to fuccour each other. *Alexander* the Great built fix Towns near the River *Oxus*, not far diftant from each other, that upon any fudden Attack from the Enemy, they might have Affiftance at Hand. The Ancients frequently made ufe of little Redoubts, which they called *Tyrfes*, fortified with very high Ramparts, like Caftles, to put a Stop to Incurfions from their Enemies. The *Perfians* ftopt up the *Tygris* with Sluices, that none of the Enemy's Veffels might get up the River: But *Alexander* took them away and opened the Stream, alledging that it was a mean and cowardly Defence, and exhorting them rather to truft to their own Valour for their Security. Some have overflowed their Country and

made

made it a perfect Marſh, like *Arabia*, which by means of a Number of Lakes and Bogs occaſioned by the River *Euphrates*, was not to be approached by an Enemy. Thus by ſuch Fortifications they both ſecured their own Country againſt the Attacks of an Enemy, and at the ſame Time made their Enemy's Country weaker and more defenceleſs. What are the Cauſes which make the Air unhealthy, we have already ſhewn ſufficiently at Length in the proper Place. We may only obſerve here in general, that for the moſt Part thoſe Cauſes are either the too great Power of the Sun, or too much Shade; ſome infectious Winds from neighbouring Parts, or peſtilent Vapours from the Soil itſelf, or elſe ſomething in the very Climate itſelf that is noxious. To mend the Air when it is unhealthy or corrupted, is a Work ſcarce thought poſſible to be done by any human Contrivance; unleſs by appeaſing the Wrath of Heaven by Prayers and Supplications, which, like the Nail driven by the Conſul, have ſometimes, as we read, put a Stop to the moſt deſtructive Contagions. Againſt the Inconveniencies of the Sun or Wind to the Inhabitants of ſome little Town or Villa, perhaps ſome Remedy may be found: But to alter the Climate of a whole Region or Province, is a Task too great; not that I deny the Poſſibility of amending a great many of thoſe Defects which proceed from the Air, by curing the Earth of exhaling noxious Vapours. In order to ſhew how this may be done, it is not neceſſary that I ſhould here ſpend Time in debating whether it is by means of the Power of the Sun, or by ſome natural inward Heat, that the Earth emits thoſe two Vapours, of which one mounting up into the Air is condenſed by the Cold, into Rain and Snow; and the other, which is a dry Vapour, is ſuppoſed to be the Cauſe of Winds: It is enough that we are aſſured, that both theſe ariſe out of the Earth; and as we find that thoſe Steams which proceed from the Bodies of Animals, partake of the Nature of the Bodies from which they ariſe, peſtiferous from peſtilentious Bodies, and ſweet from wholeſome and cleanly ones, and that ſometimes where the Sweat or Vapour is not bad in itſelf, it is rendered offenſive by the Naſtineſs of the Garment through which it paſſes; ſo it is with the Earth: For when the Ground is neither well covered with Water, nor perfectly dry, but lies like a Marſh or Bog, it muſt for ſeveral Reaſons emit noxious and unwholeſome Vapours. Thus we find, that where the Sea is deep, the

Water is cold, and warm where it is ſhallow; the Reaſon of which, we are told, is becauſe the Rays of the Sun cannot ſtrike to the Bottom of a deep Water: As if you plunge a red-hot Iron into Oil, if the Oil be but a ſmall Quantity, it will raiſe a ſtrong thick Smoke, but if there is Oil enough to cover it quite over, it will preſently quench the Iron, and make no Smoke at all. But to proceed briefly with the Subject which we have begun to take in Hand. *Servius* tells us, that a Marſh near a certain Town being almoſt dried up, and a Plague ſucceeding, the Inhabitants went for Counſel to *Apollo*, who commanded them to dry it up entirely. Near *Tempe*, there was a large ſtanding Lake, which *Hercules* made dry Ground, by cutting a Trench to let out the Water, and he is ſaid to have burnt the Serpent *Hydra* in a Place from whence frequent Eruptions of Water uſed to ravage the neighbouring City; by which means the ſuperfluous Moiſture being conſumed, and the Soil rendered firm and dry, thoſe over-abounding Channels of Water were entirely ſtopt. In ancient Times the *Nile* having once ſwelled higher than uſual, when the Waters went off, beſides the Mud, they left a great Number of different Animals, which as the Ground became dry, rotted and infected the Air with a dreadful Plague. *Strabo* ſays, that the City *Mazaca*, near the Hill *Argæus*, abounds in good Water; but if in Summer it has not a Way made for it to run off, it renders the Air unwholeſome and infectious. Moreover, towards the northern Parts of *Africa*, and alſo in *Æthiopia*, it never Rains; ſo that the Lakes are often dried up, and left like Bogs of Mud, abounding with infinite Numbers of Animals that breed by Corruption, and particularly with great Swarms of Locuſts. Againſt theſe Inconveniencies, both the Remedies uſed by *Hercules* are very proper, namely, cutting a Trench that the Water may not ſtagnate and make a Bog, and then laying the Ground open to the Sun, which I take to be the Fire uſed by *Hercules* for burning the *Hydra*. It may alſo be of Service to fill up the Place with Stones, Earth or Sand: And in what Manner you may fill up a ſtanding Water with River-ſand, we ſhall ſhew in the proper Place. *Strabo* ſays, that in his Time the Country about the City of *Ravenna*, being continually overflowed by the Sea, uſed to be incommoded with noiſome Vapours, which yet did not make the Air unwholeſome, and it ſeems ſtrange how this ſhould happen, unleſs

264 unless it be as it is at *Venice*, that the Lakes being kept in constant Agitation by the Winds and Tides, never subside, and so cannot corrupt: The Country of *Alexandria* is said to have been much of the same Nature; but the constant overflowing of the *Nile* in Summer, cured it of that Defect. Thus we are instructed by Nature what is proper to be done, and that where the Ground is marshy, we ought either to dry it up entirely, or else to bring a constant Supply of running Water into it, either from some Stream or River, or from the Sea; or lastly, to dig it so deep as to come to some living Spring. Of which we shall say no more in this Place.

CHAP. II.

That Water is the most necessary Thing of all, and of its various Sorts.

WE are now to take care that nothing be wanting, which may be necessary for our Use. What Things are necessary I shall not waste much Time in recounting, because they are manifest, as Food, Raiment, Shelter, and, above all Things, Water. *Thales* the *Milesian* affirmed, that Water was the first Principle of all Things, and even of Communities among Men. *Aristobulus* says, that he saw above a thousand Towns left quite desart, because the River *Indus* had turned his Course another Way. I own it to be my Opinion, that Water is to Animals the Source of natural Heat and the Nourisher of Life ; not to mention its Consequence to Plants, and to every Thing else which is intended for the Use of Mankind ; to all which I imagine it to be so absolutely necessary, that, without Water, nothing which grows or is nourished in the Earth would be capable even of existing. In the Country, along the River *Euphrates*, the People do not suffer their Cattle to feed as long as they would, for fear of their growing too fat in Pastures too luxurious, occasioned, as is supposed, by the Exuberance of Moisture: And some believe, that such huge Bodies as Whales are produced in the Sea, because of the great Abundance of Nourishment which is afforded by Water. *Xenophon* tells us, that the Kings of *Sparta* were allowed, by way of Dignity, to have a Lake of Water before the Doors of their Houses. Water is used by us in the Ceremonies of our Nuptials, Sacrifices, and almost all other sacred Rites, according to the Practice of our Fore-fathers ; all which shews what a high Esteem ancient Times had of Water. But indeed who can deny the great Use and Service which it is of to Mankind, insomuch that it is always thought to be deficient, where there is not a very large Abundance of it for all Manner of Occasions. With this great Necessary therefore, we shall here begin, since, according to the old Saying, we want it whether sick or well. The *Messagetæ*, a Nation of *Scythia*, made their Country abound in Water by opening the River *Aragus* in several Places. The *Tygris* and *Euphrates* were brought by Labour to *Babylon*, which was built originally in a dry Place. Queen *Semiramis* cut a Passage through a high Hill for the Space of five-and-twenty Furlongs to make Way for a Canal, fifteen Foot broad, by which she brought Water to the City of *Ecbatana*. An *Arabian* King brought Water from the *Chorus*, a River of *Arabia*, into that droughty Desart where he waited for *Cambyses*, in an Aqueduct made of the Hides of Bulls, if we may believe every thing that we read in *Herodotus*. In the Country of the *Samians*, among other surprizing Works, the most extraordinary of all was a Trench seventy Furlongs in Length, made through a Mountain which was an hundred and fifty Paces high. *Megareus*'s Conduct was also mightily admired, which brought the Water of a Spring to the City in a Frame twenty Foot high. But in my Judgment the ancient City of *Rome* far excelled all the Cities in the World in the Grandeur and Contrivance of her Aqueducts, and the great Plenty of Water conveyed in them. But you are not every where sure to find Springs or Rivers from whence Water can be brought. *Alexander*, to supply his Fleet with Water, dug a Number of Wells along the Sea Shore of *Persia*. *Appian* tells us, that *Hannibal*, when he was close pressed by *Scipio*, near the Town of *Cilla*, not being able to find Water in the Field where he was encamped, provided for the Necessities of his Troops by digging Wells. Besides, it is not all Waters which you find, that are good and proper for the Use of Men ; for besides that, some are hot, some cold, some sweet,
some

some sharp, some bitter, some perfectly clear, others muddy, viscous, oily, tinctured with Pitch, or of a petrifying Quality; some running partly clear, and partly foul, and sometimes in the same Place part sweet, and part salt or bitter: There are also several other Particulars, well worth Note, which make Waters very different from one another, as well in Nature as in Effect, and of no small Consequence to the Preservation or Prejudice of the Health. And here let us be allowed just to mention some miraculous Properties of Water, by Way of Amusement. The River *Arsione* in *Armenia*, rots the Cloaths which are washed in it. The Water of *Diana*'s Fountain, near *Camerinum*, will mix with nothing Male. At *Debri*, a Town of the *Garamanthes*, is a Spring which is cold in the Day, and warm in the Night. The *Helbesus*, a River in the Country of the *Segestani* in *Sicily*, in the Middle of its Course grows of a sudden hot. There is a sacred Well in *Epirus*, which extinguishes any Thing which is put into it burning, and lights that which is extinguished. In *Eleusina* near *Athens*, is a Spring which leaps and rejoices at the Sound of a Flute. Foreign Animals that drink at the River *Indus*, change their Colour: And upon the Shore of the *Red Sea* there is a Spring, at which if Sheep drink, their Wool presently turns Black. At *Laodicea* in *Asia*, there are Springs, near which all the fourfooted Animals that are conceived are of a yellow Hue. In the Country of *Gadara*, is a Water, of which if the Cattle drink, they lose their Hair and Nails. Near the *Hyrcanian* Sea, is a Lake, wherein all that bathe grow scabby, and can be cured with nothing but Oil. At *Susa*, is a Water which makes the Teeth fall out of the Head. Near the Lake *Zelonium*, is a Spring which makes Women barren, and another which makes them fruitful. In the Island of *Chios*, there is one which makes those that drink of it foolish: And in some other Place, which I do not now recollect, is one which not only upon drinking, but upon the bare Tasting makes the Person die laughing, and there is another wherein only Batheing is immediate Death. And near *Nonacris* in *Arcadia*, is a Water perfectly clear to the View, but of so poisonous a Quality, that it cannot be contained in any Metal whatsoever. On the contrary, there are others which are admirable for restoring the Health, such as the Waters of *Pozzuolo*, *Siena*, *Volterra*, *Bologna*, and many others of great Fame all over *Italy*. But it is yet more extraordinary which we are told of a Water in *Corsica*, namely, that it will reconsolidate broken Bones, and prevent the Effect of the most dangerous Poisons. In other Places there are Waters which mend the Wit and even inspire Divination. In *Corsica*, also there is another Spring very good for the Eyes, which if a Thief dares to deny a Theft with an Oath, and to wash his Eyes with its Water, immediately makes him blind. Of these we have said enough. Lastly, in some Places no Water at all is to be found, neither good nor bad. To remedy this, it was the Custom all over the Country of *Apulia* to receive and preserve the Rain-water in Cisterns.

C H A P. III.

Four Things to be considered with Relation to Water; also whence it is engendered or arises, and its Course.

THERE are four Things therefore which are to our Purpose with Relation to Water; namely, the finding, the conveying, the chusing, and the preserving. Of these we are to treat: But we may first premise some few Things concerning the Nature of Water in general. I am of Opinion that Water cannot be contained in any Thing but a Vessel, and therefore I agree with those, who upon that Account, affirm the Sea itself to be nothing but a Vessel of vast Capacity, and Rivers to be great oblong Vessels too. But there is this Difference between the Waters of the Sea and those of Rivers, that these latter have a Current and Motion by their own Nature, whereas the former would easily subside and be at Rest, if they were not put in Agitation by the Force of the Winds. I shall not here discuss those philosophical Questions, whether all Waters make their Way to the Sea, as to a Place of Rest, and whether the regular Flux and Reflux of the Ocean be owing to the Impulse of the Moon: Those Points not being to our Purpose: but we must not omit to take Notice of what we

see

see with our Eyes, that Water naturally tends downwards; that it cannot suffer the Air to be any where beneath it; that it hates all Mixture with any Body that is either lighter or heavier than itself; that it loves to fill up every Concavity into which it runs; that the more you endeavour to force it, the more obstinately it strives against you, nor is ever satisfied till it obtains the Rest which it desires, and that when it is got to its Place of Repose, it is contented only with itself, and despises all other Mixtures; lastly, that its Surface is always an exact Level. There is another Enquiry relating to Water, which I remember to have read in *Plutarch*; namely, whether upon digging a Hole in the Earth, the Water springs up like Blood out of a Wound; or whether it distills out like Milk engendering by Degrees in the Breast of a Nurse. Some are of Opinion, that perpetual Springs do not run from any full Vessel from whence they have their supply, but that in the Places from whence they flow, the Water is continually engendering of Air, and not of all Sorts of Air, but only of such as is most apt to be formed into Vapour, and that the Earth, and especially the Hills, are like Spunges, full of Pores, through which the Air is sucked in and condensed and so turned into Water by the Cold: For Proof of which they alledge, that the greatest Rivers spring from the greatest Hills. Others do not agree with this Opinion, observing that several Rivers, and particularly the *Pyramus*, one of no small Note, being navigable, does not take its Rise from any Hill, but from the Middle of a Plain. For this Reason, he who supposes that the Ground imbibes the Moisture of the Rain, which by its Weight and Subtilty penetrates through the Veins and so distills into the Cavities of the Earth, may perhaps be not much mistaken in his Conjecture: For we may observe, that those Countries which have least Rain, have the greatest Scarcity of Springs. *Libya* is said to

266 have been so called *quasi Lipygia*, as wanting Rain, by which means it is scantily supplied with Water. And, indeed, who can deny, that where it Rains much, there is the greatest Plenty of it? It is also to our present Purpose to observe, that a Man who digs a Well never meets with Water, till he has sunk it to the Level of the next River. At *Volsconio*, a Town standing upon a Hill in *Tuscany*, they dug a

Well no less then two hundred and twenty Foot deep before they came to any Vein of Water, not meeting with any till they came to the Level of the Springs which rise from the Side of the Hill; and you will generally find the same Observation hold good of all Wells dug upon Hills. We find by Experiment that a Spunge will grow wet by the Humidity of the Air, upon which I have made a Pair of Scales to determine the Heaviness or Dryness of the Air and Winds. I cannot indeed deny that the Moisture of the nocturnal Air is attracted from the Superficies of the Earth, and so consequently may return again into its Pores, and be easily converted once more into Humour; but I cannot pretend to determine any thing certain with Relation to this Question, finding so much Variety among Authors upon the Subject, and so many different Considerations offering themselves to the Mind when we think upon it. Thus it is certain that in many Places, either by some Earthquake, or even from no apparent Cause, Springs have burst out of a sudden, and continued a great While, and again, that others have failed in different Seasons, some growing dry in Summer, others in Winter, and that those which have dried up have afterwards again afforded great Plenty of Water: Nay, and that Springs of fresh Water not only arise from the Earth, but have been found even in the Middle of the Sea; and it has been affirmed, that Water also issues from the Plants themselves. In one of those Islands which are called *Fortunate*, we are told there grows a Sort of Cane as high as a Tree, some black, some white; from the black comes a bitter Juice, and from the white distills a fine clear Water, very beautiful to the Eye and good to drink. *Strabo*, a very grave Author, says that in the Mountains of *Armenia*, they find a Sort of Worms bred in the Snow, which are full of a Water excellent to drink. At *Fiezole* and *Urbino*, though both Towns standing upon Hills, there is Plenty of Water to be had for the least digging, which is because those Hills are formed of a stony Soil mixed with a Chalk. We are told further, that there are certain Clods of Earth which within their Coats contain a Quantity of the finest Water. Amidst all this wonderful Variety, the Knowledge of the Nature of Springs cannot be otherwise than extremely difficult and obscure.

CHAP.

CHAP. IV.

By what Marks to find any hidden Water.

LET us now return to our Subject. Hidden Waters are to be found out by certain Marks. These Marks are the Form and Face of the Spot of Ground, and the Nature of the Soil where you are to search for the Water, and some other Methods discovered by the Industry and Diligence of Men. According to the ordinary Course of Nature, a Place which is sunk down into a Hollow, or into a Sort of concave Pit, seems to be a Kind of Vessel ready prepared for the retaining of Water. In those Places where the Sun has much Power, all Humidity is so much dried up by the Force of his Rays, that few or no Veins of Water are to be found; or if any are discovered in a very open Place, they are heavy, thick and brackish. On the north Side of Hills, and where-ever there is a very thick Shade, you may very soon meet with Water. Hills whose Tops are used to be long covered with Snow, afford great Plenty of Springs. I have observed, that Hills which have a flat Meadow at the Top, never want Water; and you will find almost all Rivers have their Rise from some such Place. I have also observed, that their Springs seldom flow from any other Spot of Ground, but where the Soil beneath or about them is found and firm, with either an even Slope over them, or soft loose Earth: So that if you consider the Matter, you will be of Opinion with me, that the Water which has been gathered there, runs out as from the Side of a broken Bason. Hence it happens that the closest Soil has the least Water, and what there is, lies very near the Surface: But the loosest Earth has the most Humidity; but then the Water generally lies pretty deep. *Pliny* writes, that in some Places, upon cutting down the Woods, Springs burst out: And *Tacitus* says, that when *Moses* journeyed through the Desart, and his Followers were fainting with Thirst, he discovered Springs of Water, only by taking Notice where there were fresh Spots of Grass. *Æmilius*, when his Army suffered a Dearth of Water near Mount *Olympus*, found out a Supply by the fresh Verdure of the Woods. Some Soldiers who were in quest of Water were directed to some little Veins by a young Girl in the *Via Collatina*, where, upon

digging they found a very plentiful Spring, over which they built a little Chapel, and in it left the Memory of the Accident described in Painting. If the Earth easily gives Way to the Tread, or cleaves to the Foot, it shews that there is Water under it. One of the most certain Marks of concealed Water, is the Growth and Flourishing of those Plants which love Water, or are used to be produced by it, such as Willows, Rushes, Withes, Ivy, or any others which without Plenty of Moisture could never have attained the Perfection in which we find them. *Columella* tells us, that the Ground which produces Vines very thick of Leaves, and especially that which bears Dwarf-elder, Trefoil and wild Plumbs is a good Soil, and does not want Veins of sweet Water. Moreover great Quantities of Frogs, Earth-worms, with Gnats and other small Flies swarming together in the Air, are Tokens of Water concealed beneath. The Methods for finding Water invented by the Diligence of Men are as follows: The curious Searchers into Nature have observed, that the Earth, and especially the Hills, consist of different Coats or Layers, some closer, some looser, and others thinner; and they have found, that the Hills were composed of these Coates placed one above the other, in such a Manner that towards the Surface or outside these Layers or Coats, and their several Junctures lie level from the Right to Left: But on the Inside, towards the Center of the Hill the Layers incline downwards in an oblique Line, with all their upper Superficies inclining equally, but then the same Line does not continue on, quite to the Center of the Hill, for, suppose at the Distance of every hundred Foot the Line is broken off by a Kind of transverse Step, which makes a Discontinuance in the Layer; and so with these Breaks and Slopes the Coats run from each Side to the Center of the Hill. From an Observation of these Particulars, Men of acute Understanding soon perceived that the Waters were either engendered, or rather that the Rains gathered between these Strata, and in the Junctures of the several Coats, by which means the Middle of the Hill must needs have Water in it. Hence they concluded that in order to come at
that

267

that concealed Water, they muſt pierce into the Body of the Hill, and eſpecially in one of thoſe Parts where the Lines or Junctures of the ſeveral Strata met together, which was likely to be the moſt proper Place for what they wanted, becauſe the Muſcles of the Hill meeting together muſt in all Probability form a natural Reſervoir. Beſides the ſeveral Coats themſelves ſeemed to be of different Natures, ſome likely to imbibe, others to retain the Water. Thus the reddiſh Stone is hardly ever without Water; but then it is apt to deceive you, for it often runs out through the Veins with which that Stone abounds. The moiſt and living Flint which lies about the Roots of the Hill, broken and very ſharp, ſoon affords Water. The light Soil too gives you an eaſy Opportunity of finding Plenty of Water; but then it is of a bad Savour. But the Male-ſand and the hard Grit are ſure to afford the beſt of Water, and with the leaſt Danger of being exhauſted. It is quite the contrary with Chalk, which being too cloſe, yields no Water; but it is very good for retaining that which diſtills into it. In common Sand we find but very ſmall Veins, and thoſe foul, and apt to have a Sediment. From white Clay we have but ſmall Veins, but thoſe ſweeter than any other. The ſoft Stone yields a very cold Water; the black Earth a very clear one. In Gravel, if it is looſe, we cannot dig with any very great Hope; but if it grows cloſer as we come deeper, there is no Danger of finding Water, and when found, in either of them, there is no doubt of its being well taſted. It is alſo certain, that by the Help of Art there is no great Difficulty in finding out the Spot under which the Vein lies: And the Method by which we are taught to do it, is as follows. In the Morning extremely early, when the Air is perfectly clear and ſerene, lay yourſelf flat with your Chin reſting upon the Ground: Then take a careful Survey of the Country all round you, and where-ever you ſee a Vapour riſing out of the Earth, and curling up into the Air like a Man's Breath in a clear Froſt, there you may be pretty certain of finding Water. But in order to be ſtill more ſure of it, dig a Pit four Cubits deep and as many broad, and in this Pit, about the Time of Sun-ſet, put either an earthen Pot juſt freſh taken out of the Furnace, or a ſmall Quantity of unwaſhed Wool, or an earthen Pot unbaked, or a braſs Pot with the Mouth downwards and rubbed over with Oil; then make up the Mouth of the Pit with Boards and cover it with Earth: If next Morning the baked Pot be much heavier than it was over Night; if the Wool be moiſtened; if the unbaked Pot be wet; if the braſs Pot have Drops hanging upon it, and if a Lamp left in the ſame Pit have not conſumed much Oil, or if upon making a Fire in it, the Earth emits a good deal of Smoke, you may be very ſure that there are Veins of Water concealed. In what Seaſon it is beſt to make theſe Trials has not been ſo clearly declared; but in ſome Writers I find the following Obſervations. In the Dog-days, not only the Earth, but alſo the Bodies of Animals are very full of Humidity: Whence it happens, that in this Seaſon the Trees grow very moiſt under the Bark with Exceſs of Humour; about this Time alſo Men are very ſubject to Fluxes of the Belly, and through exceſſive Humectation, fall into frequent Fevers; and the Waters ſpring out more abundantly at this Time of the Year, than any other. *Theophraſtus* thinks the Reaſon of this to be, that about this Time we have generally ſoutherly Winds, which in their Nature are moiſt and cloudy. *Ariſtotle* affirms, that in this Seaſon the Ground is forced to emit Vapours by means of the natural Fire which lies mixed in the Bowels of the Earth. If this be true, thoſe Times muſt be beſt for the above-mentioned Trials, when thoſe Fires are moſt potent, or leaſt oppreſſed with Exuberance of Humour, as alſo when the Earth is not too much burnt up and too dry. The Seaſon therefore which I would recommend for this Purpoſe, ſhould be the Spring in dry Places, and Autumn in Places of more Shade. When your Hopes of not being diſappointed are confirmed in the Manner before ſhewn, you may begin to dig.

CHAP. V.

Of the digging and walling of Walls and Conduits.

THE Work of Digging is performed in two Manners; for either we dig a Well perpendicularly down, or we dig a Conduit horizontally. The Workmen in digging are ſometimes expoſed to Danger, either from unwholeſome Vapours, or from the falling in of the

the Sides of the Pit. The Ancients used to send their Slaves, upon their being convicted of some Crime, to dig in their Mines, where the noisome Air soon dispatched them. Against such Vapours we are taught to secure ourselves, by keeping the Air in continual Motion, and by the Burning of Lamps, to the Intent, that if the Vapour be very subtile, it may be consumed by the Flame, or if it be more gross, the Workmen may know when to get out of Harm's Way, because such a heavy Vapour will give them Notice by extinguishing the Light. But if these Damps multiply upon you, and continue for any Time, we are advised to dig Vents on each Side, to give the Vapour a free Passage to exhaust itself. To prevent the falling in of the Sides, work your Well in the following Manner. Upon the Level of the Ground where you resolve to make your Well, lay a circular Course of Work, either of Marble, or some other stout Material, of the Diameter which you intend for the Breadth of your Well. This will be the Basis or Foundation of your whole Work. Upon this build the Sides of your Well to the Height of three Cubits, and let it stand till it is thoroughly dry. When this is dry, go to digging your Well, and remove the Earth from the Inside of it; by which means, as you dig away the Earth, the Sides already raised will sink by Degrees, and make their own Way downwards; and thus adding to the Sides as you go deeper, you may sink your Work to what Depth you please. Some are for Building the Sides of the Well without Mortar, that the Veins of Water may not be stopt from getting through them. Others are for inclosing it with no less than three different Walls, that the Water rising all up from the Bottom, may be the clearer. But the main Point is the Nature of the Place where you dig; for as the Earth consists of different Strata placed one above the other, it sometimes happens, that the Rain-water, soaking thro' the upper soft Coat, lodges in the first hard Bed; and this never being pure, is unfit for Use: At other Times, on the contrary, it happens, that after you have actually found Water, upon digging deeper, it slips away and is lost. The Reason of this is, that you have dug thro' the Bottom of the Vessel which contained it. Upon this Account I very much approve of those who make their Well in the following Manner. They encompass the Sides of the Well, which is ready dug, with two Circles of Wood or Plank, as if they were making a great Tub, leaving the Space of about a Cubit between the two Circles. This Interspace between the Planks, they fill up with coarse Gravel, or rather with broken Fragments of Flint or Marble, swimming in Mortar, and then leave this Work to dry and harden for six Months. This forms so entire a Vessel, that the Water can get in no other Way but by bubbling up from the Bottom, by which Means it must be thoroughly purged and be perfectly clear and light. If you are to make an horizontal Conduit under Ground, let the Diggers observe the before-mentioned Precautions against noxious Vapours; and in order to keep the Ground from falling down upon them, let them make use of Props, and afterwards support it with a regular Arch. The Conduit should have frequent Vents, some perpendicular, others oblique, not only for the exhaling of unwholesome Vapours, but chiefly for the more convenient bringing out the Earth as it is dug, and any Obstruction which may get in. When we are digging for Water, if we do not, the lower we go, meet with moister Clods of Earth, and if our Tools do not find more and more easy Entrance, we shall certainly be disappointed of our Hopes of finding what we dig for.

Chap. VI.

Of the Uses of Water; which is best and most wholesome; and the contrary.

WHEN Water is found, it ought not to be rashly applied to the Uses of Men. But as the City requires a very great Plenty of Water, not only for drinking, but also for washing, for supplying the Gardens, for Tanners, and Fullers; for the Drains, and for extinguishing sudden Fires: The best is to be chosen for drinking, and the others are to be allotted to the other Uses, according as they are found to be respectively proper for them. *Theophrastus* was of Opinion, that the colder the Water, the more serviceable to Plants; and it is certain, that the foul and muddy, especially if it takes its Thickness

K k k

from

from a fruitful Soil, enriches the Ground. Horfes do not love a very clear Water, but grow fat with any that is moffy and warm. The hardeft is beft for Fullers. The Phyficians fay, that the Neceffity of Water to the Health and Life of Man is of two Sorts; one for quenching the Thirft, and the other, to ferve as a Vehicle to carry the Nutriment extracted from the Food into the Veins, that being there purified and digefted it may fupply the Members with their proper Juices. Thirft they tell us is an Appetite of Moifture, and chiefly of a cold one ; and therefore they think that cold Water, efpecially after Meals, fortifies the Stomach of thofe that are in good Health; but if it be exceffively cold it will throw the moft robuft into a Numbnefs, occafion Gripes in the Bowels, fhake the Nerves, and by its Rawnefs extinguifh the digeftive Faculty of the Stomach. The Water of the River *Oxus* being always turbid, is very unwholefome to drink. The Inhabitants of *Rome*, from the frequent Changes of the Air, and the nocturnal Vapours which arife from the River, as alfo from the Winds which commonly blow in the Afternoon, are very fubject to dangerous Fevers ; for thefe Winds generally blow very cold about three o' Clock in Summer, at which Time Mens Bodies are extreamly heated, and even contract the very Veins. But in my Opinion thefe Fevers, and indeed moft of the worft Diftempers there proceed, in a great Meafure, from the Water of the *Tyber*, which is commonly drank when it is foul ; to which Purpofe it may not be amifs to obferve, that the ancient Phyficians, for the Cure of thefe *Roman* Fevers, order the Ufe of the Juice of Squills and of Incifives. But to return. We are upon the Search of the beft Water. *Celfus* the Phyfician, fays of Waters, that of all the different Sorts the Rain-water is the lighteft ; the fecond is that of the Spring ; in the third Place is the River-water ; in the fourth, that of a Well; in the fifth and laft, that which diffolves from Snow or Ice. The Lake-water is heavier than any of thefe, and that of a Marfh is the worft of all. The *Mazaca*, which ftands under the Hill *Argæus*, abounds with good Water; but having no Way to run off in Summer, it grows unwholefome and peftiferous. The Definition which the beft Philofophers give us of Water, is, that it is naturally a Body fimple and unmixed, whereof Coldnefs and Humidity are two Properties. We may therefore conclude that to be the beft, which

deviates the leaft from its own Nature ; becaufe, if it be not perfectly pure, and entirely free from Mixture, Tafte, or Smell, it will certainly very much endanger the Health, by loading the inward Paffages of the Lungs, choaking up the Veins, and clogging the Spirits, the Minifters of Life, For this Reafon we are told that the Rain-water, as it confifts of the lighteft Vapours, is the beft of all, provided it be not of fuch a Sort as eafily corrupts and ftinks, which when it grows foul is very apt to harden the Belly. Some believe that the Occafion of this is, that it falls from Clouds formed of a Mixture of too many different Vapours compounded together, drawn, for Inftance, from the Sea, which is the great Receptacle of all the different Sorts of Springs; becaufe indeed nothing can be more liable to Corruption, than a confufed Medley of Things in their Nature diffimilar. Thus the Juice of different Sorts of Grapes mixed together, will never keep.

It was an ancient Law among the *Hebrews*, that no Man fhould fow any Seed but what was pick'd and unmixed; it being their Notion, that Nature totally abhorred a Medley of different Particles. Thofe who follow *Ariftotle*, thinking that the Vapours which are extracted from the Earth, when they are raifed up to the cold Region of the Air, are by the Cold compreffed into Clouds, and afterwards diffolve in Rain, are of quite a different Opinion. Thus *Theophraftus* fays, that cultivated and Garden Fruits fall more eafily into Diftempers than wild ones, which being of a tough Contexture never tamed, more vigoroufly refift any Injury from without; whereas the other being made tender by Culture, have not the fame hardy Conftitution. The fame he tells us will hold good as to Waters, and the more tender we make them (to ufe his own Words) the more liable they will be to fuffer Alteration. For this Reafon fome fay, that Water which has been boyled and foften'd by the Fire will fooneft grow cold, and fo be fooneft made hot again. Thus much of Rain-water. Next to this the Spring-water is certainly the beft. Thofe who prefer the River to the Spring, fay, what elfe is a River, but an Abundance and Concourfe of many different Springs united together, and maturated by the Sun, Winds and Motion? So they tell us too, that a Well is nothing but a Spring lying very deep: from whence they infer, if we will allow the Rays of the Sun to be of any Service to Water, that it is no hard matter to judge which of thefe Springs muft be the moft most undigested: unless we will suppose, that there is a fiery Spirit in the Bowels of the earth, by which subterraneous Waters are concocted. *Aristotle* says that the Water in Wells grows warm in the Summer in the Afternoon.   Accordingly some will have it that Well-water seems cold in Summer, only by comparison with the hot Air which surrounds us.   Accordingly we find, contrary to the old received Opinion, that Water just fresh drawn, does not bedew the Glass into which it is put, if the Glass be perfectly clean and not greasy.   But as of the first Principles whereof all Things consist, especially according to the *Pythagorean* Notion, there are two which may be called male, which are Heat and Cold ; and it being the Property of Heat to penetrate, dissolve, break, attract and suck up all Moisture, as it is that of Cold to compress, contract, harden and consolidate: both these have in a great Measure the same Effects, and particularly upon Water, provided they are excessive and of too long Continuance; because they both equally consume the more subtile Parts, which occasions exactly the same adust Dryness.   Thus we say, that Plants are burnt up, not only by extreme Heat but also by extreme Cold ; because when the more tender Parts of the Substance of the Wood are consumed and dried up either by Frost or Sun, we see the Tree look rusty and chapt as by Fire.   From the same Causes Water grows viscous by the Sun's Heat, and looks as if it were full of Ashes in extreme Frost.   But there is another Difference even among Waters allowed to be good; for particularly as to Rain-water, it is of great Importance in what Season of the Year, at what Time of the Day, and in what Winds you collect it, as also in what Place you preserve it, and what Time it has been kept.   The Rain which falls after the Middle of Winter is thought to afford the heaviest Water ; and that which is collected in the Winter is said to be sweeter than that collected in the Summer.   The first Rains after the Dog-days are bitter and unwholesome, being corrupted with a Mixture of some of the adust Particles of the Earth, and we are told that the Earth itself has a bitter savour at that Time of the Year, from being burnt up by the Heat of the Sun.   Hence we are advised, that the Rain-water gathered from the House-top, is better than that which is collected in the Ground ; and of that which is gathered from the House-top, the most wholesome is said to be that which is got after the Roof has been

well washed by the first Rain.   The *African* Physicians tell us, that the Rain which falls in Summer, especially when it thunders, is not pure, and is unwholesome from its Saltness. *Theophrastus* thinks, that the Night Rains are better than those in the Day.   Hence that is accounted the most wholesome which falls in a North Wind.   *Columella* is of Opinion, that Rain-water would not be bad if it were carried through earthen Pipes into covered Cisterns, because it easily corrupts when it stands uncovered to the Sun, and soon spoils, if it is kept in any Vessel made of Wood. Springs also are very different from one another.   *Hippocrates* judged those which rise from the Roots of Hills to be the best.   The Opinion of the Ancients concerning Springs was as follows.   They thought the very best of all were those which lay either to the North, or fronting the Sun-rise about the Equinox ; and the worst they supposed to be those which lay to the South.   The next best they thought were those which fronted the Sun-rise in Winter, nor did they disapprove of those on the West Side of the Hill, which generally is very moist with a great Abundance of light Dew, and consequently must afford a very sweet Water, because the Dew does not fall but in quiet, clear Places, and where there is a temperate Air.   *Theophrastus* thinks that Water gets a Taste from the Earth, as in Fruits, Vines, and other Trees, which all have a Savour of the Earth from which they draw their Juices, and from whatever happens to lie near their Roots.   The Ancients used to say, that there were as many different Sorts of Wines, as there were of different Soils wherein the Vineyards were planted.   Thus *Pliny* tells us, that the Wines of *Padua* tasted of the Willows to which the Inhabitants of that Country used to bind their Vines.   *Cato* teaches to medicate the Vines with the Herb *Hellebore*, by laying Bundles of it at the Roots, at the same Time that you open them, in order to make them loosen the Belly without Danger.   For these Reasons the Ancients thought, that the Water which issued out of the living Rock, was better than that which rose from the Ground.   But the best of all was thought to be that which distilled from such an Earth, which being put into a Bason with Water, and stirr'd together with it, would the soonest subside and leave the Water the least tainted either in Colour, Smell, or Taste.   For the same Reasons *Columella* was of Opinion, that Water which ran down stony Precipices

must

muſt be the beſt, being leſs likely to be ſpoil'd by any foreign Mixture. But it is not every Water which runs among Stones that is to be approved of, becauſe if it runs in a deep Bed under a dark Shade, it will be too crude; and on the contrary, if its Channel be too open, I ſhould be inclined to ſubſcribe to *Ariſtole*'s Opinion, that the too great Heat of the Sun conſuming the more ſubtle Parts, would make it viſcous. Authors prefer the *Nile* to all other Rivers, becauſe it deſcends with a very extenſive Courſe; becauſe it cuts through the fineſt Sorts of Soil which are not either infected with Corruption by Damps, nor tainted with Contagion by being burnt up; becauſe it flows towards the North: And laſtly, becauſe its Channel is always full and clear. And indeed it cannot be denied, that Waters which have the longeſt and the gentleſt Current, are the leaſt crude, and are moſt refined and purged by their eaſy Motion, leaving all the Weight of their Sediment behind them in their long Courſe. Moreover, all the Ancients agree in this, that Waters not only receive a Tincture, as we obſerved before, from the Ground in which they lie as in their Mother's Lap, but alſo borrow ſomewhat from the Soils thro' which they flow, and from the Juices of the different Plants which they waſh; not merely becauſe they lick thoſe Plants in their Courſe, but rather becauſe any peſtiferous Plant will taint them with the Mixture of the Steams of the unwholſome Soil in which they grow. This is the Reaſon that unwholſome Plants are ſaid to yield unwholeſome Water. You ſhall ſometimes obſerve the Rain itſelf to have an ill Smell, and perhaps a bitter Taſte. This we are told proceeds from the Infection of the Place from whence the Steam or Vapour firſt aroſe. Thus it is affirmed, that the Juices of the Earth, when ſufficiently maturated and concocted by Nature, produce every Thing ſweet, and on the contrary, when they are crude and undigeſted, they make every Thing bitter with which they mix. Thoſe Waters which run towards the North may perhaps be ſuppoſed to be the moſt uſeful, becauſe they are the coldeſt, as flying from the Rays of the Sun, and being rather viſited than ſcorched by him; and thoſe which flow towards the South the contrary, as throwing themſelves into the very Mouth of the Flame. *Ariſtotle* taught, that the fiery Spirit which was mixed up by Nature in all Bodies, was repelled by the Coldneſs of the North Wind, and confined

within, from evaporating, and that this gave the Water its due Concoction: And it is certain, that this Spirit is exhauſted and diſſipated by the Heat of the Sun. *Servius*, upon the Authority of experienced Perſons, ſays, that Wells and Springs which lie under a Roof, do not emit any Vapour: That light ſubtle Breath riſing from the Well, not being able to penetrate or make its Way through the denſe and groſs Air which the Roof compreſſes together over it; whereas, when it lies under the clear and open Sky, it has free Play, and extends and purges itſelf without Obſtruction: For which Reaſon, Wells under the open Air are accounted more wholeſome than thoſe under Cover. In other reſpects, all the ſame Properties are to be wiſhed for in a Well that are required in a Spring; for both ſeem to have a very near Relation to each other, and hardly differ in any Thing but in Point of Current; though you ſhall very frequently meet even with Wells which run with a very large Vein of Water; and we are told, that no Water can poſſibly be perpetual which is abſolutely without Motion; and Water without Motion, let it lie in what Soil it will, cannot be wholeſome. If a great deal of Water is continually and conſtantly drawn out of a Well, that Well may be looked upon rather as a deep Spring; and on the other hand, if a Spring does not run over its Sides, but ſtands quiet and ſtill, it may be accounted a ſhallow Well rather than a Spring. Some are of Opinion, that no Water can be perpetual, or of very long Duration, which does does not move with the riſing and falling of the next River or Torrent; and I believe the ſame. The ancient Lawyers made this Diſtinction between a Lake and a Marſh, that the Lake has a perpetual Water, whereas that of the Marſh is only temporary, and what it gathers in the Winter. Lakes are of three Sorts. One, if we may ſo call it, ſtationary, content with its own Waters, always keeping within its Bed, and never overflowing. The ſecond, which is as it were the Father of the River, diſcharges its Waters at ſome Paſſage; and the laſt receives ſome Stream from abroad, and ſends it out again into ſome River. The firſt partakes ſomewhat of the Nature of a Marſh: the ſecond is a direct Spring: and the third, if I miſtake not, is only a River ſpreading out into Breadth in that particular Place. We need not therefore upon this Occaſion repeat what we have already ſaid of the Spring and the River. We may only add, that all Water that is covered with

with a Shade, is colder and clearer, but more undigefted, than thofe warmed by the Sun; and, on the contrary, Waters too much heated by the Sun, are brackifh and vifcous. The being deep is of Service to either Sort, becaufe it prevents the latter from being made too hot, and the former from being too eafily affected by Froft. Laftly it is thought that even the Marfh is not always to be defpifed: becaufe where-ever Eels are found, the Water is reckoned to be not very bad. Of all Marfh-water that is accounted the very worft which breeds Horfe-leeches, which is fo abfolutely without Moti-on that it contracts a Scurf on the Top, which has an offenfive Smell, which is of a black or livid Colour, which being put into a Veffel will continue foul a great while, which is heavy and clammy with a moffy Slime, and which being ufed in wafhing your Hands, they are a long Time before they dry. But as a fhort Summary of what has been faid of Water, it fhould be ex-tremely light, clear, thin and tranfparent, to which muft be added thofe Particulars which we have flightly touched in the firft Book. Laftly it will be a ftrong Confirmation to you of the Goodnefs of your Water, if you find that the Cattle which have wafhed and drank in it for feveral Months together, are in good Con-dition and perfectly healthy; and you have a fure Way to judge whether they are found or not by infpecting their Livers; for what is noxious injures with Time, and the Injury which is lateft felt is of the worft Confequence.

C H A P. VII.

Of the Method of conveying Water and accommodating it to the Ufes of Men.

HAVING found Water and approved it to be good, the next Work is to convey it artfully and accommodate it properly to the Ufes of Men. There are two Ways of convey-ing Water, either by a Trench or Canal, or by Pipes or Conduits. In either of thefe Methods, the Water will not move, unlefs the Place to which you would convey it be lower than that from which it is to be brought. But then there is this Difference, that the Water which is brought by a Canal muft defcend all the Way with a continued Slope, whereas that which is conveyed in Pipes may afcend in fome Part of the Way. Of thefe two Methods we are now to treat. But firft we muft premife fome Things for the clearer Explication of our Subject. The Searchers into Nature tell us, that the Earth is Spherical, tho' in many Places it rifes into Hills, and in many others finks into Seas: but in fo vaft a Globe this Roughnefs is not per-ceptible; as in an Egg, which tho' it is far from being of a fmooth Superficies, yet its lit-tle Inequalities bearing but an inconfiderable Proportion to its whole Circumference, they are fcarce obferved. *Eratofthenes* tells us, that the Compafs of this great Globe is two hun-dred and fifty two thoufand Furlongs, or about thirty one thoufand five hundred Miles, and that there is no Hill fo high or Water fo deep as to be above fifteen thoufand Cubits perpen-dicular; not even Mount *Caucafus*, whofe Top enjoys the Sun three Hours in the Night. There is a prodigious high Mountain in *Ar-cadia* called *Cyllene*; and yet thofe who have meafured its perpendicular, affirm, that it does not exceed twenty Furlongs. Even the Sea it-felf is thought to be no more upon this Globe of Earth, than the Summer's Dew is upon the Body of an Apple. Some have wittily faid, that the Creator of the World made ufe of the Concavity of the Sea as of a Seal with the Im-preffion whereof he ftampt the Hills. What the Geometers teach us upon this Head is very much to our prefent Purpofe. They fay, that if a ftraight Line touching the Globe of the Earth at one End were to be drawn on exactly horizontal a Mile in Length, the Space be-tween the other End and the Surface of the Globe would not be above ten Inches. For this Reafon Water will never move on in a Canal, but ftand ftill like a Lake, unlefs every eight Furlongs the Trench has a Slope of one whole Foot from the Place where the Water was firft found and its Bed cut; which Place the ancient Lawyers called Incile, from the In-cifion which is made either in the Rock or Bank for conveying the Water: But if in this Space of eight Furlongs it had a Slope of more than fix Foot, it is fuppofed that the Rapidity of its Current would make it inconvenient for Boats. In order to find whether the Trench which is to convey the Water be lower than this

this Incile or Sluice or no, and what the Slope is, certain Rules and Instruments have been invented, which are of excellent Use. Ignorant Workmen try their Slope by laying a Ball in the Trench, and if this Ball rowls forwards they think the Slope is right for their Water. The Instruments of dexterous Artists are the Square, Level, Plumb-line, and, in a Word, all such as are terminated with a right Angle. This Art is a little more abstruse; but however I shall open no more of it than is necessary for the Purpose in Hand. The Practice is performed by means of the Sight and of the Object, which we shall call the Points. If the Place through which we are to convey our Water be an even Plain, there are two Ways of directing our Sight: For we must set up certain Marks or Objects, which we may place either nearer or at a greater Distance from each other. The nearer the Points of the Sight and the Mark or Object are to each other, the less the straight Line of the Direction of the Sight will depart from the Superficies of the Globe; the further those Points are from each other, the lower the Superficies of the Globe will fall from the Level of the Sight. In both these you must observe to allow ten Inches slope for every Mile of Distance. But if you have not a clear Plain, and some Hill interferes, then again you have two Ways of Proceeding: One by taking the Height from the Incile or Sluice, on the one Side, and the Height of the Slope from the Head on the other. The Head I call that appointed Place to which you would bring the Water, in order to let it run from thence free, or to appropriate it to some particular Uses. We find these Heights by taking different Steps of Measurement. I call them Steps because they are like those Steps by which we ascend to a Temple. One Line of these Steps is the Ray of Sight which goes from the Beholder's Eye along the same Level with his Eye; which is made by the Square, the Level and the Plumb-line; and the other Line is that which falls from the Beholder's Eye down to his Feet, in a Perpendicular. By means of these Steps you note how much one Line exceeds the other, by casting up the Amount of their Perpendiculars, and so find which is the Highest, that which rises from the Sluice to the Top of the Eminence, or that which rises from the Head. The other Method, is by drawing one Line from the Sluice to the Top of the Hill which interferes, and another Line from thence to the Head, and by computing the Proporti-

ons of their Angles, according to the Rules of Geometry. But this Method is difficult in Practice, and not extremely sure, because in a large Distance the least Error occasioned by the Eye of the Measurer is of very great Consequence. But there are some Things which seem to bear some Relation to this Method, as we shall shew by and by, which, if we have occasion to cut a Passage through a Hill to bring Water to a Town, may be of great Use for obtaining the right Directions. The Practice is as follows: On the Summit of the Hill, in a Place where you can have a View both of the Sluice on one Side and of the Head on the other, having laid the Ground exactly level, describe a Circle ten Foot in Diameter. This Circle we shall call the Horizon. In the Center of the Circle stick up a Pike exactly perpendicular. Having made this Preparation, the Artist goes round the Outside of the Circle, in order to find in what Part of its Circumference his Eye being directed to one of the Points of the Water which is to be conveyed, touches the lower Part of the Pike which stands in the Center. Having found out and marked this exact Place in the Circumference of his Horizon, he draws a Line for this Direction from that Mark quite to the opposite Side of his Circle. Thus this Line will be the Diameter of that Circle, as it will pass through the Center, and cut through both Sides of the Circumference. If this Line, upon taking opposite Views leads the Eye on one Side directly to the Sluice, and on the other directly to the Head of our Water, it affords us a straight Direction for our Channel. But if the two Lines of Direction do not happen to meet in this Manner, and the Diameter which leads to the Sluice, falls on one Part of the Circumference, and that which leads to the Head, on another; then from the mutual Intersection of these Lines at the Pike in the Center of the Circle, we shall find the Difference between the two Directions. I use the Help of such a Circle to make Platforms and draw Maps of Towns and Provinces, as also for the digging subterraneous Conduits, and that with very good Effect. But of that in another Place. Whatever Canal we make, whether for bringing only a smaller Quantity of Water for Drinking, or a larger for Navigation, we may follow the Directions which we have here taught. But the Preparation of our Canal must not be the same for a large Quantity of Water, as for a small. We shall first go on with the Subject which we have

27

have begun concerning Water only for Drinking, and proceed afterwards to Canals for Navigation. Canals are either worked up with Masonry, or else are only Trenches dug. Trenches are of two Sorts, cut either through an open Country, or through the Bowels of a Hill, which is called a Mine or subterraneous Conduit. In both these, when you meet with either Stone, Chalk, or compact Earth that does not imbibe the Water, you will have no Occasion for Masonry; but where the Bottom or Sides of the Canal are not sound, then you must fortify them. If you are obliged to carry your Canal through the Heart of a Hill, you must observe the Rules above laid down. In subterraneous Conduits, at the Distance of every hundred Foot, you should open Ventiges like Wells fortified according as the Nature of the Earth through which you dig requires. I have seen such Ventiges in the Country of the *Marsi* near *Roma*, where the Water falls into the ancient Lake *Fucinus* (now called the *Pie di Luco*) built very finely with burnt Brick, and of an incredible Depth. 'Till the four hundred and forty-first year after the building of the City, there was no such thing as an Aqueduct built at *Rome*; but afterwards those Works were brought to such a Pitch, that whole Rivers were conveyed to it through the Air, and we are told, that there were so many of them, that every single House was abundantly supplied with Water. At first they began with subterraneous Conduits; which indeed had a great many Conveniencies. This hidden Work was less subject to Injuries and being exposed neither to the Severity of Frosts, nor to the scorching Dog-day Sun brought the Water fresher and cooler, nor could easily be destroyed or turned away by Enemies that might happen to make Inroads into the Country. These Works were afterwards brought to such a Magnificence, that in order to have high Jets of Water in their Gardens and in their Bathes, they built vaulted Aqueducts, in some Places above an hundred and twenty Foot high, and carried on for above threescore Miles together. From these too they reaped Conveniencies. In several Places, and particularly beyond the *Tyber*, the Water of these Aqueducts served to grind their Corn, and upon their being destroyed by the Enemy, they were forced to make Mills for that Purpose in Ships. To this add, that by means of this Plenty of Water the City was kept cleaner and the Air made fresher and more wholesome. The Architects also added some ingenious Inventions to shew the Hours of the Day to the great Recreation of the Beholders, by the Contrivance of some little moving Statues of Brass, placed in the Front of the Head of the Aqueduct, which represented the publick Games and the Ceremony of the Triumph. At the same Time, the Sound of musical Instruments and sweet Voices was heard, which were caused by the Motion of the Water. These Aqueducts were covered in with an Arch of a good Thickness, to prevent the Water from being heated by the Sun; and this Vault was plaistered on the Inside with such a Composition as we have formerly in this Book recommended for Floors, to the Thickness of at least six Inches. The Parts of the ancient Aqueduct were these. Joining to the Incile was the *Septum*; along the Course of the Conduit were the *Castella*; where any higher Ground interfered the *Specus* was dug; lastly, to the Head was annexed the *Calix*. An ancient Lawyer gives us the following Description of these several Parts. An Aqueduct is a Conduit for conveying Water to a certain Place by means of a gentle Slope. The *Septum* is a Flood-gate or Water-stop made at the Sluice for letting the Water into the Aqueduct. The *Castella* are Water-houses or Conduit-heads for the Reception of the publick Water. The *Specus* is a Kind of Mill-dam dug in the Earth. The *Calix* is the End or Mouth of the Aqueduct, which discharges the Water. All these must be made of very stout Work, the Bottom as strong as possible, the Plaistering tight and by no means subject to crack. The Mouth of the Sluice must be stopt with a Flood-gate, with which you may shut out the Water when it happens to be turbid, and by means whereof you may have an Opportunity to mend any Part of the Aqueduct which is decayed, without being prevented by the Water; and this Flood-gate must have a Grate of Brass to it, that Water may flow into the Aqueduct clearer and more refined, leaving behind it the Leaves, Boughs and other Trash that fall into it. At every hundred Cubits must be either a Conduit-head, or a Mill-dam twenty Foot broad, thirty long, and fifteen deep below the Bottom of the Channel; and these are made to the Intent that those Waters which either fall into the Aqueduct from the Earth, or are thrown into it too violently, may have a Place to subside below the other Stream, which by that means will have room to flow on more refined and clear. The Mouth of the Aqueduct for discharging

the

the Water, must vary according to the Quantity of the Stream, and the Situation of the Pipe by which it makes it discharge. The greater and more rapid the Stream is from whence the Water is brought, the more direct Way it is brought, and the more it has been confined, the more the Mouth of the Conduit must be enlarged. If the discharging Pipe be placed direct to the Stream and Level, it will maintain an equal Discharge. It has been found by Experience, that this Pipe is wasted away by the continual Spray of the Water, and that no Metals stand it so well as Gold. Thus much of Conduits and Aqueducts. Water may also be brought in leaden Pipes, or rather in earthen ones, because the Physicians tell us, that those of Lead occasion an Excoriation of the Bowels, and so too will Brass.

The Learned tell us, that whatever we either drink or eat, is best preserved in Vessels of baked Earth, which the least alters their Taste; alledging that the Earth is the natural Place of Repose, as well of Water as of every Thing else which is produced by the Earth. Wooden Pipes give Water in Time an ill Colour, and an unpleasant Taste. Whatever Material they are made of, the Pipes ought to be as strong as possible. Vessels of Brass are apt to give the Epilepsy, Canker, and so breed Disorders in the Liver and Spleen. The Sides of the Pipes must be in Thickness at least one fourth Part of the Diameter of the Hollow, and the Joints of the Bricks of which they are made be mortised into one another, and cemented with unslaked Lime mixed with Oil; they should also be fortified all round with strong Brick Work, and strengthened a good Weight of Work over them, especially where you bring the Water about winding, or where after a Descent it is to rise upwards again, or where the Pipe upon a short Turn is straitened and made narrower. For the Weight and continual Pressure of the Water, with the Force and Impetuosity of its Current, would easily carry away or break the Bricks. Experienced Workmen, in order to guard against this Danger, and especially about the Windings, made use of a living Stone, and particularly of the red Sort, bored through for the Purpose. I have seen Pieces of Marble above twelve Foot long bored through from one End to the other with a Bore of four Inches Diameter, which by plain Marks in the Stone itself appeared to have been made with an Instrument of Brass turned with a

Wheel and with Sand. In order to prevent the Effects of this Impetuosity, you may slacken the Current of the Water, by making it run winding, not indeed with a sharp Elbow, but with an easy Sweep, turning sometimes to the Right, sometimes to the Left, sometimes rising, sometimes descending with a frequent Variety. To this you may add somewhat in the Nature of a Conduit-head or Mill-dam, in order for the Water to purify there, and also if any Defect should happen, that you may the more easily come to see how and where it must be repaired. But these Heads should not be placed in the Bottom of the Sweep of a Valley, nor where the Water is forced upwards, but where it keeps on its Course more equally and gently. If you are obliged to carry your Conduit-pipes through a Lake or Marsh, you may do it with a very small Expence, in the following Manner. Provide some good Timbers of Scarlet Oak, and in them Lengthways cut a Gutter in Breadth and Depth in Proportion to your Pipes, which you must lay into this Gutter well cemented with Mortar, and bound down with good Cramps of Brass. Then having laid these Timbers upon a Float across the Lake, fasten the Ends of them together as follows. You must have Pipes of Lead of the same Diameter as those upon your Timbers, and of such a Length as to allow for bending as much as may be necessary. These leaden Pipes, you must insert into your earthen ones, and cement their Joints with Lime slacked with Oil, and fortified with Plates of Brass. Thus join the Ends of the Timber together, as they hang over your Float, till you bring them from one Shore quite to the other, and their Heads rest upon the dry Ground on each Side. Then withdraw your Float, and having secured the whole Work with good Ropes, where the Lake is deepest, let it go down by little and little to the Bottom, as equally as possible, all the rest sinking by proper Degrees along with it, by which Means the leaden Pipe will bend according to the Occasion, and the whole will place itself conveniently at the Bottom of the Lake. When the Conduit is prepared in this Manner with the first Water which you send into it throw in some Ashes, that if any of the Joints should happen not to be perfectly close, they may stop them up, and help to cement them. You should also let in the Water by gentle Degrees, lest rushing in too precipitately, it should struggle with the Wind which is in the Pipe.

It

274

It is incredible the Violence and Impetuosity of Nature when the Wind in such a Pipe is restrained and compressed too close. I have read in the Works of the Physicians, that the Bone of a Man's Leg has been broken by the sudden Irruption of a Vapour so confined. The Artists in Hydraulics can force Water to leap up out of a Vessel, by confining a Quantity of Air between two Waters.

CHAP. VIII.

Of Cisterns, their Uses and Conveniencies.

I Now come to speak of Cisterns. A Cistern is a large Vessel for holding Water, not unlike the Water-house or Conduit-head. Its Bottom and Sides therefore must be perfectly strong and well compacted. There are two Sorts, one for containing Water for Drinking, and the other for preserving it for other Uses, as particularly against sudden Fires. The first we shall call a Drinking-cistern, the other a Reservoir. The Drinking-cistern ought to preserve its Water in the greatest Purity; because when it is impure it is the Cause of a great many Inconveniencies. In both we are to take care that the Water is properly admitted, preserved and dispensed. Water is brought into the Cistern by Pipes from the River or Spring, and sometimes Rain-water from the House-top or from the Ground. I was extremely pleased with the Invention of an Architect, who in a large bare Rock on the Summit of a Hill cut a round Bason ten Foot deep, which received all the Rain-water which ran into it from that naked Rock. Then in the Plain under the Hill he erected a Water-house, open on every Side, and built of Brick and Mortar, thirty Foot high, forty long and forty broad. Into this Water-house he brought the Rain-water from the upper Reservoir by a subterraneous Conduit of brick Pipe; that Reservoir lying much higher than the Top of the Water-house. If you strew the Bottom of your Cistern with good round Pebbles, or large Gravel from the River very well washed, or rather fill it with it to a certain Height, suppose of three Foot, it will make your Water clear, cool and pure; and the Higher you make this Strewing, your Water will be the more limpid. The Water sometimes runs out at the Joints and Cracks of the Cistern if it is ill made; and sometimes the Water is spoiled by Filth. And indeed it is no easy Matter to keep Water imprisoned, unless the Reservoir be strongly built, and even of good square Stone. It is also particularly necessary, that the Work should be perfectly

dry before you let the Water into it; which pressing hard upon it with its Weight, and Sweating through it by means of its Humidity, if it can but make a small Crack, will be continually working its Way till it has opened itself a large Passage. The Ancients guarded against this Inconvenience, and especially in the Corners of their Reservoirs, by several Coats of strong Plaistering, and sometimes by Incrustations of Marbles. But nothing better prevents this oozing out of the Water, than Chalk close rammed in between the Wall of the Cistern and the Side of the Trench in which it is made. We order the Chalk which we use for this Purpose to be thoroughly dried and beat into Powder. Some think, that if you fill a Glass Vessel with Salt, and stop it up close with a Plaister of Mortar tempered with Oil, that no Water may get in, and then hang it down in the Middle of the Cistern, it will prevent the Water from corrupting, let it be kept ever so long. Some add Quick-silver to the Composition. Others say, that if you take a new earthen Vessel full of sharp Vinegar, stopt up as above, and set it in the Water, it will entirely clear it from all Slime. They tell us too, that either a Cistern or a Well are purified by putting some small Fish into them, thinking that the Fish feed upon the Slime of the Water and of the Earth. We are told of an old Saying of *Epigenes*, that Water which has been once corrupted, will in Time recover and purify itself, and after that never spoil any more. Water which is beginning to corrupt, if it is stirred about, and poured often out of one Vessel into another, will lose its ill Smell, which will also hold good of Wine and Oil that is mothery. *Josephus* relates, that when *Moses* came to a dry Place, where there was only one Spring of Water, and that foul and bitter, he commanded the Soldiers to draw it; and upon their beating and stirring it about heartily, it became drinkable. It is certain that Water may be purified by boiling and straining; and we are told that Water which is nitrous and bitter, by throwing Barley-flower into it may be so sweetened, as to be fit to drink in two Hours Time. But in order to refine the Water of your Drinking-cisterns more effectually, make a little Well close to your Cistern enclosed with its own proper Wall, and its Bottom a small matter lower than the Bottom of the Cistern. This Well on the Side next the Cistern must have some small Openings filled up either with Spunge or with Pumice-stone, that the Water which gets out of the Cistern into the Well may be thoroughly strained and leave all its coarse Mixture behind it. In the Territory of *Tarragona* in *Spain*, is found a white Pumice-stone very full of small Pores, through which Water is presently strained to the greatest Clearness. It will also come out extremely limpid if you fill up the Aperture, through which the Water must pass, with a Pot bored full of Holes on every Side, and filled with River-sand, in order for the Water to make its Way through this fine Strainer. At *Bologna*, they have a soft sandy Stone of a yellow Colour, through which the Water distills Drop by Drop till it is wonderfully refined. Some make Bread of Sea-water; than which nothing can be more unwholesome. But yet those Strainers which we have mentioned are so effectual that they will make even Sea-water wholesome and sweet. *Solinus* says, that if Sea-water is passed through a white Clay it will become sweet; and we find by Experience that when it has been often strained through a fine Sand, it loses its Saltness. If you sink an earthen Pot close stopped, into the Sea, it will be filled with fresh Water. Nor is it foreign to our Purpose what we are told, that when the Water of the *Nile* is taken up into any Vessel proves foul, if you rub the Vessel just about the Edge of the Water with an Almond, it will presently make it clear. When your Conduit Pipes begin to be stopt with Slime or Dirt, take a Gall-nut, or a Ball made of the Bark of Cork, tied to a long thin Pack-thread. When the Current of the Water has carried this Ball to the other End of the Pipe, tie to the Pack-thread another stronger Cord with a Wisp of Broom fastened to it, which being drawn backwards and forwards in the Pipe, will clear away the Dirt that stopt it up.

CHAP. IX.

Of planting a Vineyard in a Meadow, or a Wood in a Marsh; and how we may amend a Region which is molested with too much Water.

I Now proceed to other Conveniencies. We observed that Food and Rayment was to provided for the Inhabitants. With these we are to be supplied by Agriculture, an Art which it is not our Business to treat of here. Yet there are some Cases wherein the Architect may be of Service to the Husbandman: As particularly when a Piece of Ground being either too dry or too wet, is not in a good Condition for Tillage. A Vineyard may be planted in a moist Meadow in the following Manner: Dig Trenches running from East to West in straight Lines, at equal Distances from each other, and as deep as may be, each nine Foot broad and fifteen Foot distant from one another, and throw up the Earth which you dig out of the Trenches on the Intervals between them, in such a Manner, that the Slope may lie open to the Mid-day Sun: and these little artificial Hills will be very proper for Vines and very fruitful. On the contrary, upon a dry Hill you may make a Meadow by the following Method: Dig a long square Trench in the upper Part of the Hill, with its Sides all equally high and exactly level. Into this Trench bring Water from the next Springs above it, which running over on the lower Side will equally and continually water the Ground beneath. In the Country of *Verona*, a Soil full of round Stones, very naked and barren, the Inhabitants in some Places, by continual watering it, have raised very fine Grass and so turned it into a beautiful Meadow. If you desire to have a Wood grow in a Marsh, turn up the Ground with the Plough, and entirely grub up all Brambles, and then sow it with Acorns about the Time of Sun-rise. This Plantation will grow into a thick Wood, and the Trees will draw to themselves most of the superfluous Moisture: And the spreading of the Roots together with the falling of the Leaves and Sprigs, will raise the Ground higher. Afterwards if you bring
down

down some Land-flood upon it, which may subside there, it will make a Crust over the whole. But of this in another Place. If the Region is subject to Inundations, as *Lombardy* along the Banks of the *Po*; *Venice*, and some other Place; in that Case, several Particulars are to be considered: For the Water is troublesome either from its over-abundance, or from its Motion, or from both these. Upon these we shall make some brief Observations. The Emperor *Claudius* bored through a Hill near the Lake *Fucinus*, and so carried away the superfluous Water into the River; and perhaps it was for the same Reason, that *M. Curius* opened a Way for the Lake *Velinus* to discharge itself into the Sea. Thus we see the Lake *Nemorensis*, carried into the Lake *Laurentina* through a Hill bored on purpose; to which we owe those pleasant Gardens and that fruitful Grove which lie below the Former of those Lakes.

Cæsar had Thoughts of cutting a Number of Trenches near *Herda* in *Spain*, in order to discharge some Part of the Water of the River *Sicoris*. The *Erymanthus*, a River of *Arcadia*, very full of Windings, is almost exhausted by the Inhabitants in watering their Lands, by which means his Remains fall into the Sea without so much as preserving his Name. *Cyrus* cut the *Ganges* into a vast Number of Canals, *Eutropius* says, no less than four hundred and sixty, by which he so sunk that River, that it might easily be forded, and sometimes even drishod. Near the Tomb of King *Halyattes*, in the Country of the *Sardes*, built chiefly by the female Slaves, is the Lake *Coloe*, dug by Art on purpose to receive Inundations. *Myris* dug a Lake in *Mesopotamia* above the City, three hundred and forty Furlongs in Circumference, and threescore Cubits deep, to receive the *Nile* whenever it rose higher than usual. Besides the strong Banks made for keeping in the *Euphrates*, that it might not overflow and wash away the Houses, some Lakes were also dug, together with some vast hollow Caves, that the standing Water in those might receive and break the Fury of Inundations. Thus much may suffice of Waters which are apt to overflow, or to do Mischief by the Impetuosity of their Motion. If any thing is wanting to this Head, we shall insert it immediately, when we come to speak of Rivers and the Sea.

CHAP. X.

Of Roads; of Passages by Water, and of artificial Banks to Rivers.

THE next Business is to get as conveniently as is possible from abroad, those Necessaries which we cannot be supplied with at home. To this Purpose are Roads and Highways, which are to be made such, that whatever is wanting may be easily brought, in its proper Season. There are two Sorts of Highways, one by Land, the other by Water, as we hinted in the former Part of this Work. Care is to be taken that the Highway by Land is not too deep, nor too much broke by Carriages; and besides those Causeways which we have spoken of formerly, we should be sure to let them be open to a good deal of Sun and to a free Air, and that they be not covered with too much Shade. In our Days, near the Wood by *Ravenna*, the Road which used to be very bad, has been made extremely convenient by cutting down the Trees, and admitting the Sun to it. We may generally observe little Puddles under Trees which stand by the Side of the Road, occasioned by the Tread of Cattle, and the Shade preventing the Ground from drying so fast as it otherwise would do, so that the Rain always settles and lies there. Highways (if we may so call them) by Water are of two Sorts: One which may be corrected and forced; as Rivers or Canals; the other which cannot; as the Sea. We may venture to say, that there happen the same Faults in a River as we find in a smaller Vessel for containing Water; that is, that perhaps either the Sides, or the Bottom are defective or not sound and convenient. For as a large Quantity of Water is necessary for the carrying of Ships, if it is not contained in stout Banks, it may break its Way through them and drown all the Country, and so even spoil the Highways on Shore. If the Bottom be very steep, how can we imagine that a Ship can make its Way up against the Rapidity of the Stream? and if it rises into Shelves, it will spoil the Navigation. Upon bringing the famous Obelisk from *Ægypt* to *Rome*, it was found that the *Tyber* was a more convenient River for Navigation than the *Nile*. The latter indeed was much broader, but the

former

former was of a more convenient Depth: For it is not so much a great Plenty as a good Depth of Water that is necessary for Navigation. Though a handsome Breadth is very convenient too, because by that means the Streams comes slower against the Banks. A River that has not a sound Bottom, will scarce have strong Banks; and scarce any Bottom can be called sound, which has not such a Strength as we have formerly required in the Foundations of Buildings, namely, to be so solid as in a Manner to defy even Tools of Iron. Thus the Bottom will be uncertain if the Banks are chalky, or if the River runs along a flat Plain, or if the Soil is covered with loose round Stones. When the Banks of a River are unfirm, its Channel will be stopt up with Shelves, Ruins, broken Trunks of Trees, and soft Stones: The weakest Sides of all, and the most variable, are those thrown up by some sudden Inundation. From this Weakness of the Sides follows what is said of the *Meander* and the *Euphrates*, the former of which we are told, used easily to cut through his soft Banks and be daily running into new Windings, and the *Euphrates* on the other Hand was continually stopping up the Canals, through which he was conveyed, with the Ruins of his Shore. These Defects in the natural Banks the Ancients used to remedy with artificial ones; the Rules for which are much the same with those for other Kinds of Structures; for we are to consider well with what Lines we erect it, and with what Kind of Work. If the artificial Bank is built in a parallel Line with the Current of the River, the Force of the Stream will never bear against it: But if it is built so as to stand against the Current, if it is not very strong it will be overthrown by it; or if it be too low the Water will overflow it. If such a Bank be not overthrown, it will be continually growing higher and higher at the Bottom, because there every Thing which the Stream brings along with it will stop, till at last having made a Hill against it which it can remove no further, it will be apt to turn its Course another Way. If the Force of the Water throws down the Bank, then it will have those Effects natural to it, which we observed before, by filling all the Hollows, driving out the Air, and sweeping away every Thing that it meets in its Passage: But still leaving behind it by Degrees as it slackens the Violence of its own Course, such heavy Things as are not easily carried far. Thus in the Mouth of the Breach which the

River makes in its Banks, the Inundation will leave a Shelf of coarse Sand of a considerable Height; but as it goes further it will only cover the Ground with a small Slime. If the River does not immediately break down its Bank, but only overflows the Top of it, the Violence with which it falls upon the Ground on the other Side of it will wash away the Earth, till by Degrees it undermines and brings down the whole Bank itself. If the Current neither is parallel with the Bank, nor sets against it directly, but only strikes it obliquely, it will bear no less, in Proportion to the Angle of its Obliquity, against the Sides to which it is thrown off, than against that which it meets with first. And indeed this Flexion will give it somewhat of the Nature of a Bank that fronts the Current directly; so that it will be liable to the very same Injuries as the latter. Thus the Bank will be washed away so much the sooner, as the Eddies of the Water will be more vehement and furious, foaming, and in a Manner boiling with Violence: For these Whirls and Eddies in a River seem to have somewhat of the Nature and Force of a Screw, which no Strength or Solidity can long resist. We may observe as well under Stone Bridges, how deep the Channel is dug by the Fall of the Water; as in those Part of the River where after having been some Time confined within narrower Banks, it finds a broader Channel to extend itself in, with what Fury it breaks out, rowling into Variety of Eddies, and tearing away every Thing that it meets with, either from the Banks or from the Bottom. I dare venture to affirm, that *Hadrian*'s Bridge at *Rome*, is one of the stoutest Pieces of Work that perhaps ever was performed; and yet the Fury of the Water has so decay'd it, that I dread its Destruction: For the Land-floods every Year load its Piers with Boughs and Trunks of Trees which they bring down along with them, and in a great Measure stop up the Arches. This makes the Water rise still higher, and then it falls down percipitately into wild Eddies, which undermine the Back of the Piers and endanger the whole Structure. Thus much of the Banks: Let us now say something of the Bottom of the River. *Herodotus* relates, that *Nitocris*, King of the *Assyrians*, slackened the Course of the River *Euphrates* near *Mesopotamia*, which before was too impetuous, by making its Channel wind about more than it used to do. It is also reasonable to suppose that the Water which has
the

the flowest Current will be the most lasting: Which may be somewhat illustrated by the Comparison of a Man that descends from a steep Hill, and who comes down not direct and as fast as he can, but fetching different Compasses about the Sides, sometimes to the right Hand, and sometimes to the Left. The Rapidity of the Stream proceeds from the Steepness of the Channel. A Current either too swift or too flow, is inconvenient. The former demolishes the Banks; the latter produces Weeds, and is easily frozen. Making the River narrower may perhaps force the Water to rise higher, and another Way to make it deeper is digging the Channel, lower. Deepening the Channel, removing Impediments, and clearing the River are all done by the same Methods and for the same Purposes, whereof we shall speak presently: But deepening the Bottom of a River will be in vain, unless we go on to do it quite away to the Sea, in order to give the Stream its due Slope all the Way.

CHAP. XI.

Of Canals; how they are to be kept well supplied with Water, and the Uses of them not obstructed.

WE now proceed to speak of Canals. What we are to provide for in these, is that they be well supplied with Water, and that the Uses for which they are intended be not obstructed. There are two Ways of preventing their failing. The first is to have a large Quantity of Water constantly running into them from some other Stream; the second is to contrive that they keep what does come into them as long as can be. The Water is to be brought into Canals in the manner above set down: and our Diligence must prevent their Uses from being obstructed, by often cleaning them, and removing whatever Incumbrances may be brought into them. A Canal is said to be a sleeping River; and it should therefore have all the same Properties which a River has, and especially its Bottom and Sides should be perfectly found, that the Water may neither be sucked up, nor run out at any Cracks. It should be more deep than broad, as well for the better carrying off all Sorts of Vessels, as that it may be less exhausted by the Sun and breed the fewer Weeds. A great many Canals were cut from the *Euphrates* to the *Tygris*, because the Channel of the former lay higher than that of the Latter. *Lombardy* lying between the *Po* and the *Adige*, is every where navigable by Canals; an Advantage which it gains by lying all upon a Flat. *Diodorus* tells us, that when *Ptolomey* went out of the Mouth of the *Nile*, he opened a Canal on Purpose, and had it stopp'd up as soon as he was got through it. The Remedies for the several Faults of either Canals or Rivers are confining, clearing and stopping them. Rivers are confined by artificial Banks. The Line of such Banks should not restrain the River at once, but by degrees, by means of an easy Slope. When you would set it at Liberty again from a narrow Channel into a wider Breadth, you must observe the same Method, not let it out at once, but gently, left upon too sudden an Enlargment it does Mischief by Eddies and Whirlpools. The River *Melas* used of old to run into the *Euphrates*; but King *Artanatrix*, perhaps out of a Desire to make his Name famous, stopp'd it up and overflowed the Country all round: but soon afterwards the Waters return'd with such Eddies and so much Fury that they tore up all that resisted them, washed away a great many Estates, and laid Waste a great Part of *Phrygia* and *Galatia*. The *Roman Senate* fined the King for this audacious Attempt, in thirty Talents. Nor is it foreign to our Purpose just to mention what we read of *Iphicrates* the *Athenian*, that when he was besieging *Stymphalus* in *Arcadia* he attempted with a vast Quantity of Spunge to stop up the River *Erasinus* which enters into the Hill and rises up again in the Country of *Argos*; but by the Admonition of *Jupiter* he laid aside the Design. I advise therefore, that your artificial Bank be made as strong as possible. This Strength must be owing to the Solidity of your Materials, your Method of putting them together, and the Breadth of the whole Work. Where it is necessary that the Water should run over this Bank, do not let the Outside of it be a Perpendicular, but fall in an easy Slope, that the Water may run down it easily and not form any Eddies. If in its Fall it begins to dig up the

the Bank, fill up the Holes immediately, not with trifling Materials, but with large, solid, square Stone. It may alſo be of Service to lay Bundles of Bruſhwood underneath the Fall of the Water, to break its Force before it comes to the Bottom. We ſee that the *Tyber* at *Rome* is for the moſt Part confined with ſolid Maſonry. *Semiramis*, not contented with a ſtrong Bank of Brick, covered it with a Coat of Plaiſter made of Bitumen, no leſs than four Cubits in Thickneſs, with Walls for many Furlongs together equally high with thoſe of the City. But theſe are Royal Works. For us, we may be contented with a Bank of Earth, like that of *Nitocris* in *Aſſyria*, which was of Mud, or like thoſe Banks in *France* which confine ſome very great Rivers, in ſuch a Manner that they ſeem to hang in the Air, the Water in ſome Places being above the Level of the Tops of the Cottages: and we may be ſatisfied if we can have our Bridges of Stone. Some commend the Graſs Turfs cut out of a Meadow for making up of Banks: and I think they will do very well, becauſe the interweaving of their Roots will fortify the Work, provided they be rammed very cloſe together: for the whole Bank, and eſpecially that Part of it which is waſhed by the Water, ought to be ſo ſolid as not to be penetrated or diſunited. Some interlace Rods of Ozier in the Bank; and this makes a very firm Bank, but then it will laſt but for a Time, for as ſuch Rods eaſily rot, little Rills of Water will penetrate into the Places of the Twigs which are decayed, and working their Way onwards, will be apt to enlarge their Paſſage till the whole River may break through in great Streams. There will not indeed be ſo much Danger of this if we take the Oziers when they are green. Others plant Willows, Elder, Poplars and ſuch other Trees as love the Water along the Shores in cloſe Rows. This has ſome Advantages; but then it is attended with the ſame Inconvenience which we juſt now mentioned; for when the Roots decay, the Water will work its Way into their Cavities. Others (which I am very well pleaſed with) plant the Shore with all Manner of Shrubs that flouriſh in the Water, and ſtrike out more Root than Branches, ſuch as Lavender, Bulruſh, Reeds, and eſpecially Withes; the laſt of which puſhes out a great deal of Root, and pierces down into the Earth with very long Fibres, which are continually making new Shoots, while at the ſame Time its Head is but ſmall, is very pliant, and does not reſiſt the Stream; and which adds to the Advantage, this Plant, out of its particular Love to Water, advances on continually even into the Current. But where the Bank runs on parallel with the ſtrong Current of the River, the Shore ought to be entirely naked and clear, that nothing may diſturb or enrage the Stream, but that it may run on peaceably. Where the Bank winding about ſtands againſt the Set of the Current, that it may make the ſtouter Reſiſtance, let it be fortified with good Plank. But if the whole Force of the River is to be withſtood and oppoſed; then, in the Summer, when the Water is loweſt, and the Shore is left dry, make Hurdles bound about ſtrong Stakes of a good Length, and faſtened to them very tight with ſtout Braces; lay theſe Hurdles with the Heads of the Stakes againſt the Current of the Stream, and drive Piles through them, by Holes made in them before-hand for that Purpoſe, as deep as the Nature of the Bottom will permit. When this is knit together, join other Beams to them croſſways, and fill up this Frame with large Stones cemented together with Mortar; or where the Expence of Mortar cannot be afforded, you may knit them together by throwing Bavins of Juniper in amongſt them. This great Weight will prevent the Water from ſtirring the Frame; and if any Eddies ſhould get within it, they will do rather Good than Harm, for by endeavouring to work downwards they will make the whole Weight of Stone ſink ſtill lower, and ſo ſtrengthen the Foundation ſtill more. But if the River always keeps at ſuch a Height, that there is no Opportunity to make ſuch a Frame, then we muſt make uſe of thoſe Methods which we formerly taught for erecting the Piers of a Bridge.

CHAP. XII.

Of the Sea Wall; of ſtrengthening the Port; and of Locks for confining the Water of a River.

THE Sea-ſhore alſo is to be fortified with artificial Banks, but not in the ſame Manner as the River, whoſe Streams does Miſchief in a different Manner from the Waves of the Sea. We are told, that the Sea in its own Nature is quiet and peaceable, but it is agitated

tated and drove about by the Winds, which push on the Waves in great Rows to the Shore, where if they meet with Oppofition, efpecially from any hard rugged Body they beat againft them with their whole Strength, and being dafhed back again they break, and falling from on high with continual Repetition dig up and demolifh whatever refifts their Fury. A full Proof of this is the great Depth of Water which we conftantly find under high Rocks by the Sea-fide. But when the Shore runs off with an eafy Defcent, the raging Sea not finding any Thing to exert its Force againft, grows quiet, and falls back lefs furious upon itfelf; and if it has brought any Sand along with it, leaves it there; by which Means we fee fuch Shores growing higher and higher into the Sea every Day. But when the Sea meets with a Promontory, and afterwards with a Bay, the Current runs impetuoufly along the Shore, and turns back again upon itfelf; which is the Reafon that in fuch Places we frequently meet with deep Channels cut under the Shore. Others maintain, that the Sea hath a Breath and Refpiration of its own, and pretend to obferve, that no Man ever dies naturally but when the Tide is going off, whence they would infer, that our Life has fome Connection and Relation with the Motion and Life of the Sea: but this is not worth Dwelling upon. It is certain, that the Tides rife and fall varioufly in different Places. The *Negropont* has no lefs than fix Tides every Day. At *Conftantinople* it has no other Change but by flowing into the *Pontus*. In the *Propontis* the Sea naturally throws upon the Shore every Thing that is brought down into it by the Rivers: becaufe every Thing which is put into an unnatural Agitation refts of Courfe where-ever it finds a Place which is not difturbed. But as upon almoft all Shores we fee Heaps of Sand or Stones thrown up, it may not be a mifs juft to mention the Conjectures of the Philofophers upon this Occafion. I have faid elfewhere, that Sand is form'd of Mud dried by the Sun, and feparated by the Heat into very minute Particles. Stones are fuppofed to be engendered by the Sea-water; for they tell us, that by Means of the Sun's Heat and of Motion, the Water grows warm, dries, and its lighter Parts evaporating hardens into a Confiftence, which grows to have fo much Solidity, that if the Sea is but a little while at reft, it by degrees contracts a flimy Cruft, of a bituminous Nature; this Cruft in Time is afterwards broken, and by new Motion

and Collifion the new-made Subftance becomes globular, and grows fomewhat like a Spunge: Thefe globular Spunges are carried to the Shore, where by their Sliminefs they lick up the Sand which is put into Agitation, which again is dried and concocted by the Heat of the Sun, and by the Salts, till by Length of Time it hardens into Stone. This is the Conjecture of the Philofophers. We frequently fee the Shore grow higher and higher towards the Mouth of Rivers, efpecially if they flow through loofe Grounds, and are much fubject to Landfloods; for fuch Rivers throw up vaft Quantities of Sand and Stones before their Mouths into the Sea, and fo lengthen out the Shore. This manifeftly appears from the *Danube*, the *Phafis* in *Colchis*, and others, and efpecially in the *Nile*. The Ancients called *Ægypt* the *Nile*'s Houfe, and tell us, that it was formerly covered by the Sea quite as far as the *Pelufian* Marfhes. So it is related, that a great Part of *Cilicia* was added to it by the River. *Ariftotle* fays, that all Things are in perpetual Motion, and that in length of Time the Sea and the Hills will change Places with one another. Hence the Saying of the Poet:

All that the Earth in her dark Womb conceals,
Time fhall dig up and drag to open Light.

BUT to return. The Waves have this particular Property, that when they meet with any Bank which refifts them, they dafh againft it with the more Fury; and being beaten back, according to the Height they fall from, the more Sand they root up. This appears from the great Depth of the Sea under the Rocks, againft which they beat with much more Violence, than they fall upon a foft and floping Sand. This being the Cafe, it requires great Diligence and the moft careful Contrivance to reftrain the Rage and Strength of the Sea, which will many Times defeat all our Art and Ability, and is not eafily fubdued by the Power of Man. However, the Sort of Work which we formerly recommended for the Foundations of a Bridge may be of fome Service in this Cafe. But if it is neceffary for us to carry out a Pier into the Sea in order to fortify a Port, we muft begin our Work upon the dry Ground, and fo by Additions work it forwards into the Sea. Our firft and greateft Care muft be to chufe a firm Soil for this Structure; and where-ever you raife it, raife it up with a Slope of the lighteft Stones that can be got, in order

order to break the Fury of the Waves, that not finding any Thing to beat against with their whole Strength, they may fall back gently and not with too violent a Precipitation. Thus the Wave which is upon Return will meet that which is coming on, and deaden its Force. The Mouths of Rivers seem to be of the same Nature with the Port, as they afford Shelter to Vessels against Storms. They ought therefore to be fortified and made narrower to exclude the Fury of the Sea. *Propertius* says,

Resolve to conquer or be o'ercome,
This is the Wheel of Love ——

It is the same in this Case; for the Mouths of Rivers by the incessant Attacks of the Sea are either overcome and filled up with Sand; or else by a constant and obstinate Resistance, they conquer and keep their Passages clear. For this Reason it is an admirable Method to open the River a double Discharge into the Sea by two different Branches, if you have but Water enough to supply them; not only that Ships may be able to get in at one of them, though the Wind be contrary for the other; but also that if one of them be stopt up, either by some Storm at Sea, or by some strong Wind blowing into it, in such a Manner that the Land-floods would be driven back again into the Country, they may have another Passage open to discharge themselves into the Sea. But of this enough. The next Point is how to clean a River. *Cæsar* took a great deal of Care about cleaning the *Tyber*, which was stopt up with Rubbish, and there are vast Heaps of the Stuff that was taken out still to be seen not far from the River, as well within the City as without. By what Methods he got so much Rubbish out of so swift a River, I do not remember to have read: But I suppose he made use of Frames to shut out the River and then emptying the Water out of them, he might easily take out the Rubbish. These Frames are made in the following Manner: Prepare some strong Timbers cut square, with Grooves cut in the Sides of them from Top to Bottom four Inches deep, and in Breadth equal to the Thickness of the Planks which you intend to use in this Work; and prepare your Planks also of equal Length and Thickness with one another. Having got these Things ready, drive down your Timbers so as they may stand perpendicular, at Distances from each other equal to the Length of your Planks. When

your Timbers are well fixed, let your Planks into the Grooves and drive them down to the Bottom. Our Workmen call these Frames Cataracts. Go on in the same Manner to fill up the Spaces between the Timbers with Planks and drive them as close together as possible. Then go to work immediately with your Pumps, Syphons, Buckets and all your other Implements for emptying out the Water, putting on as many Hands as you can, and labouring without Intermission till you have thrown out all the Water within your Inclosure. If it leaks in any Part, stop up the Crack with any old Rags: And thus the Business may be done. Between this Frame and that which we mentioned as necessary in the Building of Bridges, there is this Difference; that the latter must be stable and lasting, being to stand not only till the Piers are built, but even till the Superstructure is settled; whereas this is only temporary, and as soon as the Dirt is got out to be presently removed to another Place. But I advise you, whether you clean your River by the Help of this Frame, or by turning the Course of the Water, that you do not pretend to strive against the whole Force of the Stream at a Time in any one Place, but go on Step by Step and by Degrees. All Works raised against the Violence of Waters, if they are made in the Form of Arches, with their Backs turned against the Weight of the Water, they will be able to make the stouter Resistance. You may level a Torrent or Water-fall by laying a Barrier across the Stream in such a Manner that the Water is obliged to rise a good deal higher than usual: For the Water running over from the Top of this Barrier, will dig up the Ridge in the Channel by its fall; and then even the Channel above the Torrent, quite to the Spring will be levelled in Proportion to the lower Part of the Channel; for the Water in its Descent will be continually moving and carrying away the Earth. You may clean your Channel by turning Oxen into it in the following Manner: Stop it up that the Water may swell; then drive your Cattle about in it so that they may disturb all the Mud, and then opening the Stream that the Water may pour in rapidly, it will wash and carry away all the Dirt. If any thing lies buried and fixed in the Stream so as to spoil the Navigation, besides the common Machines used by Workmen for removing such Obstructions, it is a very good Method to load a Barge deep, and to it fasten with Ropes the Impediment which you would pull up: Then unload

unload the Barge, which by that Means rising higher in the Water, will pull up what is tyed to it. It will be a Help to the Operation, if you keep the Veſſel ſtirring about by moving the Rudder backwards and forwards while you are unloading it; to ſhew the Uſe of which, I ſhall juſt mention, that in the Country of *Præneſte* I have ſeen a moiſt Sort of Clay into which if you run a Stick or a Sword but the Depth of a ſingle Cubit, it was not by the Force of a Man's Arm to be got out again by pulling; but if as you pulled you wriggled your Arm backwards and forwards as Men do that are turning a Skrew, it would eaſily come forth. At *Genoa* there was a Rock lying under the Surface of the Water ſo as to ſtop up the Entrance into the Port. A Man was found in our Age, endued with ſurprizing Qualifications both of Art and Nature, who broke it away, and laid the Paſſage very wide. It is ſaid, that this Man uſed to ſtay under Water many Hours together, without ever coming up to take Breath. You may take up the Mud from the Bottom by means of an Oyſter-net covered with Tarpawlins; for as you draw it along it will fill itſelf. You may alſo fetch it up from the Bottom, where the Sea is ſhallow, with the following Contrivance. You muſt have two Smacks, like thoſe of Fiſhermen; in the Stern of one of theſe you muſt have an Axis upon which a very long Pole muſt ſwing like the Beam of a Balance; to that End of the Pole which lies out from the Stern muſt be faſten'd a Shovel three Foot broad and ſix long. By lowering down this Shovel to the Bottom you ſcoop up the Mud, and ſo throw it into the other Smack which lies by for that Purpoſe. From theſe Principles many other Engines yet more uſeful may be contrived; but to ſpeak of them here would be too tedious. And thus much may ſuffice for cleaning any Channel. The Locks in a River are made either by Sluices or Flood-gates. For either of theſe the Sides muſt be made full as ſtrong as the Piers of a Bridge. We may draw up the heavieſt Sluice without Danger to our Men, by applying to the Spindle or Windleſs which is to draw up the Sluice Wheels notch'd with Teeth like the Wheels in a Clock, which muſt take hold of the Teeth of the other Spindle which is to be put in Motion by them. But the moſt convenient of all is the Flood-gate, which in the Middle has a Spindle that turns upon a perpendicular Axis; to this Spindle is faſtened a broad ſquare Valve, like the ſquare Sail of a Barge which may be eaſily turned about to which Side of the Veſſel the Maſter pleaſes; but the two Sides of this Valve ſhall not be exactly equal to one another in Breadth, but let one be above three Inches narrower than the other; by which means it may be opened by a Child, and will ſhut again of itſelf; becauſe the Weight of the broader Side will exceed that of the Narrower. To each Lock you ought to make two Stops, cutting the River in two Places, and leaving a Space between them equal to the Length of a Veſſel, to the Intent, that if the Veſſel is to aſcend, when it comes to the Stop the lower Sluice may be ſhut the upper one opened; or if it be to deſcend, the upper one may be ſhut and the lower opened; for by this means the Veſſel will run down with the lower Part of the Stream, while the reſt of the Water is ſtopp'd by the upper Sluice. There is one Thing which I muſt not omit concerning publick Ways, that I may have no Occaſion for Repetition; namely, that the Streets of a Town ought never to be heaped up with any Sort of Rubbiſh, as it is grown a bad Cuſtom to do under the Notion of mending them, which ſhould rather be done by removing and carrying away all the Superfluities; leſt the Houſes come in Time to be buried, and the Level of the Town to be ſunk under Rubbiſh.

CHAP. XIII.

Of the Remedies for ſome other Inconveniencies.

I Shall now proceed to the Remedies for ſome other Inconveniencies of ſmaller Moment; in which I ſhall be as brief as poſſible. In ſome Places, upon bringing Water to them, the Country has been made warmer; in others, colder. Near *Lariſſa* in *Theſſaly* there was a Field covered with a ſtanding Water, which made the Air heavy and hot. Upon carrying off this Water, and laying the Field dry, the Country became cooler. The contrary hap-

pened

pened at *Philippi*, where, as we are informed by *Theophraſtus*, upon drawing off the Water and drying up a Lake, the Country was made warmer. The Cauſe of theſe Alterations is ſuppoſed to have lain in the Purity or Groſſneſs of the Air; for a thick Air is more difficultly moved, and longer retains either the Heat or the Cold than a thin one, which is ſoon apt to be frozen with Cold, or on a Change of Weather, to be warmed again with the Sun's Heat. A Country which lies uncultivated and neglected is ſaid to afford a thick and unhealthy Air; and in Places ſo much covered with Wood, that neither Sun nor Wind can eaſily get through, the Air is generally crude. The Caves about the Lake *Avernus* were ſo ſurrounded with thick Woods that the Sulphur which exhaled from them uſed to kill the Birds which flew over them: But *Cæſar*, by cutting down thoſe Woods, made that peſtilential Spot of Ground very healthy. At *Leghorn* a Sea-port Town in *Tuſcany*, the Inhabitants uſed always to be afflicted with ſevere Fevers in the Dog-days: By banking off the Sea with a good Wall, the Town was freed from thoſe Diſtempers; but afterwards, when they let the Water again into their Ditches, for the better Fortification of the Place, their Fevers return'd. *Varro* writes, that when his Camp lay in the Iſland of *Corcyra* (now *Corfu*) and his Soldiers died apace of Peſtilence; by keeping all the Windows towards the South cloſe ſhut, he preſerved his Army. At *Murano*, a famous Town belonging to the *Venetians*, they are very ſeldom touched with the Plague, though, their neighbouring Metropolis, *Venice*, is frequently and ſeverely afflicted with it. The Reaſon of this is ſuppoſed to be the great Number of Glaſs-houſes there; for it is very certain that the Air is wonderfully purged by Fire. And for a Proof that all Manner of Poiſons hate the Fire, it is obſerved, that the dead Bodies of poiſonous Animals do not breed Worms, like others; becauſe it is the Nature of Poiſon to deſtroy and totally to extinguiſh the Principles of Life: But if ſuch Bodies are touched by Lightening they will engender Worms, becauſe then their Poiſon is deſtroyed by Fire; for Worms are bred in the dead Bodies of Animals from no other Cauſe than a certain fiery Power in Nature working upon a Humidity which is apt to be put in Motion by a Heat which it is the Property of Poiſon to extinguiſh, where it prevails, as it is itſelf extinguiſhed by it, where that Heat is the moſt

powerful. If you root out poiſonous Herbs, and eſpecially Squills, the good Plants will draw to themſelves the bad Nouriſhment which they uſed to imbibe from the Earth, by which means our Food will be corrupted. It may be of Service to ſhelter your Houſe from unwholeſome Winds by a Grove and eſpecially of Apple-trees; for it is of a good deal of Conſequence out of the Shade of what Leaves you receive your Air. Pitch-trees are ſaid to be very good for Phthyſical Folks, or for thoſe who are recovering their Health ſlowly after long Sickneſs. It is contrary with Trees which have a bitter Leaf, for they yield an unwholeſome Air. Thus where-ever the Country is low, cloſe and maſhy, it will be of Service to lay it quite open to the Sun and Air; becauſe the Damps and noxious Animals which ariſe from ſuch Places will be preſently deſtroyed by Dryneſs and Winds. At *Alexandria* is a publick Place to which the Filth and Rubbiſh of the Town is carried, and it is now grown up to ſuch a Hill, that it ſerves as a Land-mark to Mariners to find their Way into the Port. How much more convenient would it not be to fill up low hollow Places with ſuch Stuff? Thus at *Venice*, (for which I highly applaud them) they have in my Time filled up ſeveral of their Marſhes with the Rubbiſh of the Town. *Herodotus* tells us, that the People who live among the Marſhes in *Ægypt*, in order to avoid the Gnats, lie a Nights in very high Towers. At *Ferrara* by the *Po* few or no Gnats appear within the City; but out of Town, to thoſe who are not uſed to them, they are execrable. It is ſuppoſed that they are driven from the Town by the great Quantity of Smoke and Fire. Flies do not haunt Places which are cold or expoſed to much Wind, and eſpecially where the Windows are very high. Some ſay that Flies will not enter where the Tail of a Wolf is buried, and that a Squill hung up will alſo drive away venomous Animals. The Ancients made uſe of a great many Defences againſt the violent Heats; among which I am very well pleaſed with their Crypts or ſubterraneous Porticoes, Vaults, which received Light no where but from the Top. They were alſo fond of Halls with large Windows turned away from the South, open to a cool Air, and ſhaded by ſome neighbouring Edifice. *Metellus*, the Son of *Octavia*, *Auguſtus*'s Siſter, made an Awning over the Forum with Sails, that the People might follow their Cauſes without prejudicing their Healths. But Air is more

effectual

effectual to cooling any Place than Shade, as you may find by hanging a Sail upright before that Place to keep out the Air. *Pliny* tells us, that they used to make Places in their Houses on purpose for Shade; but in what Manner they were contrived he does not describe. Whatever they were, Nature must be the best Pattern to imitate. We find, that when we gape with our Mouths wide open, our Breath issues out warm; but when we blow with our Lips pretty close together, the Air comes out cool. Thus in an Edifice, when the Air comes through a very wide Aperture, especially if the Sun lies upon that Aperture, it is warm; but if it passes through a straiter and more shady Passage, it comes quicker and cooler. If warm Water be carryed in a Tube through cold Water, it will be refrigerated. The same will hold good of Air. It is a Question what is the Reason that those that walk in the Sun do not tan so soon as those that sit in it; but the Answer is easy: For by our Motion the Air too is moved, whereby the Sun's Rays are thrown aside. Moreover, in order to make the Shade the Cooler, we may add Roof to Roof, and Wall to Wall, and the greater Space that is left between these, the Cooler, will be our Shade and the more impenetrable to the Heat; for this Interval between has almost the same Effect for this Purpose as a Wall of the same Thickness would have; and in one Respect it is better, because a Wall would retain either the Heat of the Sun or the Cold that had once penetrated it much longer; whereas these double Walls will preserve an equal Temperature of the Air. In Places where the Sun is excessively scorching, a Wall built of Pumice Stone will admit the least Heat and retain it the least Time. If the Doors to the private Apartments are double, that is to say, if there be two Doors, one opening inwards and the other outwards, with a Space of about two Foot between them, what is said within cannot be over-heard by those who are without.

CHAP. XIV.

Some more minute Particulars relating to the Use of Fire.

IF we build in a very cold Place, we shall be obliged to make use of Fire, which is done several Ways, but the most convenient of all is to have it in an open Place, where we can see it shine while we feel its Warmth; for when it is enclosed, as in Stoves, the Smoke is apt to affect the Eyes and injure the Sight. To this add, that the very Sight of the Flame and Light of a Brick Fire, is a chearful Companion to the old Men that are chatting together in the Chimney Corner. But then up towards the Middle of the Funnel of the Chimney there ought to be a transverse Iron Door, which you may shut when all the Smoke is exhausted, and the Fire burns perfectly bright, and so stop up the Tunnel, in order to prevent any Wind from getting down that Way into the Room. Walls built of Flint or Marble are both cold and damp; for by their Chilness they compress the Air into Moisture. Soft Stone and Brick are more convenient, when they are thoroughly dried. Those who venture to sleep between Walls that are new and wet, especially if the Cieling be arched, are sure to catch some very dangerous Illness, Pains, Fevers, or Rheums. Some by that Folly have lost their Eye-sight, others the Use of their Limbs, some their Senses. In order that they may dry the sooner, the Windows and Doors should be left open to give the Winds a thorough Passage. The best Walls for the Health of the Inhabitants are those built of Brick not burnt but dried in the Sun two Years before. Incrustations of Stuc thicken the Air and make it unwholsome and prejudicial to the Lungs and Brain. If you wainscot your Walls with Fir or even Poplar, it will make the House the wholsomer, warmer in Winter, and not very hot in Summer; but then you will be troubled with Mice and Bugs. This you may prevent by stuffing the Interspace with Reeds, or stopping up all the Holes and Retreats of those Vermin with Chalk and Hair tempered together with Lees of Oil: for all Sorts of Oil are mortal Enemies to those Vermin which breed of Corruption.

CHAP. XV.

By what Methods to deftroy or drive away Serpents, Gnats, Bugs, Flies, Mice,
Fleas, Moths, and the like troublefome Vermin.

SINCE we are fallen upon this Subject, I
fhall venture to fet down fome Things
which we find in very grave Authors. It
were certainly to be wifhed, that a Building
could be free from all Manner of Inconveniencies. The Inhabitants of Mount *Ætna* infti-
tuted a Sacrifice to *Hercules*, becaufe he delivered them from the Gnats; as did alfo the
Milefians for clearing their Vineyards from the
Caterpillars. The *Æolians* facrificed to *Apollo*
for deftroying their Swarms of Mice. Thefe
were doubtlefs great Benefits; but by what
Means they were done, has not been recorded.
However, in fome Authors I find what follows:
The *Affyrians* by means of a burnt Liver, together with an Onion and a Squill hanging
over the Tranfom of the Door, drove away all
poifonous Animals. *Ariftotle* fays, that Serpents may be driven from a Houfe by the
Smell of Rue, and that by laying fome Flefh
in a Pot you will draw great Numbers of
Wafps into it, where you may fhut them in,
and that by laying Sulphur and Baftard-mar-
joram upon the Holes of Ants-nefts, you may
exterminate the Ants, *Sabinus Tyro* wrote to
Mæcenas, that if their Holes were ftopt up
with Sea-mud, or Afhes, it would deftroy
them. *Pliny* fays, that the Herb Wart-wort
will effectually do it. Others think that pouring in Water where unbaked Brick has been
fteept, is a great Enemy to them. The Ancients affirm, that Nature has made mortal En-
mities between certain Animals and certain
Things, infomuch, that the one is fure Deftruction to the other. Hence the Weafel flies
from the Smell of a roafted Cat, and Serpents
from that of a Leopard. Thus they tell us,
that when a Leech fticks the moft obftinately
to a Man's Flefh, if you apply a Bug to its
Head, it will immediately quit its Hold, and
fall off languid; as, on the other hand, the
Smoke of a burning Leech will drive the Bug
out of his moft private lurking Places. *Solinus*
fays, that ftrewing a Place with fome of the
Duft of the Ifle of *Thanet*, in *Britain*, will
prefently drive away Serpents: And Hiftorians
relate, that the fame may be done by the

Earth of feveral other Places, and particularly
of the Ifland *Ebufus*. The Earth of the Ifland
Galeon belonging to the *Garamanthes* kills
both Serpents and Scorpions. *Strabo* fays, that
the *Africans*, when they went to reft, ufed to
rub the Feet of their Beds with Garlick, to
keep off the Scorpions. *Safernas* tells us how
to kill Bugs, in the following Words. Boil a
wild Cucumber in Water; then pour it where-
ever you think fit; they will never come near
the Place; or elfe rub your Bedftead with an
Ox's Gall mixed with Vinegar. Others direct
us to fill up all the Cracks with Lees of Wine.
The Root of the Holm-oak, fays *Pliny*, is an
Enemy to Scorpions, and the Afh too is excellent againft fuch noxious Animals and efpecially
Serpents; which alfo will never retire under
Fern. Serpents are likewife driven away by
the Burning of a Woman's Hair or of a Goat's
Horn, or of that of a Stag, or of the Sawduft of
Cedar, or of fome Drops of *Galbanum*, or of
Ofier, green Ivy or Juniper; and thofe who
are rubbed with Juniper-feed are perfectly fecure from Hurt by Serpents. The Smell of
the Herb *Haxus* inebriates Afpics, and lays
them fo faft afleep that they are quite be-
numbed. Againft Canker-worms we are directed only to ftick the Skeleton of a Mare's
Head upon a Poft in the Garden. The Palm-
tree is an Enemy to Bats. Where-ever you
fprinkle Water wherein Elder-flowers have been
boiled, you will kill all the Flies; but this is
fooner done with Hellebore, efpecially with
the black Sort. Burying a Dog's Tooth, together with his Tail and Feet in the Hill, will
they fay rid you of Flies. The *Tarantula*
cannot endure the Smell of Saffron. The
Smoke of burning Hops will kill the Gnats.
Mice are killed by the Smell of Wolf-bane,
though it be at a Diftance. So both Mice
and Bugs are deftroyed by the Smoke of
Vitriol. Fleas, if you fprinkle the Place with
a Decoction of Coloquintida or of the Caltrop-
thiftle, will all vanifh. If you fprinkle a Place
with Goat's-blood, they will march to it in
whole Swarms; but they are driven away by
the Smell of Colewort, and yet more effectually

ally by that of Oleander. Broad flat Veſſels full of Water ſet about the Floor are dangerous Traps for Fleas that take their Leaps too daringly. Moths are driven away by Wormwood, Aniſe-ſeed, or the Smell of the Herb Savin : Nay we are told, that Cloaths are ſafe from them ſo long as they hang upon Ropes. But upon this Subject we have dwelt long enough, and perhaps longer than a very grave Reader may like; but he will pardon it, if he conſiders, that what we have ſaid may be of ſome Service for ridding a Situation of Inconveniencies, and that all is little enough againſt the inceſſant Plague of theſe intolerable Vermin.

Chap. XVI.

Of making a Room either warmer or cooler, as alſo of amending Defects in the Walls.

I NOW return to my Subject. It is a wonderful Thing, that if you cover a Wall with Hangings woven of Wool it will make the Room warmer, and if they are of Flax, colder. If the Platform be damp, dig Pits and Drains under it, and fill them up either with Pumice-ſtone or Gravel, to prevent the Water from rotting in them. Then ſtrew the Ground with Coal to the Height of one Foot, and cover that with Sand or rather with Tiles, and over all this lay your Floor. It will be all to no Purpoſe if there is Room for the Air to paſs under the firſt Pavement or Floor. But againſt the Heat of the Sun in Summer, and the Severity of the Cold in Winter, it will be of very great Service, if the Soil thereabouts in general is not damp but dry. Under the Area of your Parlour dig away the Earth to the Depth of twelve Foot, and then floor it with nothing but naked Boards; the Space beneath which is floored only with Plaiſter will make the Air in your Parlour much cooler than you would imagine, inſomuch that you ſhall find it make your Feet cold even when your Shoes are on, nothing being over the ſubterraneous Pavement but plain Boards. The Ceiling of this Parlour ſhould be arched; and then you will be ſurprized how warm it will be in Winter and how cold in Summer. If you are troubled with the Inconvenience which the Satyriſt complains of the Noiſe of Carriages paſſing through a narrow Street, together with that of the rough Language of their bruitiſh Drivers, ſo dreadful to the poor Man in his ſick Bed; *Pliny* the younger tells us, in one of his Epiſtles, how to prevent this Diſturbance, in the following Words. Next to this Room lies the Chamber of Night and of Repoſe, in which was never heard the Voice of Servants, nor the hollow Murmur of the Sea, nor the Crack of Tempeſt, nor can you here perceive the Gleam of Lightening, nor even the Light of the Sun, unleſs you open the Windows, ſo retired is the Place. The Reaſon is, that there is a Lobby between this Chamber and the Garden, in which intermediate Space all the Sounds are loſt, let us now come to the Walls. The Defects in theſe are as follows; either they ſcale off, or they crack, or the Ribs give Way, or they lean from their Perpendicular. The Cauſes of theſe Defects are various, and ſo are their Remedies. Some of the Cauſes indeed are manifeſt, others more concealed, ſo that often we know not what Remedies to apply, till we have ſeverely felt the Miſchief. Others are not in the leaſt obſcure; but then perhaps the Negligence of Men makes them inclined to hope that they may not do ſo much Hurt as they certainly will do. The manifeſt Cauſes of Defects in the Wall are, when it is too thin, when it is not well knit together, when it is full of improper dangerous Apertures, or laſtly, when it is not ſufficiently ſtrengthened with Ribs againſt the Violence of Storms. Thoſe Cauſes which happen unexpected or unforeſeen, are Earthquakes, Lightening, the Inconſtancy of the Foundation, and indeed of Nature itſelf. But in ſhort, the greateſt Injury to all Parts of a Building is the Negligence and Heedleſſneſs of Men. A certain Author ſays, that a Weed is a ſecret Battering-ram againſt a Wall; nor is it to be believed what vaſt Stones I have myſelf ſeen removed and puſhed out of their Places by the Force, or indeed by the Wedge of a little Root that grew between the Joints; which if you had only pulled out while it was young, the Work would have been preſerved from that Injury. I greatly commend the Ancients, who kept a Number of People in

Pay, only to preferve and look after the pub-lick Buildings. *Agrippa* left Pay for two hun-dred and fifty for this Purpofe, and *Cæfar* for no lefs than four hundred and fixty; and they dedicated the next fifteen Feet to the Structure to lie quite clear by their Aqueducts, that their Sides or Arches might not breed any Weeds to demolifh them. The fame feems to have been done even by private Perfons, with re-lation to thofe Edifices which they were de-firous to have eternal; for we find, that the Infcription upon their Sepulchres generally mentioned how many Foot of Ground was confecrated to Religion in that Structure; fometimes it was fifteen, fometimes twenty. But not to fall into a Repetition of thefe Things, the Ancients thought, that you might entirely deftroy a Tree even after it was pretty well grown, if in fome Part of the Dog-days you cut it down to the Height of one Foot, and boring a Hole through the Heart, pour into it Oil of Vitriol mixed with Powder of Brimftone, or elfe fprinkling it plentifully with a Decoc-tion of burnt Bean-fhells. *Columella* fays, that you may deftroy a Wood with the Flower of Hops fteept one Day in Juice of Hemlock, ftrewed about the Roots. *Solinus* fays, that a Tree touched with the Menftrua will lofe its Leaves, and fome affirm, that it will even kill the Tree. *Pliny* fays, that a Tree may be killed by touching the Root with a wild Car-rot. But to return to the Defects of a Wall. If a Wall be thinner than it ought to be, we muft either apply a new Wall to the old one, in fuch a Manner that they may make but one; or, to avoid the Expence of this, we may only ftrengthen it with Ribs, that is to fay, with Pilafters or Columns. A new Wall may be fuperinduced to an old one, as follows. In feveral Parts of the old Wall fix ftrong Catches made of the foundeft Stone, fticking out in fuch a Manner as to enter into the Wall which you are going to join to the other, and to be in the Nature of Bands between the two Walls; and your Wall in this Cafe fhould al-ways be built of fquare Stone. You may for-tify an old Wall with a new Pilafter, in the following Manner. Firft mark out its future Breadth upon the Wall with red Oker. Then open a Break in the Bottom of the Wall quite down below the Foundation, in Breadth fome fmall Matter more than your Pilafter, but not very high. Then immediately fill up this Break with fquare Stone worked together ftrong and even. By this Means that Part of the Wall which is between the red Marks will be fhored up by the Thicknefs of the Pilafter, and fo the whole will be made ftronger. Then in the fame Manner that you have laid the Bottom of this Pilafter you muft go on to work up the Body of it quite to the Top. Thus much of a Wall that is too thin. Where the Wall has not made good Bond, we muft ufe Cramps or Spars of Iron, or rather of Brafs; but you muft take great Care that you do not weaken the Ribs by boring the Holes from them. If the Weight of any crumbling Earth pufhes againft fome Part of the Wall, and threatens Injury to it by its Humidity, dig a Trench along the Wall as broad as you find it necef-fary, and in this Trench build fome Arches to fupport the Weight of the Earth which is falling in, with a Current or Drain through thefe Arches for the Humidity to purge off by; ot elfe lay fome Girders along the Ground with the Heads fetting againft the Wall which is fhoved out by the Weight of the Earth, and let the Heads of thefe Girders into Summers, which you may cover over with new Earth. This will ftrengthen the Foundation, becaufe this new Earth will confolidate, and grow compact, before the Strength of the Girders will give Way.

281

CHAP. XVII.

Of fome Defects which cannot be provided againft, but which may be repaired after they have happened.

I NOW proceed to thofe Defects which can-not be forefeen, but which when they have happened may be repaired. Cracks in the Wall and Inclination from the Perpendicular, are fometimes occafioned by the Arches over it, which pufh out the Wall, or becaufe it is not fufficiently ftrong to bear the Weight which is laid upon it. But the greateft Defects of this Sort almoft conftantly proceed from fome Faults in the Foundation; however we may eafily
difcover

discover whether they are from thence, or from some other Cause by certain Symptoms. Thus to begin with Cracks in the Wall; to which foever Side the Crack runs in its Ascent, on that Side you may be sure the Cause of the Defect lies somewhere in the Foundation. If it does not verge to either Side, but runs up in a direct Line, and grows wider at the Top, then let us take a careful View of the Courses of Stone-work on each Side; for on which ever Side they sink from their Level, on that Side we may be sure the Foundation has failed. But if the upper Part of the Wall is entire, and there are Cracks in several Places towards the Bottom, which in their Ascent run together close at Top; then we may be satisfied that the Corners of the Building stand firm, and that the Defect is somewhere about the Middle in the Foundation. If there is but one Crack of this Sort, the higher up it goes, the the more it shews the Corners to have given Way. In order to strengthen the Foundations in any of these Cases, according to the Magnitude of the Structure and the Solidity of the Ground, dig a narrow Pit near the Wall, but so deep as to come to a firm Soil, and there breaking through the Bottom of the Wall, immediately work up to it with square Stone, and then leave it to settle. When that is settled, dig another Pit in another Part, and underprop it in the same Manner, and in the same Manner give it Time to settle. By this Means you will make a Kind of new Foundation to the whole Wall. But if even by digging you cannot come at any firm Ground, then make Holes in certain Places not too near the Corners, but pretty close to the Foundation of the Wall, on both Sides, that is to say, as well under the Roof as under the open Air, and into those Holes drive Piles as close as they will stick, and over them lay the stoutest Summers you can get lengthways, with the Sides of the Wall. Then across these Summers lay the strongest Girders running under the Bottom of the Foundation, which must rest with their whole Weight upon these Girders, as it were upon a Bridge. In all these Reparations great Care must be taken that no Part of the new Work be too weak to support the Weight which is to bear upon it, and that for ever so long Time: because the whole Pile bearing towards that weaker Part, would immediately fall to Ruins. But where the Foundation has given Way somewhere about the Middle of the Wall, and the upper Part does not appear to be affected by the Crack, then upon the Face of the Wall mark out with your Oker an Arch as large as the Case requires, or, in other Words, so big as to take in all that Part of the Wall which is sunk. Then beginning at one End of this Arch, break into the Wall with an Opening not bigger than one Stone of your intended Arch will fill up; which Stones in an Arch we formerly called Wedges; and immediately insert one of these Wedges in such a Manner that its Lines may exactly answer to the Center to which you have described your Arch. Then make another Break close above it, and fill it up with another such Wedge; and so continuing the Work successively, compleat your whole Arch: and thus you may fortify your Wall without Danger. If a Column or any other of the Ribs of the Building is weakened, you may restore it in the following Manner. Underprop the Architrave with a strong Arch of Tile and Plaister beat together, as also with Piers of Plaister rais'd for this Purpose, in such a Manner that this new Arch may quite fill up the old Intercolumnation, or Aperture between the Ribs: and let this underproping be run up as fast as possible, and without the least Intermission. It is the Nature of Plaister to swell as it dries: so that this new Work, though quite fresh, will be able to take upon itself and sustain the Weight of the old Wall Vault. Then, having before got ready all your Materials, take out the defective Column, and supply its Place with a sound one. If you chuse rather to rest the old Wall upon Timbers, then undershore it with Levers made of strong Beams, and load the longer Ends of those Levers with Baskets filled with Sand, which will raise up the Weight by degrees equally and without any Shocks. If the Wall is swerved from its Perpendicular, fix Planks or Timbers upright against it, and against each of these set a strong Timber by Way of Shore, with its Foot stretching at some Distance from the Wall. Then either with Levers or with Wedges, drive forwards the Feet of the Shores by degrees, so as they may press against the Wall, and so by distributing this Force equally in all Parts, you will raise the Wall again to its perpendicular. If this cannot be done, prop it up with Shores of Timber fixed well in the Ground, with their Ends well daubed over with Pitch and Oil to prevent their being corroded by the Touch of Mortar; then erect Buttresses of square Stone, built so as to enclose those Shores of Timber.

Perhaps

Perhaps a Coloſſus or ſome ſmall Church is ſunk to one Side in its whole Foundation. In this Caſe, you muſt either raiſe that Part which is ſunk, or take away that Part which is too high; both very bold Attempts. The firſt Thing you are to do, is to bind and faſten together, as ſtrongly as poſſible, the Foundation and thoſe Parts which will be in Danger of being ſeparated by Motion, with good Timbers and the ſtrongeſt Braces. There are no better Sort of Braces than ſtrong Hoops of Iron with Wedges drove in between them to keep them tight. Then we raiſe up the Side of the Wall which is ſunk with ſtrong Timbers put under it after the Manner of Levers, as above. If you would rather rectify the Fault by taking away from the Side which is too high, you may do it in the following Manner: Dig away the Ground about the Middle of that Side quite below the Foundation, in the Bottom of which you muſt there open a Break, not very wide, but high enough for you to make it good with ſtrong ſquare Stone. In making good this Break you muſt not work it up quite to the reſt of the Building, but leave ſome Inches ſpace between the new Work and the Old; and this Space you muſt fill up with Wedges of the tougheſt Oak drove in at very ſmall Diſtances from each other. In this Manner you muſt go on to ſhore up all that Side which you want to let down lower. When the whole Weight is thus ſupported, knock out the Wedges by degrees, as gently and cautiouſly as poſſible, till the Wall is ſunk to its juſt Perpendicular. Then fill up the Spaces between the Wedges which are left, with other Wedges of the ſtrongeſt Stone that can be got. In the

283 great Baſilique of St. *Peter* at *Rome*, ſome Parts of the Wall which were over the Columns being ſwerved from their Uprights, ſo as to threaten even the Fall of the whole Roof; I contrived how the Defect might be remedied as follows. Every one of thoſe Parts of the Wall which had given Way, let it reſt upon what Column it would, I determined ſhould be taken clear out, and made good again with ſquare Stone which ſhould be worked true to its Perpendicular, only leaving in the old Wall ſtrong Catches of Stone to unite the additional Work to the former. Laſtly, I would have ſupported the Beam under which thoſe uneven Parts of the Wall were to be taken out, by

means of Engines, called *Capra's*, erected upon the Roof, ſetting the Feet of thoſe Engines upon the ſtrongeſt Parts of the Roof and of the Wall. This I would have done at different Times over the ſeveral Columns where theſe Defects appear. The *Capra* is a naval Engine conſiſting of three Timbers, the Heads of which meet and are ſtrongly braced or bound together, and the Feet ſtretch out to a Triangle. This Engine, with the Addition of Pullies and a Capſtern is very uſeful for raiſing great Weights. If you are to lay a new Coat over an old Wall or an old plaiſtered Floor, firſt waſh it well with clean Water, and then with a Bruſh whiten it over with Whiting diſſolved and mixed with marble Duſt; and this will prepare it for holding the new Coat of Plaiſter or Stuc. If a Pavement which is expoſed to the open Air has any Cracks in it, you may ſtop them up with Aſhes ſifted fine, and tempered Oil, eſpecially of Linſeed. But the beſt Material for this Sort of Reparation is Chalk mixed with quick Lime well beat together and thoroughly burnt in the Kiln, and then ſlaked immediately with Oil; taking Care before you fill up the Cracks with it to clean them from all manner of Duſt, which you may do with Feathers, or by blowing it out with Bellows. Nor let us under this Article of Amendments, quite forget all Ornament. If any Wall looks unhandſome from being too high, embelliſh it either by faſtening on a Cornice of Stuc-work, or by Painting it like Pannels, in order to divide its Height into more decent Proportions. If a Wall be too long, adorn it with Columns reaching from the Top to the Bottom, not ſet too cloſe to each other, which will be a kind of Reſting-places to the Eye, and make the exceſſive Length appear leſs offenſive. There is another Thing not foreign to our preſent Purpoſe. Many Parts of a Building, from being either placed too low or encompaſſed with Walls not high enough, ſeem leſs, and more contracted than they really are; whereas when they are either raiſed upon a higher Platfom, or have ſome Addition made to the Height of their Walls, they ſeem at a Diſtance much larger than they did before. It is alſo certain, that a handſome Diſpoſition of the Apertures, and placing the Door and Windows gracefully, gives all the Aparments a greater Share both of Dignity and Elegance than is to be imagined.

The End of Book X.

1 This contrasts pointedly with Vitruvius' lengthy description of the functions of the architect. Cf. Vitruvius I, 1.

2 Vitruvius II, 1. Alberti disagrees with Vitruvius, as he will frequently continue to do throughout the book.

3 This passage probably refers to the exile of the Alberti family from Florence which lasted from January 1401 until October 1428. The members of the family did not receive back their full rights as citizens until 1434.

4 Raphael Trichet du Fresne (Bordeaux 1611–Paris 1661) was an antiquarian, numismatist and bibliophile. After a period as official of the newly established Imprimerie Royale, he was appointed librarian to Queen Christina of Sweden. He is said to have filched the best medals and books in her collection, by advising her to get rid of them because they were not really good enough for her. In 1651 he published in Paris an anthology of writings on art (cf. Bibliography). Leoni has taken the life of Alberti from that edition.

5 In fact, on the 14th January 1401.

6 Alberto was the son of Giovanni degli Alberti; Lorenzo, the father of Battista and Ricciardo (this last not mentioned by du Fresne) was the son of Benedetto degli Alberti. Du Fresne does not enter into the discussion on the date of Battista's birth. This matter has recently been settled by the publication of some fresh documentary evidence. Battista was born in Genoa on the 30th January 1404 (18th February old style), the son of Lorenzo de' Benedetto degli Alberti and the widow Bianca (Bianchina) Grimani. Battista's mother died in 1406 during an epidemic, and it was then that Lorenzo Alberti left Genoa for Venice, though he returned for his wedding to Margherita di Messer Pietro Benini which took place on the 22nd May, 1408. Cf. C. Ceschi, *La Madre di Leon Battista Alberti*, in BOLLETTINO D'ARTE, XXXIII, 2; April 1948, p. 191.

7 'Dubitare possis utrum ad oratoriam magis, an ad poeticen factus, utrum gravior illi sermo fuerit, an urbanior . . .' Angelo Poliziano (1454–94), in the dedicatory letter prefaced to the original edition of 1485 addressed to Lorenzo de' Medici.

8 The *Camaldulensian Disputations* were printed in 1508, but had been written earlier. They were chiefly concerned with the relative merits of the active life (represented by Lorenzo de' Medici) and the contemplative (represented by Alberti)—the scales being weighted in favour of the latter.

9 The *Apologi* (Michel XXI) were printed in French in 1693 as *Fables diverses de Léon Battiste Alberti, en italien et en françois*, by Louis Pompe. It may be to this work, whose text was taken by Pompe from the 1568 Italian edition of the *Opuscoli Morali* by Bartoli, that du Fresne is referring.

10 Biondo di Antonio Biondi di Forlí, known as Flavio Biondo (1392–1463), was a humanist historian. He is now remembered for his charming topographical book *Roma Ristaurata & Italia Illustrata* in which he mentions Alberti on several occasions.

11 Presumably 1450, the date inscribed on the building, and mentioned in this context by Vasari

12 Between 1470 and 1477.

13 This dome was added in the eighteenth century by the Turin architect Filippo Juvara.

14 Or S. Pancrazio; the chapel of the Holy Sepulchre.

15 Paolo Giovio, Bishop of Nocera and Pagani (1483–1552); in his *Lives of Famous Men*.

16 ' Modus ' is here ' measure ' rather than ' proportion '.

17 This is an extension of the description of the origins of building in the preface.

18 In Book X, 1.

19 ' As far as ', not ' beyond '.

20 Dinocrates, not Policrates; Vitruvius II, Preface.

21 In Book VIII.

22 This treatment was described by Aulus Gellius in his *Noctes Atticae* VI, xiii. In the case of poisonous bites it is, according to him, recommended by Democritus. Its peculiar effect is supposed to be the origin of the Tarantella. Theophrastus

had recommended the same remedy for sciatica. Athenaeus corroborates Aulus Gellius.

23 Ceraunia, i.e. κεραυνεα ὄρη, the mountain of thunder. Achaia, i.e. αεγια λεια, the sea-country; or perhaps an even more direct pun, Achaia/Acquaia.

24 For Demetrius, read Vitruvius. Cf. Vitruvius I, 4, ix.

25 This section of the radius is still known by its Latin name.

26 This circular temple is in fact the tomb of Theodoric, which at that time was being used as a church — S. Maria Rotonda; hence the reference to a ' temple '. The sea has now receded near Ravenna, and the ground round the building been cleared.

27 Alatri is one of the most remarkable cyclopean monuments in Italy. The sharply projecting corner of the walls described by Alberti has remained intact.

28 Cf. V, 4. This form of construction was later developed by Leonardo for military purposes. Ignazio Calvi, *Architettura Militare di Leonardo da Vinci*, pp. 34–6, Figs. 66–74.

29 Known more commonly as the *Agger Servii Tulii*, the inner wall of Rome, of which fragments still remain. A section of it has been preserved by the entrance of the railway terminus.

30 Although there is no record of a temple dedicated to Latona anywhere in Rome, the Basilica of Constantine was known as ' Templum Pacis ' until 1819, and was occasionally described in Mediaeval documents as ' Templum Pacis et Latonae '. The north-west angle of the basement of the basilica is in fact fortified and impinges on the ruins of the Forum of Peace and of Nero's palace. Theuer has suggested that the connection with Latona was due to the existence of an arched passage way called ' Arcus Latronis '—the Thief's arch—through this corner of the basilica. It was not bricked up until 1565, and must have been known to Alberti. Cf. Theuer, p. 611, and Lanciani, *Ruins and Excavations of Ancient Rome*, p. 203ff.

31 The definition of a house as the microcosm of a city became extremely influen-

tial, especially in the planning of villas and country houses. Cf. Wittkower, p. 67.

32 Vitruvius was also of this opinion. II, 3 (iii); Alberti makes further use of this quotation in II, 10.

33 *Usus honestavit*—dignified by use.

34 As in his attitude to the imitation of nature, so in imitating the ancients Alberti is always opposed to direct copying. Cf. IX, 5.

35 Books VII, VIII, IX *passim*.

36 Book VII, 6ff. This description of the column demonstrates Alberti's treatment of the column as part of the wall. This notion is one of the most important elements of his theory. Alberti must have formulated it with reference not only to Classical, but also Byzantine and Early Christian architecture. He was certainly familiar with the buildings of Ravenna and the early Roman basilicas and circular churches such as S. Stefano Rotondo and S. Costanza (the Temple of Bacchus). Even the Baptistery and S. Miniato in Florence were spoken of as Classical buildings during the fifteenth century. This whole passage is interpreted in detail by Wittkower, pp. 31ff.

37 The south clerestory wall of the nave of S. Peter's. In Alberti's time the fabric of the Constantinian basilica was in a very bad condition, and the choir was being rebuilt. Work had, in fact, been interrupted on the choir in 1452 on Alberti's advice. This wall is again referred to in X, 17 below.

38 Wreaths, garlands.

39 Area is here quite simply the floor.

40 Book VI, 2.

41 Most editors have accepted the reading of the original text. But Ammianus speaks of an *Apollo Comaeus;* a hairy, or rustic Apollo.

42 This empirical advice directly belies the commonly accepted idea about the quattrocento architect's ' academic ' attitude to design. On planning, cf. also above, I, 9.

43 The diagonal of the square is the only irrational proportion recommended by Alberti. See below, footnote 247.

44 Book VI, 12 and IX, 13.

45 Book VII, 2 and 5.

46 In Alberti's day the Basilica of Constantine (the Temple of Latona of I, 8) bore out his remark. Unfortunately the remaining columns were removed during the fifteenth and sixteenth centuries.

47 I.e., the heavenly spheres. There were seven spheres, one for each of the planets, an outer fixed sphere, and the sphere of the earth.

48 Cf. Vitruvius III, 4 (iv). Alberti has followed him precisely : risers nine to ten inches, treads eighteen inches to two feet. It is Bartoli's editing which is at fault, rather than Leoni's translation.

49 There are two stories about such bridges told by Classical writers : that of Xerxes over the Hellespont and that of Caligula over the Gulf of Pozzuoli. Both stories must have been known to Alberti.

50 This tomb is the third pyramid at Gizeh.

51 The theatre of Pompey was built *c.* 55 B.C. near the present Campo dei Fiori. It was reputed to be the first stone theatre in Rome. Its exact location was disputed in Alberti's day. The ruins were used as a quarry, and all that remains now is its outline, which is preserved in the plan of the Palazzo Pio.

52 Cf. this passage with Vitruvius VI, 8 (x).

53 Eugenius IV commissioned the new centre doors for S. Peters from Filarete in 1443, the year in which Alberti returned to Rome as a member of the Papal Court. S. Hadrian III was only pope for a few months (884/5) and no building activities of any importance are recorded in his reign. The doors are said to have been restored, after the sack of Rome by the Saracens, by Leo IV in 845. They are usually attributed to the reign of Honorius I.

54 This chapter is based on Vitruvius II, 3, and Pliny XXXV (xlix). But there is also direct evidence of Alberti's practical concern with brickmaking, in a letter written to him by Lodovico Gonzaga in June 1460, regarding the brickwork for S. Sebastiano in Mantua.

55 This schedule follows Vitruvius II, 3 (iii) ; as is Alberti's practice, however, the Greek technical terms used by Vitruvius are omitted. Cf. VI, 1, where

Alberti gives his reasons for this omission.

56 Inlays of this kind of soft limestone were probably used for the sculptured wall decorations of the interior of the Tempio Malatestiano. Theuer (p. 613), arguing from this passage and the fact that the main front had not been finished by 1454, suggests that this part of the work could not have been written earlier. In view, however, of Alberti's rule that stone should be seasoned for two years at least before use (II, 8) and the fact that Sigismondo Malatesta had already rifled some marble slabs from S. Apollinare in Classe in Ravenna in 1449, Theuer's evidence cannot be accepted as conclusive. Cf. also Mitchell, *op. cit.*

57 Although this contempt for omens and superstition was frequently expressed by Alberti, he attached a great deal of importance both to ' seasonability '—a notion much more akin to astrology than he would allow one to suppose—and to the sound and charm of a name. He had added Leone to his own baptismal name of Battista late in life (Michel suggests that he did so on entering Pomponio Leto's Academy) ; there is a further passage on the importance of names in VI, 4. Cf. Michel pp. 51, 501–3. The custom of Latinizing names or of taking a new name with a Classical allusion, was, of course, common among the humanists.

58 Virgil, *Eclogues* III, 60. ' With Jove I begin, you Muses ; all things are filled with Jove.' Michel discusses this line (pp. 538–40) without mentioning the fact that it is a direct quotation from Virgil, and has little reference to Alberti's belief in Divine immanence.

59 Vitruvius (IX, Introduction, vi) attributes the invention of this tool to Pythagoras, and, of course, it is an obvious application of Pythagoras' theorem. But the knotted rope was probably known throughout the ancient East.

60 ' Vuolsi aiutare quel che fatto é, non guastare quello che s'abbia a fare ', wrote Alberti to Matteo de' Pasti, the site architect of S. Francesco in Rimini. ' We should improve that which has already been done, not wreck that which

we are going to replace.' Wittkower
(p. 37) discusses Alberti's application of
this principle.

61 Theuer has suggested that this is the only
reference to a lost treatise, *Commentarii
Rerum Mathematicarum*, which, however,
is not included in Michel's bibliography.

62 Compare with the descriptions of such
ducts in S. Marco in Venice in I, 8.
Also below in III, 6.

63 I.e., the Mausoleum of Hadrian, which
has a concrete base.

64 Near the Tarpeian Rock; this was
usually assumed to be a part of the Capitol
to the south-west of the Tablinium.

65 Books IV, 8, and X, 10.

66 Bartoli translates ' South-West ', Theuer
' South ', Leoni ' North-West '. The
precise situation of this passage is uncertain. The temple of Vespasian which
backs on to the Capitol did not reach its
present ruined state until the end of the
sixteenth century, and as long as most
of the inscription on the entablature
remained intact, it was correctly identified. Palladio (IV, 70–2) restored it as
the temple of Jupiter Tonans, Desgodetz
records the same identification, while a
late sixteenth-century engraving by du
Pérac says that its dedication is unknown.
Palladio, in his reconstruction, records a
passage between temple and the wall of
the basement of the Tablinium, the west
side of the temple.

67 Cf. above I, 8, and III, 3.

68 Such staircases may be seen in the Basilica
of Constantine—which Alberti has mentioned before (I, 8).

69 ' Ossa.' This organic metaphor is used
by Alberti consistently throughout his
discussion of the structure.

70 Although Vituivius (II, 8) begins by
dividing masonry into two species, he
describes seven; these are subdivisions
of three principal species : ashlar, rubble
and mixed. Alberti systematizes somewhat differently, *opus reticulatum* being
unusual practice in his time.

71 VI, 6.

72 ' Nigriscans '—darkened, rather than
' turned black '.

73 Heavy wooden mallet.

74 This is almost philological procedure ;

a present abuse is corrected by reference
to the practice of the ancients.

75 Book V, 6, and VII, 15.

76 The dome of Florence Cathedral was
built in this way by Brunelleschi.

77 Vitruvius II, 1 (v); though Vitruvius
calls them Phrygenses, the Phrygians.

78 Cf. Vitruvius VII, 1.

79 Book VIII, 10.

80 This gloss on I, 1, is followed by a distinction of building according to its function
and the class of the occupier.

81 This division tallies with that of Vitruvius I, 2 (viii).

82 The city is subject to the same criteria
of excellence as all other works of art.
Cf. VI, 2.

83 This chapter is parallel to Vitruvius I, 4;
there are, however, considerable differences.

84 The example quoted but criticised is that
found in Vitruvius I, 5 (ii) and (v).

85 Perugia.

86 This advice, supported by the quotation
from Tacitus, contradicts Vitruvius'
opinion in I, 5 (iii) that the city should
have an unbroken circuit of walls. However, much material in this and the following chapter is drawn from Vitruvius
I, 5.

87 67° 30' and 60°.

88 Book X, 6.

89 Books V, 12, and X, 10.

90 Books VII and VIII.

91 This apparently fanciful piece of ety-
mology appears to be an interpretation
of Macrobius, *Saturnalia* II, 10.

92 Book V, 17.

93 Below, Book IV, 4.

94 In his dialogue *Pontifex* composed in
1437, Alberti expresses his views of the
duties of bishops in particular and priests
in general through the mouths of the two
interlocutors Paolo Bishop of Ascoli,
and Alberto di Giovanni Bishop of
Camerino, both members of the Alberti
family. The dialogue may well have
been the account of a discussion which
actually took place. Michel, p. 25 ;
bibl. XX.

95 ' Nigregeneus ' has remained uncorrecten
in all editions but Theuer's. Hoffmdn
(p. 42) pointed out that this passage oa

the location of temples is drawn from a treatise *De Limitibus*—'About Boundaries', by Hyginus Gromaticus.

96 In Book VII.

97 Described in Vitruvius V, 11.

98 Book VIII, 8. These two passages are Dehio's basis for his attribution of Nicholas V's scheme for the restoration of the Borgo Leonino to Alberti on this passage and that in VIII, 8. These plans have been discussed at length, and a new restoration attempted by Torgil Magnuson. Cf. Bibliography.

99 So also Vitruvius I, 2 (vii).

00 Alberti does not keep his promise in this case. It has been suggested by Theuer (p. 616) that Alberti had intended to write a separate book about siegeworks, following Vitruvius (X, 10–16), but the treatise was never written.

01 The raising of a part of one of the ships which had lain at the bottom of Lake Nemi since the time of Trajan was one of Alberti's most famous exploits. 'All the finest spirits (i più belli ingegni) of the Roman court came to examine it', wrote Flavio Biondo (*op. cit.*). This event took place in 1446, and consequently the book must already have been begun at that early date. See below X, 7, and note 274.

02 This treatise was known until the middle of the sixteenth century, but is now lost. Michel, p. 32; XXXI.

03 'Ponte' in the Black Sea.

04 VIII, 9.

05 In I, 9.

06 Vitruvius V, 5, makes similar distinctions.

07 The term 'Villa' in this passage refers both to country retreats and to farmhouses. A short treatise *Villa*, published for the first time recently (RINASCIMENTO IV, 1953, No. 1), by Cecil Grayson, provides an interesting commentary on this passage.

08 An interpretation and criticism of Vitruvius VI, 4.

09 'Nos autem sinum appelabimus' (we however shall call the heart). Vitruvius (VI, 3) calls it Atrium or Cavaedium.

10 Book VII, 4 (iv).

11 Book X, 11.

12 Much information in this chapter is drawn from Vitruvius VI, 4.

113 Theuer has taken this passage to indicate the long interruption between the writing of Books I–V and the rest of the work (p. 605, n. 13). A sentence on the following page would seem to support Theuer's contention: 'Thus I stood doubtful, and knew not how to resolve . . .'.

114 This reads like a general condemnation of Vitruvius. But Alberti has so far quoted him several times with approval, even if he has been somewhat critical. On one point, however, Alberti has been consistent: he has refused the help of Vitruvius' Greek terminology as in II, 10. This refusal to make use of Greek technical terms will be particularly noticeable in the second half of the work. In fact, Alberti has attempted to create a purely Latin terminology. Cf. for instance VI, 13, and VII, 5.

115 This rather negative definition of beauty is characteristic of Alberti's approach to the theory of art. He does not seek an *a priori* definition, but prefers the datum of experience as a starting point. Economy, for him, is not only a moral, but also an artistic principle—since the optimum point is that after which anything added would be superfluous and anything taken away detract, disturbing the unity of the work. For a discussion of this idea in the context of Alberti's philosophy see Petrini's essay, particularly the section on *Aurea Mediocritas*. This definition is echoed throughout the book. Cf. below I, 10; IV, 2; and above VII, 10; IX, 8.

116 Alberti means Mesopotamia and Egypt.

117 Latin 'frugalitas' has no pejorative meaning—it is temperance, modesty; sometimes it is used as a synonym for virtue.

118 Roman architects were, to the mind of Alberti, superior to the ever-subtle Greeks; they approached nature more directly, having understood how nature is governed by economy. The tradition of Etruscan temple building as transmitted by Vitruvius (IV, 7) is modified by Alberti above (VII, 4).

119 For a fuller treatment of the creative process, cf. IX, 10, above.

120 Cf. footnote 20.

121 Although echoing an idea which had become a commonplace in Italian thought since Petrarch, this seems to be the first positive mention of ruins as part of a chosen or designed landscape. They were, of course, to have a didactic and not an ornamental purpose.

122 In Crete, not Ceylon.

123 Below, in Chapters 9, 10.

124 On the importance of names, cf. footnote 57.

125 Vitruvius X, 2 (xi). Vitruvius has Chersiphron, not Ctesiphon.

126 Theuer, following Mancini, suggests that he did so in the lost treatise *de Motibus Ponderis.* Cf. Michel, p. 33; XXXIII.

127 As Leonardo had already noticed, Alberti had mistakenly spoken of the sum—*collectio*—and given the numbers wrongly. Leoni, following Bartoli, has translated *collecti sunt* as 'multiplied together', but has left the numbers in the example a sum.

128 Cf. Vitruvius X, 2 and 3.

129 Theuer suggests the treatise *dei Pondi lieve e tirari* (Michel XXXIV, p. 33) which has now been ascribed to Alberti.

130 This chapter draws much on Vitruvius VII, 2–5.

131 Cf. Vitruvius VII, 1 (iv).

132 The bronze structure of the portico roof of the Pantheon—the portico of Agrippa—which Alberti admired, was removed by order of Pope Urban VIII in 1632, and the bronze melted down for the ciborium of S. Peter's and cannon for Castel Sant'Angelo.

133 Presumably a reference to II, 6; where it is the cypress doors, and not the cedar roof, which are described.

134 The following paragraph has been omitted by Bartoli, and hence by Leoni : ' I have stated that as far as I was able I would express myself in sound Latin and as clearly as possible. I must therefore invent words, when those in current use are inadequate ; and it seemed best to draw these terms, by analogy, from familiar things. We Tuscans call a fillet that narrow band with which girls dress and bind their hair ; I would therefore like, if I may, to call the band which encircles the end of the column like a hoop, the fillet. The other moulding, at the top next to the fillet, which is tied round the end of the shaft like a twisted cord, we shall call *collar*'. Leoni translates 'collar' as ' astragal ' ; the neologism ' astragal ', which has a Greek root, would hardly therefore have pleased Alberti. The promise referred to is that above, in VI, 1.

135 Below, VII, 7.

136 Vitruvius (III, 3, xiii) refers the reader to an illustration at the end of the book. No MS., however, has such an illustration. Alberti was the first to prescribe a method of forming the swelling (usually known by the Greek name by which it is described by Vitruvius, entasis). This method was not followed by subsequent theorists ; at one point indeed—the quadrant which begins the return of the lower diminution—it cannot be constructed according to Alberti's specification. It is worth noticing that Alberti describes the procedure in terms which are obviously drawn from current practice, and possibly from his own experience.

137 The translation of this passage is a little misleading ; cf. Wittkower, p. 6. The relation between human justice and the ' giving of due deserts ' to the deity is linked in Latin by a ' since '. The last phrase runs : ' For this reason a basilica may also, if you think fit, be dedicated to religion '. But this should not be taken as a justification of the use of the basilican plan for church buildings, but rather as a *post facto* justification of the use of ancient basilicas for churches. On the distinction between the Basilica and the Church, cf. below, VII, 8.

138 Vitruvius I, 7, (i) and (ii). Although describing the pagan temples as if he himself were a pagan, Alberti's religious views were orthodox, while he inclined to those who demanded a measure of reform. The pagan gods he regarded as personifications of human passions. Cf. Momus, Prohemium, and Michel, p. 543, where Alberti's religious views are discussed at some length. Cf. also *Psalmi*

Precationum (Michel, p. 33; XXXV), C. Grayson, *Alcuni Opuscoli Inediti di Leon Battista Alberti*, Preface and especially 25–41. Cf. also Mario Petrini's essay.

139 Hypaetheral temples are not, however, recommended by Alberti when he discusses the matter more fully further on in this book.

140 Vitruvius IV, 9.

141 Book VIII, 9.

142 Cf. Vitruvius I, 2 (v).

143 This and the following chapters are considered in Wittkower, pp. 3–9 and 24–8.

144 The analagous chapter in Vitruvius (IV, 4) is very different. No descriptions of circular temples are given, for instance; these are relegated to a later chapter (IV, 8). Etruscan temples also have a chapter to themselves (IV, 7). Alberti's Etruscan temple retained an analogous proportional scheme to that of Vitruvius': both have a plan consisting of a 5/6 rectangle. An interpretation of it may be seen actually carried out in his scheme for the Church of S. Andrea, at Mantua; writing to his patron Lodovico Gonzaga on the 19th October 1470, he describes the shape of the church as ' called, after the ancients, *Etruscum sacrum* '. Theuer (pp. 619–20) has pointed out certain analogies between the Basilica of Constantine (Templum Pacis—cf. I, 8, note 30) as it has been restored by Palladio Book II, pp. 12–13, and Serlio III, pp. 21–22. This reconstruction, however, involves the addition of a great portico on to the remains of the Basilica, and the narrowing of the bays by a third. But Theuer's suggestion that this passage is a compromise between Alberti's presumed reconstruction of the Basilica of Constantine and the Vitruvius description of an Etruscan temple offers the most satisfactory suggestion about the source of this passage. Cf. also above, VIII, 10, on the similarity of Etruscan temples to the halls of Thermae.

145 Cf. Vitruvius III, 2. Of the seven categories quoted by Vitruvius, Alberti has only accepted three, while omitting the Greek technical terms: prostyle, amphiprostyle and peripteral. Temples in antis, pseudodipteral, dipteral and hypaetheral temples are omitted, because Alberti was not familiar with any ruins of such temples, and perhaps also because—as Theuer suggests—they were Greek temple-types. Alberti does not discuss circular monopteral temples, nor does he mention temples with porticoes at the side.

146 Cf. Vitruvius III, 1 (iii).

147 Vitruvius III, 1 (iii).

148 Cf. Vitruvius III, 3 (x) and (xi) where exact rules are set out.

149 This passage follows, in the main, the dimensions and classification in Vitruvius III, 3. Greek technical terms have been omitted, however. The ' widest ' intercolumniation which Vitruvius calls 'aræostyle' and disapproves as being clumsy while not mentioning any specific dimensions for it, is here classified as $3\frac{3}{8}$ diameters; it may be worth noting that Vitruvius, in dealing with this intercolumniation, says (III, 3, v): '. . . and their pediments are adorned in the Tuscan fashion with statues of terracotta and gilt bronze . . .'.

150 Cf. also IX, 4, where the same principle is suggested for houses. On the relation between columns and arches in Alberti's theory, cf. Wittkower, pp. 31ff.

151 For an alternative description of the origins and division of the column, cf. I, 10.

152 Vitruvius IV, 1 (iii–ix).

153 As is clear from the text, this is the Composite, and not the Tuscan capital. Several writers (as, for instance, Mancini) have taken it to be the latter.

154 Vitruvius (IV, 3, iv) does not speak of a base for the Doric order. Alberti has also reversed the proportions of the Ionic and Corinthian order. The Latin text gives the proportion as nine diameters for the Ionic and eight for the Corinthian. This order is corrected by Bartoli according to IX, 7, below, where the more usual proportions are given, although most translators have retained the Latin order in this passage.

155 Cf. Vitruvius III, 3 (xii).

156 Cf. end of last chapter.

157 Vitruvius, in describing the Doric order
—IV, 3—speaks of it as without a base;
Alberti's Doric base is identical with
Vitruvius' Attic base. Cf. Vitruvius III,
5 (i–ii). Vitruvius, however, was true to
Greek practice, whereas Alberti's specification must be viewed in the light of
his opinions regarding the origins of the
order. Cf. above in Chapter 6 of this
book.

158 Alberti differs in several details from
Vitruvius' description of the Ionic base.
Cf. Vitruvius III, 5 (iii).

159 As, for instance, the temple at Tivoli.

160 Alberti had in his list established a
strictly Latin nomenclature (cf. above,
VI, 1). That the English version should
return to the terminology of Vitruvius
shows that later academic architects set
greater store by his authority than Alberti
had done.

161 Cf. Vitruvius III, 5 (xi).

162 The first of these two capitals follows,
while supplementing some details, the
example in Vitruvius IV, 3 (iv); the
second must be based on observation,
as suggested by Theuer (p. 623). Alberti
seems to have favoured the use of a
cymatium instead of annulets.
Alberti was taken to task by some later
writers for this second capital: Fréart de
Chambray calls it a ' chapiteau tout
gothique ' and speaks of ' ce mauvais
gout ... cette composition disgracié ...'.
Alberti made use of a similar capital in
the lowest order of the Palazzo Rucellai.

163 There are considerable differences between the capital suggested by Alberti
and that suggested by Vitruvius in III,
5 (v–viii). The most notable, perhaps,
is the drawing of the volute in semicircles
instead of quadrants, as recommended
by Vitruvius, so that the volute acquires
a more elliptical and squashed appearance. Whereas Vitruvius visualizes the
lines of the volutes as *catheti*, perpendicular lines, Alberti describes the volute as
cortex, rind. Vitruvius' linear element
has become a plane.

164 The Latin text omits the dimension here.

165 The capital is again based on that of
Vitruvius IV, 1 (xi), though again several
dimensions not specified by Vitruvius

are introduced. Following Brunelleschi's
practice, Alberti seems to have departed
from the specification of Vitruvius in
making no distinction between the
height of the inner and outer volutes of
the capital.

166 The Italian capital is now known as the
Composite. Alberti had no precedent
for this description in Vitruvius; it may
be assumed, as no contrary indication
is given, that the general proportions of
the Composite order follow that of the
Corinthian. This description may be
compared with the somewhat bizarre
capital used by Alberti on the front of
the Tempio Malatestiano.

167 Cf. Vitruvius IV, 1 (xii).

168 Cf. Vitruvius III, 5 (ix–xiii).

169 The differences between the cornices
described respectively by Vitruvius and
Alberti are even more considerable than
in the case of capitals. The most conspicuous difference in the case of the
Doric entablature is the prescription of
three instead of the usual two furrows in
the triglyph. Theuer (p. 625) has
pointed out certain resemblances between
the Doric entablature of Alberti, and the
entablature of the Basilica Æmilia which
was still standing in the fifteenth century,
and had been drawn by G. B. da Sangallo
(cf. Hulsen, *Il libro di G. da San Gallo*,
plate Q).

170 Cf. Vitruvius III, 5 (viii). Alberti has
considerably simplified Vitruvius' rule by
not specifying for columns between 15
feet and 20 feet, which Vitruvius puts
outside the series—$\frac{1}{2}$ diameter, i.e., 1/19
of the height, and reducing Vitruvius'
other proportions, 1/13, 1/12$\frac{1}{2}$, 1/12 to
1/13, 1/12, 1/11.

171 The Ionic architrave with two fascias
follows approximately that described by
Vitruvius. Owing to a mistake in the
numbering of the Latin text it is difficult
to decide on which monuments Alberti
had based his proportions. He had
made use of such an architrave himself
at the Tempio Malatestiano and S. Pancrazio in Florence.

172 Cf. Vitruvius III, 5 (x) and (xv).

173 Vitruvius does not make this distinction,
nor is it sanctioned by any remaining

examples except late Classical ones, such as the Basilica of Constantine or the temple of Vespasian.

174 Cf. Vitruvius III, 5 (xi) and IV, 4 (ii). Alberti follows Vitruvius in the main outlines, but omits much of Vitruvius' detailed specification.

175 Cf. Vitruvius III, 5 (xiv) and IV, 3 (ix). Vitruvius does not mention spiral fluting.

176 Cf. Vitruvius IV, 3 (iii). Vitruvius recommends 26–7 parts in the case of four columns, 42–4 if there are six; editors have varied the number of parts.

177 Cf. Vitruvius III, 3 (vii).

178 On the number of steps, cf. below, I, 13.

179 Theuer (p. 628) has pointed out that Alberti applied this principle in his project for the choir of the SSma. Annunziata.

180 The proportion 4 : 11 appears to be completely foreign to Alberti's theory; cf. Wittkower, p. 7. Theuer (p. 628) has given an ingenious explanation of this ratio, based on a then-accepted value of $\pi = 13/4$. This explanation, which involves a rather coarse approximation, is more ingenious than convincing. The cross reference to the proportions of a *curial* hall in VIII, 9, does not really reinforce Theuer's case.

181 The reference is to some form of coffered decoration, such as that in the Basilica of Constantine.

182 Of Alberti's surviving building, such coffered vaults may be found under the main entrance arch of S. Maria Novella in Florence and in the porch of S. Andrea in Mantua.

183 Cf. Vitruvius III, 5 (xii). Vitruvius specified that the height of the tympanum should be one-ninth of the cornice along the Corona; Alberti's measurements give a much steeper pitch to the roof, and hence a somewhat bigger tympanum.

184 Although doors are treated much in the same way by Alberti and Vitruvius, Alberti has, as in most previous examples, ironed out the proportions specified by Vitruvius (IV, 6) whose text is, in any case, somewhat corrupt at this point. All door proportions are 1 : 2, and the method of varying the width of the whole opening in proportion to the height is

abandoned. Instead, all doors are to be narrowed by 1/14 of the width, a rule suggested by Vitruvius for the narrowing of the door jambs.

185 Cf. Vitruvius IV, 6 (iv) and (v); Alberti made the thickness of the leaves of the door identical with Vitruvius' width of the stile.

186 Vitruvius explicitly says that altars should vary in proportion, depending on the deity to which they are dedicated (IV, 9); most ancient altars are higher than they are wide. Alberti's altar is more like an early Christian than a pagan one.

187 The rebuke, which looks somewhat less startling in the Latin text, is taken by Theuer to refer to the nepotism practised by Calixtus III (1455–8), the first Borgia pope, who succeeded Nicholas V in 1455; he suggests 1455 as a *terminus a quo* for this passage.

The appeal to patristic literature, the stated desire for ecclesiastical reform, which appear here in conjunction with an all but express disapproval of more than one altar in a church, point to the close relation—at the most obvious level—between Alberti's professed religious views expressed in books such as his life of S. Potitus, and his theory of architecture. This connection had been questioned by some earlier authorities, but is reaffirmed by Wittkower, pp. 3–9 and 24–8. It may be worth noting that the following sentences were condemned by the Spanish index of 1611.

188 The dimensions have been omitted in all printed versions. The French translator, Jean Martin, has taken this description to refer to the seven-branched candlestick of the temple in Jerusalem.

189 Cf. Chapter 5 of this book.

190 Cf. below, Book VIII, 11.

191 Cf. below, VII, 2, and note. There is little reference here to Vitruvius V, 1, which deals with basilicas, and no mention of his famous basilica at Fano. The recommendation to make the height of the basilica 1½ times its width seems extremely improbable; Theuer has suggested that the Latin word *spatium* which Leoni translates 'front', be here taken to apply to the nave only. This would

give a result much more consonant with the many examples of basilican buildings with which Alberti must have been familiar.

192 A system, reconciling the arch and the column, was used by Brunelleschi in the loggia of the Foundling hospital, and later in S. Spirito and S. Lorenzo. Alberti himself, though not easy about the use of column and arch (cf. below, VII, 6; and Wittkower, p. 31) had used it in the Rucellai loggia.

193 Cf. below, Book III, 6.

194 A round church, S. Stefano Rotondo, was restored during the reign of Nicholas V. This work was probably carried out by Alberti (Mancini, pp. 338ff.), and it may be this church which he describes as a round basilica.

195 Cf. *De Statua* (Leoni), p. 30r, where the two places mentioned are Pharos and Carrara.

196 This idea is elaborated in *De Pictura* (Leoni), p. 19v.

197 Above, VI, 2.

198 The mausoleum of Augustus, between the upper end of the Corso and the bank of the Tiber, is now little more than a heap of rubble. But during the Middle Ages it had been used by the Colonna family as a fortress, and here a member of that family had Cola di Rienzi's body burnt— in derision perhaps—in 1367. But in the fifteenth century the mausoleum, like so many other monuments, was reduced to the status of a quarry. It was used more recently as a bull ring and in the nineteenth century was the site of a concert hall, which was demolished in the archaeological clean-up of the 1930's.

199 As the remark about 'enriching the column' with 'stories in relief' and interior spiral staircases indicates, Alberti had in mind the two columns of Trajan and Marcus Aurelius; Theuer suggests, in fact, that the dimensions, especially those of the pedestals separated by a plinth, were based on those of the second column.

200 Alberti must have had in mind principally, when setting out the dimensions of the mausoleum, the mausoleum of Hadrian and the tomb of Cecilia Metella;

and he probably knew many more ancient tombs now destroyed. The roads leading out of Rome were lined with some 300,000 tombs in antiquity; and there were many more left in the fifteenth century than there are now.

201 Egyptian hieroglyphs were regarded by humanists as visual equivalents of the epigram or the charm. Their interpretation of hieroglyphic inscriptions was based on a Greek treatise of the second or fourth century, the *Hieroglyphica*, which purported to be a translation of an Egyptian text by Horus Apollo or Horapollo. It was first printed by Aldus in 1505, though the text was known in Florence in the 1420's. It appears to have been familiar to Alberti, whose emblem —the winged eye, with the motto *Quid Tum*—was based on an Egyptian model. It is discussed by L. Volkmann in *Bilderschriften der Renaissance*, Leipzig 1923, pp. 10–11. Through the *Hypnerotomachia Polyphili* this passage has had an influence on subsequent emblem literature. Cf. Mario Praz, *Studies in XVIIth Century Imagery*, London 1939, pp. 19–20. An episode concerned with Bramante's interest in hieroglyphics is related in *Hypnerotomachiana* by E. H. Gombrich (Part I, Bramante, and the *Hypnerotomachia Polyphili*), JOURNAL OF THE COURTAULD AND WARBURG INSTITUTES, XIV, p. 119.

202 As, for instance, the little town of San Gimignano, in Tuscany. Though the Roman Forum seems to have been crowded with towers during the Middle Ages.

203 There are no references to superimposed orders in the chapters concerned with the ornaments of temples. The mistake is due only to a mispunctuation. The translation should, therefore, run as follows: '. . . against which we may set columns, in the same manner as in temples. At the third, as on the fourth and fifth story, we may set rotondas. We shall make our rotondas three in number, and which . . .'.

204 There must be some mistake in this specification; the dimensions have never been amended; but a calculation would

shows that the fifth story reaches the full height of the tower.

05 Alberti's theoretical tower—which has never been executed, though the description has had considerable influence on later architects—follows his principle of emulating of antiquity; the main proportions are indicated in a way analogous to the general proportions of the column.

06 On 19th December, 1450, a crown returning from S. Peter's panicked, and broke through the balustrades of the Bridge of Hadrian (Ponte Sant'Angelo). Nicholas V had the bridge restored, and erected two chapels at its head. Vasari records that he had in his possession a drawing made by Alberti of the Ponte Sant'Angelo covered by a loggia.

07 Cf. Book IV, 6.

08 Cf. Vitruvius V, 1 (i–iii).

09 Cf. above, V, 8, and Torgil Magnuson, *op. cit.*

10 This description is clearly based on the two arches of Constantine and Septimus Severus in Rome. It would be more consonant with the measurements of these arches if, as Theuer has suggested (p. 635), ' a basi infima ', here translated as ' the lowest basement ', be taken to mean the base of the column, excluding the pedestals. Alberti's use of the triumphal column is discussed by Wittkower, pp. 33ff.

11 The three theatres were those of Pompey on a site near the Campo dei Fiori, of Balbus on the site of the Palazzo Cenci some yards east, and of Marcellus a little farther on. This last is the best preserved of the three. The other two buildings mentioned are the Colosseum and the Circus Maximus, between the Aventine and the Palatine.

12 This same information is given by Flavio Biondo on the authority of Cassiodorus. *Roma Ristaurata* III, 21.

13 Cf. Vitruvius V, 3 (ii) and (v) and 9 (i).

14 Vitruvius V, 6 and 7, describes the Roman and Greek theatre, giving a chapter to each, while Alberti quotes both methods of planning, without drawing the same distinction.

15 The Latin text—' the breadth twice half the height '—is evidently corrupt, and in the corresponding passage in Vitruvius (V, 6, iii) the dimensions are given as between 1¼ feet and 1⅜ feet high, and 2 feet to 2½ feet broad.

216 Serlio illustrated these three types of scenery in the *Tutte l'Opere* II, 26–7.

217 Cf. Vitruvius V, 3, 6 and 7 for much of the above.

218 Alberti seems to be the first to use this image.

219 Alberti made no such description in connection with basilicas.

220 For the description of acoustic vases, cf. Vitruvius V, 4 and 5.

221 Since the only theatre of which enough remained to allow of restoration—that of Marcellus—was not even partially freed from post-Classical accretions until the 1520's, Alberti had had to rely more on Vitruvius than in other parts of the book, and he has had to supplement data with details taken from amphitheatres.

222 Alberti does not mention its elliptical shape.

223 The Circus of Maxentius on the via Appia near the tomb of Cecilia Metella, was the best preserved of the ancient circuses.

224 For the above passage, cf. Vitruvius V, 9 (ii–v) and 11 (i–ii).

225 Alberti has identified Vitruvius' Palæstra (V, 11) with his porticoes and covered walks connected with the theatre (V, 9) while omitting most of the subsidiary rooms, recommended by Vitruvius for the Palæstra following Greek usage. It is interesting to note that he interprets Vitruvius' recommendation to make the central row of columns of the south portico Ionic, as being done ' displuviandi tecti gratia '—to give a slope to the roof, in Leoni's words. Vitruvius was almost certainly thinking of a flat ceiling, which Alberti says he would have preferred.

226 ' Quadrangulas '—rectangular; though all other translators have ' square '. Cf. Vitruvius V, 2. The building, which was probably known as the *Curia* in Alberti's day, was the Curia Julia near the Forum, which Honorius I had dedicated as the church S. Hadrian in Tribus Fatis. Du Pérac, however, in an

engraving dated 1576, calls it the temple of Saturn, whereas the temple of Saturn was, in its turn, known as the temple of Concord both to du Pérac and to Palladio (IV, p. 124). The Curia, however, had no apse; and Theuer suggests as another likely source for Alberti's observations the temple of Venus and Rome which was known as the temple of Sol and Luna. Palladio, IV, 36ff. Theuer's further suggestion that the dissonant ratio 6/7 specified for the height of the wall by Alberti is parallel to the ratio 11/4 (total height of the Curia to half the diameter)—8/3.5=9.5, 9.5 : 3.5 is approximately 11 : 4—is rather unconvincing. This dissonant is not used by Alberti. For its use by Palladio, cf. Wittkower, p. 118, n. 2.

227 Cf. below, VII, 4, and note.

228 Alberti was familiar with the ruins of the Imperial Thermae, especially those of Caracalla and Diocletian, and therefore does not rely on Vitruvius' description of comparatively very small baths in V, 10.

229 The marbles are named in the Latin text —they are Carrara and Travertine.

230 The principle enunciated in VI, 2, is applied to architecture.

231 Such columns were, of course, much more common in Byzantine and Proto-Renaissance than in Classical building. But Piranesi records a square column with two half-columns attached 'ante Xenodochium Sanctae Mariae Consolationis' and two further ones 'in Aedibus Maximorum'. Palladio has also recorded such columns in the temple near Trevi. Cf. Palladio, IV, pp. 98–102.

232 For these measurements, cf. Vitruvius II, 8 (xvii).

233 Cf. above *loc. cit.*, the circular vestibule was not, at the time of writing nor did it ever become, a common feature of domestic architecture. Though such a suggestion would—*a priori*—have seemed agreeable to Alberti.

234 Cf. above, V, 4 and 10.

235 The last length-to-breadth dimension, 5/7 replaces the dimension specified by Vitruvius (VI, 3, iii)—diagonal of the square, the other two dimensions are as

given by Vitruvius. Alberti's hesitation in specifying the height was probably due to the fact that it seemed disproportionate to him. In fact, Vitruvius specifies 3/4, not 4/3, as the proportion of height to length.

236 Alberti writes of such problems in the *Ludi Matematici*, Michel, p. 32; XXXII.

237 In Book VIII, 7.

238 In many respects, these measurements are parallel to Vitruvius' specification for the 'scena' of a theatre (V, 6, vi). This application of the *scena* front to the facade of a private house had, both because of this passage and of Alberti's application of it in the Palazzo Rucellai in Florence, a great influence on the subsequent history of domestic architecture in Italy.

239 Cf. above, I, 9, and VI, 5.

240 Cf. also VI, 2. The distinction drawn is between 'judgement' which is a rational faculty, and the irrational 'opinion' which we would now call taste. As in his previous treatment of this problem, Alberti deliberately skirts the more complex metaphysical speculation on the origin of rational judgement, and of the notion of the beautiful his point of departure is that of the maker, not that of the spectator. Although he assumes, on the part of the readers, not only the familiarity with the important writers of classical Antiquity, but also an interest in philosophical speculation. Cf. also below, II, 9; VI, 3 and 11.

241 The three categories of number, finishing and collocation—which are subject to congruity—are further explained in this chapter (number and finishing), the next chapter (finishing) and Chapter 7 (finishing and collocation). They are recapitulated in IX, 8. These three categories correspond to the three logical categories of quantity, quality and relation. 'It is certainly true', says Alberti in IX, 8, 'that there can be no error or deformity more shocking than the mixing together either angles or lines or superficies which do not in number, size and situation answer to each other and which have not been matched, balanced, or set

out with the greatest care.' (Leoni loses the force of the retriplication by translating 'comparatas, cozquatas atque compactas' as 'blended together with the greatest care and accuracy'.) Compared with the six categories of Vitruvius (cf. Vitruvius I, 2, and J. A. Jolles, *Vitruvs Aesthetik*, Freiburg im Breisgau, 1906), Alberti's system appears more coherent.

242 This may be compared with the description of the origin of the orders later in this Book, Chapter 7, and Vitruvius IV, 2.

243 I.e., 1 + 8 + 27 + 64. Much of this material is drawn from Macrobius, *In Somnium Scipionis* I, 6. On the perfection of the numbers 6 and 10, cf. also Vitruvius III, 1 (v–ix).

There are no numerical illustrations in any of the Latin editions of Alberti. They were first introduced by Bartoli in his Italian translation of 1550.

244 It should perhaps be stressed that Alberti was not simply 'translating musical ratios into architecture, but is making use of a universal harmony apparent in music'. Cf. Wittkower, *passim*, but particularly pp. 103–10.

245 I.e., simple relations, relations built up of equal intervals, and relations built up of unequal intervals. Throughout, while treating of plan-shapes, Alberti is relying on geometrical properties—*proportio proportionum*, the proportion par excellence. Cf. Wittkower, pp. 98, 99.

246 I.e., $9/16 = (2 \times 9) - (18/16)$.

247 On the use of the irrational root of square, cf. Wittkower, p. 95. Cf. also Vitruvius, VI, 3 (iii), from whom Alberti probably drew it.

248 This is now more usually stated algebraically: $c - b = b - a$; or

$$b = \frac{c + a}{2}.$$

249 The algebraical formula is: $a/b = b/c$; or $ac = b^2$.

250 Now usually called the harmonic mean. Algebraically $b = \frac{2ac}{a+c}$; or $1/b - 1/a = 1/c - 1/b$.

251 The rule, then, stated generally, may be put this way: after determining the length and width of the room by means of the musical ratios stated in the first part of the chapter, the height is determined by taking a mean between them. This should, however, be done in 'musical' congruity with the method of determining the other two dimensions. Cf. Wittkower, p. 98. The whole chapter is discussed in pp. 100–3 where the method of generating ratios is explained.

252 A full table of the dimensions of the human body is given by Alberti at the end of *De Statua* (Leoni, p. 34 r and v). Of the two dimensions given here, one is not cited, and the other is given as 7/10 of a foot; the full height being six feet. Cf. Vitruvius III, 1 (ii).

253 Cf. above, VII, 6–8.

254 Alberti is re-tracing his steps. Cf. above, IX, 5, and note 241. The summary completes Book IX.

255 The whole passage, until the end of the chapter, is an attack on the description of the architect in Vitruvius I, 1 (ii).

256 The *Elementa Pictura* (Michel, p. 24; XIII), which deals at length with the geometrical basis of draughtsmanship.

257 Alberti is known to have worked with three such assistant architects: Matteo dei Pasti for the Tempio Malatestiano, Bernardo Rossellino for the work in Rome, and Luca Fancelli for the two churches in Mantua, for the Tribune of the SSma. Annunziata in Florence, and possibly also for the work at the church of S. Pancrazio.

258 Compare, however, above, V, 3, on tyrants.

259 Cf. Vitruvius III, Preface (ii).

260 This sentence may well have been destined to be the envoy of Alberti's treatise. The Book X is concerned with building, but with the accessories of it: repairs, post removal, waterworks, roads, some advice on farming, etc.

261 Michel, p. 28; XXIII; *Theogenio*, or *de Republica*, which deals with the changing fortunes of a state. The exact date of its composition is uncertain.

262 Following Etruscan custom, the Roman magistrates settled the date on the ides of September when, according to Livy, nails were ceremonially driven into the walls

of the temple of Jupiter on the Capitol.

263 Below, Chapter 8.

264 Paludes, marshes; the shallow parts of the Venetian Lagoon, the *Laguna morta*, still known as *Palude*.

265 This, and much information in the next chapter, is taken from Vitruvius VIII, 3.

266 This pun is borrowed from Servius' commentary on Virgil.

267 Vitruvius VIII, 1 (iii). Much of the material discussed in the remaining section of the book is drawn from Vitruvius Book VIII.

268 Cf. below, II, 7.

269 Cf. below, I, 4.

270 Cf. also Vitruvius V, 9 (vi).

271 Cf. Vitruvius I, 6 (ix).

272 Vitruvius VIII, 6 (i) recommended a fall of $\frac{1}{2}$ in. every 100 feet; Pliny, N.H. XXXI, 31, of $\frac{1}{4}$ in. every 100 feet.

273 This is the only description of surveying given in *De Re Aedificatoria*. It is further described in the *Descriptio Urbis Romae* (Michel, p. 20; X).

274 Fragments of a similar conduit were said by Flavio Biondo to have been found at the bottom of Lake Nemi; he goes on to quote Alberti's opinion that the conduits supplied spring water to pavilions built on the ships which were used as luxury boats.

275 Cf. above, III, 3, and VI, 6.

276 Cf. above, II, 12.

277 For 'pro pontibus' read 'pro portibus'; not bridges therefore, but ports. Cf. above, IV, 8, and VIII, 3.

278 Cf. Vitruvius V, 12.

279 As, for instance, Monte Giordano and Monte Citorio on the Campus Martius and Monte Testaccio on the Aventine.

280 Cf. below, I, 7.

281 Cf. below, VI, 13, where the same method of marking out work is used.

282 Cf. above, III, 13.

283 Cf. above, I, 10.

I Frontispiece.   Florence commends the image of Leon Battista Alberti (based on the woodcut in the second edition of Vasari's *Lives*) to Britannia, who is seated on a throne.   Britannia indicates the image to the personifications of Architecture and of Painting.   The putto attached to Painting, obeying Alberti's advice—'I would likewise have some one figure that may seem to address itself to the spectators of the action . . . beckoning them to come and see . . .' (Painting Book II)—is looking out of the picture and pointing also to the image held by Florence.   The putto flying above holds a streamer inscribed 'his was the greatest worth'.

II Curved lines ; p. 10.

III A. Area of a double square : B. Area of the root of a square ; p. 18.

IV The striking and bonding of triangular bricks, and a wall built of such bricks ; p. 35.

V The drawing of 'radical' lines ; pp. 42–3.

VI A. Retaining wall broken by an arcade ; p. 45 : B. Layout of foundations under columns ; p. 47.

VII A. Regular masonry : B. The bonding of *Opus Reticulatum* : C. Brickwork specially bonded every five feet ; p. 51.

VIII Various methods of effecting a joint in a beam ; p. 56.

IX Camerated (transverse) vaults and metal tie-beams ; p. 59.

X A timber bridge.   The description and the illustration are based on Caesar, *de Bello Gallico*, iv, 17.   The reconstruction in this plate is not wholly correct ; there is only one brace instead of two to hold the crosswise member in, and the protecting piles are too elegant to be true.   Bartoli's woodcut is not very clear.   Palladio had built a bridge designed on similar principles outside Vicenza and his reconstruction (III, p. 6) is much more accurate ; it was followed by Leoni in his edition of Palladio ; p. 76.

XI The suspended arrow as a demonstration of bending moment ; pp. 121–2.

XII Suspensions by single rope, which bears the whole weight ; p. 122.

XIII–XIV The weight borne by two ropes ; and by three ; p. 122.

XV The crane, described on page 123.

XVI A. The forceps ; p. 124 : B. The 'D' shaped wedge.   The 'D' is presumably a Greek 'Δ' ; p. 124.

XVII–XVIII 'Low relieve.'   Half-engaged columns and engaged pilasters ; the cornice is continuous ; p. 130.

XIX–XX 'High relieve.'   Detached columns with and without pilasters ; the cornice is broken in both cases.   The principles observed and the proportions specified are listed on page 130.

XXI The formation of the entasis (swell or belly).   It should be noted that, apart from the impossibility of drawing the lower diminution as specified (cf. footnote 136), Leoni has departed from the specification in several particulars.   So, for instance, the diameter at the widest point of the entasis is 1/12 longer than at the narrowest point of the lower part of the shaft, the lines of the lower part of the column should be parallel.   The diameter of this lower diminution should be 1/7 narrower than the bottom of the shaft, not 1/8.   And so on.   Bartoli's illustration does not specify the dimensions   p. 131.

XXII Construction of polygonal church plans ; p. 138.

XXIII Leoni's interpretation of Alberti's Etruscan temple.   This rather amorphous plan bears no relation to S. Andrea at Mantua, which is Alberti's own interpretation of the Etruscan temple.   Cf. Theuer, Fig. III, 5 and 6, and footnote 144 ; p. 139.

XXIV The Doric base ; p. 142.

XXV The Ionic base ; p. 143.

XXVI Two Doric capitals ; p. 144.

XXVII The Ionic capital ; pp. 144–5.

XXVIII The Corinthian capital ; p. 145.

XXIX The Composite capital ; p. 145.

XXX The Doric entablature ; p. 146.

XXXI The Ionic entablature ; p. 147.

XXXII The Corinthian entablature ; pp. 147–8.

XXXIII The method of setting-out flutes.   The column in the centre of the plate is reticulated to show spiral fluting ; p. 148.

XXXIV Doric intercolumniation ; p. 148.

XXXV Ionic intercolumniation ; p. 148.

XXXVI The Doric order and doorway ; p. 152.

XXXVII The Ionic order and doorway ; p. 152.

XXXVIII The Corinthian order and doorway. This illustration departs from the text and gives a somewhat stunted version of the 'sort of little portico' of page 152; pp. 152–3.

XXXIX–XL Plan and section of a basilica with single aisles. The disproportionate height in all the sections of the basilica may be due to a mistake in the text. Cf. note 191; p. 155.

XLI–XLII Plan and section of a basilica with single aisles and a 'Justiciary nave'; p. 155.

XLIII–XLIV Plan and section of a basilica with double aisles and a 'Justiciary nave'; pp. 155–6.

XLV Monumental column. It should be noted that two plinths of the column are disproportionately slender, that the lower plinth has no lower moulding at all, and that the steps are equal in height, contrary to the specification; pp. 167–8.

XLVI–XLIX Alberti's ideal tower. The structure is too 'free' an interpretation of the text. There is no plinth, for instance, and the detached columns of the lowest story do not tally with the text at all. The general proportions, however, are probably nearer Alberti's intention than in the case of the monumental column; pp. 170–1.

L The bridge. The piers are not blunted, nor do they project as much as specified.

The height is inadequate; pp. 172–3.

LI–LII Plan and section of the Forum. This is a rather pale version of Palladio's Forum of the Latins. Cf. Palladio, III, pp. 33–5. Bartoli's woodcut is very indistinct; p. 173.

LIII–LIV Plan and section of the triumphal arch. On the proportions of the attic, see pages 174–5.

LV–LVII Plan, elevation, section of the amphitheatre. Alberti has given no indication that amphitheatres were elliptical, and the plan here shows a circular amphitheatre; pp. 179–80.

LVIII The circus; p. 180.

LIX The portico for exercise. Both the north and the south sides of the portico should be free of recesses; p. 181.

LX–LXI Plan and section of the *curia*; the tribunal should have an arc and not a semicircular plan. For the square plan see note 225; p. 182.

LXII–LXIII The senate house, plan and section; p. 183.

LXIV Plan of the public baths. The plan drawn here is based on a reconstruction of the baths of Diocletian; pp. 184–5.

LXV 1. A cube, showing the two diagonals: 2. A right-angled triangle. Pythagoras' theorem; p. 199.

LXVI How to find hidden springs; p. 216.

LXVII–LXVIII Surveying; p. 222.

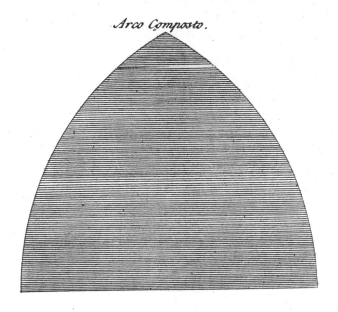

Arco Composto.

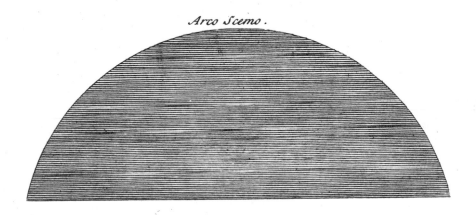

Arco Scemo.

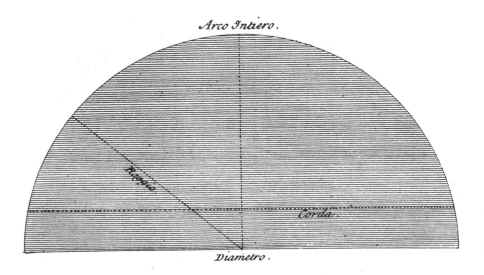

Arco Intiero.

II

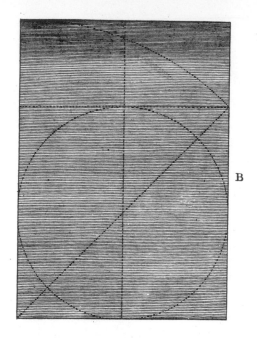

B

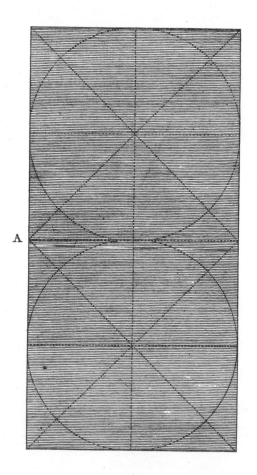

A

III

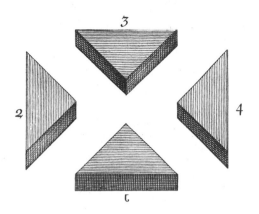

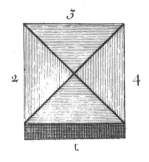

Muraglia di Mattoni Triangolari.

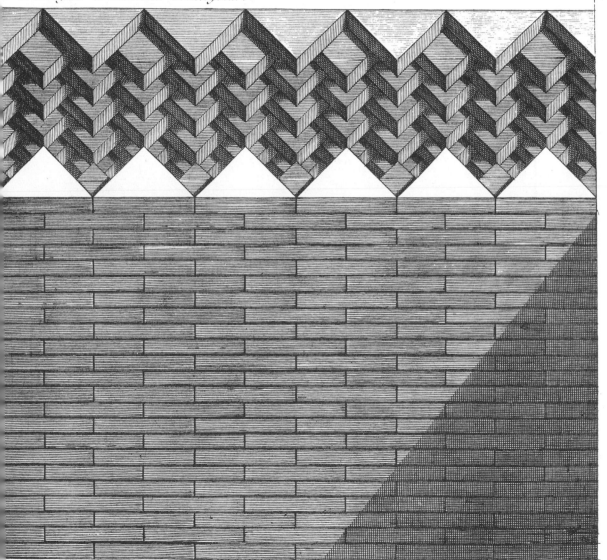

Facciata di Dietro.

Linea Prima.

Chiodo.

Linea Seconda.

Linea Prima.

Facciata d'Inanzi.

v

A.

B.

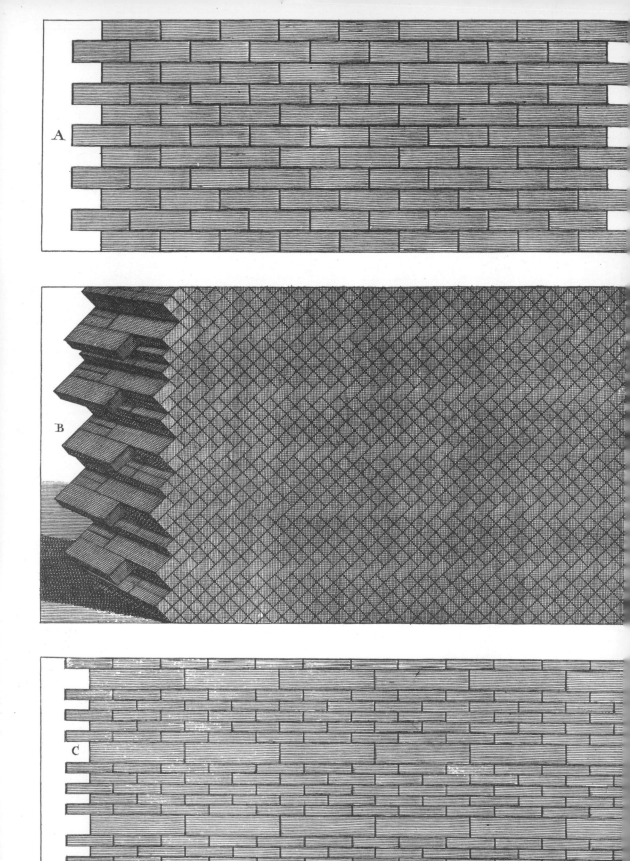

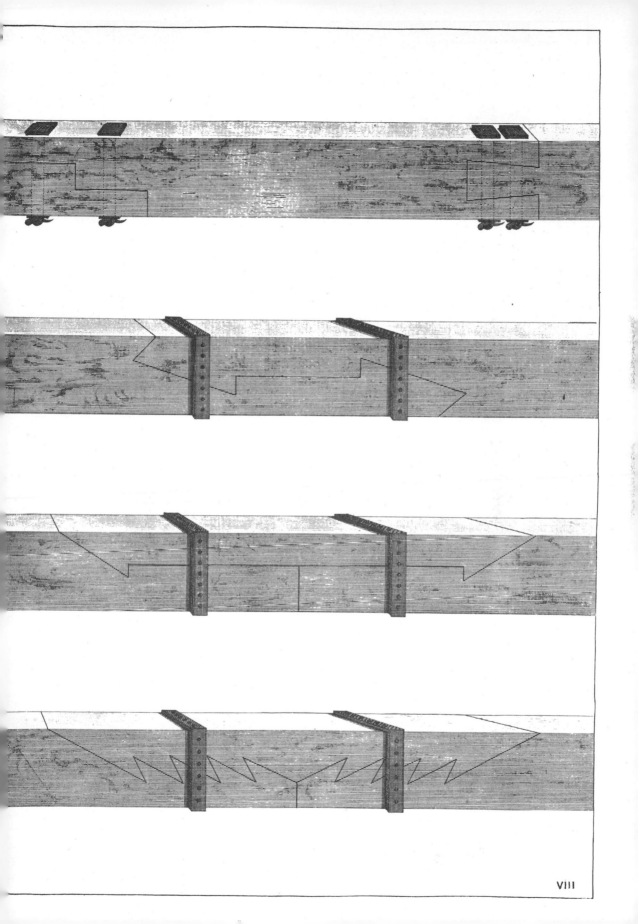

VIII

IX

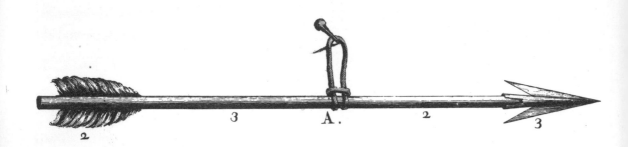

2   3   A.   2   3

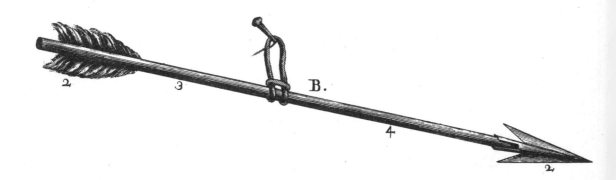

2   3   B.   4   2

XIV

A

B

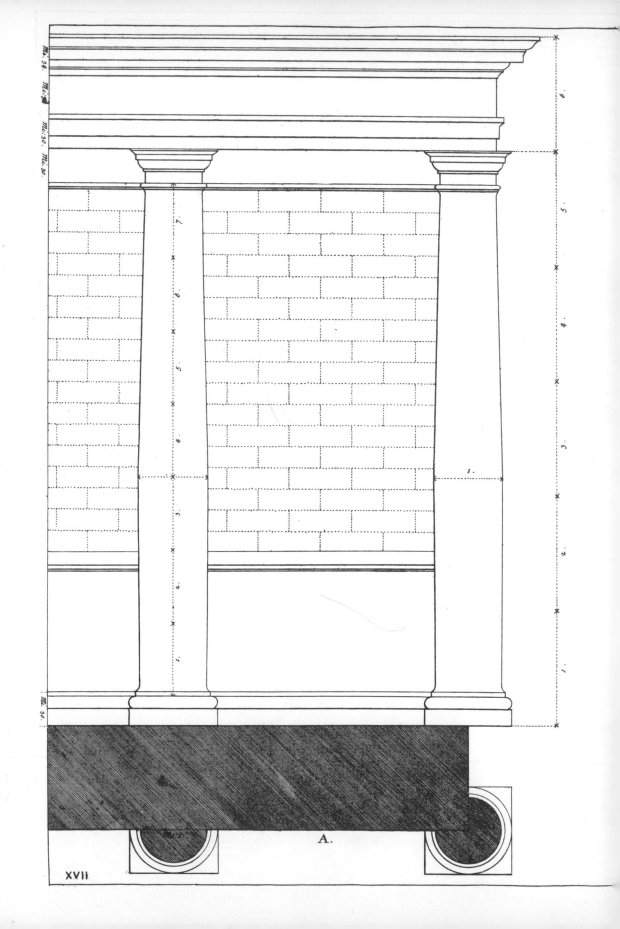

XVII

A.

XVIII

XIX

XX

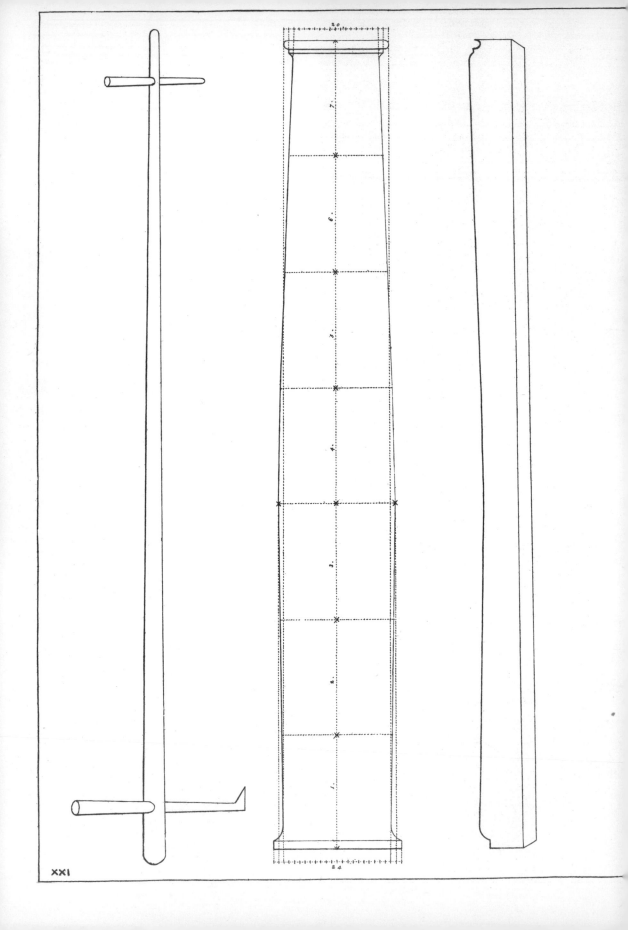

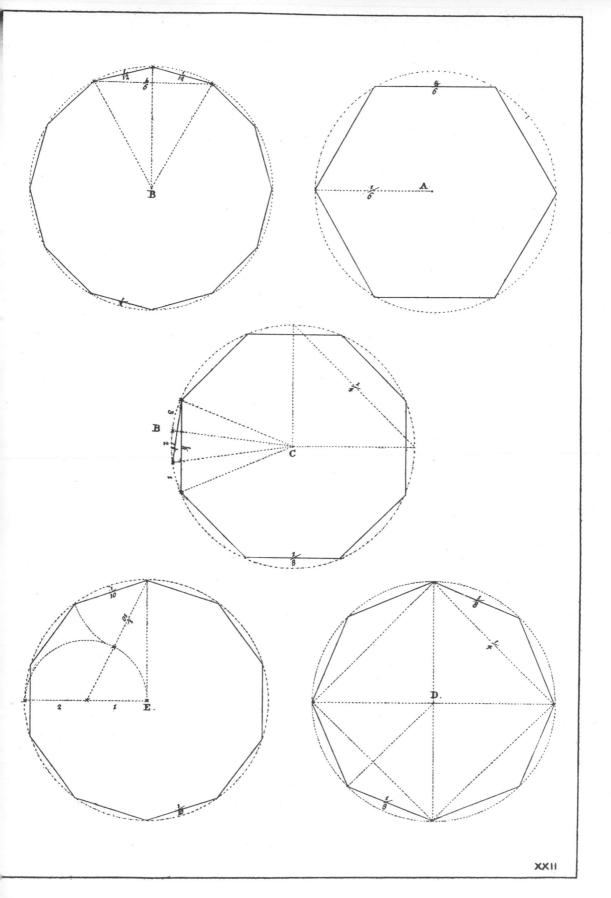

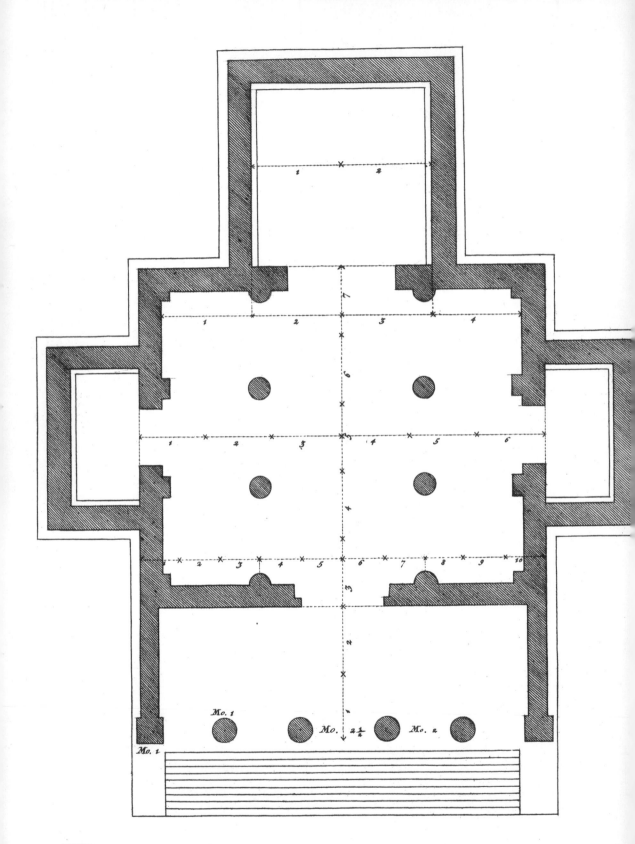

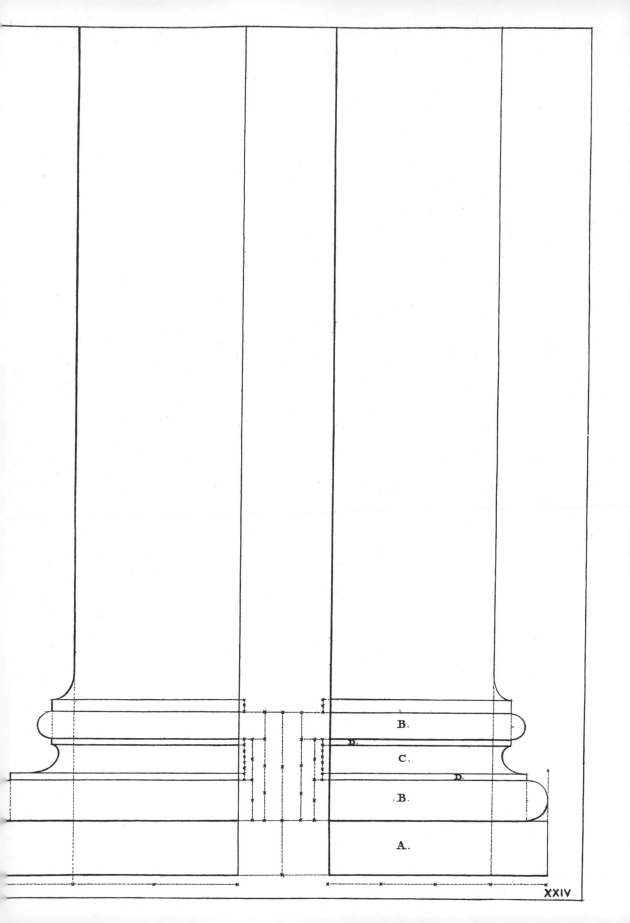

B.

D.

C.

D.

B.

A.

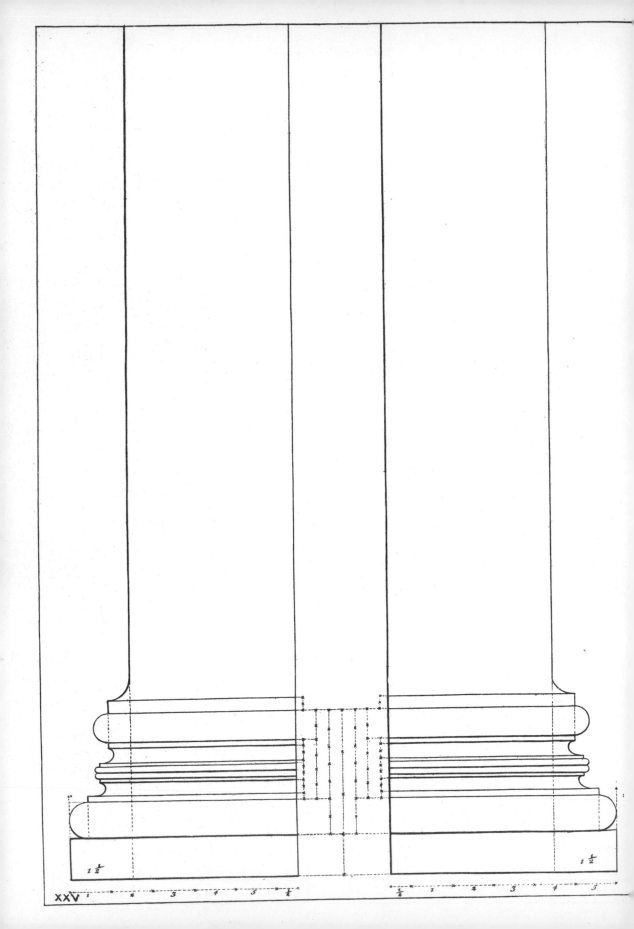

$1\frac{1}{2}$

$1\frac{1}{2}$

XXV   1   2   3   4   5   ¼   ¼   1   2   3   4   5

Capitello Dorico.

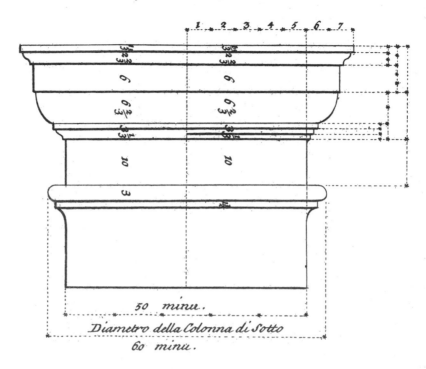

50 minu.

Diametro della Colonna di Sotto
60 minu.

Altro Capitello Dorico.

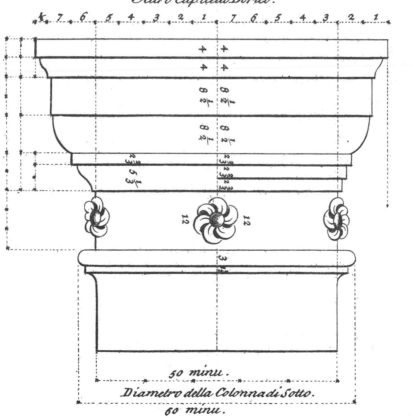

50 minu.

Diametro della Colonna di Sotto.
60 minu.

XXVI

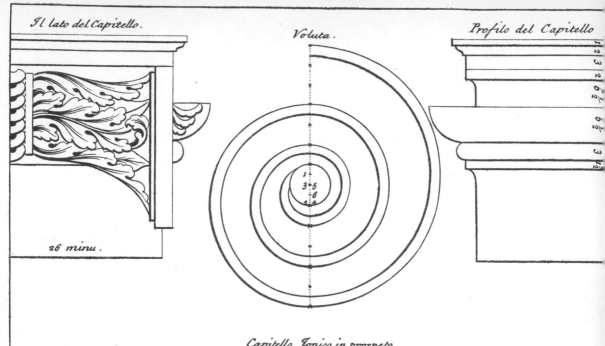

Il lato del Capitello.

Voluta.

Profilo del Capitello

26 minu.

1
3 5
6
2 4

Capitello Jonico in prospeto.

1 2 3 4 5 6 7 8 9 10 11 12 13 14 15 16 17 2

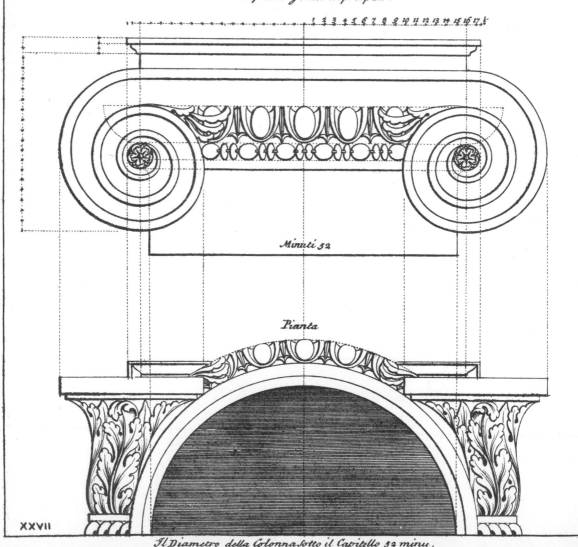

Minuti 52

Pianta

XXVII

Il Diametro della Colonna sotto il Capitello 52 minu.

Capitello Corinthio.

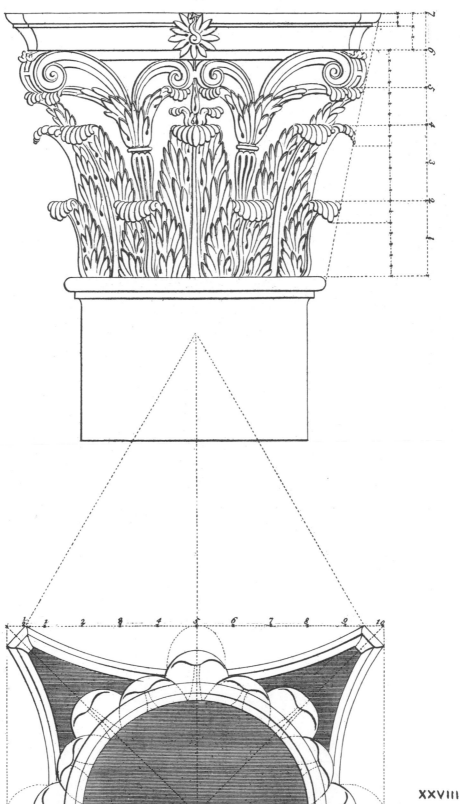

XXVIII

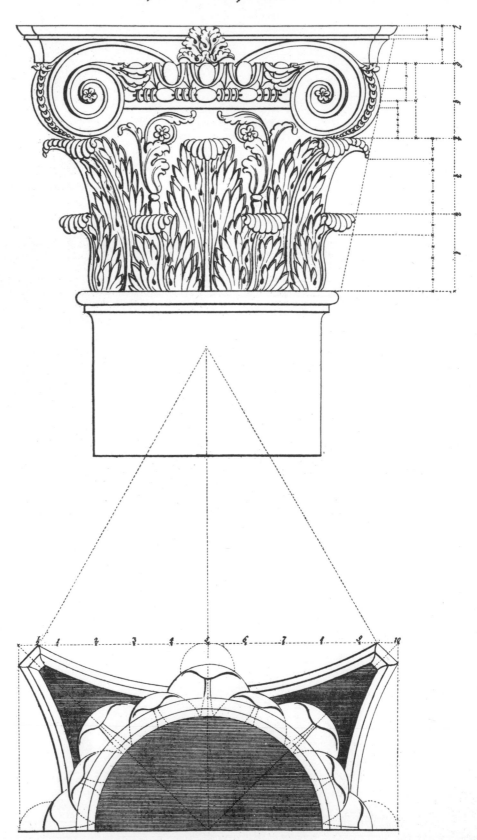

Capitello   Composito

XXIX

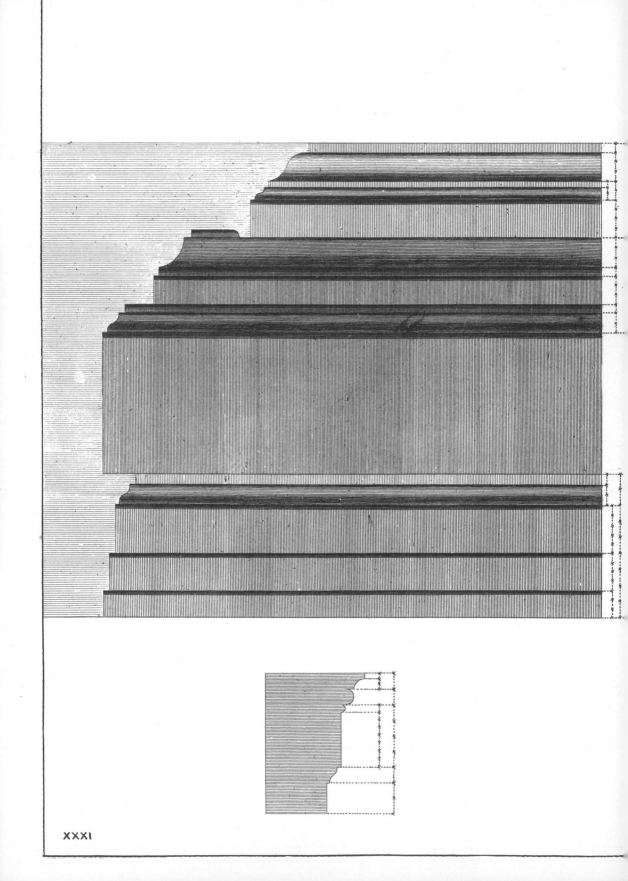

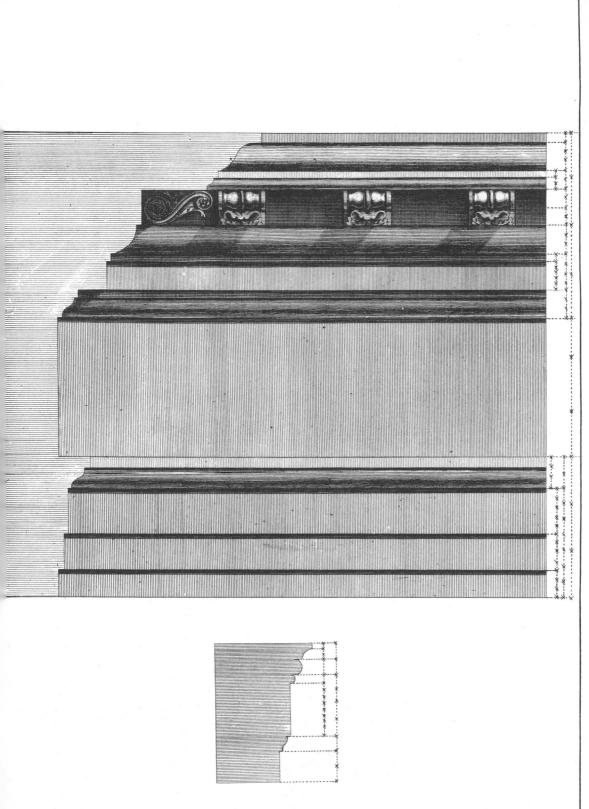

Modulo.

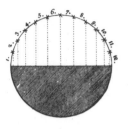

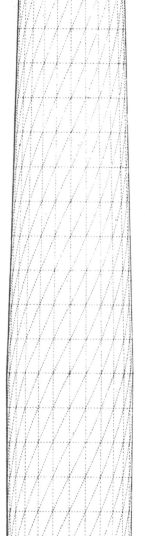

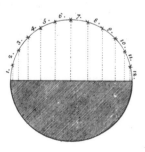

Modulo.

XXXIII

XXXV

XXXVI

Modu. 3.

Modu. 1.

14

Mod. 1.

Mod:1.

1. 2. 3. 4. 5. 6. 7. 8. 9.

XXXVIII

XXXIX

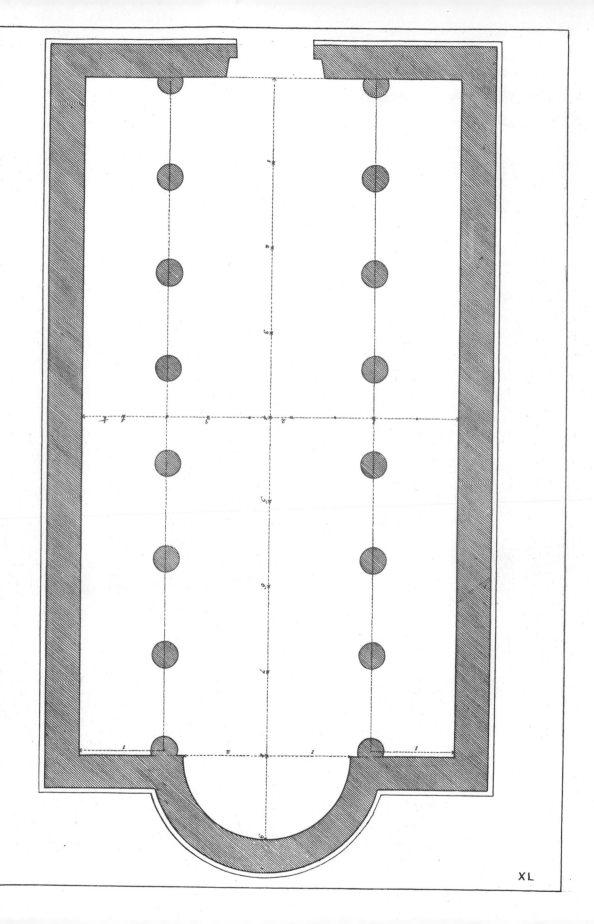

XL

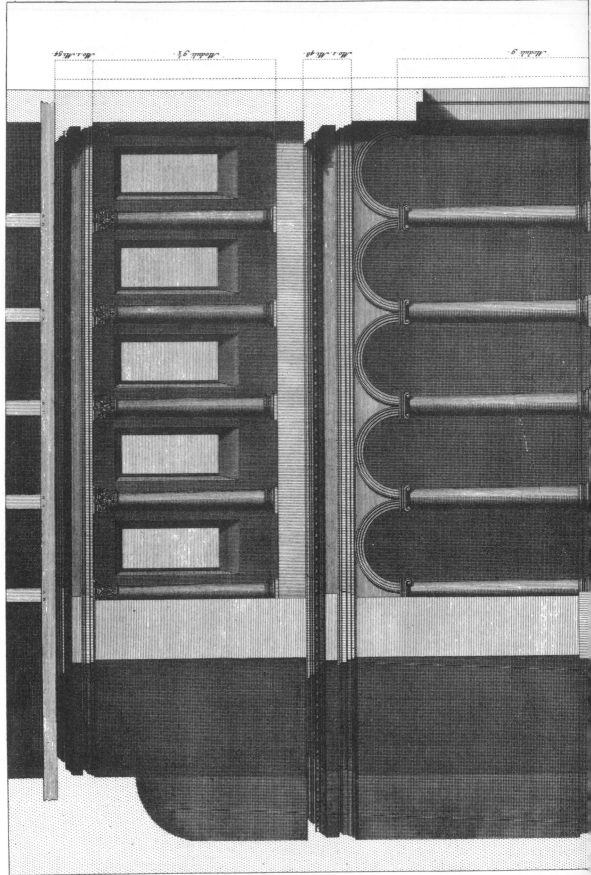

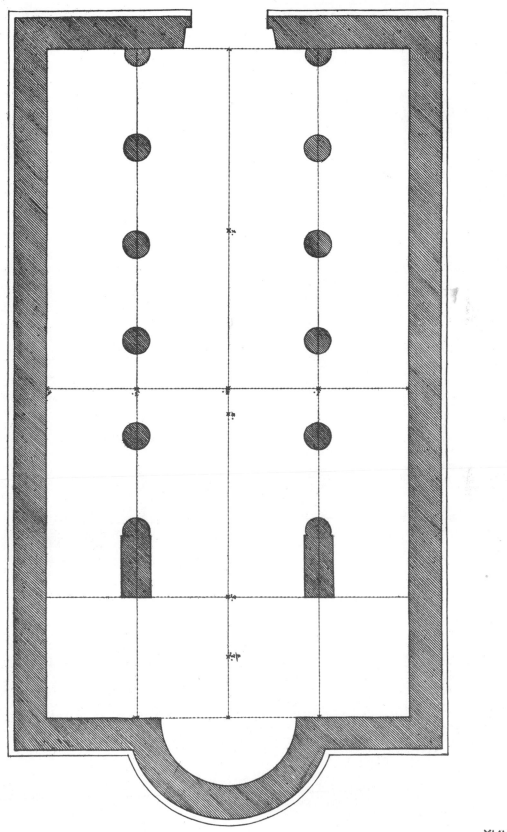

XLII

Composto 10 Moduli

8

14

9

Corintio 9 Moduli e ½

Ionico 9 Moduli

XLIII.

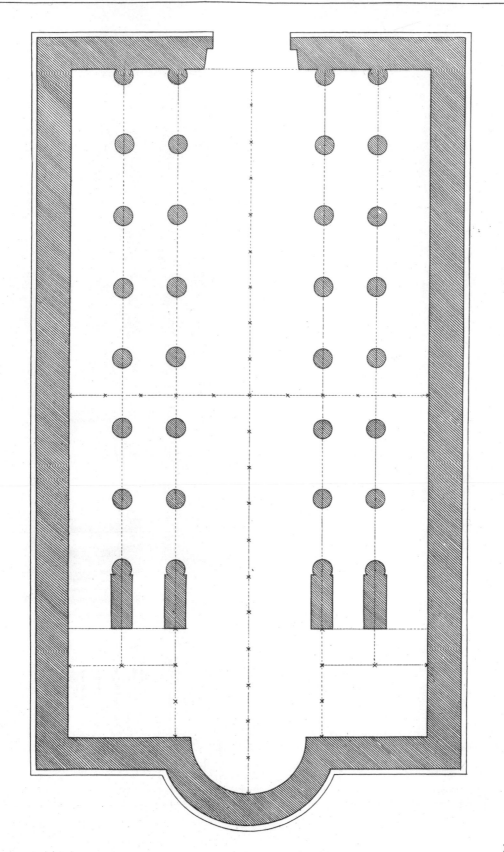

XLIV

XLV

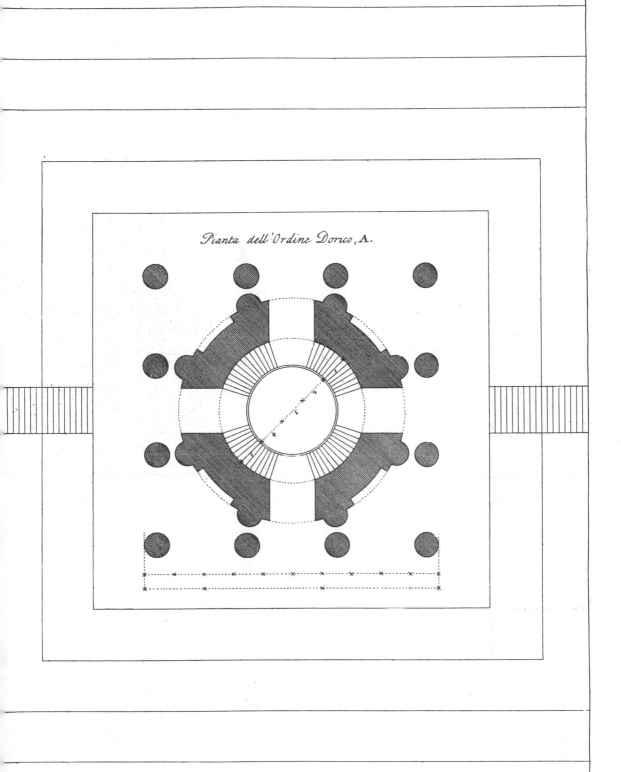

Pianta dell'Ordine Dorico, A.

XLVI

Pianta dell'Ordine Corinthio, C.

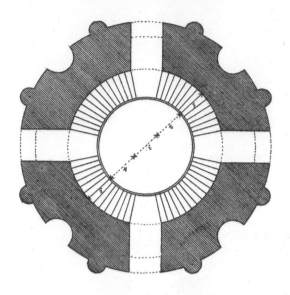

Pianta dell'Ordine Ionico, B.

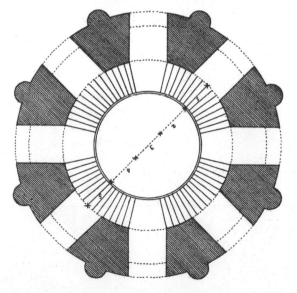

Pianta dell'Ordine Ionico, F.

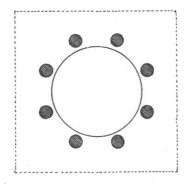

Pianta dell'Ordine Dorico, E.

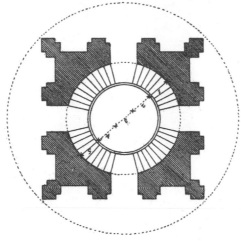

Pianta dell'Ordine Compofito, D.

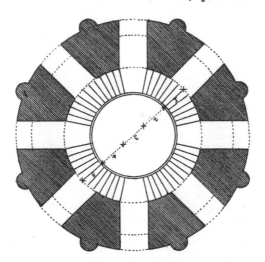

XLVIII

Moduli 2. Minuti 15.

Moduli 9.

Mod. 1.

Moduli 2.

Moduli 8.

Mod. 1.

Mod. 2. Min. 30.

Moduli 10.

Mod. 1.

Mod. 2. Min. 22 ½.

Moduli 9 ½.

Mod. 1.

Mod. 2. Min. 15.

Moduli 9.

Mo. 1.

Mo. 2.

Moduli 8.

F

E

D

C

B

A

XLIX

Super. dell'Acqua.

L

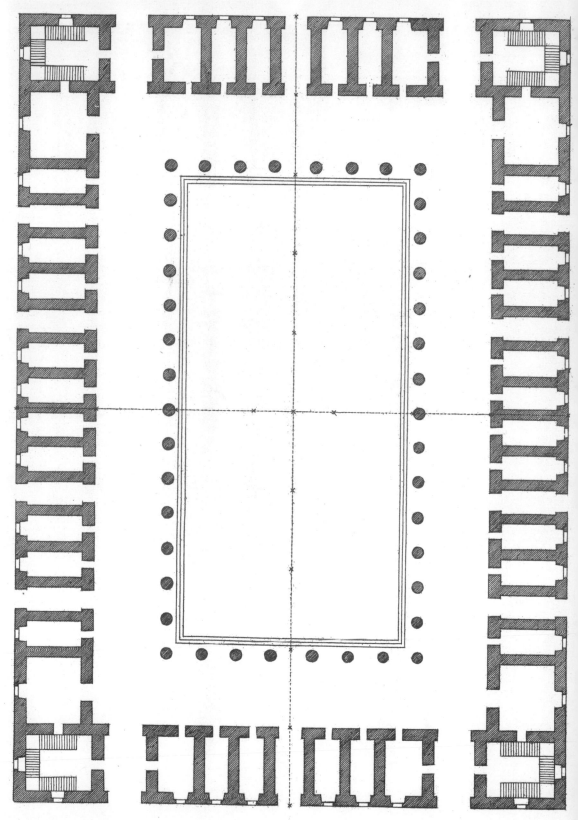

LI

Moduli 9 ½

Moduli 9

Mo: 2 ½   Mo: 1

LII

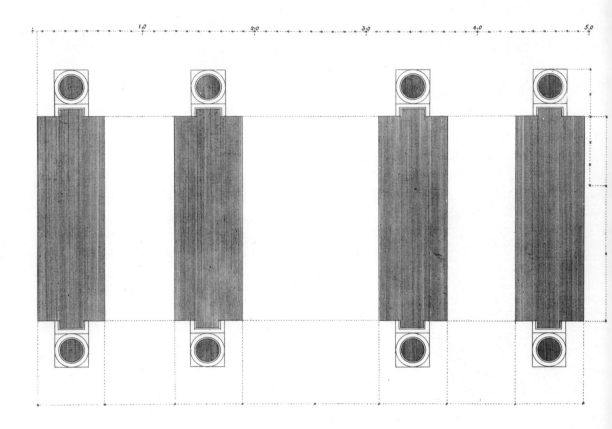

LIII

MAGNAE BRITANNIAE
EUROPAE FATA
IN
AEQUA LANCE PONENTI.

LIV

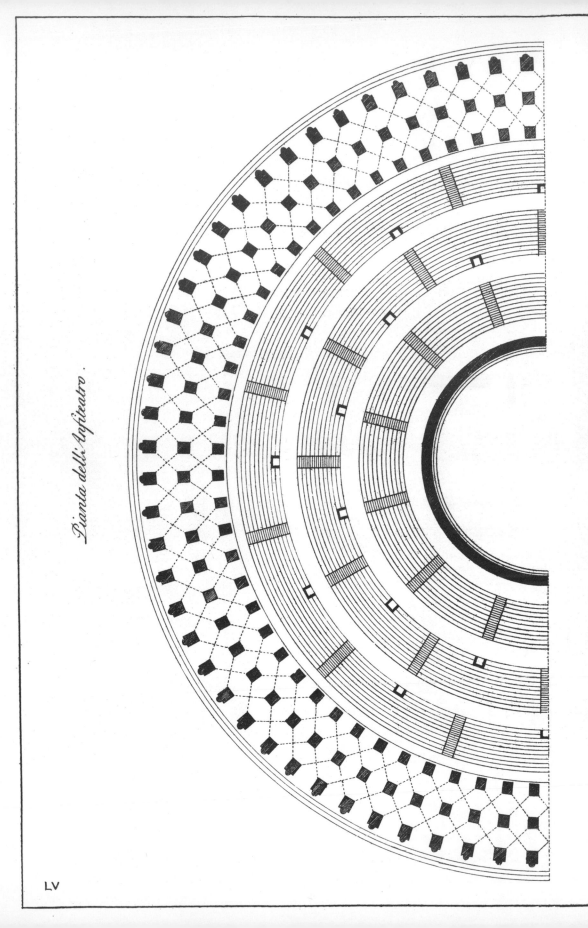

Pianta delli Anfiteatro.

LV

Corinthio

Jonico

Mod. 4

Moduli 17
Dorico

LVI

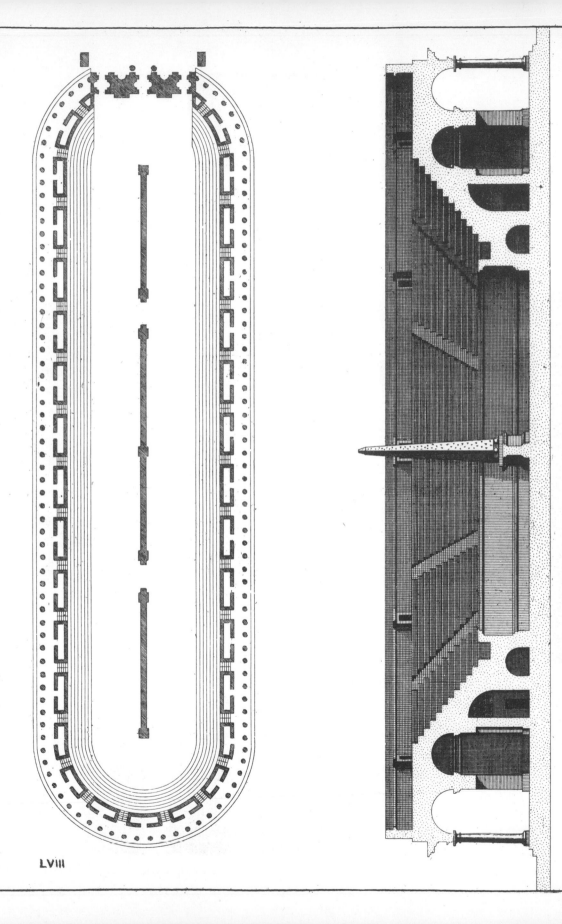

LVIII

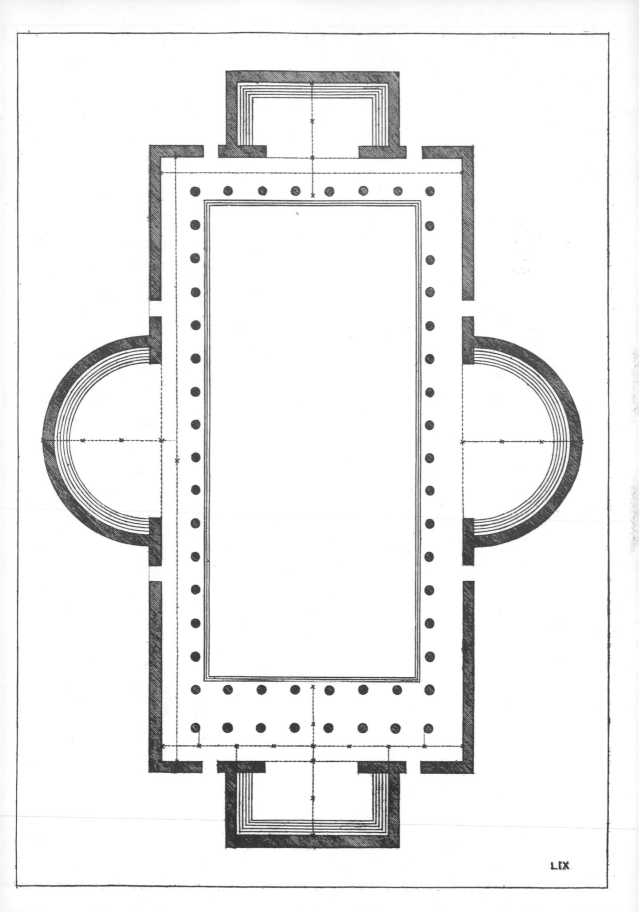

LIX.

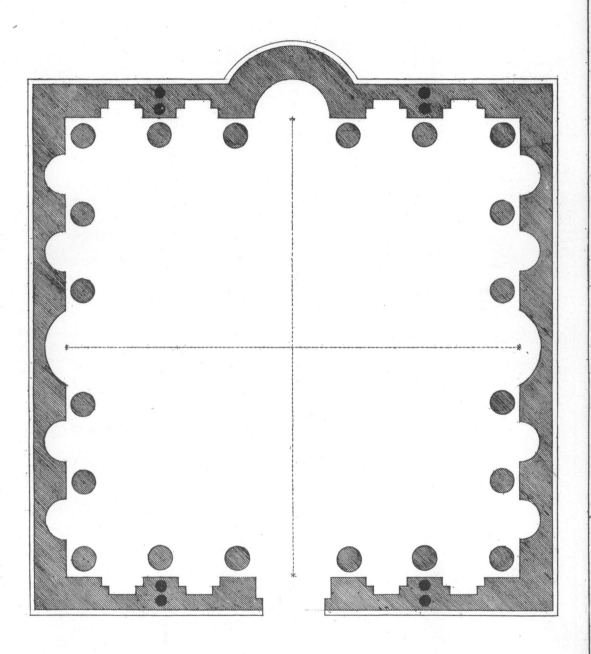

LX

LXI

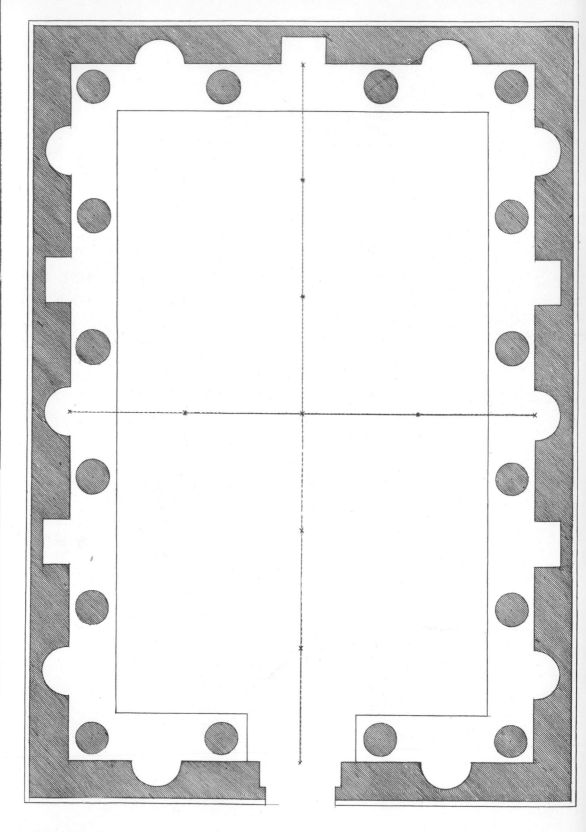

LXII

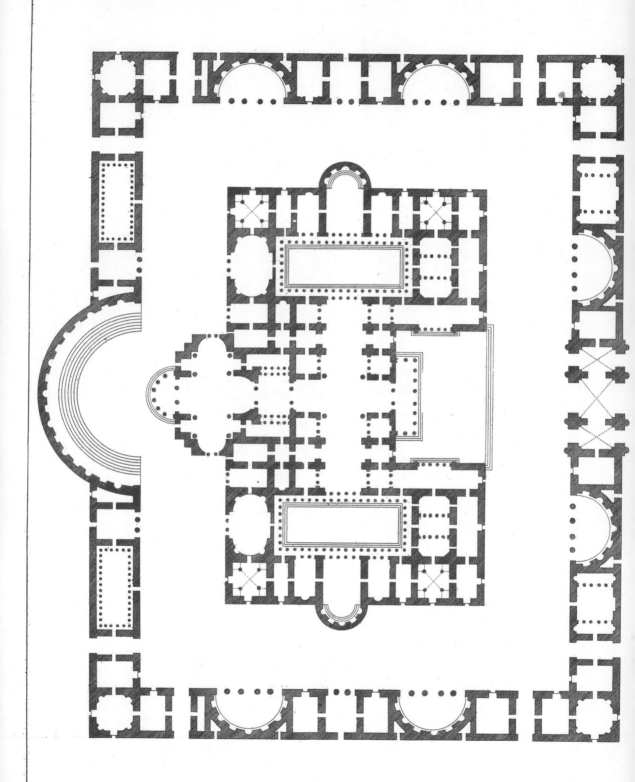

Fig. 2.

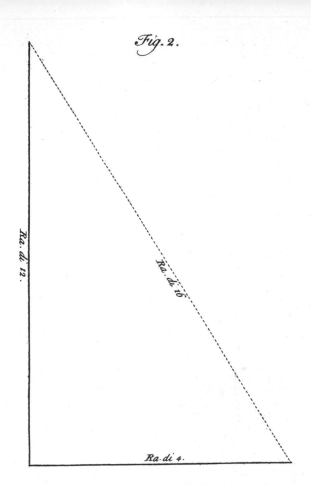

Ra. di 12.

Ra. di 16.

Ra. di 4.

Fig. 1.

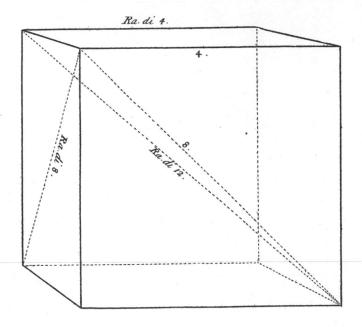

Ra. di 4.

4.

8.

Ra. di 8.

Ra. di 12.

LXV